LOCAL NETWORKS

Text/Reference Books on Data Com...
and Computer Architecture

(Available from Macmillan Publishing Co.)

DATA AND COMPUTER COMMUNICATIONS,
SECON

A broad ... ata
comm... ng,
link ... ud-
ing ... te;
(3) ... re-
late

LO
TH

An ... cal
net... on-
trol

CO
AR

A u... PU,
con... ry.
Als... on.

ISI

An ... te-
grat ... ital
net... . 7
(SS

BU

A c... om-
mu... ice,
dat... ogy
and

All of these books include a glossary, a list of acronyms, homework problems, and recommendations for further reading. These books are suitable as references, for self-study, and as textbooks.

These and other Macmillan books are available at better bookstores or can be ordered by calling 800-548-9939.

WILLIAM STALLINGS, Ph.D.

LOCAL
NETWORKS

THIRD EDITION

Macmillan Publishing Company

New York

Collier Macmillan Publishers

London

Editor(s): Ed Moura
Production Supervisor: John Travis
Production Manager: Nick Sklitsis
Cover Designer: Robert Freese
Cover Art: Piet Mondrian, *Broadway Boogie Woogie*, 1942–3.

This book was set in Times Roman by Polyglot Pte Ltd
and printed and bound by Quinn Woodbine.
The cover was printed by Phoenix Color Corp.

Macmillan Publishing Company
866 Third Avenue, New York, New York 10022

Collier Macmillan Canada, Inc.

Library of Congress Cataloging in Publication Data
Stallings, William.
    Local networks/William Stallings. -- 3rd ed.
        p.   cm.
    Bibliography: p.
    Includes index.
    ISBN 0-02-415531-4
    1. Local area networks (Computer networks)   I. Title.
TK5105.7.S78   1990   89-8139
004.6'8--dc20   CIP

Macmillan books are available at special discounts
for bulk purchases for sales promotions, premiums, fund-raising,
or educational use. For details, contact:
    College Special Sales Director
    Macmillan Publishing Company
    Front and Brown Streets
    Riverside, NJ 08075

Printing: 2 3 4 5 6 7 8   Year: 0 1 2 3 4 5 6 7 8 9

To my wife, Tricia

PREFACE

Perhaps no other major innovation in data processing or data communications has been so widely discussed or so eagerly anticipated before its maturity as local networks. Local networks are attractive for such features as high availability and the ability to support multiple vendor equipment. And, although the technology is rapidly evolving, the principal architectural forms and design approaches have emerged.

Objectives

This book focuses on the broad and constantly changing field of local networks. The aim of the text is to provide a reasoned balance among breadth, depth, and timeliness. The book emphasizes topics of fundamental importance concerning the technology and architecture of local networks. Certain key areas, such as the network interface and performance, are treated in some detail. Others, such as security and reliability, can only be treated in an introductory fashion.

The book explores the key topics in the field in the following general categories:

- *Technology and architecture:* There is a small collection of ingredients that serves to characterize and differentiate local networks, including transmission medium, network topology, communication protocols, switching technique, and hardware/software interface.

- *Network type:* It is convenient to classify local networks into three types, based partly on technology and partly on application. These are local area network (LAN), high-speed local network (HSLN), and digital switch/digital private branch exchange (PBX).
- *Design approaches:* While not attempting to be exhaustive, the book exposes and discusses important issues related to local network design.

Conspicuously missing from this list is a category with a title such as "typical systems." This book focuses on the common principles underlying the design and implementation of all local networks. It should, therefore, give the reader sufficient background to judge and compare local network products. A description of even a small sample of such systems is beyond the scope of this book. Discussions of specific systems are included herein only when they are the best vehicle for communicating the concepts and principles under discussion.

In terms of style, the book is primarily:

- *Descriptive:* Terms are defined and the key concepts and technologies are discussed in some detail.
- *Comparative:* Wherever possible, alternative or competing approaches are compared and their relative merits, based on suitable criteria, are discussed.

On the other hand, analytic and research-oriented styles are present to a much lesser degree. Virtually all of the mathematical content is confined to the chapters on performance, and even there, the emphasis is on results rather than derivations.

Intended Audience

This book is intended for a broad range of readers interested in local networks:

- *Students and professionals in computer science and data communications:* The book is intended as both a textbook for study and a basic reference volume for this exciting area within the broader fields of computer science and data communications.
- *Local network designers and implementors:* The book discusses the critical design issues and illustrates alternative approaches to meeting user requirements.
- *Local network customers and system managers:* The book alerts the reader to some of the key issues and tradeoffs, and what to look for in the way of network services and performance.

The book is intended to be self-contained. For the reader with little or no background in data communications, a brief primer is included.

Plan of the Text

The book is organized to clarify both the unifying and differentiating concepts underlying the field of local networks. The organization of the chapters is as follows:

1. *Introduction:* This chapter defines the term local network and looks at some of the applications and advantages and disadvantages.
2. *Topics in data communications and computer networking:* This necessarily brief survey explains the relevant concepts used throughout the book.
3. *Local network technology:* Focuses on the key characteristics of transmission medium and topology. The classification of local networks used in this book is presented and discussed.
4, 5. *Local area networks:* The term local area network (LAN) is often mistakenly identified with the entire field of local networks. LANs are general-purpose in nature and most of the better-known local networks fall into this class. The major types of LANs—baseband bus, broadband bus/tree, and ring—are described and compared. The important issue of medium access control protocols is explored. The standards for LANS are also described.
6. *High-speed local networks:* This chapter focuses on a special purpose high-speed type of local network, examining current technology and standards and possible future directions.
7. *Circuit-switched local networks:* Networks in this category constitute the major alternative to LANS for meeting general local interconnection needs. The category includes the data-only digital switch and the voice/data digital private branch exchange (PBX). This chapter explores the technology and architecture of these devices and examines their pros and cons relative to LANs.
8. *The network interface:* The nature of the interface between an attached device and LAN or HSLN is an important design issue. This chapter explores some alternatives.
9, 10. *Network performance:* The purpose of these chapters is to give some insight into the performance problems and the differences in performance of various local networks.
11. *Internetworking:* In the majority of cases, local networks will be connected in some fashion to other networks. Some alternatives are explored.

12. *Local network design issues:* The purpose of this chapter is to give the reader some feel for the breadth of design issues that must be addressed in implementing and operating local networks.

In addition, the book includes an extensive glossary, a list of frequently-used acronyms, and a bibliography. Each chapter includes problems and suggestions for further reading.

The book is suitable for self-study and can be conveniently covered in a one-semester course. It covers the material in Module 7 (Local Area Networks) of Subject Area 25 (Computer Communications Networks) of the 1983 IEEE Computer Society Model Program in Computer Science and Engineering. It also covers portions of CS 24 (Computer Communication Networks and Distributed Processing) of the 1981 ACM Recommendations for Master's Level Programs in Computer Science.

A final note: a considerable fraction of the material is organized with reference to the Open Systems Interconnection (OSI) model and to local network standards. This structure is suggestive of the certain future direction of local network architecture, and, equally important, it provides a terminology and frame of reference that is becoming universal in networking discourses.

Related Materials

The author has produced other material that may be of interest to students and professionals. *Local Network Technology, Second Edition* (1985, IEEE Computer Society Press, P.O. Box 80452, Worldway Postal Center, Los Angeles, CA 90080; telephone 800-272-6657) is a companion to this text, and follows the same topical organization. It contains reprints of many of the key references used herein, these are indicated by an asterisk when cited in the recommended reading section of each chapter.

A set of videotape courses specifically designed for use with this book is available from the Media Group, Professional Development Video Programs, Boston University, 565 Commonwealth Avenue, Boston, MA 02215; telephone (617) 353-3227.

Data and Computer Communications, Second Edition (Macmillan, 1987) covers fundamental concepts in the areas of data transmission, communication networks, and computer-communications protocols. *ISDN: An Introduction* (Macmillan, 1989) covers the concepts and technology of integrated services digital networks, which are all-digital networks gradually being introduced to replace existing wide-area networks.

The Third Edition

The three years since the publication of the second edition of this book have seen local networks pass an important threshold. Local networks are now an essential part of most office and factory environments. A number of factors have led to this explosion in the use of local networks.

Perhaps the most significant factor is the ubiquitous personal computer. It is the rare business today that does not have a heavy reliance on personal computers and other microcomputers. The presence of these systems in quantity leads to the need for interconnection and hence the need for local networks. Furthermore, the introduction of so-called PC LANs inevitably leads to the introduction of multiple PC LANs as well as other local networks to serve other data processing devices. This in turn creates a need for internetworking devices.

Another significant factor has been the maturing of the standards for LANs. The standards initially issued by the IEEE 802 committee are now international standards. In addition, what started as a set of standards covering a few options has blossomed into a rich array of alternatives tailored to a wide variety of applications and environments. Customers have enthusiastically embraced the standards, and vendors have produced a full set of products to meet customer needs.

Another area that has had a major impact is the increasing sophistication in the use of transmission media, most notably twisted pair and optical fiber. Unshielded twisted pair, which is found in abundance in office buildings and which is inexpensive and easy to work with, has found increasing use in a variety of topologies and at higher and higher data rates. Optical fiber costs have come down as the standards have matured.

All of these developments have expanded the range of applications that can be met at reasonable cost and have spurred the proliferation of local networks.

As the use of local networks has expanded, the technology continues to evolve. Thus the third edition represents a significant update to the second. To give some feel for the scope of the revision, approximately 27% of the figures and 25% of the references in this edition are new. Although virtually every topic and every chapter has been revised, a few areas stand out.

The most significant change in this edition is the treatment of internetworking. In recent years, there have been major advances in the technology and application of two types of internetworking devices: bridges and routers. Accordingly, Chapter 11 has been completely rewritten to reflect these developments.

Another important development is the use of unshielded twisted pair in star-topology LANs. The architecture and technology of these 1-Mbps and 10-Mbps LANs are examined. In addition, new detials on broadband technology have been added.

With respect to LAN protocols, the coverage has been updated to reflect the developments in LAN standards. Other areas of technology, such as network control, reliability, and security have also been upgraded.

All in all, this third edition constitutes a major revision. I have tried in a balanced manner to provide a comprehensive survey of the technology and architecture of local networks.

W. S.

CONTENTS

CHAPTER 1

Introduction

1.1

A DEFINITION OF LOCAL NETWORKS

To formulate a definition of the term *local network*, and to characterize the purposes of such networks, it is important to understand the trends that have brought about local networks.

Of most importance is the dramatic and continuing decrease in computer hardware costs, accompanied by an increase in computer hardware capability. Today's microprocessors have speeds, instruction sets, and memory capacities comparable to the most powerful minicomputers of a few years ago. This trend has spawned a number of changes in the way information is collected, processed, and used in organizations. There is increasing use of small, single-function systems, such as word processors and small business computers, and of general-purpose microcomputers, such as personal computers and Unix-based multiuser workstations. These small, dispersed systems are more accessible to the user, more responsive, and easier to use than large central time-sharing systems.

All of these factors lead to an increased number of systems at a single site: office building, factory, operations center, and so on. At the same time there is likely to be a desire to interconnect these systems for a variety of reasons, including:

- To share and exchange data between systems
- To share expensive resources

The ability to exchange data is a compelling reason for interconnection. Individual users of computer systems do not work in isolation, and will want to retain some of the benefits provided by a central system. These include the ability to exchange messages with other users, the ability to access data from several sources in the preparation of a document or for an analysis, and the opportunity for multiple users to share information in a common file.

To appreciate the second reason, consider that although the cost of data processing hardware has dropped, the cost of essential electromechanical equipment, such as bulk storage and line printers, remains high. In the past, with a centralized data processing facility, these devices could be attached directly to the central host computer. With the dispersal of computer power, these devices must somehow be shared.

We will elaborate on these and other reasons later in this chapter. For now, the discussion above should be enough to motivate the following definition of a *local network*:

A local network is a communications network that provides interconnection of a variety of data communicating devices within a small area.

There are three elements of significance in this definition. First, a local network is a communications network. That is, it is a facility for moving bits of data from one attached device to another. The application-level software and protocols that are required for attached devices to function cooperatively are beyond the scope of this book. As a corollary to this definition, note that a collection of devices interconnected by individual point-to-point links is not included in the definition nor in this book.

Second, we interpret the phrase *data communicating devices* broadly, to include any device that communicates over a transmission medium. Examples:

- Computers
- Terminals
- Peripheral devices
- Sensors (temperature, humidity, security alarm sensors)
- Telephones
- Television transmitters and receivers
- Facsimile

Of course, not all types of local networks are capable of handling all of these devices.

Third, the geographic scope of a local network is small. The most common occurrence is a network that is confined to a single building. Networks that span several buildings, such as on a college campus or military base, are also common. A borderline case is a network with a radius of a few tens of kilometers. With appropriate technology, such a system will behave like a local network.

Another element that could be added to the definition is that a local network is generally privately owned rather than a public or commercially available utility. Indeed, typically, a single organization will own both the network and the attached devices.

Some of the typical characteristics of local networks are:

- High data rates (0.1 to 100 Mbps)
- Short distances (0.1 to 25 km)
- Low error rate (10^{-8} to 10^{-11})

The first two parameters serve to differentiate local networks from two cousins: multiprocessor systems and long-haul networks. This is illustrated in Figure 1.1. The figure indicates three types of local networks: local area networks, high speed local networks, and digital private branch exchanges. These will be defined in Chapter 3.

Other distinctions can be drawn between local networks and its two cousins, and these have a significant impact on design and operation. Local networks generally experience significantly fewer data transmission errors

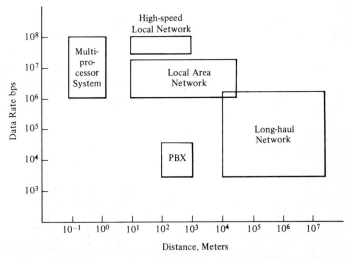

FIGURE 1-1. Comparison of Multiprocessor Systems, Local Networks, and Long-Haul Networks

and significantly lower communications costs than those of long haul networks. Cost-performance tradeoffs are thus significantly different. Also, because local networks are generally owned by the same organization as the attached devices, it is possible to achieve greater integration between the network and the devices; this topic is explored in Chapter 8.

A distinction between local networks and multiprocessor systems is the degree of coupling. Multiprocessor systems are tightly coupled, usually have some central control, and completely integrate the communications function. Local networks tend to exhibit the opposite characteristics.

1.2

BENEFITS AND PITFALLS

Table 1.1 lists some of the major benefits of a local network. Whether these are realized or not, of course, depends on the skill and wisdom of those involved in selecting and managing the local network.

One of the most important potential benefits of a local network relates to system evolution. In a non-networked installation such as a time-sharing system, all data processing power is in one or a few systems. In order to upgrade hardware, existing applications software must be either converted to new hardware or reprogrammed, with the risk of error in either case.

TABLE 1.1 Benefits and Pitfalls of Local Networks

Potential Benefits

System evolution: incremental changes with contained impact

Reliability/availability/survivability: multiple interconnected systems disperse
  functions and provide backup capability

Resource sharing: expensive peripherals, hosts, data

Multivendor support: customer not locked in to a single vendor

Improved response/performance

User needs single terminal to access multiple systems

Flexibility of equipment location

Integration of data processing and office automation

Potential Pitfalls

Interoperability is not guaranteed: software, data

A distributed data base raises problems of integrity, security/privacy

Creeping escalation: more equipment will be procured than is actually needed

Loss of control: more difficult to manage and enforce standards

Even adding new applications on the same hardware, or enhancing those that exist, involves the risk of introducing errors and reducing the performance of the entire system. With a local network it is possible to gradually replace applications or systems, avoiding the "all-or-nothing" approach. Another facet of this capability is that old equipment can be left in the system to run a single application if the cost of moving that application to a new machine is not justified.

A local network tends to improve the reliability, availability, and survivability of a data processing facility (see Section 12.2). With multiple interconnected systems, the loss of any one system should have minimal impact. Further, key systems can be made redundant so that other systems can quickly take up the load after a failure.

We have already mentioned resource sharing. This includes not only expensive peripheral devices, but data. Data can be housed and controlled from a specific facility but, via the network, be available to many users.

A local network provides at least the potential of connecting devices from multiple vendors, thus giving the customer greater flexibility and bargaining power. However, a local network will provide only a rather low or primitive level of interconnection. For the network to function properly, higher levels of networking software must be supplied within the attached devices (see Section 2.3 and Chapter 8).

These are, in most cases, the most significant benefits of a local network. Several others are also listed in Table 1.1.

Alas, there are also some pitfalls, or at least potential pitfalls. As we mentioned, a local network does not guarantee that two devices can be used cooperatively, a concept known as *interoperability*. For example, two word processors from different vendors can be attached to a local network, and can perhaps exchange data. But they probably will use different file formats and different control characters, so that it is not possible, directly, to take a file from one and begin editing it on the other. Some sort of format-conversion software is needed.

With a local network, it is likely that data will be distributed or, at least, that access to data may come from multiple sources. This raises questions of integrity (e. g., two users trying to update the data base simultaneously) and security and privacy.

Another pitfall is what Martin refers to as "creeping escalation" [MART8lb]. With the dispersal of computer equipment and the ease of incrementally adding equipment, it becomes easier for managers of sub-organizations to justify equipment procurement for their department. Although each procurement may be individually justifiable, the totality of procurements throughout an organization may well exceed the total requirements.

There is also a loss of control problem. The prime virtue of networking—distributed systems—is also its prime danger. It is difficult to manage

TABLE 1.2 Organizational Effects of Local Networks

Affected Area	Positive Effects	Negative Effects
Work quality	Wider data accessibility; fewer "lost" items. Wider participation in creating and reviewing work	Indeterminate or mediocre data quality; reduced independence and initiative
Productivity	Increased work load handled by more powerful office-systems equipment	Greater resources used to perform inconsequential work
Employee changes	Improved skill levels in current staff More challenging work Reduced status distinctions	Fewer jobs for marginal performers Less personal interaction Insufficient status distinctions
Decision-making effectiveness	Quicker availability of relevant facts Greater analytic capability More people involved in hypothesis building and testing	Factual component of decision making becomes too high "Forest and trees" problem could encourage "group think"
Organizational structure	More effective decentralization	Decentralization can get out of control
Costs	Overall cost reduction	Overall cost increase; soft benefits used as justification
Total impact	Permits the planning of new business approaches	Creates increased complexity and poorly functioning dependence relationships

Source: [EDN82].

this resource, to enforce standards for software and data, and to control the information available through a network.

We close this discussion with a sobering summary in Table 1.2 based on a recent survey of local network users. While some users noted positive effects from the installation of a local network, a similar number reported negative effects. The conflicting and exaggerated claims of vendors plus the multiplicity of choices has led to confusion and disappointment. Local networks will aid an organization only if they are chosen and managed properly.

1.3

APPLICATIONS

The range of applications for local networks is wide, as indicated by the broad definition given above. Table 1.3 lists some of the potential applications. Again, we emphasize that not all local networks are capable of sup-

TABLE 1.3 Local Network Applications

Data Processing	Energy management
Data entry	Heating
Transaction processing	Ventilation
File transfer	Air conditioning
Inquiry/response	Process control
Batch/RJE	
Office automation	Fire and security
Document/word processing	Sensors/alarms
Electronic mail	Cameras and monitors
Intelligent copying/facsimile	Telephones
Factory automation	Teleconferencing
CAD/CAM	Television
Inventory control/order entry/shipping	Off-the-air
Monitor and control of factory floor	Video presentations
equipment	

porting all applications. To give some feeling for the use of local networks, we discuss in this section five rather different types of applications.

Personal Computer Networks

We start at one extreme, a system designed to support microcomputers, such as personal computers. With the relatively low cost of such systems, individual managers within organizations are independently procuring personal computers for standalone applications, such as spreadsheet and project management tools. Today's personal computers put processor, file storage, high-level languages, and problem-solving tools in an inexpensive, "user-friendly" package. The reasons for acquiring such systems are compelling.

But a collection of standalone processors will not meet all of an organization's needs; central processing facilities are still required. Some programs, such as econometric forecasting models, are too big to run on a small computer. Corporate-wide data files, such as accounting and payroll, require a centralized facility but should be accessible to a number of users. In addition, there are other kinds of files that, although specialized, must be shared by a number of users. Further, there are sound reasons for connecting individual intelligent workstations not only to a central facility but to each other as well. Members of a project or organizational team need to share work and information. By far the most efficient way to do so is electronically.

Figure 1.2 is an example of a local network of personal computers for a hypothetical aerospace engineering group or department [SCHW82].

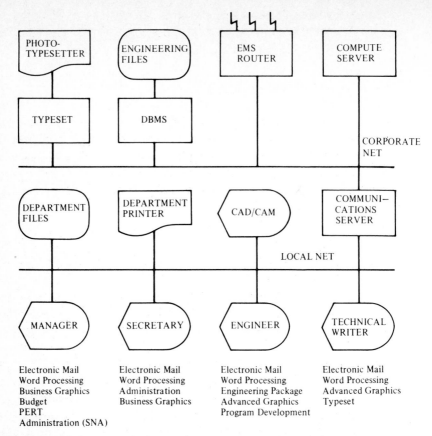

FIGURE 1-2. Personal Computers in Support of a Working Team

The figure shows four types of users who have personal computers, each equipped with particular applications.

Each type of user is provided with electronic mail and word processing to improve the efficiency of creating and distributing messages, memos, and reports. Managers are also given a set of program and budget management tools. With the amount of automation that personal computers supply, the role of secretaries becomes less that of a typist and more that of an administrative assistant. Tools such as electronic calendar and graphics support become valuable for these workers. In the same fashion, engineers and technical writers can be supplied with tailored systems.

Certain expensive resources, such as a disk and printer, can be shared by all users of the departmental local network. In addition, the network can tie into larger corporate network facilities. For example, the corporation may have a building-wide local network (see Office Automation below) and a long-haul corporate-wide network using, for example, IBM's SNA. A communications server can provide controlled access to these resources.

A key requirement for the success of such a network is low cost. The cost of attachment to the network for each device should be on the order of one to a few hundred dollars; otherwise, the attachment cost will approach the cost of the attached device. However, the capacity and data rate need not be high, so this is a realizable goal. For example, see [THUR85].

Computer Room Networks

At the other extreme from a personal computer local network is one designed for use in a computer room containing large, expensive mainframe computers. This is an example of what we will refer to as a *high-speed local network* (HSLN). The HSLN is likely to find application at very large data processing sites. Typically, these sites will be large companies or research installations with large data processing budgets. Because of the size involved, a small difference in productivity can mean millions of dollars. Further, although HSLNs are few in number, the collective cost of the equipment they support is very high. Consequently, the HSLN deserves a close look.

Consider a site that uses a dedicated mainframe computer. This implies a fairly large application or set of applications. As the load at the site grows, the existing model may be replaced by a more powerful one, perhaps a multiprocessor system. At some sites, a single-system replacement will not be able to keep up; equipment growth rates will be exceeded by demand growth rates. The facility will eventually require multiple independent computers. Again, there are compelling reasons for interconnecting these systems. The cost of system interrupt is high, so it should be possible, easily and quickly, to shift applications to backup systems. It must be possible to test new procedures and applications without degrading the production system. Large bulk storage files must be accessible from more than one computer. Load leveling should be possible to maximize utilization.

An example of an HSLN installation is the one at the National Center for Atmospheric Research (NCAR), shown in Figure 1.3. The NCAR facility is used for atmospheric research. This entails storage of massive amounts of data and the use of huge number-crunching simulation and analysis programs. There is also an extensive on-site graphics facility.

Initially, the NCAR facility consisted of a single mainframe run in batch mode. When it became clear that additional batch machines were needed, NCAR investigated the requirements for a new configuration to meet their needs. The result was four objectives:

- Provide front-end processors to remove job and file preparation tasks from the batch computers.
- Provide an efficient method for interactive processing.
- Design a system architecture which would allow different services for special needs and purposes.
- Provide a system that would allow configuration flexibility without excessive modification to existing resources.

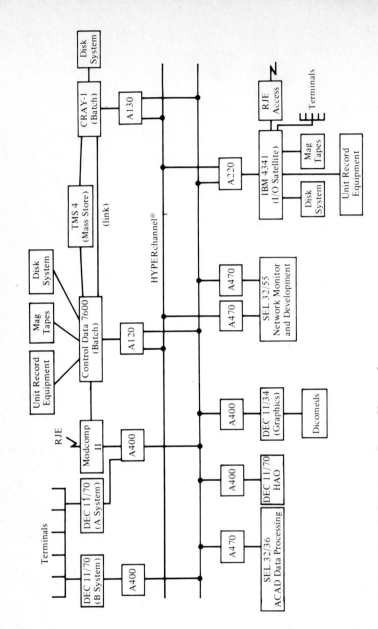

FIGURE 1-3. A Computer Room Network

The result of this study was a plan that called for the procurement of front-end processors, special-purpose computers, and bulk storage systems. A network was needed that met two requirements:

- Easy addition and subtraction of equipment
- High sustained data transfer speeds

These requirements were met by an HSLN system [CHR179].

It can be seen that some key requirements for HSLNs are the opposite of those for personal computer local networks. High data rates are required to keep up with the work, which typically involves the transfer of large blocks of data. The electronics for achieving high speeds are expensive, on the order of tens of thousands of dollars per attachment. Fortunately, given the much higher cost of attached devices, such costs are reasonable.

Office Automation

Most local network applications will fall between these two extremes. Moderate data rates and moderate attachment costs are requirements. In some cases, the local network will support one or a few types of devices and rather homogeneous traffic. Others will support a wide variety of device and traffic types.

A good generic example of the latter is an office automation system, which can be defined as the incorporation of appropriate technology to help people manage information.

The key motivation for the move to office automation is productivity. As the percentage of white-collar workers has increased, the information and paper-work volume has grown. In most installations, secretarial and other support functions are heavily labor intensive. Increased labor costs combined with low productivity and increasing work load have caused employers to seek effective ways of increasing their rather low capital investment in this type of work.

At the same time, principals (managers, skilled "information workers") are faced with their own productivity bind. Work needs to be done faster with less wait time and waste time between segments of a job. This requires better access to information and better communication and coordination with others.

Table 1.4 lists elements of a hypothetical integrated office automation system. A study of this list gives some idea of the range of devices and information types that are part of the system. For this system to work and be truly effective, a local network is needed that can support the various devices and transmit the various types of information. A discussion of the use of local networks to tie together office automation equipment such as this can be found in [DERF83].

TABLE 1.4　Elements of an Integrated Office Automation System

Basic IOAS Components

Action elements
　Word management (keying and
　　editing)
　Terminal-oriented computer-based
　　message system
　Automated file indexing
　Electronic filing and retrieval
　Off-line connection to
　　computer-operated micrographics
　　(for system purging)
Control elements
　Electronic calendar
　Electronic tickler file
Inquiry elements
　Automated file searching and retrieval
　Directory of users (names, addresses,
　telephones numbers, etc.)
　Capability for open-loop
　　computer-aided retrieval (CAR) of
　　micrographics
　Capability for input/output control of
　　physical files

**Extended-Application IOAS
Components**

Action elements
　Automated departmental billing for
　　IOAS usage
　Individual applications
　Personal computing (permits individual
　　to program)
　Unit applications
　Departmental applications
　Divisional applications
　Regional applications
　Line-of-business applications
　Functional applications (mathematical
　　formulas)
Control elements
　System usage monitoring
　　(departmental level)
　Specialized applications (as above)
Inquiry elements: specialized applications
　(as above)

Optional IOAS Components

Action elements
　Interconnection to other
　　terminal-oriented,
　　computer-based message systems
　Interconnection to public
　　teletypewriter systems
　OCR (optical character
　　recognition) input
　Digitized, hard-copy input
　　(temporary; for incoming mail)
　Store-and-forward fax
　Soft-copy fax
　Interconnection to external fax
　　devices and networks
　Audio output electronic mail
　　(digital-to-audio conversion)
　Business graphics
　　(black-and-white)
　Electronic calculator
　Sorting capabilities
　Photocomposer output
　On-line output of
　　computer-operated
　　micrographics (COM)
　Computer teleconferencing
Control elements
　COM format previewing
　Project management and control
　Management of multiauthord
　　document preparation
Inquiry elements
　Soft-copy CAR
　Electronic publishing (manuals,
　　price lists, news, etc.)
　Interconnection to other internal
　　systems and data bases
　Interconnection to external
　　research data base services

Source: [BARC81].

Factory Local Networks

The factory environment is increasingly being dominated by automated equipment: programmable controllers, automated materials handling devices, time and attendance stations, machine vision devices, and various forms of robots. To manage the production or manufacturing process, it is essential to tie this equipment together. And, indeed, the very nature of the equipment facilitates this. Microprocessor devices have the potential to collect information from the shop floor and accept commands. With the proper use of the information and commands, it is possible to improve the manufacturing process and to provide detailed machine control.

The more that a factory is automated, the greater is the need for communications. Only by interconnecting all of the devices and by providing mechanisms for their cooperation can the automated factory be made to work. The means of interconnection is the factory local area network [SCHO84, MCGA85, HALL85].

To get some feeling for the requirements for a factory local network, consider the requirements developed by General Motors [STAL88]. GM's specification of a communication network is driven by the sophisticated communications strategy it has evolved to meet its requirements. These requirements reflect those that obtain in other factory and robotics environments. Among the key areas are the following:

- Work force involvement has proven to be a valuable tool for GM's quality and cost-improvement effort. In an attempt to provide facts about the state of the business, employees are told GM's competitive position in relation to quality and costs. This information is communicated by video set-ups at numerous locations in the plant complex.
- An indirect effect on manufacturing costs has been the escalating cost of utilities. To try to control this area, GM measures usage of water, gas, pressurized air, steam, electricity and other resources—often by means of computers and programmable controllers.
- GM is investigating and, in some cases, implementing asynchronous machining and assembly systems that are much more flexible than the traditional systems of the past. To faciliate flexibility, the communication requirements increase an order of magnitude.
- To protect its large investment in facilities, GM uses closed circuit TV surveillance and computerized monitoring systems to warn of fires or other dangers.
- Accounting systems, personnel systems, material and inventory control systems, warranty systems and others use large mainframe computers with remote terminals located throughout the manufacturing facility.
- The nature of process-control and factory environments dictates that communications be extremely reliable and that the maximum time

required to transmit critical control signals and alarms be bounded and known.

To interconnect all of the equipment in a facility, a local network is needed. The requirements listed above dictate the following characteristics of the local network:

- High capacity
- Ability to handle a variety of data traffic
- Large geographic extent
- High reliability
- Ability to specify and control transmission delays.

Integrated Voice and Data Local Networks

In virtually all offices today, the telephone system is separate from any local network that might be used to interconnect data processing devices. With the advent of digital voice technology, the capability now exists to integrate the telephone switching system of a building with the data processing equipment, providing a single local network for both.

Such integrated voice/data networks might simplify network management and control. It will also provide the required networking for the kinds of integrated voice and data devices to be expected in the future. An example is an executive voice/data workstation that provides verbal message storage, voice annotation of text, and automated dialing.

Summary

This section has only scratched the surface of possible applications of local networks. This book focuses on the common principles underlying the design and implementation of all local networks, and so will not pursue the topic of specific applications. Nevertheless, in the course of the book, the reader will gain an appreciation of the variety of uses of local networks.

1.4

INFORMATION DISTRIBUTION

In determining the requirements for local networking, it is important to examine the traffic patterns that are reasonable to expect. Figure 1-4 illustrates the distribution of nonvoice information that has been consistently reported in a number of studies. About half of the information generated within a small unit of an organization (e. g., a department)

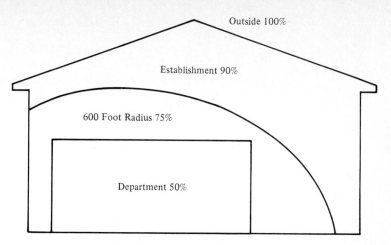

FIGURE 1-4. Information Distribution

remains within that unit. Typically only summary-type information or consolidated data is disseminated beyond the basic unit of an organization. Another 25% is normally shared with peer departments within a somewhat larger grouping (e. g., a division) and the immediate superior of the department. In a typical office layout, this would translate to a radius of about 600 feet. Another 15% goes elsewhere within the organization, such as to other departments within other divisions, central staff organizations, and top management. Finally, only about 10% of the total generated information is distributed beyond the confines of a single building or cluster of buildings. Example destinations include remote corporate headquarters, customers, suppliers, and government agencies.

Another way of looking at local network requirements is to consider the kinds of data processing equipment to be supported. In rough terms, we can group this equipment into three categories:

- *Personal computers and terminals:* the workhorse in most office environments is the microcomputer, including personal computers and workstations. Additionally, when shared systems are present in an organization, terminals are also to be found. Most of this equipment is found at the departmental level, used by individual professionals and secretarial personnel. When used for network applications, the load generated tends to be rather modest.
- *Minicomputers:* minicomputers may function as servers within a department or be shared by users in a number of departments. In many organizations, a number of commonly-used applications will be provided on time-shared minicomputers. Because of this shared use, these machines may generate more substantial traffic than microcomputers.

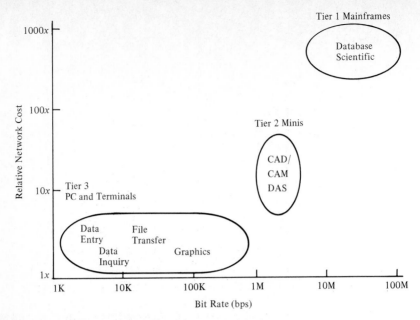

FIGURE 1-5. Office Network Performance Spectrum

- *Mainframes:* for large database and scientific applications, the mainframe is still the machine of choice. When the machines are networked, bulk data transfers dictate that a high-capacity network be used.

Figure 1-5 illustrates the performance spectrum involved. Larger, more expensive machines tend to require a higher data rate on the local network to support them. The higher the data rate, the greater the cost of the network.

The requirements indicated by Figures 1-4 and 1-5 suggest that a single local network will not, in many cases, be the most cost-effective solution. A single network would have to be rather high speed to support the aggregate demand. However, the cost of attachment to a local network tends to increase as a function of the network data rate. Accordingly, a high-speed local network would be very expensive for attachment of low-cost personal computers.

An alternative approach, which is becoming increasingly common, is to employ two or three tiers of local networks (Figure 1-6). Within a department, a low-cost, low-speed local network supports a cluster of microcomputers and terminals. These departmental local networks are then lashed together with a backbone local network of higher capacity. In addition, shared systems are also supported off of this backbone. If mainframes are also part of the office equipment suite, then a separate high-speed local network supports these devices and may be linked, as a whole, to the backbone local network to support a modest amount of traffic

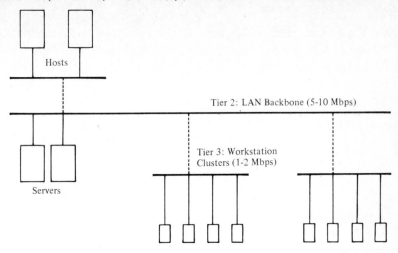

Tier 1: Computer-to-Computer (20-100 Mbps)

Hosts

Tier 2: LAN Backbone (5-10 Mbps)

Tier 3: Workstation
Clusters (1-2 Mbps)

Servers

FIGURE 1-6.   Tiered Local Networks

between the mainframes and other office equipment. We will see that local network standards and products address the need for all three types of local networks.

1.5

OUTLINE OF THE BOOK

This chapter, of course, serves as an introduction to the entire book. A brief synopsis of the remaining chapters follows.

Topics in Data Communications and Computer Networking

This book focuses on a specific aspect of data communications and computer networking. In order to provide context, and to make the book as self-contained as possible, Chapter 2 provides a basic overview of the entire field. The chapter begins with a look at some data communications concepts, including techniques for encoding analog and digital data for both analog and digital signaling, and the concept of multiplexing; the concepts of asynchronous and synchronous transmission are also discussed. The chapter then examines the properties of circuit switching and packet switching. Finally, communications architecture is discussed, using the OSI model as a basis for discussion.

Local Network Technology

The essential technology underlying all forms of local networks comprises topology, transmission medium, and medium access control technique. Chapter 3 provides an overview of the first two of these elements. Four topologies are in common use: star, ring, bus, tree. The most common transmission media for local networking are twisted pair (unshielded and shielded), coaxial cable (baseband and broadband), and optical fiber. These topologies and transmission media are discussed, and the most promising combinations described. The chapter closes with a discussion of various types of local networks.

Local Area Networks

In this book, the term *local area networks* (LAN) is used to refer to local networks that employ a packet broadcasting technique and that have a limited data rate (less than 20 Mbps). Chapter 4 is concerned with the topologies and transmission media used in LANs. The use of twisted pair and coaxial cable in bus/tree LANs is examined first, followed by a discussion of twisted-pair ring LANs. Finally, the chapter examines the emerging use of optical fiber in LANs. The discussion of LANs continues in Chapter 5, which focuses on the protocols needed for stations attached to a LAN to cooperate with each other in the exchange of packets. Specifically, the chapter deals with link control and medium access control protocols. The latter include token-passing and contention-based protocols. An appendix to Chapter 5 summarizes the standard for LANs that have been issued by the IEEE 802 committee.

High-Speed Local Networks

High-speed local networks (HSLNs) are special-purpose local networks designed to meet some specific high-performance requirements, including the support of mainframe computers and providing a backbone for interconnecting a number of LANs. Chapter 6 looks at both coaxial cable and fiber HSLNs, and examines transmission medium and medium access control issues.

Circuit-Switched Local Networks

There is a class of local networks based on the use of circuit switching, including the digital data switch and digital private branch exchange (PBX). Circuit-switching is achieved by the use of time-division switching techniques. Chapter 7 begins with an overview of time-division switching techniques, and then examines their application in digital data switches and digital PBXs.

The Network Interface

A local network is a communications facility that supports a number of attached devices. Each device attaches to the network via a *network interface*. Chapter 8 examines the logic required at this interface. A number of issues, including the use of host-to-front-end protocols, is discussed. The differences in handling terminals and computers are also described.

Network Performance

In a LAN or HSLN, the data rate, length, and medium access control technique of the network are the key factors in determining the effective capacity of the network. Chapter 9 examines performance on LANs and HSLNs, and introduces a key parameter, a, that provides a concise but powerful means of characterizing network performance. The issue of end-to-end performance is also considered. Chapter 10 looks at the rather different issues involved in assessing performance on circuit-switched local networks.

Internetworking

The increasing deployment of local networks has led to an increased need to interconnect local networks with each other and with wide-area networks. Chapter 11 focuses on the three most important devices used in internetworking involving local networks: bridges, routers, and application-level gateways. The protocols and techniques involved in each are examined in some detail.

Local Network Design Issues

Chapter 12 looks at three important design issues related to local networks. First, the issue of network management is examined. The key tasks involved in network management are monitoring and control. Next, reliability is considered. The techniques used with the various types of local networks to improve reliability are examined. Finally, security is discussed. Because a local network is a shared facility, network security becomes a major challenge to the organization. At the same time, the increasing reliance on local networks increases the need for effective network security.

RECOMMENDED READING

There have been a number of survey articles on local networks. Examples are [STAL84]*, [IBM84b], [TSAO84], and [GREG86]. Annotated bibliographies can be found in [STAL88b] and [SHOC80b].

There have been several collections of articles. [STAL88b] is a companion to this text and contains many of the key references used herein; these are indicated by an asterisk when mentioned in the recommended reading section of each chapter. The articles in [KUMM87] cover a variety of topics, including fiber optics, performance, and internetworking. The articles in [PICK86] deal mainly with performance. [FREE85b] is a collection of article about specific commercially-available systems.

[STAL90a] provides a more detailed discussion of applications of local networks. [DERF83] is a less technical treatment of the topic than presented in this text.

1.7

PROBLEMS

1.1   A computer network is an interconnected set of computers and other devices (terminals, printers, etc.) that can communicate and cooperate with each other to perform certain applications. A subset of a computer network is a communications network (sometimes called a subnetwork) that provides the necessary functions for transferring data between network devices. List functions and capabilities that should be part of the subnetwork and those that should be part of the computer network outside the subnetwork.

1.2   On what grounds should a collection of devices connected by point-to-point links be excluded from the definition of local network?

1.3   For each of the items listed in Table 1.2, what factors are key in determining whether the effects will be mostly positive or mostly negative?

1.4   An alternative to a local network for meeting local requirements for data processing and computer applications is a centralized time-sharing system plus a large number of terminals dispersed throughout the local area. What are the major benefits and pitfalls of this approach compared to a local network?

1.5   What are the key factors that determine the response time and throughput performance of a local network? Of a centralized system?

1.6   In what ways is the man-machine interface of a local network likely to differ from that of a centralized system for:

- Application users?
- System operator/manager?

CHAPTER 2

Topics in Data Communications and Computer Networking

The purpose of this chapter is to make this book self-contained for the reader with little or no background in data communications. For the reader with greater interest, references for further study are supplied at the end of the chapter.

2.1

DATA COMMUNICATIONS CONCEPTS

Analog and Digital Data Communications

The terms *analog* and *digital* correspond, roughly, to continuous and discrete, respectively. These two terms are used frequently in data communications in at least three contexts:

- Data
- Signaling
- Transmission

Very briefly, we define *data* as entities that convey meaning. A useful distinction is that data have to do with the form of something; *information*

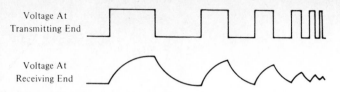

Voltage At
Transmitting End

Voltage At
Receiving End

FIGURE 2-1. Attenuation of Digital Signals

has to do with the content or interpretation of those data. *Signals* are electric or electromagnetic encoding of data. *Signaling* is the act of propagating the signal along some suitable medium. Finally, *transmission* is the communication of data by the propagation and processing of signals. In what follows, we try to make these abstract concepts clear, by discussing the terms "analog" and "digital" in these three contexts.

The concepts of analog and digital data are simple enough. *Analog data* take on continuous values on some interval. For example, voice and video are continuously varying patterns of intensity. Most data collected by sensors, such as temperature and pressure, are continuous-valued. *Digital data* take on discrete values; examples are text and integers.

In a communications system, data are propagated from one point to another by means of electric signals. An *analog signal* is a continuously varying electromagnetic wave that may be transmitted over a variety of media, depending on frequency; examples are wire media, such as twisted pair and coaxial cable, fiber optic cable, and atmosphere or space propagation. A *digital signal* is a sequence of voltage pulses that may be transmitted over a wire medium; for example, a constant positive voltage level may represent binary 1 and a constant negative voltage level may represent binary 0.

The principal advantages of digital signaling are that it is generally cheaper than analog signaling and is less susceptible to noise interference. The principal disadvantage is that digital signals suffer more from attenuation than do analog signals. Figure 2.1 shows a sequence of voltage pulses, generated by a source using two voltage levels, and the received voltage some distance down a conducting medium. Because of the attenuation or reduction of signal strength at higher frequencies, the pulses become rounded and smaller. It should be clear that this attenuation can rather quickly lead to the loss of the information contained in the propagated signal.

Both analog and digital data can be represented, and hence propagated, by either analog or digital signals. This is illustrated in Figure 2.2. Generally, analog data are a function of time and occupy a limited frequency spectrum. Such data can be directly represented by an electromagnetic signal occupying the same spectrum. The best example of this is voice data. As sound waves, voice data have frequency components in the range 20 Hz

Analog Signals — Represent data with continuously varying electromagnetic wave

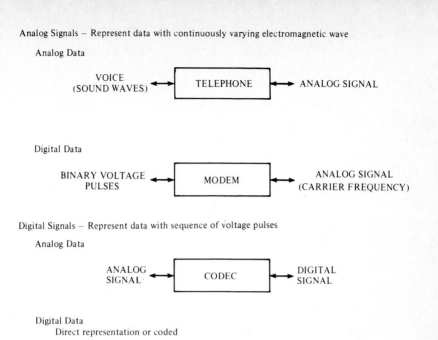

FIGURE 2-2. **Analog and Digital Signaling for Analog and Digital Data**

to 20 kHz. However, most of the speech energy is in a much narrower range. The standard spectrum of voice signals is 300 to 3400 Hz, and this is quite adequate to propagate speech intelligibly and clearly. The telephone instrument does just that. For all sound input in the range of 300 to 3400 Hz, an electromagnetic signal with the same frequency-amplitude pattern is produced. The process is performed in reverse to convert the electromagnetic energy back into sound.

Digital data can also be represented by analog signals by use of a *modem* (modulator/demodulator). The modem converts a series of binary (two-valued) voltage pulses into an analog signal by modulating a *carrier frequency*. The resulting signal occupies a certain spectrum of frequency centered about the carrier and may be propagated across a medium suitable for that carrier. The most common modems represent digital data in the voice spectrum and hence allow those data to be propagated over ordinary voice-grade telephone lines. At the other end of the line, a modem demodulates the signal to recover the original data. Various modulation techniques are discussed below.

In an operation very similar to that performed by a modem, analog data can be represented by digital signals. The device that performs this function for voice data is a *codec* (coder-decoder). In essence, the codec takes an analog signal that directly represents the voice data and approximates that signal by a bit stream. At the other end of a line, the bit stream is used to reconstruct the analog data.

Finally, digital data can be represented directly, in binary form, by two voltage levels. To improve propagation characteristics, however, the binary data are often encoded, as explained below.

A final distinction remains to be made. Both analog and digital signals may be transmitted on suitable transmission media. The way these signals are treated is a function of the transmission system. Table 2.1 summarizes the methods of data transmission. Analog transmission is a means of transmitting analog signals without regard to their content; the signals may represent analog data (e. g., voice) or digital data (e. g., data that pass through a modem). In either case, the analog signal will attenuate after a certain distance. To achieve longer distances, the analog transmission system includes amplifiers that boost the energy in the signal. Unfortunately, the amplifier also boosts the noise components. With amplifiers cascaded to achieve long distances, the signal becomes more and more distorted. For analog data, such as voice, quite a bit of distortion can be tolerated and the data remain intelligible. However, for digital data, cascaded amplifiers will introduce errors.

Digital transmission, in contrast, is concerned with the content of the signal. We have mentioned that a digital signal can be transmitted only a limited distance before attenuation endangers the integrity of the data. To achieve greater distances, repeaters are used. A repeater receives the digital signal, recovers the pattern of 1's and 0's, and retransmits a new signal. Thus the attenuation is overcome.

TABLE 2.1   Analog and Digital Transmission

(a) Treatment of Signals

	Analog Transmission	Digital Transmission
Analog Signal	Is propagated through amplifiers; same treatment for both analog and digital data	Assumes digital data; at propagation points, data in signal are recovered and new analog signal is generated
Digital Signal	Not used	Repeaters retransmit new signal; same treatment for both analog and digital data

(b) Possible Combinations

	Analog Transmission	Digital Transmission
Analog Signal	Analog signal	Digital signal
Digital Signal	Analog signal	Digital signal Analog signal

The same technique may be used with an analog signal if it is assumed that the signal carries digital data. At appropriately spaced points, the transmission system has retransmission devices rather than amplifiers. The retransmission device recovers the digital data from the analog signal and generates a new, clean analog signal. Thus noise is not cumulative.

For long-haul communications, digital signaling is not as versatile and practical as analog signaling. For example, digital signaling is impossible for satellite and microwave systems. However, digital transmission is superior to analog, both in terms of cost and quality, and wide-area communications systems are gradually converting to digital transmission for both voice and digital data.

We will see that, in local networks, the trade-offs do not always lead to the same solutions as for wide-area communications. It is still true, within the local context, that digital techniques tend to be cheaper because of the declining cost of digital circuitry. However, the limited distances of local networks limit the severity of the noise and attenuation problems, and the cost and quality of analog techniques approach those of digital. Consequently, there is a secure place for analog signaling and analog transmission in local networks.

Data Encoding Techniques

As we have pointed out, data, either analog or digital, must be converted into a signal for purposes of transmission.

In the case of **digital data**, different signal elements are used to represent binary 1 and binary 0. The mapping from binary digits to signal elements is the *encoding scheme* used for transmission. To understand the significance of the encoding scheme, consider that there are two important tasks in interpreting signals (analog or digital) that carry digital data at the receiver. First, the receiver must know when a bit begins and ends, so that the receiver may sample the incoming signal once per bit time. Second, the receiver must recognize the value of each bit. A number of factors determine how successful the receiver will be in interpreting the incoming signal. For example, the greater the strength of the signal, the more it will withstand attenuation and the more it will stand out from any noise that is present. Also, the higher the data rate, the more difficult the receiver's task is, since each bit occupies a smaller amount of time: the receiver must be more careful about sampling properly and will have less time to make decisions. Finally, the encoding scheme will affect receiver performance. We will describe a number of different encoding techniques for converting digital data to both analog and digital signals.

In the case of **analog data**, the encoding scheme will also affect transmission performance. In this case, we are concerned about the quality, or fidelity, of the transmission. That is, we would like the received data to be as close as possible to the transmitted data. For the purposes of this text, we are concerned about the encoding of analog data in digital form, and techniques for this encoding are presented below.

Digital Data, Analog Signals

The basis for analog signaling is a continuous constant-frequency signal known as the *carrier signal*. Digital data are encoded by modulating one of the three characteristics of the carrier: amplitude, frequency, or phase, or some combination of these. Figure 2.3 illustrates the three basic forms of modulation of analog signals for digital data:

- Amplitude-shift keying (ASK)
- Frequency-shift keying (FSK)
- Phase-shift keying (PSK)

In all these cases, the resulting signal contains a range of frequencies on both sides of the carrier frequency. That range is referred to as the *bandwidth* of the signal.

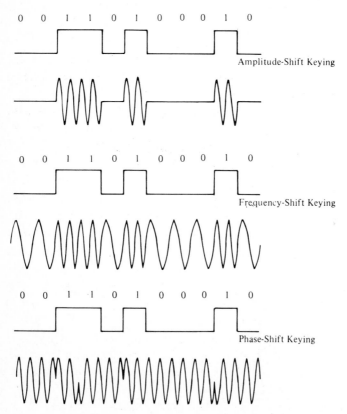

FIGURE 2-3.   Modulation of Analog Signals for Digital Data

**TOPICS IN DATA COMMUNICATIONS AND
COMPUTER NETWORKING**

In ASK, the two binary values are represented by two different amplitudes of the carrier frequency. In some cases, one of the amplitudes is zero; that is, one binary digit is represented by the presence, at constant amplitude, of the carrier, the other by the absence of the carrier. ASK is susceptible to sudden gain changes and is a rather inefficient modulation technique. On voice-grade lines, it is typically used only up to 1200 bps.

In FSK, the two binary values are represented by two different frequencies near the carrier frequency. This scheme is less susceptible to error than ASK. On voice grade lines, it is typically used up to 1200 bps. It is also commonly used for high frequency (3 to 30 MHz) radio transmission. It can also be used at even higher frequencies on local networks that use coaxial cable.

Figure 2.4 shows an example of the use of FSK for full-duplex operation over a voice-grade line. *Full duplex* means that data can be transmitted in both directions at the same time. To accomplish this, one bandwidth is used for sending, another for receiving. The figure is a specification for the Bell System 108 series modems. In one direction (transmit or receive), the modem passes frequencies in the range 300 to 1700 Hz. The two frequencies used to represent 1 and 0 are centered on 1170 Hz, with a shift of 100 Hz on either side. Similarly, for the other direction (receive or transmit) the modem passes 1700 to 3000 Hz and uses a center frequency of 2125 Hz. The shaded area around each pair of frequencies indicates the actual bandwidth of each signal. Note that there is little overlap and thus little interference.

In PSK, the phase of the carrier signal is shifted to represent data. Figure 2.3 shows an example of a two-phase system. In this system, a 0 is represented by sending a signal burst of the same phase as the previous signal burst sent. A 1 is represented by sending a signal burst of opposite phase to the previous one. PSK can use more than two phase shifts. A four-phase system would encode two bits with each signal burst. The PSK technique is more noise resistant and efficient than FSK; on a voice-grade line, rates up to 9600 bps are achieved.

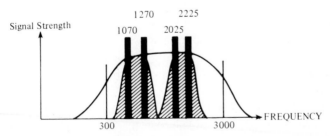

FIGURE 2-4.   Full-Duplex FSK Transmission on a Voice-Grade Line

Finally, the techniques discussed above may be combined. A common combination is PSK and ASK, where some or all of the phase shifts may occur at one of two amplitudes.

Digital Data, Digital Signals

Although a common means of transmitting digital data is to pass it through a modem and transmit it as an analog signal, we will see that the transmission of digital data as digital signals is the technique used in a number of local networks. The use of digital signals may be less expensive and, under some circumstances, provide better performance than analog signaling. In this subsection, we consider two families of coding techniques: NRZ codes and biphase codes.

With **Nonreturn-to-Zero (NRZ) codes**, two different voltage levels, one positive and one negative, are used as the signal elements for the two binary digits. The name refers to the fact that the voltage level never returns to zero, but is always positive or negative. NRZ is the most common, and easiest, way to transmit digital signals. However, we shall see that its use is not appropriate for local networks.

Figure 2-5a shows the use of a constant negative voltage to represent binary 1 and a constant positive voltage to represent binary 0. This code is known as **NRZ-L** (NRZ-level). This code is often used for very short connections, such as between a terminal and a modem or a terminal and a nearby computer.

A variation on NRZ is **NRZI** (NRZ, invert on ones). As with NRZ-L, NRZI maintains a constant voltage pulse for the duration of a bit time. The data itself is encoded as the presence or absence of a signal transition at the beginning of the bit time. A transition (low-to-high or high-to-low) at the beginning of a bit time denotes a binary 1 for that bit time; no transition indicates a binary 0 (Figure 2-5b).

NRZI is an example of differential encoding. In differential encoding, the signal is decoded by comparing the polarity of adjacent signal elements rather than determining the absolute value of a signal element. One benefit of this scheme is that it may be more reliable to detect a transition in the presence of noise than to compare a value to a threshold. Another benefit is that with a complex transmission layout, it is easy to lose the sense of the polarity of the signal. For example, on a twisted-pair medium, if the leads from an attached device to the twisted pair are accidentally inverted, all ones and zeros will be inverted. This cannot happen with differential encoding.

There are several disadvantages to NRZ transmission. It is difficult to determine where one bit ends and another begins. To picture the problem, consider that with a long string of 1's or 0's for NRZ-L, the output is a

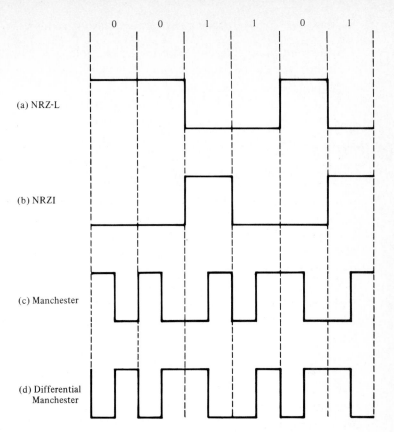

FIGURE 2-5. Digital Signal Encoding

constant voltage over a long period of time. Under these circumstances, any drift between the timing of transmitter and receiver will result in the loss of synchronization between the two. Also, there is a direct-current (dc) component during each bit time that may accumulate if positive or negative pulses predominate. Thus, alternating-current (ac) coupling, which uses a transformer and provides excellent electrical isolation between data communicating devices and their environment, is not possible. Furthermore, the dc component can cause plating or other deterioration at attachment contacts.

There is a set of alternative coding techniques, grouped under the term **biphase codes**, which overcomes these problems. Two of these techniques, Manchester and Differential Manchester, are in common use for local networks. All of the biphase techniques require at least one transition per bit time and may have as many as two transitions. Thus, the maximum modulation rate is twice that for NRZ; this means that the bandwidth or transmission capacity required is correspondingly greater. To compensate for this, the biphase schemes have several advantages:

- *Synchronization:* Because there is a predictable transition during each bit time, the receiver can synchronize on that transition. For this reason, the biphase codes are known as self-clocking codes.
- *No dc component:* Because of the transition in each bit time, biphase codes have no dc component, yielding the benefits just described.
- *Error detection:* The absence of an expected transition can be used to detect errors. Noise on the line would have to invert both the signal before and after the expected transition to cause an undetected error.

In the **Manchester** code (Figure 2-5c), there is a transition at the middle of each bit period. The mid-bit transition serves as a clock and also as data: a low-to-high transition represents a 1, and a high-to-low transition represents a 0. In **Differential Manchester** (Figure 2-5d), the mid-bit transition is used only to provide clocking. The encoding of a 0 is represented by the presence of a transition at the beginning of a bit period, and a 1 is represented by the absence of a transition at the beginning of a bit period. Differential Manchester exhibits the further advantage of being a differential encoding technique.

Analog Data, Digital Signals

The most common example of the use of digital signals to encode analog data is *pulse code modulation* (PCM), which is used to encode voice signals. This section describes PCM and then looks briefly at a similar, less used scheme, *Delta Modulation* (DM).

PCM is based on the sampling theorem, which states [JORD85]:

If a signal $f(t)$ is sampled at regular intervals of time and at a rate higher than twice the highest significant signal frequency, then the samples contain all the information of the original signal. The function $f(t)$ may be reconstructed from these samples by the use of a low-pass filter.

If voice data are limited to frequencies below 4000 Hz, a conservative procedure for intelligibility, then 8000 samples per second would be sufficient to completely characterize the voice signal. Note, however, that these are analog samples. To convert to digital, each of these analog samples must be assigned a binary code. Figure 2.6 shows an example in which each sample is approximated by being "quantized" into one of 16 different levels. Each sample can then be represented by four bits. Of course, it is now impossible to recover the original signal exactly. By using a 7-bit sample, which allows 128 quantizing levels, the quality of the recovered voice signal is comparable to that achieved via analog transmission. Note that this implies that a data rate of 8000 samples per second $\times$ 7 bits per sample = 56 kbps is needed for a single voice signal.

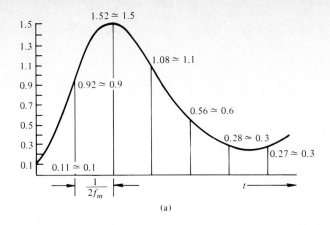

(a)

Digit	Binary equivalent	Pulse-code waveform
0	0000	
1	0001	
2	0010	
3	0011	
4	0100	
5	0101	
6	0110	
7	0111	
8	1000	
9	1001	
10	1010	
11	1011	
12	1100	
13	1101	
14	1110	
15	1111	

(b)

FIGURE 2-6.   Pulse Code Modulation

Typically, the PCM scheme is refined using a technique known as *non-linear encoding*, which means, in effect, that the 128 quantization levels are not equally spaced. The problem with equal spacing is that the mean absolute error for each sample is the same, regardless of signal level. Consequently, lower-amplitude values are relatively more distorted. By using a greater number of quantizing steps for signals of low amplitude, and a small number of quantizing steps for signals of large amplitude, a marked reduction in overall signal distortion is achieved.

PCM can, of course, be used for other than voice signals. For example, a color TV signal has a useful bandwidth of 4.6 MHz, and reasonable quality can be achieved with 10-bit samples, for a data rate of 92 Mbps.

With DM, a bit stream is produced by approximating the derivative of an analog signal rather than its amplitude. A 1 is generated if the current sample is greater in amplitude than the immediately preceding sample; a 0 is generated otherwise. For equal data rates, DM is comparable to PCM in terms of signal quality. Note that for equal data rates, DM requires a higher sampling rate: a 56-kbps voice signal is generated from 8000 PCM samples per second but 56,000 DM samples per second. In general, DM systems are less complex and less expensive than comparable PCM systems. A discussion of these and other encoding schemes can be found in [CROC83] and [JAYA84].

Multiplexing

In both local and long-haul communications, it is almost always the case that the capacity of the transmission medium exceeds that required for the transmission of a single signal. To make cost-effective use of the transmission system, it is desirable to use the medium efficiently by having it carry multiple signals simultaneously. This is referred to as *multiplexing*, and two techniques are in common use: frequency-division multiplexing (FDM) and time-division multiplexing (TDM).

FDM takes advantage of the fact that the useful bandwidth of the medium exceeds the required bandwidth of a given signal. A number of signals can be carried simultaneously if each signal is modulated onto a different carrier frequency, and the carrier frequencies are sufficiently separated that the bandwidths of the signals do not overlap. A simple example of FDM is full-duplex FSK transmission (Figure 2.4). A general case of FDM is shown in Figure 2.7a. Six signal sources are fed into a multiplexer, which modulates each signal onto a different frequency $(f_1, \ldots, f_6)$. Each signal requires a certain bandwidth centered around its carrier frequency, referred to as a *channel*. To prevent interference, the channels are separated by guard bands, which are unused portions of the spectrum.

An example is the multiplexing of voice signals. We mentioned that the useful spectrum for voice is 300 to 3400 Hz. Thus a bandwidth of 4 kHz is adequate to carry the voice signal and provide a guard band. For both North America (Bell System standard) and internationally [Consultative Committee on International Telegraphy and Telephony (CCITT) standard], a standard voice multiplexing scheme is twelve 4-kHz voice channels from 60 to 108 kHz. For higher-capacity links, both Bell and CCITT define larger groupings of 4-kHz channels.

TDM takes advantage of the fact that the achievable bit rate (sometimes, unfortunately, called bandwidth) of the medium exceeds the required data rate of a digital signal. Multiple digital signals can be carried on

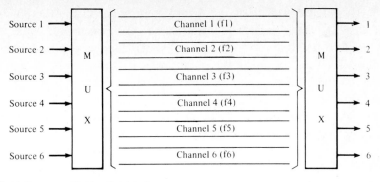

(a) Frequency-Division Multiplexing

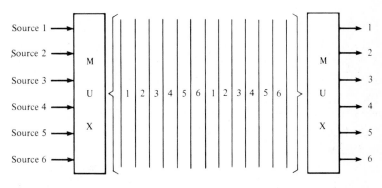

(b) Time-Division Multiplexing

FIGURE 2-7.   Multiplexing

a single transmission path by interleaving portions of each signal in time. The interleaving can be at the bit level or in blocks of bytes or larger quantities. For example, the multiplexer in Figure 2.7b has six inputs which might each be, say, 9.6 kbps. A single line with a capacity of 57.6 kbps could accommodate all six sources. Analogously to FDM, the sequence of time slots dedicated to a particular source is called a *channel*. One cycle of time slots (one per source) is called a *frame*.

The TDM scheme depicted in Figure 2.7 is also known as *synchronous TDM*, referring to the fact that time slots are preassigned and fixed. Hence the timing of transmission from the various sources is synchronized. In contrast, asynchronous TDM allows time on the medium to be allocated dynamically. Examples of this will be discussed later. Unless otherwise noted, the term TDM will be used to mean synchronous TDM only.

One example of TDM is the standard scheme used for transmitting PCM voice data, known in Bell parlance as *T1 carrier*. Data are taken from each source, one sample (7 bits) at a time. An eighth bit is added for signaling and supervisory functions. For T1, 24 sources are multiplexed, so there are

$8 \times 24 = 192$ bits of data and control signals per frame. One final bit is added for establishing and maintaining synchronization. Thus a frame consists of 193 bits and contains one 7-bit sample per source. Since sources must be sampled 8000 times per second, the required data rate is $8000 \times 193 = 1.544$ Mbps. As with voice FDM, higher data rates are defined for larger groupings.

TDM is not limited to digital signals. Analog signals can also be interleaved in time. Also, with analog signals, a combination of TDM and FDM is possible. A transmission system can be frequency-divided into a number of channels, each of which is further divided via TDM. This technique is possible with broadband local networks, discussed in Chapter 4.

Asynchronous and Synchronous Transmission

A fundamental requirement of digital data communication (analog or digital signal) is that the receiver knows the starting time and duration of each bit that it receives.

The earliest and simplest scheme for meeting this requirement is asynchronous transmission. In this scheme, data are transmitted one character (of 5 to 8 bits) at a time. Each character is preceded by a start code and followed by a stop code (Figure 2.8a). The *start code* has the encoding for 0 and a duration of one bit time; in other words, the start code is one bit with a value of zero. The *stop code* has a value of 1, and a minimum duration, depending on the system, of from one to two bit times. When there are no data to send, the transmitter sends a continuous stop code. The receiver identifies the beginning of a new character by the transition from 1 to 0. The receiver must have a fairly accurate idea of the duration of each bit in order to recover all the bits of the character. However, a small amount of drift (e.g., 1% per bit) will not matter since the receiver resynchronizes

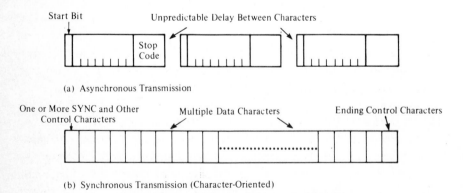

(a) Asynchronous Transmission

(b) Synchronous Transmission (Character-Oriented)

FIGURE 2-8. Asynchronous and Synchronous Transmission

with each stop code. This means of communication is simple and cheap, but requires an overhead of 2 to 3 bits per character. This technique is referred to as *asynchronous* because characters are sent independently from each other. Thus characters may be sent at a nonuniform rate.

A more efficient means of communication is synchronous transmission. In this mode, blocks of characters or bits are transmitted without start and stop codes, and the exact departure or arrival time of each bit is predictable. To prevent timing drift between transmitter and receiver, their clocks must somehow be synchronized. One possibility is to provide a separate clock line between transmitter and receiver. Otherwise, the clocking information must be embedded in the data signal. For digital signals, this can be achieved with biphase encoding. For analog signals, a number of techniques can be used; the carrier frequency itself can be used to synchronize the receiver based on the phase of the carrier.

With synchronous transmission, there is another level of synchronization required, to allow the receiver to determine the beginning and end of a block of data. To achieve this, each block begins with a *preamble* bit pattern and ends with *postamble* bit pattern. The data plus preamble and postamble is called a *frame*. The nature of the preamble and postamble depends on whether the block of data is character-oriented or bit-oriented.

With *character-oriented* schemes, each block is preceded by one or more "synchronization characters" (Figure 2.8b). The synchronization character, usually called *SYNC*, is chosen such that its bit pattern is significantly different from any of the regular characters being transmitted. The postamble is another unique character. The receiver thus is alerted to an incoming block of data by the SYNC characters and accepts data until the postamble character is seen. The receiver can then look for the next SYNC pattern.

Character-oriented schemes, such as IBM's BISYNC, are gradually being replaced by more efficient and flexible *bit-oriented schemes*, which treat the block of data as a bit stream rather than a character stream. The preamble-postamble principle is the same, with one difference. Since the data are assumed to be an arbitrary bit pattern, there is no assurance that the preamble or postamble pattern will not appear in the data. This event would destroy the higher-level synchronization.

For example, two common bit-oriented schemes, HDLC and SDLC, use the pattern 01111110 (called a *flag*) as both preamble and postamble. To avoid the appearance of this pattern in the data stream, the transmitter will always insert an extra 0 bit after each occurrence of five 1's in the data to be transmitted. When the receiver detects a sequence of five 1's, it examines the next bit. If the bit is 0, the receiver deletes it. This procedure is known as *bit stuffing*. HDLC is examined in more detail in Section 2.3.

COMMUNICATION SWITCHING TECHNIQUES

So far we have discussed how data can be encoded and transmitted over a communication link. In its simplest form, data communication takes place between two devices that are directly connected by some form of transmission medium (many of these media are described in Chapter 3). Often, however, it is impractical for two devices to be directly connected. This is so for one (or both) of the following contingencies:

- The devices are very far apart. It would be inordinately expensive, for example, to string a dedicated link between two devices thousands of miles apart.
- There is a set of devices, each of which may require a link to many of the others at various times. Examples are all of the telephones in the world and all of the terminals and computers owned by a single organization. Except for the case of a very few devices, it is impractical to provide a dedicated wire between each pair of devices.

The solution to this problem is to attach each device to a communication network. Communication is achieved by transmitting data from source to destination through a network of intermediate nodes. These nodes are not concerned with the content of the data; rather, their purpose is to provide a switching facility that will move the data from node to node until they reach their destination. Figure 2.9 illustrates the situation. We have a

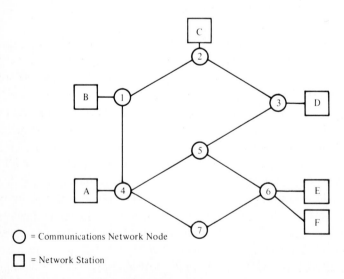

FIGURE 2-9. Generic Switching Network

collection of devices that wish to communicate; we will refer to them generically as *stations*. The stations may be computers, terminals, telephones, or other communicating devices. We also have a collection of devices whose purpose is to provide communications, which we will refer to as *nodes*. The nodes are connected to each other in some fashion by transmission links. Each station attaches to a node. The collection of nodes is referred to as a *communications network*. If the attached devices are computers and terminals, then the collection of nodes plus stations is referred to as a *computer network*.

Three switching techniques are in common use:

- Circuit switching
- Message switching
- Packet switching

Circuit Switching

Communication via circuit switching implies that there is a dedicated communication path between two stations. That path is a connected sequence of links between nodes. On each physical link, a channel is dedicated to the connection. The most common example of circuit switching is the telephone network.

Communication via circuit switching involves three phases, which can be explained with reference to Figure 2.9.

1. *Circuit establishment:* Before any data can be transmitted, an end-to-end (station-to-station) circuit must be established. For example, station A sends a request to node 4 requesting a connection to station E. Typically, the circuit from A to 4 is a dedicated line, so that part of the connection already exists. Node 4 must find the next leg in a route leading to node 6. Based on routing information and measures of availability and perhaps cost, node 4 selects the circuit to node 5, allocates a free channel (using TDM or FDM) on that circuit and sends a message requesting connection to E. So far, a dedicated path has been established from A through 4 to 5. Since a number of stations may attach to 4, it must be able to establish internal paths from multiple stations to multiple nodes. How this is done is explained in Chapter 7. The remainder of the process proceeds similarly. Node 5 dedicates a channel to node 6 and internally ties that channel to the channel from node 4. Node 6 completes the connection to E. In completing the connection, a test is made to determine if E is busy or is prepared to accept the connection.
2. *Data transfer:* Signals can now be transmitted from A through the network to E. The data may be digital (e.g., terminal to host) or analog

(e.g., voice). The signaling and transmission may each be either digital or analog. In any case, the path is: A-4 circuit, internal switching through 4, 4-5 channel, internal switching through 5, 5-6 channel, internal switching through 6, 6-E circuit. Generally, the connection is full duplex, and data may be transmitted in both directions.

3. *Circuit disconnect:* After some period of data transfer, the connection is terminated, usually by the action of one of the two stations. Signals must be propagated to 4, 5, and 6 to deallocate the dedicated resources.

Note that the connection path is established before data transmission begins. Thus channel capacity must be available and reserved between each pair of nodes in the path, and each node must have internal switching capacity to handle the connection. The switches must have the intelligence to make these allocations and to devise a route through the network.

Circuit switching can be rather inefficient. Channel capacity is dedicated for the duration of a connection, even if no data are being transferred. For a voice connection, utilization may be rather high, but it still does not approach 100%. For a terminal-to-computer connection, the capacity may be idle during most of the time of the connection. In terms of performance, there is a delay prior to data transfer for call establishment. However, once the circuit is established, the network is effectively transparent to the users. Data are transmitted at a fixed data rate with no delay other than the propagation delay through the transmission links. The delay at each node is negligible.

Message Switching

Circuit switching is an appropriate and easily used technique in the case of data exchanges that involve a relatively continuous flow, such as voice (telephone) and some forms of sensor and telemetry input. However, circuit switching does have two drawbacks:

- Both stations must be available at the same time for the data exchange.
- Resources must be available and dedicated through the network between the two stations, with the inefficiency mentioned above.

An alternative approach, which is generally appropriate to digital data exchange, is to exchange logical units of data, called messages. Examples of messages are telegrams, electronic mail, computer files, and transaction queries and responses. If one thinks of data exchange as a sequence of messages being transmitted in both directions between stations, then a very different approach, known as message switching, can be used.

With *message switching*, it is not necessary to establish a dedicated path between two stations. Rather, if a station wishes to send a message (a logical unit of information) it appends a destination address to the message. The message is then passed through the network from node to node. At each node, the entire message is received, stored briefly, and then transmitted to the next node.

In a circuit-switching network, each node is an electronic or perhaps electromechanical switching device (as described in Chapter 7) which transmits bits as fast as it receives them. A message-switching node is typically a general-purpose minicomputer, with sufficient storage to buffer messages as they come in. A message is delayed at each node for the time required to receive all bits of the message plus a queuing delay waiting for an opportunity to retransmit to the next node.

Again using Figure 2.9, consider a message from A to E. A appends E's address to the message and sends it to node 4. Node 4 stores the message and determines the next leg of the route (say to 5). Then node 4 queues the message for transmission over the 4-5 link. When the link is available, the message is transmitted to node 5, which will forward the message to node 6, and finally to E. This system is also known as a *store-and-forward* message system. In some cases, the node to which the station attaches, or some central node, also files the message, creating a permanent record.

A number of advantages of this approach over circuit switching are listed in [MART76]:

- Line efficiency is greater, since a single node-to-node channel can be shared by many messages over time. For the same traffic volume, less total transmission capacity is needed.
- Simultaneous availability of sender and receiver is not required. The network can store the message pending the availability of the receiver.
- When traffic becomes heavy on a circuit-switched network, some calls are blocked. On a message-switched network, messages are still accepted, but delivery delay increases.
- A message-switching system can send one message to many destinations. This facility is not easily provided by a circuit-switched network.
- Message priorities can be established.
- Error control and recovery procedures on a message basis can be built into the network.
- A message-switching network can carry out speed and code conversion. Two stations of different data rates can be connected since each connects to its node at its proper data rate. The message-switching network can also easily convert format (e.g., from ASCII to EBCDIC). These features are less often found in a circuit-switched system.
- Messages sent to inoperative terminals may be intercepted and either stored or rerouted to other terminals.

The primary disadvantage of message switching is that it is not suited to real-time or interactive traffic. The delay through the network is relatively long and has relatively high variance. Thus it cannot be used for voice connections. Nor is it suited to interactive terminal-host connections.

Packet Switching

Packet switching represents an attempt to combine the advantages of message and circuit switching while minimizing the disadvantages of both. In situations where there is a substantial volume of traffic among a number of stations, this objective is met.

Packet switching is very much like message switching. The principal external difference is that the length of the units of data that may be transmitted is limited in a packet-switched network. A typical maximum length is 1000 to a few thousand bits. Message switching systems accommodate far larger messages. From a station's point of view, then, messages above the maximum length must be divided into smaller units and sent out one at a time. To distinguish the two techniques, the data units in the latter system are referred to as *packets*.

Again using Figure 2.9 for an example, consider the transfer of a single packet. The packet contains data plus a destination address. Station A transmits the packet to 4, which stores it briefly and then passes it to 5, which passes it to 6, and on to E. One difference from message switching is that packets are typically not filed. A copy may be temporarily stored for error recovery purposes, but that is all.

On its face, packet switching may seem a strange procedure to adopt, with no particular advantage over message switching. Remarkably, the simple expedient of limiting the maximum size of a data unit to a rather small length has a dramatic effect on performance. Before demonstrating this, we define two common procedures for handling entire messages over a packet-switched network.

The problem is this. A station has a message to send that is of length greater than the maximum packet size. It breaks the message into packets and sends these packets to its node. Question: How will the network handle this stream of packets? There are two approaches: datagram and virtual circuit.

In the *datagram* approach, each packet is treated independently, just as each message is treated independently in a message-switched network. Let us consider the implications of this approach. Suppose that station A has a 3-packet message to send to E. It pops the packets out, 1-2-3, to node 4. On *each* packet, node 4 must make a routing decision. Packet 1 comes in and node 4 determines that its queue of packets for node 5 is shorter than for node 7, so it queues the packet for node 5. Ditto for packet 2. But for packet 3, node 4 finds that its queue for node 7 is shortest and so queues packet 3 for that node. So the packets, each with the same destination address, do not all follow the same route. Furthermore, it is just possible that packet 3 will beat packet 2 to node 6. Thus it is possible that the packets will be delivered to E in a different sequence from the one in which they were sent. It is up to E to figure out how to reorder them. In this technique each packet, treated independently, is referred to as a "datagram."

In the *virtual circuit* approach, a *logical* connection is established before any packets are sent. For example, suppose that A has one or more messages to send to E. It first sends a Call Request packet to 4, requesting a connection to E. Node 4 decides to route the request *and* all subsequent data to 5, which decides to route the request and all subsequent data to 6, which finally delivers the Call Request packet to E. If E is prepared to accept the connection, it sends out a Call Accept packet to 6. This packet is passed back through nodes 5 and 4 to A. Stations A and E may now exchange data over the logical connection or virtual circuit that has been established. Each packet now contains a virtual circuit identifier as well as data. Each node on the preestablished route knows where to direct such packets; no routing decisions are required. Thus every data packet from A traverses nodes 4, 5, and 6; every data packet from E traverses nodes 6, 5, and 4. Eventually, one of the stations terminates the connection with a Clear Request packet. At any time, each station can have more than one virtual circuit to any other station and can have virtual circuits to more than one station.

So the main characteristic of the virtual circuit technique is that a route between stations is set up prior to data transfer. Note that this does *not* mean that there is a dedicated path, as in circuit switching. A packet is still buffered at each node, and queued for output over a line. The difference from the datagram approach is that the node need not make a routing decision for each packet. It is made only once for each connection.

If two stations wish to exchange data over an extended period of time, there are certain advantages to virtual circuits. They all have to do with relieving the stations of unnecessary communications processing functions. A virtual circuit facility may provide a number of services, including sequencing, error control, and flow control. We emphasize the word "may" because not all virtual circuit facilities will provide all these services completely reliably. With that proviso, we define terms. *Sequencing* refers to the fact that, since all packets follow the same route, they arrive in the original order. *Error control* is a service that assures not only that packets arrive in proper sequence, but that all packets arrive correctly. For example, if a packet in a sequence fails to arrive at node 6, or arrives with an error, it can request a retransmission of that packet from node 4. Finally, *flow control* is a technique for assuring that a sender does not overwhelm a receiver with data. For example, if station E is buffering data from A and perceives that it is about to run out of buffer space, it can request, via the virtual circuit facility, that A suspend transmission until further notice.

One advantage of the datagram approach is that call setup phase is avoided. Thus if a station wishes to send only one or a few packets, datagram delivery will be quicker. Another advantage of the datagram

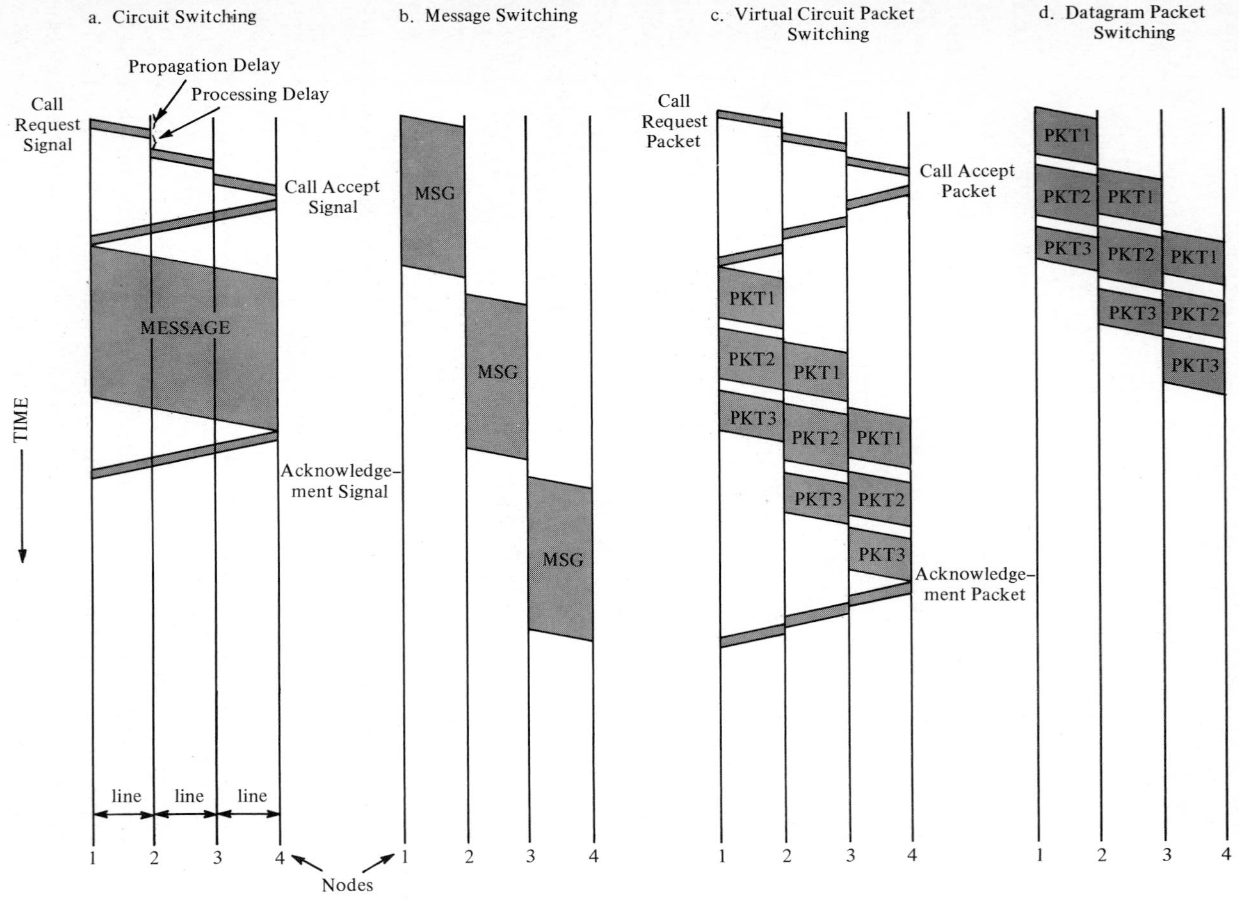

FIGURE 2-10. Event Timing for Various Communication Switching Techniques

TOPICS IN DATA COMMUNICATIONS AND COMPUTER NETWORKING

service is that, because it is more primitive, it is more flexible. A good example of this is the use of the datagram approach of internetworking, a topic explored in Chapter 11. A third advantage is that datagram delivery is inherently more reliable. If a node fails, all virtual circuits that pass through that node are lost. With datagram delivery, if a node is lost, packets may find alternate routes.

We now return to the question of performance, illustrating the techniques discussed in Figure 2.10. This figure intends to suggest the relative performance of the techniques; however, actual performance depends on a host of factors, including:

- Number of stations
- Number and arrangement of nodes
- Total load on system
- Length (in time and data) of typical exchange between two stations

And more. Given the difficulty of comparing these methods, we hazard a few observations.

- For interactive traffic, message switching is not appropriate.
- For light and/or intermittent loads, circuit switching is the most cost effective, since the public telephone system can be used, via dial-up lines.
- For very heavy and sustained loads between two stations, a leased circuit-switched line is the most cost effective.
- Packet switching is to be preferred when there is a collection of devices that must exchange a moderate to heavy amount of data; line utilization is most efficient with this technique.
- Datagram packet switching is good for short messages and for flexibility.
- Virtual circuit packet switching is good for long exchanges and for relieving stations of processing burden.

Table 2.2 summarizes the main features of the four techniques that we have discussed.

As a final point, we mention one common means of making packet-switched networks cost effective, and that is to provide a public connection service. Examples of such networks in the United States are TELENET and TYMNET. The network consists of nodes owned by the network service provider and linked together by leased channels from common carriers such as AT&T. Subscribers pay fees for attaching to the network and for transmitting packets through it. Whereas individual subscribers may not have sufficient traffic to make a packet-switched network economically feasible, the total demand of all subscribers justifies the network. These networks are referred to as value-added networks (VANs) because they take a basic long-haul transmission service (e.g., AT&T) and add value (the packet-switching logic). In most other countries, there is a single national-monopoly network, called a *public data network* (PDN).

TABLE 2.2 Comparison of Communication Switching Techniques

Circuit Switching	Message Switching	Datagram Packet Switching	Virtual Circuit Packet Switching
Dedicated transmission path	No dedicated path	No dedicated path	No dedicated path
Continuous transmission of data	Transmission of messages	Transmission of packets	Transmission of packets
Fast enough for interactive	Too slow for interactive	Fast enough for interactive	Fast enough for interactive
Messages are not stored	Messages are filed for later retrieval	Packets may be stored until delivered	Packets stored until delivered
Path is established for entire conversation	Route established for each message	Route established for each packet	Route established for entire conversation
Call setup delay; negligible transmission delay	Message transmission delay	Packet transmission delay	Call setup delay; packet transmission delay
Busy signal if called party busy	No busy signal	Sender may be notified if packet not delivered	Sender notified of connection denial
Overload may block call setup; no delay for established calls	Overload increases message delay	Overload increases packet delay	Overload may block call setup; increases packet delay
Electromechanical or computerized switching nodes	Message switch center with filing facility	Small switching nodes	Small switching nodes
User responsible for message-loss protection	Network responsible for messages	Network may be responsible for individual packets	Network may be responsible for packet sequences
Usually no speed or code conversion	Speed and code conversion	Speed and code conversion	Speed and code conversion
Fixed bandwidth transmission	Dynamic use of bandwidth	Dynamic use of bandwidth	Dynamic use of bandwidth
No overhead bits after call setup	Overhead bits in each message	Overhead bits in each packet	Overhead bits in each packet

Switching Techniques for Local Networks

Circuit switching is a widely used switching technique for local networks. The types of networks that use this technique are the digital switch and the *digital private branch exchange* (PBX). These networks are introduced in Chapter 3 and discussed in detail in Chapter 7.

Packet switching is also commonly used for local networking. In many cases, however, there is only a single, direct path from source to destination. Thus, often, there is no routing or switching function in a local network. As we shall see, packet rather than message switching is used, to facilitate techniques for preventing any source from monopolizing the medium.

Message switching is not used in any of the local networks discussed in this book.

2.3

COMPUTER NETWORKING

Communications Architecture

Motivation

In Chapter 1 we discussed some of the motivations for and benefits of local networking. Many of these factors apply equally well to computer networks in general, whether local or long-haul. Indeed, the move to distributed nonlocal computer networks predates the coming of local networks.

When work is done that involves more than one computer, additional elements are needed: the hardware and software to support the communication between or among the systems. Communications hardware is reasonably standard and generally presents few problems. However, when communication is desired among heterogeneous (different vendors, different models of same vendor) machines, the software development effort can be a nightmare. Different vendors use different data formats and data exchange conventions. Even within one vendor's product line, different model computers may communicate in unique ways.

As the use of computer communications and computer networking proliferates, a one-at-a-time special-purpose approach to communications software development is too costly to be acceptable. The only alternative is for computer vendors to adopt and implement a common set of conventions. For this to happen, a set of international or at least national standards must be promulgated by appropriate organizations. Such standards would have two effects:

- Vendors feel encouraged to implement the standards because of an expectation that, because of wide usage of the standards, their products would be less marketable without them.
- Customers are in a position to require that the standards be implemented by any vendor wishing to propose equipment to them.

It should become clear from the ensuing discussion that no single standard will suffice. The task of communication in a truly cooperative way between applications on different computers is too complex to be handled as a unit. The problem must be decomposed into manageable parts. Hence before one can develop standards, there should be a structure or *architecture* that defines the communications tasks.

This line of reasoning led the International Organization for Standardization (ISO) in 1977 to establish a subcommittee to develop such an architecture. The result was the *Open Systems Interconnection* (OSI) model, which is a framework for defining standards for linking heterogeneous computers. OSI provides the basis for connecting "open" systems for distributed applications processing. The term "open" denotes the ability of any two systems conforming to the reference model and the associated standards to connect.

The Concept of Open Systems

Open Systems Interconnection is based on the concept of cooperating distributed applications. In the OSI model, a "system" consists of a computer, all of its software, and any peripheral devices attached to it, including terminals. A distributed application is any activity that involves the exchange of information between two open systems. Examples of such activities include:

- A user at a terminal on one computer is logged onto an application such as transaction processing on another computer.
- A file management program on one computer transfers a file to a file management program on another computer.
- A user sends an electronic mail message to a user on another computer.
- A process control program sends a control signal to a robot.

OSI is concerned with the exchange of information between open systems and not with the internal functioning of each individual system. Specifically, it is concerned with the capability of systems to cooperate in the exchange of information and in the accomplishment of tasks.

The objective of the OSI effort is to define a set of standards that will enable open systems located anywhere in the world to cooperate by being interconnected through some standardized communications facility and by executing standardized OSI protocols.

An open system may be implemented in any way provided that it conforms to a minimal set of standards that allow communication to be achieved with other open systems. An open system consists of a number of applications, an operating system, and system software such as a data base management system and a terminal handling package. It also includes the communications software that turns a closed system into an open system. Different manufacturers will implement open systems in different ways, in order to achieve a product identity, which will increase their market share or create a new market. However, virtually all manufacturers are now committed to providing communications software that behaves in conformance with OSI in order to provide their customers with the ability to communicate with other open systems.

The Model

A widely accepted structuring technique, and the one chosen by ISO, is layering. The communications functions are partitioned into a hierarchical set of layers. Each layer performs a related subset of the functions required to communicate with another system. It relies on the next lower layer to perform more primitive functions and to conceal the details of those functions. It provides services to the next higher layer. Ideally, the layers should be defined so that changes in one layer do not require changes in the other layers. Thus we have decomposed one problem into a number of more manageable subproblems.

The task of ISO was to define a set of layers and the services performed by each layer. The partitioning should group functions logically, and should have enough layers to make each layer manageably small, but should not have so many layers that the processing overhead imposed by the collection of layers is burdensome. The resulting OSI architecture has seven layers, which are listed with a brief definition in Table 2-3.

Table 2-3 defines, in general terms, the functions that must be performed in a system for it to communicate. Of course, it takes two to communicate, so the same set of layered functions must exist in two systems. Communication is achieved by having the corresponding ("peer") layers in two systems communicate. The peer layers communicate by means of a set of rules, or conventions, known as a protocol. The key elements of a protocol are:

- *Syntax:* The form in which information is exchanged (format, coding)
- *Semantics:* The interpretation of control information for coordination and error handling
- *Timing:* The sequence in which control events occur

TABLE 2.3   The OSI Layers

Layer	Definition
1. Physical	Concerned with transmission of unstructured bit streaam over physical link; involves such parameters as signal voltage swing and bit duration; deals with the mechanical, electrical, and procedural characteristics to establish, maintain, and deactivate the physical link (RS-232-C, RS-449, X.21)
2. Data link	Provides for the reliable transfer of data across the physical link; sends blocks of data (frames) with the necessary synchronization, error control, and flow control (HDLC, SDLC, BiSync)
3. Network	Provides upper layers with independence from the data transmission and switching technologies used to connect systems; responsible for establishing, maintaining, and terminating connections (X.25, layer 3)
4. Transport	Provides reliable, transparent transfer of data between end points; provides end-to-end error recovery and flow control
5. Session	Provides the control structure for communication between applications; establishes, manages, and terminates connections (sessions) between cooperating applications
6. Presentation	Performs generally useful transformations on data to provide a standardized application interface and to provide common communications services; examples: encryption, text compression, reformatting
7. Application	Provides services to the users of the OSI environment; examples: transaction server, file transfer protocol, network management

Figure 2-11 illustrates the OSI architecture. Each computer contains the seven layers. Communication is between applications in the two computers, labeled application X and application Y in the figure. If application X wishes to send a message to application Y, it invokes the application layer (layer 7). Layer 7 establishes a peer relationship with layer 7 of the target computer, using a layer 7 protocol (application protocol). This protocol requires services from layer 6, so the two layer 6 entities use a protocol of their own, and so on down to the physical layer, which actually transmits bits over a transmission medium.

The figure also illustrates the way in which the protocols at each layer are realized. When application X has a message to send to application Y, it transfers those data to an application layer module. That module appends an application header to the data; the header contains the control informa-

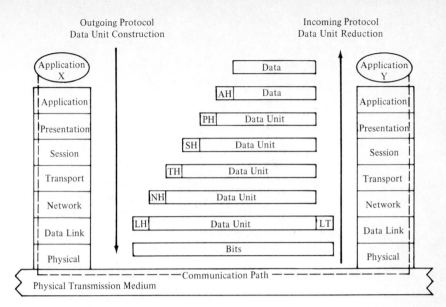

FIGURE 2-11. The OSI Environment

tion needed by the peer layer on the other side. The original data plus the header, referred to as an application protocol data unit (PDU), is passed as a unit to layer 6. The presentation module treats the whole unit as data, and appends its own header. This process continues down through layer 2, which generally adds both a header and a trailer. This layer-2 protocol data unit, usually called a *frame*, is then transmitted by the physical layer onto the transmission medium. When the frame is received by the target computer, the reverse process occurs. As we ascend the layers, each layer strips off the outermost header, acts on the protocol information contained therein, and passes the remainder up to the next layer.

We have already seen several examples of the use of control information in headers and trailers. With synchronous communication, a preamble and postamble are added to each block of data. For packet-switched networks, each packet includes not only data but also (at least) an address.

Note that there is no direct communication between peer layers except at the physical layer. Even at that layer, the OSI model does not stipulate that two systems be directly connected. For example, a packet-switched or circuit-switched network may be used to provide the communications link. This point should become clearer below, when we discuss the network layer.

The attractiveness of the OSI approach is that it promises to solve the heterogeneous computer communications problem. Two systems, no matter how different, can communicate effectively if they have the following in common:

- They implement the same set of communications functions.
- These functions are organized into the same set of layers. Peer layers must provide the same functions, but note that it is not necessary that they provide them in the same way.
- Peer layers must share a common protocol.

To assure the above, standards are needed. Standards must define the functions and services to be provided by a layer (but not how it is to be done—that may differ from system to system). Standards must also define the protocols between peer layers (each protocol must be identical for the two peer layers). The OSI model, by defining a 7-layer architecture, provides a framework for defining these standards.

Protocols

In this section we discuss briefly each of the layers and, where appropriate, give examples of standards for protocols at those layers. Table 2.4 shows the relationship to the OSI model of some of the most important standards. Remember that the OSI layers are not standards; they merely provide a framework for standards.

The International Consultative Committee on Telegraphy and Telephony (CCITT) has developed standards for connecting *data terminal*

TABLE 2.4 Some Well-Known Layers

OSI	CCITT	ISO	DOD	IEEE 802	ANS X3T9.5
7. Application		Various	Various		
6. Presentation					
5. Session		Session			
4. Transport		Transport (TP)	TCP		
3. Network	X.25	Internet Sublayer	IP		
2. Link	LAP-B			Logical link control	Data link
				Medium access control	Physical
1. Physical	X.21			Physical	

equipment (DTE) to a packet-switched network that provides *data circuit-terminating equipment* (DCE). These terms correspond to the stations and nodes of Figure 2.9. The standard, X.25, specifically addresses layer 3 and subsumes standards for layers 2 and 1. (Observers are fond of saying that X.25 is an interface, not a protocol. This point is discussed under Network Layer below.) Layer 2 is referred to as LAP-B (Link Access Protocol—Balanced) and is almost identical with ISO's HDLC (High-Level Data Link Control) and ANSI's ADCCP (Advanced Data Communication Control Procedures).

ISO has issued standards for layers 4 and 5 and is in the process of issuing a variety of standards that cover layers 6 and 7. ISO has also developed a sublayer of layer 3 that deals with internetworking, which involves communication across multiple networks.

An internetworking protocol, called IP, has been developed by the Department of Defense (DOD) for its own needs, plus a Transmission Control Protocol (TCP). TCP subsumes all the functions of layer 4 plus some of layer 5. DOD intends to mandate these standards for its procurements. In addition, DOD has issued various standards at the upper layers [STAL86b]. The mismatch with the ISO protocols is, unfortunately, unresolved.

For the type of local network that we refer to as a *local area network* (LAN), the Institute of Electrical and Electronics Engineers (IEEE), through its 802 committee, has developed a 3-layer architecture that corresponds to layers 1 and 2 of the OSI model. A number of standards have been developed by the committee for these layers. Similarly, a subcommittee responsible to the American National Standards Institute (ANSI), known as ANS X3T9.5, has developed standards for the type of local network we refer to as a *high-speed local network* (HSLN). These standards, one per layer, correspond nicely to layers 1 and 2 of the OSI model.

This variety may be disheartening, given the alleged benefit of standards, which is to put everyone on the same road. There is certainly room for pessimism. The DOD-ISO disparity makes a uniform federal government position unlikely. For LANs, the 802 committee has produced a number of options and alternatives at each layer.

However, the picture is not as bleak as Table 2.4 makes it seem. With the exception of local networks, which must be treated separately, standards have settled out quite well for layers 1 through 3. Above that, there is considerable cooperation among the various groups, so that uniform or nearly uniform standards are possible in many cases.

Physical Layer

The *physical layer* covers the physical interface between devices and the rules by which bits are passed from one to another. The physical layer has four important characteristics [BERT80, MCCL83]:

- Mechanical
- Electrical
- Functional
- Procedural

The most common standard in use today is RS-232-C. A typical use of RS-232-C is to connect a digital device to a modem, which in turn connects to a voice-grade telephone line. We will refer to this standard in describing these four characteristics.

The *mechanical characteristics* pertain to the point of demarcation. Typically, this is a pluggable connector. RS-232-C specifies a 25-pin connector, so that up to 25 separate wires are used to connect the two devices.

The *electrical characteristics* have to do with the voltage levels and timing of voltage changes. These characteristics determine the data rates and distances that can be achieved.

Functional characteristics specify the functions that are performed by assigning meaning to various signals. For RS-232-C, and for most other physical layer standards, this is done by specifying the function of each of the pins in the connector. For example, pin CA (Request to Send) is used for the device to signal the modem that it has data to send, and that a carrier should be established for modulation. Pin CF (Received Line Signal Detector or Carrier Detect) is used for the modem to alert the device that a carrier is present on the line.

Procedural characteristics specify the sequence of events for transmitting data, based on the functional characteristics. For RS-232-C, the use of the various pins is defined. For example, when a device asserts Request to Send, the modem will assert Clear to Send if it is ready to transmit data. The device can then send data from pin BA (Transmitted Data) over that line to the corresponding pin on the modem.

Data Link Layer

The physical layer provides only a raw bit stream service. The *data link layer* attempts to make the physical link reliable and provides the means to activate, maintain, and deactivate the link [CONA83, CONA80, CARL80]. The asynchronous and synchronous transmission techniques discussed in Section 2.1 are examples.

In this subsection we will spend some time defining HDLC, which is a synchronous bit-oriented protocol. We do so for two reasons:

- HDLC is the ancestor of the link layer protocol standard for LANs (IEEE 802).
- Many of the concepts concerning protocols are illustrated.

HDLC, and bit-oriented protocols in general, are intended to provide the following capabilities [CARL80]:

- *Code-independent operation (transparency):* The protocol and the data it carries are independent.
- *Adaptability to various applications, configurations, and uses in a consistent manner:* For example, point-to-point, multidrop, and loop configurations should be supported.
- *Both two-way alternate and two-way simultaneous (full-duplex) data transfer.*
- *High efficiency:* The protocol should have a minimum of overhead bits. Also, it should work efficiently over links with long propagation delays and links with high data rates.
- *High reliability:* Data should not be lost, duplicated, or garbled.

With these requirements in mind, we turn to a description of HDLC.

Three modes of operation are defined: The *normal response mode* (NRM), *asynchronous response mode* (ARM), and *asynchronous balanced mode* (ABM). Both NRM and ARM can be used in point-to-point or multipoint configurations. For each there is one *primary station* and one or more *secondary stations*. The primary station is responsible for initializing the link, controlling the flow of data to and from secondary stations, recovering from errors, and logically disconnecting secondary stations. In NRM, a secondary station may transmit only in response to a poll from the primary; in ARM, the secondary may initiate a transmission without a poll. NRM is ideally suited for a multidrop line consisting of a host computer and a number of terminals. ARM may be needed for certain kinds of loop configurations.

ABM is used only on point-to-point links and each station assumes the role of both primary and secondary. ABM is more efficient for point-to-point lines since there is no polling overhead and both stations may initiate transmissions.

Data are transmitted in frames which consist of six fields (Figure 2.12).

- FLAG: Used for synchronization, this field indicates the start and end of a frame. The flag pattern, 01111110, is avoided in the data by bit stuffing.
- ADDRESS: This field identifies the secondary station for this transmission.
- CONTROL: This field identifies the function and purpose of the frame. It is described below.
- DATA: This field contains the data to be transmitted.
- CRC: This is a frame check sequence field. It uses a 16-bit *cyclic redundancy check* (CRC). The CRC field is a function of the contents of the address, control, and data fields. It is generated by the sender and again by the receiver. If the receiver's result differs from the CRC field, a transmission error has occurred (see Appendix 2A).

Frame Structure:

8 bits	8	8	⩾ 0	16	8
FLAG	ADDRESS	CONTROL	DATA	CRC	FLAG

Control Field Structure

	1	2	3	4	5	6	7	8
Information	0		N(S)		P/F		N(R)	
Supervisory	1	0	TYPE		P/F		N(R)	
Unnumbered	1	1	TYPE		P/F		MODIFIER	

FIGURE 2-12. The HDLC Frame Structure

Three types of frames are used, each with a different control-field format. Information frames carry the data. Supervisory frames provide basic link control functions, and unnumbered frames provide supplemental link control functions.

The P/F (poll/final) bit is used by a primary station to solicit a response. More than one frame may be sent in response, with the P/F bit set to indicate the last frame. The P/F may be used with supervisory and unnumbered frames to force a response.

The N(S) and N(R) fields in the information frame provide an efficient technique for both flow control and error control. A station numbers the frames that it sends sequentially modulo 8, using the N(S) field. When a station receives a valid information frame, it acknowledges that frame with its own information frame by setting the N(R) field to the number of the next frame it expects to receive. This is known as a *piggybacked acknowledgment*, since the acknowledgment rides back on an information frame. Acknowledgments can also be sent on a supervisory frame. This scheme accomplishes three important functions.

- *Flow control:* Once a station has sent seven frames, it can send no more until the first frame is acknowledged.
- *Error control:* If a frame is received in error, a station can send a "NAK" (negative acknowledgment) via a supervisory frame to specify which frame was received in error. This is done in one of two ways. In the *go-back-n protocol*, the sending station retransmits the NAK'ed frame and all subsequent frames that had already been sent. In the *selective repeat technique*, the sending station retransmits only the frame in error.
- *Pipelining:* More than one frame may be in transit at a time; this allows more efficient use of links with high propagation delay, such as satellite links.

The N(S)/N(R) technique is known as a *sliding-window protocol* because the sending station maintains a window of messages to be sent which gradually moves forward with transmission and acknowledgment. The process is depicted in Figure 2.13.

There are four types of supervisory frames:

- *Receive Ready (RR):* used to acknowledge correct receipt of frames up through N(R)−1. Alternatively, this is a poll command instructing secondary to begin transmission with sequence number N(R).
- *Receive Not Ready (RNR):* used to indicate a temporary busy condition. N(R) is used for a possibly redundant acknowledgment.
- *Reject (REJ):* used to indicate an error in frame N(R) and to request retransmission of that and all subsequent frames.
- *Selective Reject (SREJ):* used to request retransmission of a single frame.

The unnumbered frames have no sequence number and are used for a number of special purposes, such as to initialize a station, set the mode, disconnect a station, and reject a command.

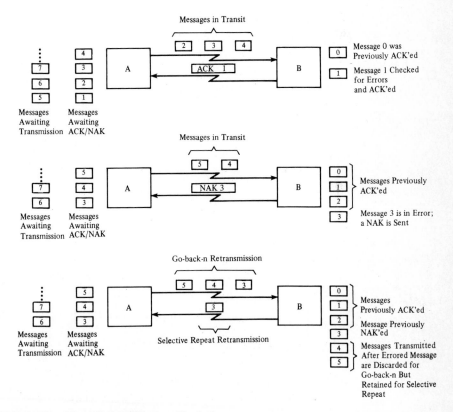

FIGURE 2-13. The Sliding-Window Technique

Network Layer

The *network layer* is designed to facilitate communication between systems across a communications network. It is at this layer that the concept of a protocol becomes a little fuzzy. This is best illustrated with reference to Figure 2.14, which shows two systems (DTEs) that are communicating, not via direct link, but via a network. The DTEs have direct links to the network nodes (DCEs). The layer 1 and 2 protocols are DTE-DCE protocols (local). Layers 4 through 7 are clearly protocols between (N) entities in the two DTEs. Layer 3 is a little bit of both.

For X.25, layer 3 has been designed for both virtual circuits and datagrams. The principal dialogue is between the DTE and its DCE; the DTE sends addressed packets to the DCE for delivery across the network. It may also request a virtual circuit connection, use the connection to transmit data, and terminate the connection. The DCE faces toward the DTE for this dialogue, but it must also face inward to the network for routing, virtual circuit establishment, and packet delivery. The X.25 standard refers to itself as an interface between a DTE and a DCE. In the terminology we have been using, it is actually a protocol between DTE and DCE. However, because packets are exchanged and virtual circuits are set up between two DTEs, there are aspects of a DTE-DTE protocol as well.

Nevertheless, the X.25 layer 3 is basically a protocol with local (DTE-DCE) significance. It does not guarantee end-to-end (DTE-DTE) reliability nor does it provide end-to-end control. Of course, this is not an inherent limitation of layer 3; it is possible to provide a layer 3 protocol that does have end-to-end significance. We will return to this point in the next subsection.

A brief description of the X.25 layer 3 is given in Chapter 8.

The basic service of the network layer is to provide for the transparent transfer of data between transport entities. It relieves the transport layer of the need to know anything about the underlying communications medium.

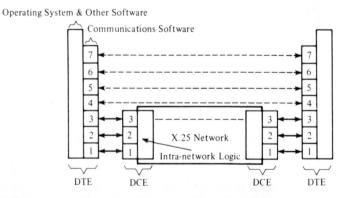

FIGURE 2-14. Communication Across a Network

At one extreme, when there is a direct link between stations, there may be no need for a network layer. Between extremes, the most common use of layer 3 is to handle the details of using a packet-switched network. At the other extreme, two devices might wish to communicate but are not even connected to the same network. Rather, they are connected to networks which, directly or indirectly, are connected to each other. This situation is explored in some detail in Chapter 11. For now is suffices to say that one approach to providing for data transfer in such a case is to use an *Internet Protocol* (IP) that sits on top of a network protocol and is used by a transport protocol. IP is responsible for internetwork routing and delivery, and relies on a layer 3 at each network for intranetwork services. IP is described in Chapter 11; it is sometimes referred to as "layer 3.5."

Transport Layer

Layers 4 and above of the OSI model are generally referred to as the higher layers [RAUC83]. Protocols at these levels are end-to-end and not concerned with the details of the underlying communications facility.

The purpose of layer 4 is to provide a reliable mechanism for the exchange of data between processes in different systems. The *transport layer* ensures that data units are delivered error-free, in sequence, with no losses or duplications. Typical features of the transport layer are:

- *Type of service:* It is connection-oriented or connectionless, analogous to virtual circuits and datagrams.
- *Grade of service:* This would allow the (5) entity to specify acceptable error and loss levels, desired delay, priority, and security.
- *Connection management:* Layer 4 will set up and manage connections between (5) entities via (4) CEPs for connection-oriented service.

The size and complexity of a transport protocol depends on the type of service it can get from layer 3. For a reliable layer 3 with a virtual circuit capability, a minimal layer 4 is required. If layer 3 is unreliable and/or only supports datagrams, then the layer 4 protocol should include extensive error detection and recovery. Accordingly, ISO has defined five classes of transport protocol, each oriented toward a different underlying network layer service.

Session Layer

The session layer provides the mechanism for controlling the dialogue between the two end systems. In many cases, there will be little or no need for session-layer services, but for some applications, such services are used. The key services provided by the session layer include:

- *Dialogue discipline:* this can be two-way simultaneous (full-duplex) or two-way alternate (half-duplex).

- *Grouping:* the flow of data can be marked to define groups of data. For example, if a retail store is transmitting sales data to a regional office, the data can be marked to indicate the end of the sales data for each department. This would signal the host computer to finalize running totals for that department and start new running counts for the next department.
- *Recovery:* the session layer can provide a checkpointing mechanism, so that if a failure of some sort occurs between checkpoints, the session entity can retransmit all data since the last checkpoint.

ISO has issued a standard for the session layer that includes as options services such as those described above.

Presentation Layer

The presentation layer defines the format of the data to be exchanged between applications, and offers application programs a set of data transformation services. For example, data compression or data encryption could occur at this level.

Application Layer

The application layer provides a means for application programs to access the OSI environment. This layer contains management functions and generally useful mechanisms to support distributed applications. In addition, general-purpose applications such as file transfer, electronic mail, and terminal accesss to remote computers are considered to reside at this layer.

Perspective on the OSI Model

Figure 2-15 provides a useful perspective on the OSI architecture. The annotation suggests viewing the seven layers in three parts. The lower three layers contain the logic for a computer to interact with a network. The host is attached physically to the network, uses a data link protocol to reliably communicate with the network, and uses a network protocol to request data exchange with another device on the network and to request network services. The X.25 standard for packet-switching networks encompasses these three layers. Continuing from this perspective, the transport layer provides a reliable end-to-end service regardless of the intervening network facility; in effect, it is the user's liaison to the communications facility. Finally, the upper three layers, taken together, are involved in the exchange of data between end users, making use of a transport service for reliable data transfer.

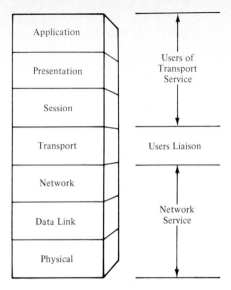

FIGURE 2-15. A Perspective on the OSI Architecture

2.4

RECOMMENDED READING

[STAL88a] covers all the topics in this chapter. Martin provides his usual readable treatment in [MART76] which covers most of the topics in Sections 2.1 and 2.2. A thorough treatment of both analog and digital communications can be found in [COUC83] and two companion books: [FREE80] and [FREE81]. [FREE81] concentrates on issues involved with the transmission of data. [FREE80] looks at design issues for communications systems, particularly circuit-switched systems. A more electronically oriented treatment can be found in [BELL82a]. [MCNA82] also covers the topics of Section 2.1, focusing on digital data communications. [DOLL78] is a good overall survey book, with a particularly good chapter on multiplexing.

A thorough discussion of the OSI model can be found in [TANE81], which averages about one chapter per layer. A more informal account can be found in [MART81]. [STAL87] contains reprints of key articles covering OSI and the standards at each layer.

2.5

PROBLEMS

2.1   Write a program to do bit stuffing.

2.2   A user may wish to use a character-oriented synchronous transmission protocol to send arbitrary bit streams. How can the protocol ensure that none of its control characters (e.g., SYNC) appear in the character stream? Write a program to do this.

2.3 Write a program that implements the sliding window technique for (1) selective repeat and (2) go-back-n.

2.4 Consider a transmission link between stations A and B with a probability of error in a frame of p.

    a. Assume a selective repeat protocol and assume that station A is sending data and station B is sending acknowledgments only (RR, SREJ) and that it individually acknowledges each frame. Assume that acknowledgments are never lost. What is the mean number of transmissions required per frame?

    b. Now assume a go-back-n protocol and that the link is such that A will transmit three additional frames before receiving RR or REJ for each frame. Also assume that acknowledgments are never lost. What is the mean number of transmissions required per frame?

2.5 Are the modem and the codec functional inverses (i.e., could an inverted modem function as a codec, and vice versa)?

2.6 List the major disadvantages with the layered approach to protocols.

2.7 Compare bit-oriented and character-oriented data link protocols in terms of advantages and disadvantages.

2.8 Among the principles used by ISO to define the OSI layers were:

- The number of layers should be small enough to avoid unwieldly design and implementation, but large enough so that separrate layers handle functions which are different in process or technology.
- Layer boundaries should be chosen to minimize the number and size of interactions across boundaries.

Based on these principles, design an architecture with eight layers and make a case for it. Design one with six layers and make a case for that.

2.9 Another form of digital encoding of digital data is known as delay modulation or *Miller coding*. In this scheme, a logic 1 is represented by a midbit transition (in either direction). A logic 0 is represented by a transition at the end of the bit period if the next bit is 0, and is represented by the absence of a transition if the next bit is a 1. Draw a Miller code waveform for the bit stream of Figure 2.5. Why might this technique be preferable to NRZ? To Manchester?

2.10 What is the percentage of overhead in a T1 carrier (percentage of bits that are not user data)?

2.11 Define the following parameters for a switching network:

N = number of hops between two given stations
L = message length, in bits
B = data rate, in bps, on all links
P = packet size, in bits
H = overhead (header) bits per packet

S = call setup time (circuit-switched or virtual circuit) in seconds

D = propagation delay per hop in seconds

a. For $N = 4$, $L = 3200$, $B = 9600$, $P = 1024$, $H = 16$, $S = 0.2$, $D = 0.001$, compute the end-to-end delay for circuit switching, message switching, virtual circuit packet switching, and datagram packet switching. Assume that there are no acknowledgments.

b. Derive general expressions for the four techniques, taken two at a time (six expressions in all) showing the conditions under which the delays are equal.

2.12 What value of P, as a function of N, B, and H results in minimum end-to-end delay on a datagram network? Assume that L is much larger than P, and D is zero.

2.13 Two stations communicate via a 1-Mbps satellite link. The satellite serves merely to retransmit data received from one station to the other, with negligible delay. The up-and-down propagation delay for a synchronous orbit is 270 ms. Using HDLC frames of length 1024 bits, what is the maximum possible data throughput (not counting overhead bits)?

APPENDIX 2A: THE CYCLIC REDUNDANCY CHECK

In HDLC and other data link control protocols, an error-detection technique is required so that the receiver can detect any bit errors in received frames and request that the sender retransmit those frames. This technique requires the addition of a **frame check sequence (FCS)**, or **error-detecting code**, to each frame. On transmission, a calculation is performed on the bits of the frame to be transmitted; the result is inserted as an additional field in the frame. On reception, the same calculation is performed on the received bits and the calculated result is compared to the value stored in the incoming frame. If there is a discrepancy, the receiver assumes that an error has occurred.

One of the most common, and one of the most powerful, of the error-detecting codes is the cyclic redundancy check (CRC). For this technique, the message to be transmitted is treated as one long binary number. This number is divided by a unique prime binary number (a number divisible only by itself and 1), and the remainder is attached to the frame to be transmitted. When the frame is received, the receiver performs the same division, using the same divisor, and compares the calculated remainder with the remainder received in the frame. The most commonly used divisors are a 17-bit divisor, which produces a 16-bit remainder, and a 33-bit divisor, which produces a 32-bit remainder.

The measure of effectiveness of any error-detecting code is what percentage of errors it detects. It can be shown that all of the following errors are not divisible by a prime divisor and hence are detectable [STAL88a]:

- All single-bit errors.
- All double-bit errors, as long as the divisor has at least three ones.
- Any odd number of errors, as long as the divisor contains a factor 11.
- Any burst error for which the length of the burst is less than the length of the divisor polynomial; that is, less than or equal to the length of the FCS.
- Most larger burst errors.

These results are summarized in Table 2-5. As you can see, this is a very powerful means of error detection and requires very little overhead. As an example, if a 16-bit FCS is used with frames of 1000 bits, then the overhead is only 1.6 percent. With a 32-bit FCS, the overhead is 3.2 percent.

TABLE 2.5 Effectiveness of the Cyclic Redundancy Check (CRC)

Type of Error	16-bit CRC Probability of Detection	32-bit CRC Probability of Detection
Single bit errors	1.0	1.0
Two bits in error (separate or not)	1.0	1.0
Odd number of bits in error	1.0	1.0
Error burst of length less than the length of the CRC (16 or 32 bits, respectively)	1.0	1.0
Error burst of length equal to the length of the CRC	$1-\frac{1}{2^{15}}$	$1-\frac{1}{2^{31}}$
Error burst of length greater than the length of the CRC	$1-\frac{1}{2^{16}}$	$1-\frac{1}{2^{32}}$

CHAPTER 3

Local Network Technology

The principal technology ingredients that determine the nature of a local network are:

* topology
* transmission medium
* medium access control technique

Together, they in large measure determine the type of data that may be transmitted, the speed and efficiency of communications, and even the kinds of applications that a network may support.

This chapter surveys the topologies and transmission media that, within the state of the art, are appropriate for local networks. The issue of access control is also briefly raised. With this survey as background, three classes of local networks are defined. The discussion is brief, with the objective of providing a context for the material in Chapters 4 through 7.

TOPOLOGIES

The term *topolgy*, in the context of a communications network, refers to the way in which the end points or stations of the network are interconnected. A topology is defined by the layout of communications links and switching elements, and it determines the data paths that may be used between any pair of stations.

To begin this discussion of topology, consider the question of why a communications network is needed at all. According to our definition in Chapter 1, the local network provides a means for interconnecting devices in a small area. Why not provide a direct connection between any pair of devices that need to communicate? Then no intermediate network of communications devices is required.

The problem with this approach is illustrated in Figure 3.1. Each device has a direct, dedicated link, called a *point-to-point link*, with each other device. If there are N devices, then $N(N - 1)$ links are required, and each device requires $(N - 1)$ input/output (I/O) ports. Thus the cost of the system, in terms of cable installation and I/O hardware, grows with the square of the number of devices.

The infeasibility of this approach, sometimes known as the *mesh topology*, was recognized early for wide-area communications. The solution, as shown in Figure 2.9, was to introduce a network of swtiching nodes with the ability to route messages, creating logical links and eliminating the need for so many direct physical connections. In this approach, each device

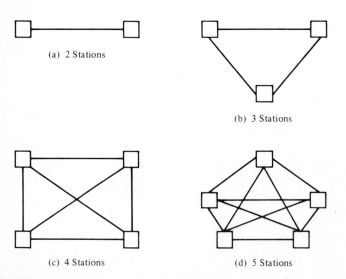

(a) 2 Stations

(b) 3 Stations

(c) 4 Stations

(d) 5 Stations

FIGURE 3-1. The Problem with Direct Connection or Mesh Topology

or station connects directly to a communication network node and communicates to other stations via the network.

This approach—the use of a collection of switching nodes—is not generally used for local networks. Because the distances involved are small, the expense of the switching nodes can be avoided. Topologies have been developed which require no or only one intermediate switching node, and yet avoid the problems of the mesh topology.

Four simple topologies are described below: bus, tree, ring, and star. These are commonly used, as is, to construct local networks. They can also be used as building blocks for networks with more complex topologies. These refinements are discussed in later chapters.

The Star Topology

In the *star topology*, each station is connected by a point-to-point link to a common central switch (Figure 3.2). Communication between any two stations is via circuit switching. For a station to transmit data, it must first send a request to the central switch, asking for a connection to some destination station. Once the circuit is set up, data may be exchanged between the two stations as if they were connected by a dedicated point-to-point link.

This topology exhibits a centralized communications control strategy. All communications are controlled by the central switch, which must set up

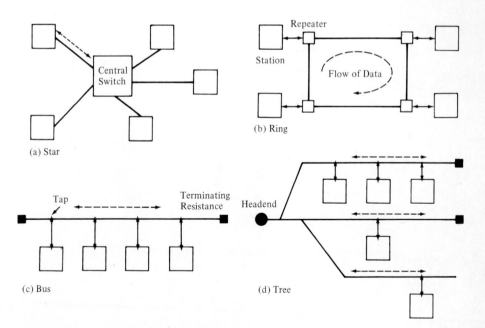

FIGURE 3-2.　Local Network Topologies

and maintain a number of concurrent data paths. Consequently, the central switch node is rather complex. On the other hand, the communications processing burden on the stations is minimal. Other than some rudimentary logic for requsting and accepting connections, the stations need only be concerned with the simple communications requirements of a point-to-point link.

The Ring Topology

In the *ring topology*, the local network consists of a set of *repeaters* joined by point-to-point links in a closed loop. Hence each repeater participates in two links. The repeater is a comparatively simple device, capable of receiving data on one link and transmitting it, bit by bit, on the other link as fast as it is received, with no buffering at the repeater. The links are unidirectional; that is, data are transmitted in one direction only, and all oriented in the same way. Thus data circulate around the ring in one direction (clockwise or counterclockwise).

Each station attaches to the network at a repeater. Data are transmitted in packets. So, for example, if station X wishes to transmit a message to station Y, it breaks the message up into packets. Each packet contains a portion of the data plus some control information, including Y's address. The packets are inserted into the ring one at a time and circulate through the other repeaters. Station Y recognizes its address and copies the packets as they go by.

Since multiple devices share the ring, control is needed to determine at what time each station may insert packets. This is almost always done with some form of distributed control. Each station contains access logic that controls transmission and reception; various techniques are explored in Chapter 5.

Note the contrast between the ring and star topologies. The star topology involves rather complex network processing functions with minimal burden on the stations. In the ring topology, the network devices are the relatively simple repeaters. However, the stations must provide the packetizing and access control logic.

The Bus and Tree Topologies

With the *bus topology*, the communications network is simply the transmission medium—no switches and no repeaters. All stations attach, through appropriate hardware interfacing, directly to a linear transmission medium, or *bus*. A transmission from any station propagates the length of the medium and can be received by all other stations.

The tree topology is a generalization of the bus topology. The transmission medium is a branching cable with no closed loops. The tree layout begins at a point known as the *headend*. One or more cables start at the headend, and each of these may have branches. The branches in turn may have additional branches to allow quite complex layouts. Again, a transmission from any station propagates throughout the medium and can be received by all other stations. For both bus and tree topologies, the medium is referred to as *multipoint*.

Because all nodes on a bus or tree share a common transmission link, only one station can transmit at a time. Some form of access control is required to determine which station may transmit next. Again, we examine this topic in Chapter 5.

As with the ring, packet transmission is typically used for communication. A station wishing to transmit breaks its message into packets and sends these one at a time. For each packet that a station wishes to transmit, it waits for its next turn and then transmits the packet. The intended destination station will recognize its address as the packets go by, and copy them. There are no intermediate nodes and no switching or repeating is involved.

With the bus or tree topology, the trend described for the ring topology is carried to the extreme. The network is relieved of the entire communications processing burden; it is simply a passive (from the point of view of communications) transmission medium. The processing burden on the attached stations is of roughly the same order of magnitude as for ring attachment.

Choice of Topology

The choice of topology depends on a variety of factors, including reliability, expandability, and performance. This choice is part of the overall task of designing a local network. As the text proceeds, the trade-offs between the various approaches should become clear. A few general observations follow.

The bus/tree topology appears to be the most flexible one. It is able to handle a wide range of devices, in terms of number of devices, data rates, and data types. High bandwidth is achievable. Because the medium is passive, it would appear at first blush to be highly reliable. As we shall see, this is not necessarily the case. In particular, a break in the cable can disable a large part or all of the network.

Very high speed links (e.g., optical fiber) can be used between the repeaters of a ring. Hence, the ring has the potential of providing the best throughput of any topology. There are practical limitations, in terms of numbers of devices and variety of data types. Finally, the reliability problem is obvious: a single link or repeater failure could disable the entire network.

The star topology, using circuit switching, readily integrates voice with data traffic. It lends itself well to low-data-rate (≤64 kbps) devices. The star topology is good for terminal-intensive requirements because of the minimal processing burden that it imposes on the attached devices.

3.2

TRANSMISSION MEDIA

The *transmission medium* is the physical path between transmitter and receiver in a communications network. Figure 3.3 shows the basic elements of a transmission system. The most common configuration is a point-to-point link between two transmitting/receiving devices, which, through appropriate interfaces, insert analog or digital signals onto the medium. One or more intermediate devices may be used to compensate for attenuation or other transmission impairments. Point-to-point links are used in the ring topology to connect adjacent repeaters, and in the star topology to connect devices to the central switch. Point-to-point links may also be used to connect two local networks in different buildings; we elaborate on this point below. Multipoint links are used to connect multiple devices, as in

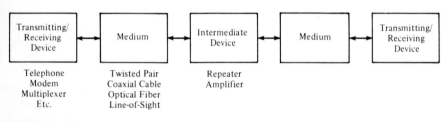

(a) Point-to-point

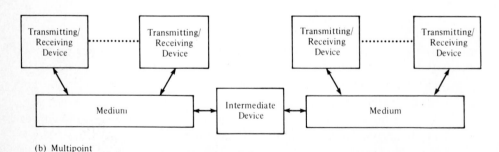

(b) Multipoint

FIGURE 3-3. **Simplified Transmission System Block Diagram (After [BELL82a])**

the bus and tree topologies. Devices attach to the medium at various points; again, repeaters (digital signals) or amplifiers (analog signals) may be used to extend the length of the medium.

Transmission media may be classified as guided or unguided. In both cases, communication is in the form of electromagnetic waves. With *guided media*, the waves are guided along a physical path. Examples of guided media are twisted pair, coaxial cable, and optical fiber, all of which are used in local networks. The atmosphere and outer space are examples of *unguided media*, which provide a means for transmitting electromagnetic waves but do not guide them. Various forms of transmission through the atmosphere are employed for building-to-building connections.

In this section, we describe these media using a set of characteristics based on that proposed in [ROSE82]. The characteristics are:

- *Physical description:* the nature of the transmission medium.
- *Transmission characteristics:* include whether analog or digital signaling is used, modulation technique, capacity, and the frequency range over which transmission occurs.
- *Connectivity:* point-to-point or multipoint.
- *Geographic scope:* the maximum distance between points on the network; whether suitable for intrabuilding, interbuilding, and/or intracity use.
- *Noise immunity:* resistance of medium to contamination of the transmitted data.
- *Relative cost:* based on cost of components, installation, and maintenance.

Twisted Pair

By far the most common transmission medium, for both analog and digital data, is *twisted pair*. The wiring within a building to connect the telephones is twisted pair, as are the "local loops" that connect all of the phones in a limited geographic area to a central exchange.

Physical Description

A twisted pair consists of two insulated wires arranged in a regular spiral pattern. The wires are copper or steel coated with copper. The copper provides conductivity; steel may be used for strength. A wire pair acts as a single communication link. Typically, a number of these pairs are bundled together into a cable by wrapping them in a tough protective sheath. Over longer distances, cables may contain hundreds of pairs. The twisting of the individual pairs minimizes electromagnetic interference between the pairs. The wires in a pair have thicknesses of from 0.016 to 0.036 inch.

Transmission Characteristics

Wire pairs may be used to transmit both analog and digital signals. For analog signals, amplifiers are required about every 5 to 6 km. For digital signals, repeaters are used every 2 or 3 km.

The most common use of wire pair is for analog transmission of voice. Although frequency components of speech may be found between 20 Hz and 20 kHz, a much narrower bandwidth is required for intelligible speech reproduction [FREE81]. The standard bandwidth of a full-duplex voice channel is 300 to 3400 Hz. Multiple voice channels can be multiplexed, using FDM, on a single wire pair. A bandwidth of 4 kHz per channel provides adequate separation between channels. Twisted pair has a capacity of up to 24 voice channels using a bandwidth of up to 268 kHz.

Digital data may be transmitted over an analog voice channel using a modem. With a current modem design, speeds of up to 19.2 kbps using phase-shift keying (PSK) are practical. On a 24-channel wire pair, the aggregate data rate is 230 kbps.

It is also possible to use digital or baseband signaling on a wire pair. Bell offers a T1 circuit using twisted pair which handles 24 PCM voice channels, for an aggregate data rate of 1.544 Mbps. Higher data rates, depending on distance, are possible. A data rate of four megabits per second represents a reasonable upper limit.

Connectivity

Twisted pair can be used for point-to-point and multipoint applications. As a multipoint medium, twisted pair is a less-expensive, lower-performance alternative to coax cable but supports fewer stations. Point-to-point usage is far more common.

Geographic Scope

Twisted pair can easily provide point-to-point data transmission to a range of 15 km or more. Twisted pair for local networks is typically used within a single building or just a few buildings.

Noise Immunity

Compared to other guided media, twisted pair is limited in distance, bandwidth, and data rate. The medium is quite susceptible to interference and noise because of its easy coupling with electromagnetic fields. For example, a wire run parallel to an ac power line will pick up 60-Hz energy. Signals on adjacent pairs of cables may interfere with each other, a phenomenon known as cross-talk.

Several measures can be taken to reduce impairments. Shielding the wire with metallic braid or sheathing reduces interference. The twisting of the wire reduces low-frequency interference, and the use of different twist lengths in adjacent pairs reduces crosstalk. These measures are effective for wavelengths much greater than the twist length of the cable. Noise immunity can be as high or higher than for coaxial cable for low frequency transmission. However, above 10 to 100 kHz, coaxial cable is typically superior.

Cost

Twisted pair is less expensive than either coaxial cable or fiber in terms of cost per foot. However, because of its connectivity limitations, installation costs may approach that of other media.

Coaxial Cable

The most versatile transmission medium for local networks is *coaxial cable*. Indeed, many people think of coaxial cable as the *only* local network transmission medium, despite the widespread use of twisted pair.

In this section we discuss two types of coaxial cable currently in use for local network applications: 75-ohm cable, which is the standard used in *community antenna television* (CATV) systems, and 50-ohm cable. As Table 3.1 illustrates, 50-ohm cable is only used for digital signaling, called *baseband*; 75-ohm cable is used for analog signaling with FDM, called *broadband*, and for high-speed digital signaling and analog signaling in which no FDM is possible. The latter is sometimes referred to as *single-channel broadband*.

Physical Description

Coaxial cable, like twisted pair, consists of two conductors, but it is constructed differently to permit it to operate over a wider range of frequencies. It consists of a hollow outer cylindrical conductor which surrounds a single inner wire conductor. The inner conductor can be either solid or stranded; the outer conductor can be either solid or braided. The inner conductor is held in place by either regularly spaced insulating rings or a solid dialectric material. The outer conductor is covered with a jacket or shield. A single coaxial cable has a diameter of from 0.4 to about 1 inch.

Transmission Characteristics

The 50-ohm cable is used exclusively for digital transmission. Manchester encoding is typically used. Data rates of up to 10 Mbps can be achieved.

CATV cable is used for both analog and digital signaling. For analog signaling, frequencies up to 300 to 400 MHz are possible. Analog data, such as video and audio, can be handled on CATV cable in much the same way as free-space radio and TV broadcasting. TV channels are each allocated 6 MHz of bandwidth; each radio channel requires much less. Hence a large number of channels can be carried on the cable using FDM.

When FDM is used, the CATV cable is referred to as "broadband." The frequency spectrum of the cable is divided into channels, each of which carries analog signals. In addition to the analog data referred to above, digital data may also be carried in a channel. Various modulation schemes have been used for digital data, including ASK, FSK, and PSK. The efficiency of the modem will determine the bandwidth needed to support a given data rate. A good rule of thumb [STAH82] is to assume 1 Hz per bps for rates of 5 Mbps and above and 2 Hz per bps for lower rates. For example, a 5-Mbps data rate can be achieved in a 6-MHz TV channel, whereas a 4.8-kbps modem might use about 10 kHz. With current technology, a data rate of about 20 Mbps is achievable; at this rate, the bandwidth efficiency may exceed 1 bps/Hz.

To achieve data rates above 20 Mbps, two approaches have been taken. Both require that the entire bandwidth of the 75-ohm cable be dedicated to this data transfer; no FDM is employed. One approach is to use digital signaling on the cable, as is done for the 50-ohm cable. A data rate of 50 Mbps has been achieved with this scheme. An alternative is to use a simple PSK system; using a 150-MHz carrier, a data rate of 50 Mbps has also been achieved. Much lower data rates are achieved using FSK.

Connectivity

Coaxial cable is applicable to point-to-point and to multipoint configurations. Basehand 50-ohm cable can support on the order of 100 devices per segment, with larger systems possible by linking segments with repeaters. Broadband 75-ohm cable can support thousands of devices. The use of 75-ohm cable at high data rates (50 Mbps) introduces technical problems, discussed in Chapter 6, that limit the number of devices to 20 to 30.

Geographic Scope

Maximum distances in a typical baseband cable are limited to a few kilometers. Broadband networks can span ranges of tens of kilometers. The difference has to do with the relative signal integrity of analog and digital signals. The types of electromagnetic noise usually encountered in industrial and urban areas are of relatively low frequencies, where most of the energy in digital signals resides. Analog signals may be placed on a carrier of sufficiently high frequency to avoid the main components of noise.

High-speed transmission (50 Mbps), digital or analog, is limited to about 1 km. Because of the high data rate, the physical distance between signals on the bus is very small. Hence very little attenuation or noise can be tolerated before the data are lost.

Noise Immunity

Noise immunity for coaxial cable depends on the application and implementation. In general, it is superior to that of twisted pair for higher frequencies.

Cost

The cost of installed coaxial cable falls between that of twisted pair and optical fiber.

Optical Fiber Cable

The most exciting developments in the realm of local network transmission media are in the area of *fiber optics*. Because the technology is changing rapidly, this section can provide only a current snapshot of fiber optic capability.

Physical Description

An optical fiber is a thin (2 to 125 μm), flexible medium capable of conducting an optical ray. Various glasses and plastics can be used to make optical fibers [JORD85]. The lowest losses have been obtained using fibers of ultrapure fused silica. Ultrapure fiber is difficult to manufacture; higher-loss multicomponent glass fibers are more economical and still provide good performance. Plastic fiber is even less costly and can be used for short-haul links, for which moderately high losses are acceptable.

An optical fiber cable has a cylindrical shape and consists of three concentric sections: the core, the cladding, and the jacket. The *core* is the innermost section, and consists of one or more very thin strands, or fibers, made of glass or plastic. Each fiber is surrounded by its own *cladding*, a glass or plastic coating that has optical properties different from those of the core. The outermost layer, surrounding one or a bundle of cladded fibers, is the *jacket*. The jacket is composed of plastic and other materials layered to protect against moisture, abrasion, crushing, and other environmental dangers.

Transmission Characteristics

Optical fiber transmits a signal-encoded beam of light by means of total internal reflection. Total internal reflection can occur in any transparent medium that has a higher index of refraction than the surrounding medium. In effect, the optical fiber acts as a waveguide for frequencies in the range 10^{14} to 10^{15} Hz, which covers the visible spectrum and part of the infrared spectrum.

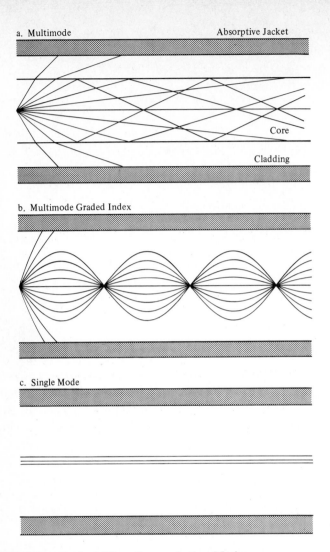

FIGURE 3-4. Optical Fiber Transmission Modes

Figure 3-4 shows the principle of optical fiber transmission. Light from a source enters the cylindrical glass or plastic core. Rays at shallow angles are reflected and propagated along the fiber; other rays are absorbed by the surrounding material. This form of propagation is called multimode, referring to the variety of angles that will reflect. When the fiber core radius is reduced, fewer angles will reflect. By reducing the radius of the core to the order of a wavelength, only a single angle or mode can pass: the axial ray. This provides superior performance to multimode for the following reason. With multimode transmission, multiple propagation paths exist, each with a different path length and hence time to traverse the fiber.

This causes signal elements to spread out in time and limits the rate at which data can be accurately received. Since there is a single transmission path with single-mode transmission, such distortion cannot occur. Finally, by varying the index of refraction of the core, a third type of transmission, known as multimode graded index, is possible. This type is intermediate between the other two in characteristics. The variable refraction has the effect of focusing the rays more efficiently than ordinary multimode, also known as multimode step-index. Table 3.1 compares the three fiber transmission modes. As can be seen, tremendous capacities can be achieved, far exceeding those of coaxial cable or twisted pair.

Two different types of light source are used in fiber optic systems [WERN86]: the *light-emitting diode* (LED) and the *injection laser diode* (ILD). The LED is a solid-state device that emits light when a current is applied. The ILD is a solid-state device that works on the laser principle in which quantum electronic effects are stimulated to produce a superradiant beam of narrow bandwidth. The LED is less costly, operates over a greater temperature range, and has a longer operational life. The ILD is more efficient and can sustain greater data rates.

The detector used at the receiving end to convert the light into electrical energy is a *photodiode*. Two solid-state devices have been used [FORR86]: the PIN detector and the APD detector. The PIN photodiode has a segment of intrinsic (I) silicon between the P and N layers of a diode. The APD, avalanche photodiode, is similar in appearance but uses a stronger electric field. Both devices are basically photon counters. The PIN is less expensive and less sensitive than the APD.

TABLE 3.1 Comparison of Three Types of Optical Fibers

	Step-index Multimode	Graded-index Multimode	Single-mode
Light Source	LED or laser	LED or laser	laser
Bandwidth	wide (up to 200 MHz/km)	very wide (200 MHz to 3 GHz/km)	extremely wide (3 GHz to 50 GHz/km)
Splicing	difficult	difficult	difficult
Typical Application	computer data links	moderate-length telephone lines	telecommunication long lines
Cost	least expensive	more expensive	most expensive
Core Diameter (μm)	50 to 125	50 to 125	2 to 8
Cladding Diameter (μm)	125 to 440	125 to 440	15 to 60

Source: [SHUF84].

The amplitude-shift keying technique is commonly used to transmit digital data over optical fiber; in this context, it is known as *intensity modulation*. For LED transmitters, binary one is represented by a short pulse of light and binary zero by the absence of light. Laser transmitters normally have a fixed "bias" current that causes the device to emit a low light level. This low level represents binary zero, while a higher-amplitude lightwave represents another signal element.

Data rates as high as a few gigabits per second have been demonstrated in the laboratory. Current practical applications are in the range of a few hundreds of megabits per second over a few kilometers.

There is a relationship among the wavelength employed, the type of transmission, and the achievable data rate [MIER86]. Both single mode and multimode can support several different wavelengths of light and can employ laser or LED light sources. In glass-composition fiber, light propagates best in three distinct wavelength "windows", centered on 850, 1300, and 1500 nanometers (nm). The loss is lower at higher wavelengths, allowing greater data rates over longer distances (Table 3.2). Most local applications today use 850-nm LED light sources. Although this is relatively inexpensive, this combination is generally limited to data rates under 100 Mbps and distances of a few kilometers. To achieve higher data rates and longer distances, a 1300-nm LED or laser source is needed. Thus although the 850-nm source is attractive for LANs, the 1300-nm source is more appropriate for HSLNs. The highest transmission capacities and longest distances achievable today require 1500-nm light sources. These require lasers and are used in some long-distance applications, but are currently too expensive for local networks.

Currently, a single carrier frequency is used for optical fiber transmis-

TABLE 3.2   Transmission Losses of Various Types of Optical Fiber [FREE85]

Mode	Material Core/Cladding	Transmission Loss, dB/km		
		850 nm	1300 nm	1500 nm
Single mode	Silica glass/silica glass	2	0.5	0.2
Step-index multimode	Silica glass/silica glass	2	0.5	0.2
	Silica glass/plastic	2.5	High	High
	Multicomponent glass/multicomponent glass	3.4	High	High
Graded-index multimode	Silica glass/silica glass	2	0.5	0.2
	Multicomponent glass/multicomponent glass	3.5	High	High

sion. Future advance will permit practical FDM systems, also referred to as wavelength division multiplexing or color division multiplexing.

Connectivity

The most common use of optical fiber is for point-to-point links. Experimental multipoint systems using a bus topology have been built, but are too expensive to be practical today. In principle, however, a single segment of optical fiber could support many more drops than either twisted pair or coaxial cable, due to lower power loss, lower attenuation characteristics, and greater bandwidth potential.

Geographic Scope

Present technology supports transmission over distances of 6 to 8 km without repeaters. Hence optical fiber is suitable for linking local networks in several buildings via point-to-point links.

Noise Immunity

Optical fiber is not affected by electromagnetic interference or noise. This characteristic permits high data rates over long distance and provides excellent security.

Cost

Fiber optic systems are more expensive than twisted pair and coaxial cable in terms of cost per foot and required components (transmitters, receivers, connectors). While costs of twisted pair and coaxial cable are unlikely to drop, engineering advances should reduce the cost of fiber optics to be competitive with these other media.

Line-of-Sight Media

In this section we look at three techniques for transmitting electromagnetic waves through the atmosphere: microwave, infrared, and laser. All three require a *line-of-sight path* between transmitter and receiver.

Because of the high frequency ranges at which these devices operate (microwave, 10^9 to 10^{10} Hz; infrared, 10^{11} to 10^{14} Hz; laser, 10^{14} to 10^{15} Hz), there is the potential for very high data rates. Practical systems for short links have been built with data rates of several megabits per second.

These transmission techniques are primarily useful for connecting local networks that are in separate buildings. It is difficult to string cable between buildings, either underground or overhead on poles, especially if the intervening space is public property. The line-of-sight techniques only require equipment at each building.

The *infrared* link consists of a pair of transmitter/receivers (transceivers) that modulate noncoherent infrared light. Transceivers must be within the line of sight, installed on either a rooftop or within a building with data transmitted through adjacent exterior windows. The system is highly directional; it is extremely difficult to intercept, inject data, or to jam such systems. No licensing is required, and the system can be installed in just a few days. Data rates of a few megabits per second over a few kilometers are practical [SEAM82].

A similar system can be installed with *laser* transceivers using coherent light modulation. The major difference is that the Food and Drug Administration (FDA) requires that laser hardware, which emits low-level radiation, be properly shielded. The licensing process takes from 2 to 6 months [CELA82].

Both infrared and laser are susceptible to environmental interference, such as rain and fog. A system with less sensitivity is *microwave*. As with laser and infrared, installation is relatively easy; the major difference is that microwave transceivers can only be mounted externally to a building. Microwave is less directional than either laser or infrared; hence there is a security problem of data eavesdropping, insertion, or jamming. As with all radio-frequency systems, microwave requires Federal Communications Commission (FCC) licensing, which takes about 2 to 3 months. Comparable data rates and distances to laser and infrared can be achieved [RUSH82].

Table 3.3 summarizes the key characteristics of these techniques and includes, for comparison, the use of cable for building-to-building links.

Choice of Transmission Medium

The choice of transmission medium is determined by a number of factors. It is, we shall see, constrained by the topology of the local network. Other factors come into play, such as [ABRA83]:

- *Capacity:* to support the expected local network traffic.
- *Reliability:* to meet availability requirements.
- *Types of data supported:* tailored to the application.
- *Environmental scope:* to provide service over the range of environments required.

And so on. The choice is part of the overall task of designing a local network, which is addressed in a later chapter. Here we can make a few general observations.

Twisted pair is an inexpensive, well-understood medium. Typically, office buildings are wired to meet the anticipated telephone system demand

TABLE 3.3 Transmission Media for Local Networks: Point-to-Point Across Public Property

Medium	Easy of Installation	Regulatory Licensing (months)	Data Rate (Mbps)	Ease of Maintenance	Cost
Infrared	1–2 days, easy	None	1–3	Excellent	Low
Laser	1–2 days, easy	2–6	1–3	Excellent	Low
Microwave	1 week, easy	2–3	1–3	Excellent	Low
Underground coax/optical fiber	1–18 months, moderate to hard	6–18	10+	Fair to good	Moderate to high
Aerial coax/optical fiber	1–6 months, moderate	6–18	10+	Good	Moderate to high

Source: [CELA82].

plus a healthy margin. Compared to coax, the bandwidth is limited. Twisted pair is likely to be the most cost effective for a single building, low-traffic, local network installation. An office automation system, with a preponderance of dumb terminals and/or intelligent workstations plus a few minis, is a good example.

Coaxial cable is more expensive than twisted pair, but has greater capacity. For the broad range of local network requirements, and with the exception of terminal-intensive systems, it is the medium of choice. For most requirements, a coaxial-based local network can be designed to meet current demand with plenty of room for expansion, at reasonable cost. Coaxial systems excel when there are a lot of devices and a considerable amount of traffic. Examples include large data processing installations and sophisticated office automation systems, which may include facsimile machines, intelligent copiers, and color graphics devices.

At the current state of the art, fiber optic links are suited for point-to-point communications. Hence they do not compete with coaxial cable. The exception is for ring topology networks. However, when the cost of multi-drop fiber cable becomes competitive with that of coaxial cable, its advantages—low noise susceptibility, low loss, small size, light weight—will make it a serious contender for many local network applications.

The line-of-sight media are not well suited to local network requirements. They are, however, good choices for point-to-point links between buildings, each of which has a twisted-pair or coaxial-based local network.

RELATIONSHIP BETWEEN MEDIUM AND TOPOLOGY

Combinations

The choices of transmission medium and topology are not independent. Table 3-4 shows the preferred combinations. The ring topology requires point-to-point links between repeaters. Twisted-pair wire, baseband coaxial cable, and optical fiber can all be used to provide the links. However, broadband coaxial cable would not work well in this topology. Each repeater would have to be capable of receiving and transmitting data simultaneously on multiple channels. It is doubtful that the expense of such devices could be justified. Table 3-5 summarizes representative parameters for transmission media for commercially available ring LANs.

For the bus topology, twisted pair and both baseband and broadband coaxial cable are appropriate. At the present time, optical fiber cable is not

TABLE 3.4 Relationship Between Medium and Topology

	Topology			
Medium	Bus	Tree	Ring	Star
Twisted pair	×		×	×
Baseband coaxial cable	×		×	
Broadband coaxial cable	×	×		
Optical fiber			×	

TABLE 3.5 Characteristics for Transmission Media for Local Networks: Ring

Transmission Medium	Data Rate (Mbps)	Repeater Spacing (km)	Number of Repeaters
Unshielded Twisted Pair	4	0.1	72
Shielded Twisted Pair	16	0.3	250
Baseband Coaxial Cable	16	1.0	250
Optical Fiber	100	2.0	240

feasible, as the multipoint configuration is not cost-effective, due to the difficulty in constructing low-loss optical taps. The tree topology can be employed with broadband coaxial cable. The unidirectional nature of broadband signaling allows the construction of a tree architecture. On the other hand, the bidirectional nature of baseband signaling, on either twisted pair or coaxial cable, is not suited to the tree topology. Again, optical fiber is not now cost effective for the multipoint nature of the tree topology. Table 3-6 summarizes representative parameters for transmission media for commercially available bus and tree LANs.

The reader will note that the performance for a given medium is considerably better for the ring topology compared with the bus/tree topology. In the bus/tree topology, each station is attached to the medium by a tap, and each tap introduces some attenuation and distortion to the signal as it passes by. In the ring, each station is attached to the medium by a repeater, and each repeater generates a new signal to compensate for effects of attenuation and distortion.

The star topology requires a single point-to-point link between each device and the central switch. Twisted pair is admirably suited to the task. The higher data rates of coaxial cable or fiber would overwhelm the switches of today's technology.

Layout

One very practical issue is related to the selection of both medium and topology, and that is the actual layout of the transmission medium in the building. To address this issue, we need to make a distinction between topology and geometry. The net illustrations in Figure 3-2 depict the various topologies of local networks; this defines the way in which the devices are interconnected. But, as a practical matter, the actual path that the cable follows is constrained by physical characteristics of the building. The cable must follow routes that accomodate the walls and floors of the

**TABLE 3.6 Characteristics for Transmission Media for
Local Networks: Bus**

Transmission Medium	Data Rate (Mbps)	Range (km)	Number of Taps
Unshielded Twisted Pair	1–2	<2	10's
Baseband Coaxial Cable	10/70	<3/<1	100's/10's
Broadband Coaxial Cable	20 per channel	<30	100's–1,000's

building. Typically, predefined cable paths are used, sometimes defined by the existence of conduits. Thus the geometry, or actual layout of the cable, will be distorted to some extent relative to the intended topology.

Let us consider some of the requirements that dictate the layout of the installed cable. Of prime importance is the need to minimize cost while providing the required capacity. One determinant of cost, of course, is the medium itself. As was mentioned, twisted pair is cheaper than coaxial cable, which is in turn cheaper than optical fiber. It is often the case, however, that the installation costs, which are primarily labor costs, far exceed the cost of the materials. This is particularly true in existing buildings, which may present difficulties in finding pathways for new cable. In new buildings, the problems and costs can be minimized if the cable layout for a local network can be designed ahead of time. Then the cable can be installed during construction.

A second important requirement is that the layout be suitable for accommodating equipment relocation and network growth. It is not unusual for 50% of the installed data terminals in an office building to be moved each year [IBM84a]. And, with the continued proliferation of personal and other microcomputers, virtually any local network can be expected to grow. The safest way to plan for both relocation and growth is to install a network that reaches every office, or at least to install a smaller network that can easily be expanded to include additional offices with little or no disruption of the existing network. Finally, the layout should be such as to facilitate servicing and maintenance. When a fault occurs somewhere in the network, we would like to be able to locate the fault, isolate it from the rest of the network, and fix it as soon as possible.

With the above considerations in mind, we can identify two general strategies for laying out the local network transmission medium: linear and star. Table 3.7 summarizes the relationship of the layout strategy to the transmission media and topologies of local networks.

The linear strategy attempts to provide the desired topology with the

TABLE 3.7   The Use of Alternative Wiring Strategies

Medium	Topology		
	Star	Ring	Bus
Twisted pair	S	L, S	L, S
Coaxial cable		L	L
Optical fiber		L	L

L = linear wiring strategy
S = star wiring strategy

minimum cable, subject to the physical constraints of the building. The medium is propagated to the subscriber locations, which may be some or all of the offices in the building. Any of the guided media which have been described can be used, and either a bus or ring topology can be provided.

The star layout strategy uses an individual cable from a concentration point to each subscriber location. This is clearly the proper approach for the star topology local network. It can also be used for bus and ring topologies, as depicted in Figure 3-5. In the case of the bus topology, the bus is very short and resides at the concentration point; the drop cables to the attached devices are relatively long. In the case of the ring topology, the ring is distorted so that each link of the ring loops through the concentration point. Typically, this layout is used separately on each floor of a building. The concentration point is referred to as a wiring closet; some or all of the offices on the floor are connected to the closet. Connections between floors are provided by linking the closets. This type of layout is invariably used to support telephones in an office building, and is becoming increasingly popular for local networks.

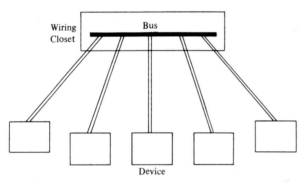

a. Bus Using Star Wiring

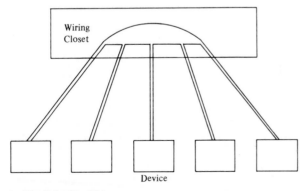

b. Ring Using Star Wiring

FIGURE 3-5. Bus and Ring Topologies Using Star Wiring

**3.3 RELATIONSHIP BETWEEN
MEDIUM AND TOPOLOGY**

Although the star strategy is logical for the star topology, it may seem inappropriate for the ring and bus topologies. Its main disadvantage is that, for the ring and bus, the star strategy will require more cable than the linear strategy, increasing cost and cable congestion. For this reason, the star strategy is rarely used for coaxial cable or optical fiber local networks. However, the star approach is well-suited for twisted-pair local networks, where the cost penalty is lower. Some of the advantages of the star strategy are:

1. It lends itself to prewiring of the building. The layout is a regular one and conforms to normal installation practice in office buildings. Furthermore, most existing buildings are prewired with excess unshielded twisted pair. Thus, for local networks that employ unshielded twisted pair, it may be possible to use existing wiring. Even in the case of shielded twisted pair, installation will be easier since the paths for the new cable are well-defined.
2. The system can be easily expanded, simply by patching additional cables into the network at the wiring closet.
3. Servicing and maintenance are easier. Diagnosis of problems can be performed from centralized points. Faults can easily be isolated by patching cables out of the network.

Further discussuion of the star strategy will be provided as we look at some specific uses in the next two chapters.

3.4

CLASSES OF LOCAL NETWORKS

This section presents a classification of local networks into three categories: local area network (LAN), high-speed local network (HSLN), and circuit-switched local networks. Table 3.8 summarizes representative characteristics. As with any classification, this one is useful to the extent that it provides a clear differentiation among categories and serves to organize the field in a meaningful way. The three classifications were chosen on the following grounds:

- *Technology:* The architectural and design issues differ significantly for the three classes. This will be seen in such areas as performance, communication protocols, switching technique, and hardware/software interface, as well as transmission media and topologies.
- *Applications:* Although there is some overlap, the three classes of local networks have by and large been developed independently to meet different sets of requirements.

TABLE 3.8 Classes of Local Networks

Characteristic	Local Area Network	High Speed Local Network	Circuit-switched Local Network
Transmission medium	Twisted pair, coaxial (both), fiber	CATV coaxial	Twisted pair
Topology	Bus, tree, ring	Bus	Star
Transmission speed	1–20 Mbps	50 Mbps	9.6–64 kbps
Maximum distance	25 km	1 km	1 km
Switching technique	Packet	Packet	Circuit
Number of devices supported	100's–1000's	10's	100's–1000's
Attachment cost	$500–$5000	$40,000–$50,000	$250–$1000

- *Standards:* Communication protocol standards are being developed separately for LANs and HSLNs.

Local Area Network

The term *local area network* (LAN) is typically used to refer to a general-purpose local network, which can serve a wide variety of devices over a large area. LANs support minis, mainframes, terminals, and peripherals. In many cases, these networks can carry not only data, but voice, video, and graphics. The office automation and factory automation examples of Chapter 1 fall into this category. A common type of LAN is a bus or tree using coaxial cable. Rings using twisted pair, coax, or even fiber are an alternative. The data transfer rates on LANs (1 to 20 Mbps) are high enough to satisfy most requirements and provide sufficient capacity to permit large numbers of devices to share the network.

A subcategory of LANs consists of low-cost networks intended primarily for microcomputers and inexpensive peripherals, such as the personal computer example in Chapter 1. Typically, these networks have data rates of 1 Mbps or less and usually use twisted pair. Because of their low cost, and the growing use of personal computers, these are the most prevalent local networks today and probably will continue to be so [KILL82].

The LAN is probably the best choice when a variety of devices and a mix of traffic types are involved. The LAN, alone or as part of a hybrid local network with one of the other types, is becoming a common feature of many office buildings and other installations.

Standards for LANs have been developed by a committee of the Institute for Electrical and Electronic Engineers (IEEE), known as the IEEE 802 committee.

High-Speed Local Network

The *high-speed local network* (HSLN) is designed to provide high end-to-end throughput between expensive, high-speed devices such as mainframes and mass storage devices. The computer room network example of Chapter 1 falls into this category.

Until recently, work on HSLNs has concentrated on the bus topology using CATV coaxial cable. Very high data rates are achievable—50 Mbps is standard—but both the distance and the number of devices are limited. More recent work has focused on optical fiber rings in the 80- to 100-Mbps range.

The HSLN is typically found in a computer room setting. Its main function is to provide I/O channel connections among a number of devices. Typical uses include file and bulk data transfer, automatic backup, and load leveling. Because of the current high prices for HSLN attachment, they are generally not practical for minicomputers, microcomputers, and less expensive peripherals.

Standards for HSLNs have been developed by a committee sponsored by the American National Standards Institute (ANSI), known as the ANS X3T9.5 committee.

Circuit-Switched Local Networks

In contrast to the LAN and HSLN, which use packet switching, there is another approach to local networking using circuit switching. Typically, circuit-switched local networks have a star or hierarchical star topology using twisted-pair wire to connect end points to the switch. In the hierarchical star, high-speed trunks of coaxial cable or optical fiber may be used to connect satellite switching units to the central switching unit. Data rates to individual stations are typically low ($\leq$64 kbps), but bandwidth is guaranteed and there is essentially no network delay once a connection is made.

One form of circuit-switched local network is the digital private branch exchange (PBX). This is an on-premise switch designed to handle both voice and data connections. Although the strength of these systems is their support for telephones, they are also well suited to terminal-to-host data traffic. Another form is the digital data switch. Devices in this category are designed to handle data only, not voice, and are typically lower in cost than a digital PBX of comparable size.

Choice of Network Type

Because the types of local networks are differentiated, at least partly, by transmission medium and topology, the observations of previous sections apply here. In general, the choice of network type represents a balance between requirements and cost [DERF83].

For applications requiring frequent high throughput between expensive devices, the HSLN currently controls the market. Although the attachment cost is high ($40,000 to $50,000), it is still only a fraction of the cost of the mainframes typically connected to the HSLN. High-speed service on a broadband LAN may, in the future, compete with the HSLN. This topic is explored in Chapter 6.

For most other applications, the choice facing the user is between the circuit-switched local network and the LAN. Both will handle a wide variety of devices. Currently, circuit-switched local network service is limited to about 64 kbps for each attachment. However, this speed is typical of devices that attach to the LAN. Only in certain instances, such as the use of a high-speed graphics device or the need to support heavy traffic between minis, are higher data rates required.

3.5

RECOMMENDED READING

An excellent overview of local network technology is [ROSE82]; it includes a discussion of the pros and cons of various media and topologies. Detailed description of the transmission characteristics of the media discussed in this section can be found in [FREE81] and [BELL82a]; a briefer survey with a good list of references is contained in [CHOU83]. [PERS83] and [KECK85] provide good introductions to optical fiber transmission. [THUR79] provides an interesting classification of local networks based on architecture.

3.6

PROBLEMS

3.1 What functions should be performed by the network layer (layer 3) in a bus topology local network? Ring topology? Star topology?

3.2 Could HDLC be used as a link layer for a bus topology local network? If not what is missing? Answer for ring and star.

3.3 An asynchronous device, such as a teletype, transmits characters one at a time with unpredictable delays between characters. What problems, if any, do you foresee if such a device is connected to a local network and allowed to transmit at will (subject to gaining access to the medium)? How might such problems be resolved? Answer for ring, bus, and star.

3.4 Which combination or combinations of medium and topology would be appropriate for the following applications, and why?
   a. Terminal intensive: many terminals throughout an office; one or a few share central computers.
   b. Small network: fewer than 50 devices, all low speed (<56 kbps).
   c. Office automation: a few hundred devices, mostly terminals and minicomputers.

3.5 Consider the transfer of a file containing one million characters from one section to another. What is the total elapsed time and effective throughput for the following cases:

a. A circuit-switched, star topology local network. Call setup time is negligible, and the data rate on the medium is 64 kbps.

b. A bus topology local network with two stations a distance D apart, a data rate of B bps, and a packet size P with 80 bits of overhead. Each packet is acknowledged with an 88-bit packet before the text is sent. The propagation speed on the bus is 200 m/μsec. Solve for:

(1): $D = 1$km, $B = 1$ Mbps, $P = 256$ bits
(2): $D = 1$km, $B = 10$ Mbps, $P = 256$ bits
(3): $D = 10$km, $B = 1$ Mbps, $P = 256$ bits
(4): $D = 1$km, $B = 50$ Mbps, $P = 10,000$ bits

c. A ring topology with a total circular length of $2D$, with the two stations a distance D apart. Acknowledgment is achieved by allowing a packet to circulate past the destination station, back to the source station. There are N repeaters on the ring, each of which introduces a delay of one bit time. Repeat the calculation for each of b1 through b4 for $N = 10; 100; 1000$.

3.6 A 10-story office building has the floor plan of Figure 3.6 for each floor. A local network is to be installed that will allow attachment of a device from each office on each floor. Attachment is to take place along the outside wall at the baseboard. Cable or wire can be run vertically through the indicated closet and horizontally along the baseboards. The height of each story is 10 ft. What is the minimum total length of cable or wire required for bus, tree, ring, and star topologies?

3.7 A tree-topology local network is to be provided that spans two buildings. If permission can be obtained to string cable between the two buildings, then one continuous tree layout will be used. Otherwise, each building will have an independent tree topology network and a point-to-point link will connect a special communications station on one network with a communications station on the other network. What functions must the communications stations perform? Repeat for ring and star.

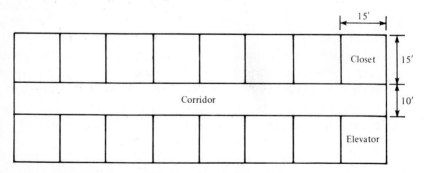

FIGURE 3-6. Building Layout for a Local Network

CHAPTER 4

Local Area Networks: Topologies and Transmission Media

Local area networks (LANs) are the most general purpose of the three types of local networks. They range from small, inexpensive systems that support personal computers to broadband coaxial cable systems spread over small cities supporting wide ranges of devices.

Recall that the three principal characteristics of a local network are transmission medium, topology, and medium access control. In this chapter, we examine the first two of these in some detail, leaving medium access control to Chapter 5. The chapter begins with an examination of bus/tree LANs, followed by an examination of ring LANs. In both cases, we confine ourselves to a consideration of copper media (coaxial cable, twisted pair). Finally we look at the design issues related to optical fiber LANs and describe alternative topologies that have been used or proposed. Throughout, reference is made to the IEEE 802 LAN standard. This is a standard developed by a committee of the Institute of Electrical and Electronic Engineers and discussed more fully in Chapter 5.

BUS/TREE TOPOLOGY

Characteristics of Bus/Tree LANs

Of the topologies discussed in the preceding chapter, only the bus/tree topology is a multipoint medium. That is, there are more than two devices connected to and capable of transmitting on the medium.

The operation of this type of LAN can be summarized briefly. Because multiple devices share a single data path, only one may transmit at a time. A station usually transmits data in the form of a packet containing the address of the destination. The packet propagates throughout the medium and is received by all other stations. The addressed station copies the packet as it goes by.

Two transmission techniques are in use for LANs: baseband and broadband. Baseband, using digital signaling, can be employed on twisted-pair or coaxial cable. Broadband, using analog signaling in the radio-frequency (RF) range, employs coaxial cable. Some of the differences are highlighted in Table 4.1, and this section explores the two methods in some detail. There is also a variant, known as "single-channel broadband," that has the signaling characteristics of broadband but some of the restrictions of baseband. This is also covered below.

The multipoint nature of the bus/tree topology gives rise to several rather stiff problems. First is the problem of determining which station on the medium may transmit at any point in time. With point-to-point links (only two stations on the medium), this is a fairly simple task. If the line is full-duplex, both stations may transmit at the same time; if the line is half-duplex, a rather simple mechanism is needed to ensure that the two stations take turns. Historically, the most common shared access scheme has been the multidrop line, in which access is determined by polling from a controlling station. The controlling station may send data to any other

TABLE 4.1 Bus/Tree Transmission Techniques

Baseband	Broadband
Digital signaling	Analog signaling (requires RF modem)
Entire bandwidth consumed by signal— no FDM	FDM possible—multiple data channels, video, audio
Bidirectional	Unidirectional
Bus topology	Bus or tree topology
Distance: up to a few kilometers	Distance: up to tens of kilometers

station, or it may issue a poll to a specific station, asking for an immediate response. This method, however, negates some of the advantages of a distributed system and is awkward for communication between two non-controller stations. A variety of distributed strategies, referred to as medium access control protocols, have now been developed for bus and tree topologies. These are discussed in Chapter 5.

A second problem has to do with signal balancing. When two devices exchange data over a link, the signal strength of the transmitter must be adjusted to be within certain limits. The signal must be strong enough so that, after attenuation across the medium, it meets the receiver's minimum signal strength requirements. It must also be strong enough to maintain an adequate signal to noise ratio. On the other hand, the signal must not be so strong that it overloads the circuitry of the transmitter, which creates harmonics and other spurious signals. Although easily done for a point-to-point link, signal balancing is no easy task for a multipoint line. If any device can transmit to any other device, then the signal balancing must be performed for all permutations of stations taken two at a time. For n stations that works out to $n \times (n - 1)$ permutations. So for a 200-station network (not a particularly large system), 39,800 signal strength constraints must be satisfied simultaneously. With interdevice distances ranging from tens to thousands of meters, this is an impossible task for any but small networks. In systems that use radio-frequency (RF) signals, the problem is compounded because of the possibility of RF signal interference across frequencies. The solution is to divide the medium into segments within which pairwise balancing is possible, using amplifiers or repeaters between segments.

Baseband Systems

The principal characteristics of a baseband system are listed in Table 4.1. As mentioned earlier, a baseband LAN is defined as one that uses digital signaling. (This is a restricted use of the word "baseband," which has become accepted in local network circles. More generally, "baseband" refers to the transmission of an analog or digital signal in its original form, without modulation.) Digital signals are inserted on the line as voltage pulses, usually using either Manchester or Differential Manchester encoding. The entire frequency spectrum of the medium is used to form the signal; hence frequency-division multiplexing (FDM) cannot be used. Transmission is bidirectional. That is, a signal inserted at any point on the medium propagates in both directions to the ends, where it is absorbed (Figure 4.1a). The digital signaling requires a bus topology. Unlike analog signals, digital signals cannot easily be propagated through the splitters and joiners required for a tree topology. Baseband systems can extend only a

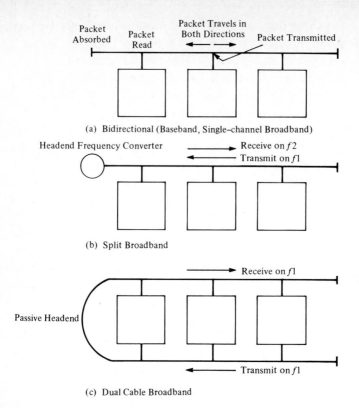

(a) Bidirectional (Baseband, Single–channel Broadband)

(b) Split Broadband

(c) Dual Cable Broadband

FIGURE 4-1. Baseband and Broadband Transmission Techniques

limited distance, about 1 km at most. This is because the attenuation of the signal, which is most pronounced at higher frequencies, causes a blurring of the pulses and a weakening of the signal to the extent that communication over larger distances is impractical.

Baseband Coax

The most well-known form of baseband bus LAN uses coaxial cable. We concentrate on those systems in this section. Unless otherwise indicated, the discussion is based on the Ethernet system [METC76, SHOC82, DIGI80] and the almost-identical IEEE standard [IEEE85b].

Most baseband coaxial cable systems use a special 50-ohm cable rather than the standard CATV 75-ohm cable. These values refer to the impedance of the cable. Roughly speaking, impedance is a measure of how much voltage must be applied to the cable to achieve a given signal strength (see Appendix 4A). For digital signals, the 50-ohm cable suffers less intense reflections from the insertion capacitance of the taps, and provides better immunity against low-frequency electromagnetic noise. The simplest baseband coaxial bus LAN consists of an unbranched length of coaxial cable with a terminating resistance at each end. The value of the resistance is set equal to the impedance of the cable; this prevents reflection by absorbing any signal on the cable.

As with any transmission system, there are engineering trade-offs involving data rate, cable length, number of taps, and the electrical characteristics of the transmit and receive components for a baseband coaxial system. For example, the lower the data rate, the longer the cable can be. That latter statement is true for the following reason: when a signal is propagated along a transmission medium, the integrity of the signal suffers due to attenuation, noise, and other impairments. The longer the length of propagation, the greater the effect, increasing the probability of error. However, at a lower data rate, the individual pulses of a digital signal last longer and can be recovered in the presence of impairments more easily than higher-rate, shorter pulses.

With the above in mind, we give one example that illustrates some of the tradeoffs. The Ethernet specification and the original IEEE standard specified the use of 50-ohm cable with a 0.4-inch diameter, and a data rate of 10 Mbps. With these parameters, the maximum length of the cable is set at 500 meters. Stations attach to the cable by means of a tap, with the distance between any two taps being a multiple of 2.5 m; this is to ensure that reflections from adjacent taps do not add in phase [YEN83]. A maximum of 100 taps is allowed. In IEEE jargon, this system is referred to as "10base5". The first two digits give the data rate in megabits per second; the four letters are an abbreviation for the medium (baseband); and the final digit is the maximum cable length in hundreds of meters.

To provide a lower-cost system for personal computer local networks, IEEE later added a 10base2 specification [METC83, FLAT84, JONE85]. Table 4.2 compares this system, dubbed Cheapernet, with the 10base5 specification. The key difference is the use of a thinner (0.25 in) cable, which is used in products like public address systems. The thinner cable is more flexible; thus it is easier to bend around corners and bring to a workstation cabinet rather than installing the cable in the wall and having to provide a drop cable to the station. The cable is easier to install and

TABLE 4.2   IEEE Specifications for 10-Mbps Baseband Coaxial Bus Local Networks

Parameter	10base5	10base2
Data Rate	10 Mbps	10 Mbps
Maximum Segment Length	500 m	200 m
Network Span	2500 m	1000 m
Nodes per Segment	100	30
Node Spacing	2.5 m	0.5 m
Cable Diameter	0.4 in	0.25 in

requires cheaper electronics than the thicker cable. On the other hand, the thinner cable suffers greater attenuation and lower noise resistance than the thicker cable. Thus it supports fewer taps over a shorter distance.

Figure 4.2, from the Ethernet specification, illustrates typical components and their functions. The main components are:

- Transceiver
- Transceiver cable
- Controller
- 50-ohm coaxial cable
- 50-ohm terminators

The transceiver taps into the coaxial cable. It transmits signals from the station to the cable, and vice versa. It also contains the electronics neces-

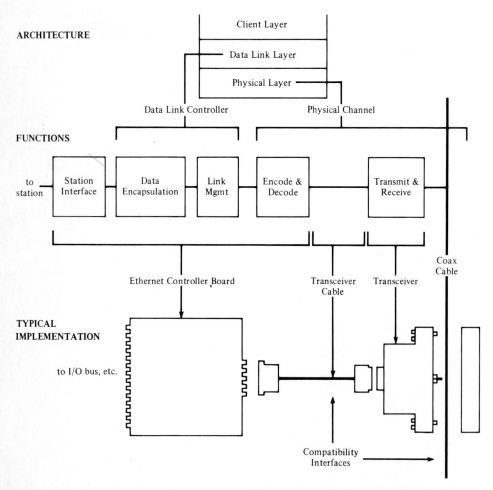

FIGURE 4-2. Ethernet Architecture and Typical Implementation (from [DIGI80])

sary to recognize the presence of a signal on the coaxial cable and to recognize a collision of two signals. This last function is needed for Ethernet and 802 because of the CSMA/CD protocol that they use (discussed in Chapter 5). A baseband bus LAN using some other protocol would not require this complexity. The transceiver also provides ground isolation between the signals from the station and the signals on the cable. Since two local grounds may differ by several volts, connection of local grounds to the cable could cause a large current to flow through the cable's shield, introducing noise and creating a safety hazard.

The transceiver cable comprises two twisted pair (referred to as twin pair) and connects the transceiver to the controller, which contains the bulk of the intelligence required to communicate over the LAN. This split is arbitrary: all of the electronics could be included at the transceiver end. The split is motivated by the assumption that the station will be located some distance from the cable and that the cable tap may be in a relatively inaccessible location. Hence the electronics at the tap should be as simple as possible to reduce maintenance costs. The cable supplies power to the transceiver and passes data signals between the transceiver and the controller as well as control signals. The latter includes a collision presence signal from transceiver to controller. Other signals are possible. For example, the 802 standard has isolate and cease-to-isolate signals, which allow the controller to enable and disable the transceiver.

The controller is an implementation of all the functions (other than those performed by the transceiver) needed to manage access to the coax cable for the purpose of exchanging packets between the coax cable and the attached station. More will be said about the particular functions in Chapter 5.

Finally, the transmission system consists of 50-ohm coaxial cable and terminators. The terminators absorb signals, preventing reflection from the ends of the bus.

These five types of components are sufficient for building a baseband bus LAN of up to about 1 km with up to about 100 stations. In many cases, this will be enough, but for greater requirements, an additional component is needed: the repeater.

The repeater is used to extend the length of the network. It consists, in essence, of two transceivers joined together and connected to two different segments of coaxial cable. The repeater passes digital signals in both directions between the two segments, amplifying and regenerating the signals as they pass through. A repeater is transparent to the rest of the system; since it does no buffering, it in no sense isolates one segment from another. So, for example, if two stations on different segments attempt to transmit at the same time, their packets will interfere with each other (collide). To avoid multipath interference, only one path of segments and repeaters is allowed between any two stations. The 802 standard allows a

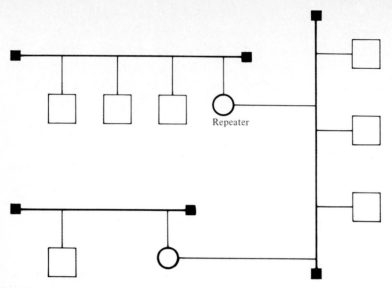

FIGURE 4-3. **Baseband Configuration**

maximum of four repeaters in the path between any two stations, extending the effective cable length to 2.5 km. Figure 4.3 is an example of a baseband system with three segments and two repeaters.

Unshielded Twisted Pair Baseband

In recent years, there has been increasing interest in the use of twisted pair as a transmission medium for LANs. From the earliest days of commercial LAN availability, twisted-pair bus LANs have been popular. However, such LANs suffer in comparison with a coaxial cable LAN. First of all, the apparent cost advantage of twisted pair is not as great as it might seem, when a linear bus layout is used. True, twisted-pair cable is less expensive than coaxial cable. On the other hand, much of the cost of LAN wiring is the labor cost of installing the cable, which is no greater for coaxial cable than for twisted pair. Secondly, coaxial cable provides superior signal quality, and therefore can support more devices over longer distances at higher data rates than twisted pair.

The renewed interest in twisted pair, at least in the context of bus/tree type LANs, is in the use of unshielded twisted pair in a star wiring arrangement (see discussion in Section 3.3). The reason for the interest is that unshielded twisted pair is simply telephone wire, and virtually all office buildings are equipped with spare twisted pairs running from wiring closets

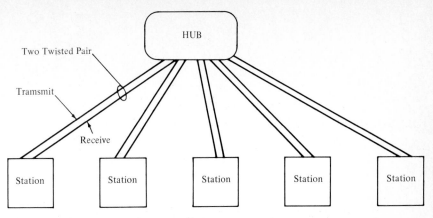

FIGURE 4-4. Twisted-Pair, Star-Wiring, Logical-Bus Arrangement

to each office. This yields several benefits when deploying a LAN:

1. There is essentially no installation cost with unshielded twisted pair, since the wire is already there. Coaxial cable has to be pulled. In older buildings, this may be difficult since existing conduits may be crowded.
2. In most office buildings, it is impossible to anticipate all the locations where network access will be needed. Since it is extravagantly expensive to run coaxial cable to every office, a coaxial-cable based LAN will typically only cover a portion of a building. If equipment subsequently has to be moved to an office not covered by the LAN, a significant expense is involved in extending the LAN coverage. With telephone wire, this problem does not arise, since all offices are covered.

The most popular approach to the use of unshielded twisted pair for a LAN is therefore a star-wiring approach. In Figure 3-5 we indicated how a star-wiring approach was compatible with a bus topology. In general, however, the products on the market use a scheme suggested by Figure 4-4, in which central element of the star is an active element, referred to as the **hub**. Each station is connected to the hub by two twisted pairs (transmit and receive). The hub acts as a repeater: When a single station transmits, the hub repeats the signal, on the outgoing line to each station.

Note that although this scheme is physically a star, it is logically a bus: A transmission from any one station is received by all other stations, and if two stations transmit at the same time there will be a collision.

Multiple levels of hubs can be cascaded in a hierarchical configuration. Figure 4-5 illustrates a two-level configuration. There is one **header hub** (HHUB) and one or more **intermediate hubs** (IHUB). Each hub may have a mixture of stations and other hubs attached to it from below. This layout fits well with building wiring practices. Typically, there is a wiring closet on

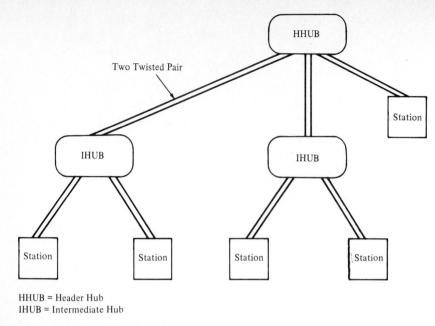

Two Twisted Pair

HHUB

Station

IHUB

IHUB

Station

Station

Station

Station

HHUB = Header Hub
IHUB = Intermediate Hub

FIGURE 4-5. Two-Level Hierarchy

each floor of an office building, and a hub can be placed in each one. Each hub could service the stations on its floor.

Figure 4-6 shows an abstract representation of the intermediate and header hubs. The header hub performs all the functions described previously for a single-hub configuration. In the case of an intermediate hub, any incoming signal from below is repeated upward to the next higher level. Any signal from above is repeated on all lower-level outgoing lines. Thus, the logical bus characteristic is retained: A transmission from any

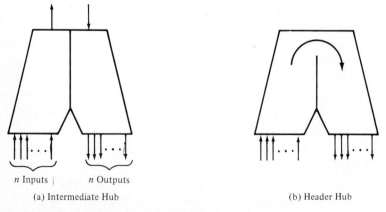

n Inputs n Outputs

(a) Intermediate Hub

(b) Header Hub

FIGURE 4-6. Intermediate and Header Hubs

one station is received by all other stations, and if two stations transmit at the same time there will be a collision.

The initial version of the above scheme employed a data rate of 1 Mbps, and was dubbed StarLAN [PARL85, GOLB86]. More recently, products operating at 10 Mbps have begun to appear [SCHM88, BREN87, MULQ88b]. These are intended to be compatible with the 10-Mbps baseband coaxial cable bus systems, requiring only a change of transceiver. Although there is now a fair amount of practical experience with these higher-speed systems, there remains a controversy about their practicality [CLAI88, ORLO88]. Several reasons for this controversy can be stated:

- Existing telephone wire in buildings can be inadequate for data transmission. Problems include twisted pair that isn't twisted, splicing and other connections, and other faults that are not noticeable for voice transmission but that would produce very high error rates at 10 Mbps.
- Twisted-pair cables are rather tightly packed together in conduits. The mutual capacitance from adjacent pairs adversely affects attenuation, crosstalk, and velocity of propagation. The effects on data transmission may not be noticeable at 1 Mbps, but become a problem at 10 Mbps.

These problems can to some extent be overcome by the use of signal processing techniques and by careful design of the transceiver. However, just as we saw with the 10-Mbps coaxial cable bus, there are trade-offs to be made. In this case, IEEE recommends a maximum distance between station and hub of 250 meters at 1 Mbps and 100 meters at 10 Mbps.

Broadband Systems

Like the term *baseband*, the term *broadband* is co-opted into the local network vocabulary from the telecommunications world, with a change in meaning. In general, broadband refers to any channel having a bandwidth greater than a voice-grade channel (4 kHz). In the local network context, the term refers to coaxial cable on which analog signaling is used. A further restriction to transmission techniques that allow frequency-division multiplexing (FDM) on the cable is usually applied. We will mean systems capable of FDM when using the term broadband. Systems intended to carry only a single analog signal will be referred to as *carrierband*.

Table 4-1 summarizes the key characteristics of broadband systems. As mentioned, broadband implies the use of analog signaling. FDM is possible: the frequency spectrum of the cable can be divided into channels or sections of bandwidth. Separate channels can support data traffic, television, and radio signals. Broadband components allow splitting and joining operations; hence both bus and tree topologies are possible. Much greater distances—tens of kilometers—are possible with broadband compared to baseband. This is because the analog signals that carry the digital data can propagate greater distances before the noise and attenuation damage the data.

Dual and Split Configurations

As with baseband, stations on a broadband LAN attach to the cable by means of a tap. Unlike baseband, however, broadband is inherently a unidirectional medium; the taps that are used allow signals inserted onto the medium to propagate in only one direction. The primary reason for this is that it is unfeasible to build amplifiers that will pass signals of one frequency in both directions. This unidimensional property means that only those stations "downstream" from a transmitting station can receive its signals. How, then, to achieve full connectivity?

Clearly, two data paths are needed. These paths are joined at a point on the network known as the **headend**. For a bus topology, the headend is simply one end of the bus. For a tree topology, the headend is the root of the branching tree. All stations transmit on one path toward the headend (inbound). Signals arriving at the headend are then propagated along a second data path away from the headend (outbound). All stations receive on the outbound path.

Physically, two different configurations are used to implement the inbound and outbound paths. (Figure 4-1 b and c). On a **dual-cable** configuration, the inbound and outbound paths are separate cables, with the headend simply a passive connector between the two. Stations send and receive on the same frequency.

By contrast, on a **split** configuration, the inbound and outbound paths are different frequency bands on the same cable. Bidirectional amplifiers[1] pass lower frequencies inbound, and higher frequencies outbound. Between the inbound and outbound frequency bands is a guardband, which carries no signals and serves merely as a separator. The headend contains a device for converting inbound frequencies to outbound frequencies.

The frequency-conversion device at the headend can either be an analog or digital device. An analog device, known as a **frequency translator**, converts a block of frequencies from one range to another. A digital device, known as a **remodulator**, recovers the digital data from the inbound analog signal and then retransmits the data on the outbound frequency. Thus, a remodulator provides better signal quality by removing all of the accumulated noise and attenuation and transmitting a cleaned-up signal.

---

[1] Unfortunately, this terminology is confusing, since we have said that broadband is inherently a unidirectional medium. At a given frequency, broadband is unidirectional. However, there is no difficulty in having signals in nonoverlapping frequency bands traveling in opposite directions on the cable, and in amplifying those signals.

TABLE 4.3 Common Cable Frequency Splits

Format	Inbound Frequency Band	Outbound Frequency Band	Maximum Two-way Bandwidth
Subsplit	5 to 30 MHz	54 to 400 MHz	25 MHz
Midsplit	5 to 116 MHz	168 to 400 MHz	111 MHz
Highsplit	5 to 174 MHz	232 to 400 MHz	168 MHz
Dual Cable	40 to 400 MHz	40 to 400 MHz	360 MHz

Split systems are categorized by the frequency allocation of the two paths, as shown in Table 4-3. Subsplit, commonly used by the cable television industry, was designed for metropolitan area television distribution, with limited subscriber-to-central office communication. It provides the easiest way to upgrade existing one-way cable systems to two-way operation. Subsplit has limited usefulness for local area networking because a bandwidth of only 25 MHz is available for two-way communication. Midsplit is more suitable for LANs, since it provides a more equitable distribution of bandwidth. However, midsplit was developed at a time when the practical spectrum of a cable-TV cable was 300 MHz, whereas a spectrum of 400 to 450 MHz is now available. Accordingly, a highsplit specification has been developed to provide greater two-way bandwidth for a split cable system.

The differences between split and dual configurations are minor. The split system is useful when a single cable plant is already installed in a building. If a large amount of bandwidth is needed, or the need is anticipated, then a dual cable system is indicated. Beyond these considerations, it is a matter of a trade-off between cost and size. The single-cable system has the fixed cost of the headend remodulator or frequency translator. The dual cable system makes use of more cable, taps, splitters, and amplifiers. Thus, dual cable is cheaper for smaller systems, where the fixed cost of the headend is noticeable, and single cable is cheaper for larger systems, where incremental costs dominate.

Broadband Components

Broadband systems use standard, off-the-shelf cable television components, including 75-ohm coaxial cable. All endpoints are terminated with a 75-ohm terminator to absorb signals (see Appendix 4A). Broadband is suitable for tens of kilometers radius from the headend and hundreds or even thousands of devices. The main components of the system are:

- Cable
- Terminators

- Amplifiers
- Directional couplers
- Modems
- Controllers

Cables used in broadband networks are of three types. **Trunk cable** forms the spine of a large LAN system. Trunk cables use a semi-rigid construction. As the name implies, semi-rigid cable is not flexible. The outer portion of the cable is made of solid aluminum. The cable can be bent, but not too many times and not very easily. Trunk lines come in six sizes, ranging from 0.412 to 1 inch in diameter. The greater the diameter of the cable, the lower the attenuation. Semi-rigid cable has excellent noise rejection characteristics and can be used indoors and outdoors. Typically, a trunk cable will extend from a few kilometers to tens of kilometers.

Distribution cables, or **feeder cables**, are used for shorter distances and for branch cables. They may be semirigid or flexible, and are typically 0.4 to 0.5 inch in diameter. Whereas trunk cables may be used indoors or outdoors, feeder cables are generally limited to indoor use. The choice of cable depends on a number of criteria [COOP84]:

- The physical constraints of the route: smaller-diameter cables are easier to install.
- The required signal level for the distribution network: larger-diameter cables have less signal loss.
- Local and national building codes.

The flexible cable most commonly used for feeder cable has the designation RG-11. With a diameter of 0.405 inches, and with poorer noise resistance than semi-rigid cable, distance is limited to about 800 meters.

Drop cables are used to connect outlets and stations to distribution cables. These are short (10 to 50 feet) and therefore need not be very large in diameter; although attenuation per unit length is greater for narrower cable, the short distance means that the total attenuation will be small even with a narrow cable. The cables used are flexible and include RG-59 (0.242 in diameter), RG-6 (0.332 inch), and RG-11 (0.405 inch) cables.

Amplifiers may be used on trunk and distribution cables to compensate for cable attenuation. As Figure 4-7 indicates, attenuation on a cable is an increasing function of frequency. Therefore, amplifiers must have a slope to account for the variability of attenuation. For split systems, amplifiers must be bidirectional, passing and amplifying lower frequencies in one direction and higher frequencies in the other.

Directional couplers provide a means for dividing one input into two outputs and combining two inputs into one output. **Splitters**, used to branch the cable, provide roughly equal attenuation along the split branches. **Taps**, used to connect drop cables and hence stations to the LAN,

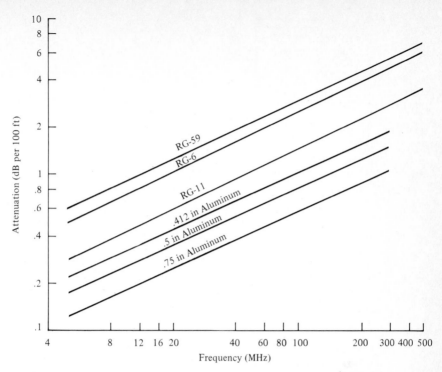

FIGURE 4-7. Cable Attenuation versus Frequency for Various Sizes of Coaxial Cable

provide more attenuation to the drop cable. Figure 4-8 illustrates these concepts.

⌐**Modems** are needed to convert between the digital data of the attached stations and the analog signal on the medium.⌐ A variety of modulation techniques are in use. The two most common, which are endorsed for use on IEEE-802-standard LANs (see Appendix 5A), are differential phase-shift keying (DPSK), used with IEEE 802.3 [ABRA86] and duobinary AM/PSK, used with IEEE 802.4 [RATN83].

In ordinary PSK, a binary zero is represented by a carrier with a particular phase, and a binary one is represented by a carrier with the opposite phase (180-degree difference). DPSK makes use of differential encoding, in which a change of phase occurs when a zero occurs, and there is no change of phase when a one occurs. The advantage of differential encoding is that it is easier for the receiver to detect the presence or absence of a change of phase than it is to determine the phase itself.

In duobinary AM/PSK, a special narrow-bandwidth pulse is created that is used to amplitude-modulate an RF carrier. Such pulse is illustrated in Figure 4-9 for a 10-Mbps data rate; the pulse of opposite polarity is also used. Note that the pulse spreads over a number of bit time. Thus, pulses that are generated in nearby bit slots will overlap. However, the overlap is

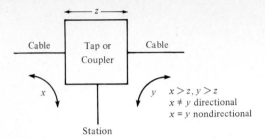

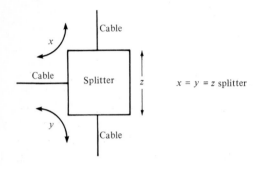

(a) Coupler

(b) Splitter
x, y, z = attenuation

FIGURE 4-8.   Directional Couplers and Splitters

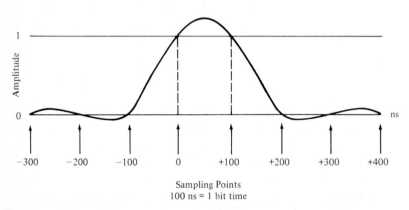

Sampling Points
100 ns = 1 bit time

FIGURE 4-9.   Input Pulse for Duobinary AM/PSK at 10 Mbps

highly predictable: At each sample point, a pulse has a value of 0 or 1. Thus, at any sample point, a 0, 1, or 2 can be detected. To encode digital data, two pulses, one bit time apart are used. A binary one is represented by two consecutive pulses of the same polarity, which will produce a sample of +2 or -2, and a binary zero is represented by two consecutive pulses of opposite polarity, which produces a sample of 0. Each pulse

**LOCAL AREA NETWORKS: TOPOLOGIES AND
TRANSMISSION MEDIA**

participates in two bits; that is, each pulse is both the second pulse of one bit and the first pulse of the next bit.

A characteristic common to virtually all broadband LAN modems is the use of scrambling. This gives the data a pseudorandom nature that helps the receiver extract bit-timing information. It also improves the spectral characteristics of the signal, giving it a more uniform power distribution, as opposed to the potentially strong discrete spectral lines in nonscrambled data. This gives the signal better noise resistance. The scrambling process is explained in Appendix 4C.

Finally, **controllers** are needed, as in baseband, to provide the basic LAN service.

Data Transmission Services

As mentioned earlier, the broadband LAN can be used to carry multiple channels, some used for analog signals, such as video and voice, and some for digital. Digital channels can generally carry a data rate of somewhere between 0.5 and 2 bps/Hz. Figure 4.10 shows a possible allocation of a 350-MHz cable.

Three kinds of digital data transfer service are possible on a broadband cable: dedicated, switched, and multiple access (Figure 4.11). For dedicated service, a small portion of the cable's bandwidth is reserved for exclusive use by two devices. No special protocol is needed. Each of the two devices attaches to the cable through a modem; both modems are tuned to the same frequency. This technique is analogous to securing a dedicated leased line from the telephone company. The dedicated service could be used to connect two devices when a heavy traffic pattern is expected; for example, one computer may act as a standby for another and need to get frequent updates of state information and file and database changes. Transfer rates of up to 20 Mbps are achievable.

The switched technique requires the use of a number of frequency bands. Devices are attached through *frequency agile modems*, capable of changing their frequency by electronic command. Initially, all attached devices, together with a controller, are tuned to the same frequency. A station wishing to establish a connection sends a request to the controller, which assigns an available frequency to the two devices and signals their modems to tune to that frequency. This technique is analogous to a dial-up line. Because the cost of frequency-agile modems rises dramatically with data rate, rates of 56 kbps or less are typical. The switched technique is used in Wang's local network for terminal-to-host connections [STAH82], and could also be used for voice service.

Finally, the multiple-access service allows a number of attached devices to be supported at the same frequency. This provides for distributed, peer communications among many devices, which is the primary motivation for

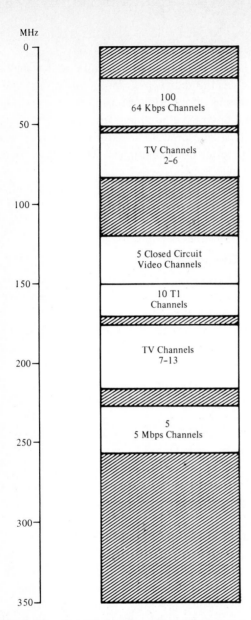

FIGURE 4-10.   Dual-Cable Broadband Spectrum Allocation

a local network. As with baseband, some form of medium access control protocol is needed to control transmission. These protocols are discussed in Chapter 5.

Baseband versus Broadband

One of the silliest aspects of the intense coverage afforded local networks in the trade and professional literature is the baseband versus broadband

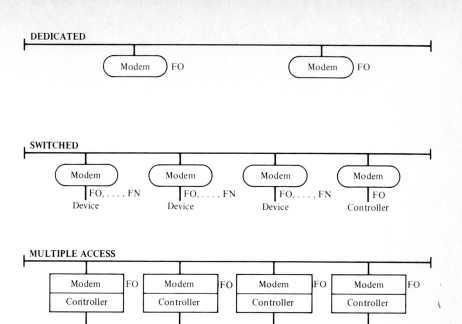

FIGURE 4-11. Broadband Data Transfer Services

debate. A *Datamation* article captured the spirit [KLEE82]:

> You almost expect to find cabbies talking about it: you've just hopped into the back seat of a Checker at O'Hare, say, and the driver turns around and offers: "Yeah, so me and the wife talked it over and we decided baseband is the way to go. None of this CSMA/CD line access, though; it won't do the job if the net gets busy. We're working on token passing. We'll probably announce it by late second quarter. It looks very promising."
>
> At this point the dispatcher sticks his head in the window. "On yeah?" he says, "What are you going to do about voice, then? What are you going to do five years down the pike when you wanna videoconference? You can go ahead and lock yourself into the office of the past if you want, but count me out. My money's on broadband."

The fact is that there is room for both technologies in the local network field. Potential customers will find themselves faced with a lot of other, more complex, decisions than this one. For the interested reader, thought-ful discussions may be found in [HOPK82] and [KRUT81].

Table 4.4 summarizes the pros and cons of the two technologies. Base-band has the advantage of simplicity, and, in principle, lower cost. The layout of a baseband cable plant is simple; there are just five rules for trunk layout in the Ethernet specification. An office-building electrician should be able to do the job.

The potential disadvantages of baseband include the limitations in capacity and distance—disadvantages only if your requirements exceed

TABLE 4.4   Baseband versus Broadband

Advantages	Disadvantages
Baseband	
Cheaper—no modem	Single channel
Simpler technology	Limited capacity
Easy to install	Limited distance
	Grounding concerns
Broadband	
High capacity	Modem cost
Multiple traffic types	Installation and maintenance complexity
More flexible configurations	Doubled propagation delay
Large area coverage	
Mature CATV technology	

those limitations. Another concern has to do with grounding. Because dc components are on the cable, it can be grounded in only one place. Care must be taken to avoid potential shock hazards and antenna effects.

Broadband's strength is its tremendous capacity; it can carry a wide variety of traffic on a number of channels. With the use of amplifiers, broadband can achieve very wide area coverage. Also, the system is based on a mature CATV technology. Components are reliable and readily available.

Broadband systems are more complex than baseband to install and maintain. The layout design must include cable type selection, and place-

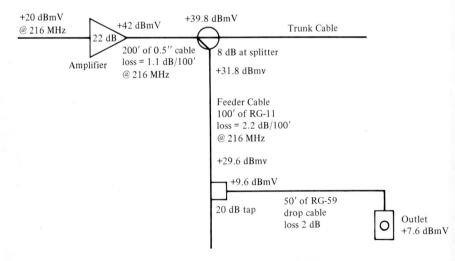

FIGURE 4-12.   Signal Levels from Trunk to Outlet [COOP84]

ment and setting of all amplifiers and taps. To get some feeling for the complexity of broadband cable layout design, consider Figure 4-12, which shows a small portion of a cable plant.[2] In order to assure that the signal level at each station or outlet is within prescribed tolerances, the engineer must consider the attenuation loss along each cable segment, the loss at each splitter and tap, and the gain at each amplifier. These losses and gains must be balanced to provide proper signal levels throughout the LAN. Maintenance involves periodic testing and alignment of all network parameters. These are jobs for experienced radio-frequency engineers.

Finally, the average propagation delay between stations on broadband is twice that for a comparable baseband system. This reduces the efficiency and performance of the broadband system, as discussed in Chapter 9.

As with all other network design choices, the selection of baseband or broadband must be based on relative costs and benefits. It is likely that some installations will have both types. Neither is likely to win the LAN war.

Carrierband Systems

There is another application of analog signaling on a LAN, known as carrierband, or single-channel broadband. In this case, the entire spectrum of the cable is devoted to a single transmission path for the analog signals; no frequency-division multiplexing is possible.

Typically, a carrierband LAN has the following characteristics [KLEI86a, RELC87]. Bidirectional transmission, using a bus topology, is employed. Hence there can be no amplifiers, and there is no need for a headend. Although the entire spectrum is used, most of the signal energy is concentrated at relatively low frequencies. This is an advantage, because attenuation is less at lower frequencies.

Because the cable is dedicated to a single task, it is not necessary to take care that the modem output be confined to a narrow bandwidth. Energy can spread over the entire spectrum. As a result, the electronics are simple and relatively inexpensive. Typically, some form of frequency-shift keying (FSK) is used.

Carrierband would appear to give comparable performance, at a comparable price, to baseband.

---

[2] The figure uses dB and dBmV units; these are explained in Appendix 4B.

RING TOPOLOGY

Description

The ring consists of a number of repeaters, each connected to two others by unidirectional transmission links to form a single closed path (Figure 4.13). Data are transferred sequentially, bit by bit, around the ring from one repeater to the next. Each repeater regenerates and retransmits each bit.

For a ring to operate as a communications network, three functions are required: data insertion, data reception, and data removal. These functions are provided by the repeaters. Each repeater, in addition to serving as an active element on the ring, serves as a device attachment point for data insertion. Data are transmitted in packets, each of which contains a destination address field. As a packet circulates past a repeater, the address field is copied to the attached station. If the station recognizes the address, then the remainder of the packet is copied.

A variety of strategies can be used for determining how and when packets are added to and removed from the ring. The strategy can be

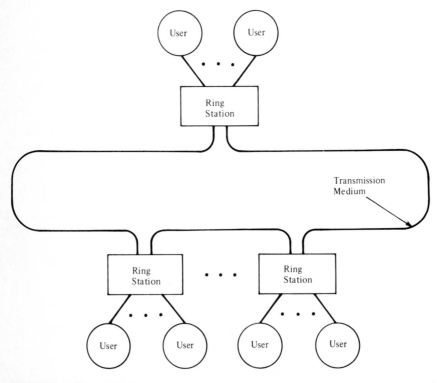

FIGURE 4-13. Ring System

viewed, at least conceptually, as residing in a medium access control layer, discussed in Chapter 5.

Repeaters perform the data insertion and reception functions in a manner not unlike that of taps, which serve as device attachment points on a bus or tree. Data removal, however, is more difficult on a ring. For a bus or tree, signals inserted onto the line propagate to the end points and are absorbed by terminators. Hence, shortly after transmission ceases, the bus or tree is clear of data. However, because the ring is a closed loop, data will circulate indefinitely unless removed. A packet may be removed by the addressed repeater. Alternatively, each packet could be removed by the transmitting repeater after it has made one trip around the loop. The latter approach is more desirable because (1) it permits automatic acknowledgment, and (2) it permits multicast addressing: one packet sent simultaneously to multiple stations.

The repeater, then, can be seen to have two main purposes: (1) to contribute to the proper functioning of the ring by passing on all the data that comes its way, and (2) to provide an access point for attached stations to send and receive data. Corresponding to these two purposes are two states (Figure 4.14): the listen state and the transmit state.

In the *listen state*, each bit that is received is retransmitted with a small delay, required to allow the repeater to perform necessary functions.

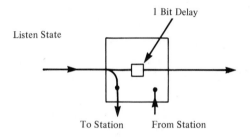

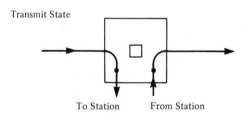

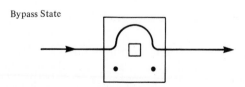

FIGURE 4-14. Ring Repeater States

Ideally, the delay should be on the order of one bit time (the time it takes for a repeater to transmit one complete bit onto the outgoing line). These functions are:

- Scan passing bit stream for pertinent patterns. Chief among these is the address or addresses of attached devices. Another pattern, used in the token control strategy explained later, indicates permission to transmit. Note that to perform the scanning function, the repeater must have some knowledge of packet format.
- Copy each incoming bit and send it to the attached station, while continuing to retransmit each bit. This will be done for each bit of each packet addressed to this station.
- Modify a bit as it passes by. In certain control strategies, bits may be modified to, for example, indicate that the packet has been copied. This would serve as an acknowledgment.

When a repeater's station has data to send and when the repeater, based on the control strategy, has permission to send, the repeater enters the *transmit state*. In this state, the repeater receives bits from the station and retransmits them on its outgoing link. During the period of transmission, bits may appear on the incoming ring link. There are two possibilities, and they are treated differently:

- The bits could be from the same packet that the repeater is still sending. This will occur if the "bit length" of the ring is shorter than the packet. In this case, the repeater passes the bits back to the station, which can check them as a form of acknowledgment.
- For some control strategies, more than one packet could be on the ring at the same time. If the repeater, while transmitting, receives bits from a packet it did not originate, it must buffer them to be transmitted later.

These two states, listen and transmit, are sufficient for proper ring operation. A third state, the *bypass state*, is also useful. In this state, a bypass relay is activated, so that signals propagate past the repeater with no delay other than medium propagation. The bypass relay affords two benefits: (1) it provides a partial solution to the reliability problem, discussed later, and (2) it improves performance by eliminating repeater delay for those stations that are not active on the network.

Ring Benefits

Until recently the ring-topology LAN was little known in the United States. While much work had been done in Europe, the emphasis in the United States was on the bus/tree topologies. The strengths of the bus/tree approach, discussed in the preceding section, are well known.

The benefits of the ring have been less well known, but interest is beginning to build. A good deal of research into overcoming some of the weaknesses of the ring has been done at M.I.T. [SALT79, SALT83] and at IBM [BUX83, STRO83, DIXO83]. The result has been a proliferation of ring-based LAN products, most notably the appearance of the IBM product in 1985, followed by a number of compatible products from other vendors [DERF86, STRO86].

Like the bus and tree, the ring is a shared-access or multiaccess network (although the medium itself is a collection of point-to-point links). Hence the benefits of this type of medium obtain, including ability to broadcast and incremental cost growth. There are other benefits provided by the ring that are not shared by the bus/tree topology.

The most important benefit or strength of the ring is that it uses point-to-point communication links. There are a number of implications of this fact. First, because the transmitted signal is regenerated at each node, greater distances can be covered than with baseband bus. Broadband bus/tree can cover a similar range, but cascaded amplifiers can result in loss of data integrity at high data rates. Second, the ring can accommodate optical fiber links, which provide very high data rates and excellent electromagnetic interference (EMI) characteristics. Finally, the electronics and maintenance of point-to-point lines are simpler than for multipoint lines.

Another benefit of the ring is that fault isolation and recovery are simpler than for bus/tree. This is discussed in more detail later in this section and in Chapter 12.

With the ring, the "duplicate address" problem is easily solved. If, on a bus or tree, two stations are by accident assigned the same address, there is no easy way to sort this out. A relatively complex algorithm must be incorporated into the LAN protocol. On a ring, the first station with an address match that is encountered by a packet can modify a bit in the packet to acknowledge reception. Subsequent stations with the same address will easily recognize the problem.

Finally, there is the potential throughput of the ring. Under certain conditions, the ring has greater throughput than a comparable bus or tree LAN. This topic is explored in Chapter 9.

Potential Ring Problems

The potential problems of a ring are, at first blush, more obvious than the benefits:

1. *Cable vulnerability:* A break on any of the links between repeaters disables the entire network until the problem can be isolated and a new cable installed. The ring may range widely throughout a building and is vulnerable at every point to accidents.

2. *Repeater failure:* As with the links, a failure of a single repeater disables the entire network. In many networks, it will be common for many of the stations not to be in operation at any time; yet all repeaters must always operate properly.

3. *Perambulation:* When either a repeater or a link fails, locating the failure requires perambulation of the ring, and thus access to all rooms containing repeaters and cable. This is known as the "pocket full of keys" problem.

4. *Installation headaches:* Installation of a new repeater to support new devices requires the identification of two nearby, topologically adjacent repeaters. It must be verified that they are in fact adjacent (documentation could be faulty or out of date), and cable must be run from the new repeater to both of the old repeaters. These are several unfortunate consequences. The length of cable driven by the source repeater may change, possibly requiring retuning. Old cable, if not removed, accumulates. In addition, the geometry of the ring may become highly irregular, exacerbating the perambulation problem.

5. *Size limitations:* There is a practical limit to the number of repeaters on a ring. This limit is suggested by the reliability and maintenance problems cited earlier, the timing jitter discussed below, and the accumulating delay of large numbers of repeaters. A limit of a few hundred repeaters seems reasonable.

6. *Initialization and recovery:* To avoid designating one ring node as a controller (negating the benefit of distributed control), a strategy is required to assure that all stations can cooperate smoothly when initialization and recovery is required. This need arises, for example, when a packet is garbled by a transient line error; in that case, no repeater may wish to assume the responsibility of removing the circulating packet.

7. *Timing jitter:* This is a subtle problem having to do with the clocking or timing of a signal in a distributed network. It is discussed below.

Problems 1 and 2 are reliability problems, which are dealt with in Chapter 12. However, these two problems, together with problems 3, 4, and 5 can be ameliorated by a refinement in the ring architecture, explained in the next section. Problem 6 is a software problem, to be dealt with by the various LAN protocols discussed in Chapter 5. Problem 7 is discussed next.

Timing Jitter

On a twisted-pair or coaxial-cable ring LAN, digital signaling is generally used with biphase encoding, typically Differential Manchester. As data circulate around the ring, each receiver must recover the binary data from the received signal. To do this, the receiver must know the starting and ending times of each bit, so that it can sample the received signal properly. This requires that all the repeaters on the ring be synchronized, or clocked, together. Recall from Chapter Two that biphase codes are self-clocking; the signal includes a transition in the middle of each bit time. Thus each repeater recovers clocking as well as data from the received signal. This clock recovery will deviate in a random fashion from the mid-bit transitions of the received signal for several reasons, including noise during transmission and imperfections in the receiver circuitry. The predominant reason, however, is delay distortion. Delay distortion is caused by the fact that the velocity of propagation of a signal through a guided medium varies with frequency. The effect is that some of the signal components of one pulse will spill over into other pulse positions; this is known as *intersymbol interference*. The deviation of clock recovery is known as *timing jitter*.

As each repeater receives data, it recovers the clocking for two purposes: first to know when to sample the incoming signal to recover the data, and second, to use the clocking for transmitting the Differential Manchester signal to the next repeater. The repeater issues a clean signal with no distortion. However, since the clocking is recovered from the incoming signal, the timing error is not eliminated. Thus the digital pulse width will expand and contract in a random fashion as the signal travels around the ring, and the timing jitter accumulates. The cumulative effect of the jitter is to cause the bit latency, or "bit length," of the ring to vary. However, unless the latency of the ring remains constant, bits will be dropped (not retransmitted) as the latency of the ring decreases or added as the latency increases.

Thus timing jitter places a limitation on the number of repeaters in a ring. Although this limitation cannot be entirely overcome, several measures can be taken to improve matters [KELL83, HONG86]; these are illustrated in Figure 4-15. First, each repeater can include a phase-locked loop (PLL). This is a device that uses feedback to minimize the deviation from one bit time to the next. Although the use of phase-locked loops reduces the jitter, there is still an accumulation around the ring. A supplementary measure is to include a buffer in one of the repeaters, usually designated as the monitor repeater or station. Bits are written in using the recovered clock and are read out using a crystal master clock. The buffer is initialized to hold a certain number of bits and expands and contracts as needed. For example, the IEEE standard specifies a 6-bit buffer, which is initialized to hold three bits. That is, as bits come in, they are placed in the buffer for three bit times before being retransmitted. If the received signal at the monitor station is slightly faster than the master clock, the buffer will expand, as required, to 4, 5, or 6 bits to avoid dropping bits. If the received signal is slow, the buffer will contract to 2, 1, or 0 bits to avoid adding bits to the repeated bit stream. Thus the cleaned-up signals that are retransmitted are purged of the timing jitter. This combination of phase-locked

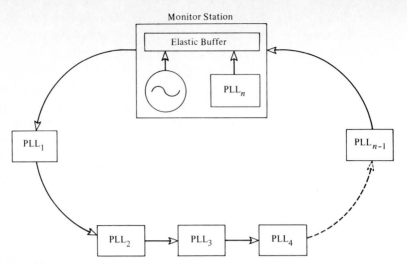

FIGURE 4-15.   Ring Synchronization

loops and a buffer significantly increases maximum feasible ring size. The actual limit will depend on the characteristics of the transmission medium, which determine the amount of delay distortion and therefore the amount of accumulated jitter. For example, the IBM ring product specifies a maximum of 72 repeaters in a ring using unshielded twisted pair, and a maximum of 260 repeaters in a ring using shielded twisted pair.

The Star-Ring Architecture

Two observations can be made about the basic ring architecture described above. First, there is a practical limit to the number of repeaters on a ring. As was mentioned above, a number of factors combine to limit the practical size of a ring LAN to a few hundred repeaters. Second, the cited benefits of the ring do not depend on the actual routing of the cables that link the repeaters.

These observations have led to the development of a refined ring architecture, the star-ring, which overcomes some of the problems of the ring and allows the construction of large local-networks [SALW83]. This architecture uses the star wiring strategy discussed in the previous chapter. It is the basis of IBM's ring product and similar products.

As a first step, consider the rearrangement of a ring into a star. This is achieved by having the interrepeater link all thread through a single site (Figure 4-16). This ring wiring concentrator has a number of advantages. Because there is access to the signal on every link, it is a simple matter to isolate a fault. A message can be launched into the ring and tracked to see how far it gets without mishap. A faulty segment can be disconnected—no

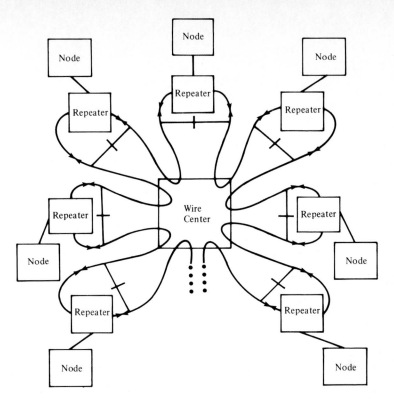

FIGURE 4-16. Ring Wiring Concentrator

pocket full of keys needed—and repaired at a later time. New repeaters can easily be added to the ring: simply run two cables from the new repeater to the site of ring wiring concentration and splice into the ring.

The bypass relay associated with each repeater can be moved into the ring wiring concentrator. The relay can automatically bypass its repeater and two links for any malfunction. A nice effect of this feature is that the transmission path from one working repeater to the next is approximately constant; thus the range of signal levels to which the transmission system must automatically adapt is much smaller.

The ring wiring concentrator greatly alleviates the perambulation and installation problems mentioned earlier. It also permits rapid recovery from a cable or repeater failure. Nevertheless, a single failure could, at least temporarily, disable the entire network. Furthermore, throughput and jitter considerations still place a practical upper limit on the number of repeaters in a ring. Finally, in a spread out network, a single wire concentration site dictates a lot of cable.

To attack these remaining problems, consider a local network consisting of multiple rings. Each ring consists of a connected sequence of wiring concentrators, and the set of rings is connected by a bridge (Figure 4-17).

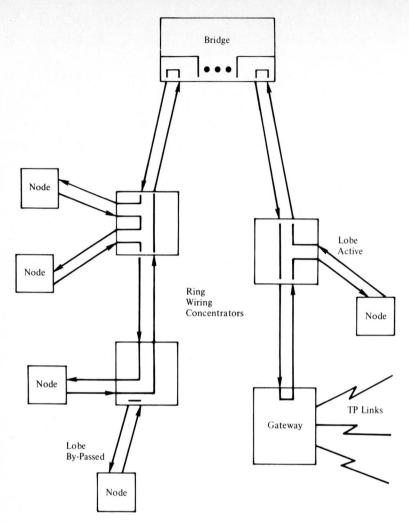

FIGURE 4-17. Ring Bridge

The bridge routes data packets from one ring subnetwork to another, based on addressing information in the packet so routed. From a physical point of view, each ring operates independently of the other rings attached to the bridge. From a logical point of view, the bridge provides transparent routing among the rings.

The bridge must perform five functions:

* *Input filtering:* For each ring, the bridge monitors the traffic on the ring and copies all packets addressed to other rings on the bridge. This function can be performed by a repeater programmed to recognize a family of addresses rather than a single address.

- *Input buffering:* Received packets may need to be buffered, either because the interring traffic is peaking, or because the target output buffer is temporarily full.
- *Switching:* Each packet must be routed through the bridge to its appropriate destination ring.
- *Output buffering:* A packet may need to be buffered at the threshold of the destination ring, waiting for an opportunity to be inserted.
- *Output transmission:* This function can be performed by an ordinary repeater.

For a small number of rings, a bridge can be a reasonably simple device. As the number of rings on a bridge grows, the switching complexity and load on the bridge also grow. For very large installations, multiple bridges, interconnected by high-speed trunks, may be needed (Figure 4-18).

Three principal advantages accrue from the use of a bridge. First, the timing jitter problem, which becomes more difficult as the number of

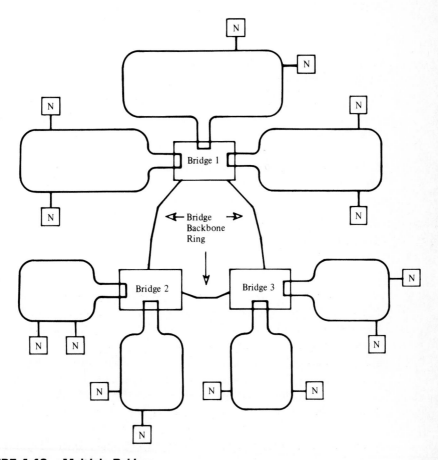

FIGURE 4-18. Multiple Bridges

repeaters on a ring grows, is bounded by restricting the size of the ring. Second, the failure of a ring, for whatever reason, will disable only a portion of the network; failure of the bridge does not prevent intraring traffic. Finally, multiple rings may be employed to obtain a satisfactory level of performance when the throughput capability of a single ring is exceeded.

There are several pitfalls to be noted. First, the automatic acknowledgment feature of the ring is lost; higher level protocols must provide acknowledgment. Second, performance may not significantly improve if there is a high percentage of interring traffic. If it is possible to do so, network devices should be judiciously allocated to rings to minimize interring traffic.

4.3

FIBER LANS

To date, the transmission media most commonly used for LANs and HSLNs have been twisted pair and coaxial cable. The use of optical fiber has lagged because of the cost and technical difficulties involved in its use. However, because of the significant advantages of optical fiber, there has in recent years been increasing interest in its use as a local network transmission medium.

In this section, we examine the benefits of optical fiber and survey the architectural approaches that have been taken. We return to the subject in Chapter 6, when we examine high-speed local networks.

Benefits

One of the most significant technological breakthroughs in data transmission has been the development of practical fiber optic communications systems. Optical fiber already enjoys considerable use in long-distance telecommunications, and its use in military applications is growing. The continuing improvements in performance and decline in prices, together with the inherent advantages of optical fiber, will result in new areas of application, such as local networks and short-haul video distribution. The following characteristics distinguish optical fiber from twisted pair and coaxial cable.

- *Greater bandwidth:* The potential bandwidth and, hence, data rate of a medium increases with frequency. At the immense frequencies of optical fiber, data rates of several Gbps over tens of kilometers have been demonstrated. Compare this to the practical maximum of hundreds of Mbps over about 1 km for coaxial cable and just a few Mbps over 1 km for twisted pair.

- *Smaller size and lighter weight:* Optical fibers are considerably smaller than coaxial cable or bundled twisted pair cable, at least an order of magnitude smaller in diameter for comparable data transmission capacity. For cramped conduits in buildings and underground along public right-of-way, the advantage of small size is considerable. The corresponding reduction in weight reduces structural support requirements.
- *Lower attenuation:* Attenuation is significantly lower for optical fiber than for coaxial cable or for twisted pair and is constant over a wide range.
- *Electromagnetic isolation:* Optical fiber systems are not affected by external electromagnetic fields. Thus, the system is not vulnerable to interference, impulse noise, or crosstalk. By the same token, fibers do not radiate energy, causing little interference with other equipment and providing a high degree of security from eavesdropping; in addition, fiber is inherently difficult to tap.
- *Greater repeater spacing:* Fewer repeaters mean lower cost and fewer sources of error. For example, Standard Elektrik Lorenz AG in Germany has developed a fiber transmission system that achieves a data rate of 5 Gbps over a distance of 111 km [ANON88] without repeaters. Coaxial and twisted-pair systems generally have repeaters every few kilometers.

There are, of course, some disadvantages. One drawback relates to the physical handling and installation of fiber cables. The techniques and tools for installing connectors, splicing, and laying the cable differ from those used for coaxial cable and twisted pair, and are in general more difficult. A second major drawback has been cost. Optical fiber equipment operates in two realms: optical and electronic. The circuitry for converting between electronic and optical signals is complex and expensive. In addition, there are cost and technical concerns peculiar to the specific architecture employed, as discussed below.

Because of the undeniable benefits of optical fiber, there has been considerable research and development effort to overcome these problems, and fiber-based local networks have begun to emerge. Nevertheless, much progress remains to be made before optical fiber is truly competitive with the other media. Perhaps the most promising area for advance is in the field of integrated optics, which is analogous to integrated circuits in the electronic realm. Over the next few years, we can expect advances in this field to significantly improve the cost and performance characteristics of optical fiber [TASS85].

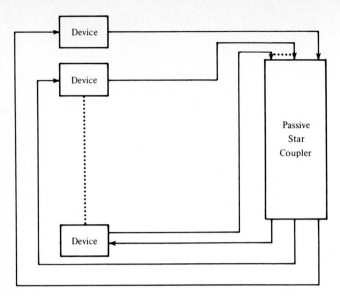

FIGURE 4-19. Optical Fiber Passive Star Configuration

Passive Star

One of the first commerically available approaches for fiber LANs was the passive star coupler [SCHO88, RAWS78, KELL84]. The passive star coupler is fabricated by fusing together a number of optical fibers. Any light input to one of the fibers on one side of the coupler will be equally divided among and output through all the fibers on the other side. To form a network, each device is connected to the coupler with two fibers, one for transmit and one for receive (Figure 4-19). All of the transmit fibers enter the coupler on one side, and all of the receive fibers exit on the other side. Thus, although the arrangement is physically a star, it acts like a bus: a transmission from any one device is received by all other devices, and if two devices transmit at the same time there will be a collision.

Two methods of fabrication of the star coupler have been pursued: the biconic fused coupler, and the mixing rod coupler. In the biconic fused coupler [STRA87], the fibers are bundled together. The bundled fibers are heated with an oxyhydrogen flame and pulled into a biconical tapered shape. That is, the rods come together into a fused mass that tapers into a conical shape and then expands back out again. The mixing road approach [OHSH86] begins in the same fashion. Then, the biconical taper is cut at the waist and a cylindrical rod is inserted between the tapers and fused to the two cut ends. This latter technique allows the use of a less narrow waist and is easier to fabricate.

Commercially available passive star couplers can support a few tens of stations at a radial distance of up to a kilometer or more. Figure 4-20

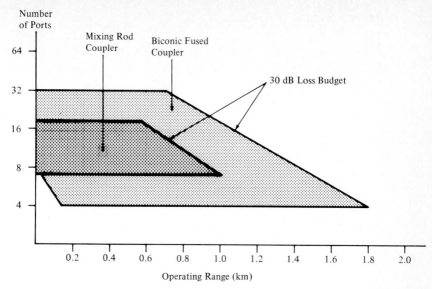

FIGURE 4-20. **Operating Range for Optical Fiber Passive Star LAN [SCHO88]**

shows the operating range of the two types of couplers. The limitations on number of stations and distances are imposed by the losses in the network. With today's equipment, the optical power loss between transmitter and receiver than can be tolerated is on the order of 25 to 30 dB. In the figure, the outer edge of each region is defined by a maximum end-to-end attenuation of 30 dB. The attenuation that will occur in the network consists of the following components:

- *Optical connector losses:* Connectors are used to splice together cable segments for increased length. Typical connector losses are 1.0 to 1.5 dB per connector. A typical passive star network will have from 0 to 4 connectors in a path from transmitter to receiver, for a total maximum attenuation of 4 to 6 dB.
- *Optical cable attenuation:* Typical cable attenuation for the cable that has been used in these systems ranges from 3 to 6 dB per kilometer.
- *Optical power division in the coupler:* The coupler divides the optical power from one transmission path equally among all reception paths. Expressed in decibels, the loss seen by any node is 10 log (number of nodes). For example, the effective loss in a 16-port coupler is about 12 dB.

As the figure indicates, the passive star coupler is quite limited. Other researchers have reached similar conclusions. It appears that passive star couplers with a large number of ports (>100) can only be made at high cost [RHOD83]. Thus, interest has turned to other approaches.

Active Star

For a number of years, work has been underway at the Xerox Palo Alto Research Center to develop an improved version of the star topology fiber LAN. The result is Fibernet II [SCHM83], which differs from the passive star only in that the central coupler is an active repeater rather than a passive device. However, like the passive star, the active star appears as a bus to the attached devices: a transmission from any one device is received by all other devices, and only one device at a time can successfully transmit.

Figure 4-21 is a schematic diagram of Fibernet II. As before, each device attaches to the central node through two optical fiber cables, one for transmit and one for receive. Figure 4-16 reveals the internal organization of the node. When a station transmits, the receiver module detects the optical signal on the inbound optical fiber and retransmits it on a backplane bus designated R. The bus is in fact a miniature 50-ohm coaxial cable. The signal on the R bus is received by the control module, which retransmits it on another 50-ohm coaxial bus designated X. The purpose of this intermediate module is to perform collision detection, a function discussed in the next chapter. Finally, the transmitter module picks up the signal from bus X and retransmits it in optical form on all output fibers. The delay for this entire process is on the order of a few bit times. It can be seen that this arrangement is in fact simply a bus topology using star wiring, as depicted in Figure 3-5a.

The active star has several advantages over the passive star. In the passive star, the incoming signal is split equally among all outgoing fibers, so that the greater the number of fibers, the greater the loss on any one path. With the active star, this loss does not occur. Thus the active star can support more devices over a greater distance. Fibernet II is designed to support up to over a hundred devices at a maximum radius of 2.5 km. The disadvantage of the active star is that it is more expensive due to the active components in the central node.

Fiber Ring

As the reader should by now be able to deduce, by far the most promising approach for fiber local networks is the ring topology. The ring consists of a series of point-to-point links, and the technology for point-to-point fiber transmission is well understood and widely available. In addition to the other advantages of fiber cited earlier, it exhibits significantly less delay distortion than coaxial cable or twisted pair and hence sufferrs less from timing jitter. This means that larger ring networks can be constructed.

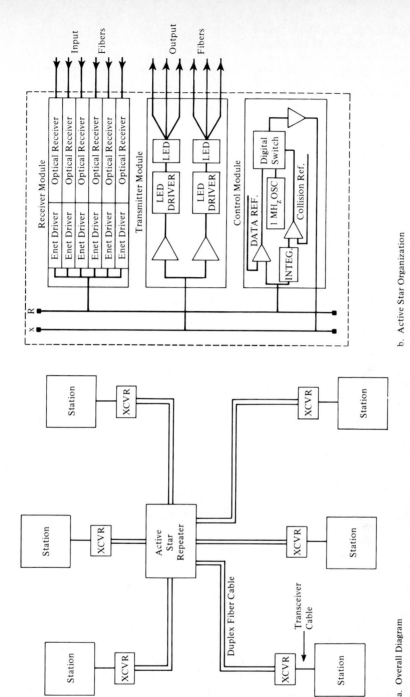

b. Active Star Organization

a. Overall Diagram

FIGURE 4-21. Fibernet II Active Star Configuration

TABLE 4.5 IBM Optical Fiber Ring Specification [SEE86]

Core Diameter	100 μm
Cladding Diameter	143 μm
Wavelength	850 nm
Attenuation	<6 dB/km
Bandwidth	>150 MHz
Data Rate	up to 20 Mbps
Distance	1.5 to 2.0 km

Because of the high data rates attainable with optical fiber, the fiber ring is a natural choice for a high-speed local network (HSLN), and this topic is pursued in Chapter 6. In this section, we will briefly look at some considerations for a fiber ring LAN. As was mentioned, cost is less of a concern with an HSLN than with a LAN because of the greater value of the attached devices. Hence, in this section, we are concerned with determining what is reasonable in terms of cost for a lower-speed (5 to 10 Mbps) fiber ring. As an example, we will use the specifications developed by IBM for its ring product [SEE86]. These are representative of what is commercially feasible.

IBM's fiber ring specification was written to satisfy current transmission requirements using a light wavelength of 850 nanometers (nm). The fiber specification also supports upward migration to higher performance networks operating at a wavelength of 1300 nm. Although the latter could support a higher data rate, the transmitters and receivers operating at that wavelength are presently five to ten times more expensive than 850-nm devices.

Table 4.5 lists the key parameters of the specification. At an 850-nm wavelength, relatively low-cost LED transmitters and PIN detectors are used. Transmission is in the graded-index mode. Data rates of up to 20 Mbps are achieveable with a maximum single-link distance of up to 1.5 to 2.0 km. The system should be able to support at least as many repeaters on a single ring as shielded twisted pair, on the order of 250.

Fiber Bus

Two approaches can be taken in the design of a fiber bus topology LAN or HSLN [NASS85]. The differences have to do with whether the taps into the bus are active or passive. In the case of an active tap (Figure 4-22a), the

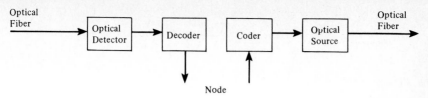

a. Active Tap

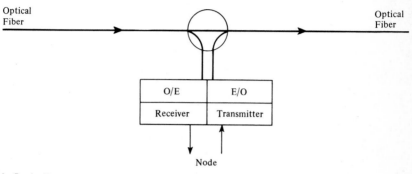

b. Passive Tap

FIGURE 4-22.   Optical Fiber Bus Taps

following steps occur:

1. Optical signal energy enters the tap from the bus.
2. Clocking information is recovered from the signal and the signal is converted to an electrical signal.
3. The converted signal is presented to the node and perhaps modified by the latter.
4. The optical output (a light beam) is modulated according to the electrical signal and launched into the bus.

In the case of a passive tap (Figure 4-22b), the tap extracts a portion of the optical energy from the bus for reception and it injects optical energy directly into the medium for transmission. In effect, the medium is not broken. This passive tap approach is equivalent to the type of taps typically used for twisted pair and coaxial cable.

Active and passive configurations are shown in Figure 4-23. For the active configuration, two optical fibers are required and each tap consists of two of the active couplers described above. This is because of the inherently unidirectional nature of the device of Figure 4-22a. For the passive configuration, each tap must again connect to the bus twice, again because the passive optical tap, like the broadband coaxial tap, is

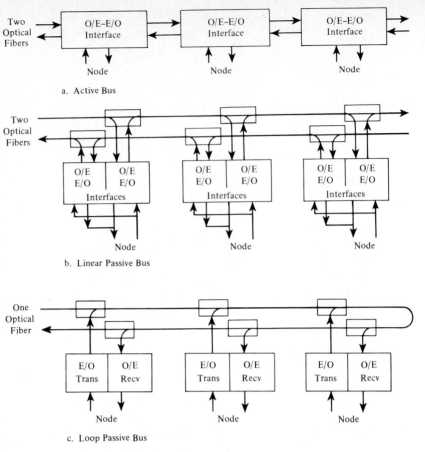

a. Active Bus

b. Linear Passive Bus

c. Loop Passive Bus

FIGURE 4-23. Optical Fiber Bus Configurations

unidirectional. Figure 4-23b shows a configuration in which two fibers are used. Each tap consists of two transmitter-receivers so that signals can be inserted and extracted from two unidirectional fibers. A better approach, illustrated in Figure 4-23c, uses a single fiber in which one end of the bus is closed. Stations transmit on one leg and receive on the other leg of the fiber, in the same fashion as a dual-cable broadband bus. This latter configuration reduces the number of required transmitters and receivers in the network by a factor of two.

The electronic complexity and interface cost are drawbacks for the implementation of the active bus. Also, each tap will add some increment of delay, just as in the case of a ring. For passive buses, the lossy nature of pure optical taps (not involving optoelectrical and electro-optical conversions) are an impediment. Low-loss taps are not yet commercially available. With a high-loss tap, only a very few taps are possible before the signal strength becomes too weak for detection [RHOD83]. However, this is an area of active research. For example, Bell Communications Research has been experimenting with a low-loss tap that its researchers believe will support up to 80 taps on a fiber bus [ALLA84].

4.4

RECOMMENDED READING

Good descriptions of baseband systems can be found in [SHOC82]* and [LEON88]. The original Ethernet article [METC76] is also informative. [FLAT84] describes Cheapernet. A description of StarLAN can be found in [GOLB86]. [STIX88] is a more general discussion of twisted-pair, star-wired LANs. Worthwhile articles on broadband LANs include [DUNB86]* and [SUNS85]*. Detailed discussions of broadband components and their use can be found in [COOP84] and [KIM88]. [RELC87] is a similarly detailed treatment of carrierband.

[STRO83]* presents IBM's ring LAN approach. [LOVE87]* provides a practical discussion. [SUH86]* and [FINL84] are good surveys of fiber LANs.

4.5

PROBLEMS

4.1 Consider a baseband bus with a number of equally-spaced stations. As a fraction of the end-to-end propagation delay, what is the mean delay between stations? What is it for broadband bus? Now, rearrange the broadband bus into a tree with N equal-length branches emanating from the headend; what is the mean delay?

4.2 Give examples of appropriate applications of the broadband dedicated service, and the switched service.

4.3 Consider a baseband bus with a number of equally-spaced stations with a data rate of 10 Mbps and a bus length of 1 km. What is the average time to send a packet of 1000 bits to another station, measured from the beginning of transmission to the end of reception? Assume a propagation speed of 200 m/μs. If two stations begin to transmit at exactly the same time, their packets will interfere with each other. If each transmitting station monitors the bus during transmission, how long before it notices an interference, in seconds? In bit times?

4.4 Repeat Problem 4.3 for a data rate of 1 Mbps.

4.5 Repeat Problems 4.3 and 4.4 for broadband bus.

4.6 Repeat Problems 4.3 and 4.4 for a broadband tree consisting of ten cables of length 100 m emanating from a headend.

4.7 Reconsider Problem 3.6. Can a baseband bus following the IEEE 802 rules

(500-m segments, maximum of four repeaters in a path) span the building? If so, what is the total cable length?

4.8 Reconsider Problem 3.6 for a broadband tree. Can the total length be reduced compared to the broadband bus?

4.9 Reconsider problem 3.6, but now assume that there are two rings, with a bridge on floor 5 and a ring wiring concentrator on each floor. The bridge and concentrators are located in closets along the vertical shaft.

4.10 At a propagation speed of 200 m/μs, what is the effective length added to a ring by a bit delay at each repeater:
   a. At 1 Mbps?
   b. At 40 Mbps?

4.11 System A consists of a single ring with 300 stations, one per repeater. System B consists of three 100-station rings linked by a bridge. If the probability of a link failure is P_l, a repeater failure is P_r, and a bridge failure is P_b, derive an expression for parts (a) through (d):
   a. Probability of failure of system A.
   b. Probability of complete failure of system B.
   c. Probability that a particular station will find the network unavailable, for systems A and B.
   d. Probability that any two stations, selected at random, will be unable to communicate, for systems A and B.
   e. Compare values of 4a through 4d for $P_l = P_b = P_r = 10^{-2}$.

4.12 Consider two rings of 100 stations each joined by a bridge. The data rate on each link is 10 Mbps. Each station generates data at a rate of ten packets of 2000 bits each per second. Let F be the fraction of packets on each ring destined for the other. What is the minimum throughput of the bridge required to keep up?

APPENDIX 4A: CHARACTERISTIC IMPEDENCE

An important parameter associated with any transmission line is its characteristic impedance. To understand its significance, we need to consider the electrical properties of a transmission line. Any transmission line has both inductance and capacitance, which are distributed along the entire length of the line. These quantities can be expressed in terms of inductance and capacitance per unit length.

An infinite transmission line has similar electrical properties to the circuit depicted in Figure 4-24a and b. Of course, the actual inductance and capacitance is distributed uniformly along the line and not lumped as shown in the figure, but the equivalent circuit is good enough to explain the behavior of an actual line.

Figure 4-24a shows a section of an infinite line connected to a voltage source. Closing the switch (Figure 4-24b) will cause current to flow. Now,

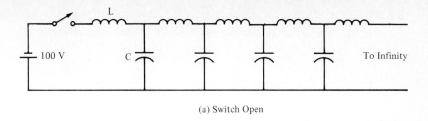

(a) Switch Open

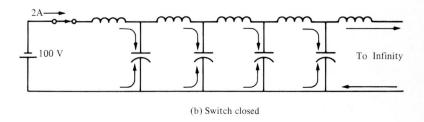

(b) Switch closed

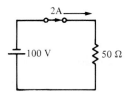

FIGURE 4-24. Characteristic Impedence

in a finite line, at steady state, the inductors will behave as short circuits (zero resistance) and the capacitors as open circuits (infinite resistance). However, at the instance that the switch is closed, current will flow and be resisted by the inductance and capacitance. The process will continue indefinitely because there are an infinite number of capacitors to be charged. There will be a definite relationship between the applied voltage and the amount of current that will flow. The relationship will depend only on the value of inductance and capacitance, which in turn depend on the physical dimensions of the line. In our example, an applied voltage of 100 volts causes a current of 2 amperes to flow into the line when the switch is closed. As far as the source is concerned, it has no way of knowing whether it is connected to a transmission line that is infinitely long or to a 50-ohm resistor, as shown in Figure 4-24. In both cases, a current of 2 amperes would flow. For this reason, we say that this particular line has a characteristic impedance, or surge impendence, of 50 ohms.

The characteristic impedance is given by the equation:

$$Z_0 = \sqrt{\frac{L}{C}}$$

where

Z = characteristic impedence of the line, in ohms

L = inductance, in henrys per unit length

C = capacitance in farads per unit length

Since the inductance and capacitance depend on the construction of the line, the characteristic impedence can also be determined from the physical dimensions of the line. In particular, for coaxial cable,

$$Z_0 = \frac{138}{\sqrt{\varepsilon}} \log \frac{D}{d}$$

where

log = logarithm to the base 10

D = diameter of outside conductor

d = diameter of inside conductor

ε = dielectric constant of the insulating material between the two conductors; for air, the value is 1

For a dielectric of 1 and an impedance of 50 ohms, the ratio D/d is 2.3, and for an impedance of 75 ohms, the ratio is 3.5.

It is important to realize that the characteristic impedance of a transmission line is a function of the construction of the line itself; it does not depend on the signal carried or on what is connected to the line.

The significance of characteristic impedance is this: When a line is terminated in its characteristic impedance, any signal on the line is absorbed when it reaches the terminating resistance. There are no reflections. Obviously, such reflections are to be avoided since they would interfere with the signal being transmitted.

More detail on these matters can be found in any text on transmission line theory, for example, [LIBO85].

APPENDIX 4B: DECIBELS

An important parameter in any transmission system is the strength of the signal being transmitted. As a signal propagates along a transmission medium, there will be a loss, or attenuation, of signal strength. Additional losses occur at taps and splitters. To compensate, amplifiers may be inserted at various points to impart a gain in signal strength. It is customary to express gains, losses, and relative levels in decibels, because:

- Signal strength often falls off logarithmically, so loss is easily expressed in terms of the decibel, which is a logarithmic unit.

- The net gain or loss in cascaded transmission path can be calculated with simple addition and subtraction.

The decibel is a measure of the difference in two signal levels:

$$N_{dB} = 10 \log \frac{P_1}{P_2}$$

where

$$N_{dB} = \text{number of decibels}$$

$$P_{1,2} = \text{voltage values}$$

For example, if a signal with a power level of 10 mw is inserted onto a transmission line and the measured power some distance away is 5 mw, the loss can be expressed as

$$\text{LOSS} = 10 \log(5/10) = 10(-.03) = -3 \text{ dB}$$

Note that the decibel is a measure of relative, not absolute difference. A loss from 1000 mw to 500 mw is also a -3 dB loss. Thus, a loss of 3 dB halves the voltage level; a gain of 3 dB doubles the magnitude.

The decibel is also used to measure the difference in voltage, taking into account that power is proportional to the square of the voltage:

$$P = \frac{V^2}{R}$$

where

$$P = \text{power dissipated across resistance } R$$

$$V = \text{voltage across resistance } R$$

Thus

$$N_{dB} = 10 \log \frac{P_1}{P_2} = 10 \log \frac{V_1^2/R}{V_2^2/R} = 20 \log \frac{V_1}{V_2}$$

Decible values refer to relative magnitudes or changes in magnitude, not to an absolute level. It is convenient to be able to refer to an absolute level of voltage in decibels so that gains and losses with reference to an initial signal level may easily be calculated. One unit in common use in cable television and broadband LAN applications is the dBmV (decibel-millivolt). This is an absolute unit with 0 dBmV equivalent to 1 mV. Thus

$$\text{Voltage(dBmV)} = 20 \log \frac{\text{Voltage(mV)}}{1 \text{ mV}}$$

The voltage levels are assumed to be across a 75-ohm resistance.

The decibel is convenient for determining overall gain or loss in a signal path. For example, Figure 4-12 shows a path from a point on a broadband trunk cable at which the signal level is 20 dBmV to an outlet. The amplifier gain, and the losses due to the cables, tap, and splitter are expressed in decibels. By using simple addition and subtraction, the signal level at the outlet is easily calculated to be 7.6 dBmV.

APPENDIX 4C: SCRAMBLING AND DESCRAMBLING

For some digital data encoding techniques, a long string of binary zeros or ones in a transmission can degrade system peformance. For example, in the differential phase shift keying (DPSK) scheme used in some broadband LAN modems, a phase shift occurs only when the input is a zero bit. If there is a long string of ones, it is difficult for the receiver to maintain synchronization with the transmitter. A similar problem arises with the other common broadband LAN modulation scheme, duobinary AM/PSK. Also, other transmission properties are enhanced if the data are more nearly of a random nature rather than constant or repetitive [BELL82a]. A technique commonly used with modems to improve signal quality is scrambling and descrambling. The scrambling process tends to make the data appear more random.

The scrambling process consists of a feedback shift register, and the matching descrambler consists of a feedforward shift register. An example is shown in Figure 4-25. In this example, the scrambled data sequence may be expressed as follows:

$$B_m = A_m \oplus B_{m-3} \oplus B_{m-5}$$

where $\oplus$ indicates the exclusive or operation. The descrambled sequence is

$$C_m = B_m + B_{m-3} \oplus B_{m-5}$$
$$= (A_m \oplus B_{m-3} \oplus B_{m-5}) \oplus B_{m-3} \oplus B_{m-5}$$
$$= A_m$$

As can be seen, the descrambled output is the original sequence.

We can represent this process with the use of polynomials. Thus, for this example, the polynomial is $P = 1 + X^{-3} + X^{-5}$. The input is divided by

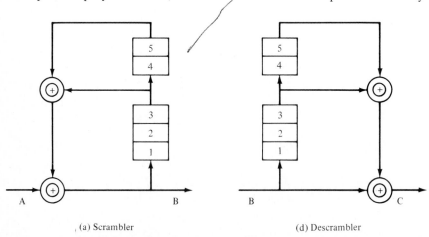

(a) Scrambler   (d) Descrambler

FIGURE 4-25.   **Scrambler and Descrambler**

this polynomial to produce the scrambled sequence. At the receiver the received scrambled signal is multiplied by the same polynomial to reproduce the original input. Figure 4-26 is an example using the polynomial P and an input of 101010100000111. The scrambled transmission, produced by dividing by P (100101) is 101110001101001. When this number is multiplied by P, we get the original input. Note that the input sequence contains the periodic sequence 10101010 as well as a long string of zeros. The scrambler effectively removes both patterns.

```
                    1 0 1 1 1 0 0 0 1 1 0 1 0 0 1  ←—B
                  _____
P  →1 0 0 1 0 1 )1 0 1 0 1 0 0 0 0 0 1 1 1 – – – – – –←—A
                1 0 0 1 0 1
                _____
                  1 1 1 1 1 0
                  1 0 0 1 0 1
                  _____
                    1 1 0 1 1 0
                    1 0 0 1 0 1
                    _____
                      1 0 0 1 1 0
                      1 0 0 1 0 1
                      _____
                            1 1 0 0 1 1
                            1 0 0 1 0 1
                            _____
                              1 0 1 1 0 1
                              1 0 0 1 0 1
                              _____
                                  1 0 0 0 0 0
                                  1 0 0 1 0 1
                                  _____
                                    1 0 1 0 0 0
```

(a) Scrambling

```
            1 0 1 1 1 0 0 0 1 1 0 1 0 0 1 ← A
                            1 0 0 1 0 1 ← P
            _____
            1 0 1 1 1 0 0 0 1 1 0 1 0 0 1
          1 0 1 1 1 0 0 0 1 1 0 1 0 0 1
        1 0 1 1 1 0 0 0 1 1 0 1 0 0 1
        _____
C = A —→ 1 0 1 0 1 0 1 0 0 0 0 0 1 1 1 – – – – –
```

(b) Descrambling

FIGURE 4-26. Example of Scrambling with $P(X) = 1 + X^{-3} + X^{-5}$

APPENDIX 4C: SCRAMBLING AND DESCRAMBLING

CHAPTER 5

Local Area Networks: Protocols

The preceding chapter examined some key issues relating to the architecture and physical properties of LANs. Because of its scope and importance, the subject of communications architecture or protocols was deferred and is presented here in its own chapter.

This chapter begins with an overall discussion of LAN protocols, and seeks to determine what layers of functionality are required. Then the specific areas of link control and medium access control are explored. Throughout, reference is made to the IEEE 802 standard. This is for two reasons:

- The standard is well thought out, providing a framework for exposing and clarifying LAN communication architectural issues.
- The standard has had a major influence on LAN products.

A brief rationale and summary of the IEEE 802 standard is contained in an appendix to this chapter.

LAN PROTOCOLS

A LAN Reference Model

Chapter 2 summarized an architecture for communications, the OSI reference model, based on seven layers of protocols. We saw in that discussion (see Figure 2.15) that layers 1 through 3 were required for the functioning of a packet-switched network. To recall, these layers were described as follows:

1. *Physical layer:* concerned with transmission of unstructured bit stream over physical link. Involves such parameters as signal voltage swing and bit duration. Deals with the mechanical, electrical, and procedural characteristics to establish, maintain, and deactivate the physical link.
2. *Data link layer:* provides for the reliable transfer of data across the physical link; sends blocks of data (frames) with the necessary synchronization, error control, and flow control.
3. *Network layer:* provides upper layers with independence from the data transmission and switching technologies used to connect systems; responsible for establishing, maintaining, and terminating connections.

We now turn to the question of what layers are required for the proper operation of the LAN. For the sake of clarity, we examine the question in the context of the OSI reference model. Two characteristics of LANs are important in this context. First, data are transmitted in addressed frames. Second, there is no intermediate switching, hence no routing required (repeaters are used in rings and may be used in baseband bus LANs, but do not involve switching or routing). One exception to the second characteristic is the ring bridge. A discussion of that and other exceptions is deferred until Chapter 11.

These two characteristics essentially determine the answer to the question: What OSI layers are needed? Layer 1, certainly. Physical connection is required. Layer 2 is also needed. Data transmitted across the LAN must be organized into frames and control must be exercised. But what about layer 3? The answer is yes and no. If we look at the functions performed by layer 3, the answer would seem to be no. First, there is routing. With a direct link available between any two points, this is not needed. The other functions—addressing, sequencing, flow control, error control, and so on—are, we learned, also performed by layer 2. The difference is that layer 2 performs these functions across a single link, whereas layer 3 may

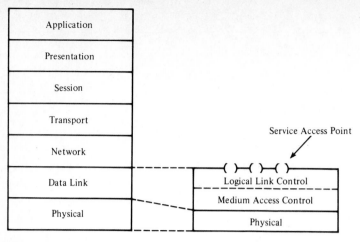

FIGURE 5-1. LAN Protocol Layers Compared to OSI

perform them across the sequence of links required to traverse the network. But since only one link is required to traverse the LAN, these layer 3 functions are redundant and superfluous!

From the point of view of an attached device, the answer would seem to be yes, the LAN must provide layer 3. The device sees itself attached to an access point into a network supporting communication with multiple devices. The layer for assuring that a message sent across that access point is delivered to one of a number of each points would seem to be a layer 3 function. So we can say that although the network provides services up through layer 3, the characteristics of the network allow these services to be implemented on two OSI layers. We shall explore this topic more fully in Chapter 8. For the purpose of this chapter it is sufficient to understand that the minimum essential communications functions that must be performed by the LAN correspond to layers 1 and 2 of the OSI model.

With the points above in mind, let us now think about the functional requirements for controlling a local network and examine these from the top down. We follow the reasoning, illustrated in Figure 5-1, used by the IEEE 802 committee [IEEE88a].

At the highest level are the functions associated with accepting transmissions from and delivering receptions to attached stations. These functions include:

- Provide one or more service access points. A service access point (SAP), recall, is a logical interface between two adjacent layers.
- On transmission, assemble data into a frame with address and CRC fields.

- On reception, disassemble frame, perform address recognition and CRC validation.
- Manage communication over the link.

These are the functions typically associated with layer 2, the data link layer. The first function, and related functions, are grouped into a logical link control (LLC) layer by IEEE 802. The last three functions are treated as a separate layer, called *medium access control* (MAC). This is done for the following reasons:

- The logic required to manage access to a multiple-source, multiple-destination link is not found in traditional layer 2 link control.
- For the same LLC, several MAC options may be provided, as we shall see.

Finally, at the lowest layer, are the functions generally associated with the physical layer. These include:

- Encoding/decoding of signals
- Preamble generation/removal (for synchronization)
- Bit transmission/reception

As with the OSI model, these functions are assigned to a physical layer in the IEEE 802 standard.

In the remainder of this section, we touch briefly on two aspects of LAN protocols. First, since the MAC layer is not found in the traditional OSI model, and to provide a context for later discussions, the characteristics and types of medium access control techniques are discussed. Then the structure for LAN frames is discussed briefly, using the IEEE 802 standard as an example.

We are then prepared to get more specific about LAN protocols. Section 5.2 discusses link control. Sections 5.3 and 5.4 provide details for various LAN medium access control techniques. Physical layer functions were discussed in Chapter 4.

Medium Access Control for Local Networks

All local networks (LAN, HSLN, circuit-switched local network) consist of collections of devices that must share the network's transmission capacity. Some means of controlling access to the transmission medium is needed so that, when required, two particular devices can exchange data.

The key parameters in any medium access control technique are where and how. "Where" refers to whether control is exercised in a centralized or distributed fashion. In a centralized scheme, a controller is designated that has the authority to grant access to the network. A station wishing to transmit must wait until it receives permission from the controller. In a decentralized network, the stations collectively perform a medium access control function to dynamically determine the order in which stations transmit. A centralized scheme has certain advantages, such as:

- It may afford greater control over access for providing such things as priorities, overrides, and guaranteed bandwidth.
- It allows the logic at each station to be as simple as possible.
- It avoids problems of coordination.

Its principal disadvantages include:

- It results in a single point of failure.
- It may act as a bottleneck, reducing efficiency.

The pros and cons for distributed control are mirror images of the points made above.

The second parameter, how, is constrained by the topology and is a tradeoff among competing factors: cost, peformance, and complexity. In general, we can categorize access control techniques as being either synchronous or asynchronous. With synchronous techniques, a specific capacity is dedicated to a connection. We will see this in the circuit-switched local networks. Such techniques are not optimal in LANs and HSLNs because the needs of the stations are generally unpredictable. It is preferable to be able to allocate capacity in an asynchronous (dynamic) fashion, more or less in response to immediate needs. The asynchronous approach can be further subdivided into three categories: round robin, reservation, and contention.

Round Robin

Round robin techniques are conceptually simple, being based on the philosophy of "give everybody a turn." Each station in turn is given an opportunity to transmit. During that opportunity, the station may decline to transmit or may transmit subject to a certain upper bound, usually expressed as a maximum amount of data or time for this opportunity. In any case, the station, when it is finished, must relinquish its turn, and the right to transmit passes to the next station in logical sequence. Control of turns may be centralized or distributed. Polling on a multidrop line is an example of a centralized technique.

When many stations have data to transmit over an extended period of time, round robin techniques can be very efficient. If only a few stations have data to transmit at any given time, other techniques may be preferable, largely depending on whether the data traffic is "stream" or "bursty." Stream traffic is characterized by lengthy and fairly continuous transmissions. Examples are voice communication, telemetry; and bulk file transfer. Bursty traffic is characterized by short, sporadic transmissions. Interactive terminal-host traffic fits this description.

Reservation

For stream traffic, reservation techniques are well suited. In general for these techniques, time on the medium is divided into slots, much as with synchronous TDM. A station wishing to transmit reserves future slots for an extended or indefinite period. Again, reservations may be made in either a centralized or distributed fashion.

Contention

For bursty traffic, contention techniques are usually appropriate. With these techniques, no control is exercised to determine whose turn it is; all stations contend for time in a way that can be, as we shall see, rather rough and tumble. These techniques are of necessity distributed in nature. Their principal advantage is that they are simple to implement and, under light to moderate load, efficient. For some of these techniques, however, performance tends to collapse under heavy load.

Although both centralized and distributed reservation techniques have been implemented in some LAN products, round robin and contention techniques are the most common.

The discussion above has been somewhat abstract, and should become clearer as specific techniques are discussed in this chapter and the next. For future reference, Table 5.1 places the techniques that will be discussed into the classification just outlined.

IEEE 802 Frame Format

This section presents the formats used for frames in the IEEE 802 standard. These formats are similar to those used by most proprietary

TABLE 5.1 Medium Access Control Techniques

	Centralized	Distributed
Round robin	Polling	Token bus Token ring Delay scheduling Implicit token
Reservation	Centralized reservation	Distributed reservation
Contention		CSMA/CD Slotted ring Register insertion

networks. They are the basis for the LLC, MAC, and physical layer functionality.

At this point it is worth reviewing the HDLC format presented in Chapter 2. The requirements for a local network frame are very similar. There must, of course, be a data or information field. A control field is needed to pass control bits and identify frame type. Starting and ending patterns are usually required to serve as delimiters. Addressing is required. Here is the main difference. Because LAN links are multiple-source, multiple-destination, both source and destination addresses are required. Further, unlike HDLC and virtually all other layer 2 protocols, the IEEE 802 LAN protocols support a form of multiplexing common in layer 3

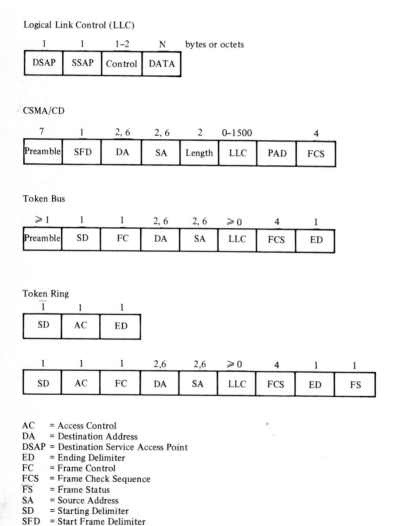

FIGURE 5-2. IEEE 802 Frame Formats

protocols. As we shall see, this is accomplished in IEEE 802 by identifying service access points at each station.

Figure 5-2 shows the IEEE 802 formats. As can be seen, a separate format is used at the LLC level, and this is then embedded in the appropriate MAC frame. IEEE 802 supports three MAC alternatives: CSMA/CD, token bus, and token ring.

5.2

LINK LAYER PROTOCOL FOR LANS

In this section we look first at the general link level requirements for a local area network, then examine the IEEE 802 specification.

Principles

The link layers for LANs should bear some resemblance to the more common link layers extant. Like all link layers, the LAN link layer is concerned with the transmission of a frame of data between two stations, with no intermediate switching nodes.

It differs from traditional link layers in three ways:

- It must support the multiaccess nature of the link (this differs from multidrop in that there is no primary node).
- It is relieved of some details of link access by the Medium Access Control (MAC) layer.
- It must provide some layer 3 functions.

Figure 5-3 will help clarify the requirements for the link layer. We consider two stations or systems that communicate via a LAN (bus or ring). Higher layers (the equivalent of transport and above) provide end-to-end services between the stations. Below the link layer, a medium

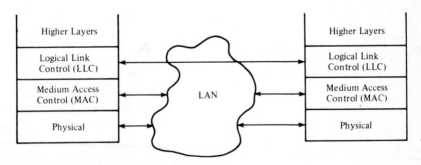

FIGURE 5-3. LAN Communication Architecture

access control (MAC) layer provides the necessary logic for gaining access to the network for frame transmission and reception.

At a minimum, the link layer should perform those functions normally associated with that layer:

- *Error control:* End-to-end error control and acknowledgment. The link layer should guarantee error-free transmission across the LAN.
- *Flow control:* End-to-end flow control.

These functions can be provided in much the same way as for HDLC and other point-to-point link protocols—by the use of sequence numbers (N(S), N(R)).

It has already been mentioned that because of the lack of intermediate switching nodes, a LAN does not require a separate layer 3; rather, the essential layer three functions can be incorporated into layer 2:

- *Connectionless:* A service that does not require the overhead of establishing a logical connection is needed for efficient support of highly interactive traffic.
- *Connection-oriented:* A connection-oriented service is also usually needed.
- *Multiplexing:* Generally, a single physical link attaches a station to a LAN; it should be possible to provide data transfer with multiple end points over that link.

Because there is no need for routing, the above functions are easily provided. The connectionless service simply requires the use of source and destination address fields, as discussed previously. The station sending the frame must designate the destination address, so that the frame is delivered properly. The source address must also be indicated so that the recipient knows where the frame came from.

Both the connection-oriented and multiplexing capabilities can be supported with the concept of the service access point (SAP), introduced in Chapter 2. An example may make this clear. Figure 5-4 shows three stations attached to a LAN. Each station has an address. Further, the link layer supports multiple SAPs, each with its own address. The link layer provides communication between SAPs. Assume that a process or application X in station A wishes to send a message to a process in station C. X may be a report generator program in minicomputer A. C may be a printer and a simple printer driver. X attaches itself to SAP 1 and requests a connection to station C, SAP 1 (station C may have only one SAP if it is a single printer). Station A's link layer then sends to the LAN a "connection-request" frame which includes the source address (A, 1), the destination address (C, 1), and some control bits indicating that this is a connection request. The LAN delivers this frame to C, which, if it is free, returns a

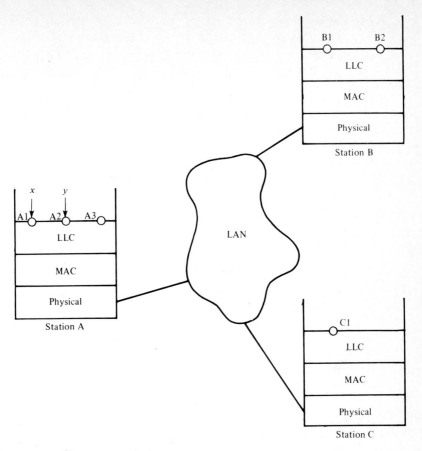

FIGURE 5-4.   LAN Link Control Scenario

"connection-accepted" frame. Henceforth, all data from X will be assembled into a frame by A's LLC, which includes source (A,1) and destination (C,1) addresses. Incoming frames addressed to (A,1) will be rejected unless they are from (C, 1); these might be acknowledgment frames, for example. Similarly, station C's printer is declared busy and C will only accept frames from (A,1).

Thus a connection-oriented service is provided. At the same time, process Y could attach to (A,2) and exchange data with (B,1). This is an example of multiplexing. In addition, various other processes in A could use (A,3) to send datagrams to various destinations.

One final function of the link layer should be included, to take advantage of the multiple access nature of the LAN:

- *Multicast, broadcast:* The link layer should provide a service of sending a message to multiple stations or all stations.

Addressing

The preceding discussion referred to both station and LLC addresses. A further elaboration of this point is warranted. To understand the function of addressing, we need to consider the requirements for exchanging data.

In very general terms, communication can be said to involve three agents: processes, stations, and networks. *Processes* are the fundamental entities that communicate. One example is a file transfer operation. In this case, a file transfer process in one station exchanges data with a file transfer process in another station. Another example is remote terminal access. In this case a user terminal is attached to one station and controlled by a terminal-handling process in that station. The user, through the terminal-handling process, is remotely connected to a time-sharing system; data is exchanged between the terminal-handling process and the time-sharing process. Processes execute on *stations*, which can often support multiple simultaneous processes. Stations are connected by a *network*, and the data to be exchanged is transmitted by the network from one station to another. From this point of view, the transfer of data from one process to another involves first getting the data to the station in which the process resides and then getting it to the process within the station.

These concepts suggest the need for two levels of addressing. To see this, consider Figure 5-5, which shows the overall format of data transmitted using the LLC and MAC protocols (compare Figure 2-11). User data to be sent is passed down to LLC, which appends a header. This header contains control information that is used to manage the protocol between the local

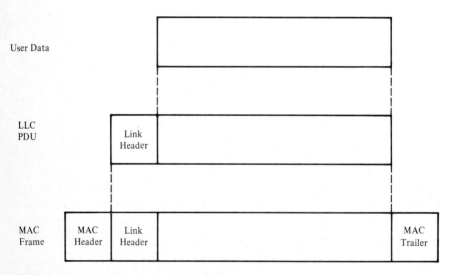

FIGURE 5-5. LAN Protocol Data Units

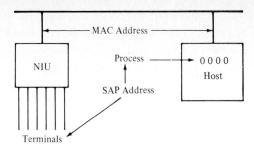

FIGURE 5-6. LAN Addressing

LLC entity and the remote LLC entity. The combination of user data and LLC header is referred to as an LLC *protocol data unit* (PDU). After the sending LLC has prepared a PDU, the PDU is then passed as a block of data down to the MAC entity. The MAC entity appends both a header and a trailer, to manage the MAC protocol. The result is a MAC-level PDU. To avoid confusion with an LLC-level PDU, the MAC-level PDU is typically referred to as a *frame*.

Now, the MAC header must contain a destination address that uniquely identifies a station on the local network. This is needed since each station on the local network will read the destination address field to determine if it should capture the MAC frame. When a MAC frame is captured, the MAC entity strips off the MAC header and trailer and passes the resulting LLC PDU up to the LLC entity. The LLC header must contain a destination SAP address so the LLC can determine to whom the data is to be delivered. Hence, two levels of addressing are needed:

- *MAC address:* Identifies a station on the local network.
- *LLC address:* Identifies an LLC user.

Figure 5-6 illustrates the two levels of addresses. The MAC address is associated with a physical attachment point on the network. The LLC SAP is associated with a particular user within a station. In some cases, the SAP corresponds to a host process. Another case relates to a common type of attached equipment, referred to as a network interface unit (NIU)[1]. Often, an NIU is used as a terminal concentration device. In this case, each terminal port on the NIU has a unique SAP.

So far, we have discussed the use of addresses that identify unique entities. In addition to these **individual addresses**, group addresses are also employed. A **group address** specifies a collection of one or more entities. For example, one might wish to send a message to all terminal users

---

[1] NIUs are examined in detail in Chapter 8.

attached to a particular NIU, or all terminal users on the entire LAN. Two types of group addresses are used. A **broadcast address** refers to all entities within some context; this is also referred to as an all-stations address. A **multicast address** refers to some subset of entities within some context.

Table 5-2 depicts the possible combinations. The first five combinations are straightforward. A specific user can be addressed. A group of users or all users at a specific station can be addressed. And all users on some stations or all users on all stations can be addressed.

The last four combination in the table are less obvious. It should be clear that LLC addresses are unique only within a single station. It is only the LLC entity within a station that examines the LLC header and determines the user. However, it is possible to assign LLC addresses uniquely across all stations; this is undesirable for several reasons:

- The total number of users on all stations would be limited by the SAP field length in the LLC header.
- Central management of SAP assignment would be required, no matter how large and heterogeneous the user population.

On the other hand, it may be desirable to assign the same SAP value to entities in different stations. For example, a station management entity in a station may always be given a SAP value of 1, to facilitate network management. Or a group of management and control entities within a station may always be given the same multicast SAP address. When such a convention is followed, then it becomes possible to address data to one SAP address or a multicast SAP address in a group of stations or all stations.

TABLE 5.2 Local Network Addressing

MAC Address	LLC User Address (Service Access Point)
Individual	Individual
Individual	Multicast
Individual	Broadcast
Multicast	Broadcast
Broadcast	Broadcast
Multicast	Individual
Multicast	Multicast
Broadcast	Individual
Broadcast	Multicast

IEEE 802 Logical Link Control

The IEEE 802 Logical Link Control (LLC) standard [IEEE85a] is a good example of a LAN link control layer. It is well thought out, and offers a variety of services. This section summarizes the features of LLC.

Figure 5-2 depicts the LLC frame. As can be seen, it specifies the source and destination service access points (thus allowing link multiplexing), a 1- or 2-byte control field, and a data field. The source and destination address fields are needed by the LLC, but are also used by MAC, and are included in the outer MAC frame. The LLC can be specified in three parts:

- The interface with the station, specifying the services that LLC (and hence the LAN) provides to the network subscriber.
- The LLC protocol, specifying the LLC functions.
- The interface with MAC, specifying the services that LLC requires to perform its function.

A variety of functions were mentioned in the previous section. Not all of these functions are needed in all environments. Accordingly, the 802 standard defines two general categories of data link control operation. The first is a connectionless operation which provides minimum service with minimum protocol complexity. This is useful and efficient when higher layers (e.g., network, transport) provide error control, flow control, and sequencing functions. It is also useful when the guaranteed delivery of data is not required. The second category is connection-oriented operation which provides the functions referred to above using a protocol similar to HDLC. These two types of operations are reflected in the specifications of both the LLC services and the LLC protocol.

LLC Services
LLC provides three services:

- *Unacknowledged connectionless service:* This is a datagram service that simply allows for sending and receiving frames. It supports point-to-point, multipoint, and broadcast.
- *Connection-oriented service:* This provides a logical connection between service access points. It provides flow control, sequencing, and error recovery.
- *Acknowledged connectionless service:* This is also a connectionless service, but provides for acknowledgment, relieving higher layers of this burden. It supports point-to-point transfers.

TABLE 5.3 Logical Link Control Primitives

UNACKNOWLEDGED CONNECTIONLESS SERVICE

DL-UNITDATA.request (source-address, destination-address, data, priority)
DL-UNITDATA.indication (source-address, destination-address, data, priority)

CONNECTION-MODE SERVICE

DL-CONNECT.request (source-address, destination-address, priority)
DL-CONNECT.indication (source-address, destination-address, priority)
DL-CONNECT.response (source-address, destination-address, priority)
DL-CONNECT.confirm (source-address, destination-address, priority)

DL-DATA.request (source-address, destination-address, data)
DL-DATA.indication (source-address, destination-address, data)

DL-DISCONNECT.request (source-address, destination-address)
DL-DISCONNECT.indication (source-address, destination-address, reason)

DL-RESET.request (source-address, destination-address)
DL-RESET.indication (source-address, destination-address, reason)
DL-RESET.response (source-address, destination-address)
DL-RESET.confirm (source-address, destination-address)

DL-CONNECTION-FLOWCONTROL.request (source-address,
  destination-address, amount)
DL-CONNECTION-FLOWCONTROL.indication (source-address,
  destination-address, amount)

ACKNOWLEDGED CONNECTIONLESS SERVICE

DL-DATA-ACK.request (source-address, destination-address, data, priority,
  service-class)
DL-DATA-ACK.indication (source-address, destination-address, data, priority,
  service-class)
DL-DATA-ACK-STATUS.indication (source-address, destination-address,
  priority, service-class, status)
DL-REPLY.request (source-address, destination-address, data, priority,
  service-class)
DL-REPLY.indication (source-address, destination-address, data, priority,
  service-class)
DL-REPLY-STATUS.indication (source-address, destination-address, data,
  priority, service-class, status)

DL-REPLY-UPDATE.request (source-address, data)
DL-REPLY-UPDATE-STATUS.indication (source-address, status)

These services are specified in terms of primitives that can be viewed as commands or procedure calls with parameters[2]. Table 5-3 summarizes the LLC primitives.

The **Unacknowledged Connectionless Service** is a datagram style of service that simply allows for sending and receiving LLC frames, with no form

---

[2] These primitives always include one of four standard modifiers: request, indication, response, confirm. The interpretation of these primitives is discussed in Appendix 5B.

of acknowledgment to assure delivery. It supports point-to-point, multi-point, and broadcast addressing.

This service provides for only two primitives across the interface between the next higher layer and LLC. DL-UNITDATA.request is used to pass a block of data down to LLC for transmission. DL-UNITDATA.indication is used to pass that block of data up to the destination user from LLC upon reception. The source-address and destination-address parameters specify the local and remote LLC users, respectively. Each of these parameters actually is a combination of LLC service access point and the MAC address. The data parameter is the block of data transmitted from one LLC user to another. The priority parameter specifies the desired priority. This (together with the MAC portion of the address) is passed down through the LLC entity to the MAC entity, which has the responsibility of implementing a priority mechanism. As we shall see, token bus and token ring are capable of this, but the 802.3 CSMA/CD system is not.

The **Connection-Oriented Service** provides a virtual-circuit style connection between service access points (between users). It provides a means by which a user can request or be notified of the establishment or termination of a logical connection. It also provides flow control, sequencing, and error recovery. It supports point-to-point addressing.

This service includes the DL-CONNECT set of primitives (request, indication, response, confirm) to establish a logical connection between SAPs. Once the connection is established, blocks of data are exchanged using DL-DATA.request and DL-DATA.indication. Because the existence of a logical connection guarantees that all blocks of data will be delivered reliably, there is no need for an acknowledgment (via indication and confirm primitives) of individual blocks of data. At any point, either side may terminate the connection with a DL-DISCONNECT.request; the other side is informed with a DL-DISCONNECT.indication.

The DL-RESET primitives are used to reset a logical connection to an initial state. Sequence numbers are reset, and the connection is reinitialized. Finally, the two flow control primitives regulate the flow of data across the SAP. The flow can be controlled in either direction. This is a local flow control mechanism which specifies the amount of data that may be passed across the SAP.

The **Acknowledged Connectionless Service** provides a mechanism by which a user can send a unit of data and receive an acknowledgment that the data was delivered, without the necessity of setting up a connection.

This service includes DL-DATA-ACK.request and DL-DATA-ACK.indication with meanings analogous to those for the Unacknowledged Connectionless Service, plus DL-DATA-ACK-STATUS.indication to provide acknowledgement to the sending user. The DL-REPLY primitives provide a data exchange service. It allows a user to request that data be returned from a remote station or that data units be exchanged with a remote station. Associated with these primitives are the DL-REPLY-UPDATE primitives. These primitives allow a user to pass data to LLC to be held, and sent out at a later time when requested to do so (by a DL-REPLY primitive) by some other station.

The specification of three types of service is intended to allow LLC to be used to support a variety of user requirements and to enable implementors to implement subsets of LLC to meet their specific needs and to optimize the implementation to those needs. The Unacknowledged Connectionless Service is the simplest and requires the minimum implementation. In cases where higher layer protocols (usually transport) provide end-to-end error control and flow control, this minimum service is all that is needed. On the other hand, when the supported devices are vey simple (e.g., terminals) it might make sense to forgo elaborate upper layers and rely on LLC to provide end-to-end control. Finally, the Acknowledged Connectionless Service may be useful in some realtime environments, such as factory LANs. For example, certain alarm or control signals may be very important and time-critical. Because of their importance, an acknowledgment is needed so that the sender can be assured that the signal got through. Because of the urgency of a signal, the user might not want to take the time to first establish a logical connection and then send the data.

LLC Protocol

The LLC protocol is modeled after the HDLC balanced mode, and has similar formats and functions. These are summarized briefly in this section. The reader should be able to see how this protocol supports the LLC services defined above.

First are the address fields. Both the DSAP and SSAP fields actually contain 7-bit addresses. The least significant bit of DSAP indicates whether this is an individual or group address. The least significant bit of SSAP indicates whether this is a command or response frame.

Figure 5-7 shows the format for the LLC control field (compare Figure 2-13). It is identical to that of HDLC and the functioning is the same, with four exceptions:

1. LLC only makes use of the asynchronous balanced mode of operation, and does not employ HDLC's normal response mode or asynchronous response mode. This mode is used to support connection-oriented service. The set asynchronous balanced mode (SABME) command is used to establish a connection, and disconnect (DISC) is used to terminate the connection.
2. LLC supports a connectionless (datagram) service by using the unnumbered information (UI) frame.

	1	2	3	4	5	6	7	8	9	10-16
Information Transfer Command/Response (I–Format PDU)	0	N(S)							P/F	N(R)
Supervisory Commands/Responses (S–Format PDUs)	1	0	S	S	X	X	X	X	P/F	N(R)
Unnumbered Commands/Response (U–Format PDUs)	1	1	M	M	P/F	M	M	M		

Where

N(S)–Transmitter Send Sequence Number (Bit 2–Low–order Bit)
N(R)–Transmitter Receive Sequence Number (Bit 10–Low–order Bit)
S–Supervisory Function Bit
M–Modifier Function Bit
X–Reserved and Set to Zero
P/F–Poll Bit–Command LLC PDU Transmissions
    Final Bit–Response LLC PDU Transmissions
    (1–Poll/Final)

FIGURE 5-7. IEEE 802 LLC Control Field Format

3. LLC permits multiplexing by the use of SAPs.
4. LLC supports an acknowledged connectionless service by using two new unnumbered frames.

A brief summary follows.

As with HDLC; three frame formats are defined for LLC: information transfer, supervisory, and unnumbered. Their use depends on the type of operation employed. The types are Type 1 (connectionless), Type 2 (connection-oriented), and Type 3 (acknowledged connectionless).

With Type 1 Operation, protocol data units (PDUs) are exchanged between LLC entities without the need to establish a logical connection. There is no acknowledgment, flow control, or error control. This type of operation supports the Unacknowledged Connectionless Service.

Three unnumbered frame formats are used. The UI (unnumbered information) frame is used to send a connectionless data frame, containing data from an LLC user. The XID (exchange identification) frame is used to convey station class (which operation types are supported). The TEST (test) frame is used to a request a TEST frame in response, to test the LLC-to-LLC path.

With Type 2 Operation, a data link connection is established between two LLC entities prior to data exchange. This type of operation supports Connection-Oriented Service and uses all three frame formats. The information transfer frames are used to send data (as opposed to control information). N(S) and N(R) are frame sequence numbers that support error control and flow control. A station sending a sequence of frames will number them, modulo 128, and place the number in N(S). N(R) is a piggybacked acknowledgment. It enables the sending station to indicate which number frame it expects to receive next. These numbers support flow control since, after sending seven frames without an acknowledgment, a station can send no more. The numbers support error control, as explained below. The P/F field is set to 1 only on the last frame in a series, to indicate that the transmission is over.

The supervisory frame is used for acknowledgment and flow control. The 2-bit SS field is used to indicate one of three commands: Receive Ready (RR), Receive Not Ready (RNR), and Reject (REJ). RR is used to acknowledge the last frame received by indicating in N(R) the next frame expected. This frame is used when there is no reverse traffic to carry a piggybacked acknowledgment. RNR acknowledges a frame, as with RR, but also asks the transmitting station to suspend transmission. When the receiving station is again ready, it sends an RR frame. REJ is used to indicate that the frame with number N(R) is rejected and that it and any subsequently transmitted frames must be sent again.

Unnumbered frames are used for control purposes in Type 2 operation. The 5-bit MMMMM field specifies a particular command or response. The commands are:

- SABME (set asynchronous balanced mode extended): used by an LLC entity to request logical connection with another LC entity.
- DISC (disconnect): used to terminate a logical connection; the sending station is announcing that it is suspending operations.

The foregoing frames are commands, initiated by a station at will. The following frames are responses:

- UA (unnumbered acknowledgment): used to acknowledge SABME and DISC commands.
- DM (disconnected mode): used to respond to a frame in order to indicate that the station's LLC is logically disconnected.
- FRMR (frame reject): used to indicate that an improper frame has arrived—one that somehow violates the protocol.

The P/F bit is used to indicate that a response is requested to a command frame.

With Type 3 Operation, each transmitted frame is acknowledged. A new unnumbered frame, the Acknowledged Connectionless (AC) Information frame, is defined. Unlike the other frames used in LLC, this frame is not defined in HDLC. User data is sent in an AC command frame and must be acknowledged using an AC response frame. To guard against lost frames, a 1-bit sequence number is used. The sender alternates the use of 0 and 1 in its AC command frames, and the receiver responds with an AC frame with the corresponding number.

LLC-MAC Interface

The IEEE 802 LLC is intended to operate with any of the three MAC protocols (CSMA/CD, token bus, token ring). A single logical interface to any of the MAC layers is defined. The 802 standard does not define an explicit interface, but provides a "model." The basic primitives are:

- MA-UNITDATA.request: to request transfer of an LLC frame from local LLC to destination LLC. This includes information transfer, supervisory, and unnumbered frames.
- MA-UNITDATA.indicate: to transfer incoming LLC frame from local MAC to local LLC.

5.3

MEDIUM ACCESS CONTROL–BUS/TREE

Of all the local network topologies, the bus/tree topologies present the greatest challenges, and the most options, for medium access control. This section will not attempt to survey the many techniques that have been proposed; good discussions can be found in [LUCZ78] and [FRAN81]. Rather, emphasis is placed on the two techniques that seem likely to dominate the marketplace: CSMA/CD and token bus. Standards for these techniques have been developed by the IEEE 802 committee.

A third technique, centralized reservation, is reviewed briefly. This is for the sake of completeness; virtually all access techniques for bus/tree are related to one of these three techniques.

Table 5.4 compares the three techniques on a number of characteristics. The ensuing discussion should clarify their significance.

TABLE 5.4   Bus/Tree Access Methods

	CSMA/CD	Token Bus	Centralized Reservation
Access determination	Contention	Token	Reservation
Packet length restriction	Greater than twofold propagation delay	None	No greater than slot size
Principal advantage	Simplicity	Regulated/fair access	Regulated/fair access
Principal disadvantage	Performance under heavy load	Complexity	Required central controller

CSMA/CD

The most commonly used medium access control technique for bus-tree topologies is carrier sense multiple access with collision detection (CSMA/CD). The original baseband version of this technique was developed and patented by Xerox [METC77] as part of its Ethernet local network [METC76]. The original broadband version was developed and patented by MITRE [HOPK80] as part of its MITREnet local network [ROMA79, HOPK77]. A baseband version inspired by Ethernet has been issued as an IEEE 802 standard [IEEE85b].

Before examining this technique, we look at some earlier schemes from which CSMA/CD evolved.

Precursors

All of the techniques discussed in this section, including CSMA/CD, can be termed *random access* or *contention* techniques. They are designed to address the problem of how to share a common broadcast transmission medium—the "Who goes next?" problem. The techniques are random access in the sense that there is no predictable or scheduled time for any station to transmit; station transmissions occur randomly. They are contention in the sense that no control is exercised to determine whose turn it is—all stations must contend for time on the network.

The earliest of these techniques, known as *ALOHA*, was developed for groundbased packet radio broadcasting networks [ABRA70]. However, it is applicable to any transmission medium shared by uncoordinated users. ALOHA, or *pure ALOHA* as it is sometimes called, is a true free-for-all. Whenever a station has a frame to send, it does so. The station then listens for an amount of time equal to the maximum possible round-trip propagation time on the network (twice the time it takes to send a frame between the two most widely separated stations). If the station hears an acknowledgement during that time, fine; otherwise, it resends the frame. After repeated failures, it gives up. A receiving station determines the correctness of an incoming frame by examining the checksum. If the frame is valid, the station acknowledges immediately. The frame may be invalid, due to noise on the channel or because another station transmitted a frame at about the same time. In the latter case, the two frames may interfere with each other so that neither gets through; this is known as a *collision*. In that case, the receiving station simply ignores the frame. ALOHA is as simple as can be, and pays a penalty for it. Because the number of collisions rises so rapidly with increased load, the maximum utilization of the channel is only about 18%.

To improve efficiency, a modification of ALOHA [ROBE75] was developed in which time on the channel is organized into uniform slots whose size equals the frame transmission time. Some central clock or other technique is needed to synchronize all stations. Transmission is permitted only to begin at a slot boundary. Thus frames that do overlap will do so totally. This increases the maximum utilization of the system to about 37%. The scheme is known as *slotted ALOHA*.

Both ALOHA and slotted ALOHA exhibit poor utilization. Both fail to take advantage of one of the key properties of both packet radio and local networks, which is that the propagation delay between stations is usually very small compared to frame transmission time. Consider the following observations. If the station-to-station propagation time is large compared to the frame transmission time, then, after a station launches a frame, it will be a long time before other stations know about it. During that time, one of the other stations may transmit a frame; the two frames may interfere with each other, and neither gets through. Indeed, if the distances are great enough, many stations may begin transmitting, one after the other, and none of their frames gets through unscathed. Suppose, however, that the propagation time is extremely small compared to frame transmission time. In that case, when a station launches a frame, all the other stations know it almost immediately. So, if they had any sense, they would not try transmitting until the first station was done. Collisions would be rare since they would occur only when two stations began to transmit almost simultaneously. Another way of look at it is that the short delay time provides the stations with better feedback about the state of the system; this information can be used to improve efficiency.

The foregoing observations led to the development of a technique known as carrier sense multiple access (CSMA) or listen before talk (LBT). A station wishing to transmit first listens to the medium to determine if another transmission is in progress. If the medium is in use, the station backs off some period of time and tries again, using one of the algorithms explained below. If the medium is idle, the station may transmit. Now, it may happen that two or more stations attempt to transmit at about the same time. If this happens, there will be a collision. To account for this, a station waits a reasonable amount of time after transmitting for an acknowledgment, taking into account the maximum round-trip propagation delay, and the fact that the acknowledging station must also contend for the channel in order to respond. If there is no acknowledgement, the station assumes that a collision has occurred and retransmits.

One can see how this strategy would be effective for systems in which the frame transmission time is much longer than the propagation time. Collisions can occur only when more than one user begins transmitting within a short time (within the period of propagation delay). If a station begins to transmit, and there are no collisions during the time it takes for the leading edge of the frame to propagate to the farthest station, then the station has seized the channel and the remainder of the frame will be transmitted without collision.

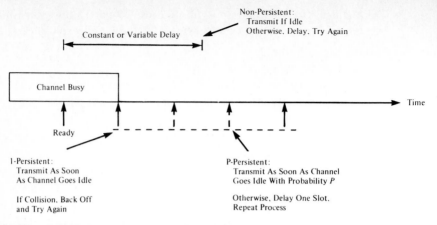

FIGURE 5-8. CSMA Persistence and Back-off

The maximum utilization achievable using CSMA can far exceed that of ALOHA or slotted ALOHA. The maximum utilization depends on the length of the frame and on the propagation time; the longer the frames or the shorter the propagation time, the higher the utilization. This subject will be explored in Chapter 9.

With CSMA, an algorithm is needed to specify what a station should do if the medium is found to be busy. Three approaches are depicted in Figure 5-8. One algorithm is *nonpersistent* CSMA. A station wishing to transmit listens to the medium and obeys the following rules:

1. If the medium is idle, transmit.
2. If the medium is busy, wait an amount of time drawn from a probability distribution (the retransmission delay) and repeat step 1.

The use of random retransmission times reduces the probability of collisions. The drawback is that even if several stations have a frame to send, there is likely to be some wasted idle time following a prior transmission.

To avoid channel idle time, the *1-persistent protocol* can be used. A station wishing to transmit listens to the medium and obeys the following rules:

1. If the medium is idle, transmit.
2. If the medium is busy, continue to listen until the channel is sensed idle; then transmit immediately.
3. If there is a collision (determined by a lack of acknowledgment), wait a random amount of time and repeat step 1.

Whereas nonpersistent stations are deferential, 1-persistent stations are selfish. If two or more stations are waiting to transmit, a collision is guaranteed. Things only get sorted out after the collision.

A compromise that attempts to reduce collisions, like nonpersistent, and reduce idle time, like 1-persistent, is *p-persistent*. The rules are:

1. If the medium is idle, transmit what probability p, and delay one time unit with probability $(1 - p)$. The time unit is typically equal to the maximum propagation delay.
2. If the medium is busy, continue to listen until the channel is idle and repeat step 1.
3. If transmission is delayed one time unit, repeat step 1.

The question arises as to what is an effective value of p. The main problem to avoid is one of instability under heavy load. Consider the case in which n stations have frames to send while a transmission is taking place. At the end of that transmission, the expected number of stations that will attempt to transmit is np. If np is greater than 1, multiple stations will attempt to transmit and there will be a collision. What is more, as soon as all these stations realize that they did not get through, they will be back again, almost guaranteeing more collisions. Worse yet, these retries will compete with new transmissions from other stations, further increasing the probability of collision. Eventually, all stations will be trying to send, causing continuous collisions, with throughput dropping to zero. To avoid this catastrophe np must be less than one for the expected peaks of n. As p is made smaller, stations must wait longer to attempt transmission but collisions are reduced. At low loads, however, stations have unnecessarily long delays.

Description of CSMA/CD

All of the techniques described above could be used in a bus/tree topology with an electrical conductor medium or in a packet radio scheme. We now introduce *carrier sense multiple access with collision detection* (CSMA/CD), which, because of the CD part, is appropriate only for a bus/tree topology [it is also referred to as *listen while talk* (LWT)]. CSMA/CD can be used with either baseband or broadband systems. Where details differ between baseband and broadband, we will use IEEE802 and MITREnet as examples for comparison.

CSMA, although more efficient than ALOHA or slotted ALOHA, still has one glaring inefficiency. When two frames collide, the medium remains unusable for the duration of transmission of both damaged frames. For long frames, compared to propagation time, the amount of wasted bandwidth can be considerable. This waste can be reduced if a station continues to listen to the medium while it is transmitting. In that case, these rules can be added to the CSMA rules:

1. If a collision is detected during transmission, immediately cease transmitting the frame, and transmit a brief jamming signal to assure that all stations know that there has been a collision.

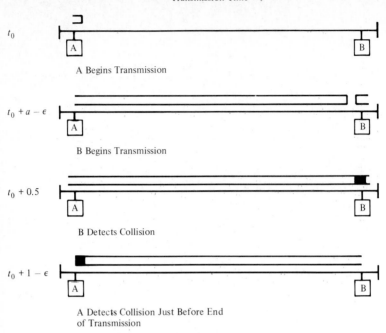

t_0

A

B

A Begins Transmission

$t_0 + a - \epsilon$

A

B

B Begins Transmission

$t_0 + 0.5$

A

B

B Detects Collision

$t_0 + 1 - \epsilon$

A

B

A Detects Collision Just Before End
of Transmission

FIGURE 5-9.   Baseband Collision Detection Timing

2. After transmitting the jamming signal, wait a random amount of time, then attempt to transmit again using CSMA.

Now the amount of wasted bandwidth is reduced to the time it takes to detect a collision. Question: How long does that take? Figure 5-9 illustrates the answer for a baseband system. Consider the worst case of two stations that are as far apart as possible. As can be seen, the amount of time it takes to detect a collision is twice the propagation delay. For broadband bus, the wait is even longer. Figure 5-10 shows a dual-cable system. This time, worst case is two stations close together and as far as possible from the head end. In this case the time required to detect a collision is four times the propagation delay from the station to the head end. The results would be the same for a midsplit system.

Both figures indicate the use of frames long enough to allow CD prior to the end of transmission. In most systems that use CSMA/CD, it is required that all frames be at least this long. Otherwise, the performance of the system is the same as the less efficient CSMA protocol, since collisions are detected only after transmission is complete.

Now let us look at a few details of CSMA/CD. First, which persistence

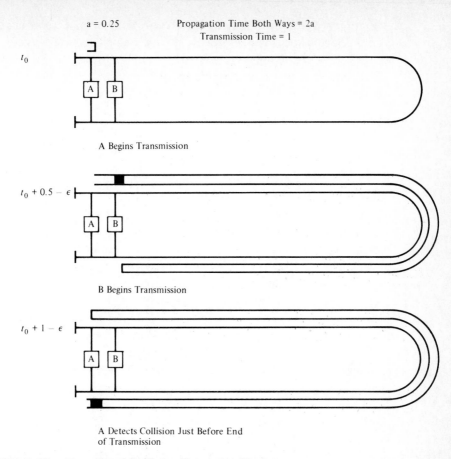

a = 0.25

Propagation Time Both Ways = 2a
Transmission Time = 1

t_0

A Begins Transmission

$t_0 + 0.5 - \epsilon$

B Begins Transmission

$t_0 + 1 - \epsilon$

A Detects Collision Just Before End
of Transmission

FIGURE 5-10. Broadband Collision Detection Timing

algorithm should we use: non-, 1-, or p-? You may be surprised to learn that the most common choice is 1-persistent. It is used by both Ethernet and MITREnet, and in the IEEE 802 standard. Recall that both nonpersistent and p-persistent have performance problems. In the nonpersistent case, capacity is wasted because the medium will generally remain idle following the end of a transmission even if there are stations waiting to send. In the p-persistent case, p must be set low enough to avoid instability, with the result of sometimes atrocious delays under light load. The 1-persistent algorithm, which after all means $p = 1$, would seem to be even more unstable than p-persistent due to the greed of the stations. What saves the day is that the wasted time due to collisions is mercifully short (if the frames are long relative to propagation delay!), and with random back-off, the two stations involved in a collision are unlikely to collide on their next tries. To ensure that back-off maintains stability, IEEE 802 and Ethernet use a technique known as binary exponential back-off. A station will attempt to transmit repeatedly in the face of repeated collisions, but after each collision, the mean value of the random delay is doubled. After 16 unsuccessful attempts, the station gives up and reports an error.

The beauty of the 1-persistent algorithm with binary exponential back-off is that it is efficient over a wide range of loads. At low loads, 1-persistence guarantees that a station can seize the channel as soon as it goes idle, in contrast to the non- and p-persistent schemes. At high loads, it is at least as stable as the other techniques. However, one unfortunate effect of the back-off algorithm is that is has a last-in, first-out effect; stations with no or few collisions will have a chance to transmit before stations that have waited longer.

Although the implementation of CSMA/CD is substantially the same for baseband and broadband, there are differences. One example is the means for performing carrier sense. For baseband systems using Manchester encoding, carrier is conveniently sensed by detecting the presence of transitions on the channel. Strictly speaking, there is no carrier to sense digital signaling; the term was borrowed from the radio lexicon. With broadband, carrier sense is indeed performed. The station's receiver listens for the presence of a carrier on the outbound channel.

Collision detection also differs for the two systems. In a baseband system, a collision should produce substantially higher voltage swings than those produced by a single transmitter. Accordingly, Ethernet and the IEEE standard dictate that a transmitting transceiver will detect a collision if the signal on the cable at the transceiver exceeds the maximum that could be produced by the transceiver alone. Because a transmitted signal attenuates as it propagates, there is a potential problem with collision detection. If two stations far apart are transmitting, each station will receive a greatly attenuated signal from the other. The signal strength could be so small that when it is added to the transmitted signal at the transceiver, the combined signal does not exceed the CD threshold. For this reason, among others, IEEE 802 restricts the maximum length of cable to 500 m. Because frames may cross repeater boundaries, collisions must cross as well. Hence if a repeater detects a collision on either cable, it must transmit a jamming signal on the other side. Since the collision may not involve a transmission from the repeater, the CD threshold is different for a nontransmitting transceiver: A collision is detected if the signal strength exceeds that which could be produced by two transceiver outputs in the worst case.

A much simpler collision detection scheme is possible with the twisted-pair star-wiring approach (Figure 4-4). In this case, collision detection is based on logic rather than sensing voltage magnitudes. For any hub, if there is activity (signal) on more than one input, a collision is assumed. A special signal called the *collision presence* signal is generated. This signal is generated and sent out as long as activity is sensed on any of the input lines. This signal is interpreted by every node as an occurrence of collision.

Figure 5-11 gives examples of the operation of a star-wired system with and without collisions. In the first example, a frame transmitted from station *A* propagates up to HHUB and is eventually received by all stations in the network. In the second example, a collision is detected by *A*'s IHUB. The collision presence signal propagates up to HHUB and is rebroadcast down to all hubs and stations. The third example shows the result of a three-way collision.

There are several possible approaches to collision detection in broadband systems. The most common of these is to perform a bit-by-bit comparison between transmitted and received data. When a station transmits on the inbound channel, it begins to receive its own transmisssion on the outbound channel after a propagation delay to the headend and back. In the IEEE 802.3 specification, the bits up through the last bit of the source address field of the transmitted and received signals are compared, and a collision is assumed if they differ. There are several problems with this approach. The most serious is the danger that differences in signal level between colliding signals will cause the receiver to treat the weaker signal as noise and fail to detect a collision. The cable system, with its taps, splitters, and amplifiers, must be carefully tuned so that attenuation effects and differences in transmitter signal strength do not cause this problem. Another problem, for dual cable systems, is that a station must simultaneously transmit and receive on the same frequency. Its two RF modems must be carefully shielded to prevent crosstalk.

An alternative approach for broadband is to perform the CD function at the headend. This is most appropriate for the split system, which has an active component at the headend anyway. This reduces the tuning problem to one of making sure that all stations produce approximately the same signal level at the headend. The headend would detect collisions by looking for garbled data or higher-than-expected signal strength.

IEEE 802 CSMA/CD

The IEEE 802 CSMA/CD standard is very close to that of Ethernet, and conforms to the preceding discussion. Figure 5-2 shows the MAC CSMA/CD frame structure. The individual fields are as follows:

- *Preamble:* a 7-byte pattern used by the receiver to establish bit synchronization and then locate the first bit of the frame.
- *Start frame delimiter (SFD):* indicates the start of a frame.
- *Destination address (DA):* specifies the station(s) for which the frame is intended. It may be a unique physical address (one destination transceiver), a multicast-group address (a group of stations), or a global address (all stations on the local network). The choice of a 16- or 48-bit address is an implementation decision, and must be the same for all stations on a particular LAN.

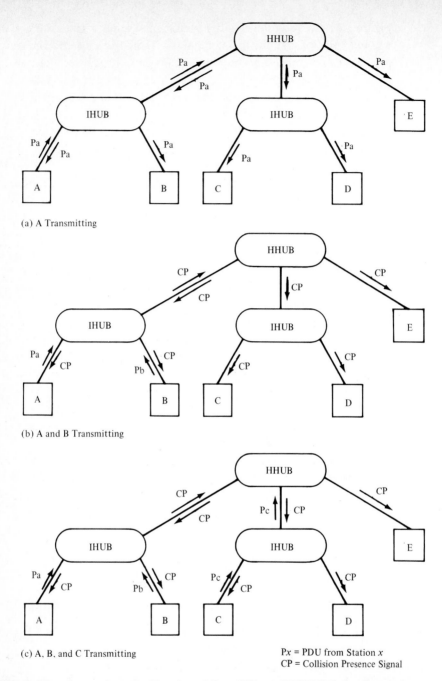

(a) A Transmitting

(b) A and B Transmitting

(c) A, B, and C Transmitting

Px = PDU from Station x
CP = Collision Presence Signal

FIGURE 5-11.   Operation of a Two-Level Star-Wired CSMA/CD Configuration

- *Source address (SA):* specifies the station that sent the frame. The SA size must equal the DA size.
- *Length:* Specifies the number of LLC bytes that follow.
- *LLC:* field prepared at the LLC level.
- *Pad:* a sequence of bytes added to assure that the frame is long enough for proper CD operation.
- *Frame check sequence (FCS):* a 32-bit cyclic redundancy check value. Based on all fields, starting with destination address.

Token Bus

This is a relatively new technique for controlling access to a broadcast medium, inspired by the token ring technique discussed later. We will first provide a general description, then look at some of the IEEE 802 details.

Description

The token bus technique is more complex than CSMA/CD. For this technique, the stations on the bus or tree form a logical ring; that is, the stations are assigned logical positions in an ordered sequence, with the last member of the sequence followed by the first. Each station knows the identity of the stations preceding and following it. The physical ordering of the stations on the bus is irrelevant and independent of the logical ordering (Figure 5-12).

A control frame known as the *token* regulates the right of access. The token frame contains a destination address. The station receiving the token is granted control of the medium for a specified time. The station may

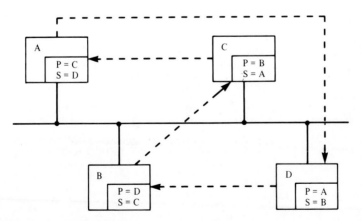

FIGURE 5-12. Token Bus

transmit one or more frames and may poll stations and receive responses. When the station is done, or time has expired, it passes the token on to the next station in logical sequence. This station now has permission to transmit. Hence steady-state operation consists of alternating data transfer and token transfer phases. Nontoken-using stations are allowed on the bus. These stations can only respond to polls or requests for acknowledgement.

This scheme requires considerable maintenance. The following functions, at a minimum, must be performed by one or more stations on the bus:

- *Ring initialization:* When the network is started up, or after the logical ring has broken down, it must be initialized. Some cooperative, decentralized algorithm is needed to sort out who goes first, who goes second, and so on.
- *Addition to ring:* Periodically, nonparticipating stations must be granted the opportunity to insert themselves in the ring.
- *Deletion from ring:* A station must be able to remove itself from the ring by splicing together its predecessor and successor.
- *Recovery:* A number of errors can occur. These include duplicate address (two stations think it is their turn) and broken ring (no station thinks that it is its turn).

IEEE 802 Token Bus

The IEEE 802 token bus protocol follows the general principles outlined above [IEEE85c]. Figure 5-2 shows the MAC frame structure for token bus. The individual fields are as follows:

- *Preamble:* a one or more byte pattern used by receivers to establish bit synchronization and locate the first bit of the frame.
- *Start delimiter (SD):* indicates start of frame.
- *Frame format (FC):* indicates whether this is an LLC data frame. If not, bits in this field control operation of the token bus MAC protocol. An example is a token frame.
- *Destination address (DA):* as with CSMA/CD.
- *Source address (SA):* as with CSMA/CD.
- *LLC:* field prepared by LLC.
- *Frame check sequence (FCS):* as with CSMA/CD.
- *End delimiter (ED):* indicates end of frame.

The details of the protocol can be grouped into the following categories, which will be considered in turn:

- Addition of a node
- Deletion of a node
- Fault management by token holder

- Ring initialization
- Classes of service

First, let us consider how *addition of a node* is accomplished, using a controlled contention process called *response windows*. Each node in the ring has the responsibility of periodically granting an opportunity for new nodes to enter the ring. While holding the token, the node issues a *solicit-successor* frame, inviting nodes with an address between itself and the next node in logical sequence to demand entrance. The transmitting node then waits for one response window or slot time (equal to twice the end-to-end propagation delay of the medium). One of four events can occur.

1. *No response:* Nobody wants in. The token holder transfers the token to its successor as usual.
2. *One response:* One node issues a *set-successor* frame. The token holder sets its successor node to be the requesting node and transmits the token to it. The requestor sets its linkages accordingly and proceeds.
3. *Multiple responses:* The token holder will detect a garbled response if more than one node demands entrance. The conflict is resolved by an address-based contention scheme. The token holder transmits a *resolve-contention* frame and waits four response windows. Each demander can respond in one of these windows based on the first two bits of its address. If a demander hears anything before its window comes up, it refrains from demanding. If the token-holder receives a valid set-successor frame, it is in business. Otherwise, it tries again, and only those nodes that responded the first time are allowed to respond this time, based on the second pair of bits in their address. This process continues until a valid set-successor frame is received, no response is received, or a maximum retry count is reached. In the latter two cases, the token holder gives up and passes the token.
4. *Invalid response:* If the token holder hears a frame other than set-successor, it assumes that some other station thinks it holds the token. To avoid conflict, the station reverts to an idle or listen state.

Deletion of a node is much simpler. If a node wishes to drop out of the logical ring, it waits until it receives the token, and then sends a set-successor frame to its predecessor (the station that transmitted the token to it) containing the address of its successor. The existing station then sends the token as usual to its successor. On the next go-round, the former predecessor of the exited node will send the token to the former successor of the exited node. Each time that a station receives a token, it automatically sets its predecessor address to equal the source address of the token frame. Thus, the exited station is spliced out of the logical ring. If a node fails, it will not pick up the token when the token is passed to it, and this will be detected by the token sender, as explained below.

TABLE 5.5 Token Bus Error Handling

Condition	Action
Multiple token	Defer/drop to 1 or 0
Unaccepted token	Retry
Failed station	"Who follows" process
Failed receiver	Drop out of ring
No token	Initialize after time-out

Fault management by the token holder covers a number of contingencies [PHIN83], listed in Table 5.5. First, while holding the token, a node may hear a frame indicating that another node has the token. If so, it immediately drops the token by reverting to listener mode. In this way, the number of token holders drops immediately to 1 or 0, thus overcoming the multiple-token problem (which could be caused by two nodes having the same address). The next three conditions listed in the table are manifested during token passing. Upon completion of its turn, the token holder will issue a token frame to its successor. The successor should immediately issue a data or token frame. Therefore, after sending a token, the token issuer will listen for one slot time to make sure that its successor is active. This precipitates a sequence of events:

1. If the successor node is active, the token issuer will hear a valid frame and revert to listener mode.
2. If the token issuer hears a garbled transmission, it waits four time slots. If it hears a valid frame, it assumes that its token got through. If it hears nothing, it assumes the token was garbled and reissues the token.
3. If the issuer does not hear a valid frame, it reissues the token to the same successor one more time.
4. After two failures, the issuer assumes that its successor has failed and issues a *who-follows* frame, asking for the identity of the node that follows the failed node. The issuer should get back a set-successor frame from the second node down the line. If so, the issuer adjusts its linkage and issues a token (back to step 1).
5. If the issuing node gets no response to its who-follows frame, it tries again.
6. If the who-follows tactic fails, the node issues a solicit-successor frame with the full address range (i.e. every node is invited to respond). If this process works, a two-node ring is established and life goes on.
7. If the solicit-successor tactic fails, it assumes that some major fault has occurred; either all other stations have failed, all stations have left the logical ring, the medium has broken, or the station's own receiver has

failed. At this point, if the station has any more data to send, it sends that data and tries passing the token again. It then ceases transmission and listens to the bus.

Logical *ring initialization* occurs when one or more stations detect a lack of bus activity of duration longer than a time-out value: the token has been lost. This can be due to a number of causes, such as the network has just been powered up, or a token-holding station fails. Once its time-out expires, a node will issue a *claim-token* frame. Contending claimants are resolved in a manner similar to the response-window process. Each claimant issues a claim-token frame padded by 0, 2, 4, or 6 slots based on the first two bits of its address. After transmission, a claimant listens to the medium and if it hears anything, drops its claim. Otherwise, it tries again, using the second pair of its address bits. The process repeats. With each iteration, only those stations who transmitted the longest on the previous iteration try again, using successive pairs of address bits. When all address bits have been used, a node that succeeds on the last iteration considers itself the token holder. The ring can now be rebuilt by the response window process described previously.

As an option, a token bus system can include *classes of service* that provide a mechanism of prioritizing access to the bus. Four classes of service are defined, in descending order: class 6, 4, 2, and 0.

Any station may have data in one or more of these classes to send. The object is to allocate network bandwidth to the higher priority frames and only send lower priority frames when there is sufficient bandwidth. To explain, let us define the following variables:

- THT = token holding time: the maximum time that a station can hold the token to transmit class 6 (synchronous) data.
- TRT4 = token rotation time for class 4: maximum time that a token can take to circulate and still permit class 4 transmission.
- TRT2 = token rotation time for class 2: as above.
- TRT0 = token rotation time for class 0: as above.

When a station receives the token, it can transmit classes of data according to the following rules (Figure 5-13):

1. It may transmit class 6 data for a time THT. Hence for an *n*-station ring, during one circulation of the token, the maximum amount of time available for class 6 transmission is $n \times$ THT.
2. After transmitting class 6 data, or if there were no class 6 data to transmit, it may transmit class 4 data only if the amount of time for the last circulation of the token (including any class 6 data just sent) is less than TRT4.
3. The station may next send class 2 data only if the amount of time for the

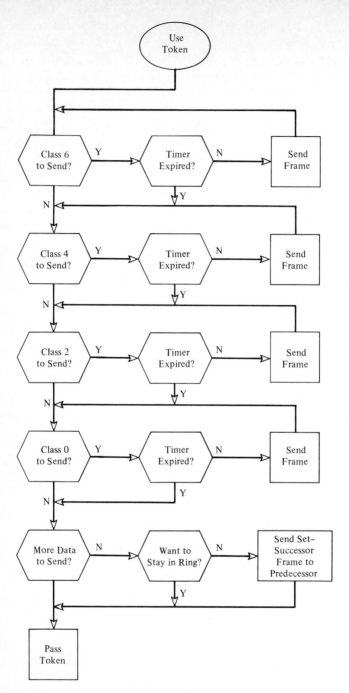

FIGURE 5-13.   Token Bus Priority Scheme

last circulation of the token (including any class 6 and 4 data just sent) is less than TRT2.

4. The station may next send class 0 data only if the amount of time for the last circulation of the token (including any class 6, 4, and 2 data just sent) is less than TRT0.

This scheme, within limits, gives preference to frames of higher priority. More definitively, it guarantees that class 6 data may have a certain portion of the bandwidth. Two cases are possible. If $n \times$ THT is greater than MAX[TRT4, TRT2, TRT0], the maximum possible token circulation time is $n \times$ THT, and class 6 data may occupy the entire cycle to the exclusion of other classes. If $n \times$ THT is less than MAX[TRT4, TRT2, TRT0], the maximum circulation time is MAX[TRT4, TRT2, TRT0], and class 6 data are guaranteed $n \times$ THT amount of that time. This analysis ignores the time it takes to transmit the token and any other overhead, such as the reaction time at a station upon receipt of a token. However, these overhead quantities will generally be small compared to data transmission time.

Figure 5-14, which is adapted from one in [JAYA87], illustrates the average behavior of the 802.4 capacity-allocation scheme. That is, the plots ignore temporary load fluctuations, instead depicting the steady-state performance. For convenience, we assume that TRT4 > TRT2 > TRT0 and that the load generated in each class of data is the same.

Figure 5-14a depicts the first case ($n \times$ THT > TRT4). At very low loads, the token circulation time is very short, and all of the data offered in all four classes is transmitted. As the load increases, the average token circulation time reaches TRT0. There is then a range, as indicated in the

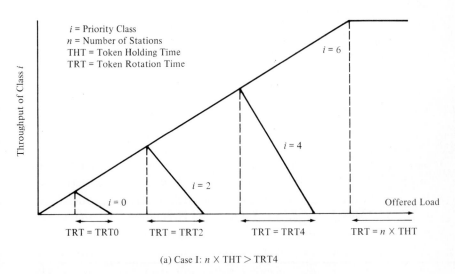

(a) Case I: $n \times$ THT > TRT4

FIGURE 5-14. Throughput of Token Bus Priority Classes

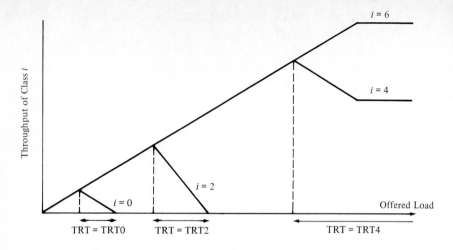

(b) Case IIa: $(TRT4/2) < n \times THT < TRT4$

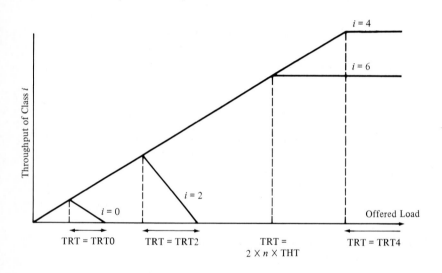

(c) Case IIb: $n \times THT < (TRT4/2)$

FIGURE 5-14. (*continued*)

figure, in which the load continues to increase but the token circulation time remains at TRT0. In this range, the other classes of data increase their throughput at the expense of Class 0 data, whose throughput declines. At some point, the load is such that the token circulation time equals TRT0, but the amount of transmission in Classes 2, 4, and 6 uses up all of that time and no Class 0 data can be transmitted. Further increase in offered load results in renewed increase in the token circulation time. The same pattern repeats for Class 2 and Class 4 data. There is a period when the load increases at a constant token circulation time of TRT2, and during that period, Class 2 data is gradually crowded out. Class 4 data is similarly crowded out at a higher level of load. Finally, a situation is reached in which only Class 6 data is being transmitted, and the token circulation time stabilizes at $n \times$ THT.

For the second case just mentioned ($n \times$ THT $<$ TRT4, we need to examine two subcases. Figure 5-14b shows the case in which $\frac{\text{TRT4}}{2} < (n \times \text{THT}) < \text{TRT4}$. As before, with increasing load, Class 0 and Class 2 traffic are eliminated and the token circulation time increases. At some point, the increasing load drives the token circulation time to TRT4. Using our simple example, when this point is reached, approximately half of the load is Class 4 data and the other half is Class 6. But, since $n \times \text{THT} > \frac{\text{TRT4}}{2}$, if the load on the network continues to increase, the portion of the load that is Class 6 traffic will also increase. This will cause a corresponding decrease in Class 4 traffic. Eventually, a point is reached at which all of the allowable Class 6 traffic is being handled during each token circulation. This will take an amount of time $n \times$ THT and still leave some time left over for Class 4 data. Thereafter, the total token circulation time remains stable at TRT4.

Finally, Figure 5-14c shows the case in which $n \times \text{THT} < \frac{\text{TRT4}}{2}$. As before, increasing load eliminates Class 0 and Class 2 traffic. A point is reached at which the token circulation time is $2 \times n \times$ THT, with half of the traffic being Class 4 and half being Class 6. This is a maximum throughput-per-token-circulation for Class 6. However, the amount of Class 4 data can continue to increase until the token circulation time is TRT4.

Figure 5-15 is a simplified example of a 4-station logical ring with THT = 610 and TRT4 = TRT2 = TRT0 = 1600. Time is measured in *octet times*. Station 9 always transmits three Class 6 frames of 128 octets each. Stations 7 and 5 send as many lower priority frames as possible, of lengths 400 and 356 octets, respectively. Station 1 transmits Class 6 frames of 305 octets each. Initially, Station 1 has two frames to transmit each time it gets the token, and later has only one frame to send per token possession. We assume that the time to pass the token is 19 octet times. In the figure, there are two columns of numbers under each station. The value in the left-hand column is the token circulation time observed at that station for the previous rotation of the token. The right-hand value is the number of frames that station transmits. Each row represents one rotation of the token.

The example begins after a period during which no data frames have been sent, so that the token has been rotating as rapidly as possible; thus

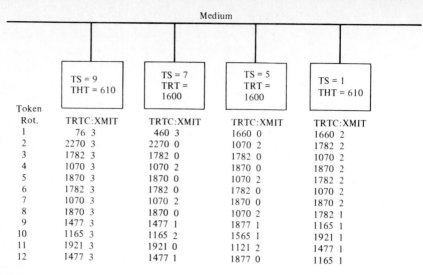

Token Rot.	TS = 9 THT = 610		TS = 7 TRT = 1600		TS = 5 TRT = 1600		TS = 1 THT = 610	
	TRTC	XMIT	TRTC	XMIT	TRTC	XMIT	TRTC	XMIT
1	76	3	460	3	1660	0	1660	2
2	2270	3	2270	0	1070	2	1782	2
3	1782	3	1782	0	1782	0	1070	2
4	1070	3	1070	2	1870	0	1870	2
5	1870	3	1870	0	1070	2	1782	2
6	1782	3	1782	0	1782	0	1070	2
7	1070	3	1070	2	1870	0	1870	2
8	1870	3	1870	0	1070	2	1782	1
9	1477	3	1477	1	1877	1	1165	1
10	1165	3	1165	2	1565	1	1921	1
11	1921	3	1921	0	1121	2	1477	1
12	1477	3	1477	1	1877	0	1165	1

FIGURE 5-15. Operation of a Multiclass Token Bus Protocol

each station measures a token circulation time of 76. In the first rotation, Station 9 transmits all of its Class 6 frames. When Station 7 receives the token, it measures a rotation time of 460 since it last received the token (3*128 + 4*19). Thus it is able to send 3 of its frames before its TRT is exhausted. Station 5 measures a rotation time of 1660 (3*400 + 3*128 + 4*19) and thus is prevented from sending any data. Finally, Station 1 sends 2 Class 6 frames.

Note that rotations 5 through 7 repeat rotations 2 through 4, showing a stable bandwidth allocation: Stations 1 and 9 use 69% of the bandwidth for Class 6 data and Stations 5 and 7 share equally the remaining bandwidth for lower-priority data. Starting on the eighth rotation, Station 1 reduces its use of the LAN. This reduces the bandwidth used for Class 6 data to 52%, and lower priority data is allowed to fill in the unused bandwidth.

CSMA/CD versus Token Bus

At present, CSMA/CD and token bus are the two principal contenders for medium access control technique on bus/tree topologies. Table 5.6 attempts to summarize the pros and cons of the two techniques. A brief discussion follows. See also [STIE81] and [MILL82].

Let us look at CSMA/CD first. On the positive side, the algorithm is simple; good news for the VLSI folks, and also good news for the user, in terms of cost and reliability. The protocol has been widely used for a long time, which also leads to favorable cost and reliability. The protocol

TABLE 5.6 CSMA/CD versus Token Bus

Advantages	Disadvantages
CSMA/CD	
Simple algorithm	Collision detection requirement
Widely used	Fault diagnosis problems
Fair access	Minimum packet size
Good performance at low to medium load	Poor performance under very heavy load
	Biased to long transmissions
Token Bus	
Excellent throughput performance	Complex algorithm
Tolerates large dynamic range	Unproven technology
Regulated access	

provides fair access—all stations have an equal chance at the bandwidth; good if you require only fair access. As we shall see in a later chapter, CSMA/CD exhibits quite good delay and throughput performance, at least up to a certain load, around 5 Mbps under some typical conditions.

There are, unfortunately, quite a few "cons" for CSMA/CD. From an engineering perspective, the most critical problem is the collision detection requirement. In order to detect collisions, the differences in signal strength from any pair of stations at any point on the cable must be small; this is no easy task to achieve. Other undesirable implications flow from the CD requirement. Since collisions are allowed, it is difficult for diagnostic equipment to distinguish expected errors from those induced by noise or faults. Also, CD imposes a minimum frame size, which is wasteful of bandwidth in situations where there are a lot of short messages, such as may be produced in highly interactive environments.

There are some performance problems as well. For certain data rates and frame sizes, CSMA/CD performs poorly as load increases. Also, the protocol is biased toward long transmissions.

For token bus, perhaps its greatest positive feature is its excellent throughput performance. Throughput increases as the data rate increases and levels off but does not decline as the medium saturates. Further, this performance does not degrade as the cable length increases. A second "pro" for token bus is that, because stations need not detect collisions, a rather large dynamic range is possible. All that is required is that each station's signal be strong enough to be heard at all points on the cable; there are no special requirements related to relative signal strength.

Another strength of token bus is that access to the medium can be regulated. If fair access is desired, token bus can provide this as well as

CSMA/CD. Indeed, at high loads, token bus may be fairer: it avoids the last in, first-out phenomenon mentioned earlier. If priorities are required, as they may be in an operational or real-time environment, these can be accommodated. Token bus can also guarantee a certain bandwidth; this may be necessary for certain types of data, such as voice, digital video, and telemetry.

An advertised advantage of token bus is that it is "deterministic"; that is, there is a known upper bound to the amount of time any station must wait before transmitting. This upper bound is known because each station in the logical ring can hold the token for only a specified time. In contrast, with CSMA/CD, the delay time can only be expressed statistically. Furthermore, since every attempt to transmit under CSMA/CD can in principle produce a collision, there is a possibility that a station could be shut out indefinitely. For process control and other real time applications, this "nondeterministic" behavior is undesirable. Alas, in the real world, there is always a finite possibility of transmission error, which can cause a lost token. This adds a statistical component to token bus.

The main disadvantage of token bus is its complexity. The reader who made it through the description above can have no doubt that this is a complex algorithm. A second disadvantage is the overhead involved. Under lightly loaded conditions, a station may have to wait through many fruitless token passes for a turn.

Which to choose? That is left as an exercise to the reader, based on requirements and the relative costs prevailing at the time. The decision is also influenced by the baseband versus broadband debate. Both must be considered together when comparing vendors.

Centralized Reservation

The CSMA/CD technique was developed to deal with bursty traffic, such as is typically produced in interactive applications (query response, data entry, transactions). In this environment, stations are not transmitting most of the time; hence, a station with data to transmit can generally seize the channel quickly and with a minimum of fuss. Token bus, on the other hand, incurs the overhead of passing the token from one idle station to another.

For applications that have a stream rather than bursty nature (file transfer, audio, facsimile), token bus can perform quite well, especially if some priority scheme is used. If the collective load is great enough, CSMA/CD has difficulty keeping up with this kind of demand.

A number of schemes have been proposed, based on the use of reservations, that appear to offer the strengths of both CSMA/CD and token bus.

In this section we look at a technique that requires centralized control. This is a likely candidate for a broadband system, with the control function performed at the headend. In Chapter 6 we will examine a decentralized control technique specifically designed for the high data rates of HSLNs.

The centralized scheme described in this section was developed by AMDAX for its broadband LAN [KARP82]. (Other centralized reservation schemes for bus systems have been described in [WILL73] and [MARK78].) Fixed-size frames of 512 bits are used, of which 72 are overhead bits. Time is organized into cycles, each cycle consisting of a set of equal-size time slots, and each time slot is sufficient for transmitting one frame. At the conclusion of one cycle, another cycle begins. The central controller at the headend may allocate slot or frame positions, within one or more future cycles, to particular stations. Frame positions not assigned to any station are referred to as *unallocated frames*. All stations must remain informed as to which frames are allocated to them and which are unallocated.

From the point of view of the station, communication is as follows. If a station has a small message to send, one that will fit in a single frame, it sends it in the next available unallocated frame on the inbound channel. The frame contains the message, source and destination addresses, and control information indicating that this is a data frame. Because the frame position used by the station is unallocated, it may also be used by another station, causing a collision. Hence the transmitting station must listen to the outbound channel for its transmission. If the station does not see its frame within a short defined time, it continues to send the frame at random times until it gets through.

To send messages too big to fit into a single frame, a station may reserve time on the bus. It does this by sending a reservation request to the central controller on the inbound channel. The request uses an unallocated frame and contains an indication that this is a request frame, the source address, and the number of frames to be sent. The station then listens to the outbound channel a short defined time, expecting to get a reservation confirmation frame containing its address and the number and order of frames in future cycles it has been allocated (if the line is too heavily loaded, it may not get all the bandwidth requested). When confirmation is received, the station may transmit its data in the frames allocated to it. If confirmation is not received, the station assumes that its reservation suffered a collision and tries again.

From the point of view of the central controller, communication is as follows. Frames are received one at a time on the inbound channel. Allocated frames are repeated on the outbound channel with no further processing. Unallocated frames must be examined. If the frame is garbled or contains an error, it is ignored. If it is a valid data frame, it is repeated on the outbound channel. If it is a valid reservation frame, the controller fills the reservation within the limits of its available frames in future cycles and sends a confirmation.

It should be clear that this technique exhibits the strengths of both CSMA/CD and token bus. Its principal disadvantage is that it requires a rather complex central controller, with the attendant reliability problems.

5.4

MEDIUM ACCESS CONTROL—RING

Over the years, a number of different algorithms have been proposed for controlling access to the ring. The three most common access techniques are discussed in this section: register insertion, slotted ring, and token ring. The first two will be briefly described; the token ring is discussed in some detail, as this is now an IEEE 802 standard.

Table 5.7 compares these three methods on a number of characteristics:

- *Transmit opportunity:* When may a repeater insert a packet onto the ring?
- *Packet purge responsibility:* Who removes a packet from a ring to avoid its circulating indefinitely?
- *Number of packets on ring:* This depends not only on the "bit length" of the ring relative to the packet length, but on the access method.
- *Principal advantage*
- *Principal disadvantage*

The significance of the table entries will become clear as the discussion proceeds.

TABLE 5.7   Ring Access Methods

Characteristic	Register Insertion	Slotted Ring	Token Ring
Transmit opportunity	Idle state plus empty buffer	Empty slot	Token
Packet purge responsibility	Receiver or transmitter	Transmitter	Transmitter
Number of packets on ring	Multiple	Multiple	One
Principal advantage	Maximum ring utilization	Simplicity	Regulated/fair access
Principal disadvantage	Purge mechanism	Bandwidth waste	Token maintenance

Register Insertion

This strategy was originally proposed in [HAFN74] and has been developed by researchers at Ohio State University [REAM75, LIU78]. It is also the technique used in the IBM Series 1 product [IBM82] and a Swiss product called SILK [HUBE83]. It derives its name from the shift register associated with each node on the ring. The shift register, equal in size to the maximum frame length, is used for temporarily holding frames that circulate past the node. In addition, the node has a buffer for storing locally produced frames.

The register insertion ring can be explained with reference to Figure 5-16, which shows the shift register and buffer at one node. First consider the case in which the station has no data to send, but is merely handling frames of data that circulate by its position. When the ring is idle, the input pointer points to the rightmost position of the shift register, indicating that it is empty. When data arrive from the ring they are inserted bit by bit in the shift register, with the input pointer shifting left for each bit. The frame begins with an address field. As soon as the entire address field is in the register, the station can determine if it is the addressee. If not, the frame is forwarded by shifting one bit out on the right as each new bit arrives from the left, with the input pointer stationary. After the last bit of the frame has arrived, the station continues to shift bits out to the right until the frame is gone. If, during this time, no additional frames arrive, the input pointer will return to its initial position. Otherwise, a second frame will begin to accumulate in the register as the first is shifted out.

Two observations are in order. First, the last few sentences imply that more than one frame may be on the ring at a time. How this can be is described below. Second, picture a series of frames, with gaps in between, passing a station. The effect of the actions described in the preceding

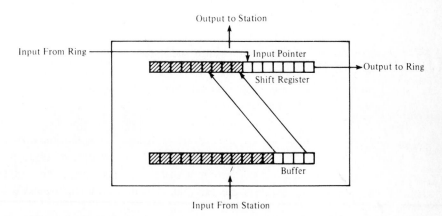

FIGURE 5-16. Register Insertion Ring

paragraph is to compress the gaps between the earlier arrivers, and stretch them out for later arrivers. As we shall see, the widening gaps provide an opportunity for new frames to be inserted into the ring.

Returning to the main line of our discussion: If an arriving frame is addressed to the station in question, the station has two choices. First, it can divert the remainder of the frame to itself and erase the address bits from the register, thus purging the frame from the ring. This is the approach taken by IBM. A moment's thought will reveal that such a strategy can result in a total bandwidth utilization that at times exceeds actual bit transmission rate. However, this may be false economy since, if the receiver rather than the transmitter purges the ring, some other means of acknowledgment must be employed, thus wasting bandwidth. The second alternative is to retransmit the frame as before, while copying it to the local station.

Now consider the case in which the station has data to transmit. A frame to be transmitted is placed in the output buffer. If the line is idle and the shift register is empty, the frame can be transferred immediately to the shift register. If the frame consists of some length n bits, less than the maximum frame size, and if at least n bits are empty in the shift register, the n bits are parallel-transferred to the empty portion of the shift register immediately adjacent to the full portion; the input pointer is adjusted accordingly.

We can see that there is a delay at each station, whose minimum value is the length of the address field and whose maximum value is the length of the shift register. This is in contrast to slotted ring and token ring, where the delay at each station is just the repeater delay—typically one or two bit times. To get a feeling for the effect, consider a station transmitting a 1000-bit frame on a 10-Mbps register insertion ring. The time it takes the station to transmit the frame is $1000/10^7 = 0.10$ ms. If the frame must pass 50 stations to reach its destination and if the address field is 16 bits, then the minimum delay, exclusive of propagation time, is $(16 \times 50)/10^7 = 0.08$ ms. This is a substantial delay compared to transmission time. Worse, if each station has a 1000-bit shift register, the maximum delay the frame could experience is $(1000 \times 50)/10^7 = 5$ ms.

The register insertion technique enforces an efficient form of fairness. As long as the ring is idle, a station with a lot of data to be sent can send frame after frame, utilizing the entire bandwidth of the ring. If the ring is busy, however, a station will find that, after sending a frame, the shift register will not accommodate another frame right away. The station will have to wait until enough intermessage gaps have accumulated before sending again. As a refinement, certain high-priority nodes can be given shift registers whose length is greater than the minimum shift register length (which is equal to the maximum frame length).

The principal advantage of the register insertion technique is that it achieves the maximum ring utilization of any of the methods. There are several other favorable features. Like the token system, it allows variable-length frames, which is efficient from the point of view of both the stations and the ring. Like the slotted ring, it permits multiple frames to be on the ring; again, an efficient use of bandwidth.

The principal disadvantage is the purge mechanism. Allowing multiple frames on the ring requires the recognition of an address prior to removal of a frame, whether it be removed by sender or receiver. If a frame's address field is damaged, it could circulate indefinitely. One possible solution is the use of an error-detecting code on the address field; IBM's Series 1 employs a parity bit. The requirement for address field recognition also dictates that each frame be delayed at each node by the length of that field. No such requirement exists in the other two methods.

Slotted Ring

For the slotted ring (Figure 5-17), a number of fixed-length slots circulate continuously on the ring. This strategy was first developed by Pierce [PIER72] and is sometimes referred to as the *Pierce loop*. Most of the development work on this technique was done at the University of Cambridge in England [HOPP83], and a number of British firms market commercial versions of the *Cambridge ring* [HEYW81]. The Cambridge ring is the basis for an ISO standard for slotted ring (ISO 8802-7).

In the slotted ring, each slot contains a leading bit to designate the slot as empty or full. All slots are initially marked empty. A station with data to transmit must break the data up into fixed-length frames. It then waits until

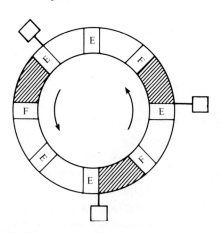

FIGURE 5-17.   Slotted Ring

an empty slot arrives, marks the slot full, and inserts a frame of data as the slot goes by. The station cannot transmit another frame until this slot returns. The full slot makes a complete round trip, to be marked empty again by the source. Each station knows the total number of slots on the ring and can thus clear the appropriate full/empty bit as it goes by. Once the now-empty slot goes by, the station is free to transmit again.

In the Cambridge ring, each slot contains room for one source address byte, one destination address byte, two, four, six, or eight data bytes, and five control bits, for a total length of 40, 56, 72, or 88 bits.

The Cambridge ring contains several interesting features. A station may decide that it wishes to receive data only from one other station. To accomplish this each station includes a source select register. When this register contains all ones, the station will receive a packet addressed to it from any source; when it contains all zeros, the station will not accept packets from any source. Otherwise the station is open to receive packets only from the source whose address is specified by the register.

The Cambridge ring specifies two response bits in each packet to differentiate four conditions:

- destination nonexistent/nonactive,
- packet accepted,
- destination exists but packet not accepted,
- destination busy.

Finally, the Cambridge ring includes a monitor, whose task it is to empty a slot that is persistently full.

Typically, there will be very few slots on a ring. Consider, for example, a 100-station ring with an average spacing of 10 m between stations and a data rate of 10 Mbps. A typical propagation velocity for signals is 2×10^8 m/s. A moment's thought should reveal that the "bit length" of the link between two stations is $(10^7 \text{ bps} \times 10 \text{ m})(2 \times 10^8 \text{ m/s}) = 0.5$ bit. Say that the delay at each repeater is one bit time. Then the total "bit length" of the ring is just $1.5 \times 100 = 150$ bits. This is enough for four slots.

The principal disadvantage of the slotted ring is that it is wasteful of bandwidth. First, each frame contains only 16 bits, resulting in a tremendous amount of overhead. Second, a station may send only one frame per round-trip time. If only one or a few stations have frames to transmit, many of the slots will circulate empty.

The principal advantage of the slotted ring appears to be its simplicity. The interaction with the ring at each node is minimized, improving reliability.

Token Ring

Token ring is probably the oldest ring control technique, originally proposed in 1969 [FARM69] and referred to as the *Newhall ring*. It has become the most popular ring access technique in the United States. This technique is the one ring access method selected for standardization by the IEEE 802 Local Network Standards Committee [PITT87, DIXO87]. IBM's product and those of a number of competitors are compatible with the standard [DERF86, STRO87, STRO89].

Description

The token ring technique is based on the use of a small frame, called a *token*, that circulates around the ring when all stations are idle. A station wishing to transmit must wait until it detects a token passing by. It then seizes the token by changing one bit in the token, which transforms it from a token to a start-of-frame sequence for a frame. The station then appends and transmits the remainder of the fields needed to construct a frame (Figure 5-18).

There is now no token on the ring, so other stations wishing to transmit must wait. The frame on the ring will make a round trip and be purged by the transmitting station. The transmitting station inserts a new token on the ring when both of the following conditions have been met:

- The station has completed transmission of its frame.
- The leading edge of its transmitted frame has returned (after a complete circulation of the ring) to the station.

If the bit length of the ring is less than the frame length, the first condition implies the second. If not, a station could release a free token after it has finished transmitting but before it begins to receive its own transmission; the second condition is not strictly necessary. However, use of the first condition alone might complicate error recovery, since several frames may be on the ring at the same time. In any case, the use of a token guarantees that only one station at a time may transmit.

When a transmitting station releases a new free token, the next station downstream with data to send will be able to seize the token and transmit.

Several implications of the token ring technique can be mentioned. Note that under lightly loaded conditions, there is some inefficiency since a station must wait for the token to come around before transmitting. However, under heavy loads, which is where it matters, the ring functions in a round-robin fashion, which is both efficient and fair. To see this, refer to Figure 5-18. Note that after station A transmits, it releases a token. The

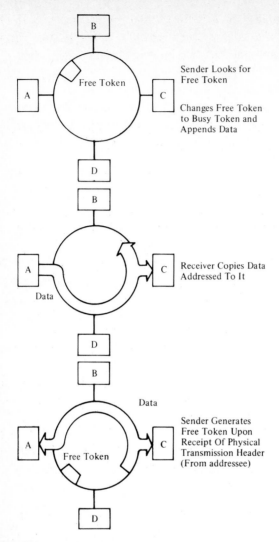

Sender Looks for
Free Token

Changes Free Token
to Busy Token and
Appends Data

Receiver Copies Data
Addressed To It

Sender Generates
Free Token Upon
Receipt Of Physical
Transmission Header
(From addressee)

FIGURE 5-18.   Token Ring

first station with an opportunity to transmit is D. If D transmits, it then
releases a token and C has the next opportunity, and so on. Finally, the
ring must be long enough to hold the token. If stations are temporarily
bypassed, their delay may need to be supplied artificially.

The principal advantage of token ring is the control over access that it
provides. In the simple scheme described above, the access is fair. As we
shall see, schemes can be used to regulate access to provide for priority and
guaranteed bandwidth services.

The principal disadvantage of token ring is the requirement for token
maintenance. Loss of the free token prevents further utilization of the ring.

Duplication of the token can also disrupt ring operation. One station must be elected monitor to assure that exactly one token is on the ring and to reinsert a free token if necessary.

IEEE 802 Token Ring

The IEEE 802 token ring specification is a refinement of the scheme just outlined. The key elements are as follows:

1. *Single-token protocol:* A station that has completed transmission will not issue a new token until the busy token returns. This is not as efficient, for small frames, as a multiple-token strategy of issuing a free token at the end of a frame. However, the single-token system simplifies priority and error-recovery functions.
2. *Priority bits:* These indicate the priority of a token and therefore which stations are allowed to use the token. In a multiple-priority scheme, priorities may be set by station or by message.
3. *Monitor bit:* Used by the ring monitor, as explained below.
4. *Reservation indicators:* They may be used to allow stations with high priority messages to request in a frame that the next token be issued at the requested priority.
5. *Token-holding timer:* Started at the beginning of data transfer, it controls the length of time a station may occupy the medium before transmitting a token.
6. *Acknowledgment bits:* There are three: error detected (E), address recognized (A), and frame copied (C). These are set to 0 by the transmitting station. Any station may set the E bit. Addressed stations may set the A and C bits.

Figure 5-2 shows the two frame formats for token ring. The individual fields are as follows:

- *Starting delimiter (SD):* a unique 8-bit pattern used to start each frame.
- *Access control (AC):* has the format 'PPPTMRRR', where PPP and RRR are 3-bit priority and reservation variables, M is the monitor bit, and T indicates whether this is a token or data frame. In the case of a token frame, the only additional field is ED.
- *Frame control (FC):* indicates whether this is an LLC data frame. If not, bits in this field control operation of the token ring MAC protocol.
- *Destination address (DA):* as in CSMA/CD and token bus.
- *Source address (SA):* as in CSMA/CD and token bus.
- *LLC:* as in CSMA/CD and token bus.
- *FCS:* as in CSMA/CD and token bus.
- *Ending delimiter (ED):* contains the error detection (E) bit, and the

intermediate frame (I) bit. The I bit is used to indicate that this is a frame other than the final one of a multiple frame transmission.

- *Frame status (FS):* contains the address recognized (A) and frame copied (C) bits.

Let us first consider the operation of the ring when only a single priority is used. In this case the priority and reservation bits are not used. A station wishing to transmit waits until a free token goes by, as indicated by a token bit of 0 in the AC field. The station seizes the token by setting the token bit to 1. The SD and AC fields of the received token now function as the first two fields of a data frame. It then transmits one or more frames, continuing until either its output is exhausted or its token-holding timer expires. When the AC field of the last transmitted frame returns, the station transmits a free token by setting the token bit to 0 and appending an ED field.

Stations in the receive mode listen to the ring. Each station can check passing frames for errors and set the E bit if an error is detected. If a station detects its own address it sets the A bit to 1; it may also copy the frame, setting the C bit to 1. This allows the originating station to differentiate three conditions:

- Station nonexistent/nonactive.
- Station exists but frame not copied.
- Frame copied.

The foregoing operation can be supplemented by a multiple-priority scheme. For example, bridges could be given higher priority than ordinary stations. The 802 specification provides three bits for eight levels of priority. For clarity, let us designate three values: P_m = priority of message to be transmitted by station; P_r = received priority; and R_r = received reservation. The scheme works as follows:

1. A station wishing to transmit must wait for a free token with $P_r \leq P_m$.
2. While waiting, a station may reserve a future token at its priority level (P_m). If a data frame goes by, it sets the reservation field to its priority ($R_r \leftarrow P_m$) if the reservation field is less than its priority ($R_r < P_m$). If a free token goes by, it sets the reservation field to its priority ($R_r \leftarrow P_m$) if $Rr < P_m$ and $P_m < P_r$. This has the effect of preempting any lower-priority reservations.
3. When a station seizes a token, it sets the token bit to 1, the reservation field to 0, and leaves the priority field unchanged.
4. Following transmission, a station issues a new token with the priority set to the maximum of P_r, R_r, and P_m, and a reservation set to the maximum of R_r and P_m.

The effect of the above steps is to sort out competing claims and allow the waiting transmission of highest priority to seize the token as soon as possible. A moment's reflection reveals that, as is, the algorithm has a ratchet effect on priority, driving it to the highest used level and keeping it there. To avoid this, two stacks are maintained, one for reservations and one for priorities. In essence, each station is responsible for assuring that no token circulates indefinitely because its priority is too high. By remembering the priority of earlier transmissions, a station can detect this condition and downgrade the priority to a previous, lower priority or reservation.

We are now in a position to summarize the priority algorithm. A station having a higher priority than the current busy token (data frame) can reserve the next free token for its priority level as the busy token passes by. When the current transmitting station is finished, it issues a free token at that higher priority. Stations of lower priority cannot seize the token, so it passes to the requesting station or an intermediate station of equal or higher priority with data to send.

The station that upgraded the priority level is responsible for downgrading it to its former level when all higher-priority stations are finished. When that station sees a free token at the higher priority, it can assume that there is no more higher-priority traffic waiting, and it downgrades the token before passing it on. Figure 5.19 is an example of the operation of the priority mechanism.

Token Maintenance

To overcome various error conditions, one station is designated as the active monitor. The active monitor periodically issues an Active-Monitor-Present control frame to assure other stations that there is an active monitor on the ring. To detect a lost-token condition, the monitor uses a valid frame timer that is greater than the time required to completely traverse the ring. The timer is reset after every valid token or data frame. If the timer expires, the monitor issues a token. To detect a persistently circulating data frame, the monitor sets a monitor bit to 1 on any passing data frame the first time it goes by. If it sees a data frame with the monitor bit already set, it knows that the transmitting station failed to abort the frame. The monitor aborts the frame and transmits a token. The same strategy is used to detect a failure in the priority mechanism: no token should circulate completely around the ring at a constant nonzero priority level. Finally, if the active monitor detects evidence of another active monitor, it immediately goes into standby monitor status.

In addition, all of the active stations on the ring cooperate to provide each station with a continuous update on the identity of its upstream neighbor. Each station periodically issues a standby-monitor-present (SMP) frame. Its downstream neighbor absorbs this frame, notes its sending address, and after a pause, sends its own SMP frame. The absence of SMP frames can be used in fault isolation.

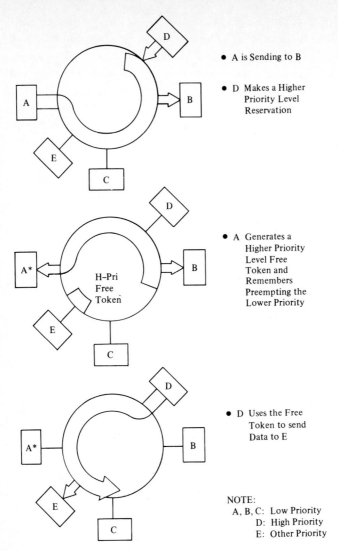

- A is Sending to B

- D Makes a Higher Priority Level Reservation

- A Generates a Higher Priority Level Free Token and Remembers Preempting the Lower Priority

- D Uses the Free Token to send Data to E

NOTE:
A, B, C: Low Priority
D: High Priority
E: Other Priority

FIGURE 5-19. Token Ring Priority Scheme

5.5

RECOMMENDED READING

A survey of bus/tree protocols can be found in [LUCZ78], and a survey of ring protocols in [PENN79]. [TROP81], which is concerned with performance, describes most bus and ring protocols. [KURO84] is a good overall survey. The rationale behind the IEEE 802 standards is contained in [CLAN82]; an opposing viewpoint is expressed in [DAHO83]. A concise

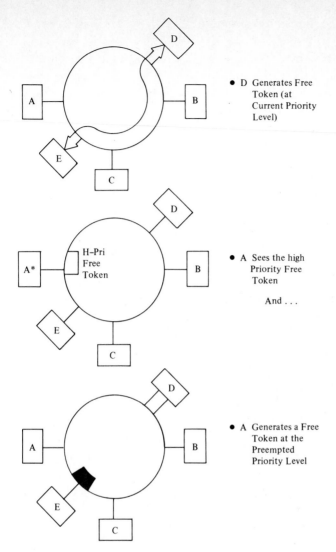

- D Generates Free Token (at Current Priority Level)

- A Sees the high Priority Free Token

  And . . .

- A Generates a Free Token at the Preempted Priority Level

FIGURE 5-19. *(continued)*

survey article of the standards is [WOOD85]*. A detailed and thorough description of the standards is contained [STAL90c].

5.6

PROBLEMS

5.1 What arguments or parameters are required for each of the LLC primitives in Table 5.1?

5.2   Why is there not an LLC primitive L-CONNECTION-FLOWCONTROL confirm?

5.3   Show, with an example, how the LLC protocol provides the LLC services as defined by the LLC primitives.

5.4   A simple medium access control protocol would be to use a fixed assignment time-division multiplexing (TDM) scheme, as described in Section 2.1. Each station is assigned one time slot per cycle for transmission. For the bus and tree, the length of each time slot is the time to transmit 100 bits plus the end-to-end propagation delay. For the ring, assume a delay of one bit time per station, and assume that a round-robin assignment is used. Stations monitor all time slots for reception. What are the limitations, in terms of number of stations, and throughput per station for:
   a. A 1-km, 10-Mbps baseband bus?
   b. A 1-km (headend to farthest point), 10-Mbps broadband bus?
   c. A 10-Mbps broadband tree consisting of a 0.5-km trunk emanating from the headend and five 0.1-km branches from the trunk at the following points: 0.05 km, 0.15 km, 0.25 km, 0.35 km, 0.45 km?
   d. A 10-Mbps ring with a total length of 1 km?
   e. A 10-Mbps ring with a length of 0.1 km between repeaters?
   f. Compute throughput per station for all of the above for 10 and 100 stations.

5.5   The binary exponential back-off algorithm is defined by IEEE 802 thus: "The delay is an integral multiple of slot time. The number of slot times to delay before the nth retransmission attempt is chosen as a uniformly distributed random interger r in the range $0 < r < 2**K$, where $K = \min(n,10)$." Slot time is, roughly, twice the round-trip propagation delay. Assume that two stations always have a frame to send. After a collision, what is the mean number of retransmission attempts before one station successfully transmits? What is the answer if three stations always have frames to send?

5.6   Consider two stations on a baseband bus at a distance of 1 km from each other. Let the data rate be 1 Mbps, the packet length be 100 bits, and the propagation velocity be 2×10^8 m/s. Assume that each station generates packets at an average rate of 1000 packets per second. For the ALOHA protocol, if one station begins to transmit a packet at time t, what is the probability of collision? Repeat for slotted-ALOHA. Repeat for ALOHA and slotted-ALOHA at 10 Mbps.

5.7   Repeat Problem 5.6 for a broadband bus. Assume that the two stations are 1 km apart and that one is very near the headend.

5.8   For a p-persistent CSMA, what is the probability that the next transmission after a successful transmission will be successful for $np = 0.1$, 1.0, and 10?

5.9   In what sense are the slotted ring and token ring protocols the complement of each other?

5.10   A promising application of fiber optics for local networks is in the ring topology. Which, if any, of the three ring protocols is inappropriate for this medium?

5.11 For a token ring system, suppose that the destination station removes the data frame and immediately sends a short acknowledgment frame to the sender, rather than letting the original frame return to sender. How will this affect performance?

5.12 Consider a Cambridge ring of length 10 km with a data rate of 10 Mbps and 500 repeaters, each of which introduces a 1-bit delay. How many slots are on the ring?

5.13 For the ring in Problem 5.12, assume a constant user data load of 4 Mbps. What is the mean number of slots that a station must wait to insert a packet?

5.14. Write a program that implements the token ring priority mechanism.

5.15 If the token ring active monitor fails, it is possible that two stations will timeout and claim that status. Suggest an algorithm for overcoming this problem.

5.16 The IEEE 802 refers to the token bus service class scheme as a "bandwidth allocation" scheme rather than a priority scheme. A priority scheme would provide that all frames of higher priority would be transmitted before any lower-priority frames would be allowed on the bus. Show by counterexample that the 802 scheme is not a priority scheme.

5.17 Compare the token bus service class scheme with the token ring and priority scheme. What are the relative pros and cons? Is it possible, with appropriate parameter settings, to achieve the same behavior from both?

APPENDIX 5A: IEEE 802 STANDARDS

The key to the development of the LAN market is the availability of a low cost interface. The cost to connect equipment to a LAN must be much less than the cost of the equipment alone. This requirement, plus the complexity of the LAN protocols, dictate a VLSI solution. However, chip manufacturers will be reluctant to commit the necessary resources unless there is a high-volume market. A LAN standard would assure that volume and also enable equipment of a variety of manufacturers to intercommunicate. This is the rationale of the IEEE Project 802 [CLAN82], a committee established by the IEEE Computer Society in February of 1980 to prepare local area network standards. In 1985, the 802 committee issued a set of four standards, which were subsequently adopted in 1985 by the American National Standards Institute (ANSI) as American National Standards [IEEE85a-d]. These standards were subsequently revised and reissued as international standards by the International Organization for Standardization (ISO) in 1987, with the designation ISO 8802.

The committee characterized its work in this way [IEEE88]:

The LANs described herein are distinguished from other types of data networks in that they are optimized for a moderate size geographic area such as a single office building, a warehouse, or a campus. The IEEE 802 LAN is a shared medium peer-to-peer communications network that broadcasts information for all stations to receive. As a consequence, it does not inherently provide privacy. The local area network enables stations to communicate directly using a common physical medium on a point-to-point basis without any intermediate switching node being required. There is always need for an access sublayer in order to arbitrate the access to the shared medium. The network is generally owned, used, and operated by a single organization. This is in contrast to Wide Area Networks (WANs) that interconnect communication facilities in different parts of a country or are used as a public utility. These LANs are also different from networks, such as backplane buses, that are optimized for the interconnection of devices on a desk top or components within a single piece of equipment.

Two conclusions were quickly reached. First, the task of communication across the local network is sufficiently complex that it needs to be broken up into more manageable subtasks. Second, no single technical approach will satisfy all requirements.

The second conclusion was reluctantly reached when it became apparent that no single standard would satisfy all committee participants. There was support for both ring and bus topologies. With the bus topology, there was

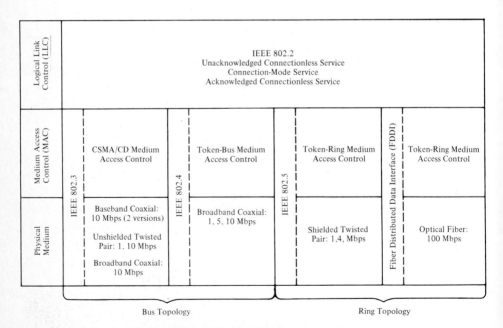

FIGURE 5-20. Local Area Network Standards

TABLE 5.8 Physical Layer Specifications for IEEE 802 LAN Standards

	Transmission Medium	Signaling Technique	Data Rate (Mbps)	Maximum Length (m)
IEEE 802.3 (CSMA/CD)				
Original (10BASE5)	Coaxial Cable (50 Ω)	Baseband (Manchester)	10	500
Cheapernet (10BASE2)	Coaxial Cable (50 Ω)	Baseband (Manchester)	10	185
StarLAN (1BASE5)	Unshielded Twisted Pair	Baseband (Manchester)	1	250
10BASE-T	Unshielded Twisted Pair	Baseband (Manchester)	10	100
Broadband (10BROAD36)	Coaxial Cable (75 Ω)	DPSK	10	3600
IEEE 802.4 (Token Bus)				
Broadband	Coaxial Cable (75 Ω)	duobinary AM/PSK	1, 5, 10	a
Carrierband	Coaxial Cable (75 Ω)	FSK	1, 5, 10	7600
IEEE 802.5 (Token Ring)				
Twisted Pair	Shielded Twisted Pair	Differential Manchester	1, 4	b

a = not specified
b = not specified; a maximum of 250 repeaters allowed

support for two access methods (CSMA/CD and token bus) and two media (baseband and broadband). The response of the committee was to standardize all serious proposals rather than to attempt to settle on just one. Figure 5-20 illustrates the results.

This chapter has described in some detail the LLC and MAC standards. It remains to briefly summarize the physical layer standards (Table 5-8). For CSMA/CD (IEEE 802.3, ISO 8802-3), the original standard specified a 10-Mbps baseband coaxial cable medium based on Ethernet.[3] A thinner coaxial cable, also at 10 Mbps and dubbed Cheapernet, was then added (Table 4-2). More recently, the committee added a 1-Mbps unshielded twisted pair standard that employs the star wiring topology, referred to as StarLAN. This was followed by a 10-Mbps broadband version. Finally, the

---

[3] The IEEE 802.3 documents make use of a shorthand notation for the various options: <data rate in Mbps><signaling type><maximum segment length (*100m)>. For example, 10BASE5 is a 10-Mbps, baseband medium, with a maximum length of 500 meters.

committee has just completed work on a 10-Mbps, star-wired LAN using unshielded twisted pair.

For token bus (IEEE 802.4, ISO 8802-4), three physical layers are provided as options. The simplest and least expensive is a carrierband system at 1 Mbps. A more expensive version of this system runs at 5 or 10 Mbps and is intended to be easily upgradable to the final option, which is broadband with channels at 1, 5, and 10 Mbps.

For token ring (IEEE 802.5, ISO 8802-5), a shielded twisted pair medium with data rates from 1 to 4 Mbps has been specified.

The range of options may surprise the reader, given the IEEE 802 rationale. However, the IEEE 802 committee has at least narrowed the alternatives. It is to be expected that the bulk of future LAN development work will be within the scope laid down by IEEE 802.

APPENDIX 5B: SERVICE PRIMITIVES AND PARAMETERS

In a communications architecture, such as the OSI model or the LAN architecture (Figure 5-1), each layer is defined in two parts: the protocol between peer (at the same layer) entities in different systems, and the services provided by one layer to the next higher layer in the same system.

We have seen a number of examples of protocols, which are defined in terms of the formats of the protocol data units that are exchanged, and the rules governing the use of those protocol data units. The services between

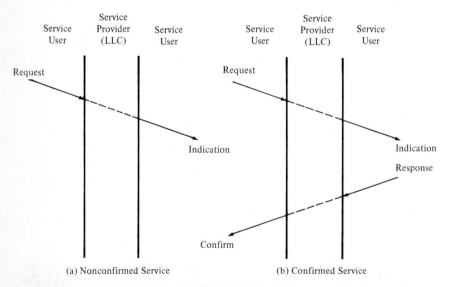

FIGURE 5-21. Relationship Among LLC Primitives

TABLE 5.9 Primitive Types

REQUEST	A primitive issued by a service user to invoke some service and to pass the parameters needed to fully specify the requested service.
INDICATION	A primitive issued by a service provided to either: 1. indicate that a procedure has been invoked by the peer service user on the connection and to provide the associated parameters, or 2. notify the service user of a provider-initiated action.
RESPONSE	A primitive issued by a service user to acknowledge or complete some procedure previously invoked by an indication to that user.
CONFIRM	A primitive issued by a service provider to acknowledge or complete some procedure previously invoked by a request by the service user.

adjacent layers are expressed in terms of primitives and parameters. A primitive specifies the function to be performed, and the parameters are used to pass data and control information. The actual form of a primitive is implementation dependent. An example is a procedure call.

Four types of primitives are used in standards to define the interaction between adjacent layers in the architecture. These are defined in Table 5-9. The layout of Figure 5-21b suggests the time ordering of these events. For example, consider the transfer of a connection request from LLC user A to a peer entity B in another system. The following steps occur:

1. A invokes the services of LLC with a DL-CONNECT.request primitive. Associated with the primitive are the parameters needed, such as the destination address.
2. The LLC entity in A's system prepares an LLC protocol data unit (PDU) to be sent to its peer LLC entity in B.
3. The destination LLC entity delivers the data to B via a DL-CONNECT.indication, which includes the source address and other parameters.
4. B issues a DL-CONNECT.response to its LLC entity.
5. B's LLC entity conveys the acknowledgment to A's LLC entity in a PDU.
6. The acknowledgment is delivered to A via a DL-CONNECT.confirm.

This sequence of events is referred to as a **confirmed service**, as the initiator receives confirmation that the requested service has had the desired effect at the other end. If only request and indication primitives are involved (corresponding to steps 1 through 3), then the service dialogue is a **nonconfirmed service**; the initiator receives no confirmation that the requested action has taken place.

APPENDIX 5B: SERVICE PRIMITIVES AND PARAMETERS

CHAPTER 6

High-Speed Local Networks

In this chapter we explore the nature of the high-speed local network. To date, HSLNs have been used primarily to satisfy requirements for high-speed data transfer among mainframes and mass storage controllers. These were referred to as computer room networks in Chapter 1.

Briefly, the key characteristics of such an HSLN are:

- *High data rate:* Both extant products and draft standards have a 50–100 Mbps data rate, higher than found with LANs.
- *High-speed interface:* HSLNs are intended to provide high throughput among computer room equipment—mainframes and high-speed peripherals. Thus the physical link between station and network must be high-speed.
- *Distributed access:* As with LANs, it is desirable for reliability and efficiency reasons to have distributed access control.
- *Limited distance:* Generally, an HSLN will be used in a computer room or a small number of rooms; hence great distances are not required.
- *Limited number of devices:* The number of expensive mainframes and mass storage devices found in the computer room is generally in the 10's of devices.

TABLE 6.1 Network Load Component Comparison

Traffic Type	Size in Bits
Compressed Page Image (400 × 400)	600,000
Compressed Page Image (200 × 200)	250,000
Word-Processing Page	20,000
Typical Memo	3,500
Data Processing Transaction	500

Although the last two characteristics are appropriate for computer room networks, they are also technical limitations of existing coaxial-cable HSLNs. However, new applications in the office environment are on the horizon for which the limitations of the traditional computer-room HSLN will be unacceptable. Desktop image processors could soon increase network data flow by an unprecedented amount [BEVA86, ROSE88, MULQ88a]. Examples of these applications include fax machines, document image processors, and graphics programs on personal computers. Resolutions as high as 400 × 400 per page are standard for these applications. Even with compression techniques, this will generate a tremendous load. Table 6.1 compares the load generated by image processing and some other office applications. In addition, optical disks are beginning to reach technical maturity and are being developed toward realistic desktop capacities exceeding 1 Gbyte. These new demands will require local networks with high speed that can support the larger numbers and greater geographic extent of office systems as compared to computer room systems. As we will see, the coaxial-able HSLN systems are inadequate for this task, and fiber-based systems appear to be required.

At present the HSLN field is dominated by the coaxial bus architecture. This is reviewed first, followed by a discussion of fiber HSLN. Then we look at issues related to link and medium access control. Emphasis will be on draft standards developed by the X3T9.5 committee of ANSI. An appendix contains a brief summary of the X3T9.5 standards.

6.1

COAXIAL CABLE SYSTEMS

In this section, we look at the three common approaches for coaxial-cable based HSLNs:

- *Single-channel broadband bus:* one of two alternatives selected for a pending ANSI standard being drafted by the X3T9.5 committee

[ANSI82, BURR83]. Both alternatives are referred to as Local Distributed Data Interface (LDDI). The single-channel broadband approach is also used in Control Data's Loosely Coupled Network [HOHN80].

- *Baseband bus:* used in the oldest and most widely use HSLN, Network Systems Corporation's HYPER channel [CHR179].
- *Passive star:* the other alternative selected by X3T9.5[ANSI87]; it is also the technique used in Digital Equipment Corporation's VAXcluster [KRON86].

All of these approaches exhibit, logically, a bus topology. That is, a transmission by any one device is received over a passive medium by all other devices, and only one device at a time can successfully transmit. Thus, they share a number of characteristics with bus-based LANs. In particular, a packet-switching technique is used and, because the medium is multiaccess, a medium access control technique is needed to determine who goes next. The key difference between a bus LAN and a bus HSLN is the higher data rate of the latter. Thus this section will concentrate on highlighting the features of bus HSLNs that result from that difference.

The first two (pure bus) approaches have much in common. Among the common characteristics:

- *Data rate of 50 Mbps:* With today's technology, this is about the highest cost-effective speed achievable.
- *Maximum length of about 1 km:* This limit is dictated by the data rate, but should be adequate for many HSLN requirements.
- *Maximum number of stations in the 10's:* Again, this is dictated by the data rate. Since HSLNs are primarily intended for expensive high-speed devices, this restriction is usually not burdensome.
- *Provisions for multiple (up to four) cables:* This increases throughput and reliability.

Single-Channel Broadband Bus

In this section we describe the system proposed by the ANS X3T9.5 committee.

As with the single-channel broadband systems described in Chapter 4, the single-channel broadband HSLN consists of the following components:

- Cable
- Terminators
- Taps
- Controllers

The cable used is 75-ohm CATV cable. Hence 75-ohm terminators are required to absorb the signal. Transmission on the cable is bidirectional, requiring the use of a nondirectional coupler or tap. Finally, a controller is needed for transmission/reception and to perform medium access control functions.

Several features of the system warrant elaboration. First, let us consider the problem of how many taps can be attached to the cable. The number is more limited with HSLNs than LANs because the higher data rates make low-error reception more difficult. To see this, consider that each bit of transmission at the higher data rate of the HSLN occupies less time and space on the cable. Therefore, a relatively small amount of attenuation or distortion can cause errors.

The draft ANSI standard provides some guidelines for number of taps based on the concept of power budget. This quantity is the ratio in decibels (dB) between the minimum signal power available at a station's transmitter and the minimum acceptable signal power at a station's receiver. For example, if the transmitter power is 1 mw and the receiver operates reliably over a signal range of 1 mw to 1 nw, then the power budget, Bp, is

$$Bp = 10 \times \log_{10}(P_0/P_1) = 10 \times \log_{10}(10^{-3}/10^{-9}) = 60 \text{ dB}$$

This says that the loss incurred between the output of one tap and the input of another must not exceed 60 dB for reliable transmission. With greater loss, it will be difficult to separate the signal from the noise.

The sources of loss are the cable and the taps, and the total loss is a function of the length of the cable and the number of taps. The relationship can be expressed as

$$B_p = L_M + L_I(N - 2) + 2L_D + L_c \tag{6.1}$$

where L_M = main trunk (cable) loss

L_I = insertion loss per tap: due to the amount of power diverted to the port

N = number of taps

L_D = isolation loss in end couplers: wasted power due to coupler

L_C = cable loss in drop cables (one transmitter, one receiver)

This equation can be solved for N, and with coupler losses and the acceptable power budget known, expressed as a function of cable length. This is done in Figure 6-1. The diagram shows how few stations can be accommodated at the 60 dB level (which is a reasonable goal). For less sensitive receivers, the number of devices that can be accommodated drops.

Equation (6.1) can also be used to determine the maximum length of the cable given the number of taps. As was mentioned, this works out to about 1 km for a few tens of devices.

Finally, let us consider the modulation scheme to be used. The technique specified by ANS X3T9.5 is to use 180 degree phase-shift-key (PSK)

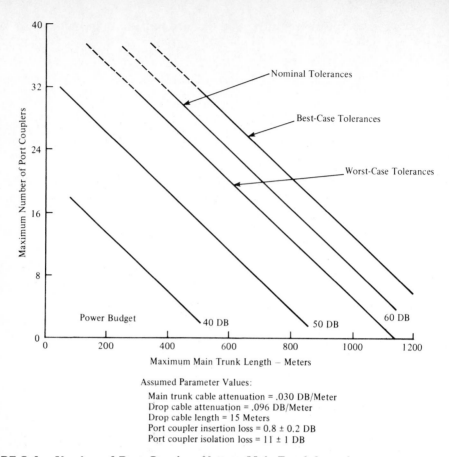

FIGURE 6-1. Number of Port Couplers Versus Main Trunk Length

modulation. For a 50 Mbps data rate, this technique uses a carrier at 150 MHz and a clock signal at 50 MHz. Figure 6-2 indicates the steps in preparing a transmission. A bit stream is encoded at two voltage levels using a "change on zero" convention; that is, at the beginning of each 0 bit, the voltage level is changed. This encoded bit stream is generated using a 50 MHz clock. To achieve phase encoding, the bit stream is modulated on a 150 Mhz digital pulse stream by taking the exclusive-or of the two signals. The result is a 150-MHz digital stream that changes phase at the beginning of each 0 bit. The modulated output is passed through a 150 MHz analog bandpass filter to produce the analog signal on the line. The 50-MHz clock is also sent out to provide synchronization. A simplified block diagram is shown in Figure 6-3.

An inverse process takes place at the receiver. The 50-MHZ signal is received and used to recover the clock. The 150-MHz signal is digitized. Two copies are produced: an inverted signal and a signal delayed by one bit time. A disagreement between these two signals corresponds to a transition from 0 to 1 or 1 to 0. A sample is shown in Figure 6-4.

HIGH-SPEED LOCAL NETWORKS

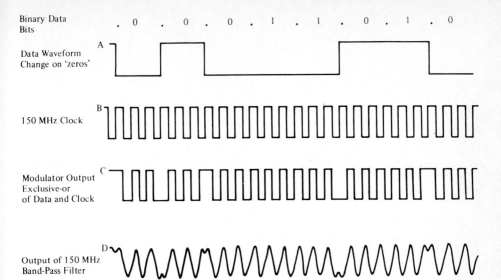

FIGURE 6-2. Idealized Transmitter Waveforms

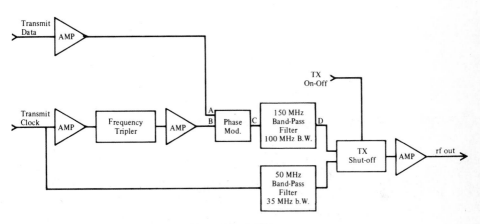

FIGURE 6-3. 50-Mbps Transmitter Block Diagram

Baseband Bus

There is little to say about a baseband HSLN that has not already been covered under the baseband LAN. Again, the main components are cable, terminators, taps, and controllers.

The only baseband system commercially available is HYPERchannel. Like the single-channel broadband, it uses a 75-ohm CATV bus with nondirectional taps. The data rate is 50 Mbps using Manchester encoding. HYPERchannel recommends a maximum length of 1.2 km and no more than about 30 stations.

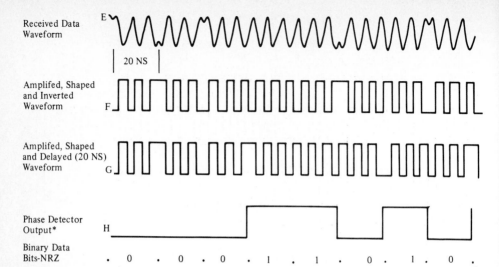

FIGURE 6-4. Idealized Receiver Waveform

It is difficult to assess the relative advantages of this scheme compared to the single-channel broadband. The broadband adherents claim that the analog signal exhibits better attenuation and distortion characteristics, but there is little empirical evidence to support this. In general, the two approaches should give comparable performances at comparable cost.

Passive Star

The coaxial cable passive star architecture is identical to that of Figure 4-14. Each station attaches to the central node via two links, in this case 50-ohm baseband coaxial cables. One cable from each station is for transmission, the other for reception. A transmission along one inbound cable is split equally by the star coupler and output to all of the outbound cables. Internally, the star uses transformer coupling to split the incoming signal. The specified data rate is 70 Mbps using Manchester encoding. As with the fiber star coupler, the number of devices that can be supported and the maximum radius are both limited by the sources of loss in the network: coaxial cable attenuation and power division in the coupler. Taking these losses into account, the specifications (both X3T9.5 and VAXcluster) allow a maximum of 16 nodes over a maximum radius of 45 meters.

Compared to the bus systems discusssed above, the passive star is clearly

HIGH-SPEED LOCAL NETWORKS

more limited. However, it does have two advantages over the bus:

- The central star coupler permits the addition and removal of stations (within the range of 1 to 16 stations) with minimum risk of electrical or mechanical disruption. This task may be more difficult on a bus.
- The passive star architecture facilitates two possible enhancements: first, an active star coupler permitting many more than 16 nodes and, second, replacement of the coaxial cable with fiber optic cables. Together, these enhancements yield the approach taken in Fibernet II (Figure 4-21), but at a much higher data rate.

6.2

OPTICAL FIBER SYSTEMS

The two main alternatives for a high-speed optical fiber local network are bus and ring. With current technology, the use of a passive fiber medium, as in a bus, is not practical for high-speed applications, because of the high loss suffered with each tap into the bus. With fiber rings, however, only point-to-point fiber links are required, and at least one system is already on the market: an 8;-Mbps system from Proteon [THUR85a]. Thus this section is devoted to a consideration of fiber ring technology. The description is based on another proposed X3T9.5 standard, the Fiber Distributed Data Interface (FDDI). The FDDI standard specifies a 100-Mbps fiber ring need to be examined:

- Data encoding
- Jitter
- Reliability

Data Encoding

Recall from our discussion in Chapter 2 that digital data need to be encoded in some form for transmission as a signal. The type of encoding will depend on the nature of the transmission medium, the data rate, and other constraints, such as cost. Optical fiber is inherently an analog medium; signals can only be transmitted in the optical frequency range. Thus we might expect that one of the popular digital-to-analog encoding techniques (ASK, FSK, PSK) would be used. Both FSK and PSK are difficult to do at high data rates and the optoelectronic equipment would be too expensive and unreliable [FREE81]. With amplitude-shift keying (ASK), recall, a constant-frequency signal is used, and two different signal levels are used to represent the two binary data values. In the simplest case, one value is represented by the absence of the carrier, and the other value by the presence, at constant value, of the signal. This technique is often called intensity modulation.

Intensity modulation, then, provides a simple means for encoding digital data for transmission over optical fiber. A binary 1 can be represented by a burst or pulse of light, and a binary 0 by the absence of optical energy. The disadvantage of this approach is its lack of synchronization. Since transitions on the fiber are unpredictable, there is no way for the receiver to synchronize its clock to the transmitter. The solution to this problem is to first encode the binary data to guarantee the presence of transitions and then to present the encoded data to the optical source for transmission. For example, the data could first be encoded using Manchester encoding; the high and low codes depicted in Figure 2-5 could then be transmitted as light and no light, respectively. This is, in fact, a common signaling technique used for optical fiber transmission. The disadvantage of this approach is that the efficiency is only 50%. That is, because there can be as many as two transitions per bit time, a signaling rate of 200 million signal elements per second (expressed as 200 Mbaud) is needed to achieve a data rate of 100 Mbps. At the high data rate of FDDI, this represents an unnecessary cost and technical burden.

To overcome the data rate burden imposed by Manchester intensity modulation, the FDDI standard specifies the use of a code referred to as 4B/5B. In this scheme, encoding is done four bits at a time; each four bits of data are encoded into a symbol with five cells such that each cell contains a single signal element (presence or absence of light). In effect, each set of 4 bits is encoded as five bits. The efficiency is thus raised to 80%; 100 Mbps is achieved with 125 Mbaud. The resulting savings is substantial: A 200-Mbaud LED and PIN pair can cost five to ten times that of a 125-Mbaud pair [JOSH85].

To understand how the 4B/5B code achieves synchronization, you need to know that there is actually a second stage of encoding [CONN87]; each element of the 4B/5B stream is treated as a binary value and encoded using a technique referred to as Nonreturn to Zero Inverted (NRZI) or Nonreturn to Zero-Mark (NRZ-M); see Figure 2-5. In this code, a binary 1 is represented with a transition at the beginning of the bit interval and a binary 0 is represented with no transition at the beginning of the bit interval; there are no other transitions. The advantage of NRZI is that it employs differential encoding. Recall from Chapter 2 that in differential encoding, the signal is decoded by comparing the polarity of adjacent signal elements rather than the absolute value of a signal element. A benefit of this scheme is that it is generally more reliable to detect a transition in the presence of noise and distortion than to compare a value to a threshold. This aids the ultimate decoding of the signal after it has been converted back from optical to the electrical realm.

Now we are in a position to describe the 4B/5B code and to understand selections that were made. Table 6.2 shows the symbol encoding used in FDDI. Since we are encoding 4 bits with a 5 bit pattern, there will be some

TABLE 6.2 4B/5B Code

Decimal	Code Group	Symbol	Assignment
Line State Symbols			
00	00000	Q	Quiet
31	11111	I	Idle
04	00100	H	Halt
Starting Delimiter			
24	11000	J	1st of sequential SD pair
17	10001	K	2nd of sequential SD pair
Data Symbols			
			Hex Binary
30	11110	0	0 0000
09	01001	1	1 0001
20	10100	2	2 0010
21	10101	3	3 0011
10	01010	4	4 0100
11	01011	5	5 0101
14	01110	6	6 0110
15	01111	7	7 0111
18	10010	8	8 1000
19	10011	9	9 1001
22	10110	A	A 1010
23	10111	B	B 1011
26	11010	C	C 1100
27	11011	D	D 1101
28	11100	E	E 1110
29	11101	F	F 1111
Ending Delimiter			
13	01101	T	Used to terminate the data stream
Control Indicators			
07	00111	R	Denoting logical ZERO (reset)
25	11001	S	Denoting logical ONE (set)
Invalid Code Assignments			
01	00001	V or H	These code patterns shall not be trans-
02	00010	V or H	mitted because they violate consecu-
03	00011	V	tive code-bit zeros or duty cycle re-
05	00101	V	quirements. Codes 01,02,08 and 16
06	00110	V	shall however be interpreted as Halt
08	01000	V or H	when received.
12	01100	V	
16	10000	V or H	

patterns that are not needed. The codes selected to represent the 16 4-bit patterns are such that a transition is present at least twice for each 5-cell code on the medium. Given an NRZI format on the fiber, no more than three zeros in a row can be allowed, since, with NRZI, the absence of a line transition indicates a zero.

We can now summarize the FDDI encoding scheme.

1. A simple intensity modulation encoding is rejected because it does not provide synchronization; a string of 1s or 0s will have no transitions.
2. The 4B/5B code is chosen over Manchester because it is more efficient.
3. The 4B/5B code is further encoded using NRZI so that the resulting differential encoding will improve reception reliability.
4. The specific codes chosen for the encoding of the 16-4 bit data patterns are chosen to guarantee no more than three zeros in a row to provide for adequate synchronization.

Only 16 of the 32 possible code patterns are required to represent the input data. The remaining symbols are either declared invalid or assigned special meaning as control symbols. For example, two of the patterns always occur in pairs and act as start delimiters for a frame.

Timing Jitter

Recall that in Chapter 4 we defined timing jitter as the deviation of clock recovery that can occur when the receiver attempts to recover clocking as well as data from the received signal. The clock recovery will deviate in a random fashion from the transitions of the received signal. If no countermeasures are taken, the jitter accumulates around the ring. We saw that the IEEE standard specifies that only one clock will be used on the ring, and that the station that has the clock is responsible for eliminating jitter by means of an elastic buffer. If the ring as a whole runs ahead of or behind the master clock, the elastic buffer expands or contracts accordingly. Even with this technique, the accumulation of jitter places a limitation on the size of the ring.

This centralized clocking approach is inappropriate for a 100-Mbps fiber ring. At 100 Mbps, the bit time is only 10 ns, compared to a bit time of 250 ns at 4 Mbps. Thus the effects of distortion are more severe, and a centralized clocking scheme would put very tough, and therefore expensive, demands on the phase-lock loop circuitry at each node. Therefore, the FDDI standard specifies the use of a distributed clocking scheme: each station uses its own autonomous clock source to transmit or repeat information onto the ring. Each station has its own elastic buffer. Data is clocked into the buffer at the clock rate recovered from the incoming stream, but is clocked out of the buffer at the station's autonomous clock rate. This distributed system is believed to be more robust and to minimize jitter. As a consequence of reclocking at each station, jitter does not limit the number of repeaters in the ring.

Reliability

Unlike the IEEE standards and the LDDI standard, the FDDI standard explicitly addresses the need for reliability and includes specifications for reliability-enhancing techniques. Three techniques are included:

- *Station bypass:* A bad or powered off station is bypassed by an automatic optical bypass switch.
- *Dual rings:* Two rings are employed to interconnect the stations in such a way that a failure of any station or repeater results in the reconfiguration of the network to maintain connectivity.
- *Wiring concentrator:* Wiring concentrators can be used in a star wiring strategy. This approach was discussed in Chapter 4.

The approaches to reliability defined in the FDDI standard have applicability to any ring. Accordingly, we defer a more detailed description to Chapter 12, where the general topic of local network reliability is examined.

6.3

HSLN LINK CONTROL

The general comments concerning link control made in Chapter 5 are equally applicable here. This section first attempts to address the unique requirements for HSLN link control and then presents the X3T9.5 LDDI draft standard as an example.

Requirements

As we mentioned in the beginning of this chapter, the characteristics that distinguish a computer-room HSLN from a LAN include fewer devices, shorter distance, and higher speed. More important, in terms of application, the HSLN is more likely to see file transfer application as opposed to interactive usage.

How do these differences manifest themselves in terms of traffic characteristics? With interactive traffic one expects to see frequent short bursts of data transfer; the HSLN is more likely to see infrequent long bursts of traffic.

We can relate this to the requirements for link control. A connection-oriented capability is desirable for the LAN, since a terminal-host interchange may extend over a long period of time. This seems less important for an HSLN. Long bulk transfers of data occur after which the connection is not needed for some time. Hence a connectionless service may be adequate.

For efficient use of the HSLN medium, the link control layer should permit sustained use of the medium either by permitting transmissions of unbounded length or permitting a pair of devices to seize the channel for an indefinite period. In the latter case, the link control layer permits a multiframe dialogue between two devices, with no other data allowed on the medium for the duration of the dialogue. This permits a long sequence of data frames and acknowledgments to be interchanged. An example of the utility of this feature is the use of the HSLN to read or write to high-performance disks. Without the ability to seize the bus temporarily, only one sector of the disk could be accessed per revolution—a totally unacceptable performance. As we shall see, the LDDI standard provides this feature at the link layer and supports it with a mechanism in the medium access control protocol.

LDDI Data Link Layer: Bus Specification

The X3T9.5 committee has produced two draft specifications for the LDDI, one for the coaxial cable bus and one for the coaxial cable passive star. At the current state of the draft, the two specifications differ not only in the physical specification but also in the medium access control and link specifications. Ultimately, these latter two specifications will probably converge, so that LDDI will consist of one link, one MAC, and two physical layer standards. In the case of both the link and the MAC draft standards, it is instructive to examine the differences in the two specifications. This section, of course, deals with the link layer. We begin with the bus specification, which is a remarkably concise specification for a data link layer, using a convention of signals and interfaces rather than procedure calls.

The features of this layer are simply explained. It is assumed that there is a network layer, not part of the HSLN, above the data link layer (DLL). The DLL exchanges packets of data with the network layer. It provides a connectionless service, with a provision for sustained dialogue. The functions of the DLL are, simply, to accept from the physical layer frames with its address, and to generate during transmission and check during reception a CRC field. The services required by the DLL from the physical layer are that it send and receive data, signal when the medium is available, and signal when the physical layer is operational.

The DLL frame has the following fields:

- D (2 bytes): destination address; may be broadcast.
- S (2 bytes): source address.
- L (2 bytes): length of I field.

- I (variable): data from the network layer, up to 64 kBytes long.
- FCS (4 bytes): frame check sequence field, containing a cyclic redundancy check code.

Figure 6-5 shows the conceptual organization of both the DLL and physical layer. Signal and data interfaces between layers are indicated. The designation conforms to the following conventions. The name of a signal or interface originating in the network, link, or physical layer begins with N, L, or P, respectively. Interface names end with an I. Table 6.3 lists the names of all the signals and interfaces in the standard.

For transmission the network layer uses four signals to the DLL and receives one from the DLL:

- NRX: asserted by network when it wishes to transmit. Transmission will be delayed until the medium is captured.
- NPRX: as above, except that this transmission follows a reception and has priority in capturing the medium. Its use is explained in the context of the medium access control protocol.
- NXSA: asserted when a frame is available for transmission or being transmitted. If a malfunction is sensed during transmission. NXSA is unasserted to abort transmission.
- NXSI: data path for transmission.
- LGXS: grants permission to network to transmit.

The DLL-physical layer interaction uses the following signals:

- LRX: passed down by DLL when NRX is asserted.
- LPRX: as above, for priority transmissions.
- LXSA: asserted when a frame is available; unasserted to abort a transmission.
- LXSI: data path for transmission.
- PGXS: grants permission; medium has been seized.

The operation of the DLL, based on the above, is almost self-explanatory. The DLL accepts the D field, inserts an S field, accepts the L and I fields, and calculates and appends an FCS field. The physical layer is responsible for medium access control and seizes the medium by transmitting a preamble.

The DLL receiver function can be explained almost as consisely. The DLL-physical layer interaction uses the following signals:

- PRSA: asserted when data are available for the DLL.
- PRSI: data path for transmission.
- PBS: asserted if received signal is bad (e.g., a collision, poor signal quality).

The network-DLL interaction consists of:

- LRSA: asserted when data are available for network. Then unasserted

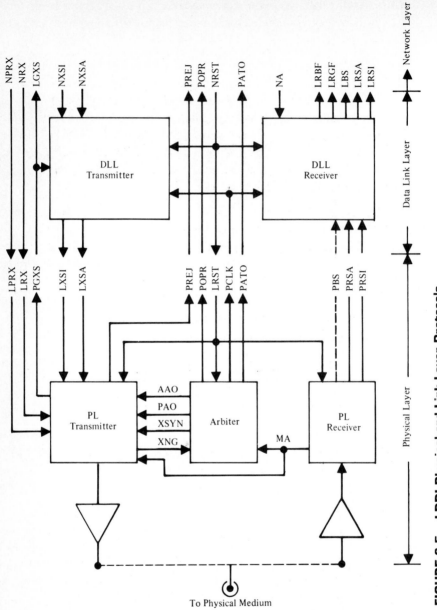

FIGURE 6-5. LDDI Physical and Link Layer Protocols

HIGH-SPEED LOCAL NETWORKS

TABLE 6.3 LDDI Signals and Interfaces

Signal	Meaning
NPRX	Network priority request to transmit
NRX	Network request to transmit
LGXS	Link grant to transmit stream
NXSI	Network transmit stream interface
NXSA	Network transmit stream available
PREJ	Physical reject
POPR	Physical operating
NRST	Network reset
PATO	Physical acknowledgment time-out
NA	Network accept
LRBF	Link receive bad frame
LRGF	Link receive good frame
LBS	Link bad signal (optional)
LRSA	Link receive stream available
LRSI	Link receive stream interface
LPRX	Link priority request to transmit
LRX	Link request to transmit
PGXS	Physical grant to transmit stream
LXSI	Link transmit stream interface
LXSA	Link transmit stream available
LRST	Link reset
PCLK	Physical clock
PBS	Physical bad signal (optional)
PRSA	Physical receive stream available
PRSI	Physical receive stream interface
AAO	Arbitrated access opportunity
PAO	Priority access opportunity
XSYN	Transmit synchronizing frame
XNG	Transmitting
MA	Medium active

to inform network that the complete received frame has been transferred and LRGF and LRBF should be examined.

- LRSI: data path for transmission.
- LRGF: asserted when received FCS indicates that a valid frame has been received.
- LRBF: as above, for invalid frame.
- NA: asserted to signal that the last frame has been received and that network is ready for a new frame.
- LBS: used by DLL to pass the PBS signal up to network.

Again, little more needs to be said. DLL receives all frames from physical and does address recognition. If the destination address is valid for this port, then DLL transfers the D, S, L, and I fields to network. Note there is at least a 2-byte delay.

Several other signals are defined which are needed for various DLL functions:

- NRST: asserted to reset lower layers to known state; any messages in process may be lost.
- LRST; asserted when it is necessary to reinitialize the port; may be precipitated by NRST.
- PREJ: asserted when an invalid physical layer operation is detected.
- PATO: asserted when the Arbitrated Access Timer expires (explained under medium access control, below).
- POPR; asserted whenever the physical layer is powered on and operating.
- PCLK: physical clock.

The simplicity of this description is in part due to the lack of a connection-oriented service, which is left to higher layers to provide. But it is, in part, also due to the conciseness of the signal/interface convention.

LDDI Data Link Layer: Passive Star Specification

At this point, the LDDI link layer specification for the passive star is not as formally defined as for the bus. First, the services to be provided to the network layer are defined.

- *Normal Service:* A single data unit supplied by the network layer is transmitted. The link entity expects to receive an acknowledgement from the destination station. The network layer is notified when an acknowledgement is received or if no acknowledgment is received within a predetermined time period.
- *Data Streaming Service:* A set of data units supplied by the network layer is transmitted. After the first frame is transmitted, the station claims

priority in the use of the medium; this function is explained under medium access control below. Each succeeding frame in the set is transmitted immediately after the reception of the acknowledgement of the previously transmitted frame. Should a frame not be acknowledged within a predetermined time limit, transmission ceases and the network layer is notified accordingly. Other stations are not able to access the medium between frames of a data streaming sequence.

Figure 6-6 illustrates the frame formats used. The fields are:

- *Type (4 bits):* Specifies whether this is an information frame, a positive acknowledgement frame, or a negative acknowledgement frame.
- *Length (12 bits):* The length of the information frame in octets, excluding the FCS field.
- *Dest (8 bits):* Identifies the destination station.
- *Dest Comp (8 bits):* Contains the ones complement of the Dest field. This serves as a simple error check to minimize the chance that a failure in address generation or recognition logic would cause an otherwise good frame to be received by the wrong station.
- *Source (8 bits): Identifies the source station.*
- *Information:* Up to 4091 octets supplied by the network layer.
- *Frame Check Sequence (32 bits):* A 32-bit cyclic redundancy check.

The specification does not include a separate MAC header. Thus the formats of Figure 6-6 indicate the complete set of local network protocol fields used. Note that there is no concept of a service access point; there is but a single user of the link layer. Any multiplexing must be accomplished at higher layers.

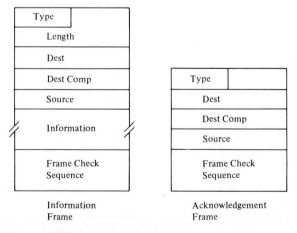

FIGURE 6-6.   LDDI Frame Formats

The two LDDI link specifications that we have reviewed are not inherently contradictory. They are essentially different approaches to defining the services and functions of the link layer.

6.4

HSLN MEDIUM ACCESS CONTROL: BUS

In this and the next section, we will examine medium access control techniques that have been either implemented or proposed for HSLNs. The design issues and objectives for medium access control are much the same for HSLNs as they are for LANs. The key difference is that we can expect higher sustained loads from individual stations.

We begin by looking at coaxial bus and passive star systems. The only type of technique that has so far gained favor for these systems is known as delay scheduling, or CSMA with collision avoidance. Several variants of this technique are described, including two proposed as part of the draft LDDI standard, and the algorithms used on HYPERchannel and VAX-cluster. Next, we examine a variety of techniques that have been proposed to match the characteristics of fiber bus HSLNs. Finally, in the next section, we look at the FDDI MAC standard for fiber ring HSLNs.

Coaxial Cable Bus

In devising a MAC algorithm for the type of system described in Section 6.1, a number of objective suggest themselves. These are briefly described next. As we shall see, these objectives are reflected in the algorithms discussed.

- Allow equal, almost immediate, access under light loading. The objective is to avoid unnecessary delay; CSMA/CD behaves in this fashion.
- Provide fair (round-robin) access with no throughput falloff under heavy loads. The objective is to avoid the instability of contention-based protocols; token bus behaves in this fashion.
- Allow uninterrupted multiframe dialogue between two stations. The necessity for this feature was described in Section 6.2.

With these objectives in mind, we now turn to a description of the LDDI MAC protocol for bus.

The protocol is based on CSMA. That is, a station wishing to transmit listens to the medium and defers if a transmission is in progress. In addition, an algorithm is used that specifically seeks to avoid collisions when the medium is found idle by multiple stations.

The scheme is remarkably similar to token bus. In both cases, the stations or ports form a logical ring (PORT0, PORT1,...PORTN, PORT0, ...). In the case of token bus, at network initialization PORT(0) has the opportunity to transmit. PORT(I + 1) waits to transmit until it receives the token from PORT(I). With the number of stations equal to N + 1, PORT(0) gets its next opportunity to transmit after PORT(N). In the ANS scheme, the network reinitializes after each transmission by any port. Each station, in turn, may transmit if none of the stations before it has done so. So PORT(I + 1) waits until after PORT(I) has had a chance to transmit. The waiting time consists of:

- The earliest time at which PORT(I) could begin transmitting [which depends on the transmission opportunity for PORT(I − 1)].
- Plus a port delay time, during which PORT(I) has the opportunity to transmit.
- Plus the propagation delay between the two ports.

As we shall see, this rather simple concept becomes complex as we consider all of its refinements.

The basic rule can be described as follows. After any transmission, PORT(0) has the right to transmit. If it fails to do so in a reasonable time, then PORT (1) has the chance, and so on. If any port transmits, the system reinitializes.

The first refinement is that we would like to permit multiframe dialogues. To accommodate this, an additional rule is added: after any transmission, the port receiving that transmission has the first right to transmit. If that port fails to transmit, then it is the turn of PORT(0), and so on. This will permit two ports to seize the medium, with one port sending data frames and the other sending acknowledgment frames.

Second refinement: What happens if nobody had a frame to transmit? HYPERchannel solves this by entering a free-for-all period, in which collisions are allowed. The LDDI protocol has a more elegant solution: If none of the stations transmits when it has an opportunity, then reinitialize the network and start over.

With these two refinements, we can depict the MAC protocol as a simple sequence of events:

1. Medium Is Active.
2. Medium Goes Idle.
    If Receiver Transmits, Then Go To 1.
                          Else Go To 3.
3. If PORT(0) Transmits, Then Go To 1.
                          Else Go To 4.
                .
                .
                .

N + 4. If No Port Transmits, Then Go To 1.

Third refinement: Note that this scheme is biased to the lower-number ports. PORT(0) *always* gets a shot, for example. To make the scheme fair, a port that has just transmitted should not try again until everyone else has had a chance.

To define the algorithm concisely, with these three refinements, we need to define some quantities:

- *Priority access opportunity:* a period of time granted to a port after it receives a frame. May be used to acknowledge frame and/or continue a multiframe dialogue.
- *Priority access timer (PAT):* used to time priority access opportunities— 64 bit times.
- *Arbitrated access opportunity:* a period of time granted to each port in sequence, during which it may initiate a transmission—16 bit times. Assigned to individual ports to avoid collisions.
- *Arbitrated access time (AAT):* used to provide each port with a unique, nonoverlapping, arbitrated access opportunity.
- *Resynchronization timer (RT):* time by which the latest possible arbitrated transmission should have been received. Used to reset all timers.
- *Arbiter wait flag (WF):* used to enforce fairness. When a port transmits, its WF is set, so that it will not attempt another arbitrated transmission until all other ports have an opportunity.

For the timers listed, we use the convention that uppercase letters refer to the variable name, and lowercase letters to a specific value. A timer that reaches a specified maximum value is said to have expired.

Now we are in a position to describe the operation of the algorithm, which is depicted in Figure 6-7. Each port on the medium has three timers (PAT, AAT, RT), which keep "local time" (i.e., time with respect to that port). When the medium is active, all timers on all ports are set to zero. When the medium goes idle, all three timers are started. Note that this event occurs at slightly different times for the various ports due to propagation delay.

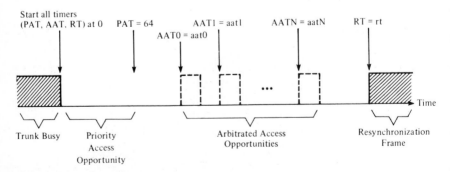

FIGURE 6-7.   Operation of the ANS X3T9.5 Medium-Access Protocol

When the medium goes idle, the port that just received a frame is granted a priority access opportunity, and may initiate a transmission until PAT expires. Of course, if the port in question chooses to transmit, then all timers on all ports are reset and the operation begins again at the beginning.

Each port is assigned a specific value of AAT which signals the beginning of its arbitrated access opportunity. These value are ordered to give PORT(0) the first opportunity, and so on (aat0<aat1 ... <aatN). When the AAT of PORT(0) expires (AAT0 = aat0), and if its WF is not set, and if it has something to transmit, then PORT(0) may transmit. It has 16 bit times to do so, which is the duration of its arbitrated access opportunity. If PORT (0) transmits, it sets its WF. The flag will not be cleared until the port's RT expires. The implication of this, as we shall see, is that the port may not transmit again during an arbitrated access opportunity until all other ports have had an opportunity to do so. However, the port may still transmit during a priority access opportunity when it receives a frame.

If PORT(0) does not transmit during its arbitrated access opportunity, either because it has nothing to send or because its WF prohibits transmission, then it is the turn of PORT(1). PORT(1) will recognize this condition as occurring when AAT1 expires (AAT1 = aat1). The general condition can be stated as follows. Following any transmission, PORT(I) may transmit when AATI expires. This will occur if and only if both of the following occur:

- The receiving port fails to transmit during its priority access opportunity.
- PORT (J) fails to transmit during its arbitrated access opportunity, for all J, $0 \leq J \leq I$.

Eventually, a transmission will occur following which the priority access opportunity is not used and none of the ports takes advantage of its arbitrated access opportunity. The latter will occur because each of the ports has nothing to send or its WF is set. At this point, the ordered transmission scheme has broken down and the system must be reinitialized or resynchronized. The easiest way to do this is to have somebody, anybody, transmit a frame, which resets all timers to zero.

The reinitialization function is facilitated by RT. When a port's RT expires, it resets its WF and AAT. If the AAT then expires, the port must send a frame, with or without data. This resets all timers at all ports.

The expiration values for the three timers at each port must be set with due regard for propagation delay. The general strategy is:

- *pat* is the same for all ports—64 bit times.
- *att0* is set to wait until after a priority transmission from any other port would have reached PORT(0).
- *aatI*, for $I>0$, is set to wait until after an arbitrated transmission from PORT (I-1) would have reached PORT(I).

- *rt* is the same for all ports, and is set to wait until after an arbitrated transmission from PORT(N) would have reached every port.

A simple technique for satisfying the foregoing conditions is to set each timer to a value greater than the previous timer by an amount equal to $2T + DP$, where T equals the end-to-end propagation delay and DP equals a port delay sufficient to allow a port to do the processing required prior to transmission. This technique is less than optimal, and the ANSI draft standard suggest a scheme based on the actual propagation delay between any pair of ports.

To explain this scheme, consider the layout of Figure 6-8. When it hears idle, PORT(0) must wait until the recipient of the last transmission has an opportunity for a priority transmission. The worse case for this is if the last transmission were addressed to PORT(2). Now, PORT(2) may not hear idle until a time later than when PORT(0) hears it by an amount equal to the propagation delay between the two, $t_{0,2}$. PORT(2) then has 64 bit times *(pat)* to transmit, and the start of that transmission will not be heard by PORT(0) until $t_{0,2}$ later. Hence when PORT(0) hears idle, it must wait until after the priority access opportunity plus twice the maximum propagation delay between it and any other port.

Next, PORT(1) must wait until after the duration of PORT(0)'s arbitrated access opportunity. Recognize, however, that the timers at the two ports differ. PORT(1) may not have heard idle until $t_{0,1}$ after PORT(0). Further, if PORT(0) chooses to transmit, PORT(1) will not hear it for $t_{0,1}$. So, PORT(1) must wait until after the arbitrated access opportunity for PORT(0) plus twice the propagation delay between the two ports.

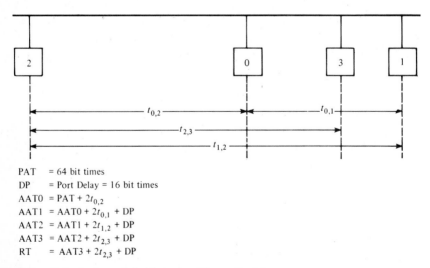

PAT	= 64 bit times
DP	= Port Delay = 16 bit times
AAT0	= PAT + $2t_{0,2}$
AAT1	= AAT0 + $2t_{0,1}$ + DP
AAT2	= AAT1 + $2t_{1,2}$ + DP
AAT3	= AAT2 + $2t_{2,3}$ + DP
RT	= AAT3 + $2t_{2,3}$ + DP

FIGURE 6-8. Calculation of Arbitration Timer Settings

The same means of computation is used for PORT(2) and PORT(3). Finally, there is RT. For simplicity, we set it the same for all ports. It is set to wait until after the arbitrated access opportunity for PORT(3) plus twice the propagation delay between PORT(3) and the port most distant from it, PORT(2).

From the above reasoning, we may derive the following general formulas:

$$pat = 64$$

$$aat0 = 64 + 2t_{0,f}$$

$$aatI = aat(I - 1) + 2t_{I,I-1} + DP, \qquad 1 \leq I \leq N$$

$$rt = aatN + 2t_{N,f}$$

where $t_{i,f}$ is the propagation delay between PORT(I) and the port most distant from it.

Note that the example in Figure 6-8 is not optimal. That is, the ordering assigned to the ports will not produce the minimum waiting times. If the ports are numbered sequentially in physical order, the waiting times will be less.

There are several strengths to the ANS MAC approach. Collisions are avoided; this reduces overhead. The priority access opportunity permits lengthy multiframe transfers. Finally, fairness is enforced.

There are some weaknesses as well. In general, this approach yields longer waiting times than CSMA/CD. This is so because PORT(I) must wait AATI to transmit when no earlier port wishes to do so. However, because the total number of ports is small, this delay has a reasonably small upper bound. Also, unlike token bus and token ring, this scheme has no concept of an inactive station. Therefore, the greater the number of ports on the network, active or not, the greater the overhead.

The HYPERchannel algorithm is very similar to the ANS scheme just described. There are two major differences:

- HYPERchannel does not use a wait flag. Hence the higher priority ports can easily dominate the medium's capacity.
- If no port transmits during an arbitration cycle, a "free for all" period is entered during which any station may transmit, as in CSMA. This permits collisions to occur.

Coaxial Cable Passive Star

While the LDDI MAC proposal for the bus is based on the MAC algorithm used in HYPERchannel, the LDDI MAC proposal for the passive star is based on the MAC algorithm for VAXcluster. The motivation is purely historical, and since the passive star is logically a bus, it is to be hoped that the two MAC specifications will converge in the final standard.

Even so, two physical differences exist between the bus and passive star specifications that can influence the chosen algorithm:

1. The passive star is limited to a fixed maximum number of devices. Thus, a fixed-slot scheme is possible, as described below.
2. In a passive star, a station, after a round-trip propagation delay, can hear its own transmission. This allows for a simple implementation of collision detection, although the algorithm described below does not exploit this property.

We begin with the somewhat simper algorithm used in VAXcluster. As before, a collision avoidance scheme is used. Time on the passive star is measured from the end of the last transmission. Each node is assigned a unique arbitrated access opportunity. Thus, there are 16 time slots defined following the end of a transmission. If a station has data to send, it may transmit during its own time slot. If a station with an earlier time slot transmits, the waiting station loses the arbitration and must begin counting time slots again.

We see that stations having shorter delay times (earlier time slots) have priority over those with longer delay times. To compensate, 32 time slots are used instead of 16. Each station is assigned one time slot in the first group of 16 and one in the second group of 16. A station must alternate between the use of its short and long-delay slots. This insures more equal access to the medium.

If all 32 slots expire with no transmission, a free-for-all period is entered and collisions may occur. However, the collision causes the medium to be resynchronized and the algorithm continues to function.

The LDDI MAC algorithm for passive star is a refinement of the VAXcluster technique. The key addition is a priority access opportunity, with function identical to that in the bus algorithm. This is followed by 32 slots, grouped as primary and secondary slots. Again a station may transmit in either its primary or secondary slot. Rather than the simple alternation described above, a more complex algorithm has been devised, and is illustrated in Figure 6-9. Each station maintains an internal flag. When the flag is true, the station may transmit during its primary slot; when it is false, the station must wait for its secondary slot. The flag is initially set to false when a new frame is ready for transmission. The station then waits for its secondary slot. If some other station transmits before the station's secondary slot comes up, then the station does the following:

1. Reset the timer.
2. Set flag to true if the last transmission was on a numerically lower time slot or if the transmission was in slot 15 and this station's primary slot number is zero. Otherwise, do not change the value of the flag.

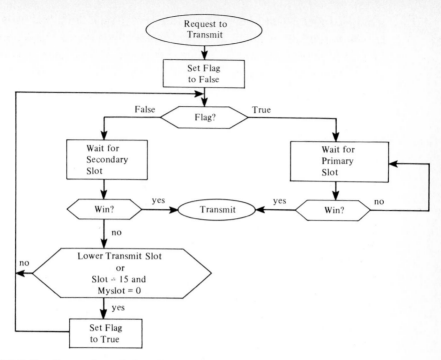

FIGURE 6-9. Operation of the LDDI MAC Passive Star Protocol

As can be seen, the LDDI passive star MAC algorithm is more complex than that of VAXcluster. The performance benefits, if any, do not seem to be dramatic, and may not justify the extrra complexity. As between the two LDDI MAC specifications, there seems little to choose between. Both appear to satisfy the HSLN requirements, and neither appears to be significantly superior.

Optical Fiber Bus

The MAC algorithm described above is, in most respects, well suited to the HSLN application. There are, of course, some limitations. Two in particular are of some concern. First, there is a practical limitation on the number of devices. As the number of devices increases, so does the number of arbitrated access opportunities, increasing the system overhead. Second, a long duration transmission can utilize the multiframe dialogue feature to lock the bus and prevent any other station from gaining access.

With current technology, these limitations may not be too serious. A 50-Mbps coaxial system accommodates only a limited number of devices anyway, and the cost of such systems dictates that most stations will be expensive high-speed devices for which long duration transmissions are the most important.

As we move to the higher data rate and larger number of attached devices potentially available with an optical fiber bus, something other than delay scheduling will be needed. Because optical fiber bus systems have not been commercially practical or available, little implementation experience exists in this area. However, a great deal of literature exists on the subject, and many proposals have been put forward. All of these proposals fall, roughly, into one of two categories: implicit token and distributed reservation. In what follows, we look at representative examples of each.

Implicit Token

In the preceding chapter, we examined in some detail an explicit token scheme for a coaxial cable bus, namely the IEEE 802.4 standard. The robustness of such a network depends on the integrity of the token, and the algorithm has to be quite complex to deal with all possible error conditions. Further, as we shall see in Chapter 9, the performance of explicit token passing (as well as delay scheduling) degrades significantly with increasing data rate. Thus an explicit token bus scheme may not be the best choice for a high-speed optical fiber bus.

In an explicit token scheme, a station transmits a token frame to the next in turn. In an implicit token bus scheme, stations rely on various events on the bus to determine when to transmit. Since the token passing is implicit, overall robustness is improved. Further, without the overhead of passing an explicit token, these schemes have greater efficiency and hence higher throughput than the explicit token schemes.

The nature of the scheme will depend in part on the bus configuration. Recall (Figure 4-23) that two passive bus configurations have been identified: linear and loop. We will examine one scheme for each configuration.

Figure 6-10 depicts the linear passive bus, with two fiber bus links, labeled A and B, and N stations. Each station has both transmit and receive taps into both buses. When a station has the opportunity to trans-

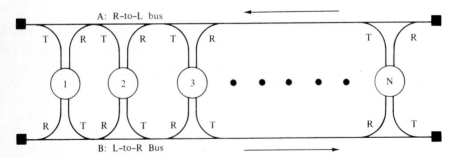

FIGURE 6-10. Linear Passive Bus

mit, it does so on both buses so that all other stations receive the transmission. We will describe a technique proposed in [RODR85].

In this scheme, the implicit token is marked by the end of a data frame, and is assumed to alternate between buses A and B. To describe the procedure, let us assume that station 1 has a frame to transmit and the permission to transmit, and that bus B is to be used for the implicit token. To begin, station 1 transmits a frame on buses B and A. All backlogged stations (stations with a frame to transmit) listen to bus B for the implicit token. Each backlogged station performs the following sequence of actions:

1. Listen to bus B for the beginning of a frame.
2. Listen for the end of the frame.
3. Wait a time d to determine if another frame is following behind the last frame. If so, go to step 2.
4. If no other frame arrives within d, transmit own frame on both buses B and A.
5. After transmission, transmit a continuous pattern, referred to as an activity signal, on A.

The result of this sequence is that all backlogged stations in order will be able to transmit one frame, so that a train of frames propagates down B and the end of that train serves as the implicit token.

The above constitutes one round of the algorithm. The next round will occur with the implicit token on bus A. To start this round, one station must be identified as end station. To accomplish this, each station performs as follows;

1. Transmit an activity signal on A as soon as the implicit token passes on B, as described above.
2. If another activity signal is heard on A, cease transmitting and wait for the implicit token on A.
3. If no other activity signal is heard within a time equal to twice the end-to-end propagation delay, assume that no other station is active to the right, and transmit a frame on A and B. This begins the new round with the implicit token on A.

This scheme is a simple and robust one, and has very little overhead.

Figure 6-11 depicts a loop bus whose configuration was proposed for a technique known as Expressnet [TOBA83, TOBA87]. Each station has a transmit tap on the lower third of the bus, called the outbound bus, and a receive tap on the upper third of the bus, called the inbound bus. Two additional details are required for the algorithm: each station has a simple tap on the lower third that allows carrier sensing, and the bus is folded twice so that stations receive in the same order that they transmit. As

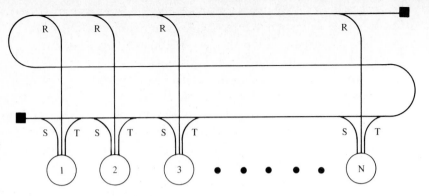

FIGURE 6-11. Loop Passive Bus

before, transmission will occur in rounds, with each station getting one chance per round and with each round consisting of a train of closely spaced frames. For each backlogged station other than the station that begins a round, the rules for transmission are:

1. Sense carrier on the outbound bus and wait until the bus goes idle.
2. Begin transmitting frame.
3. If a carrier is detected during transmission, cease transmission and go to step 1.

Each frame begins with a preamble pattern, so any aborted transmissions as a result of step 3 will merely lengthen the preamble. The result of this sequence is that all backlogged stations in order will be able to transmit one frame. This constitutes one round and results in a train of frames. To begin the next round, each station monitors the inbound bus for the end of the train, which occurs when a delay above a given threshold is detected following a frame. Step 1 above is revised to say that a station may transmit if it detects end of carrier on the outbound bus or end of train on the inbound bus. Because of the double folding of the bus, station 1 will have the first opportunity to start a new train, followed by station 2, and so on.

This scheme for the loop bus exhibits similar robustness and performance characteristics to the one described above for the linear bus.

Distributed Reservation
The advent of wider-bandwidth technologies will allow integrated networks with a wide variety of traffic types. For example, some of the stations may generate short, bursty traffic with modest throughput requirements but a need for a short delay time. Other stations may generate long streams of traffic that require high throughput, but they may be able to tolerate moderate delays prior to the start of a transmission.

A fair random access scheme, such as the ones described earlier, will not function well in these circumstances. For example, a stream transmission can cause intolerable delays for bursty traffic. If stream traffic load is stable, one solution is to dedicate certain portions of the bandwidth to various traffic types. This can be done using FDM on a broadband LAN, or by dedicating certain time slots on a TDM HSLN system. However, if the stream traffic load varies, as when file transfers are made primarily at night and interactive traffic is high during the day, then a fixed-allocation scheme lacks flexibility and is wasteful of bandwidth.

For a single-channel HSLN, a distributed reservation scheme that can dynamically allocate bandwidth to streams and bursty traffic seems well suited to the type of environment we have been describing. Such a scheme would provide, on demand, adequate bandwidth to meet the stream traffic load, and leave the rest of the bandwidth available for bursty traffic. A number of such schemes have been proposed. We will examine one in particular [HANS81] that was designed specifically for the HSLN context. Similar approaches can be found in [CHU82], [PROT82], and [SUDA83]. But first, we look at the reservation schemes that were its precursors.

All of the precursors to be discussed in this subsection share several features in common. For one, all were originally designed for a satellite network. Such a network consists of a set of ground stations and a satellite in synchronous orbit. All ground stations transmit data to the satellite, which repeats the transmission in broadcast fashion back down to all ground stations. Note the similarity to broadband LAN.

An interesting feature of satellite networks is that while carrier sensing is not practical, collision detection is. This is because of the long round trip propagation delay of 270 ms. With such delays, carrier sense is useless because packets will typically be very short compared to propagation time. Enormous packets would be needed for ground stations to hear a transmission while the originating station was still sending. For example, at a rate of 1.5 Mbps, the "bit length" of the medium is 405,000 bits. On the other hand, because of the delay, a station can easily listen to its own transmission to detect a collision.

Other features in common: They are all based in some sense on the slotted ALOHA (S-ALOHA) protocol. Also, time on the network is organized into an indefinite sequence of fixed-length "frames" (not to be confused with a link layer frame). Each frame, with a duration at least as long as the round-trip propagation delay, is divided into slots. Actual transmission is at the slot level. Because of the minimum frame length constraint, stations are aware of the usage status of time slots in the previous frame. The significance of this will be seen shortly.

Finally, all of these schemes are reservation schemes: Slots in future frames are reserved in some dynamic fashion for specific stations. They differ primarily in the way in which the reservations are made and released.

The simplest of these schemes are reservation schemes: Slots in future frames are reserved in some dynamic fashion for specific stations. They differ primarily in the way in which the reservations are made and released.

The simplest of these schemes is one proposed in [CROW73], called R-ALOHA. Reservations are implicit: Successful transmission in a slot serves as a reservation for the corresponding slot in the next frame. By repeated use of that slot position, a station can transmit a long stream of data. A station wishing to transmit one or more packets (one packet per slot) of data monitors the slots in the current frame. Any slot that is empty or contains a collision is available for the next frame; the station may contend for that slot using S-ALOHA. This approach allows a dynamic mixture of stream and bursty traffic.

The scheme described above will work with an unknown or dynamically varying number of stations. A scheme proposed in [BIND75] requires a fixed number of stations less than or equal to the number of time slots in a frame. Each station owns a particular slot position. If there are any extra slots, these are contended for by all stations using S-ALOHA. The owner may use its slot to transmit continuously. If the owner has no data to send, its slot will become empty. This is a signal to the other stations that they may contend for that slot via S-ALOHA. The owner gets its slot back simply by using it. If the transmission is successful, fine; if not, the collision causes other stations to defer and the station reclaims the slot in the next frame. This technique is superior to R-ALOHA for stream-dominated traffic, since each station is guaranteed one slot of bandwidth. However, when there are a large number of stations, this scheme can lead to a very large average delay because of the required number of slots per frame.

A different approach, proposed in [ROBE73], is to use explicit reservations. For this scheme, a frame is divided into $N + 1$ equal-length slots, one of which is further subdivided into "minislots." The minislots, acquired via S-ALOHA, function as a common queue for all users. A station wishing to transmit must send a request packet in a minislot specifying the number of slots desired, up to some maximum number. If the reservation is successful (no collison), the station then determines which future slots it has acquired and transmits in them. For this work, each station must keep track of the queue length—the number of slots reserved but not yet used. Figure 6-12 illustrates the operation. For lengthy streams, this scheme requires a user to contend for slots repeatedly, which results in significant delivery delay variances if there is much traffic. If the maximum reservation size is set high enough to allow complete stream transmission, delays to begin transmission of other traffic become long.

A sophisticated scheme that combines elements of the other schemes just described is referred to as *priority-oriented demand assignment* (PODA). This approach has been implemented in SATNET, a prototype packet satellite network [JACO78]. Each frame consists of a data sub-

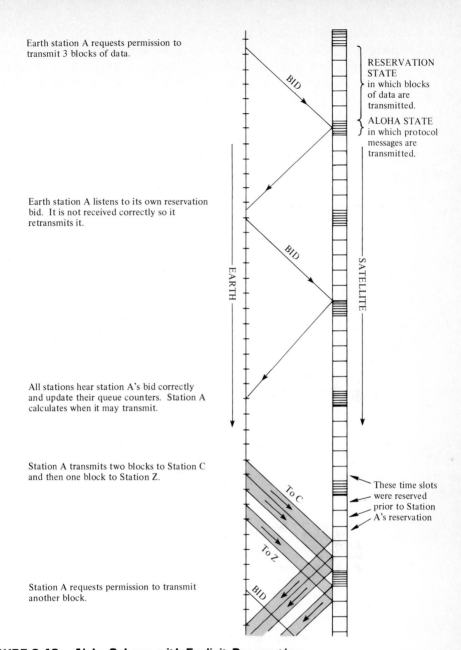

Earth station A requests permission to transmit 3 blocks of data.

BID

RESERVATION STATE in which blocks of data are transmitted.

ALOHA STATE in which protocol messages are transmitted.

Earth station A listens to its own reservation bid. It is not received correctly so it retransmits it.

BID

EARTH

SATELLITE

All stations hear station A's bid correctly and update their queue counters. Station A calculates when it may transmit.

Station A transmits two blocks to Station C and then one block to Station Z.

To C

To Z

These time slots were reserved prior to Station A's reservation

Station A requests permission to transmit another block.

BID

FIGURE 6-12.   Aloha Scheme with Explicit Reservations

frame, divided into data slots, and a control subframe divided into smaller reservation slots. A station with one or more packets to send must reserve data slots by transmitting in a reservation slot. A stream reservation is for one or more data slots per frame for the indefinite future. Further, once a station begins transmitting, additional reservations may be piggybacked onto a data packet.

If the number of stations is small, the control subframe consists of a fixed number of slots equal to the number of stations, and each station owns a reservation slot. For larger networks, the reservation slots are contended for using S-ALOHA. Also, the size of the control subframe decreases as the number of outstanding reservations increases, so that backlog can be cleared out.

All stations must keep track of all outstanding reservations. Each takes into account user-specified delay class and priority according to the same algorithm. For stream reservations, interpacket time is also specified. Each station automatically schedules future stream packets based on the single reservation. Additional reservations can be piggybacked on any transmission in the information subframe. These will be scheduled like reservations in the control subframe. Thus both reservation and information subframe messages must be monitored for content by every user. This places a heavy processing burden on each node.

Hanson et al. [HANS81] have proposed a distributed reservation MAC protocol for high-speed local networks called the *hybrid access method* (HAM). We examine HAM in some detail because it is representative of the kind of protocol that will be needed for future fiber-optic bus HSLNs, with large numbers of stations and a variety of traffic.

The protocol is designed with the following constraints in mind.

1. Stream transmissions require assurance of bandwidth without interruption.
2. Bursty traffic requires fast response time, and the number of users is large.
3. Simple user stations must have access without the burden of a heavy processing load.
4. A dynamically varying mixture of traffic must be supported.
5. Stream traffic must be restricted to ensure that it does not monopolize the bandwidth.

Constraint 1 can be satisfied with a reservation scheme. Constraint 2 suggests that decentralized control is needed to avoid a bottleneck. Constraint 3 may imply the need for a simple contention scheme for bursty traffic access control; certainly, a simple contention scheme satisfies this constraint. Constraint 4 requires a high bandwidth channel, such as optical fiber. The constraint further implies the need for a dynamic allocation technique. Finally, constraint 5 implies that some guaranteed minimum portion of the channel bandwidth must be dedicated to bursty traffic. HAM is designed to satisfy these constraints; a typical system for which it would be suited would consist of a 0.5- to 1.5-km bus and a 100- to 200-Mbps data rate.

As with the satellite networks, HAM makes use of a frame consisting of a set of slots. Each frame consists of three subframes. The *reservation subframe* consists of a set of reservation minislots. The *reserved subframe* consists of data slots that may be reserved for future use; these are intended for stream traffic. The remainder is an *unreserved subframe* of slots intended for bursty traffic. The boundary between the reserved and unreserved subframes is movable to allow up to a certain maximum number of stream slots with a certain minimum number of bursty slots.

The bursty traffic algorithm is simply explained. Any station may transmit in any bursty slot using S-ALOHA. A station needs timing and synchronization information; it must also know the location of the movable boundary.

To acquire slots in the reserved subframe, a station contends for a minislot to transmit a reservation specifying the requested number of slots per frame. Once a minislot is acquired, the requesting station continues to transmit in the minislot to hold the reservation until the stream transmission is completed. The minislots serve as a queue for the slots available to satisfy stream requests. Requests are met on a first-come, first-served basis.

The sum of the requests in all of the minislots in one frame indicates the number of slots requested for the next frame. If the number requested is less than or equal to the maximum allowable number of stream slots, then all requests are filled and the frame boundary is adjusted so that all unused slots are available for bursty transmission. Otherwise, the maximum number of stream slots is filled and remaining requests are held over. Because all of this is done without centralized control, a station needing to reserve stream slots requires quite a bit of state information. It must know which minislots are in use, to avoid colliding with an ongoing reservation. Once it has the reservation, it must have a count of request, and it must know what stream slots are available. An example of frame use over time is shown in Figure 6-13.

Slot size selection and frame duration are interrelated with each other and with the traffic mix and load. Longer frames result in greater initial delay for stream transmissions, but can handle more simultaneous streams. Too large a slot size wastes capacity if the stream traffic is not great enough to fill one slot per frame. Too small a slot size reduces effective utilization because a constant overhead for synchronization and addressing is required per slot.

The frame must be at least twice as long as the maximum propagation delay, so the reservations in one frame can be acted on in the next frame. This condition is easily met because, for synchronization, it seems advisable to require that all slots, including minislots, be as long as the propagation time plus the request or data transmission time. This allows all stations to synchronize on the leading edge of each slot, much as in the LDDI technique. Otherwise, a separate clock channel will be needed.

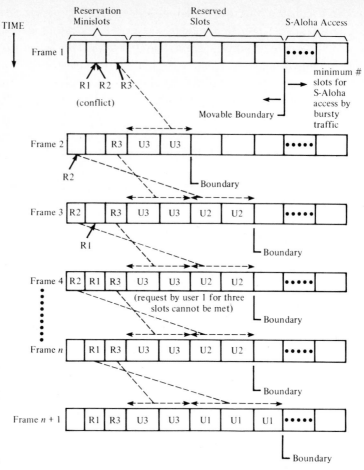

FIGURE 6-13. Frame Use Over Time for Hybrid Access Method

Finally, note that the collision detection function, which is required for the minislots, forces a listen-while-talk capability.

In summary, this scheme meets the different requirements of stream and bursty traffic. Bursty requirements are met with a simple algorithm. For stream traffic, HAM provides for zero delivery time variance unless preemptions are allowed for higher priorities. The use of minislots reduces capacity waste due to collisions.

6.5

HSLN MEDIUM ACCESS CONTROL: RING

In this section we examine what will surely be the most widely-implemented MAC technique for HSLN rings: the FDDI standard [ANSI86b]. This standard is based on the IEEE 802.5 standard. The

TABLE 6.4 Differences Between FDDI and 802.5

FDDI	802.5
Optical fiber	Shielded twisted pair
100 Mbps	4 Mbps
Reliability specification	No reliability specification
4B/5B code	Differential Manchester
Distributed clocking	Centralized clocking
Timed token rotation	Priority and reservation bits
New token after transmit	New token after receive

X3T9.5 committee decided to adopt as much of 802.5 as possible, making changes only where necessary to exploit the high speeds of a fiber ring and to provide the service to be expected on an HSLN. This strategy has several advantages:

1. The token protocol is known to work effectively, particularly at high loads (see Chapter 9); thus there is no need and some risk in adopting a different approach.
2. The use of similar frame formats facilitates the internetworking of high and low-speed rings (see Chapter 11).
3. Understanding of FDDI is facilitated for those already familiar with 802.5.
4. Implementation experience, particularly at the chip level, may be of benefit to vendors of FDDI systems and components.

Table 6.4 summarizes the key differences between 802.5 and FDDI (see also [ULLA87]). Some of these are the physical layer and have already been discussed; the remainder are at the MAC layer and it is these differences that are the focus of this section.

FDDI Frame Format

Figure 6-14 depicts the frame formats for FDDI MAC. Compare these to those of 802.5 (Figure 5-2). The fields are:

- *Preamble (PA):* synchronizes the frame with the station's clock. The originator of a frame uses a field of 64 bits; subsequent repeating stations may change the length of the field consistent with clocking requirements.
- *Starting Delimiter (SD):* a unique 8-bit pattern used to start each frame.
- *Frame Control (FC):* has the formal 'CLFFZZZZ', where C indicates whether this is a synchronous or asynchronous frame (explained below); L indicates the use of 16 or 48-bit addresses; FF indicates whether this is

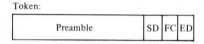

Frame:

| Preamble | SD | FC | DA | SA | INFO | FCS | E D | FS |

Token:

| Preamble | SD | FC | ED |

FIGURE 6-14. FDDI MAC Frame Formats

an LLC frame or a MAC control frame; in the latter case, the remaining bits indicate the type of control frame.

- *Destination Address (DA):* specifies the station(s) for which the frame is intended. It may be a unique physical address, a multicast address (group of stations), or a broadcast address (all stations). The ring may contain a mixture of 16-bit and 48-bit addresses.
- *Source Address (SA):* specifies the station that sent the frame.
- *Information (INFO):* LLC or station management information.
- *Frame Check Sequence (FCS):* a 32-bit cyclic redundancy check value. Based on the FC, DA, SA, and INFO fields.
- *Ending Delimiter (ED):* a unique pattern used to mark the end of the frame (except for the FS field). The ED is 8 bits long for a token and 4 bits long for all other frames.
- *Frame Status (FS):* contains the error detected (E), address recognized (A), and frame copied (F) indicators.

A comparison with the 802.5 frame format shows that the two are very similar. The FDDI frame includes a preamble to aid in clocking, which is more demanding at the higher data rate. Both 16 and 48-bit addresses fields are allowed on the same network with FDDI: this is more flexible than the scheme used on all the 802 standards. Finally, there are some differences in the control bits. For example, FDDI does not include priority and reservation bits; capacity allocation is handled in a different way, as described below.

Capacity Allocation

The token-passing protocol used in FDDI is the same as that of 802.5 in many respects. There are two main differences. The first is the timing of token issuance. In FDDI, a station emits a new token immediately following the frame, whereas in 802.5, a station emits a new token only after the leading edge of its transmitted frame returns. The FDDI scheme is thus more efficient, especially in large rings.

The second difference is the way in which capacity is allocated on the ring. For both FDDI and 802.5, it is possible to use a single token type and provide equal, fair access to all stations. For greater control over the capacity, 802.5 includes a priority and reservation scheme that encompasses eight levels of priority. For FDDI, a more powerful scheme was felt to be needed. Specifically, FDDI seeks to accommodate two requirements for HSLNs that were described earlier:

- Support for a mixture of stream and bursty traffic.
- Support for multiframe dialogue.

To accommodate the first requirement, FDDI defines two types of traffic: synchronous and asynchronous. The scheme works as follows. A target token rotation time (TTRT) is defined; each station stores the same value for TTRT. Some or all stations may be provided a synchronous allocation (SA_i), which may vary among stations. The allocation must be set such that:

$$\Sigma SA_i + D\_Max + F\_Max + Token\_Time \leq TTRT$$

where

SA_i = allocation for station i

D_Max = propagation time for one complete circuit of the ring.

F_Max = time required to transmit a maximum length frame (4500 octets.)

Token_Time = Time required to transmit a token.

Thus all stations have the same value of TTRT and a separately assigned value of SA_i. In addition, several variables that are required for the operation of the capacity-allocation algorithm are maintained at each station:

- Token-rotation timer (TRT)
- Token-holding timer (THT)
- Late counter (LC)

Each station's TRT is initialized to TTRT; when it is enabled, it counts down until it expires at TRT = 0. It is then reset to TTRT and enabled again. LC is initialized at zero and is incremented when TRT expires. Thus LC records the number of times, if any, that TRT has expired since the token was last received at that station. The token is considered to arrive early if TRT has not expired since the station received the token, that is, if LC = 0.

When a station receives the token, its actions will depend on whether the token is early or late. If the token is early, the station saves the remaining time in TRT in THT; resets TRT, and enables TRT:

$$THT \leftarrow TRT$$

$$TRT \leftarrow TTRT$$

enable TRT

The station can then transmit according to the following rules:

1. It may transmit synchronous frames for a time SA_i.
2. After transmitting synchronous frames, or if there were no synchronous frames to transmit, THT is enabled. The station may transmit asynchronous frames only so long as $THT > 0$.

If a station receives a token and the token is late, then LC is set to zero, and TRT continues to run. The station can then transmit synchronous frames for a time SA_i. The station may not transmit any asynchronous frames.

This scheme is designed to assure that the time between successive sighting of a token is on the order of TTRT or less. Of this time, a given amount is always available for synchronous traffic and any excess capacity is available for asynchronous traffic. Because of random fluctuations in traffic, the actual token circulation time may exceed TTRT[JOHN87, SEVC87], as demonstrated below.

The FDDI algorithm is similar to the 802.4 algorithm with only two classes of data, 6 and 4. Synchronous data corresponds to Class 6, and the value of SA_i in FDDI corresponds to the token holding time in 802.4. Finally, TTRT corresponds to TRT4. Since the sum of the SA_i (all the synchronous allocations) must be less than or equal to TTRT, the FDDI restrictions correspond to Case IIa in Figure 5-13.

Figure 6-15 illustrates the use of the station variables in FDDI by displaying the values of TRT, THT, and LC for a particular station. In this example, taken from [MCCO88], the TTRT is 100 milliseconds (ms). The station's synchronous capacity allocation, SA_i is 30 ms. The following events occur:

A. A token arrives early. The station has no frames to send. TRT is set to TTRT (100 ms) and begins to count down. The station allows the token to go by.
B. The token returns 60 ms later. Since TRT = 40 and LC = 0, the token is early. The station sets THT ← TRT and TRT ← TTRT, so that THT = 40 and TRT = 100. TRT is immediately enabled. The station has synchronous data to transmit and begins to do so.
C. After 30 ms, the station has consumed its synchronous allocation. It

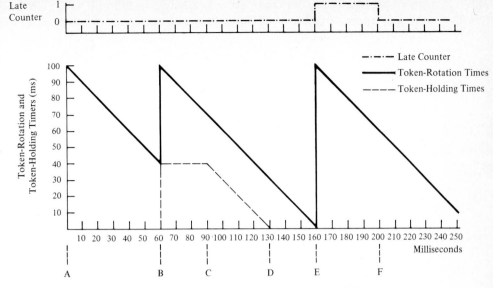

FIGURE 6-15.   FDDI Capacity Allocation Example [MCCO88]

 has asynchronous data to transmit, so it enables THT and begins transmitting.

 D. THT expires, and the station must cease transmission of asynchronous frames. The station issues a token.

 E. TRT expires. The station increments LC to 1 and resets TRT to 100.

 F. The token arrives. Since LC is 1, the token is late, and no asynchronous data may be transmitted. At this point, the station also has no synchronous data to transmit. LC is reset to 1 and the token is allowed to go by.

 Figure 6-16 provides a simplified example of a 4-station ring (compare Figure 5-15). We assume that the traffic consists of fixed-length frames, and

SA₁ = 20		SA₂ = 20		SA₃ = 20		SA₄ = 20	
TCT	XMIT	TCT	XMIT	TCT	XMIT	TCT	XMIT
4	20,94	120	20,0	140	20,0	160	20,0
180	20,0	84	20,16	100	20,0	100	20,0
100	20,0	100	20,0	84	20,16	100	20,0
100	20,0	100	20,0	100	20,0	84	20,16
100	20,0	100	20,0	100	20,0	100	20,0
84	20,16	100	20,0	100	20,0	100	20,0
100	20,0	84	20,16	100	20,0	100	20,0

FIGURE 6-16.   Operation of FDDI Capacity Allocation Scheme

6.5 HSLN MEDIUM ACCESS CONTROL: RING   **235**

that TTRT = 100 frame times and SA_i = 20 frame times for all stations. We also assume that the total overhead during one complete token circulation is 4 frame times. The value in the left-hand column is the token circulation time actually experienced at that station for the previous rotation of the token. Thus, when the token arrives early, this value is equal to $100 - TRT$. The right-hand value is the number of frames the station transmits; this is broken down into synchronous and asynchronous frames.

The example begins after a period during which no data frames have been sent, so that the token has been circulating as rapidly as possible (4 frame times). Thus, when Station 1 receives the token, it measures a circulation time of 4 (its TRT = 96). It is therefore able to send not only its 20 synchronous frames but also 96 asynchronous frames; recall that THT is not enabled until after the station has sent its synchronous frames. Station 2 experiences a circulation time of 120 (20 frames + 96 frames + 4 overhead frames), but is nevertheless entitled to transmit its 20 synchronous frames. Note that if each station continues to transmit its maximum allowable synchronous frames, then the circulation time surges to 180, but soon stabilizes at 100. With a total synchronous utilization of 80 and an overhead of 4 frame times, there is an average capacity of 16 frame times available for synchronous transmission. Note that if all stations always have a full backlog of asynchronous traffic, the opportunity to transmit asynchronous frames rotates among them.

Asynchronous traffic can be further subdivided into eight levels of priority. Each station has a set of eight threshold values, $T\_Pr(1),\ldots,$ $T\_Pr(8)$, such that $T\_PR(i)$ = maximum time that a token can take to circulate and still permit priority i frames to be transmitted. Rule 2 above is revised as follows:

2. After transmitting synchronous frames, or if there were no synchronous frames to transmit, THT is enabled and begins to run from its set value. The station may transmit asynchronous data of priority i only so long as THT > $T\_Pr(i)$. The maximum value of any of the $T\_Pr(i)$ must be no greater than TTRT.

This scheme is essentially the one used on the 802.4 token bus standard (Figure 5.13).

The above rules satisfy the requirement for support for both stream and bursty traffic and, with the use of priorities, provide a great deal of flexibility. In addition, FDDI provides a mechanism that satisfies the requirement for dedicated multiframe traffic mentioned earlier. When a station wishes to enter an extended dialogue it may gain control of all the unallocated (asynchronous) capacity on the ring by using a restricted token. The station captures a nonrestricted token, transmits the first frame of the dialog to the destination station, and then issues a restricted token. Only the station that received the last frame may transmit asynchronous frames using the restricted token. The two stations may then exchange data frames and restricted tokens for an extended period, during which no other stations may transmit asynchronous frames. Synchronous frames may be transmitted by any station upon capture of either type of token.

6.6

RECOMMENDED READING

There is not much literature on high-speed local networks, and most of it is concerned with performance, which is discussed in Chapter 9. [THOR80] provides an overall rationale and describes HYPERchannel, while [STRE84] and [KRON86]* describe VAXcluster. The LDDI standard is described in [BURR83]. The FDDI standard is described in [JOSH86]*, [BURR86]*, and [MCCO88]. Surveys of MAC techniques for fiber bus include [FINE84], [RODR85]*, and [SACH88].

6.7

PROBLEMS

6.1 Explain by example how the bit information from the 150-MHz broadband signal can be recovered by comparing an inverted output to a delayed output.

6.2 The 150-MHz carrier has a frequency three times the bit rate of 50 Mbps. Would it be possible to use a 50-MHz or 100-MHz carrier?

6.3 Using the LDDI signal and interface conventions, develop state transition diagrams for transmission and reception of frames.

6.4 For HSLN link control, why is uninterrupted multiframe dialogue preferable to one very long frame to accommodate a long transmission?

6.5 Figure 6-5 shows a combined physical and data link diagram for the LDDI standard. Describe the role of each signal and interface, in order to achieve the operation of the ANS scheme described.

6.6 Write a program that implements the MAC algorithm in the LDDI scheme.

6.7 Consider Figure 6-8. Assume propagation delays of 30 bit times between 0 and 2, 15 bit times between 0 and 3, and 5 bit times between 1 and 3. What are the values of the timers? What are the values if the ports are ordered left to right? Right to left?

6.8 Derive the formulas for the LDDI timers for a unidirectional tree network.

6.9 Write a program that calculates the LDDI timers for each port on an HSLN, given the appropriate inputs. Assume a propagation velocity of $0.9c$.

6.10 Assess token bus, CSMA/CD, and the LDDI scheme as MAC algorithms for the HSLN. Which is best suited to the nature and requirements of the HSLN?

6.11 Compare the various satellite reservation schemes to HAM when used on an HSLN. Is HAM superior to these other schemes, and why?

6.12 In the description of HAM, it was pointed out that to transmit in a bursty slot, a station needs only timing and synchronization information plus the location of the movable boundary. If a station transmits only in bursty slots, can the required information, and hence algorithm complexity, be reduced?

6.13 Suggest a bandwidth allocation scheme for HAM. Suggest a priority scheme.

APPENDIX 6A: X3T9.5 STANDARDS

Work on high-speed local network standards has been performed primarily within a subcommittee of the ANSI X3T9 technical committee on I/O interface standards. The X3T9 committee's work is aimed at developing I/O interface standards for four main areas:

- *Backplane bus:* internal computer bus connecting processors, memory, and I/O controllers.
- *Peripheral bus:* connects a single host (computer, storage director, file server) to one or more peripherals, where the peripheral includes the device (e.g., disk drive) and associated controller.
- *Device interface:* connects a "naked" device such as a floppy or rigid disk drive or a printer.
- *System bus:* connects computers, peripheral subsystems, terminal concentrators, gateways, and file servers as peers.

The system bus applies to HSLNs. Because of the expertise within X3T9 related to high-speed I/O, it was felt that this organization was better suited to developing HSLN standards than the 802 committee. A subcommittee of X3T9, called X3T9.5, has developed two HSLN standards, the Local Distributed Data Interface (LDDI) and the Fiber Distributed Data Interface (FDDI).

The LDDI standard specifies two layers, physical and link. Medium access functions are considered part of the physical layer. The data link layer specifies a simple connectionless service. At the physical layer two options are specified:

- Single-channel broadband coaxial cable bus operating at 50 Mbps, using phaseshift keying.

- Baseband coaxial cable passive star operating at 70 Mbps, using Manchester encoding.

The MAC algorithm differs for the two physical layer specifications but in both cases is a delay scheduling technique.

The FDDI standard specifies MAC and physical layers. It is assumed that the 802.2 Logical Link Control standard will be used as the data link layer. The physical layer specifies a 100-Mbps optical fiber ring, using 4B/5B coding, NRZI, and intensity modulation. The fiber specification is for a wavelength of 1300 mm and a maximum distance between repeaters of 2 km. The MAC algorithm is based on the 802.5 token ring specification. The main difference is in the technique for capacity allocation.

CHAPTER 7

Circuit-Switched Local Networks

Up until now, we have been looking at local networks that use packet switching. For many observers, this is the only kind of local network there is. But there is an alternative, based on the older circuit-switched approach. As we shall see, the differences in architecture and design issues are striking. We will also learn, perhaps to your surprise, that underneath, the similarities are equally striking.

The chapter begins by summarizing the characteristics of a star topology local network. Then we look at the digital switching concepts that underlie this type of network. Next we look at the devices most commonly used to build local networks (although these are rarely thought of as "true" local networks)—digital data switches. We are at last ready to look at the digital private branch exchange (PBX). Finally, the digital PBX and LAN are compared.

7.1

STAR TOPOLOGY NETWORKS

A star topology network, as described in Chapter 3, consists in essence of a collection of devices or stations attached to a central switching unit. Circuit switching is used; the central switch establishes a dedicated path between any two devices that wish to communicate.

Figure 7-1 depicts the major elements of a star topology network. The heart of a modern system is a digital switch. The advent of digital switching technology has dramatically improved the cost, performance, and capability of circuit-switched networks. Key to the operation of such systems are that (1) all signals are represented digitally, and (2) synchronous time-division multiplexing (TDM) techniques are used.

The network interface element represents the functions and hardware needed to connect digital devices, such as data processing devices and digital telephones, to the network. Analog telephones can also be attached if the network interface contains the logic for converting to digital signals. Trunks to external systems may also be attached. These may include analog voice trunks and digital TDM lines.

The control unit performs three general tasks. First, it establishes connections. This is generally done on demand, that is, at the request of an attached device. To establish the connection, the control unit must handle and acknowledge the request, determine if the intended destination is free, and construct a path through the switch. Second, the logic must maintain the connection. Since the digital switch uses time-division principles, this may require ongoing manipulation of the switching elements. However, the bits of the communication are transferred transparently. This is in contrast to the packet switching used on LANs and HSLNs, which are sensitive to the transmission protocol and can be considered content dependent. Third, the logic must tear down the connection, either in response to a request from one of the parties or for its own reasons.

Star networks may be either one-sided or two-sided. In a one-sided system, all attachment points are viewed the same: A connection can be

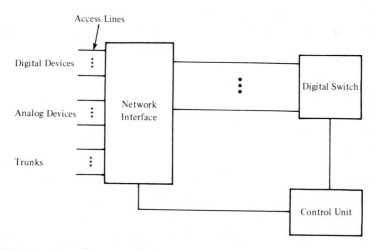

FIGURE 7-1.   Star Topology Elements

established between any two devices. In a two-sided system, attachment points are grouped into two classes and a connection can be established only between two devices from different classes. A typical application of the latter is the connection of a set of terminals to a set of computer ports; in many cases, only terminal-to-port connections are allowed.

An important characteristic of a star topology network is whether it is blocking or nonblocking. Blocking occurs when the network is unable to connect two stations because all possible paths between them are already in use. A blocking network is one in which such blocking is possible. Hence a nonblocking network permits all stations to be connected at once and grants all possible connection requests as long as the called party is free. When a network is supporting only voice traffic, a blocking configuration is generally acceptable, since it is expected that most phone calls are of short duration and that, therefore, only a fraction of the telephones will be engaged at any time. However, when data processing devices are involved, these assumptions may be invalid. For example, for a data entry application, a terminal may be continuously connected to a computer for hours at a time. [BHUS85] reports that typical voice connections on a PBX have a duration of 120 to 180 seconds, whereas data calls can have a range of from 8 seconds to 15 hours. Hence, for data applications, there is a requirement for a nonblocking or "nearly nonblocking" (very low probability of blocking) configuration.

7.2

DIGITAL SWITCHING CONCEPTS

The technology of switching has a long history, most of it covering an era when analog signal switching predominated. With the advent of PCM and related techniques, both voice and data can be transmitted via digital signals. This has led to a fundamental change in the design and technology of switching systems. Instead of dumb space-division systems, modern digital switching systems rely on intelligent control of space- and time-division elements.

This section looks at the concepts underlying contemporary digital switching (good discussions can be found in [SKAP79], [JOEL77], [JOEL79a], [JOEL79b], and [FLEM79]). We begin with a look at space-division switching, which was originally developed for the analog environment and has been carried over into digital technology. Then the various forms of time-division switching, which were developed specifically to be used in digital switches, are examined. Later sections discuss how these concepts are implemented in digital data switches and digital PBXs.

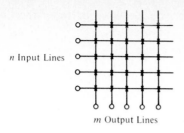

n Input Lines

m Output Lines

(a) Crossbar Matrix

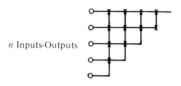

n Inputs-Outputs

(b) Triangular Switch

FIGURE 7-2.   Single-Stage Space-Division Switch

Space-Division Switching

The *space-division switch* is, as its name implies, one in which paths between pairs of devices are divided in space. Each connection requires the establishment of a physical path through the switch that is dedicated solely to the transfer of signals between the two end points. The basic building block of the switch is an electronic crosspoint or semiconductor gate [ABBO84] that can be enabled and disabled by a control unit.

Figure 7-2a shows a simple crossbar matrix with *n* inputs and *m* outputs. Interconnection is possible between any input line and any output line by engaging the appropriate crosspoint. The crossbar depicts a bilateral arrangement: there is a distinction between input and output. For example, input lines may connect to terminals, while output lines connect to computer ports. The crossbar switch is said to perform concentration, distribution, or expansion according as $n>m$, $n = m$, or $n<m$.

The crossbar matrix makes a distinction between input and output: Any input can connect to any output. It requires $n \times m$ crosspoints. However, if the inputs and outputs are the same, then $n = m$ and the requirement is that any end point can connect to any other end point. This requires only a triangular array of $n(n - 1)/2$ crosspoints (Figure 7-2b) and is referred to as a "folded" configuration.

The crossbar switch has a number of limitations or disadvantages:

- The number of crosspoints grows with n^2. This is costly for large *n*, and results in high capacitive loading on any message path.

- The loss of a crosspoint prevents connection between the two devices involved.
- The crosspoints are inefficiently utilized.

To overcome these limitations, multiple stage switches are employed. The N input lines (inlets) are broken up into N/n groups of n lines. Each group of lines goes into a first-stage matrix. The outputs of the first stage matrices become inputs to a group of second-stage matrices, and so on. Figure 7-3 depicts a 3-stage network of switches that is symmetric; that is the number of inlets to the first stage equals the number of outlets from the last stage. There are k second-stage matrices, each with N/n inlets and N/n outlets. Each first-stage matrix has k outlets so that it connects to all second-stage matrices. Each second-stage matrix has N/n outlets so that it connects to all third-stage matrices.

This type of arrangement has several advantages over the simple crossbar switch:

- The number of crosspoints is reduced (see below), increasing crossbar utilization.
- There is more than one path through the network to connect two endpoints, increasing reliability.

Of course, a multistage network requires a more complex control scheme. To establish a path in a single-stage network, it is only necessary

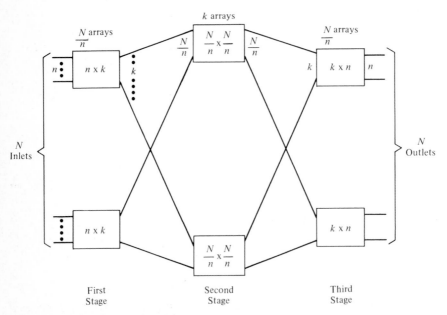

FIGURE 7-3. Three-Stage Space-Division Switch

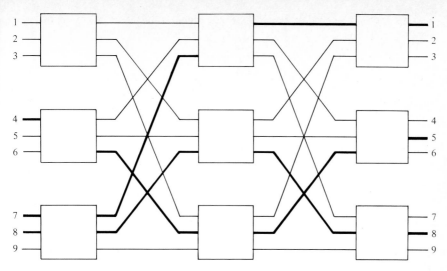

FIGURE 7-4. Example of Blocking in a Three-Stage Switch

to open a single gate. In a multistage network, a free path through the stages must be determined and the appropriate gates enabled.

A consideration with a multistage space-division switch is that it may be blocking. It should be clear from Figure 7-2 that a crossbar matrix is nonblocking; that is, a path is always available to connect an input to an output. That this is not always the case with a multiple-stage switch can be seen in Figure 7-4. The figure shows a three stage switch with $N = 9$, $n = 3$, and $k = 3$. The heavier lines indicate lines that are already in use. In this state, input line 9 cannot be connected to either output line 4 or 6, even though both of these output lines are available.

It should be clear that by increasing the value of k (the number of outlets from each first-stage switch and the number of second stage switches), the probability of blocking is reduced. What value of k is required for a nonblocking three-stage switch? The answer is depicted in Figure 7-5. Consider that we wish to establish a path from input line a to output line b. The worst case situation for blocking occurs if all of the remaining $n - 1$ input lines and $n - 1$ output lines are busy and are connected to different center-stage switches. Thus a total of $(n - 1) + (n - 1) = 2n - 2$ center switches are unavailable for creating a path from a to b. However, if one more center-stage switch exists, the appropriate links must be available for the connection. Thus, a three-stage network will be nonblocking if

$$k = 2n - 1 \tag{7.1}$$

We now return to our claim that a multiple-stage switch requires fewer crosspoints than a single-stage switch. From Figure 7-3, the total number of

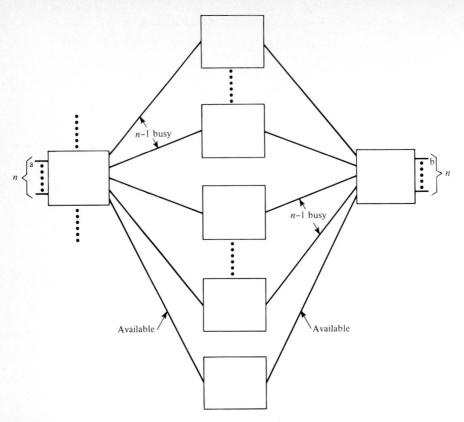

FIGURE 7-5. Nonblocking Three-Stage Switch

crosspoints N_x in a three-stage switch is

$$N_x = 2Nk + k\left(\frac{N}{n}\right)^2 \tag{7.2}$$

Substituting Equation (7-1) into (7-2),

$$N_x = 2N(2n - 1) + (2n - 1)\left(\frac{N}{n}\right)^2 \tag{7.3}$$

for a nonblocking switch. The actual value as a function of N depends on the number of arrays (N/n) in the first and third stages. To optimize, differentiate N_x with respect to n and set the result to 0. For large N, the result converges to $n = (N/2)^{1/2}$. Substituting into (7-3),

$$N_x = 4N(\sqrt{2N} - 1) \tag{7.4}$$

Table 7.1 compares this value with the number of crosspoints in a single-stage switch. As can be seen, there is a savings, which grows with the number of lines.

TABLE 7.1 Number of Crosspoints in a Nonblocking Switch

Number of Lines	Number of Crosspoints for Three-Stage Switch	Number of Crosspoints for Single-Stage Switch
128	7,680	16,384
512	63,488	262,144
3,048	516,096	4.2×10^6
8,192	4.2×10^6	6.7×10^7
32,768	3.3×10^7	1×10^9
131,072	2.6×10^8	1.7×10^{10}

A further discussion of this topic can be found in [JASJ83] and [JORD85].

Time-Division Switching

In contrast to space-division switching, in which dedicated paths are used, *time-division switching* involves the partitioning of a lower-speed data stream into pieces that share a higher-speed data stream with other data pieces. The individual pieces or slots are manipulated by the control logic to route data from input to output. Three concepts comprise the technique of time-division switching:

- TDM bus switching
- Time-slot interchange (TSI)
- Time-multiplex switching (TMS)

TDM Bus Switching

As discussed in Chapter 2, TDM is a technique that allows multiple signals to share a single transmission line by separating them in time. In this chapter we are concerned primarily with synchronous TDM, that is, a situation in which time slots are preassigned so that few or no overhead bits are required.

As shown in Figure 7-6a, synchronous TDM was designed to permit multiple low-speed streams to share a high-speed line. This permits multiple channels of data to be handled efficiently both within and outside switching systems. A set of inputs is sampled in turn. The samples are organized serially into slots (channels) to form a recurring frame of n slots. A slot may be a bit, a byte, or some longer block. An important point to note is that with synchronous TDM, the source and destination of the data

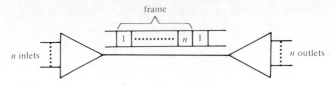

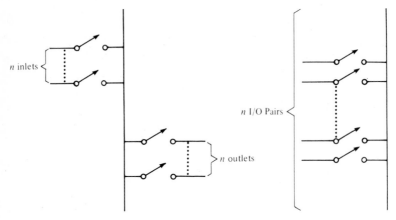

(a) Synchronous Time Division Multiplexing

(b) A Simple Time-Division Switch

(c) A Simple Folded Time-Division Switch

FIGURE 7-6. **TDM Bus Switching**

in each time slot are known. Hence there is no need for address bits in each slot.

The mechanism for synchronous TDM may be quite simple. For example, each input line deposits data in a buffer; the multiplexer scans these buffers sequentially, taking fixed size chunks of data from each buffer and sending it out on the line. One complete scan produces one frame of data. For output to the lines, the reverse operation is performed, with the multiplexer filling the output line buffers one by one.

The I/O lines attached to the multiplexer may be synchronous or asynchronous; the multiplexed line between the two multiplexers is synchronous and must have a data rate equal to the sum of the data rates of the attached lines. Actually, the multiplexed line must have a slightly higher data rate, since each frame will include some overhead bits—headers and trailers—for synchronization.

The time slots in a frame assigned to the I/O lines on a fixed, predetermined basis. If a device has no data to send, the multiplexer must send empty slots. Thus the actual data transfer rate may be less than the capacity of the system.

Figure 7-6b shows a simple way in which TDM can be used to achieve switching. A set of buffered input and output lines are connected through controlled gates to a high-speed digital bus. Each input line is assigned a

CIRCUIT-SWITCHED LOCAL NETWORKS

time slot. During that time, the line's gate is enabled, allowing a small burst of data onto the bus. For that same time slot, one of the output line gates is also enabled. Since the enabling and disabling of gates is controlled, the sequence of input and output line activations need not be in the same order. Hence a form of switching is possible. Curiously, this technique has no commonly-used name; we shall refer to it as TDM bus switching.

Of course, such a scheme need not be two-sided. As shown in Figure 7-6c, a "folded" switch can be devised by attaching n I/O pairs to the bus. Any attached device achieves full duplex operation by transmitting during one assigned time slot and receiving during another. The other end of the connection is an I/O pair for which these time slots have the opposite meanings.

The TDM bus switch has an advantage over a crossbar switch in terms of efficient use of gates. For n devices, the TDM bus switch requires $2n$ gates or switchpoints, whereas the most efficient multistage crossbar network requires on the order of $n\sqrt{n}$ switchpoints.

Let us look at the timing involved a bit more closely. First, consider a nonblocking implementation of Figure 7-6c. There must be n repetitively occurring time slots, each one assigned to an input and an output line. We will refer to one iteration for all time slots as a frame. The input assignment may be fixed; the output assignments vary to allow various connections. When a time slot begins, the designated input line may insert a burst of data onto the line, where it will propagate to both ends past all other lines. The designated output line will, during that time, copy the data if any as they go by. The time slot, then, must equal the transmission time of the input line plus the propagation delay between input and output lines. In order to keep the successive time slots uniform, time slot length should be defined as transmission time plus the end-to-end bus propagation delay. For efficiency, the propagation delay should be much less than the transmission time. Note that only one time slot or burst of data may be on the bus at a time.

To keep up with the input lines, the slots must recur sufficiently frequently. For example, consider a system connecting full-duplex lines at 19.2 kbps. Input data on each line are buffered at the gate. The buffer must be cleared, by enabling the gate, fast enough to avoid overrun. So if there are 100 lines, the capacity of the bus must be at least 1.92 Mbps. Actually, it must be higher than that to account for the wasted time due to propagation delay.

These considerations determine the traffic-carrying capacity of a blocking switch as well. For a blocking switch, there is no fixed assignment of input lines to time slots; they are allocated on demand. The data rate on the bus dictates how many connections can be made at a time. For a system with 200 devices at 19.2 kbps and a bus at 2 Mbps, about half of the devices can be connected at any one time.

The TDM bus switching scheme can accommodate lines of varying data rates. For example, if a 9600 bps line gets one slot per frame, a 19.2-kbps line would get two slots per frame. Of course, only lines of the same data rate can be connected.

Figure 7-7 is an example that suggests how the control for a TDM bus switch could be implemented. Let us assume that propagation time on the bus is zero. Time on the bus is organized into 30-μs frames of 6 5-μs slots each. A control memory indicates which gates are to be enabled during each time slot. In this example, 6 words of memory are needed. A controller cycles through the memory at a rate of one cycle every 30 μs. During the first time slot of each cycle, the input gate from device 1 and the output gate to device 3 are enabled, allowing data to pass from device 1 to device 3 over the bus. The remaining words are accessed in succeeding time slots and treated accordingly. As long as the control memory contains the contents depicted in Figure 7-7, connections are maintained between 1 and 3, 2 and 5, and 4 and 6.

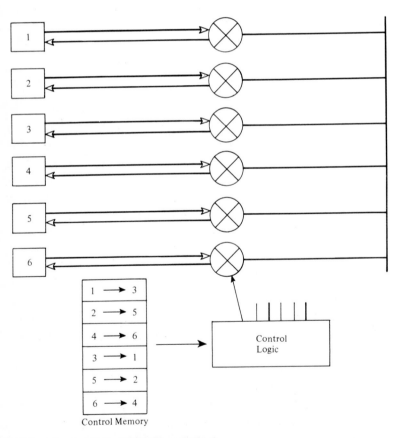

FIGURE 7-7. Control of a TDM Bus Switch

Several questions may occur to you. For one, is this circuit switching? Circuit switching, recall, was defined as a technique in which a dedicated communications path is established between devices. This is indeed the case for Figure 7-6. To establish a connection between an input and output line, the controller dedicates a certain number of time slots per frame to that connection. The appropriate input and output gates are enabled during those time slots to allow data to pass. Although the bus is shared by other connections, it is nevertheless used to create a dedicated path between input and output. Another question: Is this synchronous TDM? Synchronous TDM is generally associated with creating permanent dedicated time slots for each input line. The scheme depicted in Figure 7-6 can assume a dynamic character, with the controller allocating available time slots among connections. Nevertheless, at steady state—a period when no connections are made or broken—a fixed number of slots is dedicated per channel and the system behaves as a synchronous time-division multiplexer.

The control logic for the system described above requires the enabling of two gates to achieve a connection. This logic can be simplified if the input burst into a time slot contains destination address information. All output devices can then always connect to the bus and copy the data from time slots with their address. This scheme blurs the distinction between circuit switching and packet switching.

This point bears further comment. In the bus reservation schemes described in Chapter 6 a device with a quantity of data to send reserves sufficient future slots to handle that data. After the data are sent, the reservation goes away until the station again wants to send. In the TDM bus switching scheme, a station reserves one or more time slots per frame for the indefinite future by requesting a connection. The reservation lasts until a disconnect is requested. The logic of the two schemes is very close.

Another point: The LAN/HSLN bus and the TDM bus switch differ only in geometry, not topology. The LAN or HSLN bus involves a relatively long bus with stations attached via relatively short lines. The "star topology" of the TDM bus switch actually involves a relatively short bus with stations attached via relatively long lines. This difference is crucial, of course: The timings on the shorter bus are amenable to greater control because of the much shorter propagation delay. Also, as we shall see, not all digital switch architectures use a pure TDM bus switch. Nevertheless, the implication of the preceding discussion is valid: The differences between the technologies and architectures of the various types of networks discussed in this book are less than one might think.

Time-Slot Interchange

The basic building block of many time-division switches is the *time-slot interchange* (TSI) mechanism. A TSI unit operates on a synchronous TDM

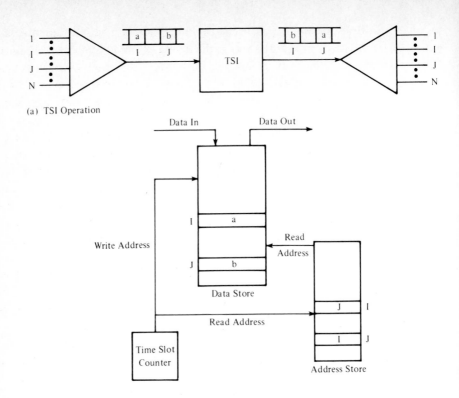

(a) TSI Operation

(b) TSI Mechanism

FIGURE 7-8.   Time-Slot Interchange (TSI)

stream of time slots, or channels, by interchanging pairs of slots to achieve full duplex operation. Figure 7-8a shows how the input line of device I is connected to the output line of device J, and vice versa.

We should note several points. The input lines of N devices are passed through a synchronous multiplexer to produce a TDM stream with N slots. To achieve interconnection, the slots corresponding to two inputs are interchanged. This results in a full-duplex connection between two lines. To allow the interchange of any two slots, the incoming data in a slot must be stored until they can be sent out on the right channel in the next frame cycle. Hence the TSI introduces a delay and produces output slots in the desired order. These are then demultiplexed and routed to the appropriate output line. Since each channel is provided a time slot in the frame, whether or not it transmits data, the size of the TSI unit must be chosen for the capacity of the TDM line, not the actual data transfer rate.

Figure 7-8b depicts a mechanism for TSI. Individual lines are multiplexed and demultiplexed. These functions can be integrated as part of the switch itself, or they may be implemented remotely, as a device clustering mechanism. A random-access data store whose width equals one time slot of data and whose length equals the number of slots in a frame is used. An incoming TDM frame is written sequentially, slot by slot, into the data store. An outgoing TDM frame is created by reading slots from the memory in an order dictated by an address store that reflects the existing connections. In the figure, the data in channels I and J are interchanged, creating a full-duplex connection between the corresponding stations.

TSI is a simple, effective way to switching TDM data. However, the size of such a switch, in terms of number of connections, is limited by the memory access speed. It is clear that, in order to keep pace with the input, data must be read into and out of memory as fast as they arrive. So, for example, if we have 24 sources operating at 64 kbps each, and a slot size of 8 bits, we would have an arrival rate of 192,000 slots per second (this is the structure of the PCM T1 carrier). Memory access time would need to be 1/192,000, or about 5 μs.

Let us look more closely at the operation of the data store; in particular, we need to view it as a function of time. As an example [DAV173], consider a system with eight input/output lines, in which the following connections exist: 1–2, 3–7 and 5–8. The other two stations are not in use. Figure 7-9 depicts the contents of the data store over the course of one frame (eight slots). During the first time slot, data are stored in location 1 and read from location 2. During the second time slot, data are stored in location 2 and read from location 1. And so on.

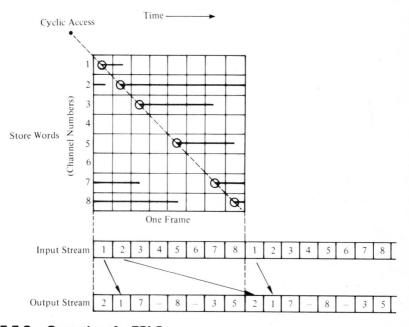

FIGURE 7-9. Operation of a TSI Store

As can be seen, the write accesses to the data store and cyclic, that is, accessing successive locations in sequential order, whereas the read accesses are acyclic, requiring the use of an address store. The figure also depicts two frames of the input and output sequences and indicates the transfer of data between channels 1 and 2. Note that in half the cases, data slots move into the next frame.

As with the TDM bus swittch, the TSI unit can handle inputs of varying data rates. Figure 7-10 suggests a way in which this may be done. Instead of presenting the input lines to a synchronous multiplexer, they are presented to a selector device. This device will select an input line based on a channel assignment provided from a store controlled by the time slot counter. Hence, instead of sampling equally from each input, it may gather more slots from some channels than others.

Time-Multiplexed Switching

As we have seen, a TSI unit can support only a limited number of connections. Further, as the size of the unit grows, for a fixed access speed, the delay at the TSI grows. To overcome both of these problems, multiple TSI units are used. Now, to connect two channels entering a single TSI unit, their time slots can be interchanged. However, to connect a channel

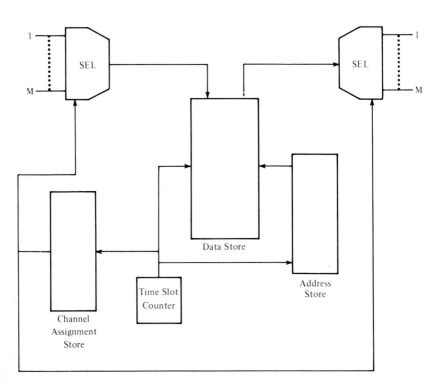

FIGURE 7-10. TSI Operation with Variable-Rate Input

on one TDM stream (going into one TSI) to a channel on another TDM stream (going into another TSI), some form of space division multiplexing is needed. Naturally, we do not wish to switch all of the time slots from one stream to another; we would like to do it one slot at a time. This technique is known as *time-multiplexed switching* (TMS).

Multiple-stage networks can be built up by concatenating TMS and TSI stages: TMS stages, which move slots from one stream to another, are referred to as S, and TSI stages are referred to as T. Systems are generally described by an enumeration of their stages from input to output, using the symbols T and S. Figure 7-11 is an example of a 2-stage TS network. Such a network is blocking. For example, if one channel in input stream 1 is to be switched to the third channel in output stream 1, and another channel in input stream 1 is to be switched to the third channel in output stream 2, one of the connections is blocked.

To avoid blocking, three or more stages are used. Some of the more common structures used in commercially available systems are [SKAP79]:

- TST
- TSSST
- STS
- SSTSS
- TSTST

The requirements on the TMS unit are stringent. The unit must provide space-division connections between its input and output lines, and these

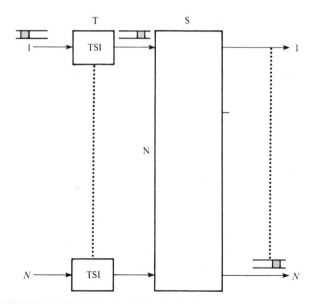

FIGURE 7-11. Two-Stage Digital Switch

connections must be reconfigured for each time slot. This requires, in effect, a control store whose width is sufficient to handle the number of ingoing and outgoing lines and whose length equals the number of time slots in a frame.

One means of implementing the TMS stage is the crossbar switch discussed earlier. This requires that the crosspoints be manipulated at each time slot. More commonly, the TMS stage is implemented by dignital selectors (SEL) which select only one input at a time on a time slot basis. These SEL devices are the same as those described in the preceding section, except that here each of their inputs is a TDM stream rather than a single line. Figure 7-12 shows STS and TST networks implemented with the SEL units.

In an STS network, the path between an incoming and outgoing channel has multiple possible physical routes equal to the number of TSI units. For

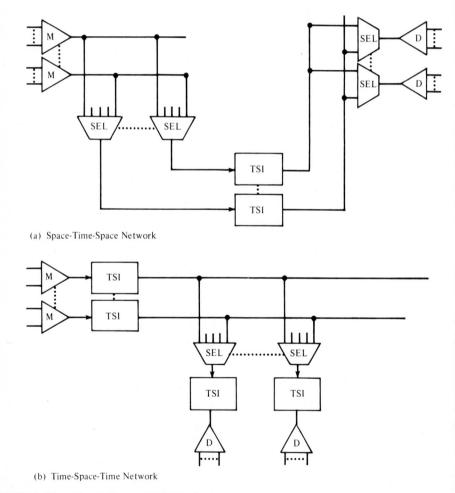

(a) Space-Time-Space Network

(b) Time-Space-Time Network

FIGURE 7-12. Three-Stage TDM Switches

a fully nonblocking network, the number of TSI units must be double the number of incoming and outgoing TDM streams. On the other hand, the multiple routes between two channels in a TST network are all in the time domain; there is only one physical path possible. Here, too, blocking is a possibility. One way to avoid blocking is by expanding the number of time slots in the space stage. In all multistage networks, a path-search algorithm is needed to determine the route from input to output.

It is interesting to compare the TDM bus switch with TSI and TMS. It does not exactly fit into either category. Compare it to a space switch. The TDM bus switch does connect any input with any output, as in a crossbar or SEL switch. The space switch operates simultaneously on all inputs, whereas the TDM bus switch operates on the inputs sequentially. However, because the frame time on the bus is less than the slot time of any input, the switching is effectively simultaneous. On the other hand, a comparison of Figures 7-8 and 7-6b reveals the similarity between TSI and TDM bus switching.

7.3

DIGITAL DATA SWITCHING DEVICES

The techniques discussed in the preceding section have been used to build a variety of digital switching products designed for data-only applications. These devices do not provide telephone service and are generally cheaper than a digital PBX for comparable capacity.

The variety of devices is wide and the distinction between types is blurred. For convenience, we categorize them as follows:

- Terminal/port-oriented switch
- Data switch

In what follows we will look at the functions performed by each type of device, and suggest an architecture that supports those functions. Keep in mind that usually any of the techniques in Section 7.2, or any combination, may be used to implement any of these switches. The discussion here is intended only to give examples.

Before turning to the specific device types, let us look at the requirements for data switching.

Data Switching Requirements

For any circuit-switching system used to connect digital data transmitting devices, certain generic requirements can be defined. These requirements apply both to pure digital data switching devices and to digital PBX systems. We begin first by looking briefly at the data transmission techniques that must be supported by a data switch, and then look at the functions to be performed.

The devices attached to a data switch will use either asynchronous or synchronous transmission. Asynchronous transmission, recall, is character-at-a-time. Each character consists of a start bit, 5 to 8 data bits, a parity bit, and a stop signal, which may be 1, 1.5, or 2 bit times in length. Logic is available which can automatically determine character length, parity, and even bit rate. Hence it is a relatively easy matter for a data switch to handle asynchronous transmission. On input, data are accumulated a character at a time, and transmitted internally using synchronous transmission. At the other end of the connection, they are buffered and transmitted a character at a time to the output line. This applies to any switch using time-division switching techniques. Of course, a pure space-division switch need not concern itself with such matters; a dedicated physical path is set up and bits are transmitted transparently.

Synchronous transmission represents a greater challenge. Synchronous communication requires either a separate clock lead from the transmission point to the reception point or the use of a self-clocking encoding scheme, such as Manchester. The latter technique is typical. With synchronous communication, the data rate must be known ahead of time, as well as the synchronization pattern (bits or characters used to signal the beginning of a frame). Thus there can be no universal synchronous interface.

Of course, for either synchronous or asynchronous transmission, full duplex operation is required. Typically, this requires two twisted pairs (known as a *twin pair*) between a device and the switch, one for transmission in each direction. This is in contrast to the case with analog signaling where a single twisted-pair suffices (see Figure 2.4). Recently, however, some vendors have begun to offer full-duplex digital signaling on a single twisted pair, using a *ping-pong protocol*. In essence, data are buffered at each end and sent across the line at double the data rate, with the two ends taking turn. So, for example, two devices may communicate, full duplex, at 56 kbps if they are attached to a 112-kbps line and the line drivers at each end buffer the device data and transmit, alternately, at 112 kbps. In fact, a somewhat higher data rate is required to account for propagation delay and control signals.

We turn now to the functions to be provided by a data switch. The most basic, of course, is the making of a connection between two attached lines. These connections can be pre-configured by a system operator, but more dynamic operation is often desired. This leads to two additional functions: port contention and port selection. *Port contention* is a function that allows a certain number of designated ports to contend or access to a smaller number of ports. Typically , this is used for terminal to host connection to allow a smaller number of host ports to service a larger number of terminal ports. When a terminal user attempts to connect, the system will scan through all the host ports in the contention group. If any of the ports is available, a connection is made.

Port selection is an interactive capability. It allows a user (or an application program in a host) to select a port for connection. This is analogous to dialing a number in a phone system. Port selection and port contention can be combined by allowing the selection, by name or number, of a contention group. Port selection devices are becoming increasingly common. A switch without this capability only allows connections that are preconfigured by a system operator. If one knows in advance what interconnections are required, fine. Otherwise, the flexibility of port selection is usually worth the additional cost.

An interactive capability carries with it an additional responsibility: the control unit of the switch must be able to talk to the requesting port. This can be done in two ways. In some cases, the manufacturer supplies a simple keypad device that attaches to and shares the terminal's line. The user first uses the keypad to dial a connection; once the connection is made, communication is via the terminal. As an alternative, the connection sequence can be effected through the terminal itself. A simple command language dialogue is used. However, this technique requires that the system understand the code and protocol being used by the terminal. Consequently, this feature is generally limited to asynchronous ASCII devices.

Terminal/Port-Oriented Switches

The devices discussed in this section were designed to address a specific problem: the connection of interactive terminals to computer ports. In many computer sites with one or more time-sharing systems and a population (usually growing) of terminals, means must be found for interconnection.

One means of connection is simply to assign each terminal to a specific computer port, even when not active. This is expensive in terms of computer ports, since generally only a fraction of the terminals are logged on. Further, the user cannot change to a different computer without making cable changes. Another approach is to use multiple dial-up telephone rotaries, for each computer and each transmission speed. The rotary allows a user to call a single number and gain access to one of several autoanswer modems; if all modems are busy, the rotary returns a busy signal. The approach ties up telephones lines for extended periods and requires the use of modems.

One early solution that avoids some of the expenses mentioned above was the patch panel. This device enabled manual connection of two lines and could also provide some system monitoring and diagnostics. The addition of intelligence to this type of device to eliminate the manual

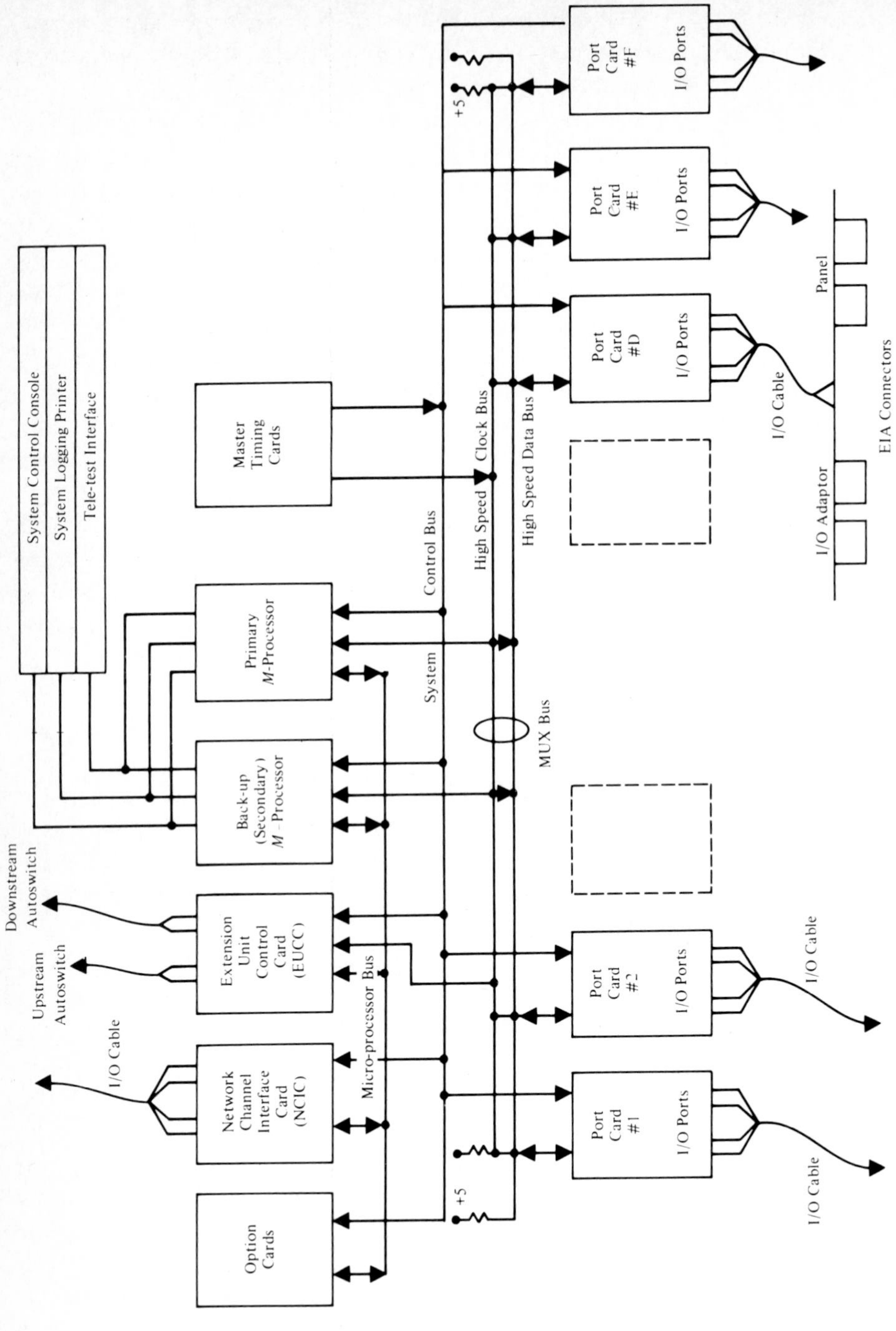

FIGURE 7-13. Example of a Port Contention System (From [BYTE85])

CIRCUIT-SWITCHED LOCAL NETWORKS

connection function has resulted in a variety of intelligent terminal/port-oriented switches. A variety of names are used, depending partly on function, including intelligent path panel, port selector, and port contention device.

At a minimum, these devices permit a set of connections to be set up and periodically updated by a system operator. Port selection and port contention functions are also provided on many products.

Figure 7-13 is an example of a noninteractive (without port selection) system. The system allows connection of one I/O port to any other I/O port on the same or a different port card. Connections are set up at system intialization time and may be changed dynamically by the system operator (not the user). The means of establishing connections is simple. Each port has associated with it a destination address register. To connect two ports, the address of each is placed in the other. To transmit data, the sending device puts its data (8 bits) and the destination address (8 bits) on the bus. All devices continually monitor the bus for their own address. The switch is nonblocking, allowing the preassignment of time slots to transmitting devices. Receiving devices need not know the time slot for reception since

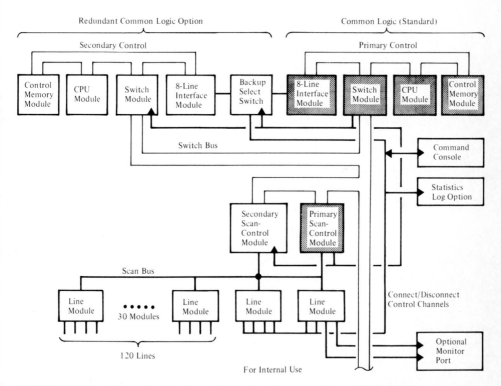

FIGURE 7-14.   Example of a Port Selection System (From [VONA80])

they are looking for an address. Thus, at the cost of 100% overhead, the control logic is greatly simplified.

Figure 7-14 is an example of a port selection system. A collection of line modules are scanned to produce a TDM stream which is passed over a bus to a switch module. The output of the switch module is a switched set of time slots that are directed to the proper port. Note the redundant architecture for reliability.

Data Switches

There is little additional that need be said about these devices. No distinction is made between terminal lines and ports. The switch simply has a set of I/O lines and is capable of establishing connections between lines. Any or a combination of the digital switching techniques described in Section 7.2 may be used. Some or all of the functions described in this section may be provided.

7.4

THE DIGITAL PRIVATE BRANCH EXCHANGE

Evolution of the Digital PBX

The digital PBX is a marriage of two technologies: digital switching and telephone exchange systems. The forerunner of the digital PBX is the *private branch exchange* (PBX). A PBX is an on-premise facility, owned or leased by an organization, which interconnects the telephones within the facility and provides access to the public telephone system. Typically, a telephone user on the premises dials a three or four digit number to call another telephone on the premises, and dials one digit (usually 8 or 9) to get a dial tone for an "outside line," which allows the caller to dial a number in the same fashion as a residential user.

The original private exchanges were manual, with one or more operators at a switchboard required to make all connections. Back in the 1920s, these began to be replaced by automatic systems, called *private automatic branch exchanges* (PABX), which did not require attendant intervention to place a call. These "first-generation" systems used electromechanical technology and analog signaling. Data connections could be made via modems. That is, a user with a terminal, a telephone, and a modem or acoustic coupler in the office could dial up an on-site or remote number that reached another modem and exchange data.

The "second-generation" PBXs were introduced in the middle 1970s. These systems use electronic rather than electromagnetic technology and the internal switching is digital. Such a system is referred to as a digital

PBX, or *computerized branch exchange* (CBX). These systems were designed primarily to handle analog voice traffic, with the codec function built into the switch so that digital switching could be used internally. The systems were also capable of handling digital data connections without the need of a modem.

The "third-generation" systems are touted as "integrated voice/data" systems, although the differences between third generation and upgraded second generaton are rather blurred. Perhaps a better term is "improved digital PBX." Some of the characteristics of these systems that differ from those of earlier systems include:

- *The use of digital phone:* This permits integrated voice/data workstations.
- *Distributed architecture:* Multiple switches in a hierarchical or meshed configuration with distributed intelligence provides enhanced reliability.
- *Nonblocking configuration:* Typically, dedicated port assignments are used for all attached phones and devices.

As new features and technologies are employed, incremental improvements make difficult the continuing classification of PBXs into generations. Nevertheless, it is worth noting recent advances in PBX products that, together, might be considered to constitute a fourth generation [JEWE85, COOV85]:

- *Integrated LAN link:* This capability provides a direct high-speed link to a LAN. This allows an optimum distribution of lower-speed devices (terminals) on the PBX and higher-speed devices (computers) on the LAN in a fashion that is fully transparent to the user.
- *Dynamic bandwidth allocation:* Typically, a PBX offers one or only a small number of different data rate services. The increased sophistication of capacity allocation within the PBX allows it to offer virtually any data rate to an attached device. This allows the system to grow as user requirements grow. For example, full-motion color video at 448 kbps or advanced voice codecs at 32 kbps could be accommodated.
- *Integrated Packet channel:* This allows the PBX to provide access to an X.25 packet-switched network.

It is worthwhile to summarize the main reasons why the evolution described above has taken place. To the untrained eye, analog and digital PBXs would seem to offer about the same level of convenience. The analog PBX can handle telephone sets directly and uses modems to accommodate digital data devices; the digital PBX can handle digital data devices directly and uses codecs to accommodate telephone sets. Some of the advantages of the digital approach are

- *Digital technology:* By handling all internal signals digitally, the digital PBX can take advantage of low-cost LSI and VLSI components. Digital technology also lends itself more readily to software and firmwave control.

- *Time-division multiplexing:* Digital signals lend themselves readily to TDM techniques, which provide efficient use of internal data paths, access to public TDM carriers, and TDM switching techniques, which are more cost effective than older, cross bar techniques.
- *Digital control signals:* Control signals are inherently digital and can easily be integrated into a digital transmission path via TDM. The signaling equipment is independent of the transmission medium.
- *Encryption:* This is more easily accommodated with digital signals.

Telephone Call Processing Requirements

The characteristic that distinguishes the digital PBX from a digital data switch is its ability to handle telephone connections. Free man [FREE80] lists eight functions required for telephone call processing:

- Interconnection
- Control
- Attending
- Busy testing
- Alerting
- Information receiving
- Information transmitting
- Supervisory

The interconnection function encompasses three contingencies. The first contingency is a call originated by a station bound for another station on the digital PBX. The switching technologies that we have discussed are used in this context. The second contingency is a call originated by a digital PBX station bound for an external recipient. For this, the PBX must not only have access to an external trunk, but must perform internal switching to route the call from the user station to the trunk interface. The PBX also performs a line to trunk concentration function to avoid the expense of one external line per station. The third contingency is a call originated externally bound for a PBX station. Referred to as *direct inward dialing*, this allows an external caller to use the unique phone number of a PBX station to establish a call without going through an operator. This requires trunk to line expansion plus internal switching.

The control function includes, of course, the logic for setting up and tearing down a connection path. In addition, the control function serves to activate and control all other functions and to provide various management and utility services, such as logging, accounting, and configuration control.

The PBX must recognize a request for a connection; this is the attending function. The PBX then determines if the called party is available (busy testing) and, if so, alerts that party (alerting). The process of setting up the connection involves an exchange of information between the PBX and the called and calling parties. Note how dramatically this differs from the distributed packet-switching approach of LANs and HSLNs.

Finally, a supervisory function is needed to determine when a call is completed and the connnection may be released, freeing the switching capacity and the two parties for future connections.

Let us look more closely at the sequence of events required to success-fully complete a call. First, consider an internal call from extension 226 to extension 280. The following steps occur:

1. 226 goes off-hook (picks up the receiver). The control unit recognizes this condition.
2. The control unit finds an available digit receiver and sets up a circuit from 226 to the digit receiver. The control unit also sets up a circuit from a dialtone generator to 226.
3. When the first digit is dialed, the dial-tone connection is released. The digit receiver accumulates dialed digits.
4. After the last digit is dialed, the connection to the digit receiver is released. The control unit examines the number for legitimacy. If it is not valid, the caller is informed by some means, such as connection to a rapid busy signal generator. Otherwise, the control unit then deter-mines if 280 is busy. If so, 226 is connected to a busy-signal generator.
5. If 280 is free, the control unit sets up a connection between 226 and a ring-back-tone generator and a connection between 280 and a ringer.
6. When 280 answers by going off-hook, the ringing and ring-back connec-tions are dropped and a connection is set up between 226 and 280.
7. When either 280 or 226 goes on-hook, the connection between them is dropped.

For outgoing calls, the following steps are required.

1–3. As above. In this case the caller will be dialing an access code number (e.g., the single digit 9) to request access to an outgoing trunk.
4. The control unit releases the connection to the digit receiver and finds a free trunk group and sends out an off-hook signal.
5. When a dial tone is returned from the central office, the control unit repeats steps 2 and 3.
6. The control unit releases the connection to the digit receiver and sends the number out to the trunk and makes a connection from the caller to the trunk.
7. When either the caller or the trunk signals on-hook, the connection between them is dropped.

There are variations on the foregoing sequence. For example, if the PBX performs least-cost routing, it will wait until the number is dialed and then select the appropriate trunk.

Finally, incoming calls, when direct inward dialing is supported, proceed as follows.

1. The control unit detects a trunk seizure signal from the central office and sends a start-dialing signal out on that trunk. It also sets up a path from the trunk to a digit receiver.
2. After the last digit is received, the control unit releases the path, examines the dialed number, and checks the called station for busy, in which case a busy signal is returned.
3. If the called number is free, the control unit sets up a ringing connection to the called number and a ring-back connection to the trunk. It monitors the called station for answer and the trunk for abandon.
4. When the called station goes off-hook, the ringing and ring-back connections are dropped and a connection is set up between the trunk and the called station.
5. When either the trunk or called station signals on-hook, the connection between them is dropped.

As you can see, the requirements for setting up a telephone connection are more complex than those for a data connection.

Advanced Services

The digital PBX is very application oriented. That is, a considerable portion of the design and development effort is spent fitting the product directly to the application.

In a digital PBX, a distinction is made between advanced services that are possible with digital control and the "plain old telephone services" (POTS) of an older PBX; the call processing functions just described are examples of the latter. Table 7-2 lists advanced services that are typically found in digital PBX products.

Data Switching Requirements

The data switching requirements for a digital PBX are the same as those for a digital data switch. Typically, a terminal user will be requesting connection to a computer port. The same issues of speed, asynchronous/synchronous, and calling technique arise.

There are several new wrinkles. The PBX may support a voice/data workstation with one twisted pair for the phone and two pairs for the terminal. In such arrangements, the destination port may be selected from the phone rather than the terminal or a keypad.

TABLE 7.2 Typical PBX Features

Automatic Call Distribution
    A call to one number is spread among a group of telephones. When a call comes in, it is routed to the next available phone in rotary fashion.

Automatic Callback
    When the caller rings a busy number, the caller is alerted and may hang up. The system will monitor the called number until it is free; it may also alert the called party with a beep on the line. When the called number is free, the system rings the caller and re-places the call. The same service can be provided for gaining access to a special outside line, such as a WATS circuit.

Call Detail Recording
    The details of telephone traffic are measured and recorded, including a history of numbers called and call duration from each phone. The record includes both internal calls and external calls plus the related charges.

Call Forwarding
    Permits a station to be set so that incoming calls are automatically referred to another telephone: (1) when the station subscriber expects to be away and/or (2) when the subscriber is using the telephone line.

Call Intercept
    When a busy number is called, the call is intercepted by a message center or operator.

Call Notification
    Enables the PBX to notify a user already engaged in a call of an incoming call. The user then has the choice of accepting, rejecting, or ignoring the waiting call. Some systems permit "executive override," permitting a calling party literally to interrupt an ongoing conversation.

Call Pickup
    This feature is useful in an office with many phones. If another phone in the room rings and there is no one to pick it up, a subscriber at a nearby phone can dial a code that transfers the call to that subscriber.

Call Transfer
    When two subscribers are connected, one may transfer the call to a third party and leave the connection. This service is different from the call forward service since, in this case, the call to be transferred must have an established end-to-end connection prior to the transfer.

Conference Call
    Permits the addition of extensions to a two-party call.

Direct Inward Dialing
    Enables an outside call to be placed directly to a PBX user without attendant intervention.

Direct Outward Dialing
    A subscriber can dial a call on the public network without assistance from an operator.

Don't Disturb
    Allows a station user to instruct the PBX not to ring through a call to the telephone.

TABLE 7.2 (*continued*)

External Number Repetition
Similar to automatic callback but to an external number. The system will repeatedly call a busy external number until the number is free and begins ringing. At that point the system rings the caller.

Outgoing Call Restriction
Certain extensions are prevented from making certain categories of calls (e.g., any outgoing call, any outgoing long-distance call).

Route Optimization
When more than one option exists for outside calls (e.g., more than one carrier, WATS, etc.) the system will pick the cheapest available route at each point in time.

Three-party Service
The possibility for a busy subscriber to hold the existing call and make a call to a third party. The following arrangements may then be possible: the ability to switch between the two calls, the introduction of a common speech path between the three parties, and the connection of the other two parties.

The PBX has the advantage of direct connection to outgoing telephone lines. The terminal user who wishes to access an external computer need not have a telephone and a modem; the PBX can provide the link-up service. Typically, the connection is to an outgoing analog voice line. To provide the proper service, the PBX maintains a pool of modems that can be used by any data device to communicate over the external lines.

The exact implementation of the modem pool depends on the architecture of the PBX, but some strange contortions may be required. Consider the case of a PBX whose switching capability consists of a TDM bus switch. Figure 7-15 illustrates this. A device wishing to communicate outside will be connected to an available modem in the pool. The modem produces analog signals which must be switched to an outgoing analog trunk. But the PBX switches only digital signals! Therefore, the modem output is routed to a codec, which digitizes the data and puts them back onto the TDM bus. They are then routed to a trunk interface, where the signal is converted back to analog and sent on its way.

The most important characteristic is the internal integration of data and digitized voice. The same switching mechanism is used for both. Therefore, both must conform to common slot size and timing conventions. This is a requirement not faced by the digital switch designer.

Digital PBX Architecture

A variety of architectures have been developed by digital PBX manufacturers. Since these are proprietary, the details are not generally known in

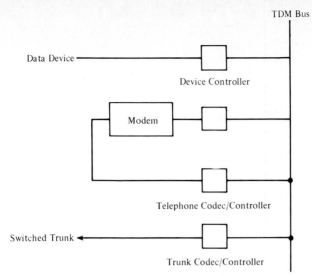

FIGURE 7-15.   Use of a Modem in a Digital PBX

most cases. In this section, we attempt to present the general architectural features common to all PBX systems.

Digital PBX Components

Figure 7-16 presents a generic PBX architecture. You should find it quite similar to the data switching architecture we have discussed. Indeed, since the requirements for the PBX are a superset of those for the data switch, a similar architecture is not surprising.

As always, the heart of the system is some kind of digital switching network. The switch is responsible for the manipulation and switching of time multiplexed digital signal streams, using the techniques described in Section 7.2. The digital switching network consists of some number of space and time switching stages. Many of the PBXs are not sufficiently large, in terms of lines or capacity, to require complex switching networks. Indeed, some have no network as such, but simply use a TDM bus switch.

Attached to the switch are a set of interface units, which provide access to/from the outside word. Typically, an interface unit will perform a synchronous time-division multiplexing function in order to accommodate multiple incoming lines. On the other side, the unit requires two lines into the switch for full duplex operation.

It is important to understand that the interface unit is performing synchronous and not asynchronous TDM, even though connections are dynamically changing. On the input side, the unit performs a multiplex operation. Each incoming line is sampled at a specified rate. For n incoming lines each of data rate x, the unit must achieve an input rate of nx. The

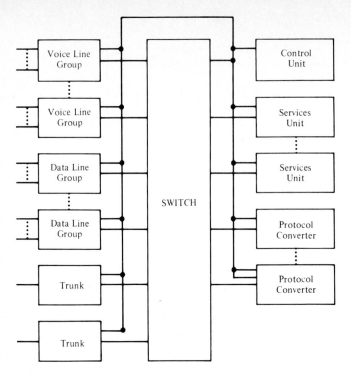

FIGURE 7-16. Generic Digital PBX Architecture

incoming data are buffered and organized into chunks of time-slot size. Then, according to the timing dictated by the control unit, individual chunks are sent out into the switch at the internal PBX data rate, which may be in the range 50 to 500 Mbps. In a nonblocking switch, n time slots are dedicated to the interface unit for transmission, whether or not they are used. In a blocking switch, time slots are assigned for the duration of a connection. In either case, the time-slot assignment is fixed for the duration of the connection, and synchronous TDM techniques may be used.

On the output side, the interface unit accepts data from the switch during designated time slots. In a nonblocking switch these may be dedicated (requiring more than a simple TDM bus switch), but are in any case fixed for the duration of the connection. Incoming data are demultiplexed, buffered, and presented to the appropriate output port at its data rate.

Several types of interface units are used. A data line group unit handles data devices, providing the functions described in Section 7.3. An analog voice line group handles a number of twisted-pair phone lines. The interface unit must include codecs for digital-to-analog (input) and analog-to-digital (output) conversion. A separate type of unit may be used for integrated digital voice/data workstations, which present digitized voice at 64 kbps and data at the same or a lower rate. The range of lines accommodated by interface units is typically 8 to 24.

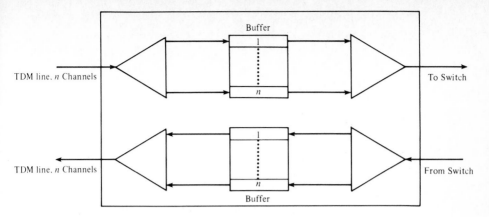

FIGURE 7-17. Operation of a Trunk Interface Unit

In addition to multiplexing interface units that accommodate multiple lines, trunk interface units are used to connect to off-site locations. These may be analog voice trunks or digital trunks, which may carry either data or PCM voice. Whereas a line interface unit must multiplex incoming lines to place on the switch, and demultiplex switch traffic to send to the lines, the trunk unit must demultiplex and multiplex in both directions (see Figure 7-17). Consider an incoming digital line with n channels of time-multiplexed data (the argument is the same for an analog trunk, which presents n channels of frequency-multiplexed voice). These data must be demultiplexed and stored in a buffer of length n units. Individual units of the buffer are then transmitted out to the switch at the designated time slots. Question: Why not pass the TDM stream directly from input to the bus, filling n contiguous time slots? Actually, in a nonblocking dedicated port system, this is possible. But for a system with dynamic time-slot assignment, the incoming data must be buffered and sent out on time slots that vary as connections are made and broken.

The other boxes in Figure 7-16 can be explained briefly. The control unit operates the digital switch and exchanges control signals with attached devices. For this purpose, a separate bus or other data path is used; control signals generally do not propagate through the switch itself. As part of this or a separate unit, network administration and control functions are implemented. Service units would include such things as tone and busy-signal generators and dialed-digit registers. Some PBX systems provide protocol convertors for connecting dissimilar lines. A connection is made from each line to the protocol convertor.

It should be noted that this generic architecture lends itself to a high degree of reliability. The failure of any interface unit means the loss of only a small number of lines. Key elements such as the control unit can be made redundant.

Distributed Architecture

For reasons of efficiency and reliability, many PBX manufacturers offer distributed architectures for their larger systems. The PBX is organized into a central switch and one or more distributed modules, with coaxial or fiber optic cable between the central switch and the modules, in a 2-level hierarchical star topology.

The distributed modules off-load at least some of the central-switch processor's real-time work load (such as off-hook detection). The degree to which control intelligence is off-loaded varies. At one extreme, the modules may be replicas of the central switch, in which case they function almost autonomously with the exception of certain overall management and accounting functions. At the other extreme, the modules are as limited as possible.

A distributed architecture means that it will often be necessary to concatenate several connections to achieve a connection between two devices. Consider Figure 7-18. A connection is desired between lines a and b. In module A, a connection is established between line a and one channel on a TDM trunk to the central switch. In the central switch, that channel is connected to a channel on a TDM trunk to module B. In module B, that channel is connected to line b.

There are several advantages to a distributed architecture:

- It permits growth beyond the practical size of a single digital switch.
- It provides better performance by off-loading of functions.
- It provides higher reliability: the loss of a single module need not disable the entire system.
- It reduces twisted-pair wiring distances.

Modular Architecture

The discussion so far has concerned what might be termed "traditional" digital switch architecture. More recently, a modular switch architecture

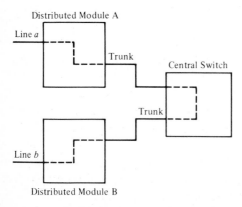

FIGURE 7-18. Circuit Establishment in a Distributed Digital PBX

has been developed based on the use of one module type for all switching stages [KAJI83]. A single module contains both time and space switching.

A major motivation for going to a modular architecture is to overcome some inherent disadvantages of the traditional multistage time-and-space switch. With the traditional switch, the designer must decide in advance the maximum exchange size in order to determine the number of stages and the switch size at each stage. These decisions, in turn, determine a lower size limit. In addition, central control is needed to set up and tear down paths through the switch. As the size of the switch grows, this task becomes increasingly complex. The modular architecture does not possess these disadvantages, as we shall see.

We can contrast the modular switch to the traditional digital switch by listing some of the advantages of the former:

- *Flexible size:* The modules serve as building blocks, allowing a large number of different switch sizes, ranging from very small to very large.
- *Simplified control:* Path setup and tear down is distributed. Each module is intelligent and control is provided via the data path.
- *Simplified manufacturing, testing, and maintenance:* There are fewer parts to build and install.

The principal disadvantage of the modular architecture is potentially increased propagation delay. Each module performs a TSI function. In a large switch, a circuit may pass through multiple modules, and the TSI delays can become substantial.

In the remainder of this section, we briefly describe one example of a modular architecture, the ITT 1240 [COTT81, KEIS85]. For another example, the reader is referred to [ENOM85].

The basic building block of the ITT switch is depicted in Figure 7-19. This module is a plug-in printed circuit board which carries 16 identical LSI *switch ports* interconnected by a TDM bus switch. Each port has an incoming and an outgoing synchronous TDM line. Each line has a data rate of 4.096 Mbps and carries 32 channels. Each channel is used for either digital data or PCM voice. One TDM frame consists of 16 bits from each of the 32 channels. Eight of these bits are control or unused bits. A little arithmetic reveals that each channel is therefore 64 kbps.

There is no common mechanism or control processor to control the modules. Each module is controlled by the individual switch ports acting together over the TDM bus to make and break connections. The receive (incoming) side of each switch port is in essence a synchronous demultiplexer. It sends the channel data, along with destination port number and channel number, out in 16-bit chunks onto the bus during assigned time slots. The transmit (outgoing) side recognizes its port number on the bus and places each slot of data in the appropriate frame slot of the outgoing

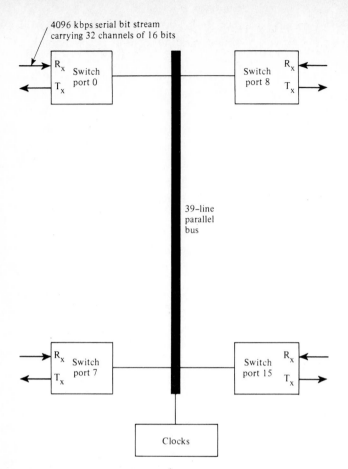

4096 kbps serial bit stream
carrying 32 channels of 16 bits

R_x Switch
T_x port 0

Switch R_x
port 8 T_x

39–line
parallel
bus

R_x Switch
T_x port 7

Switch R_x
port 15 T_x

Clocks

FIGURE 7-19.   Digital Switch Module

line. Since the slots are then transmitted in a (possibly) different order than that in which they were received from the bus, the switch port performs, in effect, a TSI operation. With this architecture, any channel on any of the 16 incoming lines can be connected to any of the 512 (16 × 32) outgoing channels. Thus the module provides a combination of time and space switching.

To begin, let us consider the operation of the simplest switch, depicted in Figure 7-20. Individual terminals (digital data or PCM voice) attach to a *terminal control element* (TCE), which produces two 32-channel TDM streams destined for the switch. Similarly, the TCE receives two 32-channel streams from the switch. Thus the TCE is nothing more than a synchronous TDM multiplexer/demultiplexer. Up to 60 terminals attach to the switch (the extra channels are used for control). The switch in this case consists of two modules which in this context are called *access switches*, with one full-duplex 32-channel link from each TCE going to each

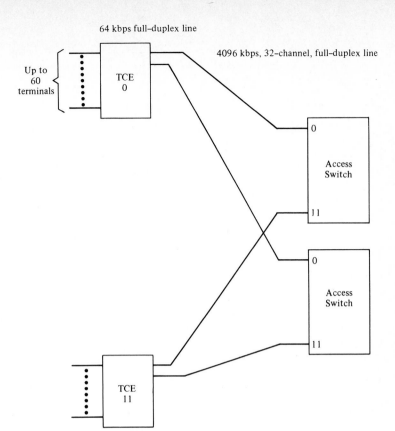

FIGURE 7-20. Single-Stage Modular Switch

module. The use of two modules provides redundancy in the case of failure. Thus any two of the 60 devices on the TCE can be connected via the switch.

Note that one TCE uses up only one port on each of the access switches. The switches support up to 12 TCEs using 12 of the available 16 ports. The remaining ports are unused in this configuration. Thus the simplest one-stage switch consists of two modules and supports 720 terminals. Switching is accomplished as follows. When a terminal requests a connection, and if the destination terminal is attached to the same TCE, the TCE completely implements the connection without involving an access switch. Otherwise, the TCE selects an available outgoing channel (out of the 64) and transmits a path setup request over that channel, which includes the destination address. The access switch responds by selecting an available channel going to the appropriate TCE.

The way in which a switch may be expanded, and the operation of a multistage switch, can be explained with reference to Figure 7-21. The single-stage switch is enclosed in a box labeled A. For a first expansion, up

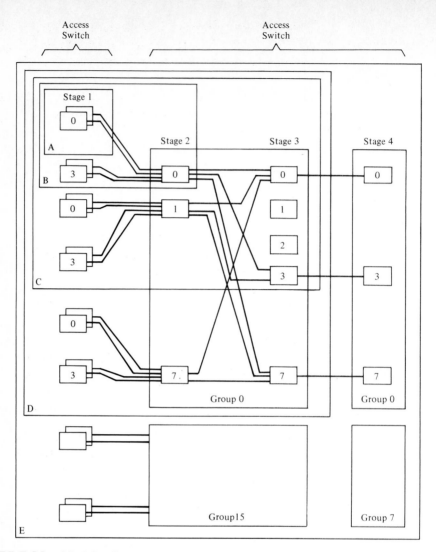

FIGURE 7-21. Modular Switch Architecture

to three more pairs of access switches may be added to the first stage, all interconnected by a second stage of switching. The four unused ports on each access switch (32 in all) connect to a second-stage switch called a *group switch*. This stage consists of up to four modules, with eight ports on each module utilized. The four ports on each access switch attach, one each, to the four modules of stage 2. Thus full connectivity is achieved. The full switch can now handle a total of 2880 terminals. Switching is accomplished as follows. If two terminals connect via TCEs to the same access switch, a path is set up that "reflects back" through the access switch without going to the second stage. Addresses have a hierarchical format, so it is easy for a module to determine if reflection is allowed. If not, an available channel to the stage 2 switch is selected and that switch in turn reflects back to a different access switch that connects to the TCE of the destination terminal.

The two-step configuration is labeled *B* in the diagram. Further expansion proceeds similarly. The eight unused ports on each second stage module are used to connect to up to eight third-stage switches. Reflection can occur at stage 1, 2, or 3 (boxes *C* and *D*). The maximum configuration consists of four stages and supports over 100,000 terminals.

Centrex

To conclude this section, we briefly describe another approach to supporting voice and data devices in an office environment. Known as Centrex, this approach provides the same service as a digital PBX, and appears the same to the user [KLIN86, BRAY85]. In contrast to the digital PBX, however, Centrex performs switching functions in equipment located in the telephone company's central office as opposed to the customer's premises. Centrex utilizes public central-office switching technology enhanced to form a virtual private switch. All telephone and voice lines are routed from the customer site to the central switch. The user can still make local calls with an extension number, giving the appearance of a local switch.

There are several benefits associated with Centrex as opposed to PBXs:

- *Reliability and availability:* The central office equipment is engineered for reliability, with extensive use of redundancy. Maintenance and technical support personnel are available at the switch at all times.
- *Flexibility:* The user is not committed to a switch of a certain size. The customer can grow or shrink the service as required.
- *Avoidance of PBX-related expenses:* These include capital investment, space requirements, and insurance.
- *Continued updating of functionality:* New hardware and software features are regularly added to Centrex offerings.

Centrex is not a true local network because of the distances involved. However, from the user's point of view, this is irrelevant, and Centrex is a major competitor to the digital PBX.

7.5

DIGITAL PBX VERSUS LAN

There is a clear overlap between the capabilities provided by a digital PBX system and a LAN. Both can support a large number and wide variety of digital devices. In order to choose between the two technologies, the potential customer should lay out all the mandatory and desirable features, and then compare the two based on a match against requirements and cost (this process is described in [DERF83]). In this section we compare briefly the two approaches, based on a checklist suggested in [PFIS82]. PBX and LAN can be compared in the following categories:

- Installation
- Reliability
- Data types
- Distance
- Speed
- Capacity
- Cost

The *installation* of the cable for a LAN in an already finished building is without question a time-consuming and expensive task. It is not out of bounds to have the wire costs of a LAN installation be 50% of the total! Consider, now the requirements for a PBX. Phone connections require a two-wire (usually twisted-pair) connection. Data connections, using digital signaling, usually require two twisted pairs for a full-duplex line. Therefore, with many PBX systems, the user who wants both a phone and a terminal in the office requires three twisted-pair lines. The third-generation PBX systems often provide integrated digital voice/data workstations that require only two twisted pairs. Some vendors, using the ping-pong protocol, offer an integrated voice/data link consisting of a single 256-kbps twisted pair (128 kbps for full duplex voice, 128 kbps for full-duplex data). In any case, just about all existing office sites are wired with twisted pairs for distribution of traditional phone services. Further, PBXs are almost always installed with two pairs of wiring per outlet—one for backup. So most PBXs have a number of available spare twisted-pair lines. This could represent a tremendous savings compared to a LAN.

With respect to *reliability*, there are problems with both PBX and LAN systems. This topic is addressed in more detail in Chapter 12. Here, let us just say that the reliability problems of the LAN may be the more severe, contrary to the usual first impression. PBX systems can be made fully redundant, virtually eliminating network-wide failures. But it is easy to postulate situations that would disable all or a substantial part of a LAN.

Both the PBX and the LAN can adequately handle most *data type* requirements. The PBX is superior for handling voice. The centralized control nature of the PBX is ideal for the variety of voice processing requirements in an office environment. Another type of transmission—video—can at present only be practically handled by a broadband LAN.

The *distances* achievable by the PBX and the LAN are about equal. With a distributed architecture, a PBX can easily span a multibuilding complex by locating a switching center in each building, thus matching the range achievable with a broadband LAN.

In terms of *data rate*, the LAN has an edge. Third-generation PBX systems generally support data up to a maximum of 64 kbps (some vendors have plans for rates of up to 256 kbps). A LAN can, with proper interfaces, accommodate attachments in the Mbps range. To many users, 64 kbps may appear to be equivalent to infinity. However, some of the newer workstations, with high-resolution graphics, require much higher data rates. Furthermore, file transfer operations can get severely bogged down at those lower rates.

Closely related to this is the question of capacity and here the picture is murkier. On its face, it would appear that the PBX has the edge. The total digital transfer capacity of a PBX can go up to about 500 Mbps (the data rate on a TDM bus, for example). Baseband bus and ring systems are far less, and even a broadband tops out at about 300 Mbps over a number of channels. However, the nature of the traffic must be taken into account. Most digital data traffic in the office is bursty in nature (terminal to host traffic). On a LAN, the network is utilized by a node only for the duration of the burst. But on a PBX, a node will consume a dedicated portion of the capacity for the duration of a connection.

Last on our checklist is the question of *cost*. For this, there is no definitive answer, partly because component costs are changing rapidly and partly because it is installation dependent. There is a final point of comparison that was not included in the checklist because it relates to detailed design strategy rather than the pros and cons of the two approaches. This point has to do with the nature of the network interface. In a circuit-switched system, the network is usually "transparent"; that is, two connected devices communicate as if they had a direct connection. In a packet-switched system, the issue of the protocol between the network and the attached device arises. Of course, with the introduction of protocol-conversion services on the PBX, the distinctions blur. In any case, it is to this issue that we turn in the next chapter.

7.6

RECOMMENDED READING

A good overview of digital switching concepts can be found in [DAVI73]. [SKAP79] provides a more detailed look. [BELL82b, Chap. 5]* provides a clear discussion of TSI and TMS.

[VONA80], [HELD87], [MULL87], and [MEHT88] describe and discuss port selection and port contention devices. A general survey of digital data switching devices can be found in [KANE80]*.

A very clear discussion of the PBX appears in [MART76, Chap. 22], which also describes the large list of features and services found in a modern PBX. A good paper is [GOEL83]*. The architecture of the digital PBX is discussed in [KASS79]. Papers that contrast the digital PBX and the LAN include [PFIS82]*, [RICH80]*, [MEHT87], and [KAUF86]*. The issues involved in the use of a PBX to handle both voice and data are examined in [COOV86]* and [BHUS85]*.

Good overall treatments of the topics in this chapter can be found in [KEIS85] and [MCDO83]. Descriptive articles on PBX products can be found in [JOEL85] and [FREE85b]. [COOV89] contains reprints of a number of useful papers on the subject.

7.7

PROBLEMS

7.1 Demonstrate that there is a high probability of blocking in a two-stage switch.

7.2 Explain the following statement in Section 7.2: "The timings on the shorter bus are amenable to greater control because of the much shorter propagation delay."

7.3 What is the magnitude of delay through a TSI stage?

7.4 For STS, give an example of blocking when the number of TSI units equals the number of incoming lines. What is the minimum number of TSI units for proper functioning (even in a blocking mode)?

7.5 In Figure 7-15, why is it not possible to route the digital data coming from the device directly to an outgoing trunk, where it will be converted to analog by the codec for transmission?

7.6 Assume that the velocity of propagation on a TDM bus is $0.7c$, its length is 10 m, and the data rate is 500 Mbps. How many bits should be transmitted in a time slot to achieve a bus efficiency of 99%?

7.7 Demonstrate that in a TSI data store at most only half of the memory is usefully occupied at any one time. Devise a means of reducing the TSI memory requirement while maintaining its nonblocking property.

7.8 Is it necessary to include address bits with each time slot in a statistical TDM stream? Is there a more efficient technique?

7.9 Justify the assertion in Section 7.2 that, for an STS network, the number of TSI units must be double the number of incoming and outgoing lines for nonblocking.

7.10 Reconsider Problem 3.6, but now assume that there is a central switching unit on floor 3 and a satellite switching unit on floor 6.

CHAPTER 8

The Network Interface

Previous chapters have looked at the capabilities and features of the various types of local networks, but little has been said of the devices that connect to those networks. The purpose of a local network is to provide a means of communication for the various attached devices. To realize this purpose, the interface between the network and attached devices must be such as to permit cooperative interaction. This section addresses the complexities implicit in that seemingly simple notion.

We began with a statement of the problem: the networking requirements for cooperative interaction. Then we consider the connection of digital devices to packet-switched networks, the common case for LANs and HSLNs; this is the area in which most of the complexity arises. The simpler issues relating to circuit-switched networks and to analog devices are then considered.

THE REQUIREMENT

To understand the network interface requirement, let us first consider, from the computer vendor's point of view, how to provide a computer networking capability. Many vendors offer some sort of networking capability. Applications such as transaction processing, file transfer, electronic mail, and so on are available to run on a network of computers and intelligent terminals. The vendor supports these applications with a networking and communications software package. Examples are IBM's SNA and DEC's DECNET. For clarity in the following discussion, we will consider a generic package based on the OSI model; the principles apply equally well to other, proprietary architectures.

It is important to note that the OSI model does not provide an architecture for the *networking* of *multiple* computers; it is a model for the *communications* between *two* computers, based on a set of protocols. Networking requires not only communications protocols but network management, a naming facility, network services, and so on. These issues are addressed later. In this chapter we are concerned with the communications protocol implications of local networking.

Communications protocols, such as those compatible with the OSI model, do provide a basis for computer networking. Traditionally, this has been done in two ways, as depicted in Figure 8-1. A common vendor offering is a private network (Figure 8-1a). Computers are connected by point-to-point links, which can be local direct connects (a special case of "local network"!) or long-haul links, either dial-up or leased. Each node in the network can act both as an end point for executing applications and as a switch for passing along data. A layer 2 protocol, such as HDLC, is sufficient to provide connectivity; the network can be viewed as a set of computers hooked together by paired, point-to-point, layer 2 links. Any given computer supports more than one link by using more than one physical port, as indicated in the diagram.

This figure is a bit misleading in that it shows a link only at one protocol layer—layer 2. Of course, there is also a layer 1 link for each layer 2 link. Furthermore, the figure suggests that there will be peer communication at higher protocol layers. However, it would be possible with this configuration for a user to write a package for exchanging data between two machines that makes use of none of these higher-layer services; the user still needs a physical connection and link control logic. Layer 2, then, is the highest *required* layer for this configuration to work.

For a long-haul network, the private network configuration can be justified if there is either a very high volume of traffic, or a very low volume. With a high volume of traffic between nodes, the expense of

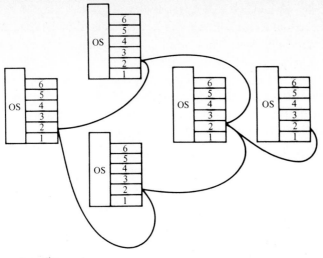

a. Private Network

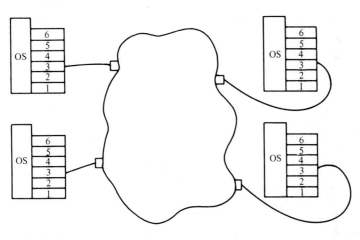

b. Public Network

FIGURE 8-1. Approaches to Computer Networking

dedicated (leased) lines is reasonable. With a low volume of traffic, dial-up lines are cost effective. Over some range between these two extremes the public or value-added network (VAN) provides the most cost-effective communications support for computer networking (Figure 8-1b). The VAN, discussed in Chapter 2, consists of switches and communication lines configured to provide connectivity among attached devices. The VAN provides, among others, three services that are relevant here:

- *Routing:* To send data, an attached device specifies the address of the destination device; the VAN is responsible for routing those data through the network to its destination.
- *Multiplexing:* An attached device does not need one physical port for

each device with which it may communicate. Rather, the VAN supports multiple virtual circuits multiplexed on a single physical line.

- *Standardized interface:* The use of a standardized interface allows the user to attach devices from a variety of vendors, since vendors readily support standards. If the VAN used a special-purpose proprietary interface, the user would be forced to develop or procure the needed hardware and software to attach to the VAN, and would have to do this for every different type of device to be attached to the VAN.

The reader will recognize that the first two items are functions requiring a layer 3 protocol. Typically, the X.25 standard is used. Most vendors who provide private networks can provide the same networking applications over a VAN. The discussion in Chapter 2 describes the mechanism by which this is accomplished.

Figure 8-1 thus serves to illustrate the network interface requirement. With a private network, the vendor's devices are directly connected to each other and the issue does not really arise. With a separate packet-switched communications network, the vendor must determine how to interface its devices to the network. The solution is to implement compatible layers 1 through 3, as with X.25.

A multiaccess local network does not fit neatly into either of the categories noted above. Devices are not attached by point-to-point links as in a private network; instead, a multipoint link exists. Neither is a local network a VAN, with a network of intermediate switching nodes. The problem for the computer vendor is how to integrate the local network into its communications and networking software. The alternatives for this integration are discussed below.

From the customer's point of view, the local network interface is also an important issue. Typically, a customer will acquire some new data processing equipment in addition to the local network. The customer probably also has existing equipment to be hooked into the network. The customer would also like the flexibility of acquiring future equipment of various types, possibly from various vendors. The problem, then, for the customer is to procure a local network whose interface accommodates a variety of equipment with little or no special software required for that equipment. What approach should the customer take?

8.2

PACKET-SWITCHED INTERFACING

Approaches to LAN/HSLN Attachment

Packet transmission is used on both LANs and HSLNs. As we have seen, packet switching implies that the data to be sent over the network by a device are organized into packets which are sent through the network one at a time. Protocols must be used to specify the construction and exchanges of these packets. At a minimum for a local network, protocols at layers 1 and 2 are needed to control the multiaccess network communication (e.g., these layers would comprise the LLC, MAC, and physical functions specified by IEEE 802).

Thus all attached devices must share these common local network protocols. From a customer's point of view, this fact structures the ways in which devices attach to a LAN or HSLN into three alternatives, depicted in Figure 8-2:

- Homogeneous/single vendor approach
- "Standards" approach
- Standard network interface approach

A homogeneous network is one in which all equipment—network plus attached devices—is provided by a single vendor. All equipment shares a common set of networking and communications software. The vendor has integrated a local network capability into its product line. Customers need not concern themselves with details of protocols and interfaces.

Undoubtedly, many customers will adopt this approach. The single-vendor system simplifies maintenance responsibility and provides an easy path for system evolution. On the other hand, the flexibility to obtain the best piece of equipment for a given task may be limited. Relying on a vendor, without consideration of their network architecture, to be able easily to accommodate foreign equipment is risky.

Another approach that a customer may take is to procure a local network that conforms to a standard and dictate that all equipment be

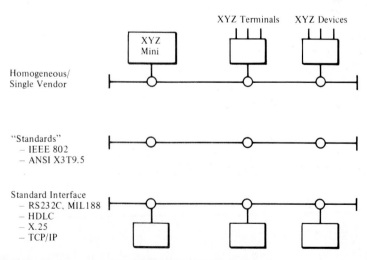

FIGURE 8-2.   Approaches to LAN/HSLN Attachment

compatible with that standard. The local network would consist of a transmission medium plus an expandable set of "attachment points." This approach, although attractive, has some problems. The IEEE standard for LANs is loaded with options, so that two devices claiming to be "IEEE-compatible" may not be able to coexist on the same network. The ANSI standard for HSLN's is still in draft form. In both cases, the standards do not address the essential function of network management. Without a standard for network management, it is unlikely that local network equipment from different vendors can be mixed successfully in a single local network. The topic of network management is explored in Chapter 12.

The promise of local networks standards lies not in the solving of the interconnect problem. Standards offer the hope that the prospect of a mass market will lead to cheap silicon implementations of local network protocols. But the interconnect problem is an architectural issue, not a protocol issue.

Now consider a local network as consisting of not only a transmission medium, but also a set of intelligent devices that implement the local network protocols *and* provide an interface capability for device attachment. We will refer to this device as a *network interface unit* (NIU). The NIUs, collectively, control access to and communications across, the local network. Subscriber devices attach to the NIU through some standard communications or I/O interface. The details of the local network operation are hidden from the device.

The NIU architecture is commonly used by independent local network vendors (those who sell only networks, not the data processing equipment that uses the network). Thus, in many cases, the NIUs in a local network configuration are supplied by a different vendor than the supplier of the terminal and computer equipment. This approach has several advantages. First, attached devices are relieved of the burden of the local network processing logic. Second, the user has more flexibility in selecting equipment to attach to the network. It is not necessary that the attached equipment support the particular type of local network that the user has implemented. It is only necessary that the NIU and the attached devices share a common, standardized interface.

Next, we look at the workings of an NIU. Following that, we consider the architectural implications for networking.

The Network Interface Unit

The NIU is a microprocessor-based device that acts as a communications controller to provide data transmission service to one or more attached devices. The NIU transforms the data rate and protocol of the subscriber device to that of the local network transmission medium and vice versa.

Data on the medium are available to all attached devices, whose NIUs screen data for reception based on address. In general terms, the NIU performs the following functions:

- Accepts data from attached device.
- Buffers the data until medium access is achieved.
- Transmits data in addressed packets.
- Scans each packet on medium for own address.
- Reads packet into buffer.
- Transmits data to attached device at the proper data rate.

The hardware interface between the NIU and the attached device is typically a standard serial communications interface, such as RS-232-C. Almost all computers and terminals support this interface. For higher speed, a parallel interface, such as an I/O channel or direct memory access (DMA) interface can be provided. For example, a number of vendors offer an NIU interface directly into the UNIBUS of DEC's minicomputer line. Figure 8-3 gives a generic architecture for an NIU.

The NIU can either be an outboard or an inboard device. As an outboard device, the NIU is a stand-alone unit, which may have one or more serial communications ports for device attachment. High-speed parallel ports are also used. As an inboard device, the NIU is integrated into the chassis of the data processing device, such as a minicomputer or terminal. An inboard NIU generally consists of one or more printed-circuit boards attached to the device's internal system bus.

From a customer's point of view, an NIU with standard interface options solves, at least at the electrical level, the interconnect problem. From a

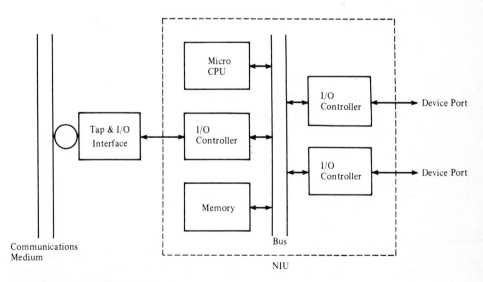

FIGURE 8-3. NIU Architecture

designer's point of view, the NIU is a useful architectural concept. Whether a network is homogeneous or not, and whether the interface provided to the local network is standard or not, there must be some distributed logic for controlling local network access. Conceptualizing this logic as an NIU clarifies some of the communications architectural issues associated with networking applications on a local network.

In what follows, we treat the NIU as a distinct device. Recognize that this device could be so integrated into the attached device as to be indistinguishable. This does not affect the reasoning involved.

8.3

THE DEVICE/NIU INTERFACE

Local Network Protocol Architecture

Having introduced the concept of the NIU, we can now turn to the problem of integrating local network protocols into the communications software of a system. Before beginning this discussion, it will be useful to examine the protocol architecture requirements for communication across a LAN.

Figure 5-3 suggests that a LAN communication architecture involves three layers: physical, medium access control (MAC), and logical link control (LLC). The physical layer provides for attachment to the medium. MAC enables multiple devices to share the medium's capacity in an orderly fashion. Finally, LLC provides for the management of a logical link across the network. The figure indicates that higher layers of software will make use of LLC. Put another way, LLC provides the service of transmitting frames of data across the LAN, and that service is invoked by a higher layer of software.

In pursuit of this line of reasoning, we need to consider what higher layers of software are appropriate in this context. In terms of the OSI model (Figure 2-11), the three IEE 802 layers correspond to the lowest two layers (physical, data link) of the OSI model. The next layer, then, would be the network layer. But, from our discussion of Section 5-1, we have determined that a network layer is not really needed in the context of a local network. Thus, we can improve efficiency by eliminating the network layer and going directly to the transport layer.

Figure 8-4a reflects this line of reasoning. The LLC layer provides a service for moving frames of data from one station on the LAN to another. The transport layer provides end-to-end reliability. Thus, the user of transport is guaranteed that its data will be delivered with no losses and no misorderings. We can trace the operation of this architecture on a single unit of user data in Figure 8-4b, which is keyed to event times marked on

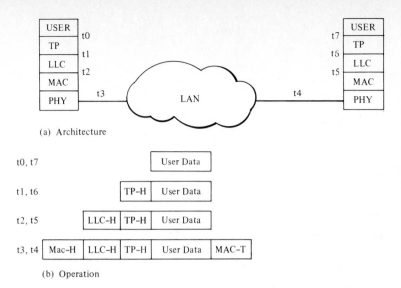

(a) Architecture

t0, t7				User Data	

t1, t6			TP–H	User Data	

t2, t5		LLC–H	TP–H	User Data	

t3, t4	Mac–H	LLC–H	TP–H	User Data	MAC–T

(b) Operation

FIGURE 8-4. Operation of a LAN Protocol Architecture

Figure 8-4a. At some time t_0, the user of transport presents a block of data to transport. The transport entity encapsulates this data with a transport header and passes the resulting unit to LLC (t_1). LLC adds its own header (Figure 5-2) and passes the resulting unit to MAC (t_2). MAC produces a frame that includes both a MAC header and a MAC trailer and this frame is transmitted across the LAN (t_3). The MAC frame includes a destination station address, and the frame will be copied by the station with that address (t_4). The user's block of data then moves up through the layers, with the appropriate headers and trailers stripped off at each layer (t_5, t_6, t_7).

Modes of Attachment

The scenario of Figure 8-4 assumes that all of the protocol layers at each station are integrated and execute on a single processor. However, in most cases, some of the lower layers will execute on an NIU, with the upper layers executing on the main processor. The remainder of this section is devoted to an examination of various approaches to achieving this split.

All of the approaches fall into one of two general categories, which are illustrated in Figure 8-5. For simplicity, the three LAN-related protocols (LLC, MAC, and Physical) are represented by the two lowest-layers of the OSI model in this figure.

To provide service to an attached device, the NIU can function as a gateway. A *gateway* is a device for connecting two systems that use different protocols: a protocol converter, if you like. In this case the NIU

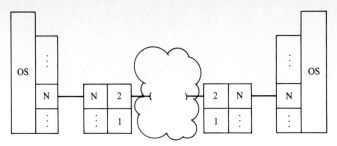

(a) THE NIU AS GATEWAY (PROTOCOL MODEL)

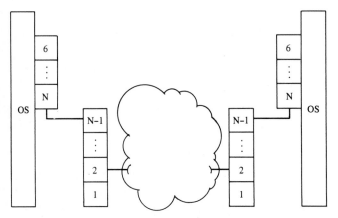

(b) THE NIU AS FRONT–END NETWORK PROCESSOR (INTERFACE MODE)

FIGURE 8-5.   Protocol Layers for Local Networks

contains logic for communicating with the attached device using some protocol native to that device; the level of communication is at some layer *n* (Figure 8-5a). The NIU converts between that protocol and that of the local network.

Compare this architecture with Figure 2-15, which describes the VAN/PDN architecture. In that figure the level of communication between the DTE and DCE is at layer 3. The operation is as follows. The data that originate at the application layer, plus all the headers generated by layers 7 through 4, are treated as a unit of data by layer 3. Layer 3 has the responsibility of routing this data unit to the destination system. It does this by means of a protocol with the *local* DCE at layer 3. Of course, to transmit a layer 3 frame from DTE to DCE, a logical link (layer 2) over a physical link (layer 1) is needed. Hence the DTE-DCE conversation consists of protocols at layers 1, 2, and 3. Now, the DCE uses a different set of protocols to route the data unit through the network to the destination DCE, which in turn has a layer 1, 2, 3 protocol conversation with the destination DTE. The result is that a layer 4 packet has been routed from source to destination through gateways which convert the protocols up through layer 3.

In Figure 8-5b we see that the NIU can function instead as a front-end network processor (FNP). An FNP is a network processor that provides communications management services to an attached information processor. In contrast to a gateway, which *converts* from one set of protocols to another, the FNP *replacces* the protocols that might be found in the attached device. The attached device contains layers 7 down through n. There is an $n/n\text{-}1$ interface to the NIU which contains layers $n\text{-}1$ to 1, with layers 2 and 1 being the local network protocols.

The typical host–FNP situation is one in which the host is a mainframe and the front end is a minicomputer. In that case, a common interface boundary is between session (5) and transport (4). This is a reasonable break: layers 1 through 4 can be thought of as "communications" management, responsible for managing physical and logical links and providing a reliable end-to-end transport service. Layers 5 and 6 can be thought of as "message management," responsible for maintaining a dialogue between end points and providing appropriate message formatting services. So the 5/4 break, although certainly not unique, is a logical one.

Within these two general categories, a number of specific approaches have been tried by various vendors and experimenters. The remainder of this section looks at those approaches that appear to be the most appropriate:

- Layer 1 Gateway (Transparent Mode)
- Layer 2 Gateway
- Layer 3 Gateway (X.25 Interface)
- Layer 4/2 FNP (LLC Interface)
- Layer 5/4 FNP (Transport Interface)

The NIU as Gateway

Layer 1 Gateway

This mode, which could be referred to as the transparent mode, permits protocol-compatible devices to communicate as if the NIUs and cable were not present. The NIU appears as a modem and provides signaling transparency. For example, for an RS-232C interface, when the originating device raises Request-to-Send to the originating NIU, the destination NIU raises Received-Line-Signal Detector (Carrier Detect) to the destination device. Data transfer is accomplished using buffering within the NIU. The transmitting NIU accumulates data from the transmitting device until either a buffer fills, a timer expires, or a control sequence is detected. The accumulated data are packaged in a frame and sent to the receiving NIU. The receiving NIU transmits the data to the receiving device.

Four parameters within each NIU control data transfer. These are: buffer size, time-out, control sequence(s), and destination address (NIU, SAP). At least the address parameter is variable and must be set using a control mode. For intelligent attached devices, a small I/O program would be needed to set NIU parameters. For dumb terminals, the associated NIU would have to provide a user interface (terminal handler) for setting parameters.

There is a lot of appeal in this approach. If the local network is truly transparent to the attached devices, any networking or communications capability that operates over traditional communications lines will operate over the local network with no modification.

Of course, this mode is not quite "transparent." There are two phases (this is true of all the modes): a control phase, for requesting a connection, and a data transfer phase. But the logic needed for the control phase is minor.

There are some disadvantages to this approach, particularly for synchronous communications, Chief among these is flow control. Flow control mechanisms for synchronous communication function at layer 2. If one device attached to the local network via its NIU is beginning to overrun the capacity of the destination device, the destination device can send, at layer 2, a message that will halt or reduce the flow of data. However, if the attached device sends data to the NIU faster than it can be accepted, there is no way for the NIU to exert flow control on the attached device. A similar problem exists with error control. If an attached device fails to receive an acknowledgment to a frame, it does not know whether the fault is in the NIU or the destination device.

These problems are not fatal, but they do present difficulties to the designer.

Layer 2 Gateway

In this mode, a layer 2 protocol is established between the attached device and the NIU. An example is HDLC.

As with a layer 1 gateway, there are two phases of communication: control and data transfer. For setting up a connection to some destination device, a dialogue is needed that is outside the layer 2 protocol. Again, this can be provided by a small I/O program. Once a connection is established, the layer 2 protocol would support data transfer.

This mode also presents a flow control problem. In this case, the NIU can excercise flow control over the attached device. However, the remote device has no means, *at layer 2*, of exercising flow control on the source device. Higher-layer protocols must be relied on in the two devices.

Another problem, common to both layer 1 and 2 protocols, is that the NIU does not support multiplexing. That is, for each logical connection to another device on the network, the attached device must have one physical connection to the network. This situation most closely resembles that of a private network using dial-up lines.

Layer 3 Gateway

In this mode, the local network presents the appearance of a VAN. Typically, the NIU provides the X.25 standard for attached intelligent devices. The advantage of this approach is that any networking capability that will work on X.25 VAN will work on the local network. The X.25 layer 3 protocol provides a multiplexing capability so that multiple virtual circuits are supported over a single physical link. In this mode, we at last get away from the necessity of a separate control dialogue. As the discussion will show, the network layer functionally includes a connection request capability.

X.25 is perhaps the best-known and most widely-used protocol standard. The standard specifies an "interface" between attached devices and a packet-switched network. The standard actually encompasses the three lowest layers of the OSI model (Figure 2-15). The physical layer makes use of a standard known as X.21, but in many cases, the RS-232-C standard is

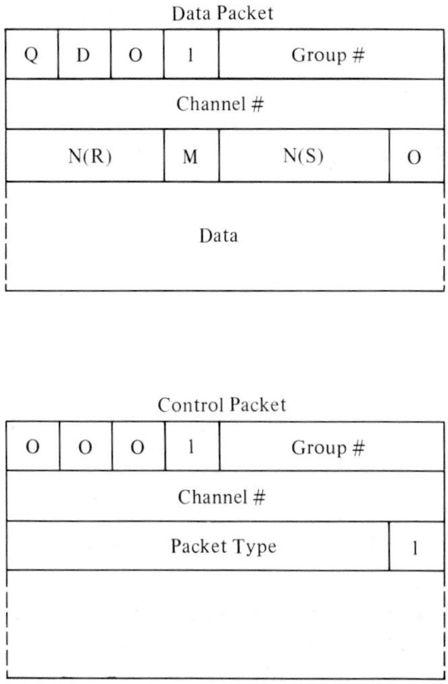

Data Packet

Q	D	O	1	Group #
Channel #				
N(R)		M	N(S)	O
Data				

Control Packet

O	O	O	1	Group #
Channel #				
Packet Type				1

FIGURE 8-6.   X.25 Layer 3 Packet Formats

substituted. The data link layer is LAP-B, which is a subset of HDLC. The network layer is referred to in the standard as the packet level; it specifies a virtual-circuit service.

Figure 8-6 shows the layer 3 packet formats used in the X.25 standard. A 24-bit header is used for data packets. The header includes a 12-bit virtual-circuit number (expressed as a 4-bit group number and an 8-bit channel number). The N(S) and N(R) fields perform the same function on a virtual-circuit basis as they do on a link basis in HDLC. The control packet has a variable-length header, depending on the specific function; some of these functions are referred to in the following discussion.

Figure 8-7 shows a typical sequence of events in a virtual call. The left-hand part of the figure shows the packets exchanged between user machine A and its DCE (the NIU plays the role of the DCE in a local network); the right-hand part shows the packets exchanged between user machine B and its DCE. The routing of packets between the DCEs is the responsibility of the internal logic of the network.

The sequence of events is as follows:

1. A requests a virtual circuit to B by sending a Call Request packet to its DCE. The packet includes a virtual circuit number (group, channel), as well as source and destination addresses. Future incoming and outgoing data transfers will be identified by the virtual circuit number.
2. B's DCE receives the call request and sends a Call Indication packet to B. This packet has the same format as the Call Request packet but a different virtual circuit number, selected by B's DCE from the set of locally unused numbers.
3. B indicates acceptance of the call by sending a Call Accepted packet specifying the same virtual circuit number as that of the Call Indication packet.
4. A receives a Call Connected packet with the same virtual circuit number as that of the Call Request packet.
5. A and B send Data and Control packets using their respective virtual circuit numbers.
6. A (or B) sends a Clear Request packet to terminate the virtual circuit and receives a local Clear Confirmation packet.
7. B (or A) receives a Clear Indication packet and transmits a Clear Confirmation packet.

Figure 8-8 depicts the operation of this architecture in transmitting one block of user data. In this case, the packet level of X.25 adds a network-layer header (t_2), and the link layer adds a link header and trailer (t_3). The resulting frame is then sent to the station's NIU, where the link header and trailer are peeled off and the packet is delivered to the network layer (t_4). Notice in the figure that there is no "user" of this layer. The NIU is an intermediate gateway whose job is to relay the data on. So the packet, or

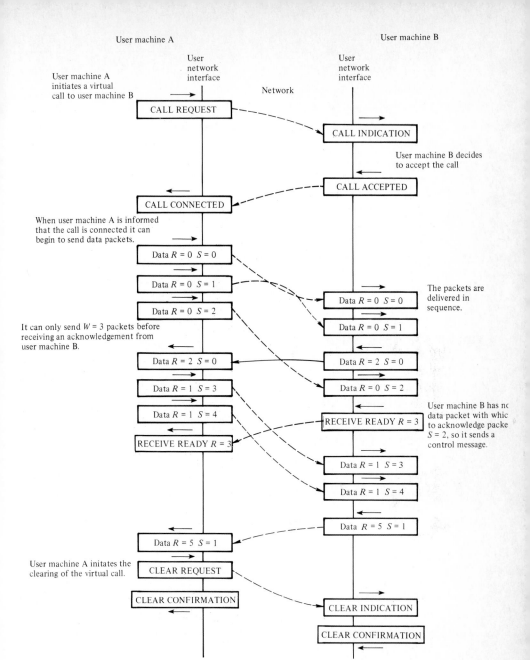

FIGURE 8-7.   Sequence of Events: X.25 Protocol

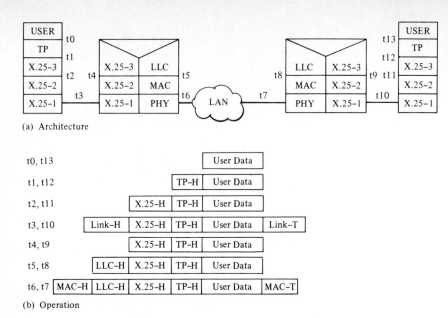

(a) Architecture

t0, t13				User Data	
t1, t12			TP-H	User Data	
t2, t11		X.25-H	TP-H	User Data	
t3, t10	Link-H	X.25-H	TP-H	User Data	Link-T
t4, t9		X.25-H	TP-H	User Data	
t5, t8	LLC-H	X.25-H	TP-H	User Data	
t6, t7	MAC-H LLC-H	X.25-H	TP-H	User Data	MAC-T

(b) Operation

FIGURE 8-8. Layer 3 Gateway

network, header is left in place to be examined at the other end. Relay logic within the NIU passes the packet to LLC, which appends its own header (t_5) and passes the result to MAC. The remainder of the figure should be self-explanatory.

The X.25 interface is already offered by a number of LAN vendors. Because this is such a common means of connecting to long-haul communications networks, its use for local networks is likely to become popular.

The NIU as Front-End Processor

Layer 4/2 FNP

Figure 8-9 illustrates a layer 4/2 FNP mode. This is an attractive option that lends itself to a high-performance inboard NIU. The two layers needed to control the local network are in the NIU: all other layers are in the attached device. This configuration also provides high "visibility" for the local network. Software executing in the attached device can directly invoke layer 2 functions provided by the local network, such as broadcasting and priorities.

The architecture of this option is not as straightforward as you might have expected. First, there is no network layer, as has already been explained. However, there are additional layers needed to link an NIU and its attached station. In the figure, we assume a serial communication link between the NIU and the attached device. Thus, a physical-layer protocol

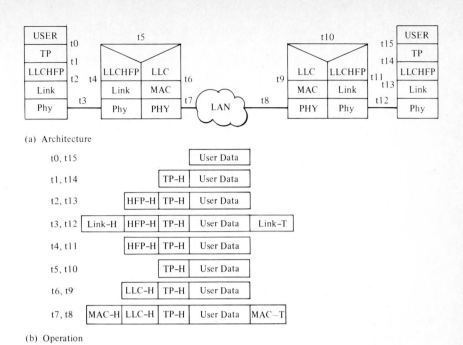

(a) Architecture

t0, t15				User Data	
t1, t14			TP–H	User Data	
t2, t13		HFP–H	TP–H	User Data	
t3, t12	Link–H	HFP–H	TP–H	User Data	Link–T
t4, t11		HFP–H	TP–H	User Data	
t5, t10			TP–H	User Data	
t6, t9		LLC–H	TP–H	User Data	
t7, t8	MAC–H	LLC–H	TP–H	User Data	MAC–T

(b) Operation

FIGURE 8-9. Layer 4/2 FNP

and a link-layer protocol are needed to exchange data across that link. One more protocol is also needed. This protocol has no universally accepted name, but is often referred to as a *host-to-front-end-protocol* (HFP). To identify this as referring to a front end whose highest layer is LLC, we shall identify it as LLC-HFP.

To understand the need for an HFP, consider again the case of an integrated architecture (Figure 8-4). At t_1, the transport entity passes a block of data to LLC for transmission. How does LLC know what to do with this data block? That information is contained in the link control primitive used by the transport layer to invoke LLC. These primitives were listed in Table 5.2. For example if the unacknowledged connectionless service is used, the transport entity would use the following primitive and associated parameters to invoke LLC:

DL-UNIDATA.request   (source-address,   destination-address,   data, priority)

where

> source address = local LLC user (service access point plus MAC address)

> destination address = remote LLC user (service access point plus MAC address)

data = block of data to be transmitted

priority = desired priority for this data transfer

Exactly how this information is passed to an LLC entity from an LLC user will depend on the implementation. For example, if LLC is invoked by a subroutine call, then the DL-UNIDATA.request call is compiled into a machine-language subroutine branch, and the parameters of the call are placed somewhere in registers or memory to be picked up by the called routine. The details are not, and should not be, part of the LLC standard.

TABLE 8.1 Example LLC-HFP PDU Header

a. Header Fields

Service Access Point	LLC User
Primitive code	LLC primitive being invoked. Codes are listed in (b)
Parameter count	Number of parameters
Parameter	This field occurs once for each parameter and consists of two subfields:
Length	Length in octets of value subfield
Value	Value of the parameter

b. Primitive codes

1	DL-UNITDATA.request
2	DL-UNITDATA.indication
3	DL-CONNECT.request
4	DL-CONNECT.indication
5	DL-CONNECT.response
6	DL-CONNECT.confirm
7	DL-DATA.request
8	DL-DATA.indication
9	DL-DISCONNECT.request
10	DL-DISCONNECT.indication
11	DL-RESET.request
12	DL-RESET.indication
13	DL-RESET.response
14	DL-RESET.confirm
15	DL-CONNECTION-FLOWCONTROL.request
16	DL-CONNECTION-FLOWCONTROL.indication
17	DL-DATA-ACK.request
18	DL-DATA-ACK.indication
19	DL-DATA-ACK-STATUS.indication
20	DL-REPLY.request
21	DL-REPLY.indication
22	DL-REPLY-STATUS.indication
23	DL-REPLY-UPDATE.request
24	DL-REPLY-UPDATE-STATUS.indication

The internal implementation of this interface depends on the machine language and operating system, and upon design choices made to optimize the implementation.

The subroutine-call approach works fine if the transport and LLC entities execute in the same processor. But in the case of Figure 8-9, they are in separate systems. We need a way for the transport and LLC entities to exchange commands (primitives) and parameters, and this is the function of the LLC-HFP. LLC-HFP provides a way for the transport and LLC entities to communicate. In the host, the LLC-HFP entity presents an interface to the transport entity that mimics LLC. This allows the transport entity to use calls such as L_DATA.request as if LLC were in the same system. In the NIU, LLC-HFP behaves like any other LLC user.

We can now trace the operation of the architecture of Figure 8-9. At t_1, the transport entity passes the user's data plus a transport header to LLC-HFP, using the L_DATA.request call. LLC-HFP appends a header and passes the result to the link layer (t_2). Table 8.1 suggests a format for the header. The remaining steps in Figure 8-9 should be clear.

Now, the above scenario assumes an outboard NIU and the use of a data link protocol such as HDLC across the host-NIU interface. If the NIU is a communications board, then there will be no link and physical layer protocols as such between the NIU and the host. In most cases, the NIU and host processor will connect to the same backplane bus and exchange information through a common main memory; the NIU typically uses direct-memory access (DMA) to access the memory. In this case, a specific area of memory is shared, and is used to construct a system control block for communication. As an example, Table 8.2 is the system control block format used in an Intel product [WEBB84].

One issue remains to be examined. Whether the host-NIU exchange is achieved by an LLC-HFP or by the exchange of system control blocks, a

TABLE 8.2 LLC-HFP System Control Block

Word	Name	Description
1	Status	NIU or host status information, such as whether or not ready to receive data
2	Directive	Management-related commands and acknowledgments
3	Command Pointer	Points to an area of memory that contains one or more commands. Each command consists of a command code and a list of parameters
4	Frame Pointer	Points to a buffer containing a block of data being passed between LLC and the LLC user
5–8	Error Counters	Error-related statistics

specification of that exchange is needed. If both the NIU and the host are provided by the same vendor, then that specification can be proprietary. If, however, the NIU and the host are from different vendors, then a standard specification would be preferable. As we have commented, it is likely that NIUs will be from a different vendor than the vendor for the attached devices. Indeed, there may be attached devices from a number of different vendors. Thus, the case for a standard for the host-NIU exchange is a strong one. Unfortunately, no such standard exists or is even contemplated by IEEE 802, ANSI X3T9.5, or ISO.

Layer 5/4 FNP

In this mode, the NIU takes on the scope and characteristics of what is normally thought of as true FNP. All of the layers normally associated with communications management are implemented in the NIU; the higher message management layers are in the attached device. For communication between two devices that implement these higher layers, this approach works well.

Figure 8-10 depicts this architecture. Note the similarity to Figure 8-9. The same reasoning applies. In this case, the user of transport executes on a different processor than the transport entity. A TP-HFP is needed to allow the transport user to exchange primitives and parameters with the transport entity. The same techniques discussed earlier can be used in this architecture. The TP-HFP header will contain a code specifying which primitive is being invoked, and the remainder of the header is a list of

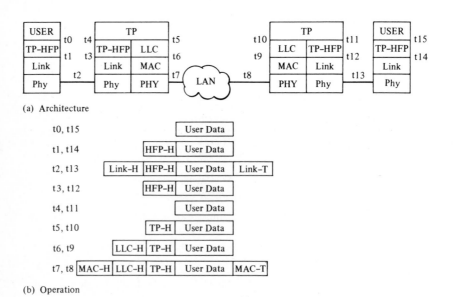

(a) Architecture

(b) Operation

FIGURE 8-10.   Layer 5/4 FNP

TABLE 8.3 ISO Transport Service Primitives

T_CONNECT.request (Called Address,Calling Address,Expedited Data
 Option,Quality of Service,Data)
T_CONNECT.indication (Called Address,Calling Address,Expedited Data
 Option,Quality of Service,Data)
T_CONNECT.response (Quality of Service,Responding Address,Expedited
 Data Option,Data)
T_CONNECT.confirm (Quality of Service,Responding Address,Expedited Data
 Option,Data)

T_DISCONNECT.request (Data)
T_DISCONNECT.indication (Disconnect Reason,Data)

T_DATA.request (Data)
T_DATA.indication (Data)

T_EXPEDITED_DATA.request (Data)
T_EXPEDITED_DATA.indication (Data)

---

parameter lengths and values. In the case of an inboard NIU, the primitives and parameters can be exchanged by means of a system control block.

Table 8.3 lists the primitives for the ISO transport protocol standard. The ISO transport protocol standard also has the concept of a service access point (SAP), so that there may be multiple users of a transport entity. The first six primitives listed in the table are used to establish and subsequently tear down a logical connection between transport SAPs. Most of the parameters are self-explanatory. The quality of service parameter allows the transport user to request specific transmission services, such as priority and security levels. The remaining primitives are concerned with data transfer. The expedited version requests that the transport entity attempt to deliver the associated data as rapidly as possible. Note the similarity of these primitives to those for LLC.

Placement of transport layer and below in the NIU is becoming a popular option (e.g., see [BAL85], [DAVI83], [WOOD79]). Again, a standard specification for TP-HFP and a transport-level system control block are desirable, but are not in sight.

Summary

The discussion in this section has dealt with the issue of which communications architecture layers should reside in the NIU, and therefore be considered part of the local network service, and which should reside in the attached device. The choice will depend on a variety of factors, including cost and performance. As yet, there is little operational experience with most of these alternatives to guide us. Consequently, we can only close this section with a few preliminary observations.

The principal advantage of placing as many layers as possible in the NIU is that this makes the task of intelligent device attachment as easy as possible. The customer or user must be assured that the various devices on the network are compatible. By placing more of the communications functionality in the network, the scope of this task is reduced. On the other hand, placing as little functionality as possible in the network may increase the network's flexibility. Functions in the attached device can be tailored to achieve certain objectives in such areas as performance, priorities, and security.

8.4

TERMINAL HANDLING FOR LANS

In the preceding section, the discussion focused on the requirements for attaching an intelligent device to a LAN or HSLN. Such devices implement the necessary communication layers and can communicate across a network as described in Chapter 2. For simplicity, we will refer to all such devices as hosts. But there are other devices that do not have the processing power to implement the OSI layers, such as dumb terminals, printers, and even limited-function intelligent terminals. We will refer to these devices generically as terminals.

From a hardware point of view, terminals attach to a LAN in the same fashion as hosts: through NIUs. An NIU for terminals will provide a number of serial communication ports for terminal attachment; support for from 4 to 32 terminals on a single NIU is typical. From a software point of view, the approaches outlined in Section 8-3 are not directly applicable to terminal support. All of the approaches discussed assumed that some number of layers would be implemented in the attached device. How, then, to attach terminals?

Two general approaches are possible. The first is to treat terminal-host communication as fundamentally different from host-host communication. This approach can be explained using the concept of a secondary network, which is discussed next. The application of this concept in the local network context is then described. The second approach relies on the use of a virtual terminal protocol. This concept is defined, following which its use in the local network context is discussed.

The Secondary Network

Let us refer to the kind of computer network we have discussed in Section 2.3 and previously in this chapter as a primary network. A primary network consists of the hardware and software required to interconnect applications executing within the OSI architecture. These include mainframes, FNPs, minicomputers, and intelligent terminals (generically, hosts). Typically a mainframe will contain the higher-order layers (5, 6, 7), and all communications functions (layers 1 through 4) are off-loaded to an FNP. Minis and intelligent terminals typically contain all the OSI layers.

Within the OSI architecture, applications execute as modules sitting on top of the presentation layer (layer 6). Interconnection is logically achieved by means of a session established by session control (layer 5). To communicate with another application, an application requests that a session be established between a "logical port" attached to itself and a "logical port" attached to the other application. This service is provided by layer 5, which can establish both local and remote connections.

This mechanism works fine for devices containing all the software needed to implement the OSI layers. However, there are a number of devices, such as dumb terminals, printers, and so on (generically, terminals), which should be accessible over a network but which do not have the functionality of the various OSI layers. The secondary network consists of the hardware and software required to connect these devices to an OSI network. Whereas the primary network uses a 7-layer architecture, secondary connections use protocols tailored to the device in question.

Conceptually, we can think of these devices being serviced by application programs that act as gateways to the primary network. We will refer to these gateways as *secondary network servers* (SNS's). Since an SNS is an application, it can establish sessions with other applications over the primary network. A device such as a terminal local to a particular computer connects directly to a local SNS and, through it, participates on the primary network.

These concepts are illustrated in Figure 8-11. Applications are represented as bubbles resting on layer 6. Sessions are represented by dashed lines. For example, consider the terminal T1 communicating with the SNS in minicomputer A. T1 could be directly connected to A or remotely via communications link or even by a network, as we will explain below. In any case, there is a connection between T1 and the SNS that does not use the OSI layers; this we refer to as a secondary network connection. Now, suppose that T1 is logged on to A vis the SNS, and wishes to access an application on minicomputer B. The SNS, as an application, can invoke the communications functions of A to establish a session with the application on B; we refer to this as to primary network connection.

With this brief background, we now look at the use of the secondary network approach for local networks. To provide a secondary network connection from terminal to host, the NIU must allow the terminal user to request a connection to an SNS in a host (alternatively, a host could set up the connection). Data transfer must occur as if the terminal were directly connected to the host. Note that the local network medium is being used to

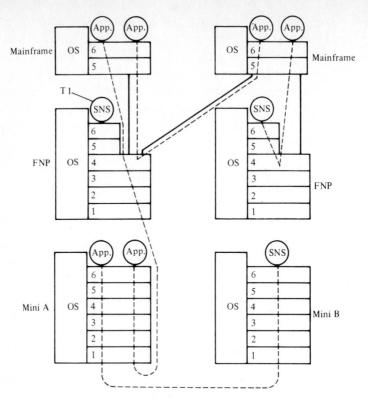

FIGURE 8-11. Primary/Secondary Network Concepts

support both primary (host-host) and secondary (terminal-host) network connections.

As we shall see, in providing secondary network connections for terminals, the NIU functions in the gateway mode (Figure 8-5a). The specific approach taken depends on whether the terminals being supported are asynchronous or synchronous.

Asynchronous Terminals: Transparent Mode

Asynchronous terminals communicate by transmitting and receiving characters one at a time. Generally, no link control protocol as such is used. Thus, there is usually no or only a primitive form of error and flow control provided.

The simplest, and most common, way of supporting asynchronous terminals on a LAN is to use a layer 1 gateway, which we referred to as a transparent mode. The architecture is illustrated in Figure 8-12a. Communication between the NIU and terminals is managed by an asynchronous handler, which simply transmits and receives using the asynchronous

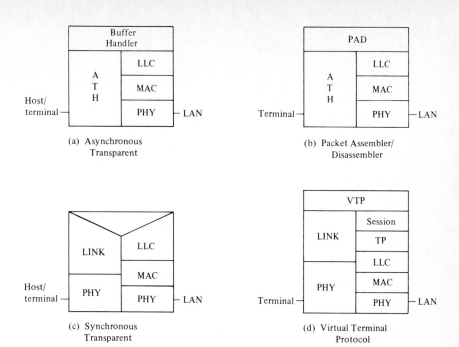

FIGURE 8-12. NIU Architectures for Terminal Handling

scheme described in Chapter 2 (Figure 2-8a). As characters come in from a terminal, they are placed in an input buffer by a buffer handler program; when a carriage return is received, or when a timeout occurs, the contents of the buffer are passed to LLC for transmission. The data are transmitted across the LAN to an NIU to which is attached the destination host. Data arriving from the host are delivered in a block by LLC to the buffer handler. These data are then transmitted to the terminal one character at a time. The host side of this architecture is identical to the terminal side. The NIU attaches to the host through one or more asynchronous communications lines. Thus, it appears to both the host and the terminal as though they were directly connected.

Asynchronous Terminals: PAD Approach

The approach just outlined is simple and effective. Its main drawback is evident in Figure 8-13. Because the connection is transparent, there must be one asynchronous port on the host for each terminal connection. This is referred to as the "milking machine" approach, and is clearly wasteful of host hardware. It would be preferable if the link to the host could be a multiplexed link that could carry traffic from a number of terminals at the same time. This approach has been standardized within the context of the X.25 standard.

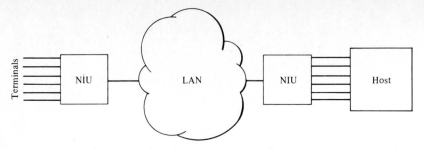

FIGURE 8-13. Asynchronous Terminal Support: Milking Machine Approach

As supplements to the X.25 standard, CCITT has developed a set of standards related to a facility known as a *packet assembler disassesmbler* (PAD). The PAD is designed to solve the two fundamental problems associated with the attachment of terminals to a network:

1. Many terminals are not capable of implementing the protocol layers for attaching in the same manner as a host. The PAD facility provides the intelligence for communicating with a host using the X.25 protocol.
2. There are differences among terminal types. The PAD facility provides a set of parameters to account for those differences. However, it only deals with asynchronous, start-stop terminals.

Three standards define the PAD facility:

- X.3: Describes the functions of the PAD and the parameters used to control its operation (Table 8.4).
- X.28: Describes the PAD–terminal protocol.
- X.29: Describes the PAD–host protocol.

Figure 8-14a indicates the architecture for use of the PAD. The terminal attached to the PAD sends characters one at a time. These are buffered in the PAD and then assembled into an X.25 packet, and sent through the network to the host. Host packets are received at the PAD, disassembled by stripping off the X.25 header, and passed to the terminal one character at a time. Simple commands between terminal and PAD (X.28), used to set parameters and establish virtual circuits, consist of character strings. Similar host–PAD control information (X.29) is transmitted in the data field of an X.25 packet, with a bit set in the X.25 header to indicate that this is control information.

Figure 8-12b shows the architecture of the NIU that provides the PAD function for terminals. The host NIU architecture is the same one shown in Figure 8-8.

TABLE 8.4 PAD Parameters (X.3)

Number	Description	Selectable Values
1	Whether terminal operator can escape from data transfer to PAD command state	0: not allowed 1: escape character 32–126: graphic characters
2	Whether PAD echoes back characters received from terminal	0: no echo 1: echo
3	Terminal characters that will trigger the sending of a partially full packet by the PAD	0: only send full packets 1: alphanumeric 2, 4, 8, 16, 32, 64: other control characters
4	Timeout value that will trigger the sending of a partially full packet by the PAD	0: no timeout 1–255: multiple of 50 ms
5	Whether PAD can exercise flow control over terminal output, using X-ON, X-OFF	0: not allowed 1: allowed
6	Whether PAD can send service signals (control information) to terminal	0: not allowed 1: allowed
7	Action(s) taken by PAD on receipt of break signal from terminal	0: nothing 1: send interrupt 2: reset 4: send break signal 8: escape 16: discard output
8	Whether PAD will discard DTE data intended for terminal	0: normal delivery 1: discard
9	Number of padding characters inserted after carriage return (to terminal)	0: determined by data rate 1–255: number of characters
10	Whether PAD inserts control characters to prevent terminal line overflow	0: no 1–255: yes, line length
11	Terminal speed (bps)	0–18: 50 to 64,000
12	Whether terminal can exercise flow control over PAD, using X-ON, X-OFF	0: not allowed 1: allowed
13	Whether PAD inserts line feed after carriage return sent or echoed to terminal	0: no line feed 1,2, 4: various conditions

TABLE 8.4 (*continued*)

Number	Description	Selectable Values
14	Number of padding characters inserted after line feed (to terminal)	0: no padding 1–255: number of characters
15	Whether PAD supports editing during data transfer (defined in parameters 16–18)	0: no 1: yes
16	Character delete	0–127: selected character
17	Line delete	0–127: selected character
18	Line display	0–127: selected character
19	Terminal type for editing PAD service signals (e.g., character delete)	0: no editing signals 1: printing terminal 2: display terminal
20	Characters that are not echoed to terminal when echo is enabled	0: no echo mask Each bit represents certain characters
21	Parity treatment of characters to/from terminal	0: no parity treatment 1: parity checking 2: parity generation
22	Number of lines to be displayed at one time	0: page wait disabled 1–255: number of lines

Sychronous Terminals: Layer 2 Gateway

For synchronous terminals, a layer 2 gateway can be used (Figure 8-12c). This gateway accepts frames of data from the synchronous terminal and transmits them across the LAN; it also accepts frames from the LAN and delivers them to the terminal.

Support for synchronous terminals is complicated by the fact that most synchronous terminals employ a poll-and-select data link protocol. With this type of protocol, all communication is initiated by the host. When the host has data to send to a terminal, it issues a select command with the terminal's address. If the terminal is ready to receive data, it responds with a positive acknowledgement, and the host sends the data. When the host is prepared to receive data, it issues a poll command with the terminal's address. If the terminal has data to send, it can then send the data. This protocol was developed to allow multiple terminals to be connected to a host over a single multipoint line.

With terminals scattered around a LAN, some mechanism is needed for

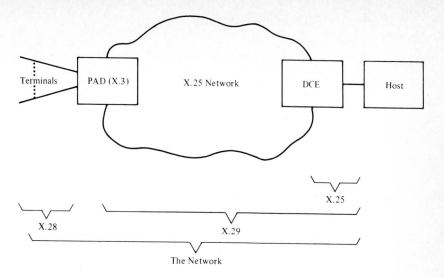

(a) Parameter-Defined Terminal

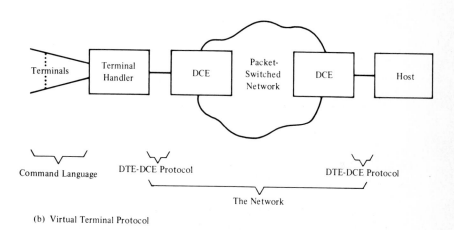

(b) Virtual Terminal Protocol

FIGURE 8-14. Two Views of Terminal-Network Architecture

performing the polling and selecting. Two approaches have been used:

1. Poll and select commands are delivered across the LAN to the various terminals.
2. Poll and select commands terminate at the host NIU. Each terminal NIU does its own polling and selecting, and the data to be exchanged is buffered at the host and terminal NIUs. Thus, when a host issues a poll, data will be delivered to the host only if there is already data in the host NIU buffer for the polled terminal.

In both cases, the NIUs must know which terminals are logically connected to which hosts in order to exercise the poll-and-select protocol.

Virtual Terminal Protocols

We have surveyed various techniques for connecting terminals to packet-switched local networks so that they can effectively communicate with host devices. There is, however, a problem buried in this approach that relates to one of the advertised benefits of a local network. Specifically, the local network user typically would like not to be locked into a single vendor. The user would like to be able to procure hosts and terminals from a variety of vendors, but also to maintain complete connectivity.

What does this imply? Usually, in order to be able to use a terminal from one vendor with a host from another vendor, a special host software package must be built to accommodate the foreign terminal. Now consider a LAN with N types of terminals and M types of hosts. For complete connectivity, each host type must contain a package for handling each terminal type. In the worst case, MN I/O packages must be developed. Furthermore, if a new type of host is acquired, it must be equipped with N new I/O packages. If a new type of terminal is acquired, each host must be equipped with a new I/O package, for a total of M new packages. This is not the type of situation designed to encourage multivendor LANs.

To solve this problem, a universal terminal protocol is needed—one that can handle all types of terminals. Such a thing exists today in name only: *virtual terminal protocol* (VTP). However, rudimentary versions do already exist. One is the TELNET protocol of ARPANET [DAVI77]. The true VTP is a fundamentally different and more flexible approach than the PAD concept. In this section we present a brief overview of VTP principles; more detail may be found in [DAY80], [DAY81], [MAGN79], and [LOWE83].

As the name implies, the VTP is a protocol, a set of conventions for communication between peer entities. It includes the following functions:

- Providing the service of establishing and maintaining a connection between two application-level entities.
- Controlling a dialogue for negotiating the allowable actions to be performed across the connection.
- Creating and maintaining a data structure that represents the "state" of the terminal.
- Translating between actual terminal characteristics and a standardized representation.

The first two functions are in the nature of session control (layer 5); the latter two are presentation control (layer 6) functions. Figure 8-14 illustrates the difference in philosophy between this approach and that of the PAD. In the VTP approach, the terminal handler, which implements the terminal side of the protocol, is considered architecturally as a host attached to the network. Thus the protocol is end-to-end in terms of reliability, flow control, and so on. On the other hand, the X.29 standard is not a protocol as such. The PAD is considered part of the network, not a separate host. From the point of view of the host, the PAD facility is part of its local DCE's X.25 layer 3 functionality. Although the PAD concept affords an easily implemented capability, it does not provide the architectural base for a flexible terminal-handling facility.

The principle purpose of the VTP is to transform the characteristics of a real terminal into a standardized form or virtual terminal. Because of the wide differences in capabilities among terminals, it is unreasonable to attempt to develop a single virtual terminal type. Four classes of interest:

- *Scroll mode:* These are terminals with no local intelligence, including keyboard-printer and keyboard-display devices. Characters are transmitted as they are entered, and incoming chracters are printed or displayed as they come in. On a display, as the screen fills, the top line is scrolled off.
- *Page mode:* These are keyboard-display terminals with a cursor-addressable character matrix display. Either user or host can modify random-accessed portions of the display. I/O can be a page at a time.
- *Form/data entry mode:* These are similar to page mode terminals, but allow definition of fixed and variable fields on the display. This permits a number of features, such as transmitting only the variable part, and defining field attributes to be used as validity checks.
- *Graphics mode:* These allow the creation of arbitrary two-dimensional patterns.

For any VTP, there are basically four phases of operation:

- *Connection management:* includes session-layer related functions, such as connection request and termination.
- *Negotiation:* used to determine a mutually agreeable set of characteristics between the two correspondents.
- *Control:* exchange of control information and commands (e.g., defining the attributes of a field).
- *Data:* transfer of data between two correspondents.

Figure 8-12d shows the terminal NIU architecture that supports a virtual terminal protocol. The VTP can be thought of as occupying layers 6 and 7 of the architecture. It interfaces to a session protocol entity at layer 5. On the host side, either of the FNP modes of attachment would work.

The ISO Virtual Terminal Service

The ISO virtual terminal service is an application-layer service defined within the framework of the open systems interconnection (OSI) model.

TABLE 8.5 Aspects of the ISO Virtual Terminal Service

Classes of Service
Basic
Forms
Graphics

Modes of Operation
Two-way alternate
Two-way simultaneous

Delivery Control
No delivery control
Simple delivery control
Quarantine delivery control

Echo Control
Local echo
Remote echo

The standard defines a model for a virtual terminal, which is an abstract representation of a real terminal. The standard defines operations that can be performed, such as reading text from the virtual keyboard, writing text on the virtual screen, and moving a cursor to a particular position on the virtual screen. The standard also defines a virtual terminal protocol for the exchange of data and control messages between a terminal and an application via the virtual terminal service. The protocol standard specifies the display data stream structure and the control messages by which the two sides can agree on the details of the terminal capabilities to be supported.

Rather than defining a single virtual terminal for all possible applications, the standard provides its users with the tools to define a virtual terminal suited to the application at hand and the physical limitations of the terminal. For example, if the physical terminal is monochrome, then the two sides agree not to use color information.

Table 8-5 lists some of the key aspects of the ISO standard. We examine each of these in turn.

Classes of Service

The ISO standard provides different classes of service. Each class meets the needs of a specific range of applications and terminal functions. So far, Basic, Forms, and Graphics classes have been identified. Of these, only the Basic class is fully defined and supported by vendors. We can expect to see the other classes available in the next few years.

The Basic class is a character-oriented service. In its simplest form, it meets the terminal access requirements of applications such as line editing and operating system command language interaction, which can be satisfied with simple scroll-mode terminals. The basic class also supports page-mode terminals and provides for the exchange of data in blocks instead of character-at-a-time. An extension to the basic class provides a primitive set of forms-related services. It allows the definition and addressing of individual fields and the transmission of selected fields. With this capability, the service can transfer just the variable fields on a form. However, there is no facility for defining or using field attributes.

The Forms class is designed to handle all of the operations associated with forms-mode terminals, such as the 3270 terminals. This would allow any forms-mode terminal from any vendor to interact with forms-mode applications on any host from any vendor. Finally, the Graphics class will deal with graphics and image-processing terminals.

Modes of Operation

The virtual terminal standard supports two modes of operation: two-way alternate (half duplex) and two-way simultaneous (full duplex). When a terminal sets up a connection to a host, the mode of operation is agreed upon between the two virtual service modules.

Two-way alternate mode enforces the discipline that only one side at a time can transmit. This prevents the situation in which data from the computer begin to appear on the terminal display screen while the user is entering text from the keyboard. The two-way alternate mode is typical of synchronous forms-mode terminals such as the 3270. Most normal enquiry/response applications are naturally two-way alternate, for example.

The two-way simultaneous mode permits both sides to transmit at the same time. An example of the utility of this would be the control terminal for a complex real-time system such as a process control plant. For such an application, the terminal must be capable of being updated rapidly with status changes even if the operator is typing in a command.

Delivery Control

Delivery control allows one side to control delivery of data to the other side to coordinate multiple actions. Normally, any data entered at a terminal are automatically delivered to the application on the other side as soon as possible, and any data transmitted by the application are delivered to the terminal as soon as possible. In some cases, however, one side may require explicit control over when certain data are delivered to its peer.

For example, suppose a user is logged on to a time-sharing system via the virtual terminal service. The time-sharing system may issue a single prompt character (e.g., ">") when it is ready for the next command. However, the terminal side of the virtual terminal service may choose to deliver data to the terminal for display only after several characters have been received, rather than one character at a time. Since this single prompt character must be displayed, and since the terminal side cannot reasonably be expected to know what the prompt character is, some mechanism is needed to force delivery. Another example is the use of special "function keys," which are often found on terminals and which can be set up to perform multiple actions, resulting in the transmission of multiple messages to the host. Sometimes it is desirable that all of the functions of the key are presented to the peer user simultaneously.

Three types of delivery control can be specified with any transmission:

- *No delivery control:* This is the default type. In this case data are made available to the peer at the convenience of the implementation of the virtual terminal service.
- *Simple delivery control:* In this case, the service user (terminal or application) can issue a request that all undelivered data be delivered. The invoking side may also, optionally, request acknowledgment of the delivery to the other side.
- *Quarantine delivery control:* This requires that the remote virtual terminal service module hold all incoming data until they are explicitly released for delivery by the other side. For example, an application could send a screenful of data in several small blocks but instruct the other side to defer delivery so that the entire screen update is displayed at once. Another example is the function key action mentioned previously.

Echo Control

Echo control is concerned with the control of how characters typed on a keyboard will cause updates to a display. In real terminals, characters typed on the keyboard may be displayed on the screen locally by the terminal as they are typed or may be "echoed back" to the display by the computer. The former option is less flexible but is often chosen when the communication link is half duplex and echoing back would therefore not be practical. The latter option is used where the communication line is full duplex and where greater control over the screen is required. For example, a time-sharing system may wish to suppress the display of the terminal user's password and identification code but display all other characters.

Virtual Terminal Parameters

In addition to the aspects of the virtual terminal service listed in Table 8-5, a major feature of the service is the use of terminal parameters. These are similar to those used in X.3 in that they provide a way of defining various characteristics of the terminal. However, the parameters available in the ISO standard are much more complex and powerful than those of X.3. They allow the user to define various characteristics of displayable characters, such as font, size, intensity, color, and so on. Control objects can be defined that are used to control formatting on the display, and to trigger various events such as ringing an alarm. Characteristics of other devices such as printers can also be specified.

CIRCUIT-SWITCHED NETWORKS

The interface issues relating to circuit-switched local networks are far simpler to deal with than those of packet-switched networks. With a circuit-switched local network, such as a digital PBX, the mode of attachment is essentially transparent, much like the layer 1 protocol mode discussed above.

As before, there are two phases of operation, a connection phase and a data transfer phase. The data transfer phase uses synchronous TDM; thus no protocols and no logic are required. As was mentioned, this is a truly transparent connection.

For the connection phase, the main issue is the means by which the attached device requests a connection. For this discussion, it is useful to refer back to Figure 7-16, which indicates that each digital data device attaches to the network via some form of data line group. At least three means of connection establishment have been used:

1. Data devices typically connect via a twisted pair; therefore, near the data device, there must be a line driver to which the device attaches. This driver can include a simple keypad for selecting a destination.
2. Either the line driver or the data line group (more likely the latter) can contain the logic for conducting a simple dialogue with a terminal. In this case, the terminal user enters the connection request via the terminal.
3. The attached device (host) could contain a simple I/O program that generates connection requests in a form understandable to the network.

Regardless of the means, the switch architecture can support the private network configuration shown in Figure 8-1a. The local network connection would appear as a dial-up line to the attached device.

Finally, we mention the protocol converter featured in Figure 7-16. This facility acts as a gateway between devices with dissimilar protocols. It is used, for example, to convert between asynchronous ASCII terminals and the synchronous IBM 3270 protocol. In the future, this might be used to implement a VTP.

ANALOG DEVICES

There are very few cases of analog device attachment to a local network to discuss. The most common is the telephone. Analog telephones are easily accommodated on a digital PBX that includes a codec in the line group (Figure 7-16). The other likely place to find analog devices is on a broadband network. As we have discussed, these networks easily accommodate video and audio attachments by dedicating channels for their use.

8.7

RECOMMENDED READING

As yet, there is not much literature on this subject. [STAC80]* is perhaps the most systematic look at NIU interfaces for LANs; other articles of interest are [BAL85]*, [CERR87]*, [SPAN86], and [CZOT87]. [OLSE83]* describes the layer 1 gateway approach for asynchronous terminals. A view of the issue for HSLNs is contained in [NESS81].

A readable description of X.3/X.28/X.29 is contained in [MART81a]. [DAY80] contains a good discussion of virtual terminal protocols.

8.8

PROBLEMS

8.1 Consider Figure 8-8. Assume that the host–NIU protocol is X.25 and the NIU–NIU protocol is IEEE 802. Describe, with an example, how the layer 3 X.25 protocol is converted to the LLC protocol for transmission over the network.

8.2 Repeat Problem 8.1, but now assume the ANS LDDI link layer for NIU–NIU.

8.3 Consider Figure 8-9. Assume that the host–NIU interface is IEEE-802 LLC. Describe, with an example, how the host layer 4 software makes use of the layer 2 services to transmit data to a destination host.

8.4 Repeat Problem 8.3, but now assume the ANS LDDI interface.

8.5 Consider a layer 1 gateway being used by devices that communicate with a synchronous layer 2 protocol, such as HDLC or BISYNC. How is the NIU overflow problem handled?

8.6 Describe how a protocol convert in a digital switch architecture can be used to implement VTP.

8.7 In Figure 8-10, the transport layer is in the NIU rather than the host and therefore part of the communications subnetwork. Since the transport layer is supposed to provide end-to-end reliability, is there cause for concern? Describe any potential problems and ways of attacking them.

CHAPTER **9**

Network Performance: LAN/HSLN

This chapter has two objectives:

- To give the reader some insight into the factors that affect performance and the relative performance of various local network schemes.
- To present analytic techniques that can be used for network sizing and to obtain first approximations of network performance.

It is beyond the scope of this book to derive analytic expressions for all of the performance measures presented; that would require an entire book on local network performance. Further, this chapter can only sketch the techniques that would be useful to the analyst in approximating performance; for deeper study, references to appropriate literature are provided.

Because of the distinctly different issues involved in packet-switched (LAN, HSLN) and circuit-switched (digital switch, digital PBX) networks, these are treated in separate chapters. This chapter begins by presenting some of the key performance considerations for LANs and HSLNs; the section serves to put the techniques and results presented subsequently into perspective. Separate sections present results for LAN and HSLN systems. Finally, the more difficult problem of end-to-end performance is broached.

LAN/HSLN PERFORMANCE CONSIDERATIONS

The key characteristics of the LAN that structure the way its performance is analyzed are that there is a shared access medium, requiring a medium access control protocol, and that packet switching is used. HSLNs share these characteristics. It follows that the basic performance considerations, and the approaches to performance analysis, will be the same for both. With the above points in mind, this section explores these basic considerations. The section begins by defining the basic measures of performance, then looks at the key parameter for determining LAN/HSLN performance, known affectionately to devotees as a [STAL86c]. Having been introduced to a, the reader is in a position to appreciate the interrelationship of the various factors that affect LAN/HSLN performance, which is the final topic.

The results that exist for the portion of performance within the local network boundary are summarized in subsequent sections. As we shall see, these results are best organized in terms of the medium access control protocol.

Measures of Performance

Three measures of LAN and HSLN performance are commonly used:

- D: the delay that occurs between the time and packet or frame is ready for transmission from a node, and the completion of successful transmission.
- S: the throughput of the local network; the total rate of data being transmitted between nodes (carried load).
- U: the utilization of the local network medium; the fraction of total capacity being used.

These measures concern themselves with performance within the local network. How they relate to the overall performance of the network and attached devices is discussed later.

The parameter S is often normalized and expressed as a fraction of capacity. For example, if over a period of 1 s, the sum of the successful data transfers between nodes is 1 Mb on a 10-Mbps channel, then $S = 0.1$. Thus S can also be interpreted as utilization. The analysis is commonly done in terms of the total number of bits transferred, including overhead (headers, trailers) bits; the calculations are a bit easier, and this approach isolates performance effects due to the local network alone. One must work backward from this to determine effective throughput.

Results for S and D are generally plotted as a function of the offered load G, which is the actual load or traffic demand presented to the local network. Note that S and G differ. S is the normalized rate of data packets successfully transmitted; G is the total number of packets offered to the network; it includes control packets, such as tokens, and collisions, which are destroyed packets that must be retransmitted. G, too, is often expressed as a fraction of capacity. Intuitively, we would expect D to increase with G: The more traffic competing for transmission time, the longer the delay for any individual transmission. S should also increase with G, up to some saturation point, beyond which the network cannot handle more load.

Figure 9-1 shows the ideal situation: channel utilization increases to accommodate load up to an offered load equal to the full capacity of the system; then utilization remains at 100%. Of course, any overhead or inefficiency will cause performance to fall short of the goal. The depiction of S versus G is a reasonable one from the point of view of the network itself. It shows the behavior of the system based on the actual load on it. But from the point of view of the user or the attached device, it may seem strange. Why? Because the offered load includes not only original transmissions but also acknowledgments and, in the case of errors or collisions, retransmissions. The user may want to know the throughput and the delay characteristics as a function of the device-generated data to be put through the system—the "input load." Or if the network is the focus, the analyst may want to know what the offered load is given the input load. We will return to this discussion later.

The reader may also wonder about the importance of U. D and S are certainly of interest, but the efficiency or utilization of the channel may seem of minor importance. After all, local networks are advertised as having very high bandwidth and low cost compared to long-haul networks.

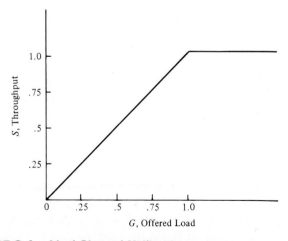

FIGURE 9-1. Ideal Channel Utilization

9.1 LAN/HSLN PERFORMANCE CONSIDERATIONS

TABLE 9.1 Example of Relationships Among LAN/HSLN Measures of Performance[a,b]

I	S	G	D	U
100	100	101	0.0505	0.1
500	500	505	0.2525	0.5
990	990	1000	0.5	0.99
2000	990	—	—	0.99

[a] Capacity: 1000 frames/sec.
[b] I, input load (frames per second); S, throughput (frames per second); G, offered load (frames per second); D, delay (seconds); U, utilization (fraction of capacity).

Although it is true that utilization is of less importance for local compared to long-haul links, it is still worth considering. Local network capacity is not free, and demand has a tendency to expand to fill available capacity.

In summary, we have introduced two additional parameters:

- G: the offered load to the local network; the total rate of data presented to the network for transmission.
- I: the input load; the rate of data generated by the stations attached to the local network.

Table 9.1 is a very simplified example to show the relationship between these parameters. Here we assume a network with a capacity of $C = 1000$ frames per second. For simplicity, I, S, and G are expressed in frames per second. It is assumed that 1% of all transmitted frames are lost and must be repeated. Thus at an input $I = 100$ frames per second, on the average 1 frame per second will be repeated. Thus $S = 100$ and $G = 101$. Assume that the input load arrives in batches, once per second. Hence, on average, with $I = 100$, $D = 0.0505$ s. The utilization is defined as $S/C = 0.1$.

The next two entries are easily seen to be correct. Note that for $I = 990$, the entire capacity of the system is being used ($G = 1000$). If I increases beyond this point, the system cannot keep up. Only 1000 frames per second will be transmitted. Thus S remains at 990 and U at 0.99. But G and D grow without bound as more and more backlog accumulates; there is no steady-state value. This pattern will become familiar as the chapter proceeds.

The Effect of Propagation Delay and Transmission Rate

Recall from Figure 1-1 that local networks are distinguished from long-haul networks on the one hand, and multiprocessor systems on the other, by the data rate (R) employed and the distance (d) of the communications path. In fact, it is the product of these two terms, $R \times d$, that can be used to characterize local networks. Furthermore, as we shall see, this term, or cousins of it, is the single most important parameter for determining the performance of a local network. We shall see that a network's performance will be the same, for example, for both a 100-Mbps, 1 km bus and a 10 Mbps, 10 km bus.

A good way to visualize the meaning of $R \times d$ is to divide it by the propagation velocity of the medium, which is nearly constant among most media of interest. A good approximation for propagation velocity is about two-thirds of the speed of light, or 2×10^8 m/s. A dimensional analysis of the formula

$$\frac{Rd}{V}$$

shows this to be equal to the length of the transmission medium in bits, that is, the number of bits that may be in transit between two nodes at any one time.

We can see that this does indeed distinguish local networks from multi-processor and long haul networks. Within a multiprocessor system, there are generally only a few bits in transit. For example, the latest IBM I/O channel offering operates at up to 24 Mbps over a distance of up to 120 m, which yields at most about 15 bits. Processor-to-processor communication within a single computer will typically involve fewer bits than that in transit. On the other hand, we saw in Chapter 6 that the bit length of a long-haul network can be hundreds of thousands of bits. In between, we have local networks. Several examples: a 500-m Ethernet system (10 Mbps) has a bit length of 25; both a 1-km HYPERchannel (50 Mbps) and a typical 5-km broadband LAN (5 Mbps) are about 250 bits long.

A useful way of looking at this is to consider the length of the medium as compared to the typical frame transmitted. Multiprocessor systems have very short bit lengths compared to frame length; long-haul nets have very long ones. Local networks generally are shorter than a frame up to about the same order of magnitude as a frame.

Intuitively, one can see that this will make a difference. Compare local networks to multiprocessor computers. Relatively speaking, things happen almost simultaneously in a multiprocessor system; when one component begins to transmit, the others know it almost immediately. For local networks, the relative time gap leads to all kinds of complications in the medium access control protocols; as we have seen. Compare long-haul networks to local networks. To have any hope of efficiency, the long-haul link must allow multiple frames to be in transit simultaneously. This places specific requirements on the link layer protocol, which must deal with a sequence of outstanding frames waiting to be acknowledged. LAN and HSLN protocol generally allow only one frame to be in transit at a time, or at the most a few for some ring protocols. Again, this affects the access protocol.

The length of the medium, expressed in bits, compared to the length of the typical frame is usually denoted by a:

$$a = \frac{\text{length of data path (in bits)}}{\text{length of frame}}$$

Some manipulation shows that

$$a = \frac{Rd}{VL}$$

where L is the length of the frame. But d/V is the propagation time on the medium (worst case), and L/B is the time it takes a transmitter to get an entire frame out onto the medium. So

$$a = \frac{\text{propagation time}}{\text{transmission time}}$$

Typical values of a range from about 0.01 to 0.1 for LANs and 0.01 to over 1 for HSLNs. Table 9.2 gives some sample values for a bus topology. In computing a, keep in mind that the maximum propagation time on a broadband network is double the length of the longest path from the headend, plus the delay, if any, at the headend. For baseband bus and ring networks, repeater delays must be included in propagation time.

The parameter a determines an upper bound on the utilization of a local network. Consider a perfectly efficient access mechanism that allows only one transmission at a time. As soon as one transmission is over, another node begins transmitting. Furthermore, the transmission is pure data—no overhead bits. (*Note:* These conditions are very close to being met in a digital switch but not, alas, in LANs and HSLNs.) What is the maximum

TABLE 9.2   Values of _a_

Data Rate (Mbps)	Packet Size (bits)	Cable length (km)	_a_
1	100	1	0.05
1	1,000	10	0.05
1	100	10	0.5
10	100	1	0.5
10	1,000	1	0.05
10	1,000	10	0.5
10	10,000	10	0.05
50	10,000	1	0.025
50	100	1	2.5

possible utilization of the network? It can be expressed as the ratio of total throughput of the system to the capacity or bandwidth:

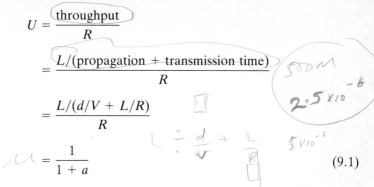

$$U = \frac{\text{throughput}}{R}$$

$$= \frac{L/(\text{propagation} + \text{transmission time})}{R}$$

$$= \frac{L/(d/V + L/R)}{R}$$

$$U = \frac{1}{1 + a} \tag{9.1}$$

So, utilization varies inversely with a. This can be grasped intuitively by studying Figure 9-2. This figure shows a baseband bus with two stations as far apart as possible (worst case) that take turns sending frames. If we normalize time such that the frame transmission time $= 1$, then $a = $ propagation time. The sequence of events can be expressed as follows.

1. A station begins transmission at t_0.
2. Reception begins at $t_0 + a$.
3. Transmission is completed at $t_0 + 1$.
4. Reception ends at $t_0 + 1 + a$.
5. The other station begins transmitting.

Propagation Time $= a < 1$ Transmission Time $= 1$

t_0
Start Of Transmission

$t_0 + a$
Start Of Reception

$t_0 + 1$
End Of Transmission

$t_0 + 1 + a$
End Of Reception

Packet Transmission Time $= 1$
Time Bus In Use $= 1 + a$
Efficiency $= 1/(1 + a)$

FIGURE 9-2a.   Effect of _a_ on Utilization: Baseband Bus (_a_ < 1)

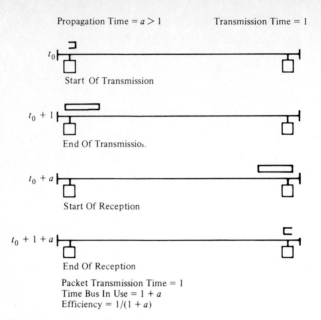

Propagation Time = $a > 1$ Transmission Time = 1

t_0 Start Of Transmission

$t_0 + 1$ End Of Transmissio٠.

$t_0 + a$ Start Of Reception

$t_0 + 1 + a$ End Of Reception

Packet Transmission Time = 1
Time Bus In Use = $1 + a$
Efficiency = $1/(1 + a)$

FIGURE 9-2b.   Effect of *a* on Utilization: Baseband Bus (*a* > 1)

Event 2 occurs *after* event 3 if $a > 1.0$. In any case the total time for one "turn" is $1 + a$, but the transmission time is only 1, for a utilization of $1/(1 + a)$.

The same effect can be seen to apply to a ring network in Figure 9-3. Here we assume that one station transmits and then waits to receive its own transmission before any other station transmits. The identical sequence of events outlined above applies.

Equation (9.1) is plotted in Figure 9-4. The implications for throughput are shown in Figure 9-5. As offered load increases, throughput remains equal to offered load up to the full capacity of the network (when $S = G = \dfrac{1}{1 + a}$), and then remains at $S = \dfrac{1}{1 + a}$ as load increases.

So we can say that an upper bound on the utilization or efficiency of a LAN or HSLN is $1/(1 + a)$, regardless of the medium access protocol used. Two caveats: First, this assumes that the maximum propagation time is incurred on each transmission. Second, it assumes that only one transmission may occur at a time. These assumptions are not always true; nevertheless, the formula $1/(1 + a)$ is almost always a valid upper bound, because the overhead of the medium access protocol more than makes up for the lack of validity of these assumptions.

The overhead is unavoidable. Frames must include address and synchronization bits. There is administrative overhead for controlling the protocol. In addition, there are forms of overhead peculiar to one or more

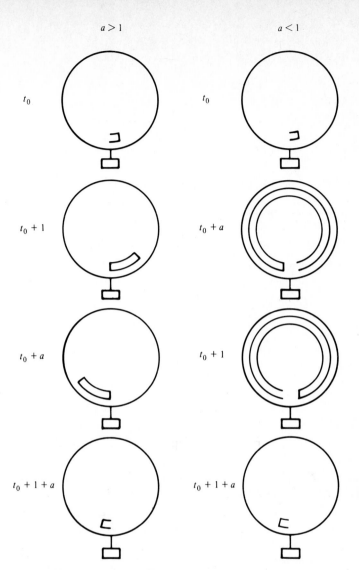

FIGURE 9-3. Effect of a on Utilization: Ring

of the protocols. We highlight these briefly for the most important protocols:

- *Contention protocols (ALOHA, S-ALOHA, CSMA, CSMA/CD):* time wasted due to collisions; need for acknowledgment frames. S-ALOHA requires that slot size equal transmission plus maximum propagation time.
- *Delay scheduling:* time spent waiting to see if other stations have data to send; acknowledgment frames.
- *Token bus:* time waiting for token if logically intervening stations have no data to send; token transmission; acknowledgment frames.

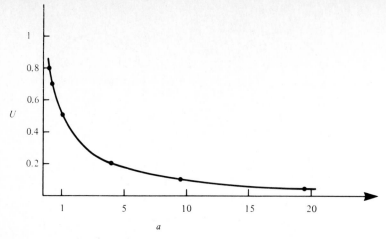

FIGURE 9-4. Utilization as a Function of *a*

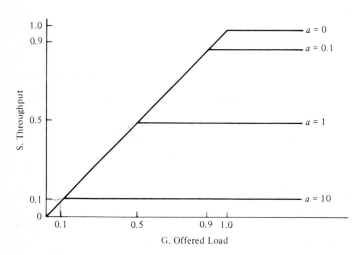

FIGURE 9-5. Effect of *a* on Throughput

- *Token ring:* time waiting for token if intervening stations have no data to send.
- *Slotted ring:* time waiting for empty slot if intervening stations have no data to send.
- *Register insertion:* delay at each node of time equal to address length. From the point of view of a single station, the propagation time and hence *a* may increase due to insertion of registers on the ring.
- *Explicit reservation:* reservation transmission, acknowledgments.
- *Implicit reservation:* overhead of protocol used to establish reservation, acknowledgments.

There are two distinct effects here. One is that the efficiency or utilization of a channel decreases as a increases. This, of course, affects throughput. The other effect is that the overhead attributable to a protocol wastes bandwidth and hence reduces effective utilization and effective throughput. By and large, we can think of these two effects as independent and additive. However, we shall see that, for contention protocols, there is a strong interaction such that the overhead of these protocols increases as a function of a.

In any case, it would seem desirable to keep a as low as possible. Looking back to the defining formula, for a fixed network a can be reduced by increasing frame size. This will only be useful if the length of messages produced by a station is an integral multiple of the frame size (excluding overhead bits). Otherwise, the large frame size is itself a source of waste. Furthermore, a large frame size increases the delay for other stations. This leads us to the next topic: the various factors that affect LAN/HSLN performance.

Factors That Affect Performance

We list here those factors that affect the performance of a LAN or a HSLN. We are concerned here with that part which is independent of the attached devices—those factors that are exclusively under the control of the local network designer. The chief factors are:

- Capacity
- Propagation delay
- Number of bits per frame
- Local network protocols
- Offered load
- Number of stations

The first three terms have already been discussed; they determine the value of a.

Next are the local network protocols: physical, medium access, and link. The physical layer is not likely to be much of a factor; generally, it can keep up with transmissions and receptions with little delay. The link layer will add some overhead bits to each frame and some administrative overhead, such as virtual circuit management and acknowledgments. This area has not been studied much, and is best considered as part of the end-to-end peformance problem discussed in Section 9.4. This leaves the medium access layer, which can have a significant effect on network performance. Sections 9.2 and 9.3 are devoted to this topic.

We can think of the first three factors listed above as characterizing the network; they are generally treated as constants or givens. The local network protocol is the focus of the design effort—the choice that must be made. The next two factors, offered load and the number of stations, are generally treated as the independent variables. The analyst is concerned with determining performance as a function of these two variables. Note that these two variables must be treated separately. Certainly, it is true that for a fixed offered load per station, the total offered load increases as the number of stations increase. The same increase could be achieved by keeping the number of stations fixed but increasing the offered load per station. However, as we shall see, the network performance will be different for these two cases.

One factor that was not listed above: the error rate of the channel. An error in a frame transmission necessitates a retransmission. Because the error rates on local networks are so low, this is not likely to be a significant factor.

9.2

LAN PERFORMANCE

A considerable amount of work has been done on the analysis of the performance of various LAN protocols for bus/tree and ring. This section will limit itself to summarizing the results for the protocols discussed in Chapter 5, those protocols that are most common for LANs.

We begin by presenting an easily-used technique for quickly establishing bounds on performance. Often, this back-of-the-envelope approach is adequate for system sizing.

Next, a comparison of the three protocols standardized by IEEE 802 (CSMA/CD, token bus, token ring) is presented. These three protocols are likely to dominate the market and an insight into their comparative performance is needed.

We then look more closely at contention protocols and devote more time here to the derivation of results. This process should give the reader a feeling for the assumptions that must be made and the limitations of the results. More time is spent on the contention protocols because we wish to understand their inherent instability. As we shall see, the basis of this instability is a positive feedback mechanism that behaves poorly under heavy load.

Finally, we revisit token ring and view it in context with the other two common ring protocols: register insertion and slotted ring.

Bounds on Performance

The purpose of this section is to present a remarkably simple technique for determining bounds on the performance of an LAN. Although a considerable amount of work has been done on developing detailed analytic and simulation models of the performance of various LAN protocols, much of this work is suspect because of the restrictive assumptions made. Furthermore, even if the models were valid, they provide a level of resolution not needed by the local network designer.

A commonsense argument should clarify this point. In any LAN or HSLN, there are three regions of operation, based on the magnitude of the offered load:

- A region of low delay through the network, where the capacity is more than adequate to handle the load offered.
- A region of high delay, where the network becomes a bottleneck. In this region, relatively more time is spent controlling access to the network and less in actual data transmission compared to the low-delay region.
- A region of unbounded delay, where the offered load exceeds the total capacity of the system.

This last region is easily identified. For example, consider the following network:

- Capacity = 1 Mbps
- Number of stations = 1000
- Frame size = 1000 bits

If, on average, each station generates data at a rate exceeding 1 frame per second, then the total offered load exceeds 1 Mbps. The delay at each station will build up and up without bound.

The third region is clearly to be avoided. But almost always, the designer will wish to avoid the second region as well. The second region implies an inefficient use to the network. Further, a sudden surge of data while in the second region would cause corresponding increases in the already high delay. In the first region, the network is not a bottleneck and, as we will discuss in Section 9.4, will contribute typically only a small amount to the end-to-end delay.

Thus the crucial question is: What region will the network operate in, based on projected load and network characteristics? The third region is easily identified and avoided; it is the boundary between the first two regions that must be identified. If the network operates below that boundary, it should not cause a communications bottleneck. If it operates above the boundary, there is reason for concern and perhaps redesign. Now, the issue is: How precisely do we need to know the boundary? The load on the network will vary over time and can only be estimated. Because the load estimates are unlikely to be precise, it is not necessary to know exactly where that boundary is. If a good approximation for the boundary can be developed, then the network can be sized so that the estimated load is well below the boundary. In the example just described, the estimated load is

1 Mbps. If the capacity of the LAN is such that the boundary is approximately 4 Mbps, then the designer can be reasonably sure that the network will not be a bottleneck.

With the above points in mind, we present a technique for estimating performance bounds, based on the approach taken by the IEEE 802 committee [STUC85]. To begin, let us ignore the medium access control protocol and develop bounds for throughput and delay as a function of the number of active stations. Four quantities are needed:

- T_{idle} = the mean time that a station is idle between transmission attempts: the station has no messages awaiting transmission.
- T_{msg} = the time required to transmit a message once medium access is gained.
- T_{delay} = the mean delay from the time a station has a packet to transmit until completion of transmission; includes queueing time and transmission time.
- THRU = mean total throughput on the network of messages per unit time.

We assume that there are N active stations, each with the same load-generating requirements. To find an upper bound on total throughput, consider the ideal case in which there is no queueing delay: Each station transmits when it is ready. Hence each station alternates between idle and transmission with a throughput of $1/(T_{idle} + T_{msg})$. The maximum possible throughput is just the summation of the throughputs of all N stations:

$$\text{THRU} \leq \frac{N}{T_{idle} + T_{msg}} \tag{9.2}$$

This upper bound increases as N increases, but is only reasonable up to the point of raw capacity of the network, which can be expressed

$$\text{THRU} \leq \frac{1}{T_{msg}} \tag{9.3}$$

The breakpoint between these two bounds occurs at

$$\frac{N}{T_{idle} + T_{msg}} = \frac{1}{T_{msg}}$$

$$N = \frac{T_{idle} + T_{msg}}{T_{msg}} \tag{9.4}$$

This breakpoint defines two regions of operation. With the number of stations below the breakpoint, the system is not generating enough load to utilize fully system capacity. However, above the breakpoint, the network is saturated: it is fully utilized and is not able to satisfy the demands of the attached stations.

To see the reasonableness of this breakpoint, consider that the capacity of the network is $1/T_{\text{msg}}$. For example, if it takes 1 μs to transmit a message, the data rate is 10^6 messages per second. The amount of traffic being generated by N stations is $N/(T_{\text{idle}} + T_{\text{msg}})$. If the traffic exceeds the network's capacity, messages get backlogged and delay increases. Note also that traffic increases either by increasing the number of stations (N) or increasing the rate at which stations transmit messages (reduce T_{idle}).

These same considerations allow us to place a lower bound on delay. Clearly,

$$T_{\text{delay}} \geq T_{\text{msg}} \qquad (9.5)$$

Now, consider that at any load the following relationship holds:

$$\text{THRU} = \frac{N}{T_{\text{idle}} + T_{\text{delay}}} \qquad (9.6)$$

since $1/(T_{\text{idle}} + T_{\text{delay}})$ is the throughput of each station. Combining (9.3) and (9.6) we have

$$T_{\text{delay}} \geq NT_{\text{msg}} - T_{\text{idle}}$$

The breakpoint calculation, combining (9.5) and the equation above yields the same result as before (see Figure 9-6). Keep in mind that these bounds are asymptotes of the true delay and throughput curves. The breakpoint delimits two regions. Below the breakpoint, capacity is under-utilized and delay is low. Above the breakpoint, capacity saturates and delay blows up. In actuality, the changes are gradual rather than abrupt.

Bounds on the other side are easily found. The delay would be maximized if all N stations had a message to transmit simultaneously:

$$T_{\text{delay}} \leq NT_{\text{msg}}$$

Combining with equation (9.6) gives us

$$\text{THRU} \geq \frac{N}{T_{\text{idle}} + NT_{\text{msg}}}$$

These bounds give one a rough idea of the behavior of a system. It allows one to do a simple back-of-the-envelope calculation to determine if a proposed system is within reasonable bounds. If the answer is no, much analysis and grief may be saved. If yes, the analyst must dig deeper.

Two examples should clarify the use of these equations. First, consider a workstation attached to a 1-Mbps local network that generates, on average, three messages per minute, with messages averaging 500 bits. With message transmission time equal to 500 μs, the mean idle time is 20 s. The breakpoint number of stations is, roughly,

$$N = \frac{20}{500 \times 10^{-6}} = 40{,}000 \text{ stations}$$

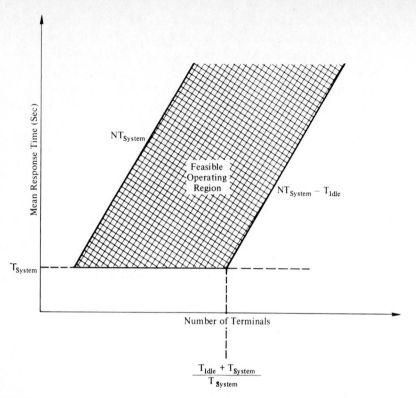

FIGURE 9-6. Feasible Operating Region, Zero-Overhead System

If the number of stations is much less than this, say 1000, congestion should not be a problem. If it is much more, say 100,000, congestion may be a problem.

Second, consider a set of stations that generate PCM digitized voice packets on a 10-Mbps local network. Data are generated at the rate of 64 kbps. For 0.1-s packets, we have a transmission time per packet of 640 μs. Thus

$$N = \frac{0.1}{640 \times 10^{-6}} = 156 \text{ stations}$$

Generally, we would not expect all voice stations (telephones) to be active at one time; perhaps one-fourth is a reasonable estimate, so the breakpoint is around 600 stations.

Note that in both these examples, we have very quickly arrived at a first-order sizing of the system with no knowledge of the protocol. All that is needed is the load generated per station and the capacity of the network.

The calculations above are based on a system with no overhead. They provide bounds for a system with perfect scheduling. One way to account for overhead is to replace T_{msg} with T_{sys}, where the latter quantity includes an estimate of the overhead per packet. This is done in Figure 9-6.

A more accurate, though still rough handle on performance can be had by considering the protocol involved. We develop the results for token passing. A similar analysis can be found in [HAYE81]. This protocol, for bus or ring, has the following characteristics:

- Stations are given the opportunity to transmit in a fixed cyclical sequence.
- At each opportunity, a station may transmit one message.
- Frames may be of fixed or variable length.
- Preemption is not allowed.

Some additional terms are needed:

- $R(K)$ = mean throughput rate (messages/second) of station K
- T_{over} = total overhead (seconds) in one cycle of the N stations
- C = duration (seconds) of a cycle
- UTIL(K) = utilization of the network due to station K.

Let us begin by assuming that each station always has messages to transmit; the system is never idle. The fraction of time that the network is busy handling requests from station K is just

$$\mathrm{UTIL}(K) = R(K)\, T_{\mathrm{msg}}(K)$$

To keep up with the work, the system must not be presented with a load greater than its capacity:

$$\sum_{K=1}^{N} \mathrm{UTIL}(K) = \sum_{K=1}^{N} R(K) T_{\mathrm{msg}}(K) \le 1$$

Now consider the overhead in the system, which is the time during a cycle required to pass the token and perform other maintenance functions. Clearly,

$$C = T_{\mathrm{over}} + \sum_{K=1}^{N} T_{\mathrm{msg}}(K)$$

From this we can deduce that

$$R(K) = \frac{1}{C} = \frac{1}{T_{\mathrm{over}} + \displaystyle\sum_{K=1}^{N} T_{\mathrm{msg}}(K)}$$

Now, let us assume that the medium is always busy but that some stations may be idle. This line of reasoning will lead us to the desired bounds on throughput and delay. Since we assume that the network is never idle, the fraction of time the system spends on overhead and transmission must sum to unity:

$$\frac{T_{over}}{C} + \sum_{K=1}^{N} R(K)T_{msg}(K) = 1$$

Thus

$$C = \frac{T_{over}}{1 - \sum_{K=1}^{N} R(K)T_{msg}(K)}$$

Note that the duration of a cycle is proportional to the overhead; doubling the mean overhead time should double the cycle time for a fixed load. This result may not be intuitively obvious; the reader is advised to work out a few examples.

With C known, we can place an upper bound on the throughput of any one source:

$$R(J) \leq \frac{1}{C} = \frac{1 - \sum_{K=1}^{N} R(K)T_{msg}(K)}{T_{over}} \tag{9.7}$$

Now let us assume that all sources are identical: $R(K) = R$, $T_{msg}(K) = T_{msg}$. Then (9-7) reduces to

$$R \leq \frac{1 - NRT_{msg}}{T_{over}}$$

Solving for R:

$$R < \frac{1}{T_{over} + NT_{msg}}$$

But, by definition, $R = 1/(T_{delay} + T_{idle})$, so we can express:

$$T_{delay} = \frac{1}{R} - T_{idle}$$

$$T_{delay} \geq T_{over} + NT_{msg} - T_{idle}$$

In practice, T_{over} may consist of some fixed amount of time C_0 for each cycle plus an amount C_1 for each station that receives the token. These numbers will differ for token ring and token bus:

$$T_{delay} \geq C_0 + N(T_{msg} + C_1) - T_{idle}$$

We also have the inequality of (9.5) and can solve for the breakpoint:

$$N = \frac{T_{msg} + T_{idle} - C_0}{T_{msg} + C_1} \tag{9.8}$$

Figure 9-7 depicts the delay-station plot, showing the two regions. Note that the slope of the line in the heavily loaded region is $T_{msg} + C_1$.

A similar analysis can be carried out for CSMA/CD. Figure 9-8 is a comparison developed in [STUC85]. The absolute positions of the various policies depend on specific assumptions about overhead and, in the case of CSMA/CD, the value of a. But the relative positions are generally true: under lightly loaded conditions CSMA/CD has a shorter delay time, but the protocol breaks down more rapidly under increasing load.

Comparative Performance of Token Passing and CSMA/CD

The purpose of this section is to give the reader some insight into the relative performance of the most important LAN protocols: CSMA/CD, token bus, and token ring. We begin with simplified models which highlight the main points of comparison. Following this, a careful analysis performed by the IEEE 802 committee is reported.

For the models, we assume a local network with N active stations. Our purpose is to estimate the maximum throughput achievable on the LAN.

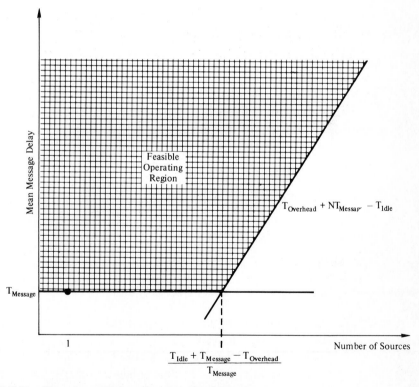

FIGURE 9-7.   Bounds on Token-Passing Performance

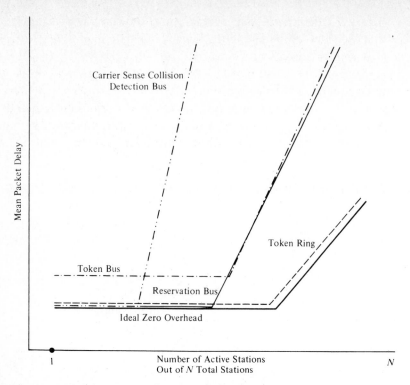

FIGURE 9-8. Comparative Bounds on LAN Protocols

For this purpose, we assume that each station is always prepared to send a frame.

First, let us consider token ring. Time on the ring will alternate between data frame transmission and token passing. Refer to a single instance of a data frame followed by a token as a cycle and define:

- C = average time for one cycle
- DF = average time to transmit a data frame
- TF = average time time to pass a token

It should be clear that the average cycle rate is just $1/C = 1/(DF + TF)$. Intuitively,

$$S = \frac{DF}{DF + TF} \tag{9.9}$$

That is, the throughput, normalized to system capacity, is just the fraction of time that is spent transmitting data.

Refer now to Figure 9-3; time is normalized such that frame transmission time equals 1 and propagation time equals a. For the case of $a < 1$, a station transmits a frame at time t_0, receives the leading edge of its own frame at $t_0 + a$, and completes transmission at $t_0 + 1$. The station then emits a token, which takes time a/N to reach the next station (assuming equally spaced stations). Thus one cycle takes $1 + a/N$ and the transmission time is 1. So $S = 1/(1 + a/N)$.

For $a > 1$, the reasoning is slightly different. A station transmits at t_0, completes transmission at $t_0 + 1$, and receives the leading edge of its frame at $t_0 + a$. At that point, it is free to emit a token, which takes a time a/N to reach the next station. The cycle time is therefore $a + a/N$ and $S = 1/[a(1 + 1/N)]$. Summarizing,

$$\text{Token:} \quad S = \begin{cases} \dfrac{1}{1 + a/N} & a < 1 \\[3mm] \dfrac{1}{a(1 + 1/N)} & a > 1 \end{cases} \qquad (9.10)$$

The reasoning above applies equally well to token bus, where we assume that the logical ordering is the same as the physical ordering and that token-passing time is therefore a/N.

For CSMA/CD, we base our approach on a derivation in [METC76]. Consider time on the medium to be organized into slots whose length is twice the end-to-end propagation delay. This is a convenient way to view the activity on the medium; the slot time is the maximum time, from the start of transmission, required to detect a collision. Again, assume that there are N active stations, each generating the same load. Clearly, if each station always has a packet to transmit, it does so, there will be nothing but collisions on the line. Therefore, we assume that each station restrains itself to transmitting during an available slot with probability p.

Time on the medium consists of two types of intervals. First is a transmission interval, which lasts $1/2a$ slots. Second is a contention interval, which is a sequence of slots with either a collision or no transmission in each slot. The throughput is just the proportion of time spent in transmission intervals [similar to the reasoning for equation (9.1)].

To determine the average length of a contention interval, we begin by computing A, the probability that exactly one station attempts a transmission in a slot and therefore acquires the medium. This is just the binomial probability that any one station attempts to transmit and the others do not:

$$A = \binom{N}{1} p^1 (1 - p)^{N-1}$$

$$= Np(1 - p)^{N-1}$$

This function takes on a maximum over p when $p = 1/N$:

$$A = \left(1 - \frac{1}{N}\right)^{N-1}$$

Why are we interested in the maximum? Well, we want to calculate the maximum throughput of the medium. It should be clear that this will be achieved if we maximize the probability of successful seizure of the medium. This says that the following rule should be enforced: During periods of heavy usage, a station should restrain its offered load to $1/N$. (This assumes that each station knows the value of N; in order to derive an expression for maximum possible throughput, we live with this assumption.) On the other hand, during periods of light usage, maximum utilization cannot be achieved because G is too low; this region is not of interest here.

Now we can estimate the mean length of a contention interval, w, in slots:

$$E[w] = \sum_{i=1}^{\infty} i \cdot \text{Pr}\,[i \text{ slots in a row with a collision or no}$$

$$\text{transmission followed by a slot with one transmission}]$$

$$= \sum_{i=1}^{\infty} i(1 - A)^i A$$

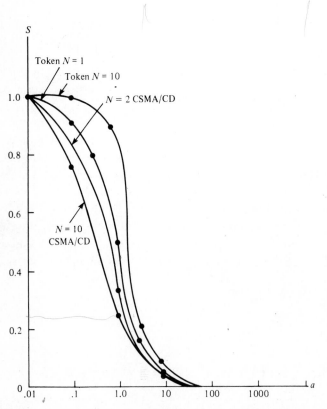

FIGURE 9-9. Throughput as a Function of a for Token Passing and CSMA/CD

The summation converges to

$$E[w] = \frac{1 - A}{A}$$

We can now determine the maximum utilization, which is just the length of a transmission interval as a proportion of a cycle consisting of a transmission and a contention interval.

$$CSMA/CD: \quad S = \frac{1/2a}{1/2a + \dfrac{1 - A}{A}} = \frac{1}{1 + 2a\dfrac{1 - A}{A}} \tag{9.11}$$

Figure 9-9 shows normalized throughput as a function of a for various values of N and for both token passing and CSMA/CD. For both protocols, throughput declines as a increases. This is to be expected. But the dramatic difference between the two protocols is seen in Figure 9-10, which shows throughput as a function of N. Token-passing performance actually improves as a function of N, because less time is spent in token passing. Conversely, the performance of CSMA/CD decreases because of the increased likelihood of collision.

$0 \cdot 4096$

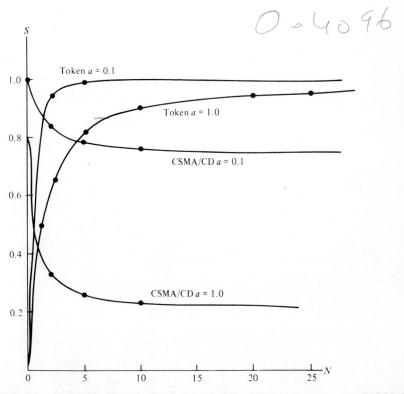

FIGURE 9-10. Throughput as a Function of _N_ for Token Passing and CSMA/CD

It is interesting to note the asymptotic value of S as N increases. For token:

$$Token: \qquad \lim_{N\to\infty} S = \begin{cases} 1 & a < 1 \\ \dfrac{1}{a} & a > 1 \end{cases}$$

For CSMA/CD, we need to know that $\lim_{N\to\infty}(1 - 1/N)^{N-1} = 1/e$. Then

$$CSMA/CD: \qquad \lim_{N\to\infty} S = \frac{1}{1 + 3.44a}$$

Continuing this example, it is relatively easy to derive an expression for delay for token passing. Once a station (station 1) transmits, it must wait for the following events to occur before it can transmit again:

- Station 1 transmits token to station 2.
- Station 2 transmits data frame.
- Station 2 transmits token to station 3.
- Station transmits data frame.

$$\cdot$$
$$\cdot$$
$$\cdot$$
$$\cdot$$

- Station $N - 1$ transmits token to station N.
- Station N transmits data frame.
- Station N transmits token to station 1.

Thus the delay consists of $(N - 1)$ cycles plus a/N, the token passing time. We have

$$Token: \qquad D = \begin{cases} N + a - 1 & a < 1 \\ aN & a > 1 \end{cases} \qquad (9.12)$$

Thus, delay increases linearly with load, and for a fixed number of stations delay is constant and finite even if all stations always have something to send. The delay for CSMA/CD is more difficult to express and depends on the exact nature of the protocol (persistence, retry policy). In general, we can say that the delay grows without bound as the system becomes saturated. As N increases, there are more collisions and longer contention intervals. Individual frames must make more attempts to achieve successful transmission. We explore this behavior further in the next station.

We now report the results of a deeper analysis done for the IEEE 802 committee [STUC85]. A similar analysis is also reported in [BUX81]. The analysis is based on considering not only mean values but second moments of delay and message length. Two cases of message arrival statistics are employed. In the first, only 1 station out of 100 has messages to transmit, and is always ready to transmit. In such a case, one would hope that the network would not be the bottleneck, but could easily keep up with one station. In the second case, 100 stations out of 100 always have messages to transmit. This represents an extreme of congestion and one would expect that the network may be a bottleneck.

The results are shown in Figure 9-11. It shows the actual data transmission rate versus the transmission speed on a 2-km bus. Note that the abscissa is not offered load but the actual capacity of the medium. The 1 station or 100 stations provide enough input to utilize the network fully. Hence these plots are a measure of maximum potential utilization. Three systems are examined: token ring with a 1-bit latency per station, token bus, and CSMA/CD. The analysis yields the following conclusions:

- For the given parameters, the smaller the mean frame length, the greater the difference in maximum mean throughput rate between token passing and CSMA/CD. This reflects the strong dependence of CSMA/CD on a.

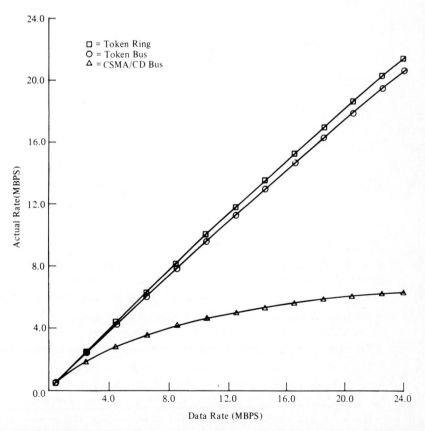

FIGURE 9-11a. Maximum potential data rate for LAN protocols: 2000 bits per packet; 100 stations active out of 100 stations total

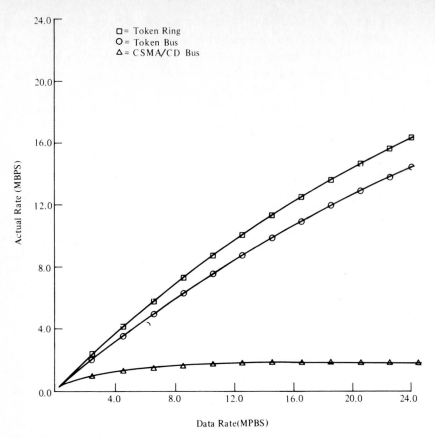

FIGURE 9-11b. 500 bits per packet,; 100 stations active out of 100 stations total

- Token ring is the least sensitive to work load.
- CSMA/CD offers the shortest delay under light load, while it is most sensitive under heavy load to the work load.

Note also that in the case of a single station transmitting, token bus is significantly less effient than the other two protocols. This is so because the assumption is made that the propagation delay is longer than for token ring, and that the delay in token processing is greater than for token ring.

Another phenomenon of interest is seen most clearly in Figure 9-11b. For a CSMA/CD system under these conditions, the maximum effective throughput at 5 Mbps is only about 1.25 Mbps. If the expected load is, say 0.75 Mbps, this configuration may be perfectly adequate. If, however, the load is expected to grow to 2 Mbps, raising the network data rate to 10 Mbps or even 20 Mbps will not accommodate the increase! The same conclusion, less precisely, can be drawn from the model presented at the beginning of this section.

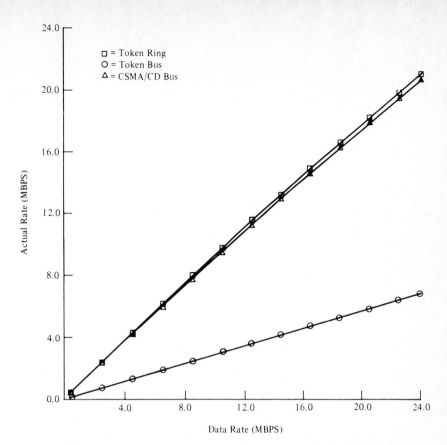

FIGURE 9-11c. 2000 bits per packets; 1 station active out of 100 stations total

As with all the other results presented in this chapter, these depend on the nature of the assumptions made and do not reflect accurately the nature of the real-world load. Nevertheless, they show in a striking manner the nature of the instability of CSMA/CD and the ability of token ring and token bus to continue to perform well in the face of overload conditions.

The Behavior of Contention Protocols

The preceding section revealed that CSMA/CD performs less well than token-passing under increasing load or increasing a. This is characteristic of all contention protocols. In this section we explore this subject in more detail, for the interested reader. To do this, we present results based on the assumption that there are an infinite number of stations. This may strike the reader as an absurd tactic, but, in fact, it leads to analytically tractable equations that are, up to a point, very close to reality. We will define that

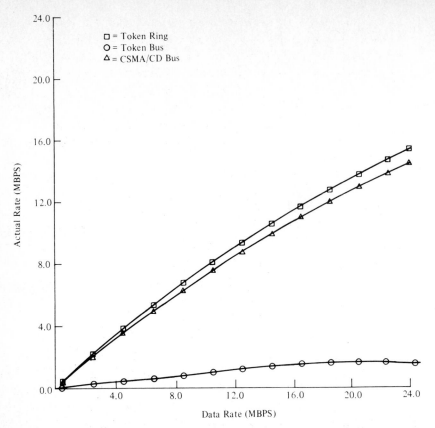

FIGURE 9-11d.   500 bits per packet; 1 station active out of 100 stations total

point shortly. For now, we state the infinite-source assumption precisely: There are an infinite number of stations, each generating an infinitely small rate of frames such that the total number of frames generated per unit time is finite.

The following additional assumptions are made:

1. All frames are of constant length. In general, such frames give better average throughput and delay performance than do variable length frames. In some analyses, an exponential distribution of frame length is used.
2. The channel is noise-free.
3. Frames do not collect at individual stations; that is, a station transmits each frame before the next arrives, hence $I = S$. This assumption weakens at higher loads, where stations are faced with increasing delays for each packet.
4. G, the offered load, is Poisson distributed.
5. For CSMA/CD, no time is lost for carrier sense and collision detection.

These assumptions do not reflect accurately any actual system. For example, higher-order moments or even the entire probability distribution of frame length or G may be needed for accurate results. These assumptions do provide analytic tractability, enabling the development of closed-form expressions for performance. Thus they provide a common basis for comparing a number of protocols and they allow the development of results that give insight into the behavior of systems. In the following discussion, we shall cite simulation and measurement studies that indicate that these insights are valid.

Let us look first at the simplest contention protocol, pure ALOHA. Traffic, of course, is generated as so many frames per second. It is convenient to normalize this to the frame transmission time; then we can view S as the number of frames generated per frame time. Since the capacity of the channel is one frame per frame time, S also has the usual meaning of throughput as a fraction of capacity.

The total traffic on the channel will consist of new frames plus frames that must be retransmitted because of collision:

$G = S + $ (number of retransmitted frames per frame transmission time)

Now, a frame must be retransmitted if it suffers a collision. Thus we can express the rate of retransmissions as $G \cdot \Pr$[individual frame suffers a collision]. Note that we must use G rather than S in this expression. To determine the probability of collision, consider as a worst case, two stations, A and B, as far apart as possible on a bus (i.e., a normalized distance a, as in Figure 9-2). A frame transmitted by station A will suffer a collision if B begins transmission prior to A but within a time $1 + a$ of the beginning of A's transmission, or if B begins transmission after A within a time period $1 + a$ of the beginning of A's transmission. Thus the vulnerable period is of length $2(1 + a)$.

We have assumed that G is Poisson distributed. For a Poisson process with rate λ, the probability of an arrival in a period of time t is $1 - e^{-\lambda t}$. Thus, the probability of an arrival during the vulnerable period is $1 - e^{-2(1+a)G}$. Therefore, we have

$$G = S + G[1 - e^{-2(1+a)G}]$$

So

$$ALOHA: \quad S = Ge^{-2(1+a)G} \qquad (9.13)$$

This derivation assumes that G is Poisson, which is not the case even for I Poisson. However, studies indicate that this is a good approximation [SCHW77]. Also, deeper analysis indicates that the infinite population assumption results closely approximate finite population results at reasonably small numbers—say, 50 or more stations [KLEI76, PATE87]. This is also true for CSMA and CSMA/CD systems [TOBA80a, TOBA82].

Another way of deriving (9.13) is to note that S/G is the fraction of offered frames that are transmitted successfully, which is just the probability that for each frame, no additional frames arrive during the vulnerable period, which is $e^{-2(1+a)G}$.

Throughput for slotted ALOHA is also easily calculated. All frames begin transmission on a slot boundary. Thus the number of frames that are transmitted during a slot time is equal to the number that was generated during the previous slot and await transmission. To avoid collisions between frames in adjacent slots, the slot length must equal frame transmission time plus propagation delay (i.e., $1 + a$). Thus the probability that an individual frame suffers collision is $1 - e^{-(1+a)G}$. Thus we have:

$$S\text{-}ALOHA: \qquad S = Ge^{-(1+a)G} \qquad (9.14)$$

Differentiating (9.13) and (9.14) with respect to G, we have that the maximum possible values for S are $1/[2e(1 + a)]$ and $1/[e(1 + a)]$ respectively. These results differ from those reported in previous accounts of local network performance [TROP81, FRAN81], which ignore a and have $S = Ge^{-2G}$ for ALOHA and $S = Ge^{-G}$ for slotted ALOHA. The discrepancy arises because these formulas were originally derived for satellite channels, for which they are valid, but are often compared with CSMA-type protocols which are derived for local networks (e.g., TOBA80b]). The results which correspond to $a = 0$ are plotted in Figure 9-12. For small values of $a(a \leq 0.01)$, these figures are adequate; but for comparison with CSMA protocols, equations (9.13) and (9.14) should be used.

Figure 9-12 provides insight into the nature of the instability problem with contention protocols. As offered load increases, so does throughput until, beyond its maximum value, throughput actually declines as G increases. This is because there is an increased frequency of collisions: more frames are offered, but fewer successfully escape collision. Worse, this

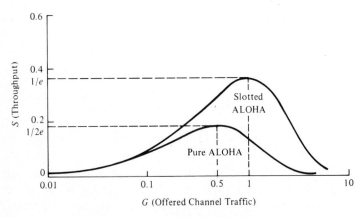

FIGURE 9-12. Performance of ALOHA, S-ALOHA with $a = 0$

situation may persist even if the input to the system drops to zero! Consider: For high G, virtually all offered frames are retransmissions and virtually none get through. So, even if no new frames are generated, the system will remain occupied in an unsuccessful attempt to clear the backlog; the effective capacity of the system is virtually zero. Thus, even in a moderately loaded system, a temporary burst of work could move the network into the high-collision region permanently. This type of instability is not possible with the noncontention protocols.

Delay is more difficult to calculate, but the following reasoning gives a good approximation. We define delay as the time interval from when a node is ready to transmit a frame until when it is successfully received. This delay is simply the sum of queueing delay, propagation delay, and transmission time. In ALOHA, the queueing delay is 0; that is, a node transmits immediately when it has a frame to transmit. However, because of collisions, we may consider the queueing delay time to be the total time consumed prior to successful transmission (i.e., the total time spent in unsuccessful transmissions). To get at this, we need to know the expected number of transmissions per frame. A little thought shows that this is simply G/S. So the expected number of retransmissions per frame is just $G/S - 1 = e^{2(1+a)G} - 1$. The delay D, can then be expressed as

$$D = [e^{2(1+a)G} - 1] \delta + a + 1$$

where δ is the average delay for one retransmission. A common algorithm used for ALOHA is to retransmit after a time selected from a uniform distribution of from 1 to K frame-transmission times. This minimizes repeated collisions. The average delay is then $(K + 1)/2$. To this, we must add the amount of time a station must wait to determine that its frame was unsuccessful. This is just the time it would take to complete a transmission $(1 + a)$ plus the time it would take for the receiver to generate an acknowledgment (w) plus the propagation time for the acknowledgment to reach the station (a). For simplicity, we assume that acknowledgment packets do not suffer collisions. Thus:

$$ALOHA: \quad D = [e^{2(1+a)G} - 1]\left(1 + 2a + w + \frac{K + 1}{2}\right) + a + 1 \quad (9.15)$$

For S-ALOHA, a similar reasoning obtains. The main difference now is that there is a delay, averaging half a slot time between the time a node is ready to send a frame and the time the next slot begins:

$$S\text{-}ALOHA: \quad D = [e^{(1+a)G} - 1]\left(1 + 2a + w + \frac{K + 1}{2}\right) + 1.5a + 1.5 \quad (9.16)$$

These formulas confirm the instability of contention-based protocols under heavy load. As the rate of new frames increases, so does the number

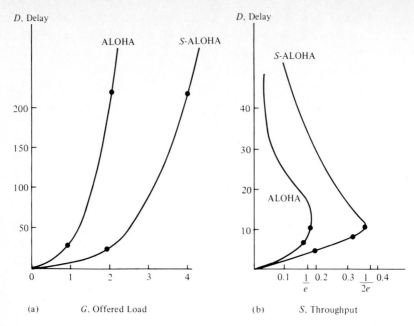

FIGURE 9-13.   Delay as a Function of G and S

of collisions. We can see that both the number of collisions and the average delay grow exponentially with G. Thus there is not only a trade-off between throughput (S) and delay (D), but a third factor enters the trade-off: stability. Figure 9-13 illustrates this point. Figure 9-13a shows that delay increases exponentially with offered load. But Figure 9-13b is perhaps more meaningful. It shows that delay increases with throughput up to the maximum possible throughput. Beyond that point, although throughput declines because of increased numbers of collisions, the delay continues to rise.

It is worth pondering Figures 9-12 and 9-13 to get a better feeling for the behavior of contention channels. Recall that we mentioned that both S and G are "derived" parameters, and what we would really like to estimate is the actual traffic generated by network devices, the "input load" I. As long as the input load is less than the maximum potential throughput, $Max_G(S)$, then $I = S$. That is, the throughput of the system equals the input load. Therefore, all frames get through. However, if $I > Max_G(S)$, Figures 9-12 and 9-13 no longer apply. The system cannot transmit frames as fast as they arrive. The result: if I remains above the threshold indefinitely, then D goes to infinity, S goes to zero, and G grows without bound.

Figure 9-13b shows that, for a given value of S, there are two possible values of D. How can this be? In both cases, $I = S$, and the system is transmitting all input frames. The explanation is as follows: As the input, $I = S$, approaches the saturation point, the stochastic nature of the input

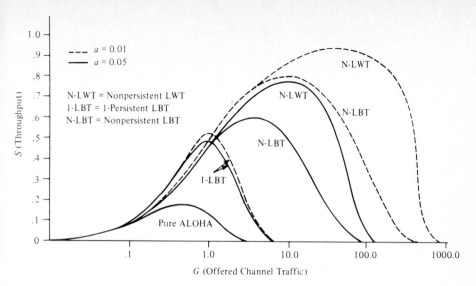

FIGURE 9-14.   Throughput for Variation Contention Protocols

will eventually lead to a period of a high rate of collisions, resulting in decreased throughput and higher frame delays.

Finally, we mention that these results depend critically on the assumptions made. For example, if there is only one station transmitting, then the achievable throughput is 1.0 not 0.18 or 0.37. Indeed, with a single user at a high data rate and a set of other users at very low data rates, utilization approaching 1 can be achieved. However, the delay encountered by the other users is significantly longer than in the homogeneous case. In general, the more unbalanced the source rates, the higher the throughput [KLEI76].

We now turn to the CSMA protocols. A similar line of reasoning can be used to derive closed-form analytic results as is done with ALOHA and S-ALOHA. Perhaps the clearest derivations can be found in [LABA78]. The same or similar results can be found in [KLEI75], [KLEI76], [SCHW77], [HERR79], [TOBA80a], [TOBA82], and [HEYM82].

Figure 9-14 compares the various contention protocols for $a = 0.01$ and 0.05. Note the dramatic improvement in throughput of the various CSMA schemes over ALOHA. Also note the decline in performance for increased a. This is seen more clearly in Figure 9-15 [TAKA85]. As expected, the performance of all CSMA schemes declines with increasing a since the period of vulnerability grows. For high enough values of a, say 0.5 to 1.0, the slotted protocols approach S-ALOHA, and the unslotted protocols approach ALOHA. At these values, neither the carrier sense nor the collision detection are of much use. Thus the distributed reservation protocol for HSLNs in Chapter 6 does not suffer by using S-ALOHA rather than CSMA to contend for reservations.

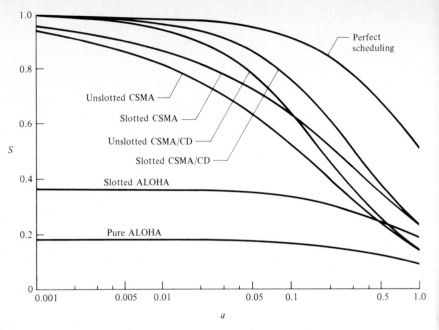

FIGURE 9-15. Maximum Channel Utilization for Various Contention Protocols

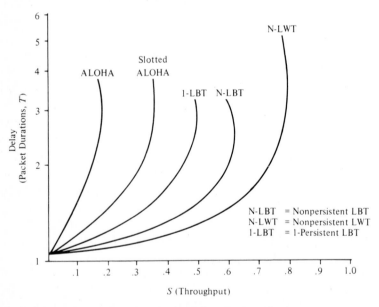

FIGURE 9-16. Delay for Various Contention Protocols

Figure 9-16 shows delay as a function of throughput. As can be seen, CSMA/CD offers significant delay and throughput improvements over CSMA at $a = 0.05$. As a increases, these protocols converge with each other and with S-ALOHA.

One of the critical assumptions used in deriving all these results is that the number of sources is infinite. The validity of the assumption can be seen in Figure 9-10. Note that for small values of a, the efficiency of the system with a finite number of stations differs little from that achieved as the number of stations grows to infinity. For larger values of a, the differences are more marked. The figure shows that the infinite-population assumption underestimates efficiency but is still a good approximation.

A second assumption that is unrealistic is that of fixed frame sizes. While a local network could enforce fixed frame sizes, this is clearly inefficient if the messages are of variable length. One common situation is to have one long frame size for file transfer and a shorter size for interactive traffic and acknowledgments. Now, as frame length decreases, a increases, so if all frames were short, then the utilization would be less than if all frames were long. Presumably, with a mixture of the two traffic types, the efficiency would be somewhere in between. This has been shown to be the case in [TOBA80a]. The analysis also showed that only a small percentage of longer frames is sufficient to achieve close to the higher throughput of the case of long frames only. However, this increased throughput is to the detriment of the thoughput and delay characteristics of the shorter frames. In effect, they are crowded out.

A final point about the foregoing derivations: All represent analytic models of local network performance. Greater validity can be achieved through simulation, where some of the assumptions may be relaxed, and through actual performance measurement. In general, these efforts tend to confirm the validity of the analytic models. Although not entirely accurate, these models provide a good feel for the behavior of the network. Interested readers may consult [TASA86, LABA78, SHOC80a, MARA82, AIME79, OREI82, BEVE88, GONS88, MOLL87]. A general discussion of CSMA/CD modeling techniques is contained in [ROUN83].

Comparative Performance of Ring Protocols

It is far more difficult to do a comparative performance of the three major ring protocols than the comparison of bus and token ring protocols. The results depend critically on a number of parameters unique to each protocol. For example:

- *Token ring:* size of token, token processing time
- *Slotted ring:* slot size, overhead bits per slot
- *Register insertion:* register size

Thus it is difficult to do a comparison, and although there have been a number of studies on each one of the techniques [TROP81, PENN79], few have attempted pairwise comparisons, much less a three-way analysis. Given this unfortunate situation, this section will merely attempt to summarize the most significant comparative studies.

The most systematic work in this area has been done by two different groups: Hammond and O'Reilly [HAMM86], and Liu and his associates [LIU78, LIU82]. We report on the results of the former; those of the latter are virtually identical. The analysis compares token ring, slotted ring, and register insertion. The following paremeters are varied:

- Number of stations: 10, 100
- Value of a: 1.0, 0.1
- Ratio of header size to data size for slotted ring: 1, 0

Figure 9-17 summarizes the results. They show that register insertion is best for a small number of stations or under low loads. Token ring seems to have the best performance under a variety of conditions. Note also that register insertion appears to be able to carry a load greater than 1.0; this is because the protocol permits multiple frames to circulate.

Bux performed an analysis comparing token ring, slotted ring, and CSMA/CD [BUX81]. This careful analysis produced several important conclusions. First, the delay-throughput performance of token ring versus CSMA/CD confirms our earlier discussion. That is, token ring suffers greater delay than CSMA/CD does at light load but less delay and stable throughput at heavy loads. Further, token ring has superior delay characteristics to slotted ring. The poorer performance of slotted ring seems to have two causes: (1) the relative overhead in the small slots of a slotted ring is very high, and (2) the time needed to pass empty slots around the ring to guarantee fair bandwidth is significant. Bux also reports several positive features of slotted ring: (1) the expected delay for a message is proportional to length (i.e., shorter packets get better service than long ones), and (2) overall mean delay is independent of packet length distribution. Bux extended his analysis to include register insertion [BUX83], achieving results comparable to Liu's.

Another study of token ring versus slotted ring is reported in [CHEN82]. Cheng's results confirm those of Bux; that is, the delay of slotted ring exceeds that of token ring. Interestingly, Cheng also showed that the performance of the ring improves as the number of slots increases at least to equal the number of nodes. However, for local area networks, which typically have $a < 1$, a multiple-slot ring is achieved only by having very small slots or artificial delays. With smaller slots, the overhead is proportionally greater.

Finally, we mention a study reported in [YU81], which also concluded that insertion ring had shorter delays than token ring. In this study, Yu

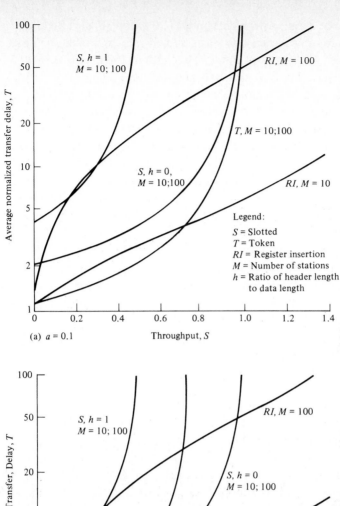

(a) $a = 0.1$

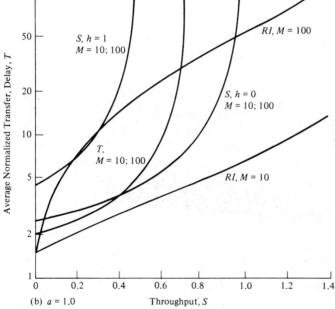

(b) $a = 1.0$

FIGURE 9-17. Delay for Various Ring Protocols

looked at a ring with a data rate of 100 Mbps over a 5-km distance. The distribution of packet size was assumed to be bimodal, with half having a length of 4 Kbytes and half with a length of 100 bytes. Thus the value of a, using average packet size, was about 0.125.

It is difficult to draw conclusions from the efforts made so far. The slotted ring seems to be the least desirable over a broad range of parameter values, owing to the considerable overhead associated with each small packet. For example, the Cambridge ring, which is the most widely available ring commerically in Europe, uses a 37 bit slot with only 16 data bits! The designers of the Cambridge ring originally started out with register insertion but rejected it for slotted ring. The sole reason seems to have been reliability: a fault developing in a shift register can disrupt the entire ring [WILK79].

As between token ring and register insertion, the evidence suggests that at least for some sets of parameter values, register insertion gives superior delay performance. Interestingly, there are very few commercially available register insertion products. On the other hand, token ring in the United States, with a boost from IEEE 802 and IBM, and slotted ring in Europe, where many firms have licensed the Cambridge slotted ring, seem destined to dominate the marketplace.

The primary advantage of register insertion is the potentially high utilization it can achieve. In contrast with token ring, multiple stations can be transmitting at a time, Further, a station can transmit as soon as a gap opens up on the ring; it need not wait for a token. On the other hand, the propagation time around the ring is not constant, but depends on the amount of traffic.

A final point in comparing token ring and register insertion. Under light loads, register insertion operates more efficiently, resulting in slightly less delay. However, both systems perform adequately. Our real interest is under heavy load. A typical LAN will have $a < 1$, usually $a < < 1$, so that a transmitting station on a token ring will append a token to the end of its packet. Under heavy load, a nearby station will be able to use the token. Thus about 100% utilization is achieved, and there is no particular advantage to register insertion.

9.3

HSLN PERFORMANCE

Although little or no modeling of the LDDI protocol has been done, there has been extensive work on modeling the similar HYPERchannel protocol. In this section we summarize some of these results. Keep in mind that, in contrast to the LDDI protocol, HYPERchannel has built-in priorities. That is, the station with the earliest time position always has the first opportunity to transmit, on down to the station with the last opportunity and hence the lowest priority.

Perhaps the most work in this area has been done by Franta and his associates at the University of Minnesota [CHLA80a, CHLA80b, CHRI81, FRAN80, FRAN82]. Similar results have also been reported in [BURK79] and [SPAN81]. The group first developed an analytic model representing a HYPERchannel system as a closed finite source queueing system, such that once a transmission request was generated by an NIU, no additional requests by that NIU are generated until the outstanding request is transmitted. Subsequently, a simulation model was developed and, finally, some actual performance measures were taken. Happily, the three approaches agree closely. Figure 9-18 shows the measured results for a 6-node, 1000-ft system. The results are for 4-Kbyte packets, so a is about 0.002. The results show that the protocol is stable in the sense that throughput does not deteriorate as load increases.

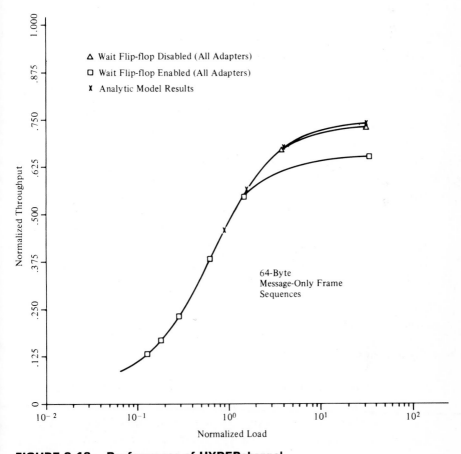

FIGURE 9-18.   Performance of HYPERchannel

The figures include a curve for the enabling of a wait flip-flop, which functions in the same manner as the wait flag for LDDI. Surprisingly, performance degrades with the use of the wait flip-flop. The reason is that the use of this mechanism increases the frequency with which the HYPER-channel contention interval occurs. Thus there are more collisions and poorer performance. Because the LDDI protocol does not have a contention interval, the use of a wait flag should have only a minor effect on performance.

A set of simulation studies of HYPERchannel have been performed at Lawrence Livermore Laboratories [DONN79, WATS80, WATS82]. These results are in close agreement with those of Franta's group. The Livermore group extended its studies to include modeling of the link layer with the interesting result that, as with CSMA/CD, HYPERchannel performance degrades under high load. The cause of this phenomenon is that, at layer 2, a HYPERchannel NIU will lock out receptions while attempting to establish a connection for transmission. This can lead to a condition approaching deadlock, and the degradation of throughput. This result points out the importance of viewing local network performance in the context of the entire network.

Finally, we mention a simulation study done at MITRE [KATK81a, KATK81b]. Again, the results were similar to those quoted above. The authors also modeled performance including layer 2 functions and found that the effective achievable data transmission rate was only 6.18 Mbps. This emphasizes the importance of not equating end-to-end throughput with raw data rate.

All of these results, by and large, are applicable to the LDDI protocol. One would expect this protocol to do somewhat better because of the lack of collisions.

9.4

END-TO-END PERFORMANCE

So far, we have been concerned with the throughput and delay performance for transmitting packets over an LAN or HSLN. Some useful insights have been gained and techniques developed for estimating that performance. Alas, this is of no concern to the local network user. The user is concerned with *end-to-end* performance. Examples:

- Two hosts regularly exchange large files. What is the end-to-end throughput rate during file transfer?
- A user at a terminal is querying a data base on a host. What is the delay from the end of query entry to the beginning of response?

Consider the steps involved in sending data from one host to another. In general terms, we have:

1. Process in source host initiates transfer.
2. Host system software transfers data to NIU.
3. Source NIU transfers data to destination NIU.
4. Destination NIU transfers data to destination host.
5. Host system software accepts data, notifies destination process.
6. Destination process accepts data.

Each of these steps involves some processing and the use of a resource potentially shared by others. What we have discussed so far, and the focus of virtually all local network performance studies, is step 3.

To get a handle on end-to-end performance, the analyst must model the NIU, the host–NIU link, and the host, as well as the NIU–NIU link. This requires the development of computer system performance models. Although these techniques have been around for a while, one of the few attempts to apply these principles systematically to local network performance has been undertaken by a group at CONTEL Information Systems [LISS81, MAGL80, MAGL81, MAGL82, MITC81, MITC86]. We summarize their approach in this section.

The discussion will be with reference to Figure 9-19. As mentioned earlier, the total delay, say, from the time a message is generated at node A by some application until it reaches node B, is just the sum of the delays encountered at each step. Each such step can be modeled using queueing theory. A queueing situation arises when a "customer" arrives at a service facility and, finding it busy, is forced to wait. The delay incurred by a customer is just the time spent waiting in the queue plus the time for service. The delay depends on the pattern of arriving traffic and the characteristics of the server. Table 9.3 summarizes some simple results. Results for more complex cases may be found in [MART67].

The system depicted in Figure 9-19 consists of a set of single-server queueing systems in tandem, that is, the output of one queue is the input to the next. In the general case, it is a complex task to characterize the behavior of this system, and closed-form analytic solutions do not exist. However, there is a theorem (Jackson's theorem) which states that under certain conditions, each node in the network of queues can be treated independently. Thus the delay at each queue can be calculated separately and summed to give an overall figure. The assumptions [JACK63]:

- Work arrives from outside the system with a Poisson distribution.
- Exponential service time at each node with first-come, first served policy.
- No saturated queues: queues are large enough to hold the maximum number of waiting customers.

TABLE 9.3 Isolated Queues

Parameters

w = mean number of items waiting for service (not including items being served)
q = mean number of items in system (waiting and being served)
t_w = mean time item spends waiting for service
t_q = mean time item spends in system, waiting and being served
ρ = utilization: fraction of time a server is busy
S = mean service time for an item

Assumption: Poisson arrivals with parameter λ, exponential service times

$$w = \frac{\rho^2}{1 - \rho}$$

$$q = \frac{\rho}{1 - \rho}$$

$$t_w = \frac{\rho S}{1 - \rho}$$

$$t_q = \frac{S}{1 - \rho}$$

$$\rho = \lambda S$$

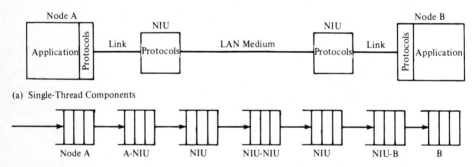

(a) Single-Thread Components

(b) Queueing Model

FIGURE 9-19. End-to-end Local Network Performance Model

There is some evidence that networks of the type we are discussing, which may violate these assumptions, are nevertheless closely approximated by the decomposition approach [MAGL81]. Furthermore, the assumption of exponential service time usually results in upper bounds to delays; thus the analysis will give conservative estimates.

Solving for total delay is thus computationally simple. Starting with the first queue, and given an arrival rate λ, the delay at that step is determined. As long as $\rho = \lambda S \leq 1$, the queue is stable and the output rate is equal to the input rate. This now becomes the input to the second stage, and so on.

For a stable system, we must have

$$\lambda \leq \frac{1}{\text{Max}[S_i]}$$

This represents the maximum achievable throughput. As long as this condition is satisfied, the total delay for a message over N stages is simply

$$D = \sum_{i=1}^{N} D_i$$

Now, let us begin with the first stage, node A. Node A must perform a number of tasks related to the passing of a message, including applications processing and the processing for the various protocol layers. These tasks may have various priorities with pre-emptive interrupts allowed. For each class of task, the queueing equation is

$$t_{qj} = \frac{1}{1 - \sum\limits_{i=1}^{j-1} \rho_i} \left\{ \frac{\sum\limits_{i=1}^{j} \rho_i S_i}{1 - \sum\limits_{i=1}^{j} \rho_i} + S_j \right\}$$

Where $\rho_i = \lambda_1 S_i$.

To solve this equation, we need values for the λ_i and S_i. The λ_i depend on the rate at which messages are generated; this should become clear in the example below. The S_i can be approximated by estimating the execution path length of each service routine and dividing by the effective instruction per second rate of the processor. Since other activities, such as disk I/O, may be handled by the processor, its raw instruction execution rate needs to be modified by some overhead factor.

The next delay encountered is the communications link between node A and its NIU. This delay will depend on the nature of the interface. As an example consider a half-duplex line with a given interface transfer rate. Here there are two classes of arrivals for a single server: node-to-NIU and NIU-to-node traffic. The λ_i ($i = 1, 2$) depend on the rate at which messages arrive for transmission across the link. The service time in either direction (S_1, S_2) is just the average message length divided by the data rate. It is easy to see that, assuming no priorities,

$$\rho = \lambda_1 S_1 + \lambda_2 S_2$$

$$S = \frac{\rho}{\lambda_1 + \lambda_2}$$

where S is the overall average service time. Then

$$t_{qj} = t_w + S_j$$

$$= \frac{\rho S}{1 - \rho} + S_j \qquad j = 1, 2$$

The NIU is the next source of delay and may be modeled in the same fashion as node A. Next comes the local network itself. The delay at this stage depends on the topology (ring, bus, or tree) and the medium access protocol. Sections 9.2 and 9.3 are devoted to developing results in this area. The remainder of the steps are symmetric with those already discussed and need not be described.

Two refinements to the model above: First, an NIU often has multiple ports. Hence the arrival rate of work at an NIU consists of the rates from multiple hosts. This must be taken into account. Second, the node-NIU link may be multiplexed so that arrivals are from multiple remote nodes.

As an example, we consider an analysis reported in [MITC81]. In this example, node A is a host and node B an intelligent workstation. Within node A, there is some application program exchanging messages with the workstation. There are five main classes of activities associated with the application. We assume that these are serviced by the host on a preemptive resume basis. The activities, in descending order of priority:

1. *Link-in:* link level functions for messages inbound from the NIU.
2. *Link-out:* link level functions for messages outbound to the NIU.
3. *Protocols-in:* higher level protocol functions for inbound messages.
4. *Protocols-out:* higher level protocol functions for outbound messages.
5. *Application:* application processing.

The host/NIU interface is assumed to have an effective transfer rate of 800 kbps, while the workstation/NIU interface is 9.6 kbps. This would be the case for an integrated host NIU and a stand-alone terminal NIU.

The NIU is assumed to implement up through the transport layer with the following priorities:

1. Network link-in
2. Node link-in
3. Network link-out
4. Node link-out
5. Higher-layer protocols

Finally, nonpersistent CSMA/CD bus system operating at 1.544 Mbps is assumed.

The results are summarized in Table 9.4, which shows that, within the moderate utilization range of the bus, the bus contributes only 5% of the delay. The implication, confirmed by the other studies referenced earlier, is that the effect of the topology and medium access control on overall delay is negligible until the medium approaches saturation. In Section 9.2, we outlined a quick and simple means of estimating the saturation point. It is clearly desirable to operate below that point and, while operating below that point, only a rough approximation of the delay due to the medium will suffice.

TABLE 9.4 End-to-End Delay, CSMA/CD Network

Traffic parameters
  Arrival rate: 0.017 message per second
  Aggregate load: 100,000 bps

CSMA/CD parameters
  Propagation: 30 μs
  Retransmission interval: 5

MSG lengths
  Input: 800 characters
  Output: 12,000 characters

I/F Transfer rates
  Host: 800,000 bps
  Workstation: 9600 bps

Protocol path-length parameters
  Node protocols
    Send: 12,000 instructions
    Receive: 12,000 instructions

  Node access link layer
    Send: 75 instructions
    Receive: 75 instructions

  Network access link layer
    Send: 75 instructions
    Receive: 75 instructions

  TCP/IP: 12,000

  Multiprogram level: 32

Processor capacities
  Host: 1.100 MIPS
  BIU: 0.615 MIPS
  Workstation: 0.115 MIPs

Host application program path length: 50,000 instructions
Cable utilization: 0.0565
Total normalized traffic, including retransmissions: 0.06

Delay Categories

Throughput	Response	Host	HI/F	WI/F	HBIU	WBIU	W/S	Cable
0.50	2.0066	0.04	0.01	0.84	0.01	0.02	0.02	0.05
1.00	2.0252	0.04	0.01	0.84	0.01	0.02	0.02	0.05
1.50	2.0444	0.04	0.01	0.84	0.01	0.02	0.02	0.05
2.00	2.0645	0.04	0.01	0.84	0.01	0.02	0.02	0.05
2.50	2.0853	0.04	0.01	0.83	0.02	0.02	0.02	0.05
3.00	2.1071	0.04	0.01	0.83	0.02	0.02	0.02	0.05
3.50	2.1298	0.04	0.01	0.83	0.02	0.02	0.02	0.05
4.00	2.1536	0.04	0.01	0.83	0.02	0.02	0.02	0.05
4.50	2.1785	0.05	0.01	0.83	0.02	0.02	0.02	0.05
5.00	2.2047	0.05	0.01	0.83	0.02	0.02	0.02	0.05
5.50	2.2324	0.05	0.01	0.83	0.02	0.02	0.02	0.05
6.00	2.2616	0.05	0.01	0.82	0.03	0.02	0.02	0.05
6.50	2.2927	0.05	0.01	0.82	0.03	0.02	0.02	0.05
7.00	2.3259	0.05	0.01	0.82	0.03	0.02	0.02	0.05
7.50	2.3615	0.06	0.01	0.82	0.03	0.01	0.02	0.05
8.00	2.4001	0.06	0.01	0.81	0.03	0.01	0.03	0.05
8.50	2.4424	0.06	0.01	0.81	0.03	0.01	0.03	0.05
9.00	2.4892	0.06	0.01	0.80	0.04	0.01	0.03	0.05
9.50	2.5423	0.07	0.01	0.79	0.04	0.01	0.03	0.05
10.00	2.6041	0.07	0.01	0.78	0.05	0.01	0.03	0.05

Source: [MITC81]

Nevertheless, we have devoted considerable space to looking at the performance of various topology/MAC approaches. This is so because the saturation points for different approaches are different. But it needs to be pointed out that beyond the determination of a saturation point, the focus of activity should be the broader end-to-end delay issue.

This section has touched only briefly on the techniques for end-to-end delay analysis. The interested reader is referred to [MART67], [SAUE81], [KOBA78], and [IBM71].

9.5

RECOMMENDED READING

Books on the subject of LAN/HSLN performance include [STUC85], [HAMM86], and [TASA86]. [LI87] is a special issue of the IEEE Journal on Selected Areas in Communications devoted to performance of broadcast networks, especially LANs. [KLEI86] presents a clever graphical technique for analyzing the effect of a. [SAST85]* is another comparison of the IEEE 802 protocols. [BOGG88] provides a good historical survey of performance models of CSMA/CD and compares these with measured performance. [GOOD88] is a careful study of CSMA/CD taking into account the use of binary exponential backoff. [TAKA88] is a rigorous analysis of polling schemes in general, with application to token bus and token ring. An interesting analysis of end-to-end performance is [MITC86]*. Similar results are reported in [MURA88], [BUX84]* and [WONG84].

9.6

PROBLEMS

9.1 Equation (9.1) is valid for token ring and baseband bus. What is an equivalent expression for
a. Broadband bus?
b. Slotted ring?
c. Register insertion ring?
d. Broadband tree (use several different configurations)?

9.2 Develop a display similar to Figure 9-6 that shows throughput as a function of N.

9.3 Derive equations similar to (9.10) and (9.11) for the case where there are two types of frames, one 10 times as long as the other, that are transmitted with equal probability by each station.

9.4 Consider a 10-Mbps, 1-km bus, with N stations and frame-size = F. Determine throughput and delay for token bus and throughput for CSMA/CD:
a. $N = 10$, $F = 1000$

b. $N = 100$, $F = 1000$

c. $N = 10$, $F = 10{,}000$

d. $N = 100$, $F = 10{,}000$.

9.5 Compare equations (9.1), (9.10), and (9.11). Under what circumstances does the throughput for the latter two equations exceed the theoretical maximum of (9.1)? Explain.

9.6 For the graphs in Figure 9-11, determine a and comment on the results.

9.7 Demonstrate that the number of stations and offered load affect performance independently for the following protocols.

   a. CSMA/CD.

   b. Collision avoidance.

   c. Token bus.

   d. Token ring.

   e. Slotted ring.

   f. Register insertion.

   g. Reservation.

9.8 Consider a S-ALOHA system with a finite number of stations N and $a = 0$. The offered load from each station is G_i, the throughput S_i. Derive an equation for S as a function of G_i. Asume that the G_i are identical; what is the equation for S? Verify that this approaches Ge^{-G} as $N \to \infty$. Above what value of N is the difference negligible?

9.9 Demonstrate that CSMA/CD is biased toward long transmissions.

9.10 Show that, for $a = 0$, the following relationship holds for 1-persistent CSMA

$$S = \frac{G(1 + G)e^{-G}}{G + e^{-G}}$$

9.11 The peformance of CSMA/CD depends on whether the collision detection is performed at the same site as the transmission (baseband) or at a time later whose average is a (broadband). What would you expect the relative performance to be?

9.12 Let $T_{msg}(K) = 0.1$ s and $T_{over} = 0.1$ s for a 50-station token system. Assume that all stations always have something to transmit. Compute C, $R(K)$, and UTIL(K). What is the percent overhead? Now let $T_{over} = 0.2$. What is the percent overhead?

9.13 Consider the conditions extant at the end of Problem 9.12. Assume that individual stations may be busy or idle. What is the cycle time C? Now halve the overhead ($T_{over} = 0.1$). What is the cycle time C?

9.14 For equation (9.7), let the number of stations be two. Plot $R(2)$ versus $R(1)$ and show the admissible mean throughput rates. Interpret the result in terms of relative static priority policies.

9.15 Do an asymptotic breakpoint analysis for CSMA/CD.

9.16 Equations (9.10) and (9.12) are valid for token ring and for token baseband bus. What are equivalent equations for broadband bus?

CHAPTER 10

Network Performance: Digital Switch/Digital PBX

The nature of the performance questions and the analytic approach are markedly different for circuit-switched systems compared to packet-switched systems. Packet-switched systems allocate their capacity using asynchronous TDM. Thus each packet that arrives for service will experience a variable amount of delay depending on the load on the system and the nature of the protocol. Further, packets in a stream of packets from a source may experience different amounts of delay, and the throughput for that source is variable.

In contrast, a circuit-switched system uses synchronous TDM. When a circuit is established between two stations, a constant amount of bandwidth is dedicated to that circuit. There are no delays other than the propagation delay through the switch, and the throughput is a fixed amount equal to the provided data rate. These values are of no analytic interest. Rather, the performance questions have to do with system sizing and availability.

Consider a switch with L attached stations and a capacity to handle N simultaneous circuits. For a space-division switch, that capacity is just the maximum number of simultaneous independent paths. For a time-division switch, capacity is determined by the internal speed of the switch. Example: For a TDM bus switch, it is just the effective bus data rate (less overhead) divided by the individual circuit data rate. Now, if $L > N/2$, the system is blocking. The fundamental performance questions we wish to ask are:

- What is the degree of blocking, that is, what is the probability that a connection request will be blocked, given L and N? Alternatively, what capacity (N) is needed given L to achieve a certain upper bound on the probability of blocking?
- If blocked calls are queued for service, what is the average delay? Alternatively, what capacity is needed to achieve a certain average delay?

For a nonblocking switch, of course, these questions do not arise. In fact, insofar as the switch itself is concerned, there are no performance questions to analyze! The only question is one of cost: Is it worth it to provide sufficient capacity so that blocking never occurs?

These questions certainly do arise for a blocking switch. They are also relevant in a different context. Recall that a common service provided by a digital switch or digital PBX is port contention. For this service, on a nonblocking switch, the questions above apply, with L the number of terminals, N the number of host ports, and $L > N$.

Both the blocking switch and port contention on a nonblocking switch are examples of multiserver queueing problems, and solution approaches will be presented in this chapter. A more complex case is a port contention service provided on a blocking switch. Either the switch or the port contention group could be the bottleneck. As a first approximation, one can treat the problems separately and size the system based on which component is the bottleneck.

The analytic techniques for addressing the issues raised above were developed for telephone switching exchanges. They are equally applicable to digital PBX and digital switch networks. In the next section we introduce the principles of telephone traffic analysis. Following that we present some formulas that have been developed for calculating key traffic variables.

10.1

CIRCUIT-SWITCHING TRAFFIC CONCEPTS

Two parameters determine the amount of load presented to a switch:

- λ: the mean rate of calls (connection requests) attempted per unit time
- h: the mean holding time per successful call

The basic measure of traffic is the traffic intensity, expressed in a dimensionless unit, the *erlang*:

$$A = \lambda h$$

A can be interpreted from several points of view. It is, in effect, a normalized version of λ: *A* equals the average number of calls arriving during the average holding period. We can view the switch as a queueing system, where the number of servers *N* is equal to the circuit capacity of a switch or to the number of host ports of a port contention unit. A moment's thought should reveal that *A* is related to the queueing system utilization, ρ, by $A = \rho N$. Thus, *A* is a measure of the average number of circuits or servers required. For example, if the calling rate averages 20 calls per minute, and the average holding time is 3 minutes, then $A = 60$. We would expect, say, a switch with a capacity of 120 circuits to be about half utilized. A switch of capacity 50 would clearly be inadequate. A capacity of 60 represents a lower bound. Because of the fluctuations around the mean rate *A*, this capacity would at times be inadequate.

To clarify these concepts, consider Figure 10-1, which shows the pattern of activity on a switch of capacity 10 circuits over a period of 1 hour. The rate of calls, per minute, is 97/60. The average holding time per call, in minutes, is 294/97. Thus $A = (97/60)(294/97) = 4.9$ erlangs. Another way of viewing this parameter is that *A* is the mean number of calls in progress. Thus, on the average, 4.9 circuits are engaged.

The latter interpretation is, however, true only for a nonblocking switch. The parameter λ was defined as the rate of calls attempted; hence *A* is a measure of offered traffic, not carried traffic. We will introduce a measure for carried traffic in the next section.

Typically, a blocking system is sized to deal with some peak level of traffic intensity. It is generally thought unreasonable to size for the highest

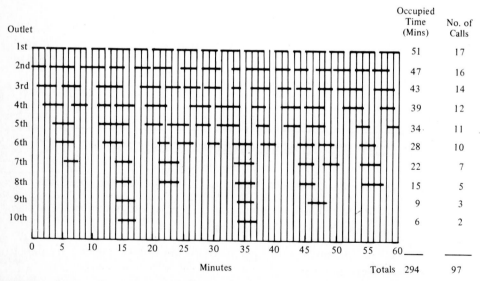

FIGURE 10-1. Distribution of Traffic on a Switch with Capacity 10

surge of traffic anticipated; rather, the common practice is to size the system to meet the average rate encountered during a busy hour. The busy hour is the 60-minute period during the day when the traffic is highest in the long run [FREE85a]. CCITT recommends taking the average of the busy hour traffic on the 30 busiest days of the year, called the "mean busy hour traffic" and using that quantity to size a system. The North American standard is to take the average of the 10 busiest days. Of course, these are typically measurements of carried rather than offered traffic and can only be used to estimate the true load.

The parameter A, as a measure of busy-hour traffic, serves as input to a traffic model. The model is used to answer questions such as those posed in the introduction to this chapter. There are two key factors that determine the nature of the model:

- The manner in which blocked calls are handled.
- The number of traffic sources.

We elaborate on these concepts briefly in this section. The next section discusses techniques for employing these models.

Blocked calls may be handled in one of two ways. First, the switch can put the blocked call in a queue awaiting a free circuit; this is referred to as *lost calls delayed* (LCD), although in fact the call is not lost. Second, the switch can simply reject the call. This in turn leads to two assumptions

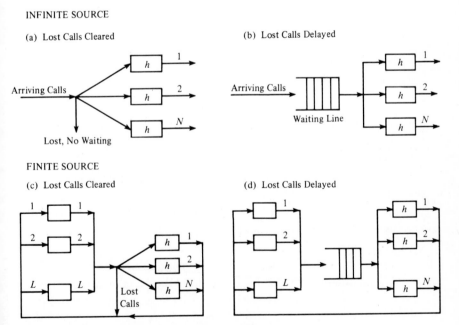

FIGURE 10-2. Multiserver Queuing Models

about the action of the user. If the user hangs up and waits some random time interval before reattempting a call, this is known as *lost calls cleared* (LCC). If the user repeatedly attempts calling, it is known as *lost call held* (LCH). In the present context, LCH is of little interest; we will focus on LCD and LCC.

The second key element of a traffic model is whether the number of sources is assumed infinite or finite. This difference can be seen in Figure 10-2. For an infinite source model, there is assumed to be a fixed arrival rate. For the finite source case, the arrival rate will depend on the number of sources already engaged. Thus, if each of L sources generates calls at a rate λ/L, then, when the switch is unoccupied, the arrival rate is λ. However, if there are K sources occupied at time t, then the instantaneous arrival rate at that time is $\lambda(L - K)/L$. Infinite source models are easier to deal with. The infinite source assumption is reasonable when the number of sources is at least 5 to 10 times the capacity of the system.

10.2

MULTISERVER MODELS

We are now ready to turn to the use of the various traffic models for system sizing. For each of the four models of Figure 10-2, formulas have been derived for the quantities of interest. These are summarized in Table 10.1. These formulas are based on the following assumptions:

- Poisson arrivals.
- Exponential holding time [not needed for formula (a)].
- Equal traffic intensity per source.
- Calls served in order of arrival (for delay calculations).

Even with these assumptions, it can be seen that the formulas involve lengthy summations. In earlier days, much of the work of traffic theorists lay in simplifying assumptions to the point that the equations could be calculated at all. The results were and are published in tables [FRAN76, FREE85a]. Clearly, the tendency would be to misuse the available tables in situations whose assumptions did not fit any of the tables. The problem is now alleviated with the use of the computer. Nevertheless, the tabular results are still useful for quick and rough sizing.

Several parameters in Table 10.1 warrant comment. For LCC systems, P is the probability that a call request will be cleared or lost. It is the ratio of calls unable to obtain service to the total call requests; in telephone traffic, it is also called grade of service. For LCD systems, an arriving call will be delayed rather than cleared. $P(>0)$ is the probability that a call request will

TABLE 10.1 Traffic Formulas[a]

(a) Infinite sources, lost calls cleared:

$$P = \frac{\dfrac{A^N}{N!}}{\displaystyle\sum_{x=0}^{N} \frac{A^x}{x!}}$$

(b) Finite sources, lost calls cleared:

$$P = \frac{\left(\dfrac{L-1}{N}\right)^{MN}}{\displaystyle\sum_{x=0}^{N} \left(\dfrac{L-1}{x}\right) M^x}$$

(c) Infinite sources, lost calls delayed:

$$P(>0) = \frac{\dfrac{A^N}{N!}\dfrac{N}{N-A}}{\displaystyle\sum_{x=0}^{N-1} \frac{A^x}{x!} + \frac{A^N}{N!}\frac{N}{N-A}}$$

$$\text{for } \left(\frac{L-1}{N}\right) = \frac{(L-1)!}{N!(L-1-N)!};$$

$$\left(\frac{L-1}{x}\right) = \frac{(L-1)!}{x!(L-1-x)!};$$

$$M = \frac{A}{L - A(1-P)}$$

The probability of delay greater than t is

$$P(>t) = P(>0)e^{-(N-A)T}$$

where $T = t/h$ is expressed as a multiple of the average holding time.

(d) Finite sources, lost calls delayed:

$$P(>0) = \frac{\displaystyle\sum_{x=N}^{L} \frac{L!}{N!}\frac{M^x}{(L-x)!N^{x-N}}}{\displaystyle\sum_{x=0}^{N-1} \left(\frac{L}{x}\right) M^x + \displaystyle\sum_{x=N}^{L} \frac{L!}{N!}\frac{M^x}{(L-x)!N^{x-N}}}$$

The average delay D_1 on all calls is

$$D_1 = P(>0)\frac{h}{N-A}$$

$$\text{for } \left(\frac{L}{x}\right) = \frac{L!}{x!(L-x)!}$$

The average delay D_2 on calls delayed is

$$D_2 = \frac{h}{N-A}$$

$$M = \frac{A}{L+1-A(1-P)} \approx \frac{A}{L+1-A}$$

The probability of delay greater than t, on calls delayed is

$$P_2(>t) = e^{-(N-A)T}$$

---

[a] A = offered traffic, Erlangs
N = number of servers
L = number of sources
h = mean holding time
P = probability of loss (blocking, delay)
$P(>0)$ = probability of delay greater than 0
$P(>t)$ = probability of delay greater than t
D_1 = mean delay, all calls
D_2 = mean delay, delayed calls

```
10 PRINT "THIS IS ERLANG-B, BY L.F.GOELLER,9-29-78."
20 PRINT "ERLANG-B SHOWS TRAFFIC ON EACH TRUNK."
30 INPUT "TRAFFIC OFFERED GROUP = ",A
40 LET N=O: LET T=1: LET T1=1: LET O=A: LET Z=10
50 PRINT "  N      OFRD  CRD      TOT    G/S"
60 LET N=N+1: LET T=T*A/N: LET T1=T1+T: LET P=T/T1
70 LET L=A*P: LET S=A-L: LET C=O-L
80 PRINT #31;N;%9F4;O;%6F4;C;%8F4;S;%6F4;P
90 LET O=L: IF P<.001 THEN 110
91 IF N<Z THEN 60
100 STOP : LET Z=Z+10: PRINT "OFFERED TRAFFIC WAS ",A: GOTO 50
110 END
```

(a) Input is offered load. Output shows carried load (TOT) and grade of service for given
    capacity (N). Output also shows incremental contribution of each additional circuit.

```
10 PRINT "ERLANG-C CALCULATES DELAY."
20 INPUT "TRAFFIC IN ERLANGS OFFERED GROUP=",A
30 PRINT "  N    P        D1      D2    Q1    Q2";
31 PRINT "   P8  P4  P2  P1  PP"
40 LET N=1: LET T=1: LET T1=1
50 IF N<=A THEN 120
60 LET T2=T*(A/N)*(N/(N-A)): LET P=T2/(T1+T2)
70 LET D2=1/(n-A): LET D1=P*D2: LET Q2=A*D2: LET Q1=P*Q2
80 LET P8=P/EXP(.125/D2): LET P4=P/EXP(.25/D2)
90 LET P2=P/EXP(.5/D2): LET P1=P/EXP(1/D2)
91 LET P0=P/EXP(2/D2)
100 PRINT %3I;N;%6F4;P;%7F2;D1;D2;Q1;Q2;%4F2;P8;P4;P2;P1;P0
110 IF P<.02 THEN 130
120 LET T=T*A/N: LET T1=T1+T: LET N=N+1: GOTO 50
130 STOP
```

(b) Input is offered load. Output shows, for capacity (N), probability of delay (P), mean
    delay on all calls (D1) and delayed calls (D2), mean queue length overall (Q1) and when
    all servers are busy (P2), and probability of delay greater than an eighth, quarter,
    half, one, and two holding times (P8, P4, P2, P1, PP).

FIGURE 10-3. Programs for Erlang B and Erlang C (From [GOEL79])

TABLE 10.2 Erlang B Table

Number of Circuits	Capacity (erlangs) for Grade of Service of:			
	0.01 (1/100)	0.005 (1/200)	0.002 (1/500)	0.001 (1/1000)
1	0.01	0.005	0.002	0.001
4	0.87	0.70	0.53	0.43
5	1.36	1.13	0.90	0.76
10	4.46	3.96	3.43	3.09
20	12.03	11.10	10.07	9.41
24	15.27	14.21	13.01	12.24
40	29.0	27.3	25.7	24.5
70	56.1	53.7	51.0	49.2
100	84.1	80.9	77.4	75.2

find the switch fully utilized and be delayed. $P(>t)$ is the probability that
any call request will be delayed by an amount greater than t, whereas
$P_2(>t)$ is the probability that a call that is delayed will be delayed by an
amount greater than t.

Infinite Sources, Lost Calls Cleared

The simplest equation is for an infinite sources, LCC model. The key parameter of interest here is the probability of loss, or grade of service. Values in the range 0.01 to 0.001 are generally considered quite good.

The equation for infinite source, LLC, known as *Erlang B*, is easily programmed, as shown in Figure 10-3a. Given the offered load and number of servers, the probability of blocking can be calculated. More often, the inverse problem is of interest: determining the amount of traffic that can be handled by a given capacity to produce a given grade of service. Another inverse problem is to determine the capacity required to handle a given amount of traffic at a given grade of service. For both these problems, tables or suitable trial-and-error programs are needed. Table 10.2 is an extract from such tables. Figure 10-4 plots the probability of loss as a function of offered load with the number of servers as a parameter.

Two important points can be noted from the table:

- A larger capacity system is more efficient than a smaller capacity one for a given grade of service.
- A larger capacity system is more susceptible to reduction of the grade of service.

To illustrate the first point, consider two switches, each with a capacity of 10 circuits. They have a joint capacity of 20 circuits and can handle an offered traffic intensity of 6.86 for a grade of service of 0.002. However, a single switch of capacity 20 circuits, will handle 10.07 erlangs at a grade of service of 0.002. To illustrate the second point, consider a switch of capacity 10 circuits giving a grade of service of 0.002 for a load 3.43 erlangs. A 30% increase in traffic reduces the grade of service to 0.01. However, for a switch of capacity 70 circuits, only a 10% increase in traffic reduces the grade of service from 0.002 to 0.01.

Of course, all of the discussion above deals with offered traffic. If sizing is being done on the basis of system measurement, all that we are likely to have is carried traffic. Figure 10-5 is a program for Erlang B which accepts carried traffic as input and then performs a seeking algorithm to work backward to offered traffic. This program reflects the relationship between carried traffic C and offered traffic:

$$C = A(1 - P)$$

For small values of P, it can be seen that A is good approximation of C.

Finite Sources, Lost Calls Cleared

In reality, of course, the number of sources is not infinite but finite, and equation (b) of Table 10.1, known as *Engset*, applies. This is a more

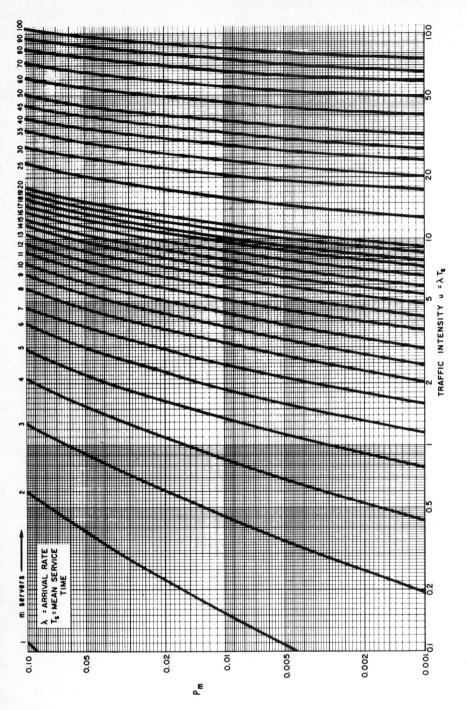

m servers →

λ = ARRIVAL RATE
T_s = MEAN SERVICE TIME

P_m

TRAFFIC INTENSITY $u = \lambda T_s$

FIGURE 10-4. Probability of Loss for Infinite Sources, LCC Systems

NETWORK PERFORMANCE: DIGITAL SWITCH/DIGITAL PBX

```
 10 PRINT "THIS IS CARRIED, BY L. F. GOELLER, 7-8-79"
 20 PRINT "CARRIED RELATES CARRIED TRAFFIC IN GROUP"
 30 PRINT "TO OFFERED TRAFFIC AND TRAFFIC ON EACH LINE."
 40 INPUT "TRAFFIC IN ERLANGS CARRIED BY GROUP = ",K
 80 INPUT "PERCENT RECALL= ",R
 90 INPUT "PERCENT OVERFLOW TO TOLL =",X
100 IF R+X<=100 THEN 120
110 PRINT "TRY AGAIN": GOTO 80
120 LET X=X/100: LET R=R/100: LET D=1-R-X
130 INPUT "CALL HOLDING TIME IN MINUTES+",M1
140 LET A=K
150 INPUT "NUMBER OF LINES IN GROUP =",W: LET I=1: LET Y=1
160 IF M1*K*W=0 THEN 600
170 IF W>K THEN 190
180 PRINT "TOO FEW LINES. TRY AGAIN.": GOTO 150
190 PRINT
200 PRINT "  N      OFRD    CRD    TOT    G/S"
210 LET T=1: LET T1=1
220 FOR N=1 TO W
230    LET T=T*A/N: LET T1=T1+T: LET P=T/T1
240 NEXT N
250 LET L=A*P: LET S=A-L
260 LET Y=S-K: IF ABS (Y)<.0001 THEN 300
270 IF Y<0 THEN 290
280 LET A=A-I: LET I=I/10
290 LET A=A+I: GOTO 210
300 LET T=1: LET T1=1: LET O=A
310 FOR N=1 TO W
320    LET T=T*A/N: LET T1=T1+T: LET P=T/T1
330    LET L=A*P: LET S=A-L: LET C=O-L
350    PRINT %3I;N;%9F3;O;%6F3;C;%8F3;S;%6F3;P
360    LET O=L
370 NEXT N
380 STOP
390 LET R1=R*L: LET X1=X*L: LET D1=D*L: LET F=A-R1
410 LET M=60/M1: LET F1=F*M: LET R2=R1*M
430 LET X2=X1*M: LET D2=D1*M: LET A1=A*M: LET K1=K*M
470 PRINT "FIRST ATTEMPT HOURS, CALLS =";%9F2;F;F1
480 PRINT "OFFERED HOURS, CALLS       =";%9F2;A;A1
490 PRINT "CARRIED HOURS, CALLS       =";%9F2;K;K1
500 PRINT "RECALLING  HOURS, CALLS    =";%9F2;R1;R2
510 PRINT "TOLL OVERFLOW HOURS, CALLS =";%9F2;X1;X2
520 PRINT "DEAD HOURS, CALLS          =";%9F2;D1;D2
530 PRINT
540 STOP : GOTO 140
550 REM: FOR HARD COPY OUTPUT, CHANGE 190 PRINT TO
560 REM: 190 PRINT: SET OF="SOL2"
570 REM: CHANGE 380 STOP TO 380 PRINT
580 REM: CHANGE 540 STOP: GOTO 140 TO
590 REM: 540 SET OF=#00: STOP: GOTO 140
600 END
```

(c) Input is carried traffic, capacity, holding time, and retry policy (LCC: Recall=0, Overflow=100; LCH: Recall=100, Overflow=0). Output is offered traffic and grade of service.

FIGURE 10-5.   Erlang B Program with Carried Traffic as Input (From [GOEL79])

complex formula and, because of the extra parameter L, the tables are more unwieldy than for Erlang B. In many cases, the infinite source assumption will suffice.

To get a handle on the relative size of the difference between finite and infinite source assumptions, let us compare two systems. One is infinite source with a calling rate of λ; the other is a finite source with a calling rate per source of λ/L. We then have

$$A_\infty = \lambda h$$

$$A_L = \frac{\lambda}{L}(L - n)h$$

$$= \lambda h\left(1 - \frac{n}{L}\right) \geq \lambda h\left(1 - \frac{N}{L}\right)$$

where

$$A\infty = \text{offered traffic, infinite source case}$$

$$A_L = \text{offered traffic, } L \text{ sources}$$

$$n = \text{number of sources currently engaged in a call}$$

The inequality results from the fact that the number of sources engaged cannot exceed the total capacity N of the system.

We have

$$A_\infty > A_L \geq A_\infty\left(1 - \frac{N}{L}\right)$$

Thus, for L much larger than N, A_∞ is a good approximation of A_L.

This conclusion is confirmed by Table 10.3, which shows that as the number of sources gets large compared to capacity, the effective capacity approaches the value for the infinite source case. Note that as the probability of loss decreases, the approximation becomes relatively less accurate. You should also be able to deduce from this table that the probability of loss is always less for a finite system than for a similar system with an infinite source. Thus the infinite source model will give conservative estimates for sizing.

Lost Calls Delayed

When queueing is allowed, the designer may be interested more in the delay characteristics than the blocking characteristics of the switch. Table 10.1c shows several formulas for the infinite source, LCD case. The

TABLE 10.3   Lost Calls Cleared, Finite and Infinite Sources (Number of Servers = 10)

Number of Sources	Offered Load (Effective Capacity)		
	$p = 0.005$	$p = 0.01$	$p = 0.05$
∞	3.96	4.46	6.22
50	4.16	4.64	6.4
25	4.6	5.1	6.81
20	4.81	5.32	7.06
15	5.27	5.78	7.41
12	5.97	6.47	8.02
10	10	10	10

designer might be interested in the probability of any delay (*Erlang C* formula), the probability of a delay greater than a given amount, or the mean value of delay. A BASIC program for calculation is shown in Figure 10-3b.

The probability of delay, the probability of delay greater than a given amount, and the average delay on all offered calls are complex functions of A and N and can be solved only with the aid of a computer or the appropriate tables. Fortunately, the average delay and the probability of delay greater than a given amount, *for calls that are delayed*, are easily calculated and of some interest.

As an example, consider this problem: What is the load that can be offered to a switch of capacity 1500 with a mean holding time of 1000 s, if the fraction of delayed calls waiting longer than 1 minute is not to exceed 10%? Thus we have $N = 1500$, $h = 1000$, $T = t/h = 60/1000 = 0.06$, and $P_2(>60) = 0.1$. Substituting, we have

$$\text{In } (0.1) = -(1500 - A)(0.06)$$

Solving for A yields $A = 1462$. Thus, for these requirements, the load on the system may be very near to the total capacity.

Our next example makes use of Figure 10-6, which shows the probability of delay for infinite source, lost calls delayed. Consider a switch with capacity 20 that experiences an average call holding time of 5 minutes. If the load on the system is 16 erlangs, what is the fraction of all calls that will be delayed greater than 2.5 minutes? First, we need the fraction of calls that will be delayed at all. From Figure 10-6, with $A = 16$ and $N = 20$, we have that $P(>0)$ is approximately 0.25. Then

$$P(>2.5) = P(>0)e^{-(N-A)t/h}$$

$$= 0.25e^{-(20-16)(2.5/5)}$$

$$= 0.03$$

The average delay on calls delayed is $h/(N-A) = 1.25$ minutes. The average delay for all calls is $P(>0) \cdot 1.25 = 0.31$ minute.

Table 10.1d shows the formula for finite source, lost calls delayed. This is the most complicated analytically, and the infinite source case should be used for a first approximation.

Summary

Using either tables or computer programs, the equations of Table 10.1 can be used in a variety of ways. For infinite sources, LCC, there are three variables: P, N, and A (which can be determined from λ and h). Given any

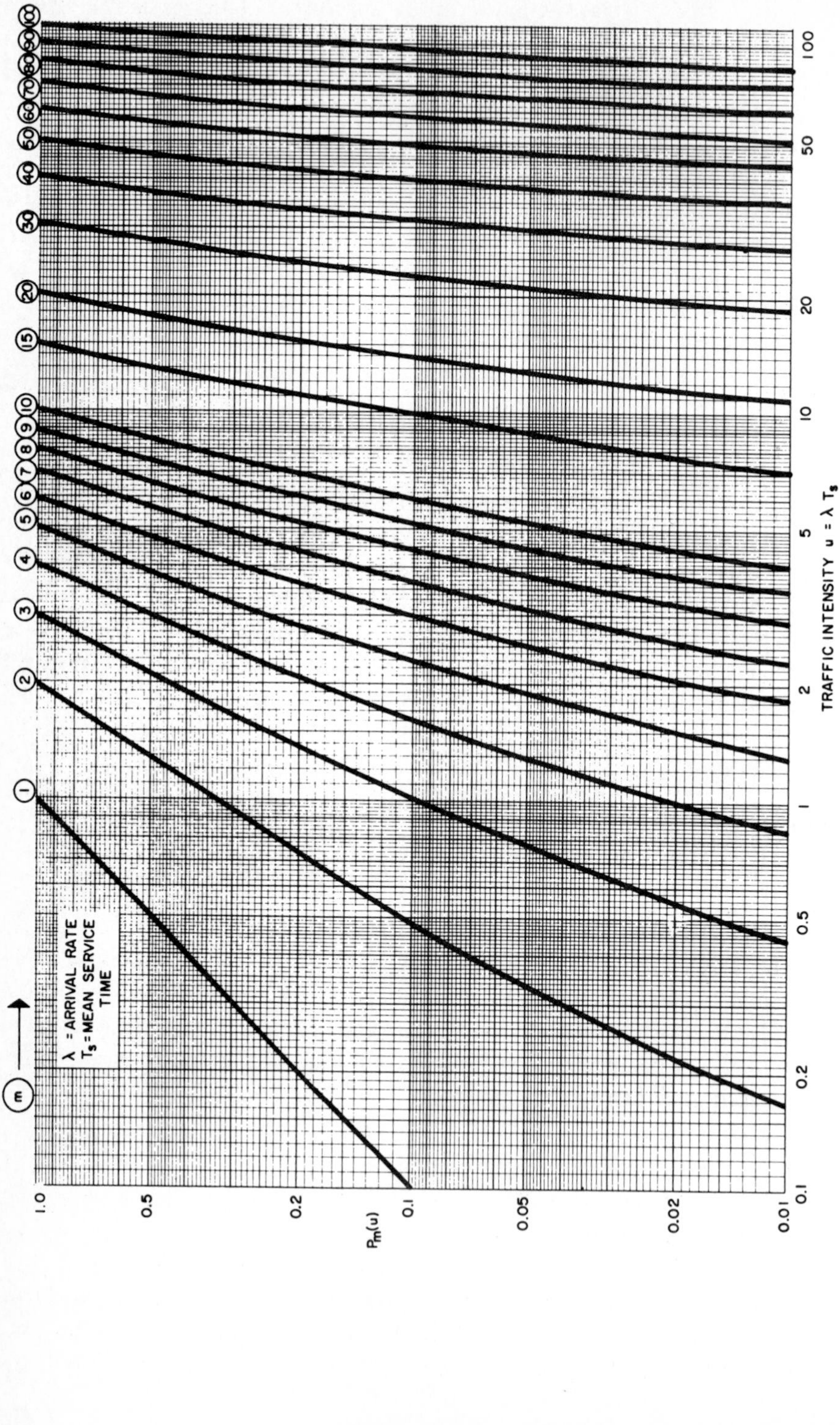

FIGURE 10-6. Probability of Delay for Infinite Sources, LCD Systems

λ = ARRIVAL RATE
T_s = MEAN SERVICE TIME

TRAFFIC INTENSITY $u = \lambda\ T_s$

$P_m(u)$

NETWORK PERFORMANCE: DIGITAL SWITCH/DIGITAL PBX

two variables, one can solve for the third. Example questions:

- Given a measured value of P for a particular N, how much must N be increased to reduce P to a given level?
- Given λ, h and a desired value for P, what capacity (N) is required?

For infinite source, lost calls delayed, there is the additional parameter, the delay. As before, among the variables $P(>0)$, N, and A, given any two the third can be found. To determine D, h must be known.

The same considerations apply for the finite-source case (LCC or LCD). In this case, a fixed L is used, and then the same types of problems can be addressed.

10.3

RECOMMENDED READING

A good introduction to the queueing theory underlying the concepts of this chapter can be found in [MART72]. A more thorough but still readable discussion is [IBM71]. One of the best textbooks on queueing theory, and one of the few that deals with the teletraffic concepts of this chapter is [COOP81]. A discussion that relates queueing theory directly to the problems of circuit-switching traffic is [BECK77]. [FRAN76] contains tables for all of the formulas presented in this book. The latter two publications are available from an organization with the unlikely name of Lee's abc of the Telephone, Box 537, Geneva, IL 60134.

Other books will useful accounts of the circuit-switched traffic problem are [ATT83], [JOLL68], [INOS79], and [SHAR82].

10.4

PROBLEMS

10.1 Using Figure 10-4, answer the following questions:
  a. Assume that the measured probability of loss is 0.05 for a system with capacity 10. How much must the capacity be increased to reduce the probability of loss to 0.005?
  b. The expected arrival rate of calls is 5 per minute, with an expected holding time of 2 minutes. What capacity switch is needed to give a probability of loss of 0.01?

10.2 A switch of capacity 25 is handling an offered load of 15 erlangs. If the load is increased by 100%, how much must the capacity be increased to maintain the same grade of service? Use the infinite sources, LCC model.

10.3 A switch of capacity 20 has engineered for a probability of delay of 0.1. The average holding time, however, turns out to be 20% greater than antici- pated. Assuming infinite sources, what is the actual probability of delay?

10.4   What capacity switch is required to handle 230 calls per hour with a probability of delay of no greater than 0.5? Assume that the average holding time is 100 s. Now add the additional requirement that the prob- ability of a delay greater than 100 s, for all calls, should be no more than 0.05. Is the capacity just calculated adequate? If not, what capacity is needed?

10.5   Why is a switch considered blocking for $L > N/2$, but a port contention unit is blocking for $L > N$?

10.6   The probability of loss for LCC systems, also known as call congestion, is the probability that an arriving call will find all circuits busy. Another quantity, the blocking probability, also known as time congestion, is the probability that, at an arbitrary time, all circuits are busy. Are these quantities the same for the infinite source case? For the finite source case? Answer using commonsense arguments, without mathematics.

10.7   For infinite source, lost calls cleared, derive an expression for the number of lost calls per unit time.

CHAPTER 11

Internetworking

In many, perhaps most, cases a local network will not be an isolated entity. An organization may have more than one type of local network at a given site, to satisfy a spectrum of needs. An organization may have local networks at various sites and need them to be interconnected for central control of distributed information exchange. And an organization may need to provide a connection for one or more terminals and hosts on a local network to other computing resources.

An interconnected set of networks, from a user's point of view, may appear simply as a larger network. However, if each of the constituent networks retains its identity, and special mechanisms are needed for communicating across multiple networks, then the entire configuration is often referred to as an **internet**, and each of the constituent networks as a **subnetwork**. These terms are briefly defined in Table 11.1.

Table 11.1 also defines three sorts of devices used to interconnect subnetworks in an internet: bridges, routers, and gateways. These devices provide a communications path and the necessary logic so that data can be exchanged between subnetworks. The differences between them have to do with the types of protocols used for the internetworking logic (Figure 11-1). In essence, a bridge operates at layer 2 of the open systems interconnection (OSI) 7-layer architecture and acts as a relay of frames

379

TABLE 11.1 Internetworking Terms

Communication Network
 A facility that provides a data transfer service among stations attached to the network.

Internet
 A collection of communication networks interconnected by bridges, routers, and/or gateways.

Subnetwork
 Refers to a consituent network of an internet. This avoids ambiguity since the entire internet, from a user's point of view, is a single network.

Bridge
 A device used to connect two LANs that use identical LAN protocols. The bridge acts as an address filter, picking up packets from one LAN that are intended for a destination on another LAN and passing those packets on. The bridge does not modify the contents of the packets and does not add anything to the packet. The bridge operates at layer 2 of the OSI model.

Router
 A device used to connect two networks that may or may not be similar. The router employs an internet protocol present in each router and each host of the network. The router operates at layer 3 of the OSI model.

Gateway
 A device used to connect two sets of computers that use two different communications architectures. The gateway maps from an application on one computer to an application that is similar in function but differs in detail on another computer. The gateway operates at layer 7 of the OSI model.

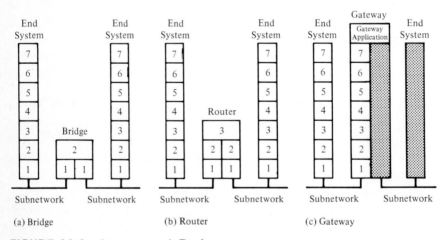

FIGURE 11-1. Internetwork Devices

between like networks. A router operates at layer 3 of the OSI architecture and routes packets between dissimilar networks. Both the bridge and the router assume that the same upper-layer protocols are in use. The gateway operates at layer 7 and provides a link between dissimilar architectures (e.g., OSI and SNA) on either the same network or different networks. In this chapter, we examine each of these devices in turn.

11.1

BRIDGES

Functions of a Bridge

The simplest of the internetworking devices is the bridge. This device is designed for use between local area networks (LANs) that use identical protocols for the physical and medium access layers (e.g., all conforming to IEEE 802.3 or all conforming to FDDI). Because the devices all use the same protocols, the amount of processing required at the bridge is minimal. The concept of a bridge was introduced in Chapter 4 as a means of linking multiple rings.

Figure 11-2 illustrates the operation of a bridge between two LANs, A and B. The bridge performs the following functions:

- Read all frames transmitted on A, and accept those addressed to stations on B.
- Using the medium access control protocol for B, retransmit the frames onto B.
- Do the same for B-to-A traffic.

In addition to these basic functions, there are some interesting design considerations:

1. The bridge makes no modifications to the content or format of the frames it receives.
2. The bridge should contain enough buffer space to meet peak demands. Over a short period of time, frames may arrive faster than they can be retransmitted.
3. The bridge must contain addressing and routing intelligence. At a minimum, the bridges must know which addresses are on each network in order to know which frames to forward. Further, there may be more than two networks in a sort of cascade configuration. The bridge must be able to pass along frames intended for networks further on. The subject of routing is explored later in this section.
4. A bridge may connect more than two networks. This was discussed in Chapter 4.

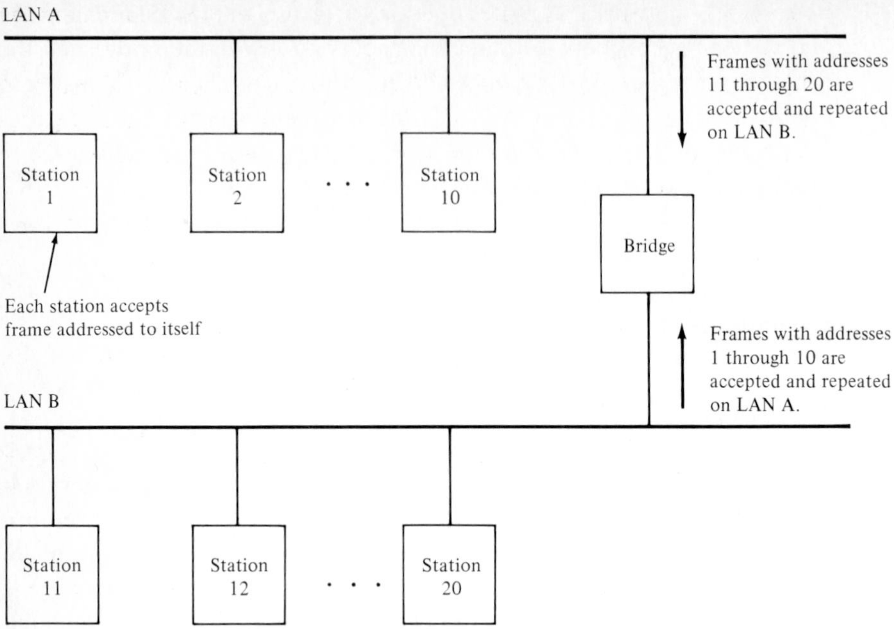

LAN A

Frames with addresses
11 through 20 are
accepted and repeated
on LAN B.

Station 1

Station 2

. . .

Station 10

Bridge

Each station accepts
frame addressed to itself

Frames with addresses
1 through 10 are
accepted and repeated
on LAN A.

LAN B

Station 11

Station 12

. . .

Station 20

FIGURE 11-2. Bridge Operation

In summary, the bridge provides an extension to the LAN that requires no modification to the communications software in the stations attached to the LANs. It appears to all stations on the two (or more) LANs that there is a single LAN on which each station has a unique address. The station uses that unique address and need not explicitly discriminate between stations on the same LAN and stations on other LANs; the bridge takes care of that.

Also, the reader will note from Figure 11-1a that the bridge encompasses only layers 1 and 2 of the OSI model. In effect, the bridge operates as a layer-2 relay. Layers 3 and above must be identical in the two end systems for successful end-to-end communications.

Since the bridge is used in a situation in which all of the LANs have the same characteristics, the reader may ask why not simply have one large LAN. Depending on circumstance, there are several reasons for the use of multiple LANs connected by bridges:

- *Reliability:* The danger in connecting all data processing devices in an organization to one network is that a fault on the network may disable communication for all devices. By using bridges, the network can be partitioned into self-contained units.
- *Performance:* In general, performance on a LAN or HSLN declines with an increase in the number of devices or the length of the medium. A number of smaller LANs will often give improved performance if de-

382   **INTERNETWORKING**

vices can be clustered so that *intra*-network traffic significantly exceeds *inter*-network traffic.

- *Security:* The establishment of multiple LANs may improve security of communications. It is desirable to keep different types of traffic (e.g., accounting, personnel, strategic planning) that have different security needs on physically separate media. At the same time, the different types of users with different levels of security need to communicate through controlled and monitored mechanisms. This topic is explored further in Chapter 12.
- *Geography:* Clearly, two separate LANs are needed to support devices clustered in two geographically distant locations. Even in the case of two buildings separated by a highway, it may be far easier to use a microwave bridge link than to attempt to string coaxial cable between the two buildings. In the case of widely separated networks, two "half bridges" are needed (see Figures 11-4 and 11-5).

The description above has applied to the simplest sort of bridge. More sophisticated bridges can be used in more complex collections of LANs. These would include additional functions, such as:

- Each bridge can maintain status information on other bridges, together with the cost and number of bridge-to-bridge hops required to reach each network. This information may be updated by periodic exchanges of information among bridges. This allows the bridges to perform a dynamic routing function.
- A control mechanism can manage frame buffers in each bridge to overcome congestion. Under saturation conditions, the bridge can give precedence to enroute packets over new packets just entering the internet from an attached LAN, thus preserving the investment in line bandwidth and processing time already made in the enroute frame.

Bridge Protocol Architecture

The IEEE 802 committee has produced two specifications for bridges [IEEE88b, IEEE88c]. In both cases, the devices are referred to as MAC-level relays. In addition, all of the MAC standards suggest formats for a globally administered set of MAC station addresses across multiple homogeneous LANs. In this subsection, we examine the protocol architecture of these bridges.

Within the 802 architecture, the endpoint or station address is designated at the MAC level. At the LLC level, only an SAP address is specified. Thus, it is at the MAC level that a bridge can function. Figure 11-3 shows the simplest case, which consists of two LANs connected by a single bridge. The LANs employ the same MAC and LLC protocols. The

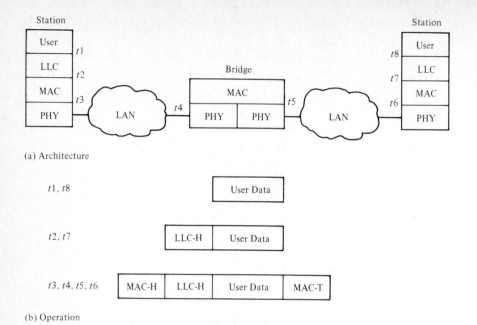

(a) Architecture

t1, t8

User Data

t2, t7

LLC-H	User Data

t3, t4, t5, t6

MAC-H	LLC-H	User Data	MAC-T

(b) Operation

FIGURE 11-3.   Connection of Two LANs by a Bridge

bridge operates as previously described. A MAC frame whose destination is not on the immediate LAN is captured by the bridge, buffered briefly, and then transmitted on the other LAN. As far as the LLC layer is concerned, there is a dialogue between peer LLC entities in the two endpoint stations. The bridge need not contain an LLC layer since it is merely serving to relay the MAC frames.

Figure 11-3b indicates the way in which data is encapsulated using a bridge. Data is provided by some user to LLC. The LLC entity appends a header and passes the resulting data unit to the MAC entity, which appends a header and a trailer to form a MAC frame. On the basis of the destination MAC address in the frame, it is captured by the bridge. The bridge does not strip off the MAC fields; its function is to relay the MAC frame intact to the destination LAN. Thus the frame is deposited on the destination LAN and captured by the destination station.

The concept of a MAC relay bridge is not limited to the use of a single bridge to connect two nearby LANs. If the LANs are some distance apart, then they can be connected by two bridges that are in turn connected by a communications facility. For example, Figure 11-4 shows the case of two bridges connected by a point-to-point link. In this case, when a bridge captures a MAC frame, it appends a link layer (e.g., HDLC) header and trailer to transmit the MAC frame across the link to the other bridge. The target bridge strips off these link fields and transmits the original, unmodified MAC frame to the destination station.

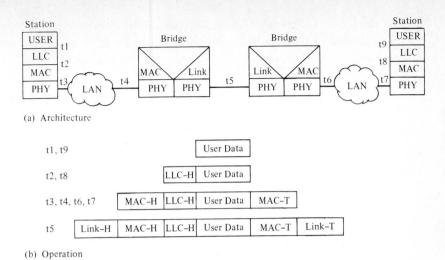

(a) Architecture

t1, t9	User Data
t2, t8	LLC-H User Data
t3, t4, t6, t7	MAC-H LLC-H User Data MAC-T
t5	Link-H MAC-H LLC-H User Data MAC-T Link-T

(b) Operation

FIGURE 11-4. Bridge Over a Point-to-Point Link

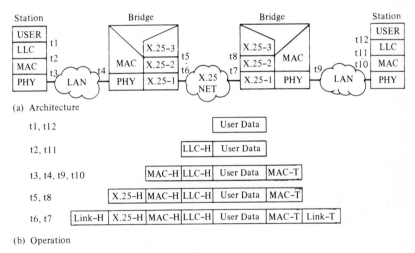

(a) Architecture

t1, t12	User Data
t2, t11	LLC-H User Data
t3, t4, t9, t10	MAC-H LLC-H User Data MAC-T
t5, t8	X.25-H MAC-H LLC-H User Data MAC-T
t6, t7	Link-H X.25-H MAC-H LLC-H User Data MAC-T Link-T

(b) Operation

FIGURE 11-5. Bridge Over an X.25 Network

The intervening communications facility can even be a network, such as a wide-area packet-switching network, as illustrated in Figure 11-5. In this case, the bridge is somewhat more complicated although it performs the same function of relaying MAC frames. The connection between bridges is via an X.25 virtual circuit. Again, the two LLC entities in the end systems have a direct logical relationship with no intervening LLC entities. Thus, in this situation, the X.25 packet layer is operating below an 802 LLC layer. As before, a MAC frame is passed intact between the endpoints. When the bridge on the source LAN receives the frame, it appends an X.25 packet layer header and an X.25 link-layer header and trailer and sends the data to the DCE (packet-switching node) to which it attaches. The DCE strips off the link layer fields and sends the X.25 packet through the network to another DCE. The target DCE appends the link layer field and sends this to the target bridge. The target bridge strips of all the X.25 fields and transmits the original unmodified MAC frame to the destination endpoint.

11.2

ROUTING WITH BRIDGES

In the configuration of Figure 11-2, the bridge makes the decision to relay a frame on the basis of destination MAC address. In a more complex configuration, the bridge must also make a routing decision. Consider the configuration of Figure 11-6. Suppose that station 1 transmits a frame on LAN A intended for station 5. The frame will be read by both bridge 101

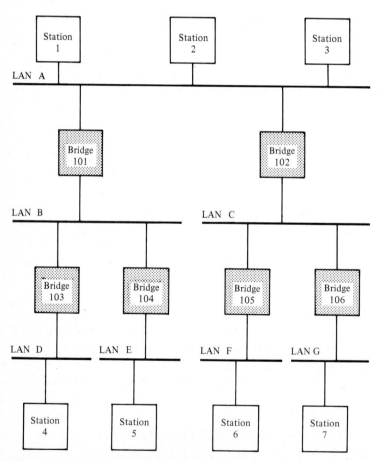

FIGURE 11-6. Internet Configuration of Bridges and LANs

and bridge 102. For each bridge, the addressed station is not on a LAN to which the bridge is attached. Therefore, each bridge must make a decision of whether or not to retransmit the frame on its other LAN, in order to move it closer to its intended destination. In this case, bridge 101 should repeat the frame on LAN B, whereas bridge 102 should refrain from retransmitting the frame. Once the frame has been transmitted on LAN B, it will be picked up by both bridges 103 and 104. Again, each must decide whether or not to forward the frame. In this case, bridge 104 should retransmit the frame on LAN E, where it will be received by the destination, station 5.

Thus we see that, in the general case, the bridge must be equipped with a routing capability. When a bridge receives a frame, it must decide whether or not to forward it. If the bridge is attached to more than two networks, then it must decide whether or not to forward the frame and, if so, on which LAN the frame should be transmitted.

The routing decision may not always be a simple one. In Figure 11-7, bridge 107 is added to the previous configuration, directly linking LAN A and LAN E. Such an addition may be made to provide for higher overall internet availability. In this case, if Station 1 transmits a frame on LAN A intended for station 5 on LAN E, then either bridge 101 or bridge 107 could forward the frame. It would appear preferable for bridge 107 to forward the frame, since it will involve only one "hop," whereas if the frame travels through bridge 101, it must suffer two hops. Another consideration is that there may be changes in the configuration. For example, bridge 107 may fail, in which case subsequent frames from station 1 to station 5 should go through bridge 101. So we can say that the routing capability must take into account the topology of the internet configuration and may need to be dynamically altered.

One final point: Figure 11-7 suggests that a bridge knows the identity of each station on each LAN. In a large configuration, such an arrangement is unwieldy. Furthermore, as stations are added to and dropped from LANs, all directories of station locations must be updated. It would facilitate the development of a routing capability if all MAC-level addresses were in the form of a network part and a station part. For example, the IEEE 802.5 standard suggests that 16-bit MAC addresses consist of a 7-bit LAN number and an 8-bit station number, and that 48-bit addresses consist of a 14-bit LAN number and a 32-bit station number.[1] In the remainder of this discussion, we assume that all MAC addresses include a LAN number and that routing is based on the use of that portion of the address only.

---

[1] The remaining bit in the 16-bit format is used to indicate whether this is a group or individual address. Of the two remaining bits in the 48-bit format, one is used to indicate whether this is a group or individual address, and the other is used to indicate whether this is a locally-administered or globally-administered address.

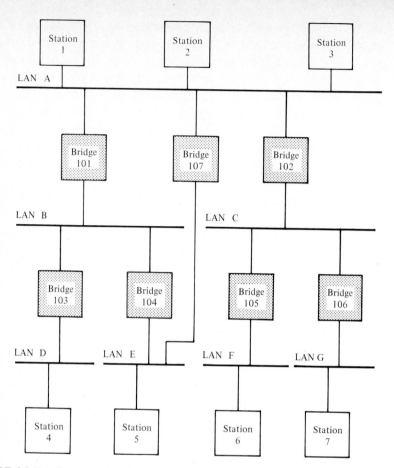

FIGURE 11-7. Internet Configuration of Bridges and LANs, with Alternate Routes

A variety of routing strategies have been proposed and implemented in recent years. The simplest, and most common strategy, is **fixed routing**. This strategy is suitable for small internets and for internets that are relatively stable. More recently, two groups within the IEEE 802 committee developed specifications for routing strategies. The IEEE 802.1 group has issued a standard for routing based on the use of a **spanning tree** algorithm. The token ring committee, IEEE 802.5, has issued its own specification, referred to as **source routing**. We examine these three strategies in turn.

Fixed Routing

For fixed routing, a route is selected for each source-destination pair of LANs in the internet. If alternate routes are available between two LANs, then typically the route with the least number of hops is selected. The routes are fixed, or at least only change when there is a change in the topology of the internet.

Figure 11-8 suggests how fixed routing might be implemented. A central routing matrix is created, to be stored perhaps at a network control center. The matrix shows, for each source-destination pair of LANs, the identity of the first bridge on the route. So for example, the route from LAN E to LAN F begins by going through bridge 107 to LAN A. Again consulting the matrix, the route from LAN A to LAN F goes through bridge 102 to LAN C. Finally, the route from LAN C to LAN F is directly through bridge 105. Thus the complete route from LAN E to LAN F is bridge 107, LAN A, bridge 102, LAN C, bridge 105.

From this overall matrix, routing tables can be developed and stored at each bridge. Each bridge needs one table for each LAN to which it attaches. The information for each table is derived from a single row of the matrix. For example, bridge 105 has two tables, one for frames arriving from LAN C and one for frames arriving from LAN F. The table shows, for each possible destination MAC address, the identity of the LAN to which the bridge should forward the frame. The table labeled "from LAN C" is derived from the row labeled C in the routing matrix. Every entry in that row that contains bridge number 105 results in an entry in the corresponding table in bridge 105.

Once the directories have been established, routing is a simple matter. A bridge copies each incoming frame on each of its LANs. If the destination MAC address corresponds to an entry in its routing table, the frame is retransmitted on the appropriate LAN.

The fixed routing strategy is widely used in commercially-available products. It has the advantage of simplicity and minimal processing requirements. However, in a complex internet, in which bridges may be dynamically added and in which failures must be allowed for, this strategy is too limited. We now turn to two more powerful alternatives.

The Spanning Tree Approach

The spanning tree approach is a mechanism in which bridges automatically develop a routing table and update that table in response to changing topology [BACK88, HART88, IEEE88b, PERL84]. The algorithm consists of three mechanisms: frame forwarding, address learning, and loop resolution.

Frame Forwarding

In this scheme, a bridge maintains a **forwarding database** for each port attached to a LAN. The database indicates the station addresses for

Central Routing Matrix
Destination LAN

<table>
<thead>
<tr><th></th><th></th><th>A</th><th>B</th><th>C</th><th>D</th><th>E</th><th>F</th><th>G</th></tr>
</thead>
<tbody>
<tr><td rowspan="7">Source LAN</td><td>A</td><td>–</td><td>101</td><td>102</td><td>101</td><td>107</td><td>102</td><td>102</td></tr>
<tr><td>B</td><td>101</td><td>–</td><td>101</td><td>103</td><td>104</td><td>101</td><td>101</td></tr>
<tr><td>C</td><td>102</td><td>102</td><td>–</td><td>102</td><td>102</td><td>105</td><td>106</td></tr>
<tr><td>D</td><td>103</td><td>103</td><td>103</td><td>–</td><td>103</td><td>103</td><td>103</td></tr>
<tr><td>E</td><td>107</td><td>104</td><td>107</td><td>104</td><td>–</td><td>107</td><td>107</td></tr>
<tr><td>F</td><td>105</td><td>105</td><td>105</td><td>105</td><td>105</td><td>–</td><td>105</td></tr>
<tr><td>G</td><td>106</td><td>106</td><td>106</td><td>106</td><td>106</td><td>106</td><td>–</td></tr>
</tbody>
</table>

Bridge 101 Table

From LAN A		From LAN B	
Dest.	Next	Dest.	Next
B	B	A	A
C	–	C	A
D	B	D	–
E	–	E	–
F	–	F	A
G	–	G	A

Bridge 102 Table

From LAN A		From LAN C	
Dest.	Next	Dest.	Next
B	–	A	A
C	C	B	A
D	–	D	A
E	–	E	A
F	C	F	–
G	C	G	–

Bridge 103 Table

From LAN B		From LAN D	
Dest.	Next	Dest.	Next
A	–	A	B
C	–	B	B
D	D	C	B
E	–	E	B
F	–	F	B
G	–	G	B

Bridge 104 Table

From LAN B		From LAN E	
Dest.	Next	Dest.	Next
A	–	A	–
C	–	B	B
D	–	C	–
E	E	D	B
F	–	F	–
G	–	G	–

Bridge 105 Table

From LAN C		From LAN F	
Dest.	Next	Dest.	Next
A	–	A	C
B	–	B	C
D	–	C	C
E	–	D	C
F	F	E	C
G	–	G	C

Bridge 106 Table

From LAN C		From LAN G	
Dest.	Next	Dest.	Next
A	–	A	C
B	–	B	C
D	–	C	C
E	–	D	C
F	–	E	C
G	G	F	C

Bridge 107 Table

From LAN A		From LAN E	
Dest.	Next	Dest.	Next
B	–	A	A
C	–	B	–
D	–	C	A
E	E	D	–
F	–	F	A
G	–	G	A

FIGURE 11-8. Fixed Routing (Using Figure 11-7)

which frames should be forwarded. We can interpret this in the following fashion. For each port, a list of stations is maintained. A station is on the list if it is on the "same side" of the bridge as the port. For example, for bridge 102 of Figure 11-6, stations on LANs C, F, and G are on the same side of the bridge as the LAN C port, and stations on LANs A, B, D, and E are on the same side of the bridge as the LAN A port. When a frame is received on any port, the bridge must decide whether that frame is to be forwarded through the bridge and out through one of the bridge's other ports. Suppose that a bridge receives a MAC frame on port x. The following rules are applied (Figure 11-9):

1. Search the forwarding database to determine if the MAC address is listed for any port except port x.

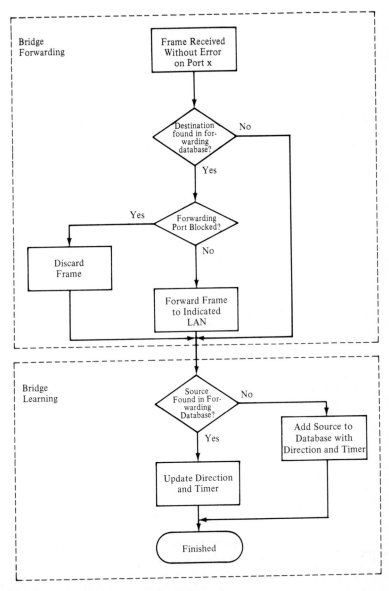

FIGURE 11-9. Bridge Forwarding and Learning

2. If the destination MAC address is not found, discard the frame.
3. If the destination address is in the forwarding database for some port y, then determine whether port y is in a blocking or forwarding state. For reasons explained below, a port may sometimes be blocked, which prevents it from receiving or transmitting frames.
4. If port y is not blocked, transmit the frame through port y onto the LAN to which that port attaches.

Address Learning

The above scheme assumes that the bridge is already equipped with a forwarding database that indicates the direction, from the bridge, of each destination station. This information can be preloaded into the bridge, as in static routing. However, an effective automatic mechanism for learning the direction of each station is desirable. A simple scheme for acquiring this information is based on the use of the source address field in each MAC frame (Figure 11-9).

The strategy is this. When a frame arrives on a particular port, it clearly has come from the direction of the incoming LAN. The source address field of the frame indicates the source station. Thus, a bridge can update its forwarding database for that port on the basis of the source address field of each incoming frame. To allow for changes in topology, each element in the database is equipped with a timer. When a new element is added to the database, its timer is set. If the timer expires, then the element is eliminated from the database, since the corresponding direction information may no longer be valid. Each time a frame is received, its source address is checked against the database. If the element is already in the database, the entry is updated (the direction may have changed) and the timer is reset. If the element is not in the database, a new entry is created, with its own timer.

The above discussion indicated that the individual entries in the database are station addresses. If a two-level address structure (LAN number, station number) is used, then only LAN addresses need to be entered in the database. Both schemes work the same. The only difference is that the use of station addresses requires a much larger database than the use of LAN addresses.

Spanning Tree Algorithm

The address learning mechanism described above is effective if the topology of the internet is a tree; that is, if there are no alternate routes in the network. The existence of alternate routes means that there is a closed loop. For example in Figure 11-7, the following is a closed loop: LAN A, bridge 101, LAN B, bridge 104, LAN E, bridge 107, LAN A.

To see the problem created by a closed loop, consider Figure 11-10. At time $t0$, station A transmits a frame addressed to station B. The

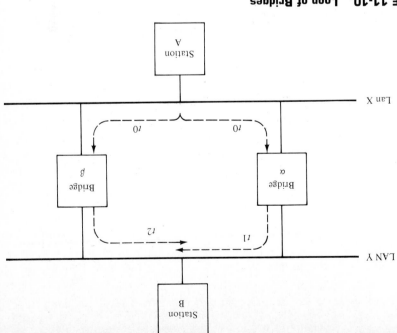

FIGURE 11-10. Loop of Bridges

frame is captured by both bridges. Each bridge updates its database to indicate that station A is in the direction of LAN X, and retransmits the frame on LAN Y. Say that bridge α retransmits at time t1 and bridge β a short time later, t2. Thus B will receive two copies of the frame. Furthermore, each bridge will receive the other's transmission on LAN Y. Note that each transmission is a MAC frame with a source address of A and a destination address of B. Thus each bridge will update its database to indicate that station A is in the direction of LAN Y. Neither bridge is now capable of forwarding a frame addressed to station A.

To overcome this problem, a simple result from graph theory is used: For any connected graph, consisting of nodes and edges connecting pairs of nodes, there is a spanning tree that maintains the connectivity of the graph but contains no closed loops. In terms of internets, each LAN corresponds to a graph node, and each bridge corresponds to a graph edge. Thus, in Figure 11-7, the removal of one (and only one) of bridges 107, 101, and 104, results in a spanning tree. What is desired is to develop a simple algorithm by which the bridges of the internet can exchange sufficient information to automatically (without user intervention) derive a spanning tree. The algorithm must be dynamic. That is, when a topology change occurs, the bridges must be able to discover this fact and automatically derive a new spanning tree.

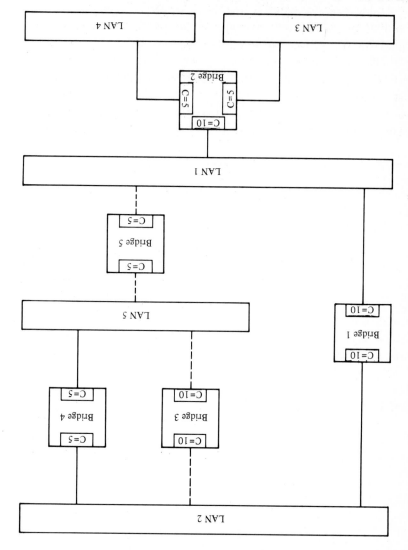

FIGURE 11-11. Example Configuration for Spanning Tree Algorithm

The algorithm is based on the use of the following:

1. Each bridge is assigned a unique identifier; in essence, the identifier consists of a MAC address for the bridge plus a priority level.

2. There is a special group MAC address that means "all bridges on this LAN." When a MAC frame is transmitted with the group address in the destination address field, all of the bridges on the LAN will capture that frame and interpret it as a frame addressed to itself.

3. Each port of a bridge is uniquely identified within the bridge, with a "port identifier."

of bridges along the path. Alternatively, costs could be assigned in a value of 1; thus the cost of a path would simply be a count of the number particular path. In the simplest case, all path costs would be assigned a bridge, the cost of transmission is added to give a total cost for a between two stations will pass through zero or more bridges. At each is the cost of transmitting a frame onto a LAN through that port. A path

- *Path cost:* Associated with each port on each bridge is a path cost, which chosen to be the root of the spanning tree.
- *Root bridge:* The bridge with the lowest value of bridge identifier is the spanning tree:

We will explain the operation of the algorithm using Figures 11-11 and 11-12 as an example. The following concepts are needed in the creation of routing information in order to determine a spanning tree of the internet. With this information established, the bridges are able to exchange

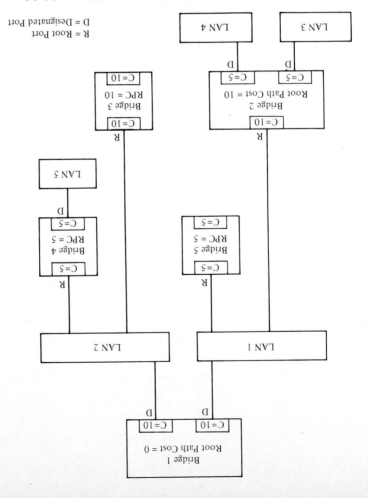

FIGURE 11-12. Spanning Tree for Configuration of Figure 11-11

R = Root Port
D = Designated Port

inverse proportion to the data rate of the corresponding LAN, or any other criterion chosen by the network manager.

- *Root port:* Each bridge discovers the first hop on the minimum-cost path to the root bridge. The port used for that hop is labeled the root port.
- *Root path cost:* For each bridge, the cost of the path to the root bridge with minimum cost (the path that starts at the root port) is the root path cost for that bridge.
- *Designated bridge, designated port:* On each LAN, one bridge is chosen to be the designated bridge. This is the bridge on that LAN that provides the minimum cost path to the root bridge. This is the only bridge allowed to forward frames to and from the LAN for which it is the designated bridge. The port of the designated bridge that attaches the bridge to the LAN is the designated port. For all LANs to which the root bridge is attached, the root bridge is the designated bridge. All internet traffic to and from the LAN passes through the designated port.

In general terms, the spanning tree is constructed in the following fashion:

1. Determine the root bridge.
2. Determine the root port on all other bridges.
3. Determine the designated port on each LAN. This will be the port with the minimum root path cost. In the case of two or more bridges with the same root path cost, then the highest-priority bridge is chosen as the designated bridge. If the designated bridge has two or more ports attached to this LAN, then the port with the lowest value of port identifier is chosen.

By this process, when two LANs are directly connected by more than one bridge, all of the bridges but one are eliminated. This cuts any loops that involve two LANs. It can be demonstrated that this process also eliminates all loops involving more than two LANs and that connectivity is preserved. Thus, this process discovers a spanning tree for the given internet. In our example, the solid lines indicate the bridge ports that participate in the spanning tree.

The steps outlined above require that the bridges exchange information. The information is exchanged in the form of bridge protocol data units (BPDUs). A BPDU transmitted by one bridge is addressed to and received by all of the other bridges on the same LAN. Each BPDU contains the following information:

- The identifier of this bridge and the port on this bridge
- The identifier of the bridge that this bridge considers to be the root
- The root path cost for this bridge

To begin, all bridges consider themselves to be the root bridge. Each bridge will broadcast a BPDU on each of its LANs that asserts this fact. On any given LAN, only one claimant will have the lowest-valued identifier and will maintain its belief. Over time, as BPDUs propagate, the identity of the lowest-valued bridge identifier throughout the internet will be known to all bridges. The root bridge will regularly broadcast the fact that it is the root bridge on all of the LANs to which it is attached. This allows the bridges on those LANs to determine their root port and the fact that they are directly connected to the root bridge. Each of these bridges in turn broadcasts a BPDU on the other LANs to which it is attached (all LANs except the one on its root port), indicating that it is one hop away from the root bridge. This activity is propagated throughout the internet. Every time that a bridge receives a BPDU, it transmits BPDUs indicating the identity of the root bridge and the number of hops to reach the root bridge. On any LAN, the bridge claiming to be the one that is closest to the root becomes the designated bridge.

We can trace some of this activity with the configuration of Figure 11-11. At startup time, Bridges 1, 3, and 4 all transmit BPDUs on LAN 2 claiming to be the root bridge. When bridge 3 receives the transmission from bridge 1, it recognizes a superior claimant and defers. Bridge 3 has also received a claiming BPDU from bridge 5 via LAN 5. Bridge 3 recognizes that bridge 1 has a superior claim to be the root bridge; it therefore assigns its LAN 2 port to be its root port, and sets the root path cost to 10. By similar actions, bridge 4 ends up with a root path cost of 5 via LAN 2; bridge 5 has a root path cost of 5 via LAN 1; and bridge 2 has a root path cost of 10 via LAN 1.

Now consider the assignment of designated bridges. On LAN 5, all three bridges transmit BPDUs attempting to assert a claim to be the designated bridge. Bridge 3 defers because it receives BPDUs from the other bridges that have a lower root path cost. Bridges 4 and 5 have the same root path cost, but bridge 4 has the higher priority and therefore becomes the designated bridge.

The results of all this activity are shown in Figure 11-12. Only the designated bridge on each LAN is allowed to forward frames. All of the ports on all of the other bridges are placed in a blocking state. After the spanning tree is established, bridges continue to periodically exchange BPDUs to be able to react to any change in topology, cost assignments, or priority assignment. Any time that a bridge receives a BPDU on a port it makes two assessments:

1. If the BPDU arrives on a port that is considered the designated port, does the transmitting port have a better claim to be designated port?
2. Should this port be my root port?

Source Routing

The source routing approach is a mechanism in which the sending station determines the route that the frame will follow and includes the routing information with the frame; bridges read the routing information to determine if they should forward the frame [DIXO88, HAMN88, PITT87, BEDE86, PITT85, IEEE88c].

Basic Operation

The basic operation of the algorithm can be described with reference to the configuration of Figure 11-13a. A frame from station X can reach station Y by either of the following routes:

- LAN 1, bridge B1, LAN 3, bridge B3, LAN 2
- LAN 1, bridge B2, LAN 4, bridge B4, LAN 2

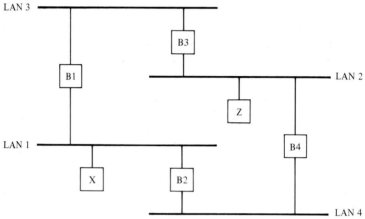

(a) Configuration

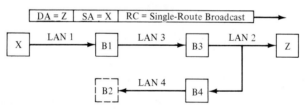

(b) Single-Route Broadcast Request

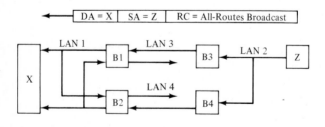

(c) All-Routes Broadcast Response

FIGURE 11-13. Route Discovery Example [DIXO88]

Station X may choose one of these two routes and place the information, in the form of a sequence of LAN and bridge identifiers, in the frame to be transmitted. When a bridge receives a frame, it will forward that frame if the bridge is on the designated route; all other frames are discarded. In this case, if the first route above is specified, bridges B1 and B3 will forward the frame; if the second route is specified, bridges B2 and B4 will forward the frame.

Note that with this scheme, bridges need not maintain routing tables. The bridge makes the decision whether or not to forward a frame solely on the basis of the routing information contained in the frame. All that is required is that the bridge know its own unique identifier and the identifier of each LAN to which it is attached. The responsibility for designating the route falls to the source station.

For this scheme to work, there must be a mechanism by which a station can determine a route to any destination station. Before dealing with this issue, we need to discuss different types of routing directives.

Routing Directives and Addressing Modes

The source routing scheme developed by the IEEE 802.5 committee includes four different types of routing directives. Each frame that is transmitted includes an indicator of the type of routing desired. The four directive types are:

- *Null:* No routing is desired. In this case, the frame can only be delivered to stations on the same LAN as the source station.
- *Nonbroadcast:* The frame includes a route, consisting of a sequence of LAN numbers and bridge numbers that defines a unique route from the source station to the destination station. Only bridges on that route forward the frame, and only a single copy of the frame is delivered to the destination station.
- *All-routes broadcast:* The frame will reach each LAN of the internet by all possible routes. Thus each bridge will forward each frame once to each of its ports in a direction away from the source node, and multiple copies of the frame may appear on a LAN. The destination station will receive one copy of the frame for each possible route through the network.
- *Single-route broadcast:* Regardless of the destination address of the frame, the frame will appear once, and only once, on each LAN in the internet. For this effect to be achieved, the frame is forwarded by all bridges that are on a spanning tree (with the source node as the root) of the internet. The destination station receives a single copy of the frame.

Let us first examine the potential application of each of these four types of routing, and then examine the mechanisms that may be employed to achieve them. First, consider null routing. In this case the bridges that share the LAN with the source station are told not to forward the frame. This will be done if the intended destination is on the same LAN as the source station. Nonbroadcast routing is used when the two stations are not on the same LAN and the source station knows a route that can be used to reach the destination station. Only the bridges on that route will forward the frame.

The remaining two types of routing can be used by the source to discover a route to the destination. For example, the source station can use all-routes broadcasting to send a request frame to the intended destination. The destination returns a response frame, using nonbroadcast routing, on each of the routes followed by the incoming request frame. The source station can pick one of these routes and send future frames on that route. Alternatively, the source station could use single-route broadcasting to send a single request frame to the destination station. The destination station could send its response frame via all-routes broadcasting. The incoming frames would reveal all of the possible routes to the destination station, and the source station could pick one of these for future transmissions. Finally, single-route broadcasting could be used for group addressings, as discussed below.

Now consider the mechanisms for implementing these various routing directives. Each frame must include an indicator of which of the four types of routing is required. For null routing, the frame is ignored by the bridge. For nonbroadcast routing, the frame includes an ordered list of LAN numbers and bridge numbers. When a bridge receives a nonbroadcast frame, it forwards the frame only if the routing information contains the sequence LAN i, Bridge x, LAN j, where

LAN i = LAN from which the frame arrived

Bridge x = this bridge

LAN j = another LAN to which this bridge is attached.

For all-routes broadcasting, the source station marks the frame for this type of routing, but includes no routing information. Each bridge that forwards the frame will add its bridge number and the outgoing LAN number to the frame's routing information field. Thus, when the frame reaches its destination, it will include a sequenced list of all LANs and bridges visited. To prevent the endless repetition and looping of frames, a bridge obeys the following rule. When an all-routes broadcast frame is received, the bridge examines the routing information field. If the field contains the number of a LAN to which the bridge is attached, the bridge will refrain from forwarding the frame on that LAN. Put the other way, the bridge will only forward the frame to a LAN that the frame has not already visited.

Finally, for single-route broadcasting, a spanning tree of the internet must be developed. This can either be done automatically, as in the 802.1 specification, or manually. In either case, as with the 802.1 strategy, one bridge on each LAN is the designated bridge for that LAN, and is the only one that forwards single-route frames.

It is worth noting the relationship between addressing mode and routing directive. Recall from Chapter 5, that there are three types of MAC addresses:

- *Individual:* the address specifies a unique destination station.
- *Group:* the address specifies a group of destination addresses; this is also referred to as *multicast.*
- *All-stations;* the address specifies all stations that are capable of receiving this frame; this is also referred to as *broadcast.* We will refrain from using this latter term since it is also used in the source routing terminology.

In the case of a single, isolated LAN, group and all-stations addresses refer to stations on the same LAN as the source station. In an internet, it may be desirable to transmit a frame to multiple stations on multiple LANs. Indeed, since a set of LANs interconnected by bridges should appear to the user as a single LAN, the ability to do group and all-stations addressing across the entire internet is mandatory.

Table 11-2 summarizes the relationship between routing specification and addressing mode. If no routing is specified, then all addresses refer only to the immediate LAN. If nonbroadcast routing is specified, then addresses may refer to any station on any LAN visited on the nonbroadcast route. From an addressing point of view, this combination is not generally useful for group and all-stations addressing. If either the all-routes or single-route specifications is included in a frame, then all stations on the internet can be addressed. Thus, the total internet acts as a single network from the point of view of MAC addresses. Since less traffic is generated by the single-route specification, this is to be preferred for group and all-stations addressing. Note also that the single-route mechanism in source routing is equivalent to the 802.1 spanning tree approach. Thus, the latter supports both group and all-stations addressing.

Route Discovery and Selection

With source routing, bridges are relieved of the burden of storing and using routing information. Thus the burden falls on the stations that wish to transmit frames. Clearly, some mechanism is needed by which the source stations can know the route to each destination for which frames are to be sent. Three strategies suggest themselves.

TABLE 11.2 Effects of Various Combinations of Addressing and Source Routing

Addressing Mode	Routing Specification			
	No Routing	**Nonbroadcast**	**All-Routes**	**Single-Route**
Individual	Received by station if it is on the same LAN	Received by station if it is on one of the LANs on the route	Received by station if it is on any LAN	Received by station if it is on any LAN
Group	Received by all group members on the same LAN	Received by all group members on all LANs visited on this route	Received by all group members on all LANs	Received by all group members on all LANs
All-Stations	Received by all stations on the same LAN	Received by all stations on all LANs visited on this route	Received by all stations on all LANs	Received by all stations on all LANs

1. Manually load the information into each station. This is simple and effective but has several drawbacks. First, any time that the configuration changes, the routing information at all stations must be updated. Secondly, this approach does not provide for automatic adjustment in the face of the failure of a bridge or LAN.

2. One station on a LAN can query other stations on the same LAN for routing information about distant stations. This approach may reduce the overall amount of routing messages that must be transmitted, compared to option 3 below. However, at least one station on each LAN must have the needed routing information, so this is not a complete solution.

3. When a station needs to learn the route to a destination station, it engages in a dynamic route discovery procedure.

Option 3 is the most flexible and the one that is specified by IEEE 802.5. As was mentioned earlier, two approaches are possible. The source station can transmit an all-routes request frame to the destination. Thus, all possible routes to the destination are discovered. The destination station can send back a nonbroadcast response on each of the discovered routes, allowing the source to choose which route to follow in subsequently transmitting the frame. This approach generates quite a bit of both forward and backward traffic, and requires the destination station to receive and transmit a number of frames. An alternative is for the source station to transmit a single-route request frame. Only one copy of this frame will reach the destination. The destination responds with an all-routes response frame, which generates all possible routes back to the source. Again, the source can choose among these alternative routes.

Figure 11-13 illustrates the latter approach. Assume that the spanning tree that has been chosen for this internet consists of bridges B1, B3, and B4. In this example, station X wishes to discover a route to station Z. Station X issues a single-route request frame. Bridge B2 is not on the spanning tree and so does not forward the frame. The other bridges do forward the frame and it reaches station Z. Note that bridge B4 forwards the frame to LAN 4, although this is not necessary; it is simply an effect of the spanning-tree mechanism. When Z receives this frame, it responds with an all-routes frame. Two messages reach X: one on the path LAN 2, B3, LAN 3, B1, LAN 1, and the other on the path LAN 2, B4, LAN 4, B2, LAN 1. Note that the frame that arrived by the latter route is received by bridge B1 and forwarded onto LAN 3. However, when bridge B3 receives this frame, it sees in the routing information field that the frame has already visited LAN 2; therefore it does not forward the frame. A similar fate occurs for the frame that follows the first route and is forwarded by bridge B2.

Once a collection of routes have been discovered, the source station needs to select one of the routes. The obvious criterion would be to select the minimum-hop route. Alternatively, a minimum-cost route could be selected, where the cost of a network is inversely proportional to its data rate. In either case, if two or more routes are equivalent by the chosen criterion, then there are several alternatives:

1. Choose the route corresponding to the response message that arrives first. One may assume that that particular route is less congested than the others since the frame on that route arrived earliest.
2. Choose randomly. This should have the effect, over time, of leveling the load among the various bridges.

Another point to consider is how often to update a route. Routes should certainly be changed in response to network failures and perhaps should be changed in response to network congestion. If connection-oriented logical link control is used (see Chapter 5), then one possibility is to rediscover the route with each new connection. Another alternative, which works with either connection-oriented or connectionless service, is to associate a timer with each selected route, and rediscover the route when its time expires.

Frame Format

With source routing, an addition must be made to the MAC frame format. Figure 11-14 shows the frame format specified by the IEEE 802.5 source routing document. A new field is added to the MAC frame, the routing information field, which consists of a routing control field followed by from 0 to 8 route designation fields. The routing control field consists of the following subfields:

- *Broadcast (3 bits):* indicates the type of routing directive (none, non-broadcast, all-routes, single-route)
- *Length (5 bits):* indicates the length of the routing information control field, in octets
- *Direction (1 bit):* indicates to a bridge whether the frame is traveling from the originating station to the target or vice versa. Its use allows the list of route designation fields to appear in the same order for frames traveling in both directions along the route.
- *Largest frame (4 bits):* specifies the largest size of the MAC information field that may be transmitted on this route. This field is encoded to indicate certain common sizes. For example: 0011 indicates a maximum size of 1500 octets, which corresponds to the IEEE 802.3 CSMA/CD and Ethernet limitations; 0111 indicates 4472 octets, which corresponds to FDDI. When a bridge receives a frame, it updates this field if the current value exceeds what the bridge can handle or its adjoining LANs allow. In this way, the route discovery process also discovers the maximum frame size that can be handled on a particular route.

The remainder of the routing information field consists of a sequence of route designators, each designator corresponding to one hop. The route

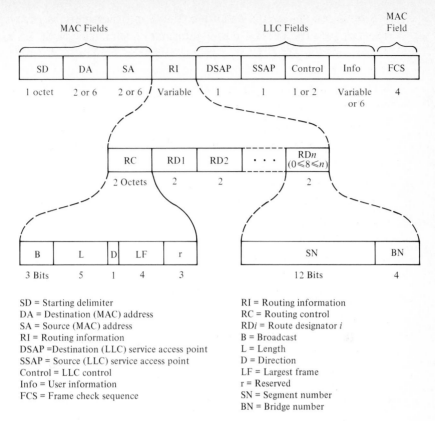

FIGURE 11-14. Source Routing Formats

SD = Starting delimiter
DA = Destination (MAC) address
SA = Source (MAC) address
RI = Routing information
DSAP =Destination (LLC) service access point
SSAP = Source (LLC) service access point
Control = LLC control
Info = User information
FCS = Frame check sequence

RI = Routing information
RC = Routing control
RDi = Route designator i
B = Broadcast
L = Length
D = Direction
LF = Largest frame
r = Reserved
SN = Segment number
BN = Bridge number

designator consists of a 12-bit segment number (LAN number) and a 4-bit bridge number.

Spanning Tree versus Source Routing

In this subsection, a brief comparison of the two approaches to bridge routing is provided. For a further discussion, see [SOHA88], [ZHAN88], and [PITT86].

The spanning tree approach requires no addition to the station logic and no changes to MAC frame format. Thus it preserves full transparency. That is, a collection of LANs interconnected by bridges using spanning-tree routing behaves, from the station's point of view, as a single LAN. The principal drawback of this approach is that it limits the use of redundant bridges to a standby role for availability. Only designated bridges forward frames, and other bridges are unused until a designated bridge fails. Thus redundant bridges cannot be used to share the traffic load, which would provide load-leveling and perhaps improved throughput.

Source routing requires additional station logic (route discovery, route selection, insertion of the routing information field in the MAC frame) and changes to the MAC frame format. Thus this method is not fully transparent. However, source routing does permit the selection of an optimal route for each source-destination pair, and permits all bridges to participate in frame forwarding, thus leveling the load. Furthermore, this method requires additional bits to be added to each frame that traverses more than one LAN, increasing the traffic burden.

The other concern relating to source routing is the magnitude of the effect of the route discovery algorithm. We will illustrate the concern with an example from [ZHAN88], which uses the configuration of Figure 11-15. The shaded bridges in the configuration are assumed to be the designated bridges if the spanning-tree approach is used. Using the spanning-tree approach, a frame sent from H2 to H1 will traverse 2 bridges and 3 LANs; only one copy of the frame will arrive at H1. In the source-routing case, the route from H1 to H2 must first be discovered. Using single-route broadcasting, a request frame is sent from H2 to H1. H1 responds with an all-routes frame. When B0, B1, and B3 receive the frame, each of them will try to forward it further to LANs it has not passed through. The original response frame will than be fabricated to multiple copies on other LANs. Specifically, four copies will be transmitted on LAN 2, five on LAN 3, and six on LAN 4, for a total of 16 transmissions of the frame (including the initial transmission on LAN 1). The result of this effort will be a route through B3 which is shorter than the spanning-tree route through B2 and B1.

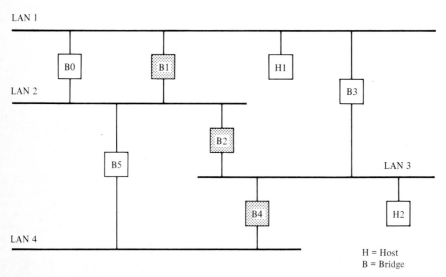

FIGURE 11-15. Internet Configuration for Comparison of Bridge Routing Approaches [ZHAN88]

Thus, while the source routing method may produce shorter routes and provides load leveling, the source discovery algorithm is very resource-intensive. Even for this small example, 16 transmissions were required. In general, the number of frame copies transmitted for route discovery is on the order of $O(N^M)$, where N is the average number of bridges on each LAN and M the number of LANs in the configuration [ZHAN88]. For example, a configuration consisting of 12 LANs with an average of 2 bridges per LAN, which is still a modest configuration, would generate on the order of $2^{12} = 4096$ frames for each route discovery.

In summary, source routing offers certain advantages in route selection at the cost of additional station logic, frame overhead, and considerable traffic overhead. In most situations, the spanning-tree approach should prove adequate and avoids the disadvantages of the source routing approach.

11.3

ROUTERS

The bridge is only applicable to a configuration involving a single type of LAN. Of course, in many cases, an organization will need access to devices on a variety of networks. For example, as Figure 1-6 illustrates, an organization may have a tiered LAN architecture, with different types of LANs

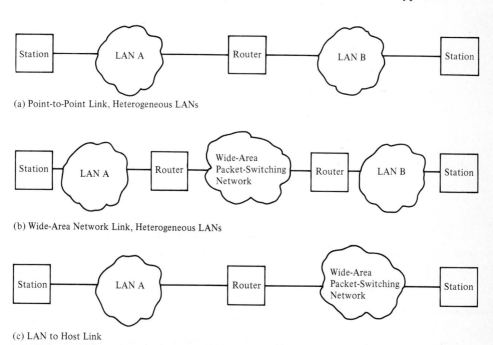

(a) Point-to-Point Link, Heterogeneous LANs

(b) Wide-Area Network Link, Heterogeneous LANs

(c) LAN to Host Link

FIGURE 11-16.   LAN Internetworking Requirements

used for different purposes within an organization. There may also need to be access to devices on a wide-area network. Examples of the latter are a public information source or data base for query and transaction applications and a customer or supplier computer for transferring ordering information.

A general-purpose device that can be used to connect dissimilar networks and that operates at layer 3 of the OSI model is known as a router.[2] We begin this section by looking at the requirements that must be satisfied by the router to support internetworking.

Requirements

Up until now, we have discussed instances in which the differences among networks were small. Now let us consider the more general problem of connecting a local network to outside resources. For now, let us limit ourselves to LANs; the principles for HSLNs are the same, and the protocol issues we are discussing do not apply to digital PBXs. For LAN connection, we can distinguish a number of cases:

1. *LAN-to-LAN:* A user or application process on one LAN desires access to a user or application process on another. The possibilities include:
   a. Point-to-point link, homogeneous networks. For example, a corporation might procure a LAN for each of its main offices from a single vendor.
   b. Network link, homogeneous networks. As above, but it is found more feasible to connect through a network (e.g., an X.25 long-haul packet-switched network).
   c. Point-to-point link, heterogeneous networks. An organization may have two LANs, in the same location, or separated, from different vendors.
   d. Network link, heterogeneous networks. As above, but linked by a packet-switched network.
2. *LAN-to-network:* In this case, some or all LAN subscribers need access to services available on a long-haul network (e.g., a data base or information utility available through a packet-swtiched network). Two possibilites are:
   a. Host-to-network link. Each host (or terminal) that requires a network link establishes one independent of the LAN.
   b. LAN-to-network link. As a service, the LAN establishes a link to the long-haul network which may be multiplexed to provide access for multiple hosts.

---

[2] A router is also referred to as an intermediate system, interworking unit, network relay, or sometimes even gateway. In this book, we have confined the use of the term *gateway* to its more common meaning of an application-level device.

Of these six cases, three are of no real interest as problems in internet-working. Case 1a can be handled with a bridge. The two halves of the bridge maintain a layer 2 point-to-point link. Case 1b is also solved by a bridge, with a special adaptation to handle the long-haul network protocol. For example, consider two LANs connected via an X.25 network. The bridge on LAN A accepts frames as before. Now, it wraps that frame in a layer 3 packet and transmits it to the bridge at LAN B, which unwraps the frame and inserts it into LAN B. For this purpose, a virtual circuit may be maintained between the two bridges. Case 2a does not involve internet-working at all! Each host on the LAN is responsible for its own link to the long-haul network and for implementing the protocols of that network; the LAN is not involved.

The remaining three cases require some kind of logic or protocol beyond that needed for intranetwork routing and delivery. This logic can be considered to reside in a router. Figure 11-16 depicts these three cases. It can be seen (or will be seen) that these three cases are fundamentally the same. The internetworking requirements are the same for all these cases. In essence, we wish to permit process-to-process communication across more than one network.

Before turning to the architectural approaches to providing the service of Figure 11-16, we list some of the requirements on the internetworking facility. These include:

1. Provide a link between networks. At minimum, a physical and link control connection is needed.
2. Provide for the routing and delivery of data between processes on different networks.
3. Provide an accounting service that keeps track of the use of the various networks and gateways and maintains status information.
4. Provide the services listed above in such a way as not to require modifications to the networking architecture of any of the attached networks. This means that the internetworking facility must accommodate a number of differences among networks. These include:
   a. Different addressing schemes. The networks may use different end-point names and addresses and directory maintenance schemes. Some form of global network addressing must be provided, as well as a directory service.
   b. Different maximum packet size. Packets from one network may have to be broken up into smaller pieces for another. This process is referred to as segmentation.
   c. Different network interfaces. For purposes of this discussion, we will assume that the interface is at layer 3, such as is found in an X.25 network. This assumption is a reasonable one since layers 1 through 3 are specific to the communications subnetwork, while layers 4 and above relate to end-to-end host process considerations.

As we discussed in Chapter 8, there are a number of protocol residency alternatives between host and NIU for LANs. In this chapter we use the DTE, DCE terminology for the communications architecture, to avoid confusion with the host-NIU architecture.

d. Different time-outs. Generally, a connection-oriented transport service will await an acknowledgment until a time-out expires, at which time it will retransmit its segment of data. Generally, longer times are required for successful delivery across multiple networks. Internetwork timing procedures must allow successful transmission that avoids unnecessary retransmissions.

e. Error recovery. Intranetwork procedures may provide anything from no error recovery up to reliable end-to-end (within the network) service. The internetwork service should not depend on nor be interfered with by the nature of the individual network's error recovery capability.

f. Status reporting. Different networks report status and performance differently. Yet it must be possible for the internetworking facility to provide such information on internetworking activity to interested and authorized processes.

g. Routing techniques. Intranetwork routing may depend on fault detection and congestion control techniques peculiar to each network. The internetworking facility must be able to coordinate these to adaptively route data between DTEs on different networks.

h. Access control. Each network will have its own user access control techniques. These must be invoked by the internetwork facility as needed. Further, a separate internetwork access control technique may be required.

i. Connection, connectionless. Individual networks may provide connection-oriented (e.g., virtual circuit) or connectionless (datagram) service. The internetwork service should not depend on the nature of the connection service for the individual networks.

Protocol Architecture

Router operation, as Figure 11-1b indicates, depends on a protocol at OSI layer 3 (network layer), sometimes known as an **internet protocol** (IP). Figure 11-17 depicts a typical example, in which two LANs are interconnected by a wide-area X.25 network. The figure depicts the operations involved for the transfer of data from station A on LAN 1 and station B on LAN 2. The two stations and the routers must share a common internet protocol. In addition, to communicate successfully, the two stations must share the same protocols above IP.

The data to be sent by A are passed down to A's internet protocol. IP attaches a header specifying, among other things, the global internet

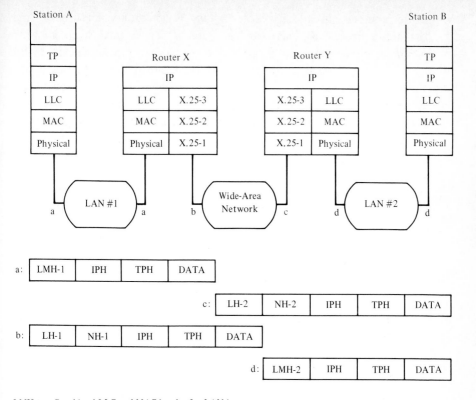

LMH-*i* : Combined LLC and MAC header for LAN i
LH-*j* : Link Header (X.25 Layer 2) for DTE = Router *j*
NH-*k* : Network Header (X.25 Layer 3) for DTE = Router *k*
IPH : Internet Protocol Header
TPH : Transport Protocol Header

FIGURE 11-17. Message Encapsulation: IP Approach

address of B. That address is in two parts: network identifier and station identifier. The result is called an internet protocol data unit, or simply a **datagram**. The datagram is then encapsulated with the LAN protocol and sent to a router that strips off the LAN header. The datagram is then encapsulated with the X.25 protocol and transmitted across the network to a router. The router strips off the X.25 fields and recovers the datagram, which is then wrapped in LAN 2 headers and sent to B. If a connection-oriented service is required, A and B must share a common layer 4 protocol.

With this example in mind, we describe briefly the sequence of steps involved in sending a datagram between two stations on different networks. This is followed by a more detailed discussion of the design issues involved.

The process starts in the sending station. Station A wants to send an IP datagram to a station B on another network. The IP module in A constructs the datagram with the global internet address of B in the datagram header and recognizes that the destination is on another network. So the first step is to send the datagram to router X. To do this, the IP module passes the datagram down to the next lower layer (in this case LLC) with instructions to send it to the router. The header at this lower layer will contain the address of the router. In our example, this is the MAC-level address of router X on LAN 1.

Next, the packet travels through LAN 1 to router X. The router strips off the MAC and LLC headers and analyzes the IP header to determine whether this datagram contains control information intended for itself, or data intended for a station farther on. In our example, the data is intended for station B. The gateway must therefore make a routing decision. There are three possibilities:

1. The destination station B is connected directly to one of the subnetworks to which the router is attached.
2. To reach the destination, one or more additional routers must be traversed.
3. The router does not know the destination address.

In case 1, the router sends the datagram directly to the destination. In case 2, a routing decision must be made: To which router should the datagram be sent? In both cases, the router sends the datagram down to the next lower layer with a destination station address. Remember, we are speaking here of a lower layer address that refers to this network (a layer 3 address for an X.25 network; a MAC address for a LAN). In case 3, the router returns an error message to the source of the datagram.

In this example, the data must be routed through router Y before reaching the destination. So router X constructs a packet by appending an X.25 header to the IP data unit containing the address of router Y. When this packet arrives at router Y, the packet header is stripped off. The router determines that this IP data unit is destined for B, which is connected directly to a network to which the router is attached. The router therefore creates a MAC frame with a destination address and sends it out onto LAN 3.

At each router, before the data can be forwarded, the router may need to segment the datagram to accommodate a smaller maximum packet size limitation on the outgoing network. The datagram is split into two or more segments, each of which becomes an independent IP datagram. Each new datagram is wrapped in a lower-layer packet and queued for transmission. The router may also limit the length of its queue for each network to which is attaches so as to avoid having a slow network penalize a faster one. Once the queue limit is reached, additional datagrams are simply dropped.

The process described above continues through as many routers as it takes for the datagram to reach its destination. As with a router, the destination host recovers the IP datagram from its network wrapping. If segmentation has occurred, the IP module in the destination host buffers the incoming data until the entire original data field can be reassembled. This block of data is then passed to a higher layer in the host.

The internet protocol does not guarantee that all data will be delivered or that the data that is delivered will arrive in the proper order. It is the responsibility of the next higher layer, the transport layer, to recover from any errors that occur. This approach provides for a great deal of flexibility.

With the internet protocol approach, each unit of data is passed from router to router in an attempt to get from source to destination. Since delivery is not guaranteed, there is no particular reliability requirement on any of the subnetworks. Thus the protocol will work with any combination of subnetwork types. Since the sequence of delivery is not guaranteed, successive data units can follow different paths through the internet. This allows the protocol to react to congestion and failure in the internet by changing routes.

Design Issues

With that brief sketch of the operation of an IP-controlled internet, we can now go back and examine some design issues in greater detail. These are:

- Addressing
- Routing
- Datagram lifetime
- Segmentation and reassembly

Addressing

Figure 11-18 illustrates that, in an internet, three levels of addressing may be required. Let us consider this addressing scheme from the bottom up. First, each network must maintain a unique address for each station

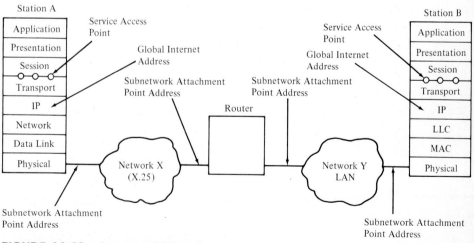

FIGURE 11-18. Internet Addressing

attached to that network. This allows the network to route packets through the network and deliver them to the intended host. Let us refer to this address as the **subnetwork attachment point address**. The term *subnetwork* is used to refer to a physically distinct network that may be part of an internet of networks interconnected by routers. Note that, from the point of view of the network, a router is just another station to which data may be delivered; hence it needs its own subnetwork attachment point address. A router will have one of these addresses for each network to which it attaches.

At the internet level, it is the responsibility of the internet protocol to deliver datagrams across one or more networks from source to destination. Hence, the internet protocol must be provided with a **global internet address** that uniquely identifies each station in the internet. It would appear convenient to provide this address in the form of (*network, station*), where the parameter *network* identifies a particular network and the parameter *station* identifies a particular station attached to that network. Thus, for routing purposes, the IP module in the sending station and in routers would need only use the network portion of the address. It would also appear convenient for the *station* parameter in the global internet address to be identical to the subnetwork attachment point address for that station. Unfortunately, this may not always be possible. Different networks use different formats and different address lengths. Furthermore, a station may enjoy more than one link into the same subnetwork. Accordingly, we must assume that the *station* parameter has global significance and the subnetwork attachment point address has significance only within a particular network. Thus, the internet protocol must translate from the global address to the locally-significant address for each network hop across the internet.

Finally, once a data unit is delivered to a station, it is passed to the upper layers for delivery to the ultimate user (process or application). Because there may be multiple users, each is identified, at the transport level, by a **service access point** number that is unique within the station. This number need not to be known to the internet layer, which is solely concerned with delivering data to the station.

Returning to the consideration of internet-level addresses, there are several features that are important when LANs are involved. One feature that is particularly useful is the support of group addressing and all-stations addressing. Table 11-3 depicts the possible combinations. A group can be defined on a specific network or scattered over a number of networks. An all-stations address can refer to all stations on one network or all stations on all networks.

Finally, an important service that must somehow be provided in the internet is a directory service. The host software must be able to determine the global address (network, station) of a desired destination. One or more

TABLE 11.3   Internet Multicasting and Broadcasting

Destination	Network Address	Host Address
Specific host	Specific	Specific
Group		
Directed	Specific	Group
Global	All	Group
All-stations		
Directed	Specific	All
Global	All	All

Source: [DALA82].

directory servers could be used. Each server would contain part or all of a name/address directory for internet hosts.

Routing

Routing is generally accomplished by maintaining a routing table in each host and router that gives, for each possible destination network, the next router to which the IP datagram should be sent.

Table 11.4 shows the routing table for the BBN router, which is part of the DARPA internet. If a network is directly connected, it is so indicated. Otherwise, the datagram must be routed through one or more routers (one or more hops). The table indicates the identity of the next router on the route (which must share a common network with this router or host) and the number of hops to the destination.

The routing table may be static or dynamic. A static table, however, could contain alternate routes if a router is unavailable. A dynamic table is more flexible in responding both to error and congestion situations. In the DARPA internet, for example, when a router goes down, all of its neighbors will send out a status report, allowing other routers and stations to update their routing tables. A similar scheme can be used to control congestion. This latter is particularly important because of the mismatch in capacity between local and wide-area networks. The interested reader may consult [POST81] and [STAL90c], which specify a variety of internet control messages used to facilitate routing.

Routing tables may also be used to support other internetworking services, such as security and priority. For example, individual networks might be classified to handle data up to a given security classification. The routing mechanism must assure that data of a given security level is not allowed to pass through networks not cleared to handle such data.

Another routing technique is source routing. The source station specifies

TABLE 11.4 INTERNET Routing Table for the BBN Router

Network Name	Net Address	Route[a]
SATNET	4	Directly connected
ARPANET	10	Directly connected
BBN-NET	3	1 hop via RCC 10.3.0.72 (ARPANET 3/72)
PURDUE-COMPUTER SCIENCE	192.5.1	2 hops via PURDUE 10.2.0.37 (ARPANET 2/37)
INTELPOST	43	2 hops via MILLS 10.3.0.17 (ARPANET 3/17)
DECNET-TEST	38	3 hops via MILLS 10.3.0.17 (ARPANET 3/17)
WIDEBAND	28	3 hops via RCC 10.3.0.72 (ARPANET 3/72)
BBN-PACKET RADIO	1	2 hops via RCC 10.3.0.72 (ARPANET 3/72)
DCN-COMSAT	29	1 hop via MILLS 10.3.0.17 (ARPANET 3/17)
FIBERNET	24	3 hops via RCC 10.3.0.72 (ARPANET 3/72)
BRAGG-PACKET RADIO	9	1 hop via BRAGG 10.0.0.38 (ARPANET 0/38)
CLARK NET	8	2 hops via MILLS 10.3.0.17 (ARPANET 3/17)
LCSNET	18	1 hop via MIT-LCS 10.0.0.77 (ARPANET 0/77)
BBN-TERMINAL CONCENTRATOR	192.1.2	3 hops via RCC 10.3.0.72 (ARPANET 3/72)
BBN-JERICHO	192.1.3	3 hops via RCC 10.3.0.72 (ARPANET 3/72)
UCLNET	11	1 hop via UCL 4.0.0.60 (SATNET 60)
RSRE-NULL	35	1 hop via UCL 4.0.0.60 (SATNET 60)
RSRE-PPSN	25	2 hops via UCL 4.0.0.60 (SATNET 60)
SAN FRANCISCO-PACKET RADIO-2	6	1 hop via C3PO 10.1.0.51 (ARPANET 1/51)

[a] Names and acronyms identify gateways in the INTERNET system.
Source: [SHEL82].

the route by including a sequential list of routers in the datagram. This, again, could be useful for security or priority requirements.

Finally, we mention a service related to routing: route recording. To record a route, each router appends its internet address to a list of addresses in the datagram. This feature is useful for testing and debugging purposes.

Datagram Lifetime

If dynamic or alternate routing is used, the potential exists for a datagram or some of its segments to circulate indefinitely through the internet.

For example, if there are sudden, significant shifts in internet traffic, the datagram might be diverted first one way and then another to avoid areas of congestion. Additionally, there might be a flaw in the routing tables of the various routers that causes the datagram to stay inside the network. These problems place an undesirable burden on the internet. To avoid these problems, each datagram can be marked with a lifetime. Once the lifetime expires, the datagram is discarded.

A simple way to implement lifetime is to use a hop count. Each time that a datagram passes through a router, the count is decremented. Alternatively, the lifetime could be a true measure of time. This requires that the router must somehow know how long it has taken for the datagram to traverse the last network, so as to know by how much to decrement the lifetime field. The advantage of using a true measure of time is that it can be used in the reassembly algorithm, which is described next.

Segmentation and Reassembly

To avoid fixing the maximum size of a packet, a constraint that is unfavorable to CSMA/CD LANs and HSLNs, segmentation must be done at the IP level by routers.

THE ISO standard, described below, specifies an efficient technique for IP segmentation. The technique requires the following fields in the datagram header:

- ID
- Length
- Offset
- More Flag

The ID is some means of uniquely identifying a station-originated datagram. It consists of the source and destination addresses, an identifier of the protocol layer that generated the datagram, and a sequence number supplied by that protocol layer. The Length is the length of the data field in octets, and the Offset is the position of a fragment in the original datagram in octets.

The source station IP layer creates a datagram with Length equal to the entire length of the data field, with Offset = 0, and the More Flag reset. To segment a long packet, an IP module in a router performs the following tasks:

1. Creates two new datagrams and copies the header fields of the incoming datagram into both.
2. Divides the data into two approximately equal portions along a 8-bit boundary, placing one portion in each new datagram.
3. Sets the Length field of the first datagram to the length of the inserted data, and sets the More Flag. The Offset field is unchanged.

TABLE 11.5 Segmentation Example

Original Datagram	First Segment	Second Segment
Length = 472	Length = 240	Length = 232
Offset = 0	Offset = 0	Offset = 240
More = 0	More = 1	More = 0

4. Sets the Length field of the second datagram to the Length of the inserted data, and adds the length of the first data portion divided by eight to the Offset field. The More Flag remains the same.

Table 11.5 gives an example. The procedure can be generalized to an *n*-way split.

To reassemble a datagram, there must be sufficient buffer space at the reassembly point. As segments with the same ID arrive, their data fields are inserted in the proper position in the buffer until the entire datagram is reassembled, which is achieved when a contiguous set of data exists starting with an Offset of zero and ending with data from a segment with a reset More Flag. Typically, reassembly is done at the destination station, to avoid burdening routers with unnecessarily large buffer space and to permit segments to arrive via different routes. However, as mentioned, it is an advantage in certain local networks to make the packet size as large as possible. Therefore, it might be a good design decision to dictate reassembly of datagrams entering a local network.

One eventuality that must be dealt with is that one or more of the segments may not get through: the IP service does not guarantee delivery. Some means is needed to decide to abandon a reassembly effort to free up buffer space. The ISO IP standard suggests two approaches. First, assign a reassembly lifetime to the first segment to arrive. This is a local, real-time clock assigned by the reassembly function and decremented while the segments of the original datagram are being buffered. If the time expires prior to complete reassembly, the received segments are discarded. A second approach is to make use of the datagram lifetime, which is part of the header of each incoming segment. The lifetime field continues to be decremented by the reassembly function; as with the first approach, if the lifetime expires prior to complete reassembly, the received segments are discarded.

11.4

THE ISO INTERNETWORKING STANDARD

In this section, we look at the internetworking standard developed by ISO [ISO87, ISO88, PISC86]. As with any layer specification, IP can be described in two parts:

- The services provided to the next higher layer (e.g., ISO transport).
- The protocol mechanisms and formats that are used to provide the service.

ISO IP Service

The ISO internetworking service is defined by two primitives at the interface between IP and an IP user. There are:

- N-UNITDATA.request (Source Address, Destination Address, Quality of Service, NS-User-Data)
- N-UNITDATA.indication (Source Address, Destination Address, Quality of Service, NS-User-Data)

The request primitive is issued by an IP user to submit data to IP for transfer across the internet. The indication primitive is issued by IP to a higher-layer user to deliver data arriving from the internet. The *source address* and *destination address* parameters are global internet addresses that uniquely identify end stations. The *quality of service* parameter consists of options drawn from the list of Table 11-6. The IP entities in the

TABLE 11.6 Quality-of-Service Parameters for the ISO Connectionless-Mode Network Service

Transit Delay	The elapsed time between an N-UNITDATA.request at the source station and the corresponding N-UNITDATA.indication at the destination station
Protection from Unauthorized Access	Four options are defined: 1. no protection features 2. protection against passive monitoring 3. protection against modification, replay, addition, or deletion 4. both (1) and (2)
Cost Determinants	Permits the user to specify: 1. that the service provider (IP) should use the least expensive means available 2. maximum acceptable cost
Residual Error Probability	Probability that a particular NS-User-Data unit will be lost, duplicated, or delivered incorrectly
Priority	Specifies the relative priority of NS-User-Data units with respect to: 1. the order in which the data units have their quality of service degraded, if necessary 2. the order in which data units are to be discarded to recover resources, if necessary

source station and the routers will endeavor, within the limitations of the network services available, to provide these additional services. Finally, *NS-User-Data* is the unit of data transferred across the internet in a datagram.

ISO IP Protocol

The ISO IP protocol is best explained with reference to the IP header format (Table 11-7). The header is largely self-explanatory. Some clarifying remarks:

- *Protocol Identifier:* When the source and destination stations are connected to the same network, an internal protocol is not needed. In that case the internet layer is null, and the header consists of this single field of 8 bits.

TABLE 11.7   ISO IP Header Format

Name	Size (bits)	Purpose
Protocol Identifier	8	Indicates if internet service is provided
Header Length	8	Header length in octets
Version	8	Version of protocol
PDU Lifetime	8	Lifetime in units of 500 ms
Flags	3	Three one-bit indicators
Type	5	Data or Error PDU
Segment Length	16	Header plus data length
Checksum	16	Applies to header only
Destination Address Length	8	Length of field in octets
Destination Address	Variable	Structure not specified
Source Address Length	8	Length of field in octets
Source Address	Variable	Structure not specified
Identifier	16	Unique for source, destination
Segment Offset	16	Offset in octets
Total Length	16	Length of original PDU
Options	Variable	Additional services

- *Lifetime:* Expressed as a multiple of 500 ms. It is determined and set by the source station. Each gateway that the IP datagram visits decrements this field by 1 for each 500 ms of estimated delay for that hop. When the lifetime value reaches 0, the datagram is discarded. This technique prevents endlessly circulating datagrams.
- *Flags:* The S/P flag indicates whether segmentation is permitted. The M/S flag is the more flag described earlier. The E/P flag indicates whether an error report is desired by the source station if a datagram is discarded.
- *Checksum:* Computed at each gateway.
- *Addresses:* Variable-length addresses are provided; the structure of the addresses is not specified in the standard.
- *Options:* The optional parameters that may be specified include: Security, defined by the user; Source Routing, which allows the source station to dictate the gateway routing; Recording of Route, used to trace the route a datagram takes; Priority; and Quality of Service, which specifies reliability and delay parameters.

11.5

APPLICATION-LEVEL GATEWAYS

Bridges and routers can be used to solve internetwork problems in an environment when all of the devices implement compatible protocols at the upper layers of the OSI model. This is the ideal situation toward which a business organization should strive. However, there will be many cases when a business has installed a proprietary network architecture such as SNA. Because of the investment in the proprietary system, it is expensive and disruptive to attempt to replace all of the communications software with OSI-based software. On the other hand, the user wants to employ OSI to gain access to products from a variety of vendors.

The gateway provides a way to permit the coexistence of OSI-based and proprietary products and gives the manager the tools needed to plan and implement a smooth migration to an exclusive OSI strategy. As Figure 11-1c illustrates, a gateway is a device that connects different network architectures by performing a conversion at the application level. The gateway itself must utilize all seven layers of the OSI model plus all of the layers of the proprietary architecture.

The gateway is used as a staging area for a two-step transfer of data. Let us consider a file transfer as an example. Figure 11-19 shows a network to which are attached two sets of devices: those that implement the OSI protocols and those that implement a proprietary architecture such as SNA. In the OSI world, the file transfer standard is file transfer, access, and management (FTAM). Two OSI stations can exchange files using

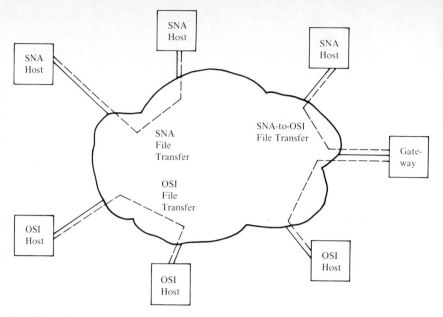

FIGURE 11-19. Gateway Operation

FTAM. Similarly, two stations with proprietary architectures can exchange files using the proprietary file transfer application. If a mixed transfer is attempted from an OSI station to a proprietary-software station, then the sending station automatically (without user intervention) sends the file to a gateway using FTAM. The gateway accepts the file and then transfers it to the intended destination using the proprietory file transfer protocol. A transfer in the reverse direction proceeds similarly. In like manner, other applications, such as electronic mail and document architecture, can also be achieved via gateway. Thus the gateway must contain both the OSI version and the proprietary version of any application requiring gateway services.

There are several key limitations with the use of a gateway:

1. The gateway is a potential bottleneck. In an environment in which there are large numbers of both types of stations, there may be considerable traffic through the gateway. To overcome performance limitations, a user might need more than one gateway. This complicates the station software, which must now make a decision of which gateway to use for each transfer.
2. The service provided for a given application is the "least common denominator." For example, FTAM supports the use of priorities. If the proprietary file transfer protocol does not, then the priority discipline is imposed only between the OSI station and the gateway. From the gateway to the other station, no priority scheme is employed.

11.6

RECOMMENDED READING

There are a number of good survey articles on internetworking; these include [CERF78], [POST80], [PISC86], [WEIS87], and [ISRA87]. Discussions that specifically deal with LANs as part of internets include [SCHN83]* and [KOSH86]*. [HAWE84]* is a thorough discussion of the bridge approach. [GERL88] is a special issue devoted to bridges, routers, and a comparison of the two.

11.7

PROBLEMS

11.1 Consider a token-passing local network configured as a single system with N stations or two systems with $N/2$ stations each connected by a bridge. Assume no delay at the bridge other than medium access delay. Do a breakpoint analysis of the type of Chapter 9 to show the relative delay characteristics of the two configurations as a function of the percentage of internetwork traffic.

11.2 Because of fragmentation, an IP datagram can arrive in pieces, not necessarily in the right order. The IP layer at the receiving host must accumulate these fragments until the original datagram is reconstituted.

    a. Consider that the IP layer creates a buffer for assembling the datagram. As assembly proceeds the buffer will consist of data and "holes" between the data. Describe an algorithm for reassembly based on this concept.

    b. For the algorithm above, it is necessary to keep track of the holes. Describe a simple mechanism for doing this.

11.3 Consider an internet which includes both gateways and routers. Further consider a site that contains multiple LANs interconnected by bridges, with one of the LANs including a router that attaches to the remainder of the internet. How can remote stations use internet addressing to address a specific station on one of the LANs? It would appear that there is no way for the internet as a whole to know of the existence of multiple networks at this site.

11.4 Would the spanning tree approach be good for an internet including routers?

11.5 What is the header overhead in the ISO IP protocol?

11.6 Describe some circumstances where it might be desirable to use source routing rather than let the routers make the routing decision.

CHAPTER 12

Local Network Design Issues

In this chapter we look at three important local network design issues. The first, and most complex, is that of network control. It is safe to say that more networks have come to grief because of inadequacies in network control than from any other problem.

Next, we look at the reliability, availability, and survivability of local networks. On the whole, local networks are rather reliable systems. However, the cost of a complete network failure to an organization is likely to be high, so this is an important area to address.

Finally, we look at the area of security. The requirements in this area vary widely from one installation to the next, but the same basic principles can be used in all cases.

All of these topics relate not just to local networks but to computer networks as well, and each is worthy of book-length treatment. All that we will attempt in this chapter is to introduce the concepts and then focus on some design issues of particular interest in the context of local networks.

NETWORK CONTROL

A computer network is a complex system that cannot create or run itself. The manager of the network must be able to configure the network, monitor its status, react to failures and overloads, and plan intelligently for future growth.

We begin by looking at and defining the overall concept of network management, which encompasses a host of human and automated tasks designed to support the network manager. These principles apply whether the network is local or not. We then focus on those aspects of network control that are unique to local networks, looking in turn at the distinctive requirements of packet-switched and circuit-switched networks. Finally, we show how these concepts relate to the somewhat different concept of computer network control.

A more general discussion of network control can be found in [TERP87].

Network Management

Network management is a broad concept that encompasses those tasks, human and automated, that "support" the creation, operation, and evolution of a network. The word support is used advisedly. Network management does not encompass the actual managerial function of controlling the development and ongoing use of a system, nor the disciplines required to actually develop and modify the system. Rather, it is the "glue" or infrastructure of techniques and procedures that assure the proper operation of a system (see [STAL80]).

In this section, we review briefly the key elements of network management. We use this to set the context for the discussion that follows, which focuses on some network control features for local networks.

Network management encompasses the following functions or disciplines:

- Operations
- Administration
- Maintenance
- Configuration management
- Documentation/training
- Data base management
- Planning
- Security

A brief discussion follows. A more thorough treatment, using somewhat different categories, can be found in [FREE82].

Operations management is responsible for the day-to-day operation of the network. A key element of operations is the status of the network, including traffic and performance status, active devices, and accounting and billing information. It should be possible to monitor response time performance, locate bottlenecks, and record information for later analysis and for customer or user accounting.

Administration deals with managing the use of the network. This includes such things as system generation, assigning user passwords, managing resource and file access, and billing users.

Maintenance is that key function which assures that the network continues to operate. It involves, first, detecting and reporting problems. Once a problem is known, it must be isolated to determine the cause. Finally, the problem must be resolved. Many of the detection and even isolation functions can be automated. Nevertheless, much of the maintenance activity is a human task. Maintenance management can support this task with a data base of events and network characteristics and components, and some automated capabilities for determining problem resolution.

The three functions discussed so far can, at least partially, be supported by a *network control center* (NCC). The following subsections will describe desirable attributes of an NCC. Before that, however, we briefly summarize the remaining network management functions.

The primary objective of configuration management (CM) is the effective management of a system's life cycle and its evolving configuration. CM identifies hardware and software components of the system at an appropriate level for control—not so aggregated that the specific functions are not visible, and not so disaggregated as to create an overwhelming amount of detail. CM tracks each component through the system life cycle, documenting and controlling any changes, and ensuring that the overall system retains its integrity and conforms to requirements. CM also maintains information on the status of each system component.

The documentation/training function is responsible for educational functions, including CAI, and for developing and maintaining documentation. Data base management provides the capability for a network management data base. Planning is responsible for ongoing requirements analysis and configuration change planning. Security is responsible for prevention and detection of unauthorized network access.

This capsule summary should give the reader some idea of the tremendous scope of network management. We narrow our focus now to those aspects of network management that can be implemented in a local network control center.

The Network Control Center: LAN/HSLN

In many LANs and HSLNs, a network control center (NCC) is provided. Typically, this device attaches to the network through an NIU and consists of a keyboard/screen interface and a microcomputer. Except for the smallest networks (fewer than 10 to 20 NIUs), an NCC is vital. It supports key operations, administration, and maintenance functions. The need for an automated set of functions with an operator interface for controlling the complexities of a network is beyond doubt. For a good discussion of some of the problems of networking, the reader is referred to [WILE82]. In this section we list some of the important NCC functions; their value should become clear as the discussion proceeds.

All of the functions of an NCC involve observation, active control, or a combination of the two. They fall into three categories:

- Configuration functions
- Monitoring functions
- Fault isolation

NCC Configuration Functions

One of the principal functions of an NCC is to control the link layer connections between NIU ports or service access points. A connection can be set up in one of two ways. First, the link layer protocol in the NIU can issue a connection request to another NIU, either in response to higher-layer software or a terminal user command. These could be referred to as "switched connections." Second, the NCC could set up a permanent connection between two NIUs.

The operation of the permanent connection is simple. The NCC sets parameters in the NIU indicating that all data received from a particular attached device are to be routed to a designated destination address. As the NIU receives the data, they are wrapped in a link layer frame with the appropriate destination address and transmitted. The NCC can also, under operator command, break a connection (permanent or switched). Another useful feature is being able to designate a backup or alternate address to be used in case the primary destination fails to respond.

A related NCC function is that of directory management. The NCC can maintain a name/address table that allows users to request a connection by name. Thus network resources can be identified by an operator-specified symbolic name rather than a fixed address. A resource may be any device or service—terminals, hosts, peripherals, application programs, or utility programs. For example, a user at a terminal who wishes to use the accounts payable package could request it with LOGON ACCTSP. This gives the operator, via the NCC, the ability to move applications around (for load balancing or because a host is down). The directory is kept at the NCC, but portions or all of it can also be down-line loaded to NIUs to reduce the network traffic required for directory look-up. An example of a directory service is described in [BASS80].

The NCC can also control the operation of the NIUs. The NCC could have the ability to shut down and start up NIUs and to set NIU parameters. For example, an NIU may be restricted to a certain set of NIUs or destination names that it can communicate with. This is a simple means of setting up a type of security system. Assuming that the MAC protocol supports it, NIUs can be assigned priorities.

NCC Monitoring Functions

A second important set of functions that can be performed by an NCC is that of network monitoring. This activity falls into three categories: performance monitoring, network status, and accounting.

Performance monitoring encompasses three components: performance measurement, which is the actual gathering of statistics about network traffic and timing; performance analysis, which consists of software for reducing and presenting the data; and synthetic traffic generation, which permits the network to be observed under a controlled load. One obvious motivation for a performance monitoring facility is that it can be used to validate analytic and simulation models of LAN/HSLN performance. This is of interest to researchers and designers. But performance monitoring has a key operational role as well. It allows the network manager to assess the current status of the network, to locate bottlenecks and other problems, and to plan for future growth.

Table 12.1 lists the types of measurements reported at one local network facility [AMER82, AMER83] and gives some idea of the kind of measurements that are of interest. Amer lists some examples of the types of questions that can be answered with these reports. Questions concerning possible errors or inefficiencies include:

- Is traffic evenly distributed among the network users or are there source-destination pairs with unusually heavy traffic?
- What is the percentage of each type of packet? Are some packet types of unusually high frequency, indicating an error or an inefficient protocol?
- What is the distribution of data packet sizes? Are variable size data packets worth the additional overhead or would fixed size packets suffice?
- What are the channel acquisition and communication delay distributions? Are these times excessive?
- Are collisions a factor in getting packets transmitted, indicating possible faulty hardware or protocols?
- What is the information utilization and throughput? How do the information statistics compare with the channel statistics?

TABLE 12.1   Performance Measurement Reports

Name	Variables	Description
Host communication matrix	Source × destination	(Number, %) of (packets, data packets, data bytes)
Group communication matrix	Source × destination	As above, consolidated into address groups
Packet type histogram	Packet type	(Number, %) of (packets, original packets) by type
Data packet size histogram	Packet size	(Number, %) of data packets by data byte length
Throughput-utilization distribution	Source	(Total bytes, data bytes) transmitted
Packet interarrival time histogram	Interarrival time	Time between consecutive carrier (network busy) signals
Channel acquisition delay histogram	NIU acquisition delay	(Number, %) of packets delayed at NIU by given amount
Communication delay histogram	Packet delay	Time from original packet ready at source to receipt
Collision count histogram	Number of collisions	Number of packets by number of collisions
Transmission count histogram	Number of transmissions	Number of packets by transmission attempts

Source: [AMER82].

A second area has to do with increasing traffic load and varying packet sizes:

- What is the effect of traffic load on utilization, throughput, and time delays? When, if ever, does traffic load start to degrade system performance?
- Defining a stable network as one whose utilization is a nondecreasing function of traffic load, what is the tradeoff among stabilty, throughput, and delay?
- What is the maximum capacity of the channel under normal operating conditions? How many active users are necessary to reach this maximum?
- Do larger packets increase or decrease throughput and delay?
- How does constant packet size affect utilization and delay?

These areas are certainly of interest to the network manager. Other questions of concern have to do with response time and throughput by user class and determining how much growth the network can absorb before certain performance thresholds are crossed.

Because of the broadcast nature of LANs and HSLNs, many of the measurement data can be collected passively at the NCC, without perturbing the network. The NCC's NIU can be programmed to accept all packets, regardless of destination address. For a heavily loaded network, this may not be possible, and a sampling scheme must be used. A local network containing bridges presents some problems; one collection point per segment is required. On a ring, passive monitoring will catch all packets only if they are removed at the source rather than the destination.

However, not all information can be centrally collected. To get end-to-end measures, even within the local network, would require knowing the time of arrival of packets from devices to the NIUs. A number of protocol-specific measures cannot be centrally collected. For example, for CSMA/CD, the following measures are of interest:

- Mean amount of time an NIU defers before transmitting.
- Number of collisions by source NIU.
- Mean number of collisions per packet.

All of these measures require some collection capability at the NIUs. From time to time, the NIUs can send the collected data to the NCC. Unfortunately, this technique increases the complexity of the NIU and requires overhead communication.

A second major area of NCC monitoring is that of network status. The NCC keeps track of which NIUs are currently activated and the connections that exist. This information is displayed to the operator on request.

Finally, the NCC can support some accounting and billing functions. This can be done on either a device or user basis. For the latter, the NCC must be aware of the identity of network users. This topic is addressed in Section 12.3.

NCC Fault Isolation Functions

The NCC can continuously monitor the network to detect faults and, to the extent possible, narrow the fault down to a single component or small group of components.

This topic is explored in Section 12.2. Here we mention two common techniques for fault isolation. The NCC can periodically poll each NIU, requesting that it return a status packet. Alternatively, each NIU can be required to periodically and automatically (without poll) emit a status packet. When an NIU fault is detected, the NCC can alert the operator and also attempt to disable the NIU so that it does not interfere with the network.

An example of an NCC used for fault isolation is reported in [CHRI78].

The Network Control Center: Digital PBX/Digital Switch

The functions that can be performed by an NCC for a digital PBX or digital switch are similar to those for a LAN or HSLN. Again, the NCC will have a keyboard/screen interface. For a switch, however, the NCC intelligence is not stand-alone but integrated into the control unit of the switch.

As before, we can organize the functions into configuration, monitoring, and fault isolation.

NCC Configuration Functions

When a new line or set of lines is added to a switch, its parameters must be defined, unless the switch is capable of handling only one kind of input. This can be done via the NCC. Examples of parameters include data rate, code (e.g., ASCII), and whether echo-back is required. These parameters would generally be the same for all lines terminating in one physical group (see Figure 7-16).

Logical groups may also be defined and parameterized. A good example of this is a port contention group. A common name must be defined. In addition, there might be a permission list, restricting access to a designated set of terminal lines. If queueing is permitted, the queue size must be defined. Other parameters, such as priorities and maximum holding time, can be included.

For switches that do not have a user port selection capability, the NCC must be used to actually configure the network (i.e., set up the connections between devices). This is generally done at system generation time and changed only occasionally. Connections can be one to one, or many to many as for port contention. In either case, the user need not (and cannot) select a port—it is done automatically.

The NCC can also dynamically force and break connections. An example of the use of the break command is to release a connection when a device has been abandoned but not turned off. The NCC should also be able to close a queue to a port (i.e., not allow any new calls to queue) and to clear a queue. This action can be used to prepare a resource to be disabled and tested.

NCC Monitoring Functions

As with a packet-switched local network, certain traffic statistics are of interest for a circuit-switched network. The parameters differ, though. Examples:

- Number of calls (connection requests) by user, user group.
- Mean connection time.
- Calls lost.

- Queue statistics: queue length, queueing time, number of queue overflows.

These statistics give the network manager a good indication of utilization and enable informed planning for future growth.

For accounting and billing purposes, more detailed information is needed, particularly if the switch has a trunk to the long-haul network. A measurement process referred to in the PBX world as *call detail recording* (CDR) is used. CDR records all pertinent information related to all calls placed by individual stations or user groups. For each call the record would include calling extension (address), called extension, date, time, and duration.

Finally, the NCC monitoring function includes status reporting. Summary information would include current number of connections and queue sizes. More detailed data may also be displayable. For example, for each data line, NCC could provide:

- Enabled/disabled
- Connection status (idle, service, ringing, connected)
- Group membership
- Data rate
- Device type
- Echo/non-echo
- ASCII/non-ASCII
- Originate-only, answer-only, or both

NCC Fault Isolation Functions

The NCC can report the status of lines, to include a line that is supposed to be active but fails to respond to a connection request. In addition, the NCC should be able to put individual devices in loop-back mode and test the device by sending a stream of data and comparing that to returned data.

ISO Network Management Standard

The International Organization for Standardization (ISO) has developed a standard for network management, referred to as the management framework. It specifies the functions to be performed by a network management system and defines protocols for the exchange of commands, responses, and measurement data. This standard is relatively new and no products are yet available. However, it is serving as the basis for network management systems being developed by computer and local area network vendors and so will assume increasing importance in the marketplace. Also, a review of the ISO framework provides a useful checklist of network management system features.

Network Management Categories

The ISO network management framework comprises the following major categories:

- Fault management
- Accounting management
- Configuration and name management
- Performance management
- Security management

Table 12-2 provides a brief definition of each category.

Fault management facilities allow network managers to detect problems in the communications network and the OSI environment. These facilities include mechanisms for the detection, isolation, and correction of abnormal operation in any network component or in any of the OSI layers. Fault management provides procedures to:

1. Detect and report the occurrence of faults. These procedures allow a managed system to notify its manager of the detection of a fault, using a standardized event reporting protocol.
2. Log the received event report. This log can then be examined and processed.
3. Schedule and execute diagnostic tests, trace faults, and initiate correction of faults. These procedures may be invoked as a result of analysis of the event log.

TABLE 12.2 Elements of the ISO Network Management Architecture

Fault management	The facilities that enable the detection, isolation, and correction of abnormal operation of the OSI environment.
Accounting management	The facilities that enable charges to be established for the use of managed objects and costs to be identified for the use of those managed objects.
Configuration and name management	The facilities that exercise control over, identify, collect data from, and provide data to managed objects for the purpose of assisting in providing for continuous operation of interconnection services.
Performance management	The facilities needed to evaluate the behavior of managed objects and the effectiveness of communication activities.
Security management	Addresses those aspects of OSI security essential to operate OSI network management correctly and to protect managed objects.

Accounting management facilities allow a network manager to determine and allocate costs and charges for the use of network resources. Accounting management provides procedures to:

1. Inform users of costs incurred, using event reporting and data manipulation software.
2. Enable accounting limits to be set for the use of managed resources.
3. Enable costs to be combined where multiple resources are used to achieve needed communication.

Configuration and name management facilities allow network managers to exercise control over the configuration of the network components and OSI layer entities. Configurations may be changed to alleviate congestion, isolate faults, or meet changing user needs. Configuration management provides procedures to:

1. Collect and disseminate data concerning the current state of resources. Locally initiated changes or changes occurring due to unpredicted occurrences are communicated to management facilities by means of standardized protocols.
2. Set and modify parameters related to network components and OSI layer software.
3. Initialize and close down managed objects.
4. Change the configuration.
5. Associate names with objects and sets of objects.

Performance management facilities provide the network manager with the ability to monitor and evaluate the performance of network and layer entities. Performance management provides procedures to:

1. Collect and disseminate data concerning the current level of performance of resources.
2. Maintain and examine performance logs for purposes such as planning and analysis.

Security management facilities allow a network manager to manage those services that provide access protection of communications resources. Security management provides support for the management of:

1. Authorization facilities.
2. Access control.
3. Encryption and key management.
4. Authentication.
5. Security logs.

OSI Management Architecture. The architectural model of OSI systems participating in network management is shown in Figure 12-1. The system on the left functions as a network control center; the system on the right is

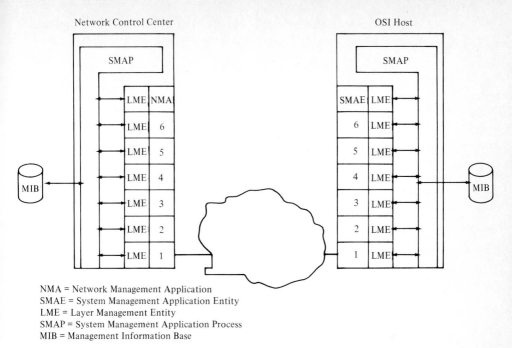

NMA = Network Management Application
SMAE = System Management Application Entity
LME = Layer Management Entity
SMAP = System Management Application Process
MIB = Management Information Base

FIGURE 12-1.   OSI Network Management Architecture

representative of other nodes in the network. The key elements of this architecture are:

- *Network-management application:* This application provides the mechanism for the network manager, a human, to read or alter data, control the network, and access reports. This application could be a very simple command interpreter or an expert system requiring very little interaction with the network manager. This application is present in the network control center.
- *System management application process (SMAP):* This is the local software within a system that is responsible for executing the network management functions on a single system (host, front-end processor, etc.). It has access to an overall view of system parameters and capabilities and can, therefore, manage all aspects of the system and can coordinate with the network-management application and SMAPs on other systems.
- *System-management application entity (SMAE):* This application is responsible for communication with other nodes, especially with the network-management application in the network control center host. Standardized application-level protocols are used for this purpose.
- *Layer-management entity (LME):* Software is embedded into each layer of the OSI architecture to provide network-management functions specific to that layer.

- *Management information base (MIB):* The collection of information at each node pertaining to network management.

By defining these particular elements, ISO has created a structure within which standards relating to network management can be developed.

12.2

RELIABILITY, AVAILABILITY, SURVIVABILITY

The purpose of this section is to introduce the reader to the concepts of reliability, availability, and survivability (RAS) as they relate to local networks. A detailed look at this topic, which would draw extensively on mathematical analysis and electrical engineering, is beyond the scope of this book. This brief discussion merely attempts to raise some architectural issues specifically related to local networks.

A more general discussion can be found in [JOHN88], [IRLA88], and [RAND78].

Basic Concepts

We begin by introducing the basic concepts of interest. This discussion is based on [KATZ78].

Reliability is the probability that a system or component will perform its specified function for a specified time under specified conditions. Component failure is expressed by the *mean time between failures* (MTBF). Typically, it is assumed that the "up" time for a component is exponentially distributed:

$$\Pr[T < t] = 1 - e^{-\lambda t}$$

Thus the MTBF is $1/\lambda$, and the variance is $1/\lambda^2$. The probability that a component will function for at least a time t is $e^{-\lambda t}$.

The reliability of a system depends on the reliability of its individual components plus the system organization. For example, some components may be redundant, such that the failure of just one component does not affect system operation. Or the configuration may be such that loss of a component results in reduced capability, but the system still functions.

Reliability is pertinent to system designers and maintenance engineers. Of much more interest to system managers and users is availability, which is the probability that a system or component is available at a given time t. The availability, A, can be expressed as

$$A = \frac{\text{MTBF}}{\text{MTBF} + \text{MTTR}}$$

where MTTR is the mean time to repair following a failure.

When dealing with the availability of a function or service (functional availability), the quantity will depend not only on the availability of system components but also the expected load on the system.

As an example, consider a dual-processor system. Nonpeak periods account for 40% of requests for service, and during those periods, either processor can handle the load. During peak periods, both processors are required to handle the full load, but one processor can handle 80% of the peak load. Functional availability for the system can be expressed as:

$$A_F = \text{(Capability when one processor is up)} \cdot \text{Pr[1 processor up]}$$
$$+ \text{(Capability when two processors are up)} \cdot \text{Pr[2 processors up]}$$

The probability that both processors are up is A^2, where A is the availability of either processor. The probability of just one processor up is $A(1 - A) + (1 - A)A = 2A - 2A^2$. Using a value for A of 0.9, and recalling that one processor is sufficient for nonpeak loads, we have

$$A_F(\text{nonpeak}) = (1.0)(0.18) + (1.0)(0.81) = 0.99$$

and, for peak periods

$$A_F(\text{peak}) = (0.8)(0.18) + (1.0)(0.81) = 0.954$$

Overall functional availability, then, is

$$A_F = 0.6A_F(\text{peak}) + 0.4A_F(\text{nonpeak}) = 0.9684$$

Thus, on the average, about 97% of requests for service can be handled by the system.

Finally, survivability is the probability that a function or service is available after a specified subset of components or systems become unavailable.

With these concepts in mind, we can now turn to the RAS concerns for local networks. Generally, two types of problems can disrupt communications. The first is transmission errors. Typically, the error rates on local network media are very low, on the order of 10^{-8} to 10^{-11}. This type of error is handled by the various protocol layers and need not concern us here.

The second kind of problem is component failure or malfunction, which is the problem that relates to RAS. We can categorize these components into network components and attached devices. We are not interested, in this section, in attached device failures. An attached device failure should not cause the loss of the entire network—only the function or service offered by that device is lost. Of course, if the device performs a network-critical role, such as a network access logon server, its loss could indeed cripple the network. But this is an application-related problem and will not be examined here.

Which leaves us with RAS concerns related to local network component failure, a topic to which we now turn.

Broadband Networks

The advantage of a broadband network is its tremendous capacity and flexibility. A great number and variety of devices dispersed over a large area can be supported on a single network. This advantage is also the most serious danger of a broadband system: loss of the network can be catastrophic. Such vulnerability is unacceptable in most organizations. Hence the architecture of the local network must overcome the inherent weakness of broadband.

Four elements of the local network need to be addressed:

1. *Headend:* This is a "single point of failure." Loss of the headend means loss of the entire network.
2. *Transmission medium:* The transmission medium consists of standard CATV cable, taps, splitters, and amplifiers. These components are highly reliable, with a typical mean time between failures (MTBF) of 18 years for amplifiers and 30 to 40 years for all other components [COOP84]. It is, however, possible for a failure to occur due to accidental or deliberate physical trauma. Also, because amplifiers draw power from the cable itself, loss of power supply can disable the cable.
3. *Network interface unit:* The NIU presents less of an availability and survivability problem than the headend or medium. In general, malfunction of an NIU does not affect the network as a whole; it merely denies access to the attached device or devices. There is, however, one way in which NIU failure can affect the entire network: jamming. If an NIU remains in a transmit mode, the affected channel or channels are useless.
4. *Network control center:* The NCC also presents a relatively minor availability problem. The NCC is actually not required during steady-state operation of the network for most systems. Individual NIUs are capable of making and breaking connections and exchanging data.

Let us now look briefly at measures that can be taken to improve broadband RAS.

Headend

The passive headend used in the dual-cable configuration is simply a length of cable joining the two portions of the system. It is as reliable as the rest of the transmission medium, treated below.

For a split-cable system, failure of the frequency converter, an active component, causes failure of the entire network. A hot backup can be supplied that can override the primary converter and control the cable. Care must be taken to assure that a malfunctioning backup does not seize control from a functioning primary converter. Schematically, the configuration is depicted in Figure 12-2.

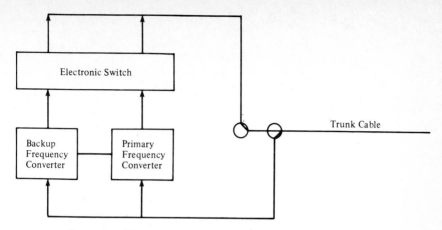

FIGURE 12-2. Redundant Headend

Transmission Medium

The next area of concern is the cable itself. An obvious means to improve reliability is by providing a backup cable (in the case of a dual cable, a dual backup cable is required). Each NIU could have two cable ports for connecting to the two cables. When a fault is detected on the primary cable, the NCC could use the backup cable to send a message to each NIU, instructing it to use the backup cable for future transmissions.

If there is a component failure, such as a tap or amplifier, the backup cable architecture is a good solution. However, the scheme seems less reliable as a means of recovering from physical cable damage. As a practical matter, the backup cable must be located near the primary cable along its entire length. This enables the NIUs to be attached to both cables with a reasonable amount of drop cable. Consequently, any physical damage sustained by the primary may also affect the backup cable.

An alternative or supplementary measure is the use of addressable taps [WILL81]. The NCC can probe the quality of the line by sending control signals to successive taps. The signal instructs the tap to return a signal which is compared with a stored value of expected magnitude. For a dual-cable system, the tap must merely be able to open and close, passing signals in an open state and returning them ("loop-back") in a closed state. For midsplit systems, the tap must be more complex, capable of accepting a control signal on one frequency and transmitting one on another frequency.

When a fault is isolated, the NCC can send another control signal to a tap, causing the tap to shut off the part of the cable beyond it. The tap selected should be the one just inbound of the tap that was unsuccessfully probed (see Figure 12-3). In this way, damage to the cable will affect only those stations downstream from the fault (away from the headend). The effectiveness of this measure can be increased by using a heavily branched

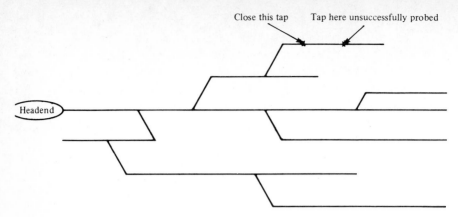

FIGURE 12-3. Use of Addressable Taps for Fault Isolation

topology rather than a single linear bus. Obviously, if damage occurs on the main trunk near the headend, the entire network will be lost.

Other than the headend, the only active CATV components are the amplifiers. Parallel redundant amplifiers can be used, with only a modest increase in attenuation.

Despite all these measures, a network manager or user can have legitimate concern about the availability of a large local network. A simple, effective measure is to partition the network into subnetworks joined by bridges and point-to-point links. Each subnetwork would have its own headend and perhaps its own NCC.

Network Interface Units

As mentioned above, a typical NIU failure affects only the attached device or devices. However, some failure in logic could cause an NIU to transmit continuously, jamming the channel. Other problems: A transmitter malfunction could produce distorted signals; a receiver failure would interfere with CSMA protocols.

To guard against the most serious problem, jamming, addressable taps can again be used. In this case, the taps must be signaled on a frequency other than that used by the NIUs (out-of-band signaling). The NCC can experimentally close taps, starting with the most remote ones, until the jamming is shut out. This also pinpoints the source of the problem. The use of subnetworks also limits the havoc that a streaming NIU can cause.

To detect more benign failures, it is useful for the NCC to monitor the status of active NIUs. This can be done in two ways. All NIUs could be required to periodically (e.g., once every second) emit a status packet addressed to the NCC. Alternatively, the NCC could periodically poll each NIU, requesting a status packet.

Network Control Center

Because of the lesser availability concerns associated with the NCC, it is reasonable to take no measures to enhance its reliability. However, a hot backup, in the same spirit as that for the headend, could be used. The backup NCC would connect to the cable via an independent NIU and would monitor all cable activity without transmitting. If it detected an NCC failure, it would instruct the NCC's NIU to shut down and would then seize control of the network.

Another simple measure to enhance NCC availability is to connect it to the LAN via two separate NIUs. Then, failure of a single NIU will not cause the loss of the NCC.

Baseband Bus Networks

The architecture of a baseband bus network entails fewer availability concerns compared to broadband. Referring back to Figure 4-3, the baseband bus has no active components (headend, amplifiers) and for large networks consists of segments connected by repeaters. Hence there is less likelihood of failure and the failure can easily be confined to a single segment.

To assure this confinement, repeaters should contain sufficient intelligence not to transmit from a cable that is being jammed. Another measure, as in broadband, is the use of multiple cables. This is, in fact, often done with HSLNs.

NIU and NCC concerns are the same as for broadband LANs and can be treated in the same fashion.

Ring Networks

IBM Approach

The subject of ring reliability was addressed initially in Section 4.2. It was pointed out that the loss of a single link or repeater on a simple ring can result in the loss of the entire network. Measures for overcoming this inherent reliability problem were depicted in Figure 4-12 and are summarized here:

- Ring wiring concentrators make it easy to isolate a fault and also to close a bypass relay to remove the problem.
- Multiple rings connected by bridges reduce the impact of a ring failure.

With the addition of some intelligence to the ring wiring concentrator [referred to as an active wiring concentrator (AWC)], fault recovery can be automated and availability improved. First, we require that each repeater generate network timing signals on its outbound link when there is no message to send. Thus failure of a link or repeater is immediately known to the next repeater on the link by the loss of input signal. This station can then generate a beacon frame to inform downstream stations of the outage. The beacon frame includes the station's address, to identify the location of the problem. Within an AWC subring, the AWC intelligence or station is the last downstream station. When the beacon frame reaches the AWC station, the AWC can identify the failed lobe (repeater plus links) and remove it by closing a bypass switch.

The procedure above works for all repeaters and for all links except those between AWCs. To recover from an inter-AWC link failure, a backup ring that connects the AWCs and circulates in the opposite direction to the primary ring is used. Figure 12-4 illustrates the architecture. As an example, the circled numbers relate to the following events.

1. The link between AWC2 and AWC1 fails.
2. Ring station 1 detects loss of input and transmits a beacon frame.
3. The AWC1 station receives the frame and determines that the failure is upstream from ring station 1.
4. Assuming that the failure is the link from AWC1 to ring station 1, AWC1 bypasses that lobe.
5. Ring station 2 now detects loss of input and transmits a beacon frame.
6. AWC1 now assumes that the problem is upstream.
7. AWC1 opens the bypass, reinserting ring station 1, and connects the backup segment from AWC3. This action breaks the flow of timing signals from AWC1 to AWC2 on the backup ring.
8. AWC2 detects the loss of timing signals and switches the primary ring flow from its own AWC ring station to the backup segment leading to AWC3.

These actions isolate the AWC2-AWC1 link fault and restore a closed ring.

The above scheme was developed by IBM for use in their 802.5-compatible product [BUX83a]. It is not a part of the 802.5 standard itself.

FDDI Standard

The FDDI standard explicitly addresses the need for reliability by including specifications for reliability-enhancing techniques. Three techniques are included:

- *Station bypass:* A bad or powered-off station may be bypassed using an automatic optical bypass switch.
- *Wiring concentrator:* Wiring concentrators can be used in a star-wiring strategy, as previously discussed.
- *Dual rings:* Two rings may be employed to interconnect the stations in

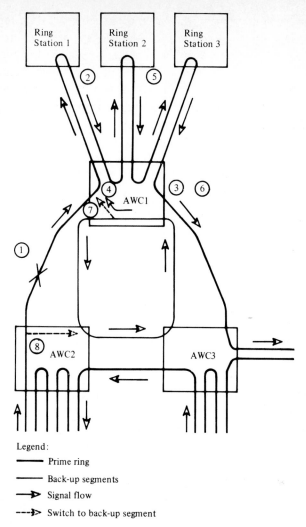

Legend:
——— Prime ring
——— Back-up segments
——▷ Signal flow
--▷ Switch to back-up segment

FIGURE 12-4. Reconfiguration of a Ring with Wiring Concentrators

such a way that a failure of any station or link results in the reconfiguration of the network to maintain connectivity.

The concept of dual rings is illustrated in Figure 12-5 [ROSS87]. Stations participating in a dual ring are connected to their neighbors by two links that transmit in opposite directions. This creates two rings: a primary ring, and a secondary ring on which data circulate in the opposite direction. Under normal conditions, the secondary ring is idle. When a link failure occurs, the stations on either side of the link reconfigure as shown in Figure 12-5b. This isolates the link fault and restores a closed ring. In this figure, a dark dot represents a MAC attachment within the station. Thus, in the counter direction, signals are merely repeated, while the MAC pro-

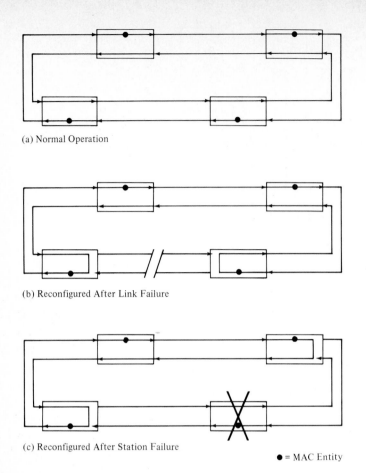

(a) Normal Operation

(b) Reconfigured After Link Failure

(c) Reconfigured After Station Failure

● = MAC Entity

FIGURE 12-5.   FDDI Dual-Ring Operation

tocol is only involved in the primary direction. Should a station itself fail, as shown in Figure 12-5c, then the stations on either side reconfigure to eliminate the failed station and both links to that station.

A network can be constructed with a mixture of single-ring and dual-ring capability. The FDDI standard defines two classes of stations:

- *Class A:* Connects to both primary and secondary rings. In the event of a failure, provisions are made within a Class A station to reconfigure the network using a combination of the operational links of the primary and secondary rings.
- *Class B:* Connects only to a primary ring. Failure can isolate a Class B station.

Figure 12-6 depicts the FDDI scheme. An active wiring concentrator, such as was described previously, is a Class A station in FDDI terminology. But the concept is not limited to wiring concentrators; any station can

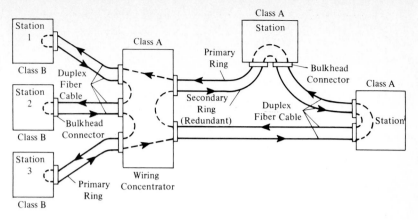

FIGURE 12-6. FDDI Ring Architecture

be equipped with dual ring connections. The two node classes allow users to tailor network complexity to meet cost objectives. The user can equip stations that are of greater importance as Class A stations, insuring their higher availability. Stations of lesser importance can be configured as Class B stations, reducing their cost.

Double Loop

In the configuration of Figure 12-4, the backup links are not used except when a failure occurs. A number of proposals have appeared which would use the backup or secondary links not only to increase availability but to improve throughput. The group at Ohio State [WOLF78] developed an enhancement to their register insertion ring, called Distributed Double Loop Computer Network (DDLCN), by providing two links between repeaters, one in each direction (Figure 12-7a). Traffic can be carried in either direction. If a fault occurs, stations on both sides can wrap around so that incoming data are repeated back out in the direction they came from. Another double-loop network, called daisy-chain loop, was proposed in [GRNA80]. Here, the backup links connect every other node (Figure 12-7b). This network was shown to be superior to DDLCN in both reliability and performance in both the fault-free and fault modes of operation.

It should be intuitively clear that the delay performance of the daisy chain is superior to DDLCN. For example, for the 15-node rings illustrated, the maximum number of "hops" for DDLCN is 7, whereas for the daisy chain, it is 6. Also, intuitively, reliability is improved because there are more alternative paths in the daisy chain.

Furthermore improvement can be had by increasing the length of the backward hop to $h = \lfloor \sqrt{N} \rfloor$, i.e. the largest integer less than or equal to $\sqrt{N}$ (for DDLCN, $h = 1$; for daisy chain, $h = 2$). Figure 12-7c shows this

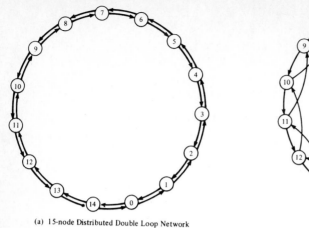

(a) 15-node Distributed Double Loop Network

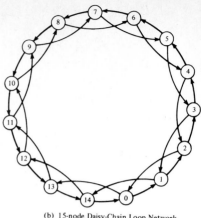

(b) 15-node Daisy-Chain Loop Network

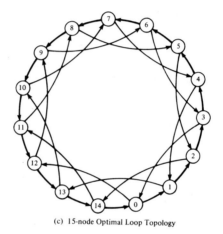

(c) 15-node Optimal Loop Topology

FIGURE 12-7. Double-Loop Configurations

architecture for a 15-station ring. It has been shown that this value of h is optimal, both in terms of throughput and availability [RAGH81, LE88].

Of course, all of these double loop arrangements require more complexity and intelligence in the repeater, which now has two incoming and two outgoing links and must make a routing decision on each host transmission. A simpler scheme would be to have a separate and independent backup ring, analogous to the technique for bus and tree topologies. This falls midway between single ring and the integrated dual ring in both reliability and complexity.

Finally we mention that NCC and NIU (excluding repeater) concerns are the same as for bus/tree LANs and can be treated in the same fashion.

Digital Switch Networks

The most common approach to improving the availability of a digital switch is the use of redundancy, as illustrated in Figure 7-14. With the exception of the individual line cards, all of the components of the switch can be made redundant: power supply, processor, and special-purpose features such as a protocol convertor. Backup battery capability is usually provided to take over automatically in the event of power failure.

The primary processor is responsible for monitoring all devices for failure and running diagnostics. When a failure is detected, the failed component is disabled so that it will not interfere with switch operation, and an operator is alerted. The backup processor maintains a duplicate of all current status and connection data and continually exchanges monitor information with the primary. Should the backup detect a failure in the primary processor, it disables the primary and assumes control.

With this architecture, the loss of any single component other than a line card will cause no disruption or loss of service. The loss of a line card affects only the attached devices, typically only 8 or 16 devices. This loss is immediately reported and card replacement normally takes only a few minutes.

Availability is further improved in the hierarchical star architecture (Figure 7-18) if each of the switches is capable of independent operation.

12.3

NETWORK SECURITY

Network security can be defined as the protection of network resources against unauthorized disclosure, modification, utilization, restriction, or destruction [CHAM80]. Security has long been an object of concern and study for both data processing systems and communications facilities. With computer networks, these concerns are combined. And for local networks, the problems may be most acute.

Consider a full-capacity local network, with direct terminal access to the network and data files and applications distributed among a variety of processors. The local network may also provide access to and from long-haul communications and be part of an internet. The complexity of the task of providing security in such an environment is clear.

The subject is a broad one, and encompasses physical and administrative controls as well as automated ones. In this section we confine ourselves to considerations of automated security controls and focus attention on three areas of specific concern for local networks:

- Access control
- Encryption
- Multilevel security

More general discussions of computer network security can be found in [WOOD83], [DENN79], and [PRIC84].

Types of Threats

A publication of the National Bureau of Standards identified some of the threats that have stimulated the upsurge of interest in security [BRAN78]:

1. Organized and intentional attempts to obtain economic or market information from competitive organizations in the private sector.
2. Organized and intentional attempts to obtain economic information from government agencies.
3. Inadvertent acquisition of economic or market information.
4. Inadvertent acquisition of information about individuals.

TABLE 12.3 Potential Network Security Threats

PASSIVE THREATS

The monitoring and/or recording of data while the data are being transmitted over a communications facility.

Release of Message Contents
Attacker can read the user data in messages.

Traffic Analysis
The attacker can read packet headers, to determine the location and identity of communicating hosts. The attacker can also observe the length and frequency of messages.

ACTIVE THREATS

The unauthorized use of a device attached to a communications facility to alter transmitting data or control signals or to generate spurious data or control signals.

Message-stream Modification
The attacker can selectively modify, delete, delay, reorder, and duplicate real messages.
The attacker can also insert counterfeit messages.

Denial of Message Service
The attacker can destroy or delay most or all messages.

Masquerade
The attacker can pose as a real host or switch and communicate with another host or switch to acquire data or services.

5. Intentional fraud through illegal access to computer data banks with emphasis, in decreasing order of importance, on acquisition of funding data, economic data, law enforcement data, and data about individuals.
6. Government intrusion on the rights of individuals.
7. Invasion of individual rights by the intelligence community.

These are examples of specific threats that an organization or an individual (or an organization on behalf of its employees) may feel the need to counter. The nature of the threat that concerns an organization will vary greatly from one set of circumstances to another. Fortunately, we can approach the problem from a different angle by looking at the generic types of threats that might be encountered.

Table 12-3 lists the types of threats that might be faced in the context of network security. The threats can be divided into the categories of passive threats and active threats (Figure 12-8).

Passive Threats
These are in the nature of eavesdropping or monitoring of the transmissions of an organization. The goal of the attacker is to obtain information

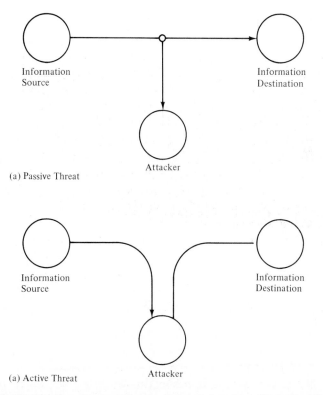

(a) Passive Threat

(a) Active Threat

FIGURE 12-8. Passive and Active Communications Security Threats

that is being transmitted. Two types of threats are involved here: release of message contents and traffic analysis.

The threat of **release of message contents** is clearly understood by most managers. A telephone conversation, an electronic mail message, a transferred file may contain sensitive or confidential information. We would like to prevent the attacker from learning the contents of these transmissions.

The second passive threat, **traffic analysis**, is more subtle and often less applicable. Suppose that we had a way of masking the contents of messages or other information traffic so that an attacker, even if he or she captured the message, would be unable to extract the information from the message. The common technique for doing this is encryption, discussed at length subsequently. If we had such protection in place, it might still be possible for an attacker to observe the pattern of these messages. The attacker can determine the location and identity of communicating hosts and can also observe the frequency and length of messages being exchanged. This information might be useful in guessing the nature of the communication that is taking place.

Passive threats are very difficult to detect since they do not involve any alteration of the data. However, it is feasible to prevent these attacks from being successful. Thus the emphasis in dealing with passive threats is on prevention and not detection.

Active Threats

The second major category of threat is active threats. These involve some modification of the data stream or the creation of a false stream. We can subdivide these threats into three categories: message-stream modification, denial of message service, and masquerade.

Message-stream modification simply means that some portion of a legitimate message is altered, or that messages are delayed, replayed, or reordered, in order to produce an unauthorized effect. For example, a message meaning "Allow John Smith to read confidential file accounts" is modified to mean "Allow Fred Brown to read confidential file accounts."

The **denial of service** prevents or inhibits the normal use or management of communications facilities. This attack may have a specific target; for example, an entity may suppress all messages directed to a particular destination (e.g., the security audit service.) Another form of service denial is the disruption of an entire network, either by disabling the network or by overloading it with messages so as to degrade performance.

A **masquerade** takes place when one entity pretends to be a different entity. A masquerade attack usually includes one of the other two forms of active attack. Such an attack can take place, for example, by capturing and replaying an authentication sequence.

Active threats present the opposite characteristics of passive threats. Whereas passive attacks are difficult to detect, measures are available to prevent their success. On the other hand, it is quite difficult to absolutely prevent active attacks, since this would require physical protection of all communications facilities and paths at all times. Instead, the goal with respect to active attacks is to detect these attacks and to recover from any disruption or delays caused by the attack. Because the detection has a deterrent effect, this may also contribute to prevention.

Access Controls

The purpose of access controls is to ensure that only authorized users have access to the system and its individual resources and that access to and modification of particular portions of data is limited to authorized individuals and programs.

Figure 12-9 depicts, generically, the measures taken to control access in a data processing system. They fall into two categories: first, those associated with the user or group of users and, second, those associated with the data. In what follows, we elaborate on these concepts and extend them to the local networking environment.

The control of access by user is referred to as authentication. A quite common example of this on a time-sharing system is the user logon, which requires both a user id and a password. The system will only allow a user to

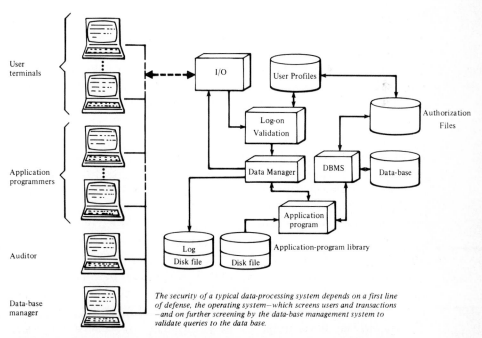

The security of a typical data-processing system depends on a first line of defense, the operating system—which screens users and transactions —and on further screening by the data-base management system to validate queries to the data base.

FIGURE 12-9. Data Processing System Security (From [BERN82])

logon if that user's id is known to the system and if the user knows the password associated by the system with that id. This id/password system is a notoriously unreliable method of access control. Users can forget their passwords, and accidentally or intentionally reveal their password. Also, the id/password file is subject to penetration attempts.

No cost-effective method of overcoming this problem exists. Exotic techniques such as voiceprints, fingerprints, and hand geometry analysis may be foolproof but are at present prohibitively expensive. Simple measures that can be taken now are to change passwords frequently and to maintain multiple tight measures of security over the id/password directory. One additional measure that is cost effective is to associate id's with terminals rather than users and hard wire the code into the terminal. This changes an administrative/software security problem into a physical security problem. However, if it is desirable to allow one-to-many and/or many-to-one relationships between users and terminals, this technique is ineffective.

The problem of authentication is compounded over a multiaccess medium LAN or HSLN. The logon dialogue must take place over the communications medium and eavesdropping is a potential threat. One approach to protection would be to certify that each NIU (except those of the NCC) can capture only data addressed to it. This is no easy task, as we discuss below. Another approach is to encrypt the id/password data. This is described below.

User and user group authentication can be either centralized or distributed. In a centralized approach the network provides a logon service, which we can think of as being associated with the NCC. In the case of a LAN or HSLN, this could be accomplished by setting up a connection between each inactive NIU and the NCC's NIU. When a user activates an NIU, the initial connection is automatically to the NCC. After a successful logon, the NCC then establishes a connection between the requesting NIU and the requested destination address. When this connection is terminated, the original user–NCC connection is reestablished. A similar technique would be used in a digital switch. A data port off-hook condition would result in a connection to a logon server; after authentication, the request connection would be made.

Distributed authentication treats the network as a transparent communication link, and the usual logon procedure is carried out by the destination host. Of course, the security concerns for multiaccess media must still be addressed.

In fact, in many local networks, two levels of authentication will probably be used. Individual hosts may be provided with a logon facility to protect host-specific resources and applications. In addition, the network as a whole may have protection to restrict network acess to authorized users. This two-level facility is desirable for the common case, currently, in which the local network connects disparate hosts and simply provides a convenient means of terminal-host access. Future integrated networks (in the OSI sense) may require only a network-level scheme.

Following successful authentication, the user has been granted access to one or a set of hosts and/or processes. This is generally not sufficient for a system that includes sensitive data in its data base. Through the authentication procedure, a user can be identified together with a profile that specifies permissible operations and file accesses. The operating system can enforce rules based on the user profile. The data base management system, however, must control access to specific portions of records. For example, it may be permissible for anyone in administration to obtain a list of company personnel, but only selected individuals may have access to salary information. The issue is more than just one of level of detail. Whereas the operating system may grant a user permission to access a file or use an application, following which there are no further security checks, the data base management system must make a decision on each individual access attempt. That decision will depend not only on the user's identity but also on the specific parts of the record being accessed, and even on the information already divulged to the user.

A general model of access control as exercised by a data base management system is that of an access matrix (Table 12-4). One axis of the table consists of identified subjects that may attempt data access. Typically, this list will consist of individual users or user groups, although access could be

TABLE 12.4 Data Base Access Matrix

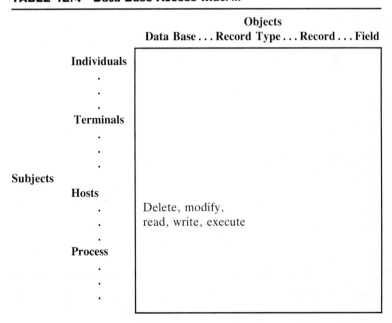

controlled for terminals, hosts, or processes instead of or in addition to users. The other axis lists the objects that may be accessed. At the greatest level of detail, objects may be individual data fields. More aggregate groupings, such as records, record types, or even the entire data base may also be objects in the matrix. Each entry in the matrix indicates the access rights of that subject for that object.

In practice, an access matrix is usually sparse, and is implemented by decomposition in one of two ways. The matrix may be decomposed by columns, yielding access control lists. Thus for each object, an access control list lists users and their permitted access opportunities. Decomposition by rows yields capability tickets. A capability ticket specifies authorized objects and operations for a user. Each user has a number of tickets and may be authorized to loan or give them to others. Because tickets may be dispersed around the system, they present a greater security management problem than access control lists.

Network considerations for access control parallel those for authentication. Encryption may be needed to provide secure communications on a LAN or HSLN. Typically, access control is decentralized, that is, controlled by host-based data base management systems. However, if a network data base server exists on a LAN or HSLN, access control becomes a network service.

Encryption

Earlier, we referred to one of the major security risks on LANs and HSLNs, which use a multiaccess medium—the risk of eavesdropping. Eavesdropping can be accomplished by programming the NIU to accept packets other than those addressed to it or by physically tapping into the medium. One countermeasure that, properly used, is very effective is to encrypt the data in each packet (i.e., send the data in code).

A number of schemes for encryption have been proposed; good discussions can be found in [KENT81] and [POPE79]. In this section, we describe two techniques that are good candidates for local network use.

Conventional Encryption

Figure 12-10a illustrates the conventional encryption process. The original intelligible message, referred to as *plaintext*, is converted into apparently random nonsense, referred to as *ciphertext*. The encryption process consists of an algorithm and a key. The key is a relatively short bit string that controls the algorithm. The algorithm will produce a different output depending on the specific key being used at the time. Changing the key radically changes the output of the algorithm.

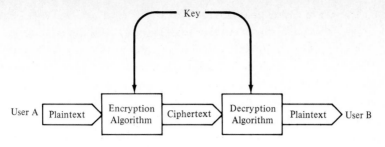

(a) Conventional Encryption

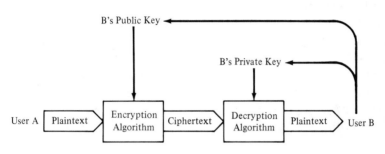

(b) Public-Key Encryption

FIGURE 12-10.   Encryption

Once the ciphertext is produced, it is transmitted. Upon reception, the ciphertext can be transformed back to the original plaintext by using a decryption algorithm and the same key that was used for encryption.

The security of conventional encryption depends on several factors. First, the encryption algorithm must be powerful enough so that it is impractical to decrypt a message on the basis of the ciphertext alone. Beyond that, the security of conventional encryption depends on the secrecy of the key, not the secrecy of the algorithm. That is, it is assumed that it is impractical to decrypt a message on the basis of the ciphertext *plus* knowledge of the encryption/decryption algorithm. In other words, we don't need to keep the algorithm secret; we only need to keep the key secret.

This feature of conventional encryption is what makes it feasible for widespread use. The fact that the algorithm need not be kept secret means that manufacturers can, and have, developed low-cost chip implementations of data encryption algorithms. These chips are widely available and incorporated into a number of products. With the use of conventional encryption, the principal security problem is maintaining the secrecy of the key. This issue is addressed here.

The Data Encryption Standard

The most widely used encryption scheme is based on the data encryption standard (DES), adopted in 1977 by the National Bureau of Standards. For DES, data are encrypted in 64-bit blocks using a 56-bit key. Using the key, the 64-bit input is transformed in a series of steps involving transposition and exclusive-or operations. The result is a 64-bit output in which each bit of output is a function of each bit of the input and each bit of the key. At the receiver, the plaintext is recovered by using the same key and reversing the steps. A precise definition of this algorithm can be found in [DAVI84].

The DES has enjoyed increasingly widespread use. Unfortunately, it has also been the subject of much controversy as to how secure the DES is. The main concern is in the length of the key, which some observers consider to be too short. To appreciate the nature of the controversy, let us quickly review the history of the DES.

The DES is the result of a request for proposals for a national cipher standard released by NBS in 1973. At that time, IBM was in the final stages of a project called Lucifer to develop its own encryption capability. IBM proposed the Lucifer scheme, which was by far the best system submitted. It was, in fact, so good that it considerably upset some people at the National Security Agency (NSA), which until that moment had considered itself comfortably ahead of the rest of the world in the still arcane art of cryptography. DES, as eventually adopted, was essentially the same as Lucifer, with one crucial difference: Lucifer's key size was originally 128 bits, whereas the final standard uses a key of 56 bits. What is the significance of the 72 dropped bits?

There are basically two ways to break a cipher. One way is to exploit properties of whatever mathematical functions form the basis of the encryption algorithm to make a "cryptoanalytic" attack on it. It is generally assumed that DES is immune to such attacks, although the role of NSA in shaping the final DES standard leaves lingering doubts. The other way is a brute force attack in which you try all possible keys in an "exhaustive search." That is, you attempt to decrypt ciphertext with every possible 56-bit key until something intelligible pops out. With only 56 bits in the DES key, there are 2^{56} different keys—a number that is uncomfortably small, and becoming smaller as computers get faster.

Whatever the merits of the case, DES has flourished in recent years and is widely used, especially in financial applications. Except in areas of extreme sensitivity, the use of DES in commercial applications should not be a cause for concern by the responsible managers.

Commercial Communications Security Endorsement Program

Although DES still has a reasonably useful life ahead of it, it is likely that nongovernment organizations will begin to look for replacements for what is seen as an increasingly vulnerable algorithm. The most likely replacement is a family of algorithms developed under the NSA Commercial COMSEC (communications security) Endorsement Program (CCEP). CCEP is a joint NSA–industry effort to produce a new generation of encryption devices that are more secure than DES, that are low-cost, and that are capable of operating at high data rates. Features of the new CCEP algorithms:

1. The CCEP algorithms are developed by NSA and are classified. Thus the algorithms themselves remain secret and are subject to change from time to time.
2. Industry participants will produce chip implementation of the algorithms, but the NSA maintains control over the design, fabrication, and dissemination of chips.

Two types of algorithms come under the CCEP heading. Type I algorithms are designed to protect classified government information. Equipment using type I CCEP will be available only to government agencies and their designated contractors. Type II algorithms are designed to protect sensitive but unclassified information. Type II gear is intended to replace DES gear. Unlike the Type I modules, which will handle classified information, the Type II equipment is controlled only to the point of sale. Presumably, after a Type II module is built into a computer or communication device and sold by a vendor, the customer can do with it as he or she pleases—short of exporting it overseas.

Although the purpose of developing the Type II equipment, as with the Type I equipment, was to provide a means of protecting government information, the Type II modules are available for use in nongovernment, private sector applications. As this equipment becomes more widely available, it is likely to become more widely used, at the expense of DES.

Key Distribution

For conventional encryption to work, the two parties to an exchange must have the same key, and that key must be protected from access by others. Furthermore, frequent key changes are usually desirable to limit the amount of data compromised if an attacker learns the key. Therefore, the strength of any cryptographic system rests with the key distribution technique, a term that refers to the means of delivering a key to two parties that wish to exchange data, without allowing others to see the key. Key distribution can be achieved in a number of ways [ABBR86]. For two parties A and B:

1. A key could be selected by A and physically delivered to B.
2. A third party could select the key and physically deliver it to A and B.

3. If *A* and *B* have previously and recently used a key, one party could transmit the new key to the other, encrypted using the old key.
4. If *A* and *B* each have an encrypted connection to a third party *C*, *C* could deliver a key on the encrypted links to *A* and *B*.

Options 1 and 2 call for manual delivery of a key, which is awkward. In a distributed system, any given host or terminal may need to engage in exchanges with many other hosts and terminals over time. Thus, each device needs a number of keys, supplied dynamically. The difficulty with Option 3 is that if an attacker ever succeeds in gaining access to one key, then all subsequent keys are revealed.

Option 4 is the most attractive and could be handled from a host facility or network control center. Figure 12-11 illustrates a possible implementation. For this scheme, two kinds of keys are identified:

• *Session key:* When two end systems (hosts, terminals, etc.) wish to communicate, they establish a logical connection (e.g., LLC connection or transport connection). For the duration of that logical connection, all user data are encrypted with a one-time session key. At the conclusion of the session, or connection, the session key is destroyed.
• *Permanent key:* A permanent key is a key used between entities for the purpose of distributing session keys.

The configuration consists of the following elements:

• *Access control center:* The access control center determines which systems are allowed to communicate with each other.

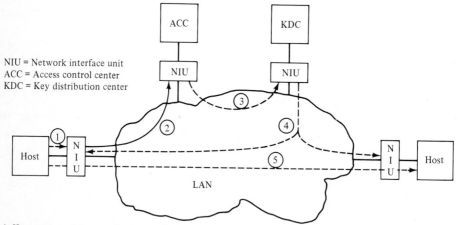

NIU = Network interface unit
ACC = Access control center
KDC = Key distribution center

1. Host sends packet requesting connection.
2. NIU buffers packet, asks ACC for session key.
3. ACC approves request, commands KDC.
4. KDC distributes session key to both NIUs.
5. Buffered packet transmitted.

FIGURE 12-11.   Key Distribution Across a LAN

- *Key distribution center:* When permission is granted by the access control center for two systems to establish a connection, the key distribution center provides a one-time session key for that connection.
- *Network interface unit:* The NIU performs end-to-end encryption and obtains session keys on behalf of its host or terminal.

The steps involved in establishing a connection are shown in Figure 12-11. When one host wishes to set up a connection to another host, it transmits a connection-request packet (1). The NIU saves that packet and applies to the access control center for permission to establish the connection (2). The communication between the NIU and the access control center is encrypted using a permanent key shared only by the access control center and the NIU. The access control center has one such unique key for each NIU and for the key distribution center. If the access control center approves the connection request, it sends a message to the key distribution center, asking for a session key to be generated (3). The key distribution center generates the session key and delivers it to the two appropriate NIUs, using a unique permanent key for each NIU (4). The requesting NIU can now release the connection request packet, and a connection is set up between the two end systems (5). All user data exchanged between the two end systems are encrypted by their respective NIUs using the one-time session key.

Several variations on this scheme are possible. The functions of access control and key distribution could be combined into a single system. The separation makes the two functions clear and may provide a slightly enhanced level of security. If we wish to let any two devices communicate at will, then the access control function is not needed at all: When two devices wish to establish a connection, one of them applies to the key distribution center for a session key.

The automated key distribution approach provides the flexibility and dynamic characteristics needed to allow a number of terminal users to access a number of hosts and for the hosts to exchange data with each other. A number of LAN vendors offer some version of the scheme shown in Figure 12-11. It is a powerful and reasonably inexpensive means of enhancing network security.

Public-Key Encryption

As we have seen, one of the major difficulties with conventional encryption schemes is the need to distribute the keys in a secure manner. A clever way around this requirement is an encryption scheme that, surprisingly, does not require key distribution. This scheme, known as public-key encryption and first proposed in 1976 [DIFF76], is illustrated in Figure 12-10b.

For conventional encryption schemes, the keys used for encryption and decryption are the same. This is not a necessary condition. Instead, it is possible to develop an algorithm that uses one key for encryption and a companion but different key for decryption. Furthermore, it is possible to develop algorithms such that knowledge of the encryption algorithm plus the encryption key is not sufficient to determine the decryption key. Thus the following technique will work.

1. Each end system in a network generates a pair of keys to be used for encryption and decryption of messages that it will receive.
2. Each system publishes its encryption key by placing it in a public register or file. This is the public key. The companion key is kept private.
3. If A wishes to send a message to B, it encrypts the message using B's public key.
4. When B receives the message, it decrypts it using B's private key. No other recipient can decrypt the message since only B knows B's private key.

As you can see, public-key encryption solves the key distribution problem, since there are no keys to distribute! All participants have access to public keys, and private keys are generated locally by each participant and therefore need never be distributed. As long as a system controls its private key, its incoming communication is secure. At any time, a system can change its private key and publish the companion public key to replace its old public key.

A further refinement is needed. Since anyone can transmit a message to A using A's public key, a means is needed to prevent impostors. To develop this scheme, you need to know that public-key encryption algorithms are such that the two keys can be used in either order. That is, one can encrypt with the public key and decrypt with the matching private key, or encrypt with the private key and decrypt with the matching public key. Now consider the following scenario: B prepares a message and encrypts it with its own private key, and then encrypts the result with A's public key. On the other end, A first uses its private key and then uses B's public key in a double decryption. Since the message was encrypted with B's private key, it could only come from B. Since it was also encrypted with A's public key, it can only be read by A. With this technique, any two stations can at any time set up a secure connection without a prior secret distribution of keys.

A main disadvantage of public-key encryption compared to conventional encryption is that algorithms for the former are much more complex. Thus, for comparable size and cost of hardware, the public-key scheme will provide much lower throughput. One possible application of public-key encryption is to use it for the permanent key portion of Figure 12-11, with conventional keys used for sessions keys. Since there are few control

TABLE 12.5 Conventional and Public-Key Encryption

Conventional Encryption	Public-key Encryption
Needed to Work:	**Needed to Work:**
1. The same algorithm with the same key can be used for encryption and decryption.	1. One algorithm is used for encryption and decryption with a pair of keys, one for encryption and one for decryption.
2. The sender and receiver must share the algorithm and the key.	2. The sender and receiver must each have one of the matched pair of keys.
Needed for Security:	**Needed for Security:**
1. The key must be kept secret.	1. One of the two keys must be kept secret.
2. It must be impossible or at least impractical to decipher a message if no other information is available.	2. It must be impossible or at least impractical to decipher a message if no other information is available.
3. Knowledge of the algorithm plus samples of ciphertext must be insufficient to determine the key.	3. Knowledge of the algorithm plus one of the keys plus samples of ciphertext must be insufficient to determine the key.

messages relative to the amount of user data traffic, the reduced throughput should not be a handicap.

Table 12-5 summarizes some of the important aspects of conventional and public-key encryption.

Multilevel Security

The techniques that we have discussed so far have been concerned primarily with security as it relates to the individual user. A somewhat different but widely applicable requirement is to protect data or resources on the basis of levels of security. This is commonly found in the military, where information is unclassified (U), confidential (C), secret (S), top secret (TS), or beyond. Discussions of the military multilevel security problem in the context of LANs can be found in [SHIR82], [GILL82], and [SHIR83].

Of course, the concept of multilevel security is equally applicable in other areas, where information can be organized into gross categories and users can be granted clearances to access certain categories of data. For example, the highest level of security might be for strategic corporate planning documents and data, accessible by only corporate officers and

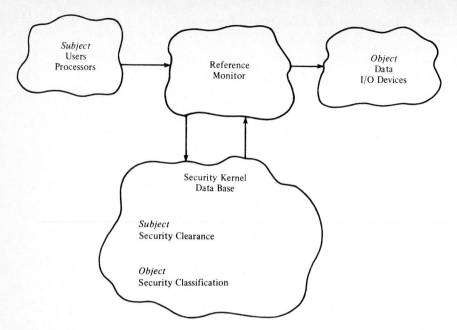

FIGURE 12-12. Reference Monitor

their staff. Next might come sensitive financial and personnel data, accessible only by administration personnel and corporate officers. And so on.

When multiple categories or levels of data are defined, the requirement is referred to as one of multilevel security. The requirement is in two parts and is simply stated. A multilevel secure system must enforce:

- *No read up:* A subject can only read an object of less or equal security level.
- *No write down:* A subject can only write into an object of greater or equal security level.

These two rules, if properly enforced, provide multilevel security. For a data processing system, the approach that has been taken, and been the object of much research and development, is based on the reference monitor or security kernel concept ([ANDE72], [AMES83]). The approach is depicted in Figure 12-12. The reference monitor controls the access of subjects to objects on the basis of security parameters of the subject and object. The reference monitor enforces the security rules (no read up, no write down) and has the following properties:

- *Complete mediation:* The security rules are enforced on every access, not just, for example, when a file is opened.
- *Isolation:* The reference monitor and data base are protected from unauthorized modification.

- *Verifiability:* The reference monitor's correctness must be provable. That is, it must be possible to mathematically demonstrate that the reference monitor enforces the security rules and provides complete mediation and isolation.

These are stiff requirements. The requirement for complete mediation means that every access to data within main memory and on disk and tape must be mediated. Pure software implementations impose too high a performance penalty to be practical; the solution must be at least partly in hardware. The requirement for isolation means that it must not be possible for an attacker, no matter how clever, to change the logic of the reference monitor or the contents of the security kernel data base. Finally, the requirement for mathematical proof is formidable for something as complex as a general-purpose computer. A system that can provide such verification is referred to as a **trusted system**.

In an effort to meet its own needs, and also as a service to the public, the U.S. Department of Defense in 1981 established the Computer Security Center within the National Security Agency (NSA) with the goal of encouraging the widespread availability of trusted computer systems. This goal is realized through the center's Commercial Product Evaluation Program. In essence, the center attempts to apply mathematical techniques to verify commercially available products as meeting the security requirements just outlined. The center classifies verified products according to the range of security features that they provide. These evaluations are needed for Department of Defense procurements but are published and freely available. Hence, they can serve as guidance to commercial customers for the purchase of commercially available, off-the-shelf equipment.

With this background, we now turn to the problem of multilevel security on a local network. It should be clear as the discussion proceeds that digital switches introduce no new problems or solutions and that LANs and HSLNs can be treated identically. For convenience, we will refer only to LANs in the following discussion.

Multilevel LAN Security

Overview
Figure 12-13a illustrates the problem: hosts and terminals at different security levels exist. To compound this situation, multilevel trusted hosts are part of the environment. With no modification to the LAN, those systems cannot be connected as shown. There are a number of approaches to correct this condition.

1. *Physical separation (Figure 12-13b):* The security problem disappears if the various LANS are kept in separate areas and protected at their

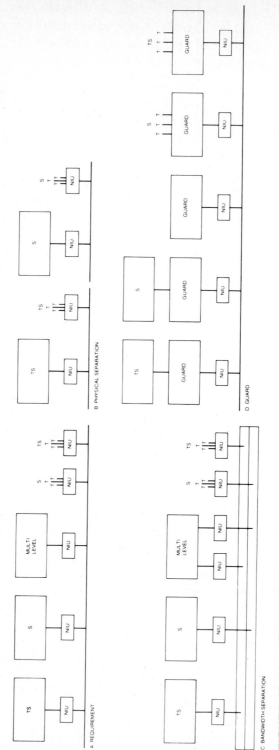

FIGURE 12-13. LAN/HSLN Security Approaches

designated security levels. This approach, however, negates most of the benefits of the LAN. Connectivity is drastically limited. Security requirements permit data to be passed upward (from a lower to a higher classification area), but this approach does not facilitate such data transfer.

2. *Bandwidth separation (Figure 12-13c):* With a broadband cable, each classification level could be assigned a separate channel. Cross-channel traffic could then be supported by a multilevel secure host. This approach requires the use of a trusted multilevel host.

3. *Encryption (not shown):* As the subject of much recent research, this is a promising approach. Each NIU would require encryption capability, and there needs to be a trusted facility for distributing keys to end points requesting a connection. This method may ultimately gain wide acceptance.

4. *Trusted hosts (Figure 12-13d):* Liberal use of trusted host machines (Guards) could satisfy the security requirement. If the trusted host were a minicomputer, mainframes could be connected by a trusted front end. Terminals would have to interface to the network via a trusted host.

5. *Trusted NIU (Figure 12-14):* The trusted NIU (TIU) is an NIU that provides the reference monitor capability. As we shall see, it is a remarkably simple device.

Of the options listed, 1 is impractical and 2 is not very flexible and is limited to braodband LANs. Options 3 and 4 have promise, but their cost effectiveness has yet to be demonstrated. The TIU concept, which has been funded by DOD and is the subject of ongoing research [SIDH82a, SIDH82b, RUSH83] is a promising and apparently cost-effective approach. It is to this topic that we now turn.

The Trusted Interface Unit

The Trusted Interface Unit (TIU) performs all the functions of an ordinary NIU. In addition, it is designed to operate at an assigned security level. Two other functions are required:

- The TIU will label each frame that it transmits with its security level.
- The TIU will accept only frames that are labeled with its own or a lesser security level.

Figure 12-14 depicts the architecture that can be supported by TIUs. Single-level hosts at a given security level connect to the LAN via a TIU of the same level. The TIU assures that the host receives only data up to the classification that it is permitted. All data transmitted by the host are labeled by the TIU with its security level, thereby ensuring that no end point of a lower classification level can receive the data.

As with hosts, terminals are also connected via TIUs. All terminals connected to the same TIU must operate at the same level.

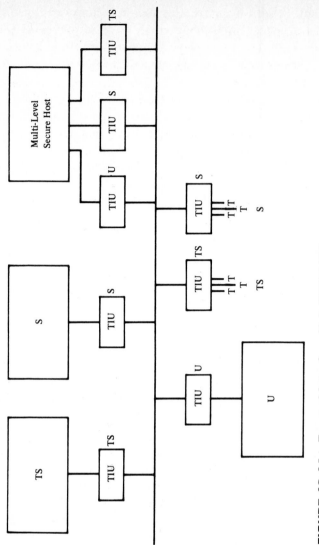

FIGURE 12-14. Trusted Interface Unit (TIU) LAN

A multilevel trusted host could connect to the LAN through a number of TIUs at various security levels. Each TIU is trusted to operate at its own security level. The trusted host is trusted to handle the communication ports to the various TIUs, again each at its own appropriate level.

Note that unclassified devices require a TIU operating at the unclassified level, not a simple NIU. The filtering function is most important for unclassified devices.

The use of TIUs requires modification of the LAN's layer 2 protocol. An additional field must be added for the security label.

The TIU approach is an attractive one because of the relative ease of building a trusted NIU. The performance penalty is slight; only a small amount of additional processing per packet is required. And compared to a general-purpose computer, the TIU is simple enough for one to feel encouraged about the verification process.

Refinements

The previous section discusses, in general terms, the architecture of a multilevel secure LAN, based on a TIU implementation. Several refinements make this a more flexible capability.

- *Variable-level TIU:* This TIU would have a manual switch enabling an an operator to select a security level other than the maximum one allowed for the TIU. Thus a terminal or host could opeate at different security levels at different times. This could be a significant convenience.
- *Multilevel TIU:* A multilevel TIU would allow a multilevel trusted host to connect to the LAN through a single TIU. The multilevel TIU would trust its host to label data appropriately for transmission. For reception, the TIU would pass all data up to the host's maximum level.
- *Subnetworks:* In a multilevel environment, the cable and all TIUs must be physically protected to the highest security level of the LAN. However, it may not be practical or desirable to protect all attached devices to that level. One solution is to break the network into subnetworks that are physically separate and protected to various levels (Figure 12-15). Each subnetwork could be multilevel and physically protected to its highest level. Subnetworks would then connect by trusted bridges with encryption devices. Consider host A in Figure 12-15. While physically protected to secret, host A may run at an unclassified level, and at that level can communicate with host B on the unclassified network, which may be in another room or building. To prepare for such a connection, host A must be "sanitized" of all classified data, and its TIU adjusted to unclassified.

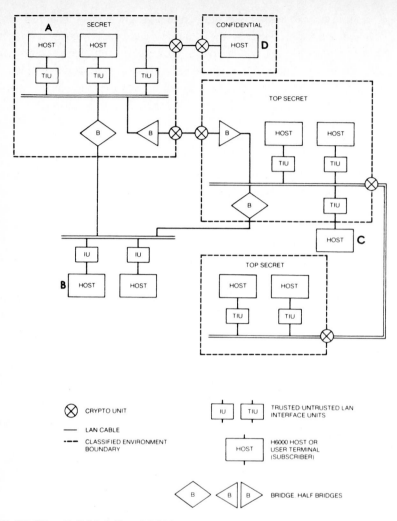

FIGURE 12-15. Full Multilevel LAN

12.4

RECOMMENDED READING

General discussions of local network management, emphasizing performance monitoring, include [PRES88], [COUC87], [JACO87], [LEBA86], and [SOHA87]*. Examples of commercially available NCCs are discussed in [MATS82] and [ESTR86]. A good example of a measurement facility is described in [AMER82]. A discussion of network management for communications networks in general can be found in [STAL90a].

Approaches to enhancing reliability and availability of bus/tree LANs are discussed in [BASS80]. A more detailed description for broadband may be found in [WILL81]. For rings, a good discussion can be found in [SALT79]. The IBM active wiring concentrator approach is described in [STRO83]*. The FDDI reliability specification is examined in detail in [JOHN86]*.

A good discussion of computer network security, covering all of the topics in Section 12.3, can be found in [KENT81]. [SIDH83]* presents the TIU concept. Discussions of the use of trusted systems in LANs include [FRAI87] and [ABRA87]. A discussion of security for communications networks in general can be found in [STAL90a].

12.5

PROBLEMS

12.1 Give some examples of useful applications of permanent link layer connections.

12.2 List useful protocol-specific performance measures for following protocols. Indicate whether collection can be centralized or must be distributed.
  a. Token bus.
  b. Collision avoidance (ANS X3T9.5).
  c. Token ring.
  d. Slotted ring.
  e. Register insertion.
  f. Distributed reservation.

12.3 For centrally collected measurement data, there is a timing bias due to the propagation delay of the medium. Give examples of performance measures that are (are not) affected by this bias.

12.4 Consider a system consisting of N identical units, only M of which are required for the system to function. Derive an expression for the availability of the system.

12.5 Consider a ring network with the following parameters:

$$N = \text{number of nodes/repeaters}$$

$$h = \text{skip distance in the backward direction}$$

$$d_{ij} = \text{shortest hop distance from node } i \text{ to node } j$$

$$d = \text{diameter} = \text{Max}_{ij}[d_{ij}]$$

Note that for DDLCN, $d = \lfloor N/2 \rfloor$, and for daisy-chain, $d = \lfloor N/3 \rfloor + 1$.
  a. For the general case, derive an expression for d as a function of N and h. Show that d is minimum for $h = \lfloor \sqrt{N} \rfloor$.

b. Assuming that the transfer of data between each combination of stations is equally likely, we have that the average number of hops is

$$K = \frac{1}{N} \sum_{i=0}^{N-1} \left[\frac{1}{N-1} \sum_{j=0}^{N-1} d_{ij} \right]$$

$$= \frac{1}{N-1} \sum_{j=0}^{N-1} d_{ij} \qquad \text{for arbitrary } i$$

Solve for K as a function of N, h. What is K for DDLCN? For daisy chain? For $h = \lfloor \sqrt{N} \rfloor$? Show that K is minimum for $h = \lfloor \sqrt{N} \rfloor$.

c. A measure of reliability is the number of alternate routes between the two farthest nodes on the network. There is exactly one forward route and a number of backward routes consisting of $b = \lfloor N/(h+1) \rfloor$ backward hops and $(h-1)$ forward hops; there are different routes depending on the different combination of forward and backward hops in the sequence. Derive an expression of the number of routes, R, as a function of N and h. What is R for DDLCN? For daisy chain? For $h = \lfloor \sqrt{N} \rfloor$? Show that R is a minimum for $h = \lfloor \sqrt{N} \rfloor$.

12.6 In Figure 12-12, host C is in an unclassified environment connected to a LAN in a TS facility. Why must its TIU be inside the TS facility? Why is host D connected to its TIU via encryption devices whereas host C is not?

12.7 List and describe some potential security and penetration problems with the TIU concept.

GLOSSARY

ALOHA. A medium access control technique for multiple access transmission media. A station transmits whenever it has data to send. Unacknowledged transmissions are repeated.

AMPLIFIER. An analog device designed to compensate for the loss in a section of transmission medium. It increases the signal strength of an analog signal over a range of frequencies.

ANS X3T9.5 A committee sponsored by the American National Standards Institute (ANSI) that is responsible for a variety of system interconnection standards. The committee has produced draft standards for high-speed coaxial cable bus and fiber optic ring local networks.

BANDWIDTH. Refers to a relative range of frequencies, that is, the difference between the highest and lowest frequencies transmitted. For example, the bandwidth of a TV channel is 6 MHz.

BASEBAND. Transmission of signals without modulation. In a baseband local network, digital signals (1's and 0's) are inserted directly onto the cable as voltage pulses. The entire spectrum of the cable is consumed by the signal. This scheme does not allow frequency-division multiplexing.

BRIDGE. A device used to link two or more homogeneous LANs or HSLNs. It accepts frames from attached networks addressed to devices on other networks, buffers them, and retransmit them in the direction of the other network. A bridge does not alter the frame content but acts merely as a relay. It operates at the MAC layer.

BROADBAND. The use of coaxial cable for providing data transfer by means of analog or radio-frequency signals. Digital signals are passed through a modem and transmitted over one of the frequency bands of the cable.

BUS. A topology in which stations are attached to a shared transmission medium. The transmission medium is a linear cable; transmissions propagate the length of the medium, and are received by all stations.

CARRIERBAND. Same as single-channel broadband.

CATV. Community Antenna Television. CATV cable is used for broadband local networks.

CENTRALIZED BUS ARCHITECTURE. A bus topology in which the bus is very short and the links to attached devices are relatively much longer.

CENTREX. A voice and data switching service that performs switching functions in the telephone company's central office as opposed to a digital PBX, which performs switching on the customer's premises.

CHEAPERNET. A baseband local area network that uses a thinner cable and less expensive components than Ethernet or the original IEEE 802.3 standard. Although the data rate is the same (10 Mbps), the network span and number of stations is less for Cheapernet.

CIRCUIT SWITCHING. A method of communicating in which a dedicated communications path is established between two devices through one or more intermediate switching nodes. Unlike packet switching, digital data are sent as a continuous stream of bits. Bandwidth is guaranteed, and delay is essentially limited to propagation time. The telephone system uses circuit switching.

COAXIAL CABLE. An electromagnetic transmission medium consisting of a center conductor and an outer, concentric conductor.

CODEC. Coder–decoder. Transforms analog voice into a digital bit stream (coder), and digital signals into analog voice (decoder), usually using pulse code modulation (PCM).

COLLISION. A condition in which two packets are being transmitted over a medium at the same time. Their interference makes both unintelligible.

CONTENTION. The condition when two or more stations attempt to use the same channel at the same time.

CRC. Cyclic Redundancy Check. A numeric value derived from the bits in a message. The transmitting station calculates a number that is attached to the message. The receiving station performs the same calculation. If the results differ, then one or more bits are in error.

CSMA. Carrier Sense Multiple Access. A medium access control technique for multiple-access transmission media. A station wishing to transmit first senses the medium and transmits only if the medium is idle.

CSMA/CD. Carrier Sense Multiple Access with Collision Detection. A refinement of CSMA in which a station ceases transmission if it detects a collision.

DATAGRAM. A packet switching service in which packets (datagrams) are independently routed and may arrive out of order. The datagram is self-contained, and carries a complete address. Delivery confirmation is provided by higher level protocols.

DCE. Data Circuit-Terminating Equipment. A generic name for network-owned devices that provide a network attachment point for user devices.

DIFFERENTIAL ENCODING. A means of encoding digital data on a digital signal such that the binary value is determined by a signal change rather than a signal level.

DIFFERENTIAL MANCHESTER ENCODING. A digital signaling technique in which there is a transition in the middle of each bit time to provide clocking. The encoding of a 0(1) is represented by the presence (absence) of a transition at the beginning of the bit period.

DIGITAL DATA SWITCH. A star topology local network using circuit-switching. Usually refers to a system that handles only data but not voice.

DIGITAL PRIVATE BRANCH EXCHANGE. A local network based on the private branch exchange architecture. Provides an integrated voice/data switching service. See PBX.

DTE. Data Terminal Equipment. A generic name for user-owned devices or stations that attach to a network.

DUAL CABLE. A type of broadband cable system in which two separate cables are used: one for transmission and one for reception.

ETHERNET. A 10-Mbps baseband local area network specification developed jointly by Xerox, Intel, and Digital Equipment. It is the forerunner of the IEEE 802.3 CSMA/CD standard.

FRAME. A group of bits that include data plus one or more addresses. Generally refers to a link layer (layer 2) protocol.

FREQUENCY-AGILE MODEM. A modem used on some broadband systems which can shift frequencies in order to communicate with stations in different dedicated bands.

FREQUENCY-DIVISION MULTIPLEXING (FDM). A technique for combining multiple signals on one circuit by separating them in frequency.

FREQUENCY TRANSLATOR. In a split broadband cable system, an analog device at the headend that converts a block of inbound frequencies to a block of outbound frequencies.

FSK. Frequency-Shift Keying. A digital-to-analog modulation technique in which two different frequencies are used to represent 1's and 0's.

GATEWAY. A device that connects two systems, especially if the two systems use different protocols. Recently, the term gateway has been reserved for the interconnection of networks at layer 7 of the OSI model.

GRADE OF SERVICE. For a circuit-switched system, the probability that, during a specified period of peak traffic, an offered call will fail to find an available circuit.

HEADEND. The end point of a broadband bus or tree network. Transmission from a station is toward the headend. Reception by a station is from the headend.

HIGH-SPEED LOCAL NETWORK (HSLN). A local network designed to provide high throughput between expensive, high-speed devices, such as mainframes and mass storage devices.

HIGHSPLIT. A type of braodband cable system in which the available frequencies are split into two groups: one for transmission (5 to 174 MHz) and one for reception (232 to 400 MHz). Requires a frequency translator.

HOST. The collection of hardware and software which attaches to a network and uses that network to provide interprocess communication and user services.

HYBRID LOCAL NETWORK. An integrated local network consisting of more than one type of local network (LAN, HSLN, digital PBX).

IEEE 802. A committee of IEEE organized to produce a LAN standard.

INBOUND PATH. On a broadband LAN, the transmission path used by stations to transmit packets toward the headend.

INFRARED. Electromagnetic waves whose frequency range is above that of microwave and below the visible spectrum: 3×10^{11} to 4×10^{14} Hz.

INJECTION LASER DIODE (ILD). A solid state device that works on the laser principle to produce a light source for optical fiber.

INTERNET. A collection of packet-switched networks that are connected together via gateways.

INTERNETWORKING. Communication among devices across multiple networks.

LASER. Electromagnetic source capable of producing infrared and visible light.

LIGHT-EMITTING DIODE (LED). A solid-state device that emits light when a current is applied. Used as a light source for optical fiber.

LISTEN BEFORE TALK (LBT). Same as Carrier-Sense Multiple Access (CSMA).

LISTEN WHILE TALK (LWT). Same as Carrier-Sense Multiple Access with Collision Detection (CSMA/CD).

LOCAL AREA NETWORK (LAN). A general-purpose local network that can serve a variety of devices. Typically used for terminals, micro-computers, and minicomputers.

LOCAL NETWORK. A communications network that provides inter-connection of a variety of data communicating devices within a small area.

MANCHESTER ENCODING. A digital signaling technique in which there is a transition in the middle of each bit time. A 1 is encoded with a high level during the first half of the bit time; a 0 is encoded with a low level during the first half of the bit time.

MEDIUM ACCESS CONTROL (MAC). For bus, tree, and ring topolo-gies, the method of determining which device has access to the transmis-sion medium at any time. CSMA/CD and token are common access methods.

MESSAGE SWITCHING. A switching technique using a message store and forward system. No dedicated path is established. Rather, each message contains a destination address and is passed from source to destination through intermediate nodes. At each node, the entire message is received, stored briefly, and then passed on to the next node.

MICROWAVE. Electromagnetic waves in the frequency range 1 to 30 GHz.

MIDSPLIT. A type of broadband cable system in which the available frequencies are split into two groups: one for transmission (5 to 116 MHz) and one for reception (168 to 400 MHz). Requires a fre-quency translator.

MODEM. Modulator/Demodulator. Transforms a digital bit stream into an analog signal (modulator) and vice versa (demodulator). The analog signal may be sent over telephone lines, or could be radio frequencies or lightwaves.

NETWORK CONTROL CENTER. The operator interface to software that observes and controls the activities in a network.

NETWORK INTERFACE UNIT. A communications controller that attaches to a local network. It implements the local network protocols and provides an interface for device attachment.

NETWORK MANAGEMENT. A set of human and automated tasks that support the creation, operation, and evolution of a network.

NONBLOCKING NETWORK. A circuit-switched network in which there is always at least one available path between any pair of idle end points regardless of the number of end points already connected.

OPTICAL FIBER. A thin filament of glass or other transparent material through which a signal-encoded light beam may be transmitted by means of total internal reflection.

OUTBOUND PATH. On a broadband LAN, the transmission path used by stations to receive packets coming from the headend.

PACKET. A group of bits that includes data plus source and destination addresses. Generally refers to a network layer (layer 3) protocol.

PACKET SWITCHING. A method of transmitting messages through a communications network, in which long messages are subdivided into short packets. The packets are then transmitted as in message switching. Usually, packet switching is more efficient and rapid than message switching.

PASSIVE HEADEND. A device that connects the two broadband cables of a dual cable system. It does not provide frequency translation.

PASSIVE STAR. A star-topology local network configuration in which the central switch or node is a passive device. Each station is connected to the central node by two links, one for transmit and one for receive. A signal input on one of the transmit links passes through the central node where it is split equally among and output to all of the receive links.

PBX. Private Branch Exchange. A telephone exchange on the user's premises. Provides a switching facility for telephones on extension lines within the building and access to the public telephone network. May be manual (PMBX) or automatic (PABX).

PCM. Pulse Code Modulation. A common method for digitizing voice. The data rate typically used for a single digitized voice channel is 64 kbps.

PROPAGATION DELAY. The delay between the time a signal enters a channel and the time it is received.

PROTOCOL. A set of rules governing the exchange of data between two entities.

REGISTER INSERTION RING. A medium access control technique for rings. Each station contains a register that can temporarily hold a circulating packet. A station may transmit whenever there is a gap on the ring and, if necessary, hold an oncoming packet until it has completed transmission.

REMODULATOR. In a split broadband cable system, a digital device at the headend that recovers the digital data from the inbound analog signal and then retransmits the data on the outbound frequency.

REPEATER. A device that receives data on one communication link and transmits it, bit by bit, on another link as fast as it is received, without buffering. An integral part of the ring topology. Used to connect linear segments in a baseband bus local network.

RING. A topology in which stations are attached to repeaters connected in a closed loop. Data are transmitted in one direction around the ring, and can be read by all attached stations.

RING WIRING CONCENTRATOR. A site through which pass the links between repeaters, for all or a portion of a ring.

ROUTER. A device used to link two or more networks. The router makes use of an internet protocol, which is a connectionless protocol operating at layer 3 of the OSI model.

SINGLE-CHANNEL BROADBAND. A local network scheme in which the entire spectrum of the cable is devoted to a single transmission path; frequency-division multiplexing is not used. Also known as carrierband.

SLOTTED ALOHA. A medium access control technique for multiple-access transmission media. The technique is the same as ALOHA, except that packets must be transmitted in well-defined time slots.

SLOTTED RING. A medium access control technique for rings. The ring is divided into slots, which may be designated empty or full. A station may transmit when an empty slot goes by, by marking it full and inserting a packet into the slot.

SPACE-DIVISION SWITCHING. A circuit-switching technique in which each connection through the switch takes a physically separate and dedicated path.

SPECTRUM. Refers to an absolute range of frequencies. For example, the spectrum of CATV cable is now about 5 Hz to 400 MHz.

SPLITTER. Analog device for dividing one input into two outputs and combining two outputs into one input. Used to achieve tree topology on broadband CATV networks.

STAR. A topology in which all stations are connected to a central switch. Two stations communicate via circuit switching.

STAR WIRING. A method of laying out the transmission medium that is installed for a local network. All cables are concentrated in a wiring closet, with a dedicated cable run from the closet to each device on the network.

STATISTICAL TIME-DIVISION MULTIPLEXING. A method of TDM in which time slots on a shared transmission line are allocated to I/O channels on demand.

SUBSPLIT. A type of broadband cable system in which the available frequencies are split into two groups: one for transmission (5 to 30 MHz) and one for reception (54 to 400 MHz). Requires a frequency translator.

SYNCHRONOUS TIME-DIVISION MULTIPLEXING. A method of TDM in which time slots on a shared transmission line are assigned to I/O channels on a fixed, predetermined basis.

TAP. An analog device that permits signals to be inserted or removed from a twisted pair of coax cable.

TDM BUS SWITCHING. A form of time-division switching in which time slots are used to transfer data over a shared bus between transmitter and receiver.

TERMINAL. A collection of hardware and possibly software which provides a direct user interface to a network.

TERMINATOR. An electrical resistance at the end of a cable which serves to absorb the signal on the line.

TIME-DIVISION MULTIPLEXING (TDM). A technique for combining multiple signals on one circuit by separating them in time.

TIME-DIVISION SWITCHING. A circuit-switching technique in which time slots in a time-multiplexed stream of data are manipulated to pass data from an input to an output.

TIME-MULTIPLEXED SWITCHING (TMS). A from of space-division switching in which each input line is a TDM stream. The switching configuration may change for each time slot.

TIME-SLOT INTERCHANGE (TSI). The interchange of time slots within a time-division multiplexed stream.

TIMING JITTER. Deviation of clock recovery that can occur when a receiver attempts to recover clocking as well as data from the received signal. The clock recovery will deviate in a random fashion from the transitions of the received signal.

TOKEN BUS. A medium access control technique for bus/tree. Stations form a logical ring, around which a token is passed. A station receiving the token may transmit data, and then must pass the token on to the next station in the ring.

TOKEN RING. A medium access control technique for rings. A token circulates around the ring. A station may transmit by seizing the token, inserting a packet onto the ring, and then retransmitting the token.

TOPOLOGY. The structure, consisting of paths and switches, that provides the communications interconnection among nodes of a network.

TRANSCEIVER. A device that both transmits and receives.

TRANSCEIVER CABLE. A twin-pair cable that connects the transceiver in a baseband coax LAN to the controller.

TRANSMISSION MEDIUM. The physical path between transmitters and receivers in a communications network.

TREE. A topology in which stations are attached to a shared transmission medium. The transmission medium is a branching cable emanating from a headend, with no closed circuits. Transmissions propagate throughout all branches of the tree, and are received by all stations.

TWISTED PAIR. An electromagnetic transmission medium consisting of two insulated wires arranged in a regular spiral pattern.

VIRTUAL CIRCUIT. A packet-switching service in which a connection (virtual circuit) is established between two stations at the start of transmission. All packets follow the same route, need not carry a complete address, and arrive in sequence. .

WIRING CLOSET. A specially designed closet used for wiring data and voice communication networks. The closet serves as a concentration point for the cabling that interconnects devices and as a patching facility for adding and deleting devices from the network.

REFERENCES

ABBO84 Abbot, G. "Digital Space Division: A Technique for Switching High-Speed Data Signals." *IEEE Communications Magazine*, April, 1984.

ABBR86 Abbruscato, C. "Choosing a Key Management Style that Suits the Application." *Data Communications*, April, 1986.

ABRA70 Abramson, N. "The ALOHA System—Another Alternative for Computer Communications." *Proceedings, Fall Joint Computer Conference*, 1970.

ABRA83 Abramson, P., and Noel, F. "Matching the Media to Local Network Requirements." *Data Communications*, July, 1983.

ABRA86 Abraham, M. "Running Ethernet Modems over Broadband Cable." *Data Communications*, May, 1986.

ABRA87 Abrams, M., and Jeng, A. "Network Security: Protocol Reference Model and the Trusted Computer Security System Evaluation Criteria." *IEEE Network*, April, 1987.

AIME79 Aimes, G.T., and Lazowska, E.D. "The Behavior of Ethernet-like Computer Communications Networks." *Proceedings, Seventh Symposium on Operating Systems Principles*, 1979.

ALLA84 Allan, R. "Low-loss Tapping Opens Door to Optical Network Buses." *Electronic Design*, October 18, 1984.

AMER82 Amer, P.D. "A Measurement Center for the NBS Local Area Computer Network." *IEEE Transactions on Computers*, August, 1982.

AMER83 Amer, P.D.; Rosenthal, R.; and Toense, R. "Measuring a Local Network's Performance." *Data Communications*, April, 1983.

AMES83 Ames, S.; Gasser, M.; and Schell, R. "Security Kernal Design and Implementation: An Introduction." *Computer*, July, 1983.

ANDE72 Anderson, J.P. *Computer Security Technology Planning Study*. Electronic Systems Division, Hanscom Field, Bedford, MA, Report ESD-TR-73-51, October, 1972.

ANON88 Anonymous. "SEL Claims Mark for Optical Transmission." *Electronics*, March 3, 1988.

ANSI82 American National Standards Institute. *Draft Proposed American National Standard Local Distributed Data Interface*, May, 1982.

ANSI86a American National Standards Institute. *Draft Proposed American National Standard for Local Distributed Data Interfaces*, February 21, 1986.

ANSI86b American National Standards Institute. *FDDI Token Ring Media Access Control (MAC); Draft Proposed American National Standard*, February 28, 1986.

ATT83 AT&T Bell Laboratories. *Engineering and Operations in the Bell System*, 1983.

BACK88 Backes, F. "Transparent Bridges for Interconnection of IEEE 802 LANs." *IEEE Network*, January 1988.

BAL85 Bal, S. "Core Modules Speed System Design." *Systems & Software*, November, 1985.

BARC81 Barcomb, D. *Office Automation: A Survey of Tools and Technology*. Bedford, MA: Digital Press, 1981.

BART85 Bartee, T. *Data Communications, Networks, and Systems*. Indianapolis, IN: Howard W. Sams and Co., 1985.

BASC87 Basch, E. *Optical-Fiber Transmission*. Indianapolis, IN: Howard W. Sams, 1987.

BECK77 Beckmann, P. *Elementary Queueing Theory and Telephone Traffic*. Geneva, IL: Lee's abc of the Telephone, 1977.

BEDE86 Bederman, S. "Source Routing." *Data Communications*, February, 1986.

BELL82a Bell Telephone Laboratories. *Transmission Systems for Communications*, 1982.

BELL82b Bellamy, J. *Digital Telephony*, New York: Wiley, 1982.

BERN82 Bernhard, R. "Breaching System Security." *IEEE Spectrum*, June, 1982.

BERT80 Bertine, H.U. "Physical Level Protocols." *IEEE Transactions on Communications*, April, 1980.

BEUE88 Beuerman, S., and Coyle, E. "The Delay Characteristics of CSMA/CD Networks." *IEEE Transactions on Communications*, May, 1988.

BEVA86 Bevan, M. "Image Processing May Cause Future Problems with Network Loading." *Data Communications*, March, 1986.

BHUS85 Bhushan, B., and Opderbeck, H. "The Evolution of Data Switching for PBX's." *IEEE Journal on Selected Areas in Communications*, July, 1985.

BIND75 Binder, R. "A Dynamic Packet Switching System for Satellite Broadcast Channels." *Proceedings of the ICC*, 1975.

BOGG88 Boggs, D.; Mogul, J.; and Kent, C." Measured Capacity of an Ethernet: Myths and Reality." *Proceedings, SIGCOMM 88 Symposium*, August, 1988.

BRAN78 Branstad, D., ed. *Computer Security and the Data Encryption Standard.* National Bureau of Standards, Special Publication No. 500-27, February, 1978.

BRAY85 Bray, J. "The Resurgence of Centrex." *Telecommunications*, September, 1985.

BURG84 Burg, F.; Chen, C.; and Folts, H. "Of Local Networks, Protocols, and the OSI Reference Model." *Data Communications*, November, 1984.

BURK79 Burke, R.G. "Eliminating Conflicts on a Contention Channel." *Proceedings, Fourth Local Computer Network Conference*, 1979.

BURR83 Burr, W. "An Overview of the Proposed American National Standard for Local Distributed Data Interfaces." *Communications of the ACM*, August, 1983.

BURR86 Burr, W. "The FDDI Optical Data Link." *IEEE Communications Magazine*, May, 1986.

BUX81 Bux, W. "Local-Area Subnetworks: A Performance Comparison." *IEEE Transactions on Communications*, October, 1981.

BUX83a Bux, W.; Closs, F.; Kummerle, K.; Keller, H.; and Mueller, H. "Architecture and Design of a Reliable Token-Ring Network." *IEEE Journal on Selected Areas in Communications*, November, 1983.

BUX83b Bux, W., and Schlatter, M. "An Approximate Method for the Performance Analysis of Buffer Insertion Rings." *IEEE Transaction on Communications*, January, 1983.

BUX84 Bux, W. "Performance Issues in Local-Area Networks." *IBM Systems Journal*, no. 4, 1984.

BYTE85 Bytex Corporation. *Autoswitch Technical Manual*, 1985.

CALL83 Callon, R. "Internetwork Protocol." *Proceedings of the IEEE*, December, 1983.

CARL80 Carlson, D.E. "Bit-Oriented Data Link Control Procedures." *IEEE Transactions on Communications*, April, 1980.

CELA82 Celano, J. "Crossing Public Property: Infrared Link and Alternative Approaches for Connecting a High Speed Local Area Network." *Proceedings, Computer Networking Symposium*, 1982.

CERF78 Cerf, V.G., and Kristein, P.T. "Issues in Packet-Network Interconnection." *Proceedings of the IEEE*, November, 1978.

CERR87 Cerruti, M., and Voce, M. "Zap Data Where It Really Counts—Direct-to-Host Connections." *Data Communications*, July, 1987.

CHAM80 Champine, G.A.; Coop, R.D.; and Heinselman, R.C. *Distributed Computer Systems: Impact on Management, Design, and Analysis.* New York: North-Holland, 1980.

CHEN82 Cheng, W. *Performance Evaluation of Token Networks.* Ph.D. thesis, University of Illinois at Urbana-Champaign, 1982.

CHER83 Cheriton, D. "Local Networking and Internetworking in the V-System." *Proceedings, Eighth Data Communications Symposium*, 1983.

CHLA80a Chlamtac, I., and Franta, W.R. "Message-Based Priority Access to Local Networks." *Computer Communications*, April, 1980.

CHLA80b Chlamtac, I.; Franta, W.R.; Patton, P.C.; and Wells, B. "Performance Issues in Back-End Storage Networks." *Computer*, February, 1980.

CHOU83 Chou, W., ed. *Computer Communications, Vol. I: Principles.* Englewood Cliffs, NJ: Prentice-Hall, 1983.

CHRI79 Christensen, G.S. "Links Between Computer-Room Networks." *Telecommunications*, February, 1979.

CHRI81 Christensen, G.S., and Franta, W.K. "Design and Analysis of the Access Protocol for HYPERchannel Networks." *Proceedings, Third USA–Japan Computer Conference*, 1981.

CHU82 Chu, W.W.; Haller, W.; and Leung, K.K. "A Contention Based Channel Reservation Protocol for High Speed Local Networks." *Proceedings, Seventh Conference on Local Computer Networks*, 1982.

CLAI88 Clair, M., and Orlov, M. "Is it Wise for Users to Run Ethernet Over Existing Nonshielded Twisted Pair?" *Network World*, January 11, 1988.

CLAN82 Clancy, G.J. et al. "The IEEE 802 Committee States Its Case Concerning Its Local Network Standards Efforts." *Data Communications*, April, 1982.

CONA80 Conard, J. "Character-Oriented Data Link Control Protocols." *IEEE Transactions on Communications*, April, 1980.

CONA83 Conard, J. "Services and Protocols of the Data Link Layer." *Proceedings of the IEEE*, December, 1983.

COOP81 Cooper, R.B. *Introduction to Queueing Theory*. New York: North Holland, 1981.

COOP84 Cooper, E. *Broadband Network Technology*. Mountain View, CA: Sytek Press, 1984.

COOV85 Coover, E. "Notes from Mid-revolution: Searching for the Perfect PBX." *Data Communications*, August, 1985.

COOV86 Coover, E. "Voice-Data Integration in the Office: A PBX Approach." *IEEE Communications Magazine*, July, 1986.

COOV89 Coover, E. *Digital Private Branch Exchanges*. Washington, DC: IEEE Computer Society Press, 1989.

COTT81 Cotton, J.; Giesken, K.; Lawrence, A.; and Upp, D. "ITT 1240 Digital Exchange: Digital Switching Network." *Electrical Communication*, No. 2/3, 1981.

COUC83 Couch, L. *Digital and Analog Communication Systems*. New York: Macmillan, 1983.

COUC87 Couch, D. Measuring the Performance of a Mixed-Vendor Ethernet." *Data Communications*, August, 1987.

CROC83 Crochiere, R.E., and Flanagan, J.L. "Current Perspectives in Digital Speech." *IEEE Communications Magazine*, January, 1983.

CROW73 Crowther, W.; Rettberg, R.; Walden, D.; Orenstein, S.; and Heart, F. "A System for Broadcast Communication: Reservation ALOHA." *Proceedings, Sixth Hawaii International System Science Conference*, 1973.

CUNN80 Cunningham, J.E. *Cable Television*. Indianapolis: Howard W. Sams, 1980.

CZOT87 Czotter, T. "Network Interface Design Guide." *Proceedings, 12th Conference on Local Computer Networks*, October, 1987.

DAHO83 Dahod, A.M. "Local Network Standards: No Utopia." *Data Communications*, March, 1983.

DALA81 Dalal, Y.K., and Printis, R.S. "48-Bit Absolute Internet and Ethernet Host Numbers." *Proceedings, Seventh Data Communications Symposium*, 1981.

DAVI73 Davies, D.W., and Barber, D.L. *Communication Networks for Computers*. New York: Wiley, 1973.

DAVI77 Davidson, J.; Hathaway, W.; Postel, J.; Mimno, N.; Thomas, R.; and Walden, D. "The ARPANET Telnet Protocol: Its Purpose, Principles, Implementation, and Impact on Host Operating System Design." *Proceedings, Fifth Data Communications Symposium*, 1977.

DAVI83 Davidson, J. "OSI Model Layering of a Military Local Network." *Proceedings of the IEEE*, December, 1983.

DAVI84 Davies, D., and Price, W. *Security for Computer Networks*. New York: Wiley, 1984.

DAY80 Day, J. "Terminal Protocols." *IEEE Transactions on Communications*, April, 1980.

DAY81 Day, J. "Terminal, File Transfer, and Remote Job Protocols for Heterogeneous Computer Networks." In *Protocols and Techniques for Data Communication Networks*, edited by F.F. Kuo, Englewood Cliffs, NJ: Prentice-Hall, 1981.

DCA85 Defense Communications Agency. *DDN Protocol Handbook*. Menlo Park, CA: DDN Information Center, December, 1985.

DENN79 Denning, D.E., and Denning, P.J. "Data Security." *Computing Surveys*, September, 1979.

DERF83 Derfler, F., and Stallings, W. *A Manager's Guide to Local Networks*. Englewood Cliffs, NJ: Prentice-Hall/Spectrum, 1983.

DERF86 Derfler, F., and Stallings, W. "The IBM Token-Ring LAN." *PC Magazine*, March 11, 1986.

DIFF76 Diffie, W., and Hellman, M.E. "New Directions in Cryptography." *IEEE Transactions on Information Theory*, November, 1976.

DIGI80 Digital Equipment Corp.; Intel. Corp.; and Xerox Corp. *The Ethernet: A Local Area Network Data Link Layer and Physical Layer Specifications*. September 30, 1980.

DINE80 Dineson, M.A., and Picazo, J.J. "Broadband Technology Magnifies Local Network Capability." *Data Communications*, February, 1980.

DINE81 Dineson, M.A. "Broadband Local Networks Enhance Communication Design." *EDN*, March 4, 1981.

DIXO83 Dixon, R.; Strole, N.; and Markov, J. "A Token-ring Network for Local Data Communications." *IBM Systems Journal*. Nos. 1/2, 1983.

DIXO87 Dixon, R. "Lore of the Token Ring." *IEEE Network*, January, 1987.

DIXO88 Dixon, R., and Pitt, D. "Addressing, Bridging, and Source Routing." *IEEE Network*, January, 1988.

DOD83 Department of Defense. *Military Standard Internet Protocol*, MIL-STD-1777.

DOLL78 Doll, D.R. *Data Communications: Facilities, Networks, and System Design*. New York: Wiley, 1980.

DONN79 Donnelly, J.E., and Yeh, J.W. "Interaction Between Protocol Levels in a Prioritized CSMA Broadcast Network." *Computer Networks*, March, 1979.

DUNB86 Dunbar, R. "Design Considerations for Broadband Coaxial Cable Systems." *IEEE Communications Magazine*, June, 1986.

EDN82 EDN Magazine. "Credibility Problems Could Block LAN Growth." *EDN*, September 1, 1982.

ENOM85 Enomoto, O.; Kohashi, T.; Aomori, T.; Kadota, S.; Oka, S.; and Fujita, K. "Distributed Microprocessors Control Architecture for Versatile

Business Communications." *IEEE Journal on Selected Areas in Communications*, July, 1985.

ESTR86 Estrin, J., and Cheney, K. "Managing Local Area Networks Effectively." *Data Communications*, January, 1986.

FARM69 Farmer, W.D., and Newhall, E.E. "An Experimental Distributed Switching System to Handle Bursty Computer Traffic." *Proceedings, ACM Symposium on Problems in the Optimization of Data Communications*, 1969.

FINE84 Fine, M., and Tobagi, F. "Demand Assignment Multiple-Access Schemes in Broadcast Bus Local Area Networks." *IEEE Transactions on Computers*, December, 1984.

FINL84 Finley, M. "Optical Fibers in Local Area Networks." *IEEE Communications Magazine*, August, 1984.

FLAT84 Flatman, A. "Low-Cost Local Network for Small Systems Grows From IEEE-802.3 Standard." *Electronic Design*, July 26, 1984.

FLEM79 Fleming, P. *Principles of Switching*. Geneva, IL: Lee's abc of the Telephone, 1979.

FORR86 Forrest, S. "Optical Detectors: Three Contenders." *IEEE Spectrum*, May, 1986.

FRAI87 Fraim, L. "Secure Office Management System: The First Commodity Application on a Trusted System." *Proceedings, 1987 Fall Joint Computer Conference*, October, 1987.

FRAN76 Frankel, T. *Tables for Traffic Management and Design*. Geneva, IL: Lee's abc of the Telephone, 1976.

FRAN80 Franta, W.R., and Bilodeau, M.B. "Analysis of a Prioritized CSMA Protocol Based on Staggered Delays." *Acta Informatica*, June, 1980.

FRAN81 Franta, W.R., and Chlamtec, I. *Local Networks*. Lexington, MA: Lexington Books, 1981.

FRAN82 Franta, W.R., and Heath, J.R. *Performance of HYPERchannel Networks: Parameters, Measurements, Models, and Analysis*. University of Minnesota, Computer Science Department, Technical Report 82-3, January, 1982.

FREE80 Freeman, R.L. *Telecommunication System Engineering*. New York: Wiley, 1980.

FREE81 Freeman, R.L. *Telecommunication Transmission Handbook*. New York: Wiley, 1981.

FREE82 Freeman, R.B. "Net Management Choices: Sidestream or Mainstream." *Data Communications*, August, 1982.

FREE85a Freeman, R. *Reference Manual for Telecommunications Engineering*. New York: Wiley, 1985.

FREE85b Freeman, H., and Thurber, K. *Local Network Equipment*. Washington, DC: *IEEE Computer Society Press*, 1985.

GERL88 Gerla, M.; Green, L.; and Rutledge, R. Special Issue on Bridges and Routers. *IEEE Network*, January, 1988.

GILL82 Gilligan, J.M., and Vasak, J.M. "A Generic Security Architecture for Distributed Systems." *Proceedings, Seventh Conference on Local Computer Networks*, 1982.

GOEL79 Goeller, L.F. "Programs for Traffic Calculation." *Business Communications Review*, May-June, 1979.

GOEL83 Goeller, L.F., and Goldston, J.A. "The ABCs of the PBX." *Datamation*, April, 1983.

GOLB86 Golbert, A., and Gandhi, S. *Implementing StarLAN with the Intel 82588*. Intel Application Note AP-236, November 1986. Reprinted in *Microcommunications Handbook*, Intel, 1988.

GONS88 Gonsales, T., and Tobagi, F. "On the Performance Effects of Station Locations and Access Protocol Parameters in Ethernet Networks." *IEEE Transactions on Communications*, April, 1988.

GOOD88 Goodman, J.; Greenberg, A.; Madras, N.; and March, P. "Stability of Binary Exponential Backoff." *Journal of the ACM*, July, 1988.

GRAN83 Grant, A.; Hutchinson, D.; and Shepherd, W. "A Gateway for Linking Local Area Networks and X.25 Networks." *Proceedings, SIGCOMM 83 Symposium*, 1983.

GRAU84 Graube, M., and Molder, M. "Local Area Networks." *IEEE Computer*, October, 1984.

GREG86 Gregory, P. "A Typology of Local Area Networks, *Data Communications*, August, 1986.

GRNA80 Grnarov, A.; Kleinrock, L.; and Gerla, M. "A Highly Reliable Distributed Loop Network Architecture." *Proceedings, International Symposium on Fault-Tolerant Computing*, 1980.

HAFN74 Hafner, E.R.; Nenadal, Z.; and Tschanz, M. "A Digital Loop Communications System." *IEEE Transactions on Communications*, June, 1974.

HALL85 "Factory Networks." *Micro Communications*, February, 1985.

HAMM86 Hammond, J., and O'Reilly, P. *Performance Analysis of Local Computer Networks*. Reading, MA: Addison-Wesley, 1986.

HAMN88 Hamner, M., and Samsen, G. "Source Routing Bridge Implementation." *IEEE Network*, January, 1988.

HANS81 Hanson, K.; Chou, W.; and Nilsson, A. "Integration of Voice, Data, and Image Traffic in a Wideband Local Network." *Proceedings, Computer Networking Symposium*, 1981.

HART88 Hart, J. "Extending the IEEE 802.1 MAC Bridge Standard to Remote Bridges." *IEEE Network*, January, 1988.

HAWE84 Hawe, B.; Kirby, A.; and Stewart, B. "Transparent Interconnection of Local Area Networks with Bridges." *Journal of Telecommunication Networks*, Summer, 1984.

HAYE81 Hayes, J.F. "Local Distribution in Computer Communications." *IEEE Communications Magazine*, March, 1981.

HELD87 Held, G. "A Dozen Ways to Beef Up Your Network with a Port Selector." *Data Communications*, June, 1987.

HERR79 Herr, D.E., and Nute, C.T. "Modeling the Effects of Packet Truncation on the Throughput of CSMA Networks." *Proceedings, Computer Networking Symposium*, 1979.

HEYM82 Heyman, D.P. "An Analysis of the Carrier-Sense Multiple-Access Protocol." *Bell System Technical Journal*, October, 1982.

HEYW81 Heywood, P. "The Cambridge Ring Is Still Making the Rounds." *Data Communications*, July, 1981.

HOHN80 Hohn, W.C. "The Control Data Loosely Coupled Network Lower Level Protocols." *Proceedings, National Computer Conference*, 1980.

HONG86 Hong, J. "Timing Jitter." *Data Communications*, February, 1986.

HOPK77 Hopkins, G.T. *A Bus Communications System.* MITRE Technical Report MTR-3515, 1977.

HOPK79 Hopkins, G.T. "Multimode Communications on the MITRENET." *Proceedings, Local Area Communications Network Symposium*, 1979.

HOPK80 Hopkins, G.T., and Wagner, P.E. *Multiple Access Digital Communications System.* U.S. Patent 4,210,780, July 1, 1980.

HOPK82 Hopkins, G.T., and Meisner, N.B. "Choosing Between Broadband and Baseband Local Networks." *Mini-Micro Systems*, June, 1982.

HOPP83 Hopper, A., and Williamson, R. "Design and Use of an Integrated Cambridge Ring." *IEEE Journal on Selected Areas in Communications*, November, 1983.

HUBE83 Huber, D.; Steinlin, W.; and Wild, P. "SILK: An Implementation of a Buffer Insertion Ring." *IEEE Journal on Selected Areas in Communications*, November, 1983.

IBM71 IBM Corp. *Analysis of Some Queueing Models in Real-Time Systems.* GF20-0007, 1971.

IBM82 IBM Corp. *IBM Series/Local Communications Controller Feature Description.* GA34-0142-2, 1982.

IBM84a IBM Corp. *A Building Planning Guide for Communication Wiring.* G320-8059, March, 1984.

IBM84b IBM Corp. *An Introduction to Local Area Networks.* GC20-8203, July, 1984.

IEEE85a The Institute of Electrical and Electronics Engineers. *Logical Link Control.* American National Standard ANSI/IEEE Std 802.2-1985.

IEEE85b The Institute of Electrical and Electronics Engineers. *Carrier Sense Multiple Access with Collision Detection (CSMA/CD) Access Method and Physical Layer Specifications.* American National Standard ANSI/IEEE Std 802.3-1985.

IEEE85c The Institute of Electrical and Electronics Engineers. *Token-Passing Bus Access Method and Physical Layer Specifications.* American National Standard ANSI/IEEE Std 802.4-1985.

IEEE85d The Institute of Electrical and Electronics Engineers. *Token Ring Access Method and Physical Layer Specifications.* American National Standard ANSI/IEEE Std 802.5-1985.

IEEE85e IEEE Computer Society. *Draft IEEE Standard 802.1 (Part A): Overview and Architecture*, October, 1985.

IEEE88a The Institute of Electrical and Electronics Engineers. *IEEE Standard 802.1: Overview and Architecture*, July, 1988.

IEEE88b The Institute of Electrical and Electronics Engineers. *IEEE Standard 802.1: Source Routing*, September, 1988.

IEEE88c The Institute of Electrical and Electronics Engineers. *IEEE 802.5, Appendix D: Multi-ring Networks (Source Routing)*, November, 1988.

INOS79 Inose, H. *An Introduction to Digital Integrated Communications Systems.* Tokyo: University of Tokyo Press, 1979.

IRLA88 Irland, E. "Assuring Quality and Reliability of Complex Electronic Systems: Hardware and Software." *Proceedings of the IEEE*, January, 1988.

ISO87 International Organization for Standardization. *Network Service Definition, Addendum 1: Connectionless-mode Transmission*, ISO 8348/Add. 1, 1987.

ISO88 International Organization for Standardization. *Protocol for Providing the Connectionless-mode Network Service (Internetwork Protocol)*, ISO 8473, 1988.

ISRA87 Israel, J., and Weissberger, A. "Communicating Between Heterogeneous Networks." *Data Communications*, March, 1987.

JACK63 Jackson, J.R. "Job Shop-like Queueing Systems." *Management Sciences*, 1963.

JACO78 Jacobs, I.; Binder, R.; and Hoversten, E. "General Purpose Packet Satellite Networks." *Proceedings of the IEEE*, November, 1978.

JACO87 Jacobson, D., et al. "A Master/Slave Monitor Measurement Technique for an Operating Ethernet Network." *IEEE Networks*, July, 1987.

JAJS83 Jajszczyk, A. "On Nonblocking Switching Networks Composed of Digital Symmetrical Matrices." *IEEE Transactions on Communications*, January, 1983.

JAYA84 Jayant, N., and Noll, P. *Digital Coding of Waveforms.* Englewood Cliffs, NJ: Prentice-Hall, 1984.

JAYA87 Jayasumana, A. "Performance Analysis of Token Bus Priority Schemes: *Proceedings, INFOCOM '87*, 1987.

JEWE85 Jewett, R. "The Fourth-Generation PBX: Beyond the Integration of Voice and Data." *Telecommunications*, February, 1985.

JOEL77 Joel, A.E. "What Is Telecommunications Circuit Switching?" *Proceedings of the IEEE*, September, 1977.

JOEL79a Joel, A.E. "Circuit Switching: Unique Architecture and Applications." *Computer*, June, 1979.

JOEL79b Joel, A.E. "Digital Switching—How it Has Developed." *IEEE Transactions on Communications*, July, 1979.

JOEL85 Joel, A., ed. *Special Issue on Serving the Business Customer Using Advances in Switching Technologies.* IEEE Journal on Selected Areas in Communications, July, 1985.

JOHN86 Johnson, M. "Reliability Mechanisms of the FDDI High Bandwidth Token Ring Protocol." *Computer Networks and ISDN Systems*, Vol 11, 1986.

JOHN87 Johnson, M. "Proof that Timing Requirements of the FDDI Token Ring Protocol are Satisfied." *IEEE Transactions on Communications*, June, 1987.

JOHN88 Johnson, A., and Malek, M. "Survey of Software Tools for Evaluating Reliability, Availability, and Serviceability." *ACM Computing Surveys*, December, 1988.

JOLL68 Jolley, E.H. *Introduction to Telephony and Telegraphy.* New York: Hart, 1968.

JONE85 Jones, K. "Cheapernet Makes Local Area Networking More Affordable." *Mini-Micro Systems*, January, 1985.

JORD85 Jordan, E., ed. *Reference Data for Engineers: Radio, Electronics, Computer, and Communications.* Indianapolis, IN: Howard Sams & Co., 1985.

JOSH84 Joshi, S., and Iyer, V. "New Standards for Local Networks Push Upper Limits for Lightwave Data." *Data Communications*, July, 1984.

JOSH85 Joshi, S. "Making the LAN Connection with a Fiber Optic Standard." *Computer Design*, September, 1985.

JOSH86 Joshi, S. "High-Performance Networks: A Focus on the Fiber Distributed Data Interface (FDDI) Standard." *IEEE Micro*, June, 1986.

KAJI83 Kajiwara, M. "Trends in Digital Switching System Architectures." *IEEE Communications Magazine*, May, 1983.

KANE80 Kane, D.A. "Data Communications Network Switching Methods," *Computer Design*, April, 1980.

KARP82 Karp, P.M., and Socher, I.D. "Designing Local-Area Networks." *Mini-Micro Systems*, April, 1982.

KASS79 Kasson, J.M. "Survey of Digital PBX Design." *IEEE Transactions on Communications*, July, 1979.

KATK81a Katkin, R.D., and Sprung, J.G. "Simulating a Cable Bus Network in a Multicomputer and Large-Scale Application Environment." *Proceedings, Sixth Conference on Local Computer Networks*, 1981.

KATK81b Katkin, R.D., and Sprung, J.G. *Application of Local Bus Network Technology to the Evolution of Large Multi-computer Systems.* MITRE Technical Report MTR-81W290, November, 1981.

KATZ78 Katzan, H. *An Introduction to Distributed Data Processing.* New York: Petrocelli Books, 1978.

KAUF86 Kaufman, H. "PBX Versus LAN." *Telecommunications*, May, 1986.

KECK85 Keck, D. "Fundamentals of Optical Waveguide Fibers." *IEEE Communications Magazine*, May, 1985.

KEIS85 Keiser, B. and Strange, E. *Digital Telephony and Network Integration.* New York: Van Nostrand Reinhold, 1985.

KELL83 Keller, H.; Meyr, H.; and Mueller, H. "Transmission Design Criteria for a Synchronous Token Ring." *IEEE Journal on Selected Areas in Communications*, November, 1983.

KELL84 Kelley, R.; Jones, J.; Bhatt, V.; and Pate, P. "Transceiver Design and Implementation Experience in an Ethernet-Compatible Fiber Optic Local Area Network." *Proceedings, INFOCOM 84*, 1984.

KENT81 Kent, S.T. "Security in Computer Networks." In *Protocols and Techniques for Data Communication Networks*, edited by F.F. Kuo. Englewood Cliffs, NJ: Prentice-Hall, 1981.

KILL82 Killen, M. "The Microcomputer Connection to Local Networks." *Data Communications*, December, 1982.

KIM88 Kim, G. *Broadband LAN Technology.* Norwood, MA: Artech House, 1988.

KLEE82 Klee, K.; Verity, J.W.; and Johnson, J. "Battle of the Networkers." *Datamation*, March, 1982.

KLEI75 Kleinrock, L., and Tobagi, F.A. "Packet Switching in Radio Channels: Part I: Carrier Sense Multiple-Access Modes and Their Throughput-Delay Characteristics." *IEEE Transactions on Communications*, December, 1975.

KLEI76 Kleinrock, L. *Queueing Systems, Vol. II: Computer Applications.* New York: Wiley, 1976.

KLEI86a Klein, M., and Balph T. "Carrierband is Low-Cost, Single-Channel Solution for MAP." *Computer Design*, February 1, 1986.

KLEI86b Kleinrock, L. "Channel Efficiency for LANs." in [PICK86].

KLIN86 Klinck, C. "Just When You Thought It Made Sense to Get Rid of Centrex." *Data Communications*, March, 1986.

KOBA78 Kobayashi, K. *Modeling and Analysis: An Introduction to System Performance and Evaluation Methodology.* Reading, MA: Addison-Wesley, 1978.

KRON86 Kronenberg, N.; Levy, H.; and Strecker, W. "VAXclusters: A Closely-Coupled Distributed System." *ACM Transactions on Computer Systems*, May, 1986.

KRUT81 Krutsch, T.E. "A User Speaks Out: Broadband or Baseband for Local Nets?" *Data Communications*, December, 1981.

KUMM87 Kummerle, K.; Limb, J.; and Tobagi, F. *Advances in Local Area Networks*. New York: IEEE Press, 1987.

KURO84 Kurose, J.; Schwartz, M.; and Yemini, Y. "Multiple-Access Protocols and Time-Constrained Communication." *ACM Computing Surveys*, March, 1984.

LE88 Le, K., and Raghavendra, C. "Fault-Tolerant Routing in a Class of Double Loop Networks." *Proceedings, IEEE INFOCOM '88*, March, 1988.

LEBA86 LeBarre, L., and Brusil, P. "Metrics and Measurements for Evaluating LAN Terminal Communications." *Proceedings, Fifth Annual International Phoenix Conference on Computers and Communications*, March, 1986.

LEON88 Leong, J. "A Practical Guide to Ethernet." in [STALL88b].

LI87 Li, V., editor. Performance Evaluation of Multiple-Access Networks. *IEEE Journal on Selected Areas in Communications*, July, 1987.

LI88 Li, T., and Linke, R. "Multigigabit-Per-Second Lightwave Systems Research for Long-Haul Applications." *IEEE Communications Magazine*, April, 1988.

LIBO85 Liboff, R., and Dalman, G. *Transmission Lines, Waveguides, and Smith Charts*. New York: Macmillan, 1985.

LISS81 Lissack, T.; Maglaris, B.; and Chin, H. "Impact of Microprocessor Architecture on Local Network Interface Adapters." *Proceedings, Conference on Local Networks and Office Automation Systems*, 1981.

LIU78 Liu, M.T. "Distributed Loop Computer Networks." In *Advances in Computers, Vol. 17*. New York: Academic Press, 1978.

LIU82 Liu, M.T.; Hilal, W.; and Groomes, B.H. "Performance Evaluation of Channel Access Protocols for Local Computer Networks." *Proceedings, COMPCON 82 Fall*, 1982.

LOVE87 Love, R., and Toher, T. "How to Design and Build a Token Ring LAN." *Data Communications*, May, 1987.

LOWE83 Lowe, H. "OSI Virtual Terminal Service." *Proceedings of the IEEE*, December, 1983.

LUCZ78 Luczak, E.C. "Global Bus Computer Communication Techniques." *Proceedings, Computer Network Symposium*, 1978.

MAGL80 Maglaris, B., and Lissack, T. "An Integrated Broadband Local Network Architecture." *Proceedings, Fifth Conference on Local Computer Networks*, 1980.

MAGL81 Maglaris, B.; Lissack, T.; and Austin, M. "End-to-End Delay Analysis on Local Area Networks: An Office Building Scenario." *Proceedings, National Telecommunications Conference*, 1981.

MAGL82 Maglaris, B., and Lissack, T. "Performance Evaluation of Interface Units for Broadcast Local Area Networks." *Proceedings, COMPCON Fall 82*, 1982.

MAGN79 Magnee, F.; Endrizzi, A.; and Day, J. "A Survey of Terminal Protocols." *Computer Networks*, November, 1979.

MARA82 Marthe, M., and Hawe, B. "Predicted Capacity of Ethernet in a University Environment." *Proceedings, SOUTHCON 82*, 1982.

MARK78 Mark, J.W. "Global Scheduling Approach to Conflict-Free Multiaccess via a Data Bus." *IEEE Transactions on Communications*, September, 1978.

MART67 Martin, J. *Design of Real-Time Computer Systems*. Englewood Cliffs, NJ: Prentice-Hall, 1967.

MART72 Martin, J. *Systems Analysis for Data Transmission*. Englewood Cliffs, NJ: Prentice-Hall, 1972.

MART76 Martin, J. *Telecommunications and the Computer, 2nd Ed.* Englewood Cliffs, NJ: Prentice-Hall, 1976.

MART81a Martin, J. *Computer Networks and Distributed Processing*. Englewood Cliffs, NJ: Prentice-Hall, 1981.

MART81b Martin, J. *Design and Strategy for Distributed Data Processing*. Englewood Cliffs, NJ: Prentice-Hall, 1981.

MATS82 Matsukane, E. "Network Administration and Control System for a Broadband Local Area Communications Network." *Proceedings, COMPCON FALL 82*, 1982.

MCCL83 McClelland, F. "Services and Protocols of the Physical Layer." *Proceedings of the IEEE*, December, 1983.

MCCO88 McCool, J. "FDDI: Getting to know the Inside of the Ring." *Data Communications*, March, 1988.

MCDO83 McDonald, J., ed. *Fundamentals of Digital Switching*. New York: Plenum, 1983.

MCGA85 McGarry, S. "Networking Has a Job To Do in the Factory." *Data Communications*, February, 1985.

MCNA82 McNamara, J.E. *Technical Aspects of Data Communication*. Bedford, MA: Digital Press, 1982.

MEHT87 Mehta, S. "Who Needs a LAN?" *LAN Magazine*, June, 1987.

MEHT88 Mehta, S. "The Big Switch." *LAN Magazine*, June, 1988.

METC76 Metcalfe, M., and Boggs, D.R. "Ethernet: Distributed Packet Switching for Local Computer Networks." *Communications of the ACM*, July, 1976.

METC77 Metcalfe, M.; Boggs, D.R.; Thacker, C.P.; and Lampson, B.W. "Multipoint Data Communication System with Collision Detection." *U.S. Patent* 4,063,220, 1977.

METC83 Metcalfe, R. "Controller/Transceiver Board Drives Ethernet into PC Domain." *Mini-Micro Systems*, January, 1983.

MIER86 Mier, E. "Light Sources and Wavelengths." *Data Communications*, February, 1986.

MILL82 Miller, C.K., and Thompson, D.M. "Making a Case for Token Passing in Local Networks." *Data Communications*, March, 1982.

MITC81 Mitchell, L.C. "A Methodology for Predicting End-to-End Responsiveness in a Local Area Network." *Proceedings, Computer Networking Symposium*, 1981.

MITC86 Mitchell, L., and Lide, D. "End-to-End Performance Modeling of Local Area Networks." *IEEE Journal on Selected Areas in Communications*, September, 1986.

MOLL87 Molle, M.; Sohraby, K.; and Venetsanopoulos, A. "Space-Time Models of Asynchronous CSMA Protocols for Local Area Networks." *IEEE Journal on*

Selected Areas in Communications, July, 1987.

MULL87 Muller, N. "Enhanced Data Switches May Outshine LAN, PBX Alternatives." *Data Communications*, May, 1987.

MULQ88a Mulqueen, J. "Flashing Images Across Networks—A Technology Whose Time is Coming." *Data Communications*, May, 1988.

MULQ88b Mulqueen, J. "Phone Wire Loses Its Wimp Image in High-Speed Ethernet LANs." *Data Communications*, December, 1988.

MURA88 Murata, M., and Takagi, H. "Two-Layer Modeling for Local Area Networks." *IEEE Transactions on Communications*, September, 1988.

MYER82 Myers, W. "Toward a Local Network Standard." *IEEE Micro*, August, 1982.

NASS85 Nassehi, M.; Tobaji, F.; and Marhic, M. "Fiber Optic Configurations for Local Area Networks." *IEEE Journal on Selected Areas in Communications*, November, 1985.

NESS81 Nessett, D.M. *HYPERchannel Architecture: A Case Study of Some Inadequacies in the ISO OSI Reference Model*. Lawrence Livermore Laboratory Report UCRL-53139, April, 1981.

OHSH86 Ohshima, S.; Ito, T.; Donuma, K.; Sugiyama, H.; and Fujii, Y. "Small Loss-Deviation Tapered-Fiber Star Coupler for LANs." *Journal of Lightwave Technology*, June, 1986.

OLSE83 Olsen, R.; Seifert, W.; and Taylor, J. "Tutorial: RS-232-C Data Switching on Local Networks." *Data Communications*, September, 1983.

OREI82 O'Reilly, P.J.; Hammond, J.L.; Schalg, J.H.; and Murray, D.N. "Design of an Emulation Facility for Performance Studies of CSMA-Type Local Networks." *Proceedings, Seventh Conference on Local Computer Networks*, 1982.

ORLO88 Orlov, M. "Another Twist: Twisted-Pair Ethernet May Not Be All It's Cracked Up to Be." *LAN Magazine*, August, 1988.

PARL85 Parlatore, P. "Hooking Into AT&T Networks." *Systems & Software*, September, 1985.

PATE87 Paterakis, M.; Georgiadis, L.; and Papantoni-Kazakos, P. "On the Relation Between the Finite and Infinite Population Models for a Class of Random Access Algorithms." *IEEE Transactions on Communications*, November, 1987.

PENN79 Penny, B.K., and Baghdadi, A.A. "Survey of Computer Communications Loop Networks." *Computer Communications*, August and October, 1979.

PERL84 Perlman, R. "An Algorithm for Distributed Computation of a Spanning Tree." Proceedings, Ninth Data Communications Symposium, 1984.

PERS83 Personick, S. "Review of Fundamentals of Optical Fiber Systems." *IEEE Journal on Selected Areas in Communications*, April, 1983.

PFIS82 Pfister, G.M., and O'Brien, B.V. "Comparing the CBX to the Local Network—and the Winner Is?" *Data Communications*, July, 1982.

PHIN83 Phinney, T. and Jelatis, G. "Error Handling in the IEEE Token-Passing Bus LAN." *IEEE Journal on Selected Areas in Communications*, November, 1983.

PICK86 Pickholz, R. *Local Area and Multiple Access Networks*. Rockville, MD: Computer Science Press, 1986.

PIER72 Pierce, J.R. "Network for Block Switches of Data." *Bell System Technical Journal*, July/August, 1972.

PISC86 Piscitello, D.; Weissberger, A.; Stein, S.; and Chapin, L. "Internetworking in an OSI Environment." *Data Communications*, May, 1986.

PITT85 Pitt, D.; Sy, K.; and Donnan, R. "Source Routing for Bridged Local Area Networks." *Proceedings, Globecom '85*, December 1985. Reprinted in [KUMM87].

PITT86 Pitt, D., and Sy, K. "Address-Based and Non-Address-Based Routing Schemes for Interconnected Local Area Networks." in [PICK86].

PITT87a Pitt, D. "Standards for the Token Ring." *IEEE Network*, January 1987.

PITT87b Pitt, D., and Winkler, J. "Table-Free Bridging." *IEEE Journal on Selected Areas in Communications*, December 1987.

POPE79 Popek, G.J., and Kline, C.S. "Encryption and Secure Computer Networks." *Computing Surveys*, December, 1979.

POST80 Postel, J.B. "Internetwork Protocol Approaches." *IEEE Transactions on Communications*, April, 1980.

POST81 Postel, J. *Internet Control Message Protocol.* RFC 792, Menlo Park, CA: DDN Network Information Center, September 1981. Reprinted in [DCA85].

PRES88 Press, L. "Benchmarks for LAN Performance Evaluation." Communications of the ACM, August, 1988.

PROT82 Protunotarios, E.N.; Sykas, E.P.; and Apostolopoulos, T.K. "Hybrid Protocols for Contention Resolution in Local Area Networks." *Proceedings, Seventh Conference on Local Computer Networks*, 1982.

RAGH81 Raghavendra, C.S., and Gerla, M. "Optimal Loop Topologies for Distributed Systems." *Proceedings, Seventh Data Communications Symposium*, 1981.

RAND78 Randell, B.; Lee, P.A.; and TreLeaven, P.C. "Reliability Issues in Computing System Design." *Computing Surveys*, June, 1978.

RATN83 Ratner, D. "How Broadband Modems Operate on Token-Passing Nets." *Data Communications*, June, 1983.

RAUC83 Rauch-Hindin, W.B. "Upper-Level Network Protocols." *Electronic Design*, March 3, 1983.

RAWS78 Rawson, E.G., and Metcalfe, R.M. "Fibernet: Multimode Optical Fibers for Local Computer Networks." *IEEE Transactions on Communications*, July, 1978.

REAM75 Reames, C.C., and Liu, M.T. "A Loop Network for Simultaneous Transmission of Variable-Length Messages." *Proceedings, Second Annual Symposium on Computer Architecture*, 1975.

RELC87 Relcom, Inc. *Carrier-Band Network Handbook, Second Edition.* Forest Grove, OR, 1987.

RHOD83 Rhodes, N. "Interaction of Network Design and Fiber Optic Component Design in Local Area Networks." *IEEE Journal on Selected Areas in Communications*, April, 1983.

RICH80 Richer, J.; Steiner, M.; and Sengoku, M. "Office Communications and the Digital PBX." *Computer Networks*, December, 1980.

ROBE73 Roberts, L.G. "Dynamic Allocation of Satellite Capacity Through Packet Reservation." *Proceedings, National Computer Conference*, 1973.

ROBE75 Roberts, L.G. "ALOHA Packet System With and Without Slots and Capture." *Computer Communications Review*, April, 1975.

RODR85 Rodrigues, P.; Fratta, L.; and Gerla, M. "Tokenless Protocols for Fiber Optic Local Area Networks." *IEEE Journal on Selected Areas in Communications*, November, 1985.

ROSE82 Rosenthal, R., ed. *The Selection of Local Area Computer Networks.* National Bureau of Standards Special Publication 500-96, November, 1982.

ROSE88 Rosenberg, R. "The Shots Seen Round the World." *Data Communications*, December, 1988.

ROSS86 Ross, F. "FDDI: A Tutorial." *IEEE Communications Magazine*, May, 1986.

ROSS87 Ross, F. "Rings are 'Round for Good!" *IEEE Network*, January, 1987.

ROUN83 Rounds, F. "Use Modeling Techniques to Estimate Local-net Success." *EDN*, April 14, 1983.

RUSH82 Rush, J.R. "Microwave Links Add Flexibility to Local Networks." *Electronics*, January 13, 1982.

RUSH83 Rushby, J., and Randell, B. "A Distributed Secure System." *Computer*, July, 1983.

SACH88 Sachs, S. "Alternative Local Area Network Access Protocols." *IEEE Communications Magazine*, March, 1988.

SALT79 Saltzer, J.H., and Pogran, K.T. "A Star-Shaped Ring Network with High Maintainability." *Proceedings, Local Area Communications Network Symposium*, 1979.

SALT83 Saltzer, J.; Pogran, K.; and Clark, D. "Why a Ring?" *Computer Networks*, March, 1983.

SALW83 Salwen, H. "In Praise of Ring Architecture for Local Area Networks." *Computer Design*, March, 1983.

SAND82 Sanders, L. "Manchester Code Gaining on NRZ" *Electronic Design*, August 5, 1982.

SAST85 Sastry, A. "Maximum Mean Data Rate in a Local Area Network with a Specified Maximum Source Message Load." *Proceedings, 1985 INFOCOM Conference*, March, 1985.

SAUE81 Sauer, C.H., and Chandy, K.M. *Computer Systems Performance Modeling*, Englewood Clliffs, NJ: Prentice-Hall, 1981.

SCHM83 Schmidt, R.; Rawson, E.; Norton, R.; Jackson, S.; and Bailey, M. "Fibernet II: A Fiber Optic Ethernet." *IEEE Journal on Selected Areas in Communication*, November, 1983.

SCHM88 Schmidt, R. "Developing Ethernet Capability on Unshielded Twisted Pair." *Telecommunications*, January, 1988.

SCHN83 Schneidewind, N. "Interconnecting Local Networks to Long-Distance Networks." *Computer*, September, 1983.

SCHO84 Schoeffler, J. "Distributed Computer Systems for Industrial Process Control." *Computer*, February, 1984.

SCHO88 Scholl, F., and Coden, M. "Passive Optical Star Systems for Fiber Optic Local Area Networks." *IEEE Journal on Selected Areas in Communications*, July, 1988.

SCHW77 Schwartz, M. *Computer-Communication Network Design and Analysis.* Englewood Cliffs, N.J.: Prentice-Hall, 1977.

REFERENCES

SCHW82 Schwartz, J., and Melling, W.P. "Sharing Logic and Work." *Datamation*, November, 1982.

SEAM82 Seaman, J. "Local Networks: Making the Right Connection." *Computer Decisions*, June, 1982.

SEE86 See, M. "Specifying Fiber." *Data Communications*, March, 1986.

SEVC87 Sevcik, K., and Johnson, M. "Cycle Time Properties of the FDDI Token Ring Protocol." *IEEE Transactions on Software Engineering*, March, 1987.

SHAR82 Sharma, R.L.; Sousa, P.T.; and Ingle, A.D. *Network Systems: Modeling, Analysis, and Design*. New York: Van Nostrand Reinhold, 1982.

SHIR82 Shirey, R.W. "Security in Local Area Networks." *Proceedings, Computer Networking Symposium*, 1982.

SHIR83 Shirey, R. *Security Architectures for Local Area Networks in Command Centers*, Mitre Technical Report MTR-83W00162.

SHOC80a Shoch, J.F., and Hupp, J.A. "Measured Performance of an Ethernet Local Network." *Communications of the ACM*, December, 1980.

SHOC80b Shoch, J.F. *An Annotated Bibliography on Local Computer Networks*. Xerox Palo Alto Research Center, April, 1980.

SHOC82 Shoch, J.F.; Dala, Y.K.; and Redell, D.D. "Evolution of the Ethernet Local Computer Network." *Computer*, August, 1982.

SIDH82a Sidhu, D., and Gasser, M. "A Multilevel Secure Local Area Network." *Proceedings of the 1982 Symposium on Security and Privacy*, 1982.

SIDH82b Sidhu, D.P. "A Local Area Network Design for Military Applications." *Proceedings, Seventh Conference on Local Computer Networks*, 1982.

SIDH83 Sidhu, D. "Local Area Military Network." *Proceedings of the IEEE International Conference on Communications*, 1983.

SOHA87 Soha, M. "A Distributed Approach to LAN Monitoring Using Intelligent High Performance Monitors." *IEEE Network*, July, 1987.

SOHA88 Soha, M., and Perlman, R. "Comparison of Two LAN Bridge Approaches." *IEEE Network*, January, 1988.

SKAP79 Skaperda, N.J. "Some Architectural Alternatives in the Design of a Digital Switch." *IEEE Transactions on Communications*, July, 1979.

SPAN81 Spaniol, O. "Analysis and Performance Evaluation of HYPERchannel Access Protocols." *Performance Evaluation*, 1981.

SPAN86 Spanier, S. "FEPs Ease Migration to New LAN Protocols." *Mini-Micro Systems*, September, 1986.

SPEC82 Spector, A. "Performing Remote Operations Efficiently on a Local Computer Network." *Communications of the ACM*, April, 1982.

STAC80 Stack, T.R., and Dillencourt, K.A. "Protocols for Local Area Networks." *Proceedings, NBS Symposium on Computer Network Protocols*, 1980.

STAH82 Stahlman, M. "Inside Wang's Local Net Architecture." *Data Communications*, January, 1982.

STAL87 Stallings, W. *Computer Communications: Architectures, Protocols, and Standards*, Second Edition. Washington, DC: IEEE Computer Society Press, 1987.

STAL88a Stallings, W. *Data and Computer Communications, Second Edition*. New York: Macmillan, 1988.

STAL88b Stallings, W. *Local Network Technology, Third Edition*. Washington, DC: IEEE Computer Society Press, 1988.

STAL90a Stallings, W. *Business Data Communications*. New York: Macmillan, 1990.

STAL90b Stallings, W. *Handbook of Computer-Communications Standards: Volume I: The Open Systems Interconnection (OSI) Model and OSI-Related Standards, Second Edition*. Indianapolis, IN: Howard W. Sams & Co., 1990.

STAL90c Stallings, W. *Handbook of Computer-Communications Standards: Volume II: Local Area Network Standards, Second Edition*. Indianapolis, IN: Howard W. Sams & Co., 1990.

STAL90d *Handbook of Computer-Communications Standards*, Second Edition. *Volume III, The TCP/IP Protocol Suite*. Indianapolis, IN: Howard W Sams & Co., 1990.

STIE81 Stieglitz, M. "Local Network Access Tradeoffs." *Computer Design*, October, 1981.

STIE85 Stieglitz, M. "X.25 Standard Simplifies Linking of Different LANs." *Computer Design*, February, 1985.

STIX88 Stix, G. "Telephone Wiring: a Conduit for Networking Standards." *IEEE Spectrum*, June, 1988.

STRA87 Straus, J., and Kawasake, B. "Passive Optical Components." in [BASC87].

STRE84 Strecker, W. "CI: A High Speed Interconnect for Computers and Mass Storage Controllers." *Proceedings, Eighth International Fiber Optics Communications and Local Area Network Exposition*, 1984.

STRO83 Strole, N. "A Local Communication Network Based on Interconnected Token-Access Rings: A Tutorial." *IBM Journal of Research and Development*, September, 1983.

STRO86 Strole, N. "How IBM Addresses LAN Requirements with the Token Ring." *Data Communications*, February, 1986.

STRO87 Strole, N. "The IBM Token Ring Network—A Functional Overview." *IEEE Network*, January, 1987.

STRO89 Strole, N. "Inside Token Ring Version II, According to Big Blue." *Data Communications*, January, 1989.

STUC85 Stuck, B., and Arthurs, E. *A Computer Communications Network Performance Analysis Primer*. Englewood Cliffs, NJ: Prentice-Hall, 1985.

SUDA83 Suda, T.; Miyahara, H.; and Hasegawa, T. "Performance Evaluation of an Integrated Access Scheme in a Satellite Communications Channel." *IEEE Journal on Selected Areas in Communications*, January, 1983.

SUNS77 Sunshine, C. "Interconnection of Computer Networks." *Computer Networks*, February, 1977.

SUNS85 Sunshine, C, and Ennis, G. "Broad-band Personal Computer LANs." *IEEE Journal on Selected Areas in Communications*, May, 1985.

TAKA85 Takagi, H., and Kleinrock, L. "Output Processes in Contention Packet Broadcasting Systems." *IEEE Transactions on Communications*, November, 1985.

TAKA88 Takagi, H. "Queuing Analysis of Polling Models." *ACM Computing Surveys*, March, 1988.

TANE81 Tanenbaum, A.S. *Computer Networks*. Englewood Cliffs, NJ: Prentice-Hall, 1981.

TASA86 Tasaka, S. *Performance Analysis of Multiple Access Protocols*. Cambridge, MA: MIT Press, 1986.

TASS85 Tassey, G. *Technology and Economic Assessment of Optoelectronics*. National Bureau of Standards, Planning Report 23, October, 1985.

TERP87 Terplan, K. *Communication Networks Management.* Englewood Cliffs, NJ: Prentice-Hall, 1987.

THOR80 Thornton, J.E. "Back-End Network Approaches." *Computer,* February, 1980.

THUR79 Thurber, K.J., and Freeman, H.A. "Architecture Considerations for Local Computer Networks." *Proceedings, First International Conference on Distributed Computer Systems,* 1979.

THUR85 Thurber, K. "Department Solutions." *Datamation,* September, 1985.

TOBA80a Tobagi, F.A., and Hunt, V.B. "Performance Analysis of Carrier Sense Multiple Access with Collision Detection." *Computer Networks,* October/November, 1980.

TOBA80b Tobagi, F.A. "Multiaccess Protocols in Packet Communications Systems." *IEEE Transactions on Communications,* April, 1980.

TOBA82 Tobagi, F.A. "Distributions of Packet Delay and Interdeparture Time in Slotted ALOHA and Carrier Sense Multiple Access." *Journal of the ACM,* October, 1982.

TOBA83 Tobagi, F.; Borgonova, F.; and Fratta, L. "Expressnet: A High-Performance Integrated Services Local Area Network." *IEEE Journal on Selected Areas in Communications,* November, 1983.

TROP81 Tropper, C. *Local Computer Network Technologies.* New York: Academic Press, 1981.

TSAO84 Tsao, D. "A Local Area Network Architecture Overview." *IEEE Communications Magazine,* August, 1984.

ULLA87 Ullal, J. and McCool, J. "Fiberoptic Network Standard Delivers Speed and Reliability." *Computer Design,* October 1, 1987.

VONA80 Vonarx, M. "Controlling the Mushrooming Communications Net." *Data Communications,* June, 1980.

WARN80 Warner, C. "Connecting Local Networks to Long-Haul Networks: Issues in Protocol Design." *Proceedings, Fifth Conference on Local Computer Networks,* 1980.

WATS80 Watson, W.B. "Simulation Study of the Configuration Dependent Performance of a Prioritized, CSMA Broadcast Network." *Proceedings, Fifth Conference on Local Computer Networks,* 1980.

WATS82 Watson, W.B. "Validation of a Discrete Event Computer Model of Network Systems Corporation's HYPERchannel." *Proceedings, Seventh Conference on Local Computer Networks,* 1982.

WEBB84 Webb, M. "Build a VLSI-Based Workstation for the Ethernet Environment." *EDN,* February 23, 1984.

WEIS87 Weissberger, A., and Israel, J. "What the New Internetworking Standards Provide." *Data Communications,* February, 1987.

WERN86 Wernli, M. "The Choices in Designing a Fiber-Optic Network." *Data Communications,* June, 1986.

WILE82 Wiley, J.M. "Achilles' Heels of Modern Networking: A User's Lament." *Data Communications,* April, 1982.

WILK79 Wilkes, M., and Wheeler, D. "The Cambridge Digital Communication Ring." *Proceedings, Local Area Communications Network Symposium,* 1979.

WILL73 Willard, D. "MITRIX: A Sophisticated Digital Cable Communications System." *Proceedings, National Telecommunications Conference,* 1973.

WILL81 Willard, D.G. "Reliability/Availability of Wideband Local Communication Networks." *Computer Design*, August, 1981.

WOLF78 Wolf, J.J., and Liu, M.T. "A Distributed Double-Loop Computer Network." *Proceedings, Seventh Texas Conference of Computing Systems*, 1978.

WONG84 Wong, J. and Bux, W. "Analytic Modeling of an Adapter to Local Area Networks." *IEEE Transactions on Communications*, October, 1984.

WOOD83 Wood, H.M., and Cotton, I.W. "Security in Computer Communications Systems." In [CHOU83].

WOOD85 Wood, D. "Local Area Network Standards." in [BART85].

YEN83 Yen, C., and Crawford, R. "Distribution and Equalization of Signal on Coaxial Cables used in 10-Mbits Baseband Local Area Networks." *IEEE Transactions on Communications*, October, 1983.

YU81 Yu, P.S. *Interconnection Structures of Backend Storage Networks.* IBM Technical Report RC 9165, December, 1981.

ZHAN88 Zhang, L. "Comparison of Two Bridge Routing Approaches." *IEEE Network*, January, 1988.

INDEX

College Division
Macmillan Publishing Company
Front & Brown Streets
Riverside, NJ 08075

ORDER FORM

Ship To:
(Please print or type)

Name _____

Co. _____

Address _____

_____

City _____ St _____ Zip _____

Bill To:
(If different from shipping address)

Name _____

Co. _____

Address _____

_____

City _____ St _____ Zip _____

Mail your order to the above address or call 800-548-9939 (in New Jersey call 609-461-6500) or Fax 609-461-9265

Shipping Method **(select one)**
_____ UPS ground _____ 2nd Day Air _____ Book Rate

Payment Method
(select one)

_____ Check   _____ Visa
_____ Bill Me   _____ MasterCard

_____
Authorized Signature

_____   _____
Card Number   Exp Date

(*continued*)

TEAR OUT THIS PAGE TO ORDER OTHER TITLES BY WILLIAM STALLINGS:

SEQ.	QTY.	ISBN NO.	TITLE	PRICE	TOTAL
1	_____	002-415491-1	Computer Organization & Architecture 2/e	$55.00	_____
2	_____	002-415451-2	Data and Computer Communications 2/e	$59.00	_____
3	_____	002-415531-4	Local Networks 3/e	$40.00	_____
4	_____	002-415431-8	Business Data Communications	$43.00	_____
5	_____	002-415471-7	ISDN	$48.00	_____

PSR-PSL 350-3500   FC# 1355

Handbooks of Computer Communications Standards (available through Howard Sams & Co.):

6	_____	0-672-22697-9	Volume 1, The Open Systems Interconnection (OSI) Model and OSI-Related Standards, 2/e	$34.95	_____
7	_____	0-672-22698-7	Volume 2, Local Area Network Standards, 2/e	$34.95	_____
8	_____	0-672-22696-0	Volume 3, The TCP/IP Protocol Suite, 2/e	$34.95	_____

GRAND TOTAL   _____

A small shipping charge will be added. Prices subject to change without prior notification.

Acronyms

ANS	American National Standard
ANSI	American National Standards Institute
ASK	Amplitude-Shift Keying
CATV	Community Antenna Television
CBX	Computerized Branch Exchange
CCITT	Consultative Committee on International Telegraphy and Telephony
CRC	Cyclic Redundancy Check
CSMA	Carrier-Sense Multiple Access
CSMA/CD	Carrier-Sense Multiple Access with Collision Detection
DCE	Data Circuit-Terminating Equipment
DES	Data Encryption Standard
DOD	Department of Defense
DTE	Data Terminal Equipment
FCS	Frame Check Sequence
FDDI	Fiber Distributed Data Interface
FDM	Frequency-Division Multiplexing
FNP	Front-End Network Processor
FSK	Frequency-Shift Keying
HAM	Hybrid Access Method
HDLC	High-Level Data Link Control
HSLN	High-Speed Local Network
IEEE	Institute of Electrical and Electronics Engineers
IP	Internet Protocol
ISO	International Standards Organization
LAN	Local Area Network